U0941058

上海市统计局·编
SHANGHAI MUNICIPAL STATISTICS BUREAU

上海统计年鉴 2007

SHANGHAI STATISTICAL YEARBOOK

《上海统计年鉴－2007》编辑委员会 EDITORIAL BOARD

编者说明

一、《上海统计年鉴——2007》是一本信息高度密集的资料工具书。本书收录了2006年上海的经济和社会等各方面的统计数据,以及重要年份和改革开放以来的主要统计数据。

二、全书内容分为24个篇目,即:1. 行政区划和自然地理;2. 综合;3. 人口和劳动力;4. 国民经济核算;5. 财政收支;6. 固定资产投资;7. 对外经济贸易和旅游;8. 价格水平;9. 人民生活;10. 城市建设;11. 农业;12. 工业;13. 建筑业;14. 交通运输、邮政和信息传输;15. 批发和零售;16. 金融业;17. 房地产业;18. 科学技术;19. 环境保护治理;20. 教育;21. 卫生、社会保障和社会福利业;22. 文化和体育;23. 法律、公证和其他;24. 浦东新区。为便于读者正确地使用资料,各篇目还附有主要统计指标解释。

三、本年鉴数据主要是由我局通过年报调查收集,不作特别说明。凡是由专业部门提供的数据均在表式的注释中说明了数据来源。

四、资料中所使用的度量衡单位均采用国际统一标准计量单位。

五、本年鉴总量指标计算所采用的价格均为现行价格。

六、本年鉴部分数据合计数或相对数由于单位取舍不同产生的计算误差均未作机械调整。

七、 本年鉴表中的符号使用说明:

“…”表示数据不足本表最小计量单位数;

“空格”表示该项统计数据不详或无该项数据;

“#”表示其中的主要项。

八、《上海统计年鉴》公开出版以来,受到了国内外广大读者的关心和支持,对本年鉴的内容和编辑工作提出了许多宝贵的意见,对此我们深表谢意。限于我们的水平,本年鉴还存在一些不足之处,欢迎读者继续给予批评和指正,帮助我们进一步改进年鉴的编辑工作,以期更好地为广大读者服务。

EDITOR'S NOTE

Ⅰ. Shanghai Statistical Yearbook 2007 contains comprehensive statistics of Shanghai's social and economic development in 2006 and selected data of some important years and of the period since China adopted the policy of reform and opening to the outside world..

Ⅱ. The book is composed of 24 parts viz. 1. Administrative Division and Physical Geography; 2. General Survey; 3. Population and Labour Force; 4. National Economic Accounting; 5. Fiscal Revenue and Expenditure; 6. Investment in Fixed Assets; 7. Foreign Economic Relations, Trade and Tourism; 8. Prices; 9. Living Standards; 10. Urban Construction; 11. Agriculture; 12. Industry; 13. Construction; 14. Transportation, Posts and Information Transmission; 15. Wholesale and Retail; 16. Finance; 17. Real Estate; 18. Science and Technology; 19. Environment Protection and Treatment; 20. Education; 21. Health, Social Security and Social Welfare; 22. Culture, Sports; 23. Laws, Notary and others; 24. Pudong New Area. In order to make readers using materials correctly, explanations of major statistical indicators are attached after every chapter.

Ⅲ. Main part of the data in this yearbook are investigated and collected by Municipal Statistical Bureau, we haven't mentioned especially. As to the data provided by professional bureaus, we especially mentioned the source of data in the notes after the tables.

Ⅳ. The international standard unit of measurement is applied in this book.

Ⅴ. The prices used for gross indicators' calculating in this yearbook are current prices.

Ⅵ. Statistical discrepancies in this book due to rounding are not adjusted.

Ⅶ. Marks in this book: … means not large enough to be rounded into the least unit of measurement; Blank space means data are not available; # indicates major item in a category.

Ⅷ. Previous editions of Shanghai Statistical Yearbook have won wide acclaim among the readers. In order to excel, we welcome all candid comments and criticism from our readers.

目录
CONTENTS

[第一篇 CHAPTER 1] 行政区划和自然地理 ADMINISTRATIVE DIVISION AND PHYSICAL GEOGRAPHY

[第二篇 CHAPTER 2] 综合 GENERAL SURVEY

目录
CONTENTS

第三篇 CHAPTER 3 人口和劳动力 POPULATION AND LABOUR FORCE

[第四篇 CHAPTER 4] 国民经济核算 NATIONAL ECONOMIC ACCOUNTING

目录
CONTENTS

第五篇 CHAPTER 5 财政收支 FISCAL REVENUE AND EXPENDITURE

第六篇 CHAPTER 6 固定资产投资 INVESTMENT IN FIXED ASSETS

目录·
CONTENTS

第七篇 CHAPTER 7 对外经济贸易和旅游 FOREIGN ECONOMIC RELATIONS, TRADE AND TOURISM

第八篇 CHAPTER8 价格水平 PRICES

第九篇 CHAPTER 9 人民生活 LIVING STANDARDS

目录
CONTENTS

第十篇 CHAPTER 10 城市建设 URBAN CONSTRUCTION

第十一篇 CHAPTER 11 农 业 AGRICULTURE

目录
CONTENTS

第十二篇 CHAPTER 12 工业 INDUSTRY

第十三篇 CHAPTER 13 建筑业 CONSTRUCTION

第十四篇 CHAPTER 14 交通运输、邮政和信息传输 TRANSPORTATION, POSTS AND INFORMATION TRANSMISSION

目录 CONTENTS

第十五篇 CHAPTER 15 批发和零售 WHOLESALE AND RETAIL

目录
CONTENTS

第十六篇 CHAPTER 16 金融业 FINANCE

第十七篇 CHAPTER 17 房地产业 REAL ESTATE

目录 CONTENTS

第十八篇 CHAPTER 18 科学技术 SCIENCE AND TECHNOLOGY

第十九篇 CHAPTER 19 环境保护治理 ENVIRONMENT PROTECTION AND TREATMENT

第二十篇 CHAPTER 20 教育 EDUCATION

目录
CONTENTS

第二十二篇 CHAPTER 22 文化和体育 CULTURE,SPORTS

目录
CONTENTS

第二十三篇 CHAPTER 23 法律、公证和其他 LAWS,NOTARY AND OTHERS

目录
CONTENTS

第二十四篇 CHAPTER 24 浦东新区 PUDONG NEW AREA

第一篇

CHAPTER 1

行政区划和自然地理

ADMINISTRATIVE DIVISION AND PHYSICAL GEOGRAPHY

表 1.1 行政区划（2006）
ADMINISTRATIVE DIVISION

单位：个（unit）

地 区 District		镇 Towns	乡 Township	街道办事处 Urban Sub-district Office	居民委员会 Neighbourhood Committees	村民委员会 Village Committees
全 市	**Total**	**106**	**3**	**104**	**3 413**	**1 862**
浦东新区	Pudong New Area	11		12	566	243
黄 浦 区	Huangpu			9	121	
卢 湾 区	Luwan			4	75	
徐 汇 区	Xuhui	1		12	303	5
长 宁 区	Changning	1		9	173	6
静 安 区	Jingán			5	72	
普 陀 区	Putuo	3		6	221	8
闸 北 区	Zhabei	1		8	207	1
虹 口 区	Hongkou			10	245	
杨 浦 区	Yangpu	1		11	304	
宝 山 区	Baoshan	9		3	246	118
闵 行 区	Minhang	9		3	309	160
嘉 定 区	Jiading	8		3	102	164
金 山 区	Jinshan	9		1	68	132
松 江 区	Songjiang	10		4	134	115
青 浦 区	Qingpu	8		3	69	184
南 汇 区	Nanhui	14		1	70	185
奉 贤 区	Fengxian	8			76	270
崇 明 县	Chongming	13	3		52	271

注：本表由市民政局提供。
Note: The figures on the table are provided by Shanghai Civil Affairs Bureau.

自然状况(2006)
NATURAL CONDITIONS

位　置:

上海,简称沪。位于北纬31度14分,东经121度29分。它北界长江,东濒东海,南临杭州湾,西接江苏、浙江两省。

上海地处长江三角洲东缘,位于我国南北海岸的中心,长江由此入海,交通便利,腹地广阔,地理位置优越,是一个良好的江海港口。

Location:

Shanghai, or "Hu" alternatively, located at 31° 14 ′ north latitude and 121°29 ′ east longtitude, with the Yangtze River to the north, the East China Sea to the east, the Hangzhou Bay to the south, Jiangsu and Zhejiang Provinces to the west.

The city situates on the eastern fringe of the Yangtze River Delta, which is in the centre of the coastline from north to south. Located at the mouth of the Yangtze River, Shanghai enjoys convenient communications and a favourable geographical location with a good harbour and a vast hinterland.

地　势:

全境除西南部有少数残丘外,全为坦荡低平的长江三角洲冲击平原的一部分,平均高度海拔4米左右。

Topography:

Shanghai averages about 4 metres above the sea level, whose territory is a part of the broad flat alluvial plain of the Yangtze River Delta with few remnant hills in the southwest.

面　积:

全市面积6 340.5平方公里,其中陆地面积6 218.65平方公里,水面面积121.85平方公里,南北长约120公里,东西宽约100公里。

Area:

Covering an area of 6 340.5 square kilometres, land area of 6 218.65 square kilometres and water area of 121.85 square kilometres. The city is about 100 kilometres wide from east to west and 120 kilometres long from north to south.

河　流:

上海地区天然河港密布,多属太湖流域,主要河流有黄浦江及其支流吴淞江(苏州河)。

River:

Shanghai is thick with natural rivers and branch streams mostly in the Taihu drainge area. The main waterways are the Huangpu River and its branch Wusong River (or Suzhou Creek).

气　候:

上海地区属亚热带季风气候,四季分明。

Climate:

Shanghai has a subtropical monsoon climate with four distinct seasons.

岛　屿:

上海的崇明岛是我国的第三大岛,由长江挟带下来的泥沙冲积而成。此外,上海所属的岛屿还有长兴岛、横沙岛等。

Islands:

Chongming Island in Shanghai is the third largest island in China, which is an alluvial island formed with soil carried by the Yangtze River. Other islands under Shanghai administration are Changxing Island and Hengsha Island etc.

河流名称	River	长度(公里) Length(km)	宽度(米) Width(m)	深度(米) Depth(m)
黄浦江	Huangpu River	80	400左右(or so)	7~9
苏州河	Suzhou Creek	125	70~80	
# 在本市境内	In Shanghai Territory	53.1		

岛屿名称	Island	面　积(平方公里) Area(sq. km)
崇明岛	Chongming Island	1 041.21
长兴岛	Changxing Island	88.54
横沙岛	Hengsha Island	55.74

指　标	Indicators	2006	指　标	Indicators	2006
平均气温(℃)	Annual Average Temperature(℃)	18.4	蒸发量(毫米)	Evaporation (mm)	862.1
极端最高气温(℃)	Utmost Highest Air Temperature(℃)	38.6	降水量(毫米)	Precipitation(mm)	1 042.6
极端最低气温(℃)	Utmost Lowest Air Temperature(℃)	-3.5	降雨日(天)	Annual Rainy Days(day)	129
日照时间(小时)	Annual Sunshine Time (h)	1 638.2	无霜期(天)	Frost-free Period(day)	333
			晴天天数(天)	Sunshine Days(day)	73

表 1.2 各月主要气象指标(2006)
MAIN CLIMATE INDICATORS

月 份 Month		平均气温(℃) Annual Average Temperature (℃)	极端最高气温(℃) Utmost Highest Air Temperature(℃)	极端最低气温(℃) Utmost Lowest Air Temperature(℃)	日照时数(小时) Annual Sunshine Time(h)
1 月	Jan.	6.5	17.7	-3.5	75.0
2 月	Feb.	6.1	22.2	-1.9	87.6
3 月	Mar.	11.6	23.7	1.2	166.5
4 月	Apr.	17.0	31.4	6.8	168.9
5 月	May.	21.3	32.2	13.7	164.8
6 月	Jun.	25.9	37.3	16.7	140.7
7 月	Jul.	29.8	37.9	22.3	154.5
8 月	Aug.	30.4	38.6	25.5	239.9
9 月	Sep.	24.2	33.5	17.6	117.0
10 月	Oct.	22.3	28.9	16.0	132.4
11 月	Nov.	15.9	26.7	7.4	98.3
12 月	Dec.	8.6	18.5	-0.7	92.6

注：资料由上海市气象局提供。
Note: Data are provided by Shanghai Meteorological Bureau.

表 1.2 续表 continued

月 份 Month		降水量(毫米) Precipitation (mm)	降雨日(天) Annual Rainy Days (day)	蒸发量(毫米) Evaporation (mm)	晴天(天) Sunny Days (day)
1 月	Jan.	15.6	13	24.4	2
2 月	Feb.	81.6	14	24.5	3
3 月	Mar.	42.8	7	65.5	8
4 月	Apr.	127.2	10	88.6	10
5 月	May.	120.1	11	94.4	9
6 月	Jun.	129.0	14	101.4	6
7 月	Jul.	217.7	14	121.3	7
8 月	Aug.	28.2	6	143.5	15
9 月	Sep.	87.5	14	72.6	4
10 月	Oct.	33.4	4	63.1	1
11 月	Nov.	142.2	14	34.9	8
12 月	Dec.	17.3	8	27.9	

上/海/统/计/年/鉴

主要统计指标解释

■ 行政区划

指国家对行政区域的划分。根据宪法规定，我国的行政区域划分如下：(1)全国分为省、自治区、直辖市；(2)省、自治区分为自治州、县、自治县、市；(3)自治州分为县、自治县、市；(4)县、自治县分为乡、民族乡、镇；(5)直辖市和较大的市分为区、县；(6)国家在必要时设立的特别行政区。

■ 气　候

指地球与大气之间长期能量交换与质量交换所形成的一种自然环境状态，它是多种因素综合作用的结果。气候既是人类生活和生产的环境要素之一，又是供给人类生活和生产的重要资源。气温、降水、湿度等气象要素的多年平均值是用来描述一个地区气候状况的主要参数，而各种气象要素某年、某月的平均值（或总量）则可以反映出该时期天气气候状况的重要特征。

■ 气　温

指空气的温度，一般以摄氏度(℃)为单位表示。气象观测的温度表是放在离地面约 1.5 米处通风良好的百叶箱里测量的，因此，通常说的气温指的是离地面 1.5 米处百叶箱中的温度。其统计计算方法为：

月平均气温是将全月各日的平均气温相加，除以该月的天数而得。

年平均气温是将 12 个月的月平均气温累加后除以 12 而得。

■ 降水量

指从天空降落到地面的液态或固态（经融化后）水，未经蒸发、渗透、流失而在地面上积聚的深度。其统计计算方法为：

月降水量是将全月各日的降水量累加而得。

年降水量是将 12 个月的月降水量累加而得。

■ 日照时数

指太阳实际照射地面的时间。其统计方法与降水量相同。

SHANGHAI STATISTICAL YEARBOOK

EXPLANATORY NOTES TO MAJOR STATISTICAL INDICATORS

□ Divisions of Administrative Areas

Divisions of Administrative Areas refer to the division o-faministrative areas by the state. The Constitution of the People's Republic of China stipulates that the administrative areas in China are divided as: 1) The whole country is divided into provinces, autonomous regions and municipalities directly under the central government; 2) Provinces and autonomous regions are divided into autonomous prefectures, counties, autonomous counties and cities; 3) Autonomous prefectures are divided into counties, autonomous counties and cities; 4) Counties and autonomous counties are divided into townships, nationality townships and towns; 5) Municipalities and large cities are divided into districts and counties, 6) The state shall, when necessary, establish special administrative regions.

□ Climate

Climate refers to the natural environmental status formed by the long-term exchange of energy and mass between the earth and the air, and is the results of interaction of many factors. Climate is both one of the environment factors and the important resources for the living and production activities of the human being. The average values across several years of meteorological factors such as temperature, rainfall and humidity are used as important parameters to describe the climate of a region, while the average values (or total values) of a given year or month of meteorological factors reflect the key characteristics of climate for that period of time.

□ Temperature

Temperature refers to the air temperature. It often uses centigrade as the unit. The thermometry used for weather observation is put in a breezy shutter, which is 1.5 meters high from the ground. Therefore, the commonly used temperature refers to the temperature in the breezy shutter 1.5 meters away from the ground. The calculation method is as follows:

Monthly average temperature is the summation of average daily temperature of one month divided by the actual days of that particular month. Annual average temperature is the summation of monthly average of a year divided by 12 months.

□ Volume of Precipitation

Volume of Precipitation refers to the deepness of liquid state or solid state (thawed) water falling from the sky to the ground that has not been evaporated, infiltrated or run off. The calculation method is as follows:

Monthly precipitation is the summation of daily precipitation of a month.

Annual precipitation is the summation of 12 months precipitation of a year.

□ Sunshine Hours

Sunshine Hours refer to the actual hours of sun irradiating the earth. The calculation method is the same as that of the precipitation.

第二篇

CHAPTER 2

综　合

GENERAL SURVEY

表 2.1 主要年份社会经济主要指标
MAJOR SOCIAL AND ECONOMIC INDICATORS IN MAIN YEARS

指标	Indicators	1990	2000	2005	2006
人口与就业	**Population and Employment**				
人　口	**Population**				
年末户籍人口(万人)	Year-end Population(10 000 persons)	1 283.35	1 321.63	1 360.26	1 368.08
#非农业人口	Non-agricultural Population	864.46	986.16	1 148.94	1 173.30
就　业	**Employment**				
从业人员(万人)	Employees(10 000 persons)	787.72	745.24	863.32	885.51
职工人数(万人)	Staff and Workers(10 000 persons)	508.10	390.14	420.12	500.94
城镇登记失业率(%)	Registered Unemployment Rate in Urban Areas (%)	1.5	3.5	4.4	4.4
宏观经济	**Macro Economy**				
国民经济核算	**Domestic Economic Accounts**				
上海市生产总值(亿元)	Gross Domestic Product(100 million yuan)	781.66	4 771.17	9 164.10	10 366.37
第一产业	Primary Industry	34.24	76.68	90.26	93.80
第二产业	Secondary Industry	505.70	2 207.63	4 452.92	5 028.37
#工　业	Industry	469.83	1 998.96	4 129.52	4 670.11
第三产业	Tertiary Industry	241.82	2 486.86	4 620.92	5 244.20
人均生产总值(元)	Per Capita Gross Domestic Product(yuan)				
按户籍人口计算	Calculated by Registered Population	6 107	36 217	67 565	75 990
按常住人口计算	Calculated by Resident Population	6 107	29 671	51 529	57 695
固定资产投资	**Investment in Fixed Assets**				
全社会固定资产投资总额(亿元)	Total Investment in Fixed Assets(100 million yuan)	227.08	1 869.67	3 542.55	3 925.09
#房地产投资	Investment in Real Estate	8.16	566.17	1 246.86	1 275.59
财　政	**Public Finance**				
全市财政收入(亿元)	Fiscal Revenue(100 million yuan)	284.36	1 752.69	4 095.81	4 798.93
#地方财政收入	Local Fiscal Revenue	166.99	497.96	1 433.90	1 600.37
地方财政支出(亿元)	Local Fiscal Expenditure(100 million yuan)	75.56	622.84	1 660.32	1 813.80
价　格	**Price**				
居民消费价格指数(上年=100)	Consumer Price Index(preceding =100)	106.3	102.5	101.0	101.2
商品零售价格指数(上年=100)	Retail Price Index(preceding =100)	104.8	96.4	99.4	100.2

注：从业人员为在岗从业人员。
Note: Employees refer to working employees.

表 2.1 续表 1　continued

指　标	Indicators	1990	2000	2005	2006
外商直接投资	**Foreign Direct Investment**				
签订合同项目（个）	Number of Contracts (unit)	203	1 814	4 091	4 061
签订合同金额（亿美元）	Contractual Foreign Investment(100 million USD)	2.14	63.90	138.33	145.74
实际到位金额（亿美元）	Foreign Investment Actually Absorbed(100 million USD)	1.77	31.60	68.50	71.07
产　业	**Industries**				
农　业	**Agriculture**				
农业总产值（亿元）	Gross Output Value of Agriculture (100 million yuan)	68.16	216.50	233.39	237.01
主要农副产品产量（万吨）	Output of Major Farm and Sideline Products (10 000 tons)				
粮　食	Grain	244.36	174.00	105.36	111.30
棉　花	Cotton	1.22	0.12	0.18	0.20
油菜籽	Rapeseed	18.17	15.71	6.51	4.91
牛　奶	Milk	22.68	25.95	23.76	22.09
蔬　菜	Vegetables	186.79	377.00	409.03	418.76
猪　肉	Pork	23.32	25.96	18.02	16.18
水产品	Aquatic Products	27.36	28.87	35.35	38.75
工　业	**Industry**				
工业总产值（亿元）	Gross Output Value of Industry (100 million yuan)	1 642.75	7 002.98	16 876.78	19 631.23
轻工业	Light Industry	846.63	2 903.40	4 299.31	4 747.28
重工业	Heavy Industry	796.12	4 119.59	12 577.48	14 883.94
主要工业产品产量	Output of Major Industrial Products				
钢　材(万吨)	Steel Products (10 000 tons)	609.59	1 544.46	1 964.16	2 129.78
发电量(亿千瓦・时)	Electric Generation(100 million kwh)	284.10	553.09	728.74	710.96
程控交换机(万线)	Program Controlled Exchanges (10 000 lines)	95.23	1 091.64	796.59	553.53
微型电子计算机(万部)	Micro-Computers (10 000 units)	0.77	42.04	2 176.17	2 670.09
移动通信设备(万部)	Mobile Communication Equipments(10 000 units)		1.60	115.03	174.16
集成电路(亿块)	Semi-conductor IC (100 million units)	0.12	23.93	67.70	64.05
汽　车(万辆)	Motor Vehicles (10 000 vehicles)	2.81	25.29	48.45	65.28
#轿　车	Cars	2.46	25.15	48.09	64.47
金属切削机床（万台）	Metal-cutting Machines(10 000 units)	1.38	2.23	1.32	1.34
民用钢质船舶（万总吨）	Civil Steel Ships (10 000 syn-tons)	39.07	118.81	235.59	295.48
建筑业	**Construction**				
总产值（亿元）	Gross Output Value (100 million yuan)	75.62	631.64	1 889.25	2 285.38
全员劳动生产率（元/人）（按总产值计算）	Overall Labor Productivity (yuan/person) (In Term of Output Value)	18 569	109 244	182 299	208 368

表2.1 续表2 continued

	指 标 Indicators	1990	2000	2005	2006
交通运输、邮政业和信息传输	**Transportation, Post and Information Transmission**				
货物运输量（万吨）	Freight Transportation Volume (10 000 tons)	26 777	52 206	71 304	75 184
旅客发送量（万人次）	Passenger Departures (10 000 person-times)	3 835	6 893	9 487	10 205
港口货物吞吐量（万吨）	Port Cargo throughput (10 000 tons)	13 959	20 440	44 317	53 748
国际标准集装箱吞吐量(万TEU)	International Container Throughput Capacity(10 000TEU)	45.60	561.20	1 808.40	2 171.90
邮电业务总量(亿元)	Revenue from Post and Telecommunications Services (100 million yuan)	10.23	171.70	414.26	555.00
年末固定电话用户（万户）	Year-end Installed Telephone Subscribers (10 000 households)	45.69	549.00	996.70	1 112.30
数字数据用户(万户)	Digital and Data Users(10 000 households)			2.4	1.8
批发和零售	**Wholesale and Retail**				
社会消费品零售总额(亿元)	Retail Sales of Consumer Goods(100 million yuan)	333.86	1 865.28	2 972.97	3 360.41
批发零售业商品销售总额(亿元)	Total Sales of Wholesale and Retail (100 million yuan)	1 305.41	7 474.81	12 943.25	15 504.05
对外经济贸易	**Foreign Trade**				
口岸进出口总额(亿美元)	Total Value of Port Imports and Exports(100 million USD)	172.89	1 093.11	3 506.78	4 287.54
进口额	Imports	86.27	477.39	1 382.48	1 621.89
出口额	Exports	86.62	615.72	2 124.30	2 665.65
外贸进出口总额(亿美元)	Total Value of Foreign Imports and Exports(100 million USD)	74.31	547.10	1 863.65	2 274.89
进口额	Imports	21.10	293.56	956.23	1 139.16
出口额	Exports	53.21	253.54	907.42	1 135.73
国际旅游	**International Tourism**				
上海入境境外旅游者人数(万人次)	Number of Foreign Tourists through Shanghai Custom (10 000 persons-times)	89.30	181.40	571.35	605.67
国际旅游(外汇)收入(亿美元)	Foreign Exchange Earnings from International Tourism(100 million USD)	2.31	16.13	36.08	39.61
金融保险	**Finance and Insurance**				
金融机构存款余额(亿元)	Total Saving Deposits of Financial Institutions(100 million yuan)		9 349.83	23 320.86	26 454.88
金融机构贷款余额(亿元)	Total Loan Balance of Financial Institutions(100 million yuan)		7 254.26	16 798.12	18 603.92
保险费收入(亿元)	Premium Income(100 million yuan)	8.99	127.23	333.62	407.04
保险赔款及给付支出(亿元)	Indemnity Payments(100 million yuan)	2.22	36.04	87.46	91.31
教育、科技、文化	**Education, Science&Technology and Culture**				
教 育	**Education**				
在校学生数(万人)	Students Enrollment(10 000 persons)				
高等学校	Institutions of Higher Education	12.13	22.68	44.26	46.63
普通中学	Regular Secondary Schools	48.31	79.54	77.02	71.17
小 学	Primary Schools	110.19	78.86	53.50	53.37
每万人拥有大学生(人)	Number of College and University Students Per 10 000 Persons(person)	94	172	325	341

表 2.1 续表 3 continued

指　标	Indicators	1990	2000	2005	2006
科　技	**Science and Technology**				
科技成果（项）	Achievements in Science and Technology(item)	2 092	1 102	1 701	1 953
研究与试验发展经费支出(亿元)	Research and Development Expenditures (100 million yuan)	10.13	76.73	213.77	256.78
研究与试验发展经费支出相当于上海市生产总值比例(%)	R&D Expenditure as Percentage of Gross Domestic Product (%)	1.36	1.61	2.33	2.48
文　化	**Culture**				
出版数量	Number of Publications				
图　书（亿册、张）	Books (100 million copies)	2.98	2.54	2.59	2.54
期　刊（亿册）	Periodicals (100 million copies)	1.73	1.85	1.90	1.83
报　纸（亿份）	Newspapers (100 million copies)	16.16	16.77	19.06	17.89
故事影片产量（部）	Feature Films Produced(film)	16	10	13	9
家庭、生活、环境	**Family, Living and Environment**				
家　庭	**Household**				
家庭总户数(万户)	Total Households (10 000 households)	415.28	475.73	496.69	499.54
平均每户家庭人口(人)	Average Persons Per Household (person)	3.1	2.8	2.7	2.7
婚　姻	**Marriages and Divorces**				
准予登记结婚（万对）	Marriage Registration Permitted (10 000 couples)	10.77	9.31	10.27	16.56
离婚人数（万人）	Divorce (10 000 persons)	3.27	6.36	7.86	9.43
离婚率（‰）	Divorce Rate (‰)	1.37	2.42	2.90	3.45
住　宅	**Housing**				
市区人均使用面积(平方米)	Per Capita Floor space of Urban Residents Land Used in Downtown (sq·m)	9.1	16.3	21.3	22.0
市区人均居住面积(平方米)	Per Capita Net Floor Space of Urban Residents(sq·m)	6.6	11.8	15.5	16.0
农村居民人均居住面积(平方米)	Per Capita Net Floor Space of Rural Residents(sq·m)	37.08	53.58	56.56	59.99
生　活	**Living**				
城市居民人均可支配收入(元)	Per Capita Annual Disposable Income of Urban Households(yuan)	2 182	11 718	18 645	20 668
城市居民人均消费支出（元）	Per Capita Annual Consumption Expenditures of Urban Households(yuan)	1 936	8 868	13 773	14 762
农村居民人均可支配收入(元)	Per Capita Annual Disposable Income of Rural Households(yuan)	1 665	5 565	8 342	9 213
农村居民人均生活消费支出(元)	Per Capita Annual Consumption Expenditure of Rural Households(yuan)	1 262	4 138	7 265	8 006
城乡居民储蓄存款余额(亿元)	Saving Deposits of Urban and Rural Households (100 million yuan)	252.16	2 627.07	8 432.49	9 480.28

注：根据国家对离婚率计算方法调整的要求，本年鉴的离婚率计算方法相应作了调整，分子为离婚对数，分母为年平均人口数。

Note: According to the adjustment of calculate method of Divorce Rate, the calculate method of Divorce Rate has been adjusted, which the molecule is the divorced couples and the denominator is the yearly average population.

表 2.1 续表 4 continued

指 标	Indicators	1990	2000	2005	2006
工 资	**Wages**				
职工工资总额(亿元)	Total Wages of Staff and Workers(100 million yuan)	146.78	614.53	1 146.97	1 475.93
职工平均工资(元)	Average Wages of Staff and Workers (yuan)	2 917	15 420	26 823	29 569
卫 生	**Health Care**				
医 院(个)	Number of Hospitals(unit)	462	459	487	505
医 生(万人)	Doctors(10 000 persons)	5.82	4.99	4.40	4.55
医院床位数(万张)	Number of Hospital Beds (10 000 beds)	6.21	7.31	8.93	9.28
每万人拥有医生(人)	Number of Doctors Per 10 000 Persons (person)	45	38	32	33
城市建设	**Urban Construction**				
城市基础设施投资额(亿元)	Investment in Urban Infrastructure (100 million yuan)	47.22	449.90	885.74	1 125.54
自来水售水量(亿立方米)	Sales Volume of Tap Water (100 million cu. m)	12.25	19.75	22.81	23.30
用电量(亿千瓦时)	Electric Power Consumption (100 million kwh)	264.74	559.42	921.97	990.15
城市煤气供应量(亿立方米)	Volume of Coal Gas Supply in Urban Areas(100 million cu. m)	12.72	21.31	22.86	21.76
年末出租车运营总数(辆)	Year-end Operating Taxi Vehicles(vehicle)	11 298	42 943	47 794	48 022
运营公交车辆数(辆)	Total Number of Public Buses (vehicle)	6 264	17 939	17 985	17 284
道路长度(公里)	Length of Roads(km)	1 631	6 641	12 227	14 619
城市人均公共绿地面积(平方米)	Public Green Areas Per Capita (sq. m)	1.02	4.60	11.01	11.50
城市绿化覆盖率(%)	Coverage Rate of Urban Green Areas(%)	12.4	22.2	37.0	37.3
森林覆盖率(%)	Coverage Rate of Forest(%)	5.5	9.2	11.6	11.6
环境保护投资相当于上海市生产总值比例(%)	Environment Protection Investment as Percentage of Gross Domestic Product(%)		3.10	3.07	3.00
环境空气质量优良率(%)	Rate of Good Ambient Air Quality (%)		80.8	88.2	88.8
火灾、交通事故	**Fires and Traffic Accidents**				
火灾发生数(起)	Number of Fires (unit)	2 146	5 164	4 288	4 526
火灾损失额(万元)	Loss of Fires (10 000 yuan)	1 868	1 919	1 731	2 292
交通事故发生数(万起)	Number of Traffic Accidents(10 000 unit)	0.76	4.13	0.92	0.66
交通事故损失额(万元)	Loss of Traffic Accidents(10 000 yuan)	1 345	20 391	7 961	3 292

①本表总量指标中的价值量指标均按当年价格计算。
②1990、2000 年邮电业务总量按 1990 年不变价格计算,2005、2006 年按 2000 年不变价格计算。
③1990 年农村居民年人均可支配收入为农村居民年人均纯收入。
④2005 年起,卫生指标按照新《中国卫生统计调查制度》统计,(以下同)。
❶The data in value terms in the table are calculated at current prices.
❷Figures of Revenue from Post and Telecommunication Services in 1990 and 2000 were calculated at constant prices of 1990, and those figures in 2005、2006 were calculated at constant prices of 2000.
❸1990, Per Capita Annual Disposable Income of Rural Households referred to per Capita annual net income of rural residents. (Same as follows)
❹Statistics of health care are based on "China Health Care Statistical Investigation System" in 2005. (same as follows)

表 2.2 主要年份社会经济主要指标发展速度
GROWTH RATE OF MAJOR SOCIAL AND ECONOMIC INDICATORS IN MAIN YEARS

单位:%

指　标	Indicators	2006 年比下列各年增长 Indicatars' Growth Rate Between Years Below and Year 2006		
		1990	2000	2005
年末户籍人口	Year-end Population	6.6	3.5	0.6
上海市生产总值	Gross Domestic Product	5.3 倍	96.2	12.0
第一产业	Primary Industry	20.1	-5.3	0.8
第二产业	Secondary Industry	5.4 倍	1.1 倍	12.3
第三产业	Tertiary Industry	6.1 倍	87.8	12.0
全市财政收入	Fiscal Revenue	16 倍	1.7 倍	17.2
# 地方财政收入	Local Fiscal Revenue	8.6 倍	2.2 倍	11.6
地方财政支出	Local Fiscal Expenditure	23 倍	1.9 倍	9.2
直接吸收外资	Foreign Direct Investment			
签订合同项目	Number of Contracts	19 倍	1.2 倍	-0.7
签订合同金额	Contractual Foreign Investment	67 倍	1.3 倍	5.4
实际到位金额	Foreign Investment Actually Absorbed	39 倍	1.2 倍	3.8
农业总产值	Gross Output Value of Agriculture	48.3	-6.4	0.7
工业总产值	Gross Output Value of Industry	10 倍	1.7 倍	13.9
轻工业	Light Industry	5.2 倍	91.0	7.1
重工业	Heavy Industry	15 倍	2.3 倍	16.3
货物运输量	Freight Transportation Volume	1.8 倍	44.0	5.4
旅客发送量	Passenger Departures	1.7 倍	48.0	7.6
港口货物吞吐量	Port Cargo Throughput	2.9 倍	1.6 倍	21.3
社会消费品零售总额	Retail Sales of Consumer Goods	9.0 倍	80.2	13.0
口岸进出口总额	Total Value of Port Imports and Exports	24 倍	2.9 倍	22.3
进口额	Imports	18 倍	2.4 倍	17.3
出口额	Exports	30 倍	3.3 倍	25.5
外贸进出口总额	Total Value of Foreign Imports and Exports	30 倍	3.2 倍	22.1
进口额	Imports	53 倍	2.9 倍	19.1
出口额	Exports	20 倍	3.5 倍	25.2
城市居民家庭人均可支配收入	Per Capita Annual Disposable Income of Urban Households	8.5 倍	76.4	10.8
城市居民家庭人均消费支出	Per Capita Annual Consumption Expenditures of Urban Households	6.6 倍	66.5	7.2
农村居民家庭人均可支配收入	Per Capita Annual Disposable Income of Rural Households	4.5 倍	65.6	10.4
农村居民家庭人均生活消费支出	Per Capita Annual Consumption Expenditures of Rural Households	5.3 倍	93.5	10.2
全社会固定资产投资总额	Total Investment in Fixed Assets	16 倍	1.1 倍	10.8
城市基础设施投资额	Investment in Urban Infrastructure	23 倍	1.5 倍	27.1
医　生	Doctors	-21.8	-8.8	3.4
高等学校在校学生	Student Enrollment of Institutions of Higher Education	2.8 倍	1.1 倍	5.4

注：本表速度指标中，上海市生产总值及三次产业、工业总产值、农业总产值均按可比价格计算。

Note: The growth rates of the following indicators are calculated at comparable prices: Gross Domestic Product, Three Industries, Gross Output Value of Agriculture and Gross Output Value of Industry.

表 2.2 续表 continued

单位:%

指　标	Indicators	平均每年增长 Indicators' Average Annual Growth Rate 1991～2006	2001～2006
年末户籍人口	Year-end Population	0.4	0.6
上海市生产总值	Gross Domestic Product	12.2	11.9
第一产业	Primary Industry	1.1	-0.9
第二产业	Secondary Industry	12.3	13.1
第三产业	Tertiary Industry	13.0	11.1
全社会固定资产投资总额	Total Investment in Fixed Assets	22.6	12.3
全市财政收入	Fiscal Revenue	19.3	18.3
#地方财政收入	Local Fiscal Revenue	15.2	21.5
地方财政支出	Local Fiscal Expenditure	22.0	19.5
农业总产值	Gross Output Value of Agriculture	2.5	-1.1
工业总产值	Gross Output Value of Industry	16.3	18.3
轻工业	Light Industry	12.1	11.4
重工业	Heavy Industry	19.0	21.7
货物运输量	Freight Transportation Volume	6.7	6.3
旅客发送量	Passenger Departures	6.3	6.8
港口货物吞吐量	Port Cargo Throughput	8.8	17.5
社会消费品零售总额	Retail Sales of Consumer Goods	15.5	10.3
口岸进出口总额	Total Value of Port Imports and Exports	22.2	25.6
进口额	Imports	20.1	22.6
出口额	Exports	23.9	27.7
外贸进出口总额	Total Value of Foreign Imports and Exports	23.8	26.8
进口额	Imports	28.3	25.4
出口额	Exports	21.1	28.4
城市居民家庭人均可支配收入	Per Capita Annual Disposable Income of Urban Households	15.1	9.9
城市居民家庭人均消费支出	Per Capita Annual Consumption Expenditures of Urban Households	13.5	8.9
农村居民家庭人均可支配收入	Per Capita Annual Disposable Income of Rural Households	11.3	8.8
农村居民家庭人均生活消费支出	Per Capita Consumption Expenditure of Rural Households	12.2	11.6
医　生	Doctors	-1.5	-1.5
高等学校在校学生	Student Enrollment of Institutions of Higher Education	8.8	12.8
城市基础设施投资额	Investment in Urban Infrastructure	24.1	14.0

表 2.3　主要年份社会经济发展结构指标
STRUCTURAL INDICATORS OF SOCIAL AND ECONOMIC DEVELOPMENT IN MAIN YEARS

单位：%

	指　标 Indicators	1990	2000	2005	2006
农业非农业人口结构	Structure of Agriculture and Non-agriculture	100	100	100	100
农　业	Agriculture	32.6	25.4	15.5	14.2
非农业	Non-agriculture	67.4	74.6	84.5	85.8
人口性别结构	Structure of Sex	100	100	100	100
男	Male	50.4	50.4	50.2	50.2
女	Female	49.6	49.6	49.8	49.8
从业人员产业结构	Industrial Structure of Employees	100	100	100	100
第一产业	Primary Industry	11.1	10.8	7.1	6.3
第二产业	Secondary Industry	59.3	44.3	37.3	37.0
第三产业	Tertiary Industry	29.6	44.9	55.6	56.7
上海市生产总值产业结构	Industrial Structure of GDP	100	100	100	100
第一产业	Primary Industry	4.4	1.6	1.0	0.9
第二产业	Secondary Industry	64.7	46.3	48.6	48.5
第三产业	Tertiary Industry	30.9	52.1	50.4	50.6
上海市生产总值所有制结构	Ownership Structure of GDP	100	100	100	100
公有制经济	Public State-owned	95.4	71.4	57.6	55.9
国有经济	State-owned	71.2	55.0	49.0	47.9
集体经济	Collective-owned	24.2	16.4	8.6	8.0
非公有制经济	Non-state-owned	4.6	28.6	42.4	44.1
全社会固定资产投资所有制结构	Ownership Structure of Total Investment	100	100	100	100
国有经济	State-owned	84.7	44.4	35.0	37.2
非国有经济	Non-State-owned	15.3	55.6	65.0	62.8
地方财政收入结构	Structure of Local Fiscal Revenue	100	100	100	100
#增值税	Value-added Tax		18.8	15.8	16.9
营业税	Business Tax		30.9	35.8	34.9
企业所得税	Enterprise Income Tax		20.7	17.4	16.9
个人所得税	Personal Income Tax		12.1	7.8	8.2
外商直接投资实际吸收外资结构	Foreign Direct Investment Structure of Foreign Investment Actually Absorbed	100	100	100	100
#合资企业	Joint Ventures	61.0	40.9	20.8	22.3
合作企业	Cooprative Enterprises	37.9	9.5	2.4	2.6
独资企业	Sole-foreign Enterprises	1.1	49.6	67.0	75.1
农业总产值结构	Structure of Gross Output Value of Agriculture	100	100	100	100
#种植业	Planting	42.7	41.5	47.7	50.6
牧　业	Animal Husbandry	44.4	40.3	23.3	19.5
渔　业	Fishery	11.8	17.5	22.1	23.3
工业总产值结构	Structure of Gross Output Value of Industry	100	100	100	100
轻工业	Light Industry	51.5	41.3	25.5	24.2
重工业	Heavy Industry	48.5	58.7	74.5	75.8

表2.3 续表 continued

	指 标 Indicators	1990	2000	2005	2006
货物运输总量结构	Structure of Freight Transportation	100	100	100	100
铁 路	Railways	19.4	10.2	5.4	5.0
公 路	Roadways	32.5	54.3	45.8	45.0
水 运	Waterways	48.0	35.3	48.5	49.7
民用航空	Civil Aviation	0.1	0.2	0.3	0.3
社会消费品零售总额结构	Structure of Retail Sales of Consumer Goods	100	100	100	100
吃	Food	42.6	39.8	39.4	39.5
穿	Clothing	15.7	13.4	12.8	12.7
用	Articles	41.1	46.0	46.7	46.6
烧	Fuels	0.6	0.8	1.1	1.2
出口商品结构	Structure of Exports		100	100	100
初级产品	Primary Goods		3.4	2.7	2.4
工业制成品	Manufactured Goods		96.6	97.3	97.6
进口商品结构	Structure of Imports		100	100	100
初级产品	Primary Goods		11.9	10.4	10.7
工业制成品	Manufactured Goods		88.1	89.6	89.3
中资金融机构人民币存款结构	Structure of RMB Saving Deposit in Chinese Financial Instituation	100	100	100	100
#企业存款	Enterprise Deposits	43.1	56.9	49.4	49.1
储蓄存款	Saving Deposits	41.1	32.5	36.9	37.1
中资金融机构人民币贷款结构	Structure of RMB Loans in Chinese Financial Instituation	100	100	100	100
#短期贷款	Short Term Loans	75.2	72.9	34.5	31.5
中长期贷款	Medium and Long Term Loans	14.8	18.0	55.7	60.5
在校学生结构	Structure of Students Enrollment	100	100	100	100
大学生	University and College Students	7.1	12.5	25.3	26.9
中学生	Secondary Students	28.3	43.9	44.1	41.8
小学生	Primary Students	64.6	43.6	30.6	31.3
城市居民消费结构	Consumption Structure of Urban Households	100	100	100	100
#食 品	Food	56.5	44.5	35.9	35.6
衣 着	Clothing	10.8	6.4	6.8	6.9
家庭设备、用品及服务	Household Facilities, Articles and Services	10.1	7.7	5.8	5.9
交通和通信	Transportation and Communications	3.0	8.6	14.4	15.8
教育文化娱乐服务	Cultural, Education and Recreation Services	11.9	14.5	16.5	16.5
居 住	Residence	4.6	9.0	10.2	9.7
农村居民消费结构	Consumption Structure of Rural Households	100	100	100	100
#食 品	Food	46.4	44.0	36.8	37.8
衣 着	Clothing	8.5	4.9	5.1	5.2
家庭设备、用品及服务	Household Facilities, Articles and Services	10.2	5.4	6.3	6.0
交通和通信	Transportation and Communications	0.5	6.7	10.2	9.7
文教娱乐用品及服务	Culture, Education, Recreation Articles and Services	4.7	13.5	12.9	11.5
居 住	Residence	21.6	17.5	18.2	20.7
卫生机构数结构	Structure of Health Care Institutions	100	100	100	100
#医 院	Hospitals	6.0	10.4	19.3	20.0
卫生技术人员结构	Structure of Medical Professionals	100	100	100	100
#医 生	Doctors	49.2	46.6	42.5	41.7
护师、护士	Senior and Junior Nurses	27.6	34.4	38.1	38.7

表 2.4　各时期社会经济主要指标
MAJOR SOCIAL AND ECONOMIC INDICATORS OF EACH FIVE-YEAR PLAN PERIOD

时　期 Period		上海市生产总值(亿元) Gross Domestic Product (100 million yuan)	其中 of which 第一产业 Primary Industry	第二产业 Secondary Industry	第三产业 Tertiary Industry	全市财政收入(亿元) Total Fiscal Revenue (100 million yuan)	地方财政收入(亿元) Local Fiscal Revenue (10 000 million yuan)
"一五"时期	"First Five-Year Plan" Period	293.26	12.56	163.89	116.81	177.51	14.93
"二五"时期	"Second Five-Year Plan" Period	568.99	21.03	412.70	135.26	430.23	304.28
	1963～1965	304.94	17.28	220.81	66.85	224.52	172.51
"三五"时期	"Third Five-Year Plan" Period	657.06	37.64	487.88	131.54	466.76	374.19
"四五"时期	"Fourth Five-Year Plan" Period	918.76	42.75	708.84	167.17	680.97	633.79
"五五"时期	"Fifth Five-Year Plan" Period	1 309.61	49.26	1 004.23	256.12	886.60	797.56
"六五"时期	"Sixth Five-Year Plan" Period	1 871.24	74.20	1 349.98	447.06	1 089.20	846.92
"七五"时期	"Seventh Five-Year Plan" Period	3 162.79	132.52	2 105.23	925.04	1 342.38	846.96
"八五"时期	"Eighth Five-Year Plan" Period	8 017.61	213.47	4 698.27	3 105.87	2 422.69	1 006.06
"九五"时期	"Ninth Five-Year Plan" Period	19 157.33	365.76	9 434.90	9 356.67	6 233.99	1 962.85
"十五"时期	"Tenth Five-Year Plan" Period	34 872.39	402.49	16 579.69	17 890.21	14 714.28	4 792.93
	1953～2006	81 510.27	1 472.68	42 194.79	37 842.80	33 468.06	13 286.98

表 2.4 续表 continued

时　期 Period		地方财政支出(亿元) Local Fiscal Expenditure (100 million yuan)	工业总产值(亿元) Gross Output Value of Industry (100 million yuan)	全社会固定资产投资总额(亿元) Total Investment in Fixed Assets (100 million yuan)	外贸出口商品总额(亿美元) Total Exports Value of Foreign Trade (100 million USD)	社会消费品零售总额(亿元) Retail Sales of Consumer Goods (100 million yuan)
"一五"时期	"First Five-Year Plan" Period	12.25	512.03	19.29	17.46	121.02
"二五"时期	"Second Five-Year Plan" Period	60.79	1 069.50	55.60	31.00	145.82
	1963～1965	19.28	596.63	20.29	20.12	79.50
"三五"时期	"Third Five-Year Plan" Period	39.41	1 334.94	34.77	43.08	153.86
"四五"时期	"Fourth Five-Year Plan" Period	86.78	1 894.01	95.79	92.86	200.62
"五五"时期	"Fifth Five-Year Plan" Period	111.30	2 550.91	151.44	150.33	302.07
"六五"时期	"Sixth Five-Year Plan" Period	138.52	3 509.15	412.74	180.08	576.32
"七五"时期	"Seventh Five-Year Plan" Period	327.68	6 498.13	1 020.34	226.96	1 383.16
"八五"时期	"Eighth Five-Year Plan" Period	775.11	17 308.90	3 994.67	403.31	3 408.52
"九五"时期	"Ninth Five-Year Plan" Period	2 421.50	29 776.04	9 620.86	880.57	7 874.26
"十五"时期	"Tenth Five-Year Plan" Period	5 762.87	59 716.74	13 261.11	2 724.27	12 254.59
	1953～2006	11 569.29	144 398.21	32 612.00	5 905.81	29 860.15

表2.5 各时期社会经济主要指标平均增长率
GROWTH RATE OF MAJOR SOCIAL AND ECONOMIC INDICATORS OF EACH FIVE-YEAR PLAN PERIOD

单位:%

时期 Period	上海市生产总值 Gross Domestic Product	其中 of which 第一产业 Primary Industry	第二产业 Secondary Industry	第三产业 Tertiary Industry	全市财政收入 Total Fiscal Revenue	地方财政收入 Local Fiscal Revenue
"一五"时期 "First Five-Year Plan" Period	13.8	3.3	18.4	8.3	18.9	12.6
"二五"时期 "Second Five-Year Plan" Period	1.6	1.3	4.1	-3.1	6.2	57.2
1963～1965	17.0	11.6	21.8	5.6	10.5	12.3
"三五"时期 "Third Five-Year Plan" Period	8.7	3.3	9.7	5.7	6.5	9.7
"四五"时期 "Fourth Five-Year Plan" Period	6.6	-1.6	7.1	6.2	5.2	6.4
"五五"时期 "Fifth Five-Year Plan" Period	8.4	0.9	8.6	8.6	6.2	5.1
"六五"时期 "Sixth Five-Year Plan" Period	9.1	4.3	8.3	12.3	5.8	1.1
"七五"时期 "Seventh Five-Year Plan" Period	5.7	1.2	5.0	8.0	1.5	-1.6
"八五"时期 "Eighth Five-Year Plan" Period	13.1	1.4	13.9	12.8	19.8	6.0
"九五"时期 "Ninth Five-Year Plan" Period	11.5	3.4	9.7	15.5	20.1	17.0
"十五"时期 "Tenth Five-Year Plan" Period	11.9	-1.3	13.3	10.9	18.5	23.6
1953～2006	9.5	2.1	10.4	8.3	10.8	12.7

表2.5 续表 continued

单位:%

时期	Period	地方财政支出 Local Fiscal Expenditure	工业总产值 Gross Output Value of Industry	全社会固定资产投资总额 Total Investment in Fixed Assets	外贸出口商品总额 Total Exports Value of Foreign Trade	社会消费品零售总额 Retail Sales of Consumer Goods
"一五"时期	"First Five-Year Plan" Period	12.3	14.5	23.1	30.6	5.6
"二五"时期	"Second Five-Year Plan" Period	0.6	4.9	26.5	4.2	1.2
	1963～1965	25.2	18.8	31.4	11.4	-0.1
"三五"时期	"Third Five-Year Plan" Period	11.2	10.2	-3.6	2.5	3.3
"四五"时期	"Fourth Five-Year Plan" Period	15.5	7.5	19.4	20.7	8.4
"五五"时期	"Fifth Five-Year Plan" Period	-6.3	7.6	-2.4	14.0	11.0
"六五"时期	"Sixth Five-Year Plan" Period	19.2	7.7	20.6	-4.7	16.6
"七五"时期	"Seventh Five-Year Plan" Period	10.4	5.9	18.7	9.6	14.0
"八五"时期	"Eighth Five-Year Plan" Period	28.8	18.0	45.4	16.8	25.8
"九五"时期	"Ninth Five-Year Plan" Period	18.4	12.3	6.2	17.0	12.2
"十五"时期	"Tenth Five-Year Plan" Period	21.7	19.2	11.9	29.0	9.8
	1953～2006	13.3	11.2	15.3	13.5	10.0

表 2.6　国民经济主要指标比上年增长(1978～2006)

GROWTH RATE OF MAJOR NATIONAL ECONOMIC INDICATORS OVER PRECEDING YEAR

单位:%

年　份 Year	上海市 生产总值 Gross Domestic Product	全　市 财政收入 Fiscal Revenue	地　方 财政收入 Local Fiscal Revenue	地　方 财政支出 Local Fiscal Expenditure	工　业 总产值 Gross Output Value of Industry	全社会固定资产 投资总额 Total Investment in Fixed Assets
1978	15.8	19.2	14.6	51.4	12.1	55.1
1979	7.4	1.1	2.1	4.0	8.6	27.5
1980	8.4	3.2	1.2	-29.1	6.5	27.7
1981	5.6	2.9	-0.2	-0.6	3.7	20.2
1982	7.2	-1.9	-3.6	8.5	4.7	30.7
1983	7.8	1.8	-6.9	8.3	7.0	6.4
1984	11.6	5.6	4.8	35.4	9.9	21.5
1985	13.4	22.3	12.4	51.9	13.5	28.5
1986	4.4	-2.3	-2.6	28.2	5.5	23.9
1987	7.5	-6.3	-5.8	-8.9	6.7	26.8
1988	10.1	8.4	-4.3	22.3	10.5	31.7
1989	3.0	13.6	3.3	11.3	3.0	-12.4
1990	3.5	-4.3	0.1	3.1	4.0	5.7
1991	7.1	14.2	5.1	13.9	14.1	13.7
1992	14.8	4.8	5.7	10.4	20.2	38.4
1993	15.1	29.2	30.6	36.1	20.0	83.0
1994	14.5	40.1	-27.7	52.3	18.2	71.8
1995	14.3	14.1	29.6	36.0	17.4	42.6
1996	13.1	24.4	26.9	27.9	15.5	21.9
1997	12.8	22.6	22.1	25.2	14.5	1.3
1998	10.3	7.0	11.3	12.1	7.8	-0.6
1999	10.4	21.3	10.1	13.7	10.5	-5.5
2000	11.0	26.0	15.3	14.0	13.5	0.7
2001	10.5	13.9	24.6	16.6	16.4	6.7
2002	11.3	25.6	44.5	40.9	14.6	9.6
2003	12.3	28.5	32.5	25.6	31.4	12.1
2004	14.2	27.0	24.5	26.6	20.3	25.8
2005	11.1	13.9	20.7	19.0	13.9	14.8
2006	12.0	17.2	11.6	9.2	13.9	10.8

表 2.6 续表 continued

单位:%

年 份 Year	外贸进出口总额 Total Value of Foreign Import and Export	其中 of which 出口总额 Export	社会消费品零售总额 Retail Sales of Consumer Goods	直接吸收外资合同金额 Contracted Foreign Direct Investment	直接吸收外资实际到位金额 Actually Absorbed Foreign Direct Investment	港口货物吞吐量 Cargo Handled at Ports	城市居民家庭人均可支配收入 Per Capita Annual Disposable Income of Urban Households
1978	30.4	30.3	9.8			30.6	
1979	28.2	27.0	26.2			5.0	
1980	16.2	16.1	17.8			1.6	
1981	-7.9	-10.8	10.3	1.0 倍	…	-1.7	
1982	-6.2	-5.3	1.2	1.8 倍	…	7.7	3.5
1983	6.3	1.2	12.1	1.8 倍	2.7 倍	2.4	4.8
1984	6.3	-1.7	22.9	3.1 倍	1.5 倍	9.5	20.7
1985	17.6	-6.3	40.1	56.4	1.2 倍	12.2	28.9
1986	0.6	6.6	13.5	-68.9	58.1	11.6	20.3
1987	15.2	16.1	14.4	35.8	1.2 倍	1.8	11.1
1988	20.8	10.7	31.3	28.7	71.7	3.8	19.9
1989	8.3	9.3	12.0	6.6	15.9	9.6	14.6
1990	-5.3	5.7	0.7	20.9	-58.1	-4.4	10.4
1991	8.2	7.9	14.4	30.4	-1.1	5.2	13.9
1992	21.3	14.2	21.7	5.7 倍	6.2 倍	11.0	21.1
1993	30.5	12.6	34.3	1.0 倍	84.1	8.0	42.1
1994	24.6	23.0	23.5	42.3	39.4	-5.8	37.2
1995	19.9	27.5	25.9	0.2	0.6	-0.1	22.2
1996	17.0	14.3	19.7	8.4	45.1	-1.0	13.8
1997	11.2	11.2	14.1	-8.4	2.0		3.4
1998	26.6	8.4	11.0	9.9	-24.3	-0.1	4.0
1999	23.2	17.7	8.1	-29.8	-16.2	13.7	24.6
2000	41.7	35.0	8.3	55.7	3.7	9.7	7.2
2001	11.3	9.0	8.1	15.4	39.0	8.1	9.9
2002	19.3	16.0	9.3	43.4	14.5	19.4	11.5
2003	54.7	51.2	9.1	23.5	30.1	19.8	12.2
2004	42.4	51.6	10.5	12.6	11.8	19.8	12.2
2005	16.5	23.4	11.9	18.3	4.7	16.9	11.8
2006	22.1	25.2	13.0	5.4	3.8	21.3	10.8

表 2.7　上海社会经济主要指标占全国比重(2006)
PERCENTAGE OF THE NATIONAL TOTAL OF SHANGHAI'S MAJOR SOCIAL AND ECONOMIC INDICATORS

指　标	Indicators	全　国 Country	上　海 Shanghai	上海占全国比重(%) Percentage of the National Total(%)
土地面积(万平方公里)	Land Area (10 000 sq. km)	960	0.63	0.1
生产总值(亿元)	Gross Domestic Product (100 million yuan)	209 407	10 366.37	5.0
第一产业	Primary Industry	24 700	93.80	0.4
第二产业	Secondary Industry	102 004	5 028.37	4.9
#工　业	Industry	90 351	4 670.11	5.2
第三产业	Tertiary Industry	82 703	5 244.20	6.3
财政收入(亿元)	Total Fiscal Revenue (100 million yuan)	39 344	4 799	12.2
港口货物吞吐量(亿吨)	Port Cargo Handled at Seaports (100 millions tons)	45.6	5.37	11.8
国际标准集装箱吞吐量(万 TEU)	International Container Throughput Capacity (10 000 TEU)	9 300	2 172	23.4
邮电业务总量(亿元)	Revenue of Post and Telecommunication (100 million yuan)	15 321	555	3.6
全社会固定资产投资总额(亿元)	Total Investment in Fixed Assets (100 million yuan)	109 870	3 925	3.6
社会消费品零售总额(亿元)	Retail Sales of Consumer Goods (100 million yuan)	76 410	3 360.41	4.4
口岸进出口商品总额(亿美元)	Total Port Exports and Imports (100 million USD)	17 607	4 287.54	24.4
进口额	Imports	7 916	1 621.89	20.5
出口额	Exports	9 691	2 665.65	27.5
外商直接投资实际到位金额(亿美元)	Foreign Direct Investment Actually Absorbed (100 million USD)	694.70	71.07	10.2
国际旅游入境人数(万人次)	Number of International Tourists (10 000 person-times)	12 494	605.67	4.8
研究与试验发展经费支出(亿元)	Research and Development Expenditure (100 million yuan)	2 943	256.78	8.7
图书出版量(亿册/张)	Books Published (100 million copies/signatures)	62	2.54	4.1
期　刊(亿册)	Periodicals (100 million copies)	30.0	1.83	6.1
报纸出版量(亿份)	Newspapers Published (100 million copies)	416	17.89	4.3
医　生(万人)	Doctors (10 000 persons)	197.0	4.55	2.3
医院床位数(万张)	Beds in Hospitals (10 000 beds)	322	9.28	2.9

表 2.8 主要年份人大情况
BASIC STATISTIC OF SHANGHAI MUNICIPAL PEOPLE'S CONGRESS IN MAIN YEARS

类 别	Types	2000	2005	2006
全国人大代表人数(人)	Number of National Congress(Person)	68	66	66
#女 性	Female	17	17	17
全国人大代表提出议案(件)	Proposals Offered by National Congress Representations (Case)		65	57
市人大代表人数(人)	Number of Municipal Congress Representatives(Person)	865	869	869
#女 性	Female	203	210	208
市人大常委人数(人)	Number of Municipal Standing Committee(Person)	65	52	64
#女 性	Female	13	9	11
市人大代表提出议案(件)	Proposals Offered by Municipal Congress Representatives (Case)		102	58
区县人大代表人数(人)	Number of District Level Congress Representatives (Person)	4 944	4 865	4 961
#女 性	Female	1 451	1 509	1 561
区县人大常委人数(人)	Number of District Level Standing Committee(Person)	432	362	416
#女 性	Female	67	83	87
区县人大代表提出议案(件)	Proposals Offered by District Level Congress Representatives(Case)		109	150

注：本表数据由市人大代表工作委员会提供。
Note: Data in this table are provided by Shanghai Committee of People's Congress.

表 2.9 主要年份政协情况
BASIC STATISTICS ON SHANGHAI MUNICIPAL PEOPLE'S POLITICAL CONSULTATIVE CONFERENCE IN MAIN YEARS

类 别	Types	2000	2005	2006
全国政协委员人数(人)	Number of National Commissary (person)	104	115	113
#女 性	Female	20	26	26
全国政协委员提出议案(件)	Proposals Offered by National Commissary (Case)		132	282
市政协委员人数(人)	Number of Municipal Commissary(person)	729	794	791
#女 性	Female	120	144	144
市政协常委人数(人)	Number of Municipal Standing Committee(person)	121	129	131
#女 性	Female	20	17	18
市政协委员提出议案(件)	Proposals Offered by Municipal Commissary (Case)	1 197	1 144	962
区县政协委员人数(人)	Number of District Level Commissary(person)	4 802	5 036	5 004
#女 性	Female	1 230	1 313	1 310
区县政协常委人数(人)	Number of District Level Standing Committee(person)	707	707	691
#女 性	Female	174	170	160
区县政协委员提出议案(件)	Offering Proposals Offered by District Level Commissary (Case)		3 666	3 480

注：本表数据由市政协提供。
Note: Data in this table are provided by Shanghai Municipal People's Political Consultative Conference.

上 / 海 / 统 / 计 / 年 / 鉴

主要统计指标解释

■ 登记注册类型

登记注册类型是以工商行政管理机关登记注册的具有法人资格的各类企业为划分对象。产业活动单位和行政机关、事业单位、社会团体及其他经济组织参照执行。

国有企业指企业全部资产归国家所有，并按《中华人民共和国企业法人登记管理条例》规定登记注册的非公司制的经济组织。不包括有限责任公司中的国有独资公司。

集体企业指企业资产归集体所有，并按《中华人民共和国企业法人登记管理条例》规定登记注册的经济组织。

股份合作企业指以合作制为基础，由企业职工共同出资入股，吸收一定比例的社会资产投资组建，实行自主经营，自负盈亏，共同劳动，民主管理，按劳动分配与按股分红相结合的一种集体经济组织。

联营企业指两个及两个以上相同或不同所有制性质的企业法人或事业单位法人，按自愿、平等、互利的原则，共同投资组成的经济组织。联营企业包括国有联营企业、集体联营企业、国有与集体联营企业和其他联营企业。

有限责任公司指根据《中华人民共和国公司登记管理条例》规定登记注册，由2个以上，50个以下的股东共同出资，每个股东以其所认缴的出资额对公司承担有限责任，公司以其全部资产对其债务承担责任的经济组织。有限责任公司包括国有独资公司以及其他有限责任公司。

股份有限公司指根据《中华人民共和国公司登记管理条例》规定登记注册，其全部注册资本由等额股份构成并通过发行股票筹集资本，股东以其认购的股份对公司承担有限责任，公司以其全部资产对其债务承担责任的经济组织。

私营企业指由自然人投资设立或由自然人控股，以雇佣劳动为基础的营利性经济组织。包括按照《公司法》、《合伙企业法》、《私营企业暂行条列》规定登记注册的私营有限责任公司、私营股份有限公司、私营合伙企业和私营独资企业。

港澳台商投资合资经营企业指港澳台地区投资者与内地的企业依照《中华人民共和国中外合资经营企业法》及有关法律的规定，按合同规定的比例投资设立、分享利润和分担风险的企业。

港澳台商投资合作经营企业指港澳台地区投资者与内地企业依照《中华人民共和国中外合作经营企业法》及有关法律的规定，依照合作合同的约定进行投资或提供条件设立、分享利润和分担风险的企业。

港澳台商独资经营企业指依照《中华人民共和国外资企业法》及有关法律的规定，在内地由港澳台商地区投资者全额投资设立的企业。

港澳台商投资股份有限公司指根据国家有关规定，经外经贸部依法批准设立，其中港、澳、台商的股本占公司注册资本的比例达25%以上的股份有限公司。凡其中港、澳、台商的股本占公司注册资本的比例小于25%的，属于内资企业中股份有限公司。

中外合资经营企业指外国企业或外国人与中国内地企业依照《中华人民共和国中外合资经营企业法》及有关法律的规定，按合同规定的比例投资设立、分享利润和分担风险的企业。

中外合作经营企业指外国企业或外国人与中国内地企业依照《中华人民共和国中外合作经营企业法》及有关法律的规定，依照合作合同的约定进行投资或提供条件设立、分享利润和分担风险的企业。

外资企业指依照《中华人民共和国外资企业法》及有关法律的规定，在中国内地由外国投资者全额投资设立的企业。

外商投资股份有限公司指根据国家有关规定，经外经贸部依法批准设立，其中外资的股本占公司注册资本的比例达25%以上的股份有限公司。凡其中外资股本占公司注册资本的比例小于25%的，属于内资企业中的股份有限公司。

■ 国民经济行业分类

《国民经济行业分类》国家标准于1984年首次发布，1994年对其进行了第一次修订，2002年为第二次修订。

本年鉴的行业分类使用2002年修订的行业分类标准。

2002年新行业分类标准按照国际通行的经济活动同质性原则划分行业，进一步打破了部门管理界限，对原标准中不符合这一原则的分类进行了调整；根据我国社会经济活动的发展状况，重点加强了第三产业的分类，新增了大量服务业方面的活动类别；对新标准的每一个行业小类，全部与国际标准产业分类的最细一层分类建立

主要统计指标解释

了对应关系。新修订的国民经济行业分类主要目的之一是与联合国的《全部经济活动的国际标准产业分类》接轨,准确反映一定时期内国民经济行业的构成状况。

■ 各个计划时期

表内所用各个"时期"代表的年份如下:恢复时期为1950到1952年;第一个五年计划时期(简称"一五"时期)为1953到1957年;第二个五年计划时期(简称"二五"时期)为1958到1962年;第三个五年计划时期(简称"三五"时期)为1966到1970年;第四个五年计划时期(简称"四五"时期)为1971到1975年;第五个五年计划时期(简称"五五"时期)为1976到1980年;第六个五年计划时期(简称"六五"时期)为1981到1985年;第七个五年计划时期(简称"七五"时期)为1986到1990年;第八个五年计划时期(简称"八五"时期)为1991到1995年;第九个五年计划时期(简称"九五"时期)为1996到2000年;第十个五年计划时期(简称"十五"时期)为2001到2005年;第十一个五年计划时期(简称"十一五"时期)为2006到2010年。

■ 可比价格

指在不同时期的价值指标对比时，扣除了价格变动的因素,以确切反映物量的变化。按可比价格计算有两种方法:一种是直接用产品产量乘某一年的不变价格计算;另一种是用价格指数换算。

■ 不变价格

指以同类产品某年的平均价格作为固定价格，用于计算各年的产品价值。按不变价格计算的产品价值消除了价格变动因素，不同时期对比可以反映生产的发展速度。新中国成立后,随着工农业产品价格水平的变化,国家统计局先后五次制定了全国统一的工业产品不变价格和农业产品不变价格。从1952年到1957年使用1952年工(农)业产品不变价格,从1957年到1970年使用1957年不变价格，从1971年到1980年使用1970年不变价格,从1981年到1990年使用1980年不变价格,从1991年到2000年使用1990年不变价格,从2001年开始使用2000年不变价格。

■ 指　数

指数是一种表明社会经济现象动态的相对数。运用指数可以测定不能直接相加和直接对比的社会经济现象的总动态；可以分析社会经济现象总变动中各因素变动的影响程度；可以研究总平均指标变动中各组标志水平和总体结构变动的作用。它是在把各个年份的产值换算成可比价格的基础上，根据定基数等于相应各个环比指数的连乘积这个换算关系计算出来的。

本年鉴所列的上海市生产总值、工业总产值、农业总产值等指标增长速度，就是分别使用上海市生产总值指数、工业总产值指数、农业总产值指数直接计算的。

■ 平均每年增长速度

在我国计算平均增长速度有两种方法。一种是习惯上经常使用的"水平法",又称几何平均法,是以间隔期最后一年的水平同基期水平对比来计算平均每年增长（或下降)速度;另一种是"累计法",又称代数平均法或方程法，是以间隔期内各年水平的总和同基期水平对比来计算平均每年增长(或下降)速度。

在一般正常情况下，两种方法计算的平均每年增长速度比较接近。但在经济发展不平衡,出现大起大落时,两种方法计算的结果差别较大。

本年鉴内所列的平均每年增长速度，除固定资产投资、直接吸收外资是用"累计法"计算以外,其余均用"水平法"计算。从某年到某年平均增长速度的年份,均不包括基期年在内。如1953~2006年平均增长速度是以1952年为基期计算的,余类推。

■ 国有企业

指企业全部资产归国家所有,并按《中华人民共和国企业法人登记管理条例》规定登记注册的非公司制的经济组织。不包括有限责任公司中的国有独资公司。

■ 集体企业

集体企业指企业资产归集体所有,并按《中华人民共和国企业法人登记管理条例》规定登记注册的经济组织。

SHANGHAI STATISTICAL YEARBOOK

EXPLANATORY NOTES TO MAJOR STATISTICAL INDICATORS

□ Registration Categories

Registration Categories are used to classify all kinds of enterprises that have the legal person status and have registered with the industrial and commercial administrations. The classification of business units, administrative and public institutions, social organizations and other economical bodies may refer to it.

The state-owned enterprises are economic organizations whose assets are solely owned by the state and whose registrations are made according to "Regulations of the People's Republic of China for Controlling the Registration of Enterprises as Legal Persons"excluding the state-owned liability limited companies.

The collective-owned enterprises are economic organizations whose assets are owned by collecting and whose registration are made according to "Regulations of the People's Republic of China for Controlling the Registration of Enterprises as Legal Persons."

Share-holding cooperative enterprises are a kind of collective economic organizations based on a cooperative system. In addition to the shares bought by their workers and staff, the enterprises also absorb a certain percentage of social capital. They enjoy the autonomy in operation and are responsible for their own losses and profits. The share-holders work together, conduct democratic management, and combine labor-based distribution with share-based dividents.

Joint-owned enterprises refer to economic organizations set up with joint investment from legal persons of two or more enterprises of different ownerships or institutions according to principle of voluntary participation, equality and mutual benefit. They include state-owned joint operation enterprises, collective joint operation enterprises, state-collective joint operation enterprises and other types of joint operation enterprises.

A company with limited liability is a company registered in accordance with the "Regulations of the People's Republic of China on Administration of Company Registration." Its investment comes from more than 2 and less than 50 shareholders. Each shareholder assumes limited liability for the company according to his subscription to capital stock. The company assumes liabilities for its debts according to all its assets. Such economic organizations include solely state-invested companies and other types of companies with limited liability.

A share-holding company with limited liability refers to economic organizations registered in accordance with the "Regulations of the People's Republic of China on Administration of Company Registration." All its registered capital is composed of shares of equal value and its capital is collected through share issuing. The shareholders bear limited liability for the company according to the amount of shares they have bought from the company and the company assumes liabilities for its debts according all its assets.

A private enterprise refers to profit-making economic organizations set up with investment from natural persons or with controlling interest in the hands of natural persons who employ laborers for operation. Such enterprises include private companies with limited liability, private joint stock companies limited, private partnership enterprises and solely individual-invested enterprises, which are registered according to the "Company Law", "Partnership Enterprises Law" and "Interim Regulations of Private Enterprises."

The joint ventures with investment from Hong Kong, Macao and Taiwan refer to those established according to the "Law of the People's Republic of China on Chinese-foreign Joint Ventures" and regulations stipulated in relevant laws, by investors from those regions and the Chinese mainland enterprises with contracted share of investment and sharing profits and ventures between the parties.

Cooperative businesses with investment from Hong Kong, Macao and Taiwan refer to enterprises jointly set up by investors from Hong Kong, Macao and Taiwan and mainland enterprises according to the "Law of the People's Republic of China on Chinese-foreign Contractural Joint Ventures" and other relevant regulations. They invest or provide conditions for establishment, decide profit distribution, and share risks according to provisions prescribed in the cooperative venture contracts.

Solely Hong Kong, Macao and Taiwan Funded enterprises refer to enterprises set up on the mainland according to the "Law of the People's Republic of China on Foreign Capital Enterprises and solely invested by investors from Hong Kong, Macao and Taiwan."

A share-holding company with limited liability with investment from Hong Kong, Macao and Taiwan refers to any joint stock company limited that is set up according relevant state regulations

EXPLANATORY NOTES TO MAJOR STATISTICAL INDICATORS

and is approved by the Ministry of Foreign Economic Relations and Trade. The investment from Hong Kong, Macao and Taiwan investors must account more than 25 percent of the company's total capital. If such investment is less than 25 percent, it shall be classified as a joint stock company limited invested by domestic investors.

A Sino-foreign joint venture refers to any enterprise that is jointly set up by foreign enterprises or foreigners with Chinese enterprises in accordance with the "Law of the People's Republic of China on Joint Ventures with Chinese and Foreign Investment." The investors shall put in investment, share profits and risks according to the contract on the joint venture.

Sino-foreign cooperative Businesses refers to the enterprises set up by foreign enterprises or foreigners with Chinese enterprises as their partners, in line with "The Sino-foreign Cooperative Ventures Law of the People's Republic of China" and other relevant laws and regulations. The partners of the cooperative ventures will invest, take profits and share risks according to the requirements of stipulated in the contract.

A Solely Foreign-Funded enterprise refers to any enterprise that is set up on the Chinese mainland according to the "Law of the People's Republic of China on Foreign-Capital Enterprises" and with all its investment coming from foreign investors.

The foreign-invested joint stock company limited refers to any joint stock company limited that is set up according to relevant state regulations and is approved by the Ministry of Foreign Economic Relations and Trade. The foreign investment must account more than 25 percent of the company's total capital. If such investment is less than 25 percent, it shall be classified as a joint stock company limited invested by Chinese investors.

□ Classification of the Sectors of the National Economy

Classification of the Sectors of the National Economy was first published in 1984 and revisions were made into it in 1994 and 2002 respectively.

This Yearbook follows standards in the 2002 version of the Classification of the Sectors of the National Economy.

In the 2002 version, economic sectors are classified in accordance with the international categories of the economic activities, abolishing in definition between different administrative departments. Given the development of China's social and economic activities, more detailed classification is made of the service sector. The further breakdown of each economic sector in the latest version is geared to the most specific categorization in international practice. The latest version aims at, among others, an objective and precise presentation of the composition of the national economy in a certain period.

□ Various Planning Periods

The conventional division of time period in this statistical yearbook is as follows: Rehabilitation Period, 1950-1952; The First Five-Year Plan period (cited as first-five period), 1953-1957; The Second Five-Year Plan period (cited as second-five period), 1958-1962; The Third Five-Year Plan period (cited as third-five period), 1966-1970; The Fourth Five-Year Plan period (cited as fourth-five period), 1971-1975; The Fifth Five-Year Plan period (cited as fifth-five period), 1976-1980; The Sixth Five-Year Plan period (cited as sixth-five period), 1981-1985; The Seventh Five-Year Plan period (cited as seventh-five period), 1986-1990; The Eight Five-Year Plan period (cited as eighth-five period), 1991-1995; The Ninth Five-Year Plan period (cited as ninth-five period), 1996-2000; The Tenth Five-Year Plan period (cited as tenth-five period), 2001-2005; The eleventh Five-Year Plan period (cited as eleventh-five period),2006-2010.

□ Comparable Prices

Comparable Prices are applied when comparing indicators over time to reflect accurately the changes in real term. Two methods are used for calculating comparable prices: 1. output by constant price of certain year; 2. output in current prices divided by relevant price index.

□ Constant Price

Constant Price refers to the average price of a given product in certain year, which is used for comparison of output value over time. As the output value at constant prices removes the factor of price changes, it reflects the trend of production development over time. Since 1949, with the changes in general price level, National Bureau of Statistics has issued nationally unified constant prices five times: the 1952 constant prices for 1949-1957; the 1957 constant prices for 1957-1971; the 1970 constant prices for 1971-1981; the 1980 constant prices for 1981-1990; the 1990 constant prices for 1991-2000; and the 2000 constant prices have been used since 2001.

□ Index

Index refers to the relative figures indicating social and eco-

EXPLANATORY NOTES TO MAJOR STATISTICAL INDICATORS

nomic phenomena and developments. Index is used to evaluate the overall development of social and economic phenomena which can not be determined by simple addition or direct comparison. It is also used to analyze the outcome of various changes in the general phenomenon movement of social and economic development, and to study the level of each sub-index in the changes of general average index and the role of the changes of the overall structure. It is calculated at the comparable prices conversed from the output value of each year, using the formula of index number with fixed base period equal to the continuous product of its relative chain index.

The increases of Shanghai Gross Domestic Product, industrial output value and agricultural output value compared with the previous year, which are listed in this yearbook, are calculated according to Shanghai GDP index, industrial output value index and agricultural output value index.

□ Average Annual Growth Rate

Two methods for calculating Average Annual Growth Rate are applied in China, one is often called "level approach" or geometry average, which is derived by comparing the growth rate for the last year of the interval with that of the beginning year; the other is called "accumulating approach" or algebraic average or equation method, which is calculated by comparing the total growth rate of each year for the interval with that of base year.

Usually the results calculated by the two methods are fairly close, but they differ sharply when imbalance occurred in economic development with striking fluctuations in growth.

The Average Annual Growth Rates listed in this statistical yearbook are calculated by "level approach" except for the growth rate of investment in fixed assets and foreign capital absorbed. The base years are not listed when the years are listed for average annual growth rates for instance, the average annual growth rate of 1953-2006 is calculated with the base year 1952, and the analogy of this is also for the rest.

□ State-owned Enterprises

State-owned Enterprises refer to non-corporation economic units where the entire assets are owned by the state and which have registered in accordance with the Regulation of the People's Republic of China on the Management of Registration of Corporate Enterprises. Excluded from this category are sole state-funded corporations in the limited liability corporations.

□ Collective-owned Enterprises

Collective-owned Enterprises refer to economic units where the assets are owned collectively and which have registered in accordance with the Regulation of the People's Republic of China on the Management of Registration of Corporate Enterprises.

第三篇

CHAPTER 3

人口和劳动力

POPULATION AND LABOUR FORCE

表3.1 户籍人口、户数、人口密度和平均期望寿命(1978～2006)
TOTAL HOUSEHOLDS, REGISTERED POPULATION, DENSITY OF POPULATION AND LIFE EXPENDENCY

年份 Year	总户数 (万户) Total Households (10 000 households)	年末户籍人口(万人) Year-end Registered Population (10 000 persons)	按性别分 Grouped by Sex		按农业非农业分 Grouped by Agriculture and Non-agriculture	
			男性 Male	女性 Female	农业 Agriculture	非农业 Non-agriculture
1978	291.69	1 098.28	542.70	555.58	453.05	645.23
1979	296.71	1 132.14	560.40	571.74	444.76	687.38
1980	303.87	1 146.52	569.30	577.22	444.09	702.43
1981	314.56	1 162.84	578.76	584.08	447.76	715.08
1982	321.71	1 180.51	588.82	591.69	449.20	731.31
1983	330.60	1 194.01	596.67	597.34	448.15	745.86
1984	340.78	1 204.78	602.59	602.19	444.03	760.75
1985	351.72	1 216.69	609.70	606.99	440.32	776.37
1986	364.92	1 232.33	618.88	613.45	429.77	802.56
1987	380.19	1 249.51	628.78	620.73	427.20	822.31
1988	394.95	1 262.42	635.82	626.60	423.49	838.93
1989	406.82	1 276.45	643.51	632.94	420.61	855.84
1990	415.28	1 283.35	647.13	636.22	418.89	864.46
1991	425.84	1 287.20	649.03	638.17	417.32	869.88
1992	431.67	1 289.37	649.97	639.40	413.82	875.55
1993	438.69	1 294.74	652.92	641.82	401.28	893.46
1994	444.38	1 298.81	655.14	643.67	388.32	910.49
1995	450.76	1 301.37	656.48	644.89	379.67	921.70
1996	457.49	1 304.43	657.86	646.57	372.29	932.14
1997	461.40	1 305.46	657.93	647.53	362.43	943.03
1998	465.72	1 306.58	658.22	648.36	352.93	953.65
1999	470.11	1 313.12	661.19	651.93	343.49	969.63
2000	475.73	1 321.63	665.51	656.12	335.47	986.16
2001	478.92	1 327.14	668.32	658.82	328.07	999.07
2002	481.77	1 334.23	672.05	662.18	315.42	1 018.81
2003	486.06	1 341.77	675.47	666.30	300.38	1 041.39
2004	490.58	1 352.39	680.38	672.01	254.79	1 097.60
2005	496.69	1 360.26	683.51	676.75	211.32	1 148.94
2006	499.54	1 368.08	686.66	681.42	194.78	1 173.30

注：户数和年末户籍人口由市公安局提供，平均期望寿命由市卫生局提供。
Note: The figures of total households and year-end registered population are provided by Shanghai Municipal Public Security Bureau, and the figures of life Expendency are provided by Shanghai Municipal Health Bureau.

表3.1 续表 continued

年份 Year	非农业人口占总人口比重(%) Percertage of Non-agriculture Population in Total(%)	平均每户人口(人) Average Persons Per Household (person)	人口密度(人/平方公里) Density of Population (person/sq·km)	平均期望寿命(岁) Life Expectancy (year)	其中 of which 男性 Male	女性 Female
1978	58.7	3.8	1 776	73.35	70.69	74.78
1979	60.7	3.8	1 830	73.14	70.64	75.48
1980	61.3	3.8	1 854	73.33	71.25	75.36
1981	61.5	3.7	1 880	73.38	71.28	75.47
1982	61.9	3.7	1 908	74.04	71.77	76.25
1983	62.5	3.6	1 930	73.23	71.15	75.26
1984	63.1	3.5	1 948	73.9	71.73	76.17
1985	63.8	3.5	1 967	74.27	72.14	76.37
1986	65.1	3.4	1 944	74.71	72.54	76.85
1987	65.8	3.3	1 971	74.46	72.32	76.60
1988	66.5	3.2	1 991	74.63	72.50	76.77
1989	67.0	3.1	2 013	74.98	72.85	77.12
1990	67.4	3.1	2 024	75.46	73.16	77.74
1991	67.6	3.0	2 030	75.79	73.58	77.95
1992	67.9	3.0	2 034	75.97	74.04	77.91
1993	69.0	3.0	2 042	75.97	74.04	77.91
1994	70.1	2.9	2 048	76.26	74.29	78.23
1995	70.8	2.9	2 052	76.03	74.11	77.97
1996	71.5	2.9	2 057	76.11	74.07	78.21
1997	72.2	2.8	2 059	77.20	75.18	79.21
1998	73.0	2.8	2 061	77.03	75.06	79.02
1999	73.8	2.8	2 071	78.44	76.38	80.53
2000	74.6	2.8	2 084	78.77	76.71	80.81
2001	75.3	2.8	2 093	79.66	77.47	81.83
2002	76.4	2.8	2104	79.52	77.36	81.63
2003	77.6	2.8	2 116	79.80	77.78	81.81
2004	81.2	2.8	2 133	80.29	78.08	82.48
2005	84.5	2.7	2 145	80.13	77.89	82.36
2006	85.8	2.7	2 158	80.97	78.64	83.29

表3.2 各区、县土地面积、户籍人口、户数及人口密度（2006）
LAND AREA, HOUSEHOLDS, REGISTERED POPULATION AND DENSITY OF POPULATION IN DISTRICTS AND COUNTIES

地 区	District	土地面积（平方公里）Land Area (sq. km)	户 数（万户）Total Households (10 000 households)	年末户籍人口（万人）Year-end Registered Population (10 000 persons)	平均每户人口（人）Average Persons Per Household (person)	人口密度（人/平方公里）Density of Population (person/sq·km)
全 市	**Total**	**6 340.50**	**499.54**	**1 368.08**	**2.7**	**2 158**
浦东新区	Pudong New Area	532.75	70.11	187.56	2.7	3 521
黄 浦 区	Huangpu	12.41	19.41	60.19	3.1	48 501
卢 湾 区	Luwan	8.05	10.82	31.37	2.9	38 969
徐 汇 区	Xuhui	54.76	31.99	88.75	2.8	16 207
长 宁 区	Changning	38.30	21.35	61.42	2.9	16 037
静 安 区	Jing'an	7.62	10.64	30.96	2.9	40 630
普 陀 区	Putuo	54.83	31.8	85.97	2.7	15 679
闸 北 区	Zhabei	29.26	25.48	69.86	2.7	23 876
虹 口 区	Hongkou	23.48	28.06	78.70	2.8	33 518
杨 浦 区	Yangpu	60.73	37.85	107.75	2.8	17 742
宝 山 区	Baoshan	270.99	31.42	81.59	2.6	3 011
闵 行 区	Minhang	370.75	33.03	85.53	2.6	2 307
嘉 定 区	Jiading	464.20	18.28	53.25	2.9	1 147
金 山 区	Jinshan	586.05	17.45	52.29	3.0	892
松 江 区	Songjiang	605.64	17.48	53.21	3.0	879
青 浦 区	Qingpu	670.14	15.35	45.63	3.0	681
南 汇 区	Nanhui	677.66	29.11	72.73	2.5	1 073
奉 贤 区	Fengxian	687.39	20.96	51.33	2.4	747
崇 明 县	Chongming	1 185.49	28.95	69.98	2.4	590

注：土地面积由市民政局提供，户数、年末户籍人口由市公安局提供。
Note: The figures of land area are provided by Shanghai Civil Affairs Bureau. The figures of total households and year-end registered population are provided by Shanghai Municipal Public Security Bureau.

表 3.3 各区、县土地面积、常住人口及人口密度（2006）
LAND AREA, RESIDENT POPULATION AND DENSITY OF POPULATION IN DISTRICTS AND COUNTIES

地区	District	土地面积（平方公里）Land Area (sq. km)	年末常住人口（万人）Year-end Resident Population (10 000 persons)	其中 of which 外来人口 Floating People	人口密度（人/平方公里）Density of Population (person/sq · km)
全　市	**Total**	**6 340.50**	**1 815.08**	**467.26**	**2 863**
浦东新区	Pudong New Area	532.75	285.30	82.12	5 355
黄浦区	Huangpu	12.41	51.45	7.62	41 459
卢湾区	Luwan	8.05	27.04	3.52	33 590
徐汇区	Xuhui	54.76	96.22	13.57	17 571
长宁区	Changning	38.30	65.39	9.74	17 073
静安区	Jing'an	7.62	25.75	3.47	33 793
普陀区	Putuo	54.83	112.11	22.81	20 447
闸北区	Zhabei	29.26	75.10	10.34	25 666
虹口区	Hongkou	23.48	78.31	10.47	33 352
杨浦区	Yangpu	60.73	118.30	12.78	19 480
宝山区	Baoshan	270.99	132.70	35.46	4 897
闵行区	Minhang	370.75	182.48	80.13	4 922
嘉定区	Jiading	464.20	98.01	42.23	2 111
金山区	Jinshan	586.05	63.46	11.43	1 083
松江区	Songjiang	605.64	94.37	40.57	1 558
青浦区	Qingpu	670.14	74.43	28.66	1 111
南汇区	Nanhui	677.66	93.05	21.88	1 373
奉贤区	Fengxian	687.39	74.55	23.16	1 085
崇明县	Chongming	1 185.49	67.06	7.30	566

注：土地面积由市民政局提供。
Note: The figures of land area are provided by Shanghai Civil Affairs Bureau.

表 3.4 主要年份常住人口
RESIDENT POPULATION IN MAIN YEARS

单位：万人（10 000 persons）

指标	Indicators	2000	2005	2006
年末常住人口	**Year-end Resident Population**	**1 608**	**1 778.42**	**1 815.08**
户籍人口	Year-end Registered Population	1 309	1 340.02	1 347.82
外来人口（半年及以上人口）	Year-end Floating Population(Above Half Year)	299	438.40	467.26
外来人口总量	Floating Population	387	581.29	627.01
半年及以上人口	Above Half Year	299	438.40	467.26
半年以下人口	Below Half Year	88	142.40	159.75

注：户籍人口不包括离开上海、外出半年以上的本市户籍人口。
Note: Registered population excludes those departed from Shanghai for over half year.

表 3.5 主要年份户籍人口出生率、死亡率、自然增长率
BIRTH RATE, DEATH RATE AND NATURAL GROWTH RATE OF REGISTERED POPULATION IN MAIN YEARS

年份 Year	出生 Birth		死亡 Death		自然增长 Natural Growth	
	人数（万人） Population (10 000 persons)	出生率（‰） Birth Rate (‰)	人数（万人） Population (10 000 persons)	死亡率（‰） Death Rate (‰)	人数（万人） Population (10 000 persons)	自然增长率（‰） Natural Growth Rate(‰)
1990	13.12	10.25	8.63	6.74	4.49	3.51
1995	7.11	5.47	9.79	7.53	-2.68	-2.06
1996	6.79	5.21	9.77	7.50	-2.98	-2.29
1997	6.42	4.92	9.57	7.33	-3.15	-2.41
1998	6.17	4.73	10.13	7.75	-3.96	-3.03
1999	6.56	5.01	9.54	7.28	-2.98	-2.27
2000	6.95	5.27	9.45	7.17	-2.50	-1.90
2001	5.76	4.34	9.34	7.05	-3.58	-2.71
2002	6.20	4.66	9.67	7.27	-3.47	-2.61
2003	5.73	4.28	10.07	7.52	-4.34	-3.24
2004	8.09	6.00	9.65	7.16	-1.56	-1.16
2005	8.25	6.08	10.23	7.54	-1.98	-1.46
2006	8.12	5.95	9.80	7.19	-1.68	-1.24

注：本表至表 3.9 由市公安局提供。
Note: This table to table 3.9 are provided by Shanghai Municipal Public Security Bureau.

表 3.6 主要年份户籍人口迁移
MIGRATION IN MAIN YEARS

年份 Year	迁入 Inflows		迁出 Outflows		机械增长 Mechanical Increase	
	人口（万人） Population (10 000 persons)	迁入率（‰） Rate of Inflows (‰)	人口（万人） Population (10 000 persons)	迁出率（‰） Rate of Outflows (‰)	人口（万人） Population (10 000 persons)	增长率（‰） Growth Rate (‰)
1990	12.18	9.52	10.72	8.38	1.46	1.14
1995	13.12	10.09	6.47	4.98	6.65	5.11
1996	13.01	9.99	6.41	4.92	6.60	5.07
1997	11.47	8.79	5.72	4.38	5.75	4.41
1998	11.73	8.98	5.04	3.86	6.69	5.12
1999	14.06	10.73	5.08	3.88	8.98	6.85
2000	15.16	11.51	5.32	4.04	9.84	7.47
2001	14.63	11.05	5.56	4.20	9.07	6.85
2002	15.41	11.58	4.38	3.29	11.03	8.29
2003	14.92	11.15	3.69	2.76	11.23	8.39
2004	13.93	10.34	2.74	2.03	11.19	8.31
2005	12.96	9.55	3.46	2.55	9.50	7.00
2006	12.86	9.43	3.50	2.57	9.36	6.86

表 3.7 各区、县户籍人口迁移(2006)
MIGRATION IN DISTRICTS AND COUNTIES

地 区	District	迁 入(人) Inflows(person)		迁 出(人) Outflows(person)	
		市内迁入 From Inside of the City	市外迁入 From Outside of the City	迁往市内 To the Inside of the City	迁往市外 To the Outside of the City
全 市	**Total**	**8 059**	**128 638**	**9 606**	**34 995**
浦东新区	Pudong New Area	910	15 715	248	3 860
黄 浦 区	Huangpu	102	4 465	83	538
卢 湾 区	Luwan	41	2 327	15	352
徐 汇 区	Xuhui	168	12 460	86	3 688
长 宁 区	Changning	88	8 628	56	3 137
静 安 区	Jing 'an	50	1 860	18	372
普 陀 区	Putuo	192	5 741	100	2 111
闸 北 区	Zhabei	340	4 822	149	803
虹 口 区	Hongkou	360	4 633	140	1 591
杨 浦 区	Yangpu	463	20 374	339	11 500
宝 山 区	Baoshan	1 599	7 833	3 233	881
闵 行 区	Minhang	464	14 125	167	2 478
嘉 定 区	Jiading	56	3 579	32	410
金 山 区	Jinshan	12	2 272	36	630
松 江 区	Songjiang	33	8 659	14	628
青 浦 区	Qingpu	25	2 548	41	646
南 汇 区	Nanhui	37	3 448	19	314
奉 贤 区	Fengxian	45	2 654	17	790
崇 明 县	Chongming	3 074	2 495	4 813	266

表3.8 各区、县户籍人口自然变动情况（2006）
NATURAL CHANGES OF REGISTERED POPULATION IN DISTRICTS AND COUNTIES

地区 District		出生 Birth		死亡 Death		自然增长 Natural Growth	
		人数（万人）Population (10 000 persons)	出生率（‰）Birth Rate (‰)	人数（万人）Population (10 000 persons)	死亡率（‰）Death Rate (‰)	人数（万人）Population (10 000 persons)	自然增长率（‰）Natural Growth Rate(‰)
全市	**Total**	**8.12**	**5.95**	**9.80**	**7.19**	**-1.68**	**-1.24**
浦东新区	Pudong New Area	1.27	6.83	1.29	6.93	-0.02	-0.10
黄浦区	Huangpu	0.31	5.08	0.51	8.51	-0.21	-3.43
卢湾区	Luwan	0.15	4.65	0.27	8.71	-0.13	-4.06
徐汇区	Xuhui	0.45	5.11	0.61	6.92	-0.16	-1.81
长宁区	Changning	0.28	4.60	0.39	6.25	-0.10	-1.65
静安区	Jing'an	0.14	4.54	0.27	8.81	-0.13	-4.27
普陀区	Putuo	0.46	5.35	0.66	7.72	-0.20	-2.37
闸北区	Zhabei	0.32	4.62	0.55	7.78	-0.22	-3.16
虹口区	Hongkou	0.37	4.74	0.62	7.83	-0.24	-3.09
杨浦区	Yangpu	0.48	4.41	0.77	7.13	-0.29	-2.72
宝山区	Baoshan	0.50	6.21	0.57	7.02	-0.07	-0.81
闵行区	Minhang	0.77	9.21	0.57	6.84	0.20	2.37
嘉定区	Jiading	0.41	7.68	0.39	7.28	0.02	0.40
金山区	Jinshan	0.30	5.71	0.34	6.59	-0.05	-0.88
松江区	Songjiang	0.35	6.69	0.34	6.47	0.01	0.22
青浦区	Qingpu	0.30	6.66	0.30	6.52	0.01	0.14
南汇区	Nanhui	0.52	7.15	0.45	6.22	0.07	0.93
奉贤区	Fengxian	0.31	6.12	0.31	6.13	…	-0.01
崇明县	Chongming	0.42	5.93	0.58	8.33	-0.17	-2.40

表 3.9 各区、县户籍人口年龄构成(2006)
AGE STRUCTURE OF POPULATION IN DISTRICTS AND COUNTIES

单位:万人(10 000 persons)

地 区	District	合 计 Total	17 岁及以下 17 and below	18 ~ 34 岁 18 ~ 34	35 ~ 59 岁 35 ~ 59	60 岁及以上 60 and above
全 市	**Total**	**1 368.08**	**154.07**	**328.86**	**609.54**	**275.62**
浦东新区	Pudong New Area	187.56	21.49	46.25	83.42	36.41
黄 浦 区	Huangpu	60.19	6.12	14.54	26.94	12.59
卢 湾 区	Luwan	31.37	2.95	7.56	13.68	7.19
徐 汇 区	Xuhui	88.75	9.85	22.26	37.45	19.19
长 宁 区	Changning	61.42	5.91	17.53	25.45	12.54
静 安 区	Jing'an	30.96	3.26	7.20	13.28	7.22
普 陀 区	Putuo	85.97	8.38	20.57	39.44	17.58
闸 北 区	Zhabei	69.86	7.16	16.21	32.29	14.21
虹 口 区	Hongkou	78.70	8.12	18.19	35.53	16.86
杨 浦 区	Yangpu	107.75	10.13	29.07	47.30	21.25
宝 山 区	Baoshan	81.59	9.16	18.78	37.91	15.74
闵 行 区	Minhang	85.53	10.37	21.80	36.79	16.57
嘉 定 区	Jiading	53.25	6.18	12.02	23.80	11.24
金 山 区	Jinshan	52.29	6.92	11.28	24.45	9.65
松 江 区	Songjiang	53.21	6.96	13.23	23.05	9.97
青 浦 区	Qingpu	45.63	5.95	9.96	20.90	8.83
南 汇 区	Nanhui	72.73	10.06	17.24	32.27	13.16
奉 贤 区	Fengxian	51.33	6.69	11.66	23.31	9.67
崇 明 县	Chongming	69.98	8.42	13.52	32.29	15.76

表3.10 各区、县计划生育基本情况(2006)
FAMILY PLANNING IN DISTRICTS AND COUNTIES

地 区	District	出生人数(万人) Birth (10 000 persons)	已婚育龄妇女人数(万人) Married Women at Childbearing Age (10 000 persons)	领独生子女证人数(万人) Married Couples with One-child Certificate (10 000 persons)	采取避孕措施人数(万人) Married People Adopting Contraception (10 000 persons)	计划生育率(%) Family Planning Rate (%)	领证率(%) Coverage of One-child Certificate (%)	避孕率(%) Comprehensive Contarception Rate (%)
全 市	**Total**	**8.12**	**226.37**	**73.25**	**195.07**	**99.2**	**32.4**	**86.2**
浦东新区	Pudong New Area	1.27	29.43	10.31	25.64	99.6	35.0	87.1
黄浦区	Huangpu	0.31	7.89	2.35	6.43	97.7	29.7	81.6
卢湾区	Luwan	0.15	4.8	1.47	3.75	99.0	30.6	78.3
徐汇区	Xuhui	0.45	14.11	4.6	11.5	98.7	32.6	81.5
长宁区	Changning	0.28	8.78	2.69	7.05	98.9	30.6	80.3
静安区	Jing'an	0.14	3.92	1.21	3.28	99.2	30.7	83.7
普陀区	Putuo	0.46	12.46	4.45	10.11	99.0	35.7	81.2
闸北区	Zhabei	0.32	10.47	3.11	8.76	98.9	29.7	83.7
虹口区	Hongkou	0.37	10.27	3.18	8.36	98.9	31.0	81.3
杨浦区	Yangpu	0.48	15.28	4.46	13.04	99.1	29.2	85.4
宝山区	Baoshan	0.50	13.21	4.20	11.35	98.6	31.8	85.9
闵行区	Minhang	0.77	13.82	4.15	11.9	99.6	30.0	86.1
嘉定区	Jiading	0.41	10.16	3.34	9.18	99.3	32.9	90.4
金山区	Jinshan	0.30	11.23	3.53	10.3	99.9	31.5	91.7
松江区	Songjiang	0.35	10.32	3.56	9.32	99.6	34.5	90.3
青浦区	Qingpu	0.30	10.01	3.17	8.86	97.4	31.7	88.6
南汇区	Nanhui	0.52	15.57	5.67	14.2	99.3	36.4	91.2
奉贤区	Fengxian	0.31	10.25	3.36	9.17	99.6	32.8	89.4
崇明县	Chongming	0.42	14.41	4.45	12.86	99.8	30.9	89.2

注：本表由市人口和计划生育委员会提供。
Note: This table is provided by Shanghai Municipal Committee of Population and Family Planning.

表 3.11 主要年份婚姻情况
MARRIAGE STATISTICS IN MAIN YEARS

年份 Year	准予登记结婚（万对）Marriage Registration Permitted (10 000 couples)	初婚（万人）First Marriage (10 000 persons)	再婚（万人）Remarriage (10 000 persons)	其中 of which 女性 Female	离婚人数（万人）Divorce (10 000 persons)	其中 of which 民政部门批准 Approved by the Civil Administration	法院调判 Mediated by the Court
1980	16.82	33.07	0.57		0.66	0.18	0.48
1985	18.24	35.47	1.01	0.48	1.39	0.46	0.93
1990	10.77	19.49	2.04	1.06	3.27	1.45	1.82
1995	8.40	14.61	2.19	1.09	4.54	1.97	2.57
1996	8.96	14.98	2.31	1.24	4.93	2.14	2.79
1997	8.84	15.12	2.57	1.27	5.46	2.38	3.08
1998	8.57	14.48	2.67	1.28	5.92	2.85	3.07
1999	9.05	15.07	2.46	1.24	6.24	3.39	2.85
2000	9.31	15.08	2.89	1.45	6.36	3.52	2.84
2001	9.30	15.23	2.68	1.40	6.29	3.36	2.93
2002	9.10	14.60	3.05	1.40	5.92	3.08	2.84
2003	10.82	17.20	3.97	2.31	6.60	3.97	2.63
2004	12.49	20.27	4.18	2.05	7.26	5.35	1.91
2005	10.27	16.44	4.09	2.05	7.86	6.21	1.65
2006	16.56	27.29	5.83	2.93	9.43	7.55	1.88

①本表由市民政局提供(下表同)。
②1999 年起，初婚、再婚仅指内地居民，不包括涉及华侨及港澳台居民登记的初婚、再婚情况。
❶The figures of this table are provided by Shanghai Civil Affairs Bureau.
❷Since 1999 figure of first marriages and remarriage covers only mainland residents, not include overseas.

表 3.12 涉外婚姻情况(1985～2006)
CHINESE-FOREIGN MARRIAGE

年份 Year	涉外婚姻(对) Chinese-Foreign Marriage (couple)	在涉外婚姻中的国内公民（人）In Chinese-Foreign Marriage: Chinese Citizens (person)	在国内公民中 Among the Chinese Citizens 男性 Male	女性 Female
1985	826	824	91	733
1986	794	793	73	720
1987	773	767	95	672
1988	802	800	92	708
1989	963	961	90	871
1990	1 345	1 345	136	1 209
1991	1 865	1 863	170	1 693
1992	2 555	2 554	214	2 340
1993	2 552	2 552	488	2 064
1994	2 549	2 457	139	2 318
1995	3 033	3 030	274	2 756
1996	3 107	3 105	307	2 798
1997	2 839	2 838	298	2 540
1998	2 926	2 923	293	2 630
1999	2 872	2 869	343	2 526
2000	3 187	3 182	374	2 808
2001	3 447	3 438	399	3 039
2002	2 705	2 690	67	2 623
2003	2 418	2 418	367	2 051
2004	2 636	2 623	417	2 206
2005	2 407	2 385	372	2 013
2006	2 943	2 943	540	2 403

表 3.13 在沪外国常住人口(2005～2006) FOREIGN IN SHANGHAI

单位:人(person)

类别	Types	2005	2006
总 计	**Total**	**100 011**	**119 876**
居留许可外国人	**Residence Permitted Foreigners**	**95 384**	**115 326**
一、按国别(地区)分	Grouped by Country and Region		
日 本	Japan	27 812	29 326
韩 国	Republic of Korea	14 047	17 020
马来西亚	Malaysia	3 480	4 097
新加坡	Singapore	5 547	6 336
德 国	Germany	4 591	5 636
英 国	United Kingdom	2 904	3 725
加拿大	Canada	4 279	4 572
美 国	United States	14 329	15 877
澳大利亚	Australia	3 729	3 927
法 国	France	4 181	5 437
二、按类别分	By Types		
#留学人员及家属	Overseas Students and Relatives	10 224	12 555
驻华机构代表及家属	Delegate and Relatives of Institutions Stationed in China	9 769	11 281
外资企业工作人员及家属	Employees and Relatives at Foreign Ventures	60 137	76 873
外国专家及家属	Foreign Experts and Relatives	4 586	4 942
永久居留外国人	Permanent Residence Foreigners		295
长期签证外国人(半年以上)	Long-term Vise Foreigners Above One Year		4 255

注:本表由市公安局出入境管理局提供。
Note: The figures from this table are provided by Bureau of Exit-Entry Administration Shanghai Municipal Public Security Bureau.

表 3.14 主要年份从业人员和职工人数 NUMBER OF EMPLOYEES AND STAFF AND WORKERS IN MAIN YEARS

单位:万人(10 000 persons)

类别	Types	2000	2005	2006
从业人员	**Employees**	**745.24**	**863.32**	**885.51**
国 有	State-owned	180.99	141.59	138.92
集 体	Collective-owned	282.18	219.33	214.77
港澳台及外商投资企业	Enterprises with Investment from Hongkong, Macco, Taiwan and Foreign Countries	51.77	89.83	92.41
其 他	Others	230.30	412.57	439.41
#有限责任公司	Companies With Limited Liability	25.77	43.93	47.39
股份有限公司	Share-holding Companies with Limited Liabilities	22.34	33.35	33.74
城镇私营	Urban Privately Run Businesses	58.23	221.50	240.76
城镇个体	Urban Self-employed Businesses	9.27	19.80	21.18
非正规就业及自由职业	Free Labor Jobs	19.90	45.31	51.44
职工人数	**Staff and Workers**	**390.14**	**420.12**	**500.94**
国 有	State-owned	229.24	155.47	146.38
集 体	Collective-owned	47.45	20.95	18.11
港澳台及外商投资企业	Enterprises with Overseas Investment	54.97	73.31	75.60
其 他	Others	58.48	170.39	260.85
#有限责任公司	Companies With Limited Liability	27.99	38.29	42.95
股份有限公司	Share-holding Companies with Limited Liabilities	21.86	30.57	30.34

注:2006 年职工人数中包括 120 人以上的私营企业职工(表 3.16～表 3.18 同)。
Note: Population of employees in 2006 includes employees work for private enterprises over 120 persons(same as table 3.16 to table 3.18).

表3.15　各行业从业人员(2006)
EMPLOYEES IN DIFFERENT SECTORS

单位:万人(10 000 persons)

行业	Sector	从业人员 Employees	按登记注册类型分 Classified According to the Categories of Registration: 国有 State-owned Units	集体 Collective-owned Units	港澳台及外商投资单位 Units with Investment from Hong Kong, Macao, Taiwan and Foreign Countries	其他 Other Ownership Units
总　计	**Total**	**885.51**	**138.92**	**214.77**	**92.41**	**439.41**
一、按产业分	**Grouped by Industry**					
第一产业	Primary Industry	55.33	0.68	53.57	0.03	1.05
第二产业	Secondary Industry	327.63	27.34	105.39	78.33	116.57
第三产业	Tertiary Industry	502.55	110.90	55.81	14.05	321.79
二、按行业分	**Grouped by Sector**					
农、林、牧、渔业	Farming, Forestry, Animal Husbandry and Fishery	55.33	0.68	53.57	0.03	1.05
采矿业	Mining	0.05	0.04			0.01
制造业	Manufacturing	279.08	17.85	93.20	77.59	90.44
电力、燃气及水的生产和供应业	Power, Gas and Water Production and Supply	5.40	3.83	0.07	0.31	1.19
建筑业	Construction	43.10	5.62	12.12	0.43	24.93
交通运输、仓储和邮政业	Transportation, Warehousing and Post Industries	49.23	11.67	9.18	2.78	25.60
信息传输、计算机服务和软件业	Information Transmission, Computer Servcie and Software Industries	9.89	1.62	0.93	1.95	5.39
#信息传输	Information Transmission	2.86	1.43	0.04	0.93	0.46
批发和零售业	Retail and Wholesale	134.66	4.05	4.63	1.75	124.23
住宿和餐饮业	Hoteling and Catering	25.90	2.91	2.55	2.75	17.69
金融业	Finance	19.57	4.30	2.43	1.42	11.42
房地产业	Real Estate	29.95	2.87	13.70	1.27	12.11
租赁和商务服务业	Leasing and Business Service Industries	50.98	7.45	4.98	0.90	37.65
科学研究、技术服务和地质勘查业	Scientific Research, Technical Service and Geological Prospecting	16.15	12.34	2.21	0.29	1.31
水利、环境和公共设施管理业	Water Conservancy, Environment and Public Facility Management	7.00	4.10	2.14	0.15	0.61
#公共设施管理业	Public Facility Management	1.57	0.98	0.07	0.14	0.38
居民服务和其他服务业	Resident Service and Other Services	83.83	1.22	3.14	0.44	79.03
教　育	Education	27.77	24.45	2.18	0.01	1.13
卫生、社会保障和社会福利业	Health, Social Security and Welfare	18.41	12.96	3.63	0.02	1.80
文化、体育和娱乐业	Culture, Sports and Entertainment	10.16	3.66	2.36	0.32	3.82
公共管理和社会组织	Public Administration and Social Organizations	19.05	17.30	1.75		

表3.16 各行业职工人数(2006)
STAFF AND WORKERS IN DIFFERENT SECTORS

单位:万人(10 000 persons)

行业 Sector		职工人数 Staff and Workers	按登记注册类型分 Classified According to the Categories of Registration			
			国有单位 State-owned Units	集体单位 Collective-owned Units	港澳台及外商投资单位 Units with Investment from Hong Kong, Macao, Taiwan and Foreign Countries	其他单位 Other Ownership Units
总　计	**Total**	**500.94**	**146.38**	**18.11**	**75.60**	**260.85**
一、按产业分	**Grouped by Industry**					
第一产业	Primary Industry	1.74	0.52	0.14	0.02	1.06
第二产业	Secondary Industry	230.63	40.59	5.15	65.75	119.14
第三产业	Tertiary Industry	268.57	105.27	12.82	9.83	140.65
二、按行业分	**Grouped by Sector**					
农、林、牧、渔业	Farming, Forestry, Animal Husbandry and Fishery	1.74	0.52	0.14	0.02	1.06
采矿业	Mining	0.06	0.04			0.02
制造业	Manufacturing	201.29	31.56	4.70	65.16	99.87
电力、燃气及水的生产和供应业	Power, Gas and Water Production and Supply	5.32	3.80	0.09	0.31	1.12
建筑业	Construction	23.96	5.19	0.36	0.28	18.13
交通运输、仓储和邮政业	Transportation, Warehousing and Post Industries	34.76	10.95	0.97	2.58	20.25
信息传输、计算机服务和软件业	Information Transmission, Computer Servcie and Software Industries	7.27	1.54	0.05	1.39	4.30
#信息传输	Information Transmission	2.25	1.36	0.04	0.44	0.40
批发和零售业	Retail and Wholesale	55.29	6.81	3.55	1.28	43.66
住宿和餐饮业	Hotel and Cateries	9.82	2.60	0.27	1.04	5.91
金融业	Financial	15.28	3.90		1.09	10.29
房地产业	Real Estate	8.68	1.96	0.16	0.61	5.94
租赁和商务服务业	Leasing and Business Service Industries	40.05	6.55	4.41	0.83	28.26
科学研究、技术服务和地质勘查业	Scientific Research, Technology Service and Geological Prospecting	13.24	11.76	0.18	0.26	1.03
水利、环境和公共设施管理业	Water Conservancy, Environment and Public Facility Management	4.40	3.37	0.35	0.14	0.54
#公共设施管理业	Public Facility Management	1.36	0.82	0.08	0.13	0.33
居民服务和其他服务业	Resident Service and Other Service	19.08	1.85	0.52	0.40	16.32
教　育	Education	23.71	22.86	0.18	0.01	0.66
卫生、社会保障和社会福利业	Health, Social Security and Welfare	14.51	11.47	1.78	0.02	1.24
文化、体育和娱乐业	Culture, Sports and Entertainment	5.88	3.29	0.14	0.17	2.28
公共管理和社会组织	Public Administration and Social Organizations	16.60	16.34	0.25		

表3.17 各行业在岗职工人数(2006)
WORKING STAFF AND WORKERS IN DIFFERENT SECTORS

单位:万人(10 000 persons)

行业	Sector	职工人数 Staff and Workers	按登记注册类型分 Classified According to the Categories of Registration			
			国有单位 State-owned Units	集体单位 Collective-owned Units	港澳台及外商投资单位 Units with Investment from Hong Kong, Macao, Taiwan and Foreign Countries	其他单位 Other Ownership Units
总计	**Total**	**446.45**	**116.67**	**10.08**	**72.84**	**246.86**
一、按产业分	**Grouped by Industry**					
第一产业	Primary Industry	1.48	0.43	0.11	0.02	0.92
第二产业	Secondary Industry	201.13	22.90	1.99	63.22	113.02
第三产业	Tertiary Industry	243.84	93.34	7.98	9.60	132.92
二、按行业分	**Grouped by Sector**					
农、林、牧、渔业	Farming, Forestry, Animal Husbandry and Fishery	1.48	0.43	0.11	0.02	0.92
采矿业	Mining	0.05	0.03			0.02
制造业	Manufacturing	173.83	15.15	1.66	62.64	94.38
电力、燃气及水的生产和供应业	Power, Gas and Water Production and Supply	5.20	3.71	0.07	0.30	1.12
建筑业	Construction	22.06	4.01	0.27	0.27	17.51
交通运输、仓储和邮政业	Transportation, Warehousing and Post Industries	30.81	9.39	0.62	2.48	18.32
信息传输、计算机服务和软件业	Information Transmission, Computer Servcie and Software Industries	7.16	1.47	0.04	1.37	4.28
#信息传输	Information Transmission	2.14	1.29	0.04	0.42	0.39
批发和零售业	Retail and Wholesale	48.01	3.30	1.38	1.26	42.06
住宿和餐饮业	Hotel and Cateries	8.77	2.10	0.15	1.01	5.51
金融业	Financial	14.82	3.66		1.06	10.10
房地产业	Real Estate	7.88	1.58	0.15	0.60	5.55
租赁和商务服务业	Leasing and Business Service Industries	33.83	4.84	2.70	0.82	25.46
科学研究、技术服务和地质勘查业	Scientific Research, Technology Service and Geological Prospecting	12.66	11.29	0.13	0.26	0.98
水利、环境和公共设施管理业	Water Conservancy, Environment and Public Facility Management	3.82	2.90	0.33	0.14	0.45
#公共设施管理业	Public Facility Management	1.27	0.76	0.07	0.13	0.31
居民服务和其他服务业	Resident Service and Other Service	17.46	0.68	0.33	0.39	16.06
教育	Education	22.83	22.07	0.11	0.01	0.65
卫生、社会保障和社会福利业	Health, Social Security and Welfare	13.89	10.94	1.69	0.02	1.24
文化、体育和娱乐业	Culture, Sports and Entertainment	5.52	2.98	0.10	0.17	2.27
公共管理和社会组织	Public Administration and Social Organizations	16.38	16.13	0.25		

注:本表包括120人以上的私营企业职工(下表同)。
Note: Data in this table includes those of employees work for private enterprises over 120 persons(same as next table).

表3.18 各行业在岗女职工人数(2006)
WORKING FEMALE STAFF AND WORKERS IN VARIOUS SECTORS

单位:万人(10 000 persons)

行业	Sector	在岗女职工人数 Working Female Staff and Workers	按登记注册类型分 Classified According to the Categories of Registration			
			国有单位 State-owned Units	集体单位 Collective-owned Units	港澳台及外商投资单位 Units with Investment from Hong Kong, Macao, Taiwan and Foreign Countries	其他单位 Other Ownership Units
总 计	**Total**	**157.86**	**46.36**	**4.18**	**32.99**	**74.33**
一、按产业分	**Grouped by Industry**					
第一产业	Primary Industry	0.38	0.11	0.02	0.01	0.24
第二产业	Secondary Industry	67.79	5.53	0.69	28.80	32.77
第三产业	Tertiary Industry	89.69	40.72	3.47	4.18	41.32
二、按行业分	**Grouped by Sector**					
农、林、牧、渔业	Farming, Forestry, Animal Husbandry and Fishery	0.38	0.11	0.02	0.01	0.24
采矿业	Mining	0.01	0.01			
制造业	Manufacturing	61.09	3.83	0.64	28.64	27.99
电力、燃气及水的生产和供应业	Power, Gas and Water Production and Supply	1.30	0.94	0.02	0.10	0.24
建筑业	Construction	5.38	0.75	0.03	0.06	4.54
交通运输、仓储和邮政业	Transportation, Warehousing and Post Industries	6.60	1.72	0.21	0.74	3.92
信息传输、计算机服务和软件业	Information Transmission, Computer Servcie and Software Industries	2.29	0.49	0.01	0.49	1.30
#信息传输	Information Transmission	0.77	0.43	0.01	0.18	0.14
批发和零售业	Retail and Wholesale	16.31	1.20	0.57	0.65	13.89
住宿和餐饮业	Hotel and Cateries	3.21	0.85	0.08	0.49	1.79
金融业	Financial	6.77	1.88		0.63	4.27
房地产业	Real Estate	2.38	0.46	0.05	0.21	1.66
租赁和商务服务业	Leasing and Business Service Industries	10.33	1.30	0.85	0.40	7.78
科学研究、技术服务和地质勘查业	Scientific Research, Technology Service and Geological Prospecting	5.31	4.86	0.05	0.08	0.31
水利、环境和公共设施管理业	Water Conservancy, Environment and Public Facility Management	1.21	0.89	0.14	0.06	0.12
#公共设施管理业	Public Facility Management	0.41	0.23	0.03	0.05	0.09
居民服务和其他服务业	Resident Service and Other Service Industries	5.48	0.24	0.18	0.33	4.74
教 育	Education	13.62	13.17	0.08	0.01	0.36
卫生、社会保障和社会福利业	Health, Social Security and Welfare	8.95	7.37	1.11	0.02	0.45
文化、体育和娱乐业	Culture, Sports and Entertainment	2.04	1.18	0.04	0.10	0.72
公共管理和社会组织	Public Administration and Social Organizations	5.21	5.10	0.11		

表3.19 主要年份城镇新就业人数
NUMBER OF NEW URBAN EMPLOYEES IN MAIN YEARS

单位：万人(10 000 persons)

指 标	Indicators	1980	1990	2000	2005	2006
总 计	**Total**	**23.05**	**14.17**	**49.74**	**68.49**	**68.99**
按主要来源分	**Grouped by Source of Employment**					
城镇劳动力	Urban Labour Force	12.36	4.55	39.14	47.55	46.98
农村劳动力	Rural Labour Force	2.67	2.51	1.76	10.75	11.15
大学、中专、技校毕业生	Graduates from Universities, Secondary Technical Schools and Worker Training Schools	5.22	5.76	4.09	6.67	7.47
其 他	Others	2.80	1.35	4.75	3.52	3.39
按安置去向分	**Grouped by Employment Assignment**					
国有经济单位	State-owned Units	16.54	11.46	7.40	6.15	10.09
城镇集体经济单位	Urban Collective-owned Units	5.82	1.46	1.42	0.83	0.88
其他经济单位	Other Ownership Units		0.76	8.60	26.47	29.25
其他劳动者	Others	0.36	0.49	32.32	35.04	28.77

注：本表至表3.24"其他单位"包括港澳台及外商投资企业。
Note: "Other" in this table to tablr 3.24 includes foreign invested and HongKong, Macau and Taiwan funded enterprises.

表3.20 主要年份城镇登记失业人数和城镇登记失业率
NUMBER OF REGISTERED URBAN UNEMPLOYED AND REGISTERED URBAN UNEMPLOYMENT RATE IN MAIN YEARS

年 份 Year	城镇从业人数(万人) Urban Employees (10 000 persons)	城镇登记失业人数(万人) Registered Urban Unemployment (10 000 persons)	其 中 of which 区 District	县 County	城镇登记失业率(%) Registered Urban Unemployment Rate(%)
1978	423.64	10.00			2.3
1980	448.39	14.75			3.2
1985	499.58	1.20	0.94	0.26	0.2
1990	519.44	7.70	6.62	1.08	1.5
1995	531.34	14.36	13.52	0.84	2.7
1996	533.00	14.54	13.69	0.85	2.7
1997	534.91	14.90	14.03	0.87	2.8
1998	551.03	15.96	15.24	0.72	2.9
1999	540.92	17.47	16.49	0.98	3.1
2000	560.60	20.08	18.86	1.22	3.5
2001	573.23	25.72	25.21	0.51	4.3
2002	576.40	28.78	27.79	0.99	4.8
2003	582.10	30.11	28.98	1.13	4.9
2004	588.97	27.43	26.63	0.80	4.5
2005	598.34	27.50	26.71	0.79	4.4
2006	605.43	27.82	27.06	0.76	4.4

①本表由市劳动和社会保障局提供(下表同)。
②本表从业人员数不包括聘用离退休人员。
❶The figures of this table are provided by Shanghai Municipal Labour and Social Security Bureau. (The same as next table)
❷Employed of retired people are not included in this table.

表 3.21 主要年份离休、退休及退职职工人数
NUMBER OF RETIRED AND RESIGNED PEOPLE IN MAIN YEARS

单位:万人(10 000 persons)

	指 标 Indicators	1980	1990	2000	2005	2006
总 计	**Total**	**96.47**	**159.14**	**234.23**	**290.73**	**294.69**
国有单位	State-owned Units	68.24	113.65	165.55	166.3	166.73
离 休	Retired Veteran Cadres		3.85	3.39	2.71	2.36
退 休	Retired	67.39	108.54	161.03	159.04	159.82
退 职	Resigned	0.85	1.26	1.13	4.56	4.55
集体单位	Collective-owned Units	28.23	44.18	50.22	46.00	46.91
离 休	Retired Veteran Cadres		0.40	0.10	0.07	0.06
退 休	Retired	27.85	42.02	48.40	44.12	44.96
退 职	Resigned	0.38	1.76	1.72	1.81	1.89
其他单位	Other Ownership Units		1.31	18.46	78.43	81.05
离 休	Retired Veteran Cadres		0.01	0.21	0.42	0.66
退 休	Retired		1.22	18.05	75.88	77.56
退 职	Resigned		0.08	0.20	2.12	2.83

表 3.22 在岗职工人数变动(2006)
CHANGES IN THE NUMBER OF WORKING STAFF AND WORKERS

单位:万人(10 000 persons)

	指 标 Indicators	合 计 Total	按登记注册类型划分 Classified According to the Categories of Registration		
			国有单位 State-owned Units	集体单位 Collective-owned Units	其他单位 Other Ownership Units
增加人数	**Increase of Staff and Workers**	**62.73**	**16.34**	**1.70**	**44.69**
从农村招收	Recruited from Rural Areas	11.15	0.60	0.32	10.23
从城镇招收	Recruited from Urban Areas	18.21	5.98	0.33	11.90
录用的复员转业军人	Demobilized Soldiers	0.30	0.19		0.11
录用的大、中专、技工学校毕业生	Graduates from Colleges, Secondary Technical Schools and Worker Training Schools	9.38	2.84	0.07	6.47
调入人数	Number Transferred in	9.15	3.78	0.35	5.02
# 市外调入	From Outside Areas	0.97	0.40	0.01	0.56
其 他	Others	14.54	2.95	0.63	10.96
减少人数	**Decrease of Staff and Workers**	**70.36**	**17.03**	**2.34**	**50.99**
离休、退休、退职	Retired and Resigned	7.05	3.75	0.50	2.80
开除、除名、辞退	Expelled and Discharged	2.23	0.30	0.11	1.82
终止、解除合同	Contract Terminated	39.91	7.31	0.72	31.88
死 亡	Death	0.29	0.10	0.02	0.17
调出人数	Number Transferred Out	8.76	2.89	0.50	5.37
# 调往市外	To Outside Areas	0.52	0.21		0.31
其 他	Others	12.12	2.68	0.49	8.95

表3.23 在岗长期职工和临时职工人数(2006)
NUMBER OF PERMANENT AND TEMPORARY WORKING STAFF AND WORKERS

单位:万人(10 000 persons)

行业	Sector	合计 Total	其中 of which 在岗长期职工 Permanent Working Staff and Workers	在岗临时职工 Temporary Working Staff and Workers
总计	**Total**	**446.45**	**403.78**	**42.67**
农、林、牧、渔业	Farming, Forestry, Animal Husbandry and Fishery	1.47	1.32	0.15
采矿业	Mining	0.05	0.05	
制造业	Manufacturing	173.83	155.84	17.99
电力、燃气及水的生产和供应业	Power, Gas and Water Production and Supply	5.20	5.20	
建筑业	Construction	22.06	19.29	2.77
交通运输、仓储和邮政业	Transportation, Warehousing and Post Industries	30.81	29.30	1.51
信息传输、计算机服务和软件业	Information Transmission, Computer Servcie and Software Industries	7.16	6.43	0.73
#信息传输	Information Transmission	2.14	2.14	
批发和零售业	Retail and Wholesale Industries	48.01	40.98	7.03
住宿和餐饮业	Hotel and Cateries	8.77	7.78	0.98
金融业	Financial	14.82	14.20	0.62
房地产业	Real Estate	7.88	7.06	0.82
租赁和商务服务业	Leasing and Business Service Industries	33.83	28.83	5.00
科学研究、技术服务和地质勘查业	Scientific Research, Technology Service and Geological Prospecting	12.66	12.64	0.02
水利、环境和公共设施管理业	Water Conservancy, Environment and Public Facility Management	3.82	3.74	0.08
#公共设施管理业	Public Facility Management	1.27	1.27	
居民服务和其他服务业	Community Service and Other Service Industries	17.46	14.09	3.37
教育	Education	22.83	22.72	0.11
卫生、社会保障和社会福利业	Health, Social Security and Welfare Industries	13.89	13.38	27.00
文化、体育和娱乐业	Culture, Sports and Entertainment	5.52	5.09	0.43
公共管理和社会组织	Public Administration and Social Organizations	16.38	15.85	0.53

表3.24 主要年份离岗职工人数
NUMBER OF LAID-OFF EMPLOYEES IN MAIN YEARS

单位:万人(10 000 persons)

指标	Indicators	2000	2005	2006
总计	**Total**	**83.11**	**63.58**	**54.49**
国有单位	State-owned Units	48.25	35.16	29.71
集体单位	Collective-owned Units	20.87	9.97	8.03
其他单位	Other Ownership Units	13.99	18.46	16.75

表 3.25 主要年份职业介绍所
EMPLOYMENT AGENCIES IN MAIN YEARS

指 标	Indicators	2000	2005	2006
机构数(个)	**Number of Institutions(unit)**	**465**	**507**	**493**
#劳动保障部门	Run by Labor Insurance Departments	346	276	266
其他组织办	Run by Other Organs	110	96	92
公民个人办	Run by Individuals	9	135	135
职工人数(人)	Staff and Workers (person)	2 807	5 207	4 673
登记招聘人数(万人次)	Number of Vacancies Registered (10 000 person times)	54.09	160.17	168.36
登记求职人数(万人次)	Number of Registered People Seeking a Job(10 000 person times)	54.69	135.69	149.13
#女 性	Females	25.45	60.52	61.26
#失业人员	Unemployed	29.86	78.25	85.44
#获得职业资格人员	Personnel with Job Qualifications		23.45	24.37
职业指导人数(万人次)	**Number of People Receiving Career Training(10 000 person times)**	**55.58**	**97.12**	**110.38**
介绍成功人数(万人次)	**Number of People that Got a Job through Employment Agencies(10000 person times)**	**28.59**	**51.36**	**59.48**
#女 性	Females	13.87	23.27	28.62
#失业人员	Unemployed	14.33	30.44	38.11
#获得职业资格人员	Personnel with Job Qualifications		14.61	16.57

注：本表由市劳动和社会保障局提供。
Note: The figures of this table are provided by Shanghai Municipal Labour and Social Security Bureau.

表 3.26 主要年份人才市场
HUMAN RESOURCE MARKET IN MAIN YEARS

指 标	Indicators	2000	2005	2006
挂牌人才市场数(个)	Number of Human Resource Markets with Registration(unit)	24	19	30
人才流动机构数(个)	Number of Human Resource Exchange Organizations(unit)	105	509	608
人才流动机构人数(人)	Number of Persons in Human Resource Excharge Organization(person)	746	5 565	7 078
举办人才交流大会次数(次)	Number of Human Resource Exchange Meetings(time)	662	957	1 998
参加人才交流大会人数(万人)	Number of Persons Attending Human Resource Exchange Meetings(10 000 persons)	134.11	378.49	249.81

注：本表由市人事局提供。
Note: Data in this table are provided by Shanghai Municipal Personel Bureau.

上 / 海 / 统 / 计 / 年 / 鉴

主要统计指标解释

■ 人　口

人口数为每年 12 月 31 日的年末总人口。根据统计口径的不同,分为户籍人口和常住人口。户籍人口是指在公安部门办理了户籍登记的人口。常住人口是指实际上经常居住在一个地方(住所)的人口,一般都以在其住所居住半年以上者为常住人口。

■ 出生率

出生率(又称粗出生率)指在一定时期内(通常为一年)一定地区的出生人数与同期平均人数(或期中人数)之比,一般用千分率表示。计算公式:

$$出生率=\frac{年出生人数}{年平均人数}\times 1000‰$$

出生人数是指活产婴儿,即胎儿脱离母体时(不管怀孕月数),有过呼吸或其他生命现象。年平均人数是年初、年底人口数的平均数,也可用年中人口数代替。

■ 死亡率

死亡率(又称粗死亡率)指在一定时期内(通常为一年)一定地区的死亡人数与同期平均人数(或期中人数)之比,一般用千分率表示。计算公式:

$$死亡率=\frac{年死亡人数}{年平均人数}\times 1000‰$$

■ 人口自然增长率

指在一定时期内(通常为一年)人口自然增加数(出生人数减死亡人数)与该时期内平均人数(或期中人数)之比,一般用千分率表示。计算公式:

$$人口自然增长率=\frac{本年出生人数-本年死亡人数}{年平均人数}\times 1000‰$$

$$人口自然增长率=人口出生率-人口死亡率$$

■ 平均期望寿命

指在一定年龄组的死亡率水平下,该年龄组人群日后平均可能继续生存的年(岁)数。通常所说的平均期望寿命是指刚出生的一批人平均一生可能存活的年数。

■ 从业人员

指从事一定社会劳动并取得劳动报酬或经营收入的人员,包括在岗职工、再就业的离退休人员、私营业主、个体户主、私营和个体从业人员、乡镇企业从业人员、农村从业人员、其他从业人员(包括民办教师、宗教职业者、现役军人等)。这一指标反映了一定时期内全部劳动力资源的实际利用情况,是研究我国基本国情国力的重要指标。

各单位的从业人员指在各级国家机关、政党机关、社会团体及企业、事业单位中工作,取得工资或其他形式的劳动报酬的全部人员。包括在岗职工、再就业的离退休人员、民办教师以及在各单位中工作的外方人员和港澳台方人员、兼职人员、借用的外单位人员和第二职业者。不包括离开本单位仍保留劳动关系的职工。各单位的就业人员反映了各单位实际参加生产或工作的全部劳动力。

■ 职　工

指在国有、城镇集体、联营、股份制、外商和港、澳、台投资、其他单位及其附属机构工作,并由其支付工资的各类人员。不包括下列人员:(1)乡镇企业就业人员;(2)私营企业就业人员;(3)城镇个体劳动者;(4)离休、退休、退职人员;(5)再就业的离、退休人员;(6)民办教师;(7)在城镇单位中工作的外方及港、澳、台人员;(8)其他按有关规定不列入职工统计范围的人员。(1998 年及以后的数据均为在岗职工数据,其他相关指标如职工工资总额,职工平均工资等指标也从 1998 年按此口径进行了相应调整)。

■ 城镇登记失业人员

指有非农业户口,在一定的劳动年龄内(16 岁以上及男 50 岁以下、女 45 岁以下),有劳动能力,无业而要求就业,并在当地就业服务机构进行求职登记的人员。

■ 城镇登记失业率

指城镇登记失业人员同城镇单位就业人员、城镇私营企业及个体就业人员(扣除使用的农村劳动力、聘用的离退休人员、港澳台及外方人员)和城镇登记失业人员、城镇单位中的不在岗职工之和的比。计算公式为:

主要统计指标解释

城镇登记失业率＝城镇登记失业人员／（城镇单位就业人员－使用的农村劳动力－聘用的离退休人员－聘用的港澳台及外方人员）＋不在岗职工＋城镇私营企业及个体就业人员＋城镇登记失业人员×100%

在岗职工

指在本单位工作并由单位支付工资的人员，以及有工作岗位，但由于学习、病伤产假等原因暂未工作，仍由单位支付工资的人员。

SHANGHAI STATISTICAL YEARBOOK

EXPLANATORY NOTES TO MAJOR STATISTICAL INDICATORS

□ Population

Population refers to the total population by December 31 every year. According to different statistical approaches, there are two definitions of population named as population with registered residence and population with permanent residence. The former refers to the population with registration in the police while the latter refers to the population that actually reside in a place (residence) permanently ,usually longer than half a year.

□ Birth Rate

Birth Rate (or gross birth rate) means the ratio of the number of births in a certain period (usually a year) to the average population in the same period (or mid-year figure). It is usually calculated in terms of permillage and its calculating formula is:

$$\text{Birth Rate} = \frac{\text{Number of Births}}{\text{Average Number of Population}} \times 1000‰$$

Number of Births refers to live births, when babies have showed any vital phenomena regardless of the length of pregnancy.

Average Number of Population is the average of the number of population at the beginning of the year and, at the end of the year and sometimes is substituted for with mid-year population.

□ Death Rate

Death Rate (or Gross Death Rate) refers to the ratio of number of deaths to the average population (or mid-year population) during a certain period of time (usually a year), which is often presented as permillage. Its calculating formula is :

$$\text{Death Rate} = \frac{\text{Number of Deaths}}{\text{Average Number of Population}} \times 1000‰$$

□ Natural Growth Rate of Population

Natural Growth Rate of Population refers to the ratio of natural increase in population (number of births minus number of deaths) in a certain period of time (usually a year) to the average population (or mid-year population) of the same period, which is often presented as permillage. The following formula are applied:

Number of Births–Number of Deaths

$$\text{Natural Growth Rate of Population} = \frac{\text{Number of Births} - \text{Number of Deaths}}{\text{Average Number of Population}} \times 1000‰$$

Natural Growth Rate of Population = Birth Rate—Death Rate

□ Average Life Expectancy

Average Life Expectancy refers to the average age that an age group may possibly live at a certain mortality rate of the group, in the common knowledge, the average age that a group of new-borns may possibly live.

□ Employees

Employees refer to the persons who are engaged in social working and receive remuneration payment or earn business income, including total staff and workers, re-employed retirees, employers of private enterprises, self-employed workers, employees in private enterprises and individual economy, employees in township enterprises, employed persons in the rural areas , and other employed persons (including teachers in the schools run by the local people, people engaged in religious profession and the servicemen, etc.). This indicator reflects the actual utilization of total labour force during a certain period of time and is often used for the research on China's economic situation and national power.

Employees in Various Units refer to all the persons working in government agencies of various levels, political and party organizations, social organizations, enterprises and institutions, and receiving wages or other forms of payment. They include fully-employed staff and workers, re-employed retirees, teachers in schools run by the local people, foreigners and Chinese compatriots from Hong Kong, Macao, and Taiwan working in various units, part-time employees, employees of other units working temporarily at current posts, and employees holding the second job, but exclude staff and workers who have left their working units while keeping their labor contract (employment relation) unchanged. This indicator reflects the total number of laborers actually engaged in production or other operations in various units.

□ Staff and Workers

Staff and Workers refer to persons working in, and receive payment from units of state ownership, collective ownership, joint ownership, share holding ownership, foreign ownership, and ownership by entrepreneurship from Hong Kong, Macao, and Taiwan, and other types of ownership and their affiliated units. They do not

EXPLANATORY NOTES TO MAJOR STATISTICAL INDICATORS

include 1) persons employed in township enterprises, 2) persons employed in private enterprises, 3) urban self-employed persons, 4) retirees, 5) re-employed retirees, 6) teachers in the schools run by the local people, 7) foreigners and persons from Hong Kong, Macao and Taiwan who work in urban units, and 8) other persons not to be included by relevant regulations. (Data of 1998 and afterward refer to fully employed staff and workers. Other related statistics such as total wages and average wage are adjusted since 1998 accordingly).

□ Registered Urban Unemployment

Registered Urban Unemployment refers to those non-agricultural population within working age (16-50 years for male and 16-45 years for females),who are able and willing to work but unemployed and have registered for job in local employment service agencies.

□ Registered Urban Unemployment Rate

Registered Urban Unemployment Rate refers to the ratio of the number of the registered unemployed to the sum of the number of persons employed in various units (minus the rural labour force, retirees, and Hong Kong, Macao, Taiwan and foreign employees they employ) laid-off workers in urban units, urban self-employed individuals and the registered urban unemployed persons . The formula is as follows:

Registered Urban Unemployment Rate = Number of Registered Urban Unemployed Persons ÷ (Number of Persons Employed in Urban Units − rural labour force employed− retirees employed − Hong Kong, Macao, Taiwan and foreign employees + laid-off workers + Self-employed Individuals in Urban Areas + Number of Registered Urban Unemployed Persons) × 100%.

□ Fully Employed Staff and Workers

Fully Employed Staff and Workers refer to persons who work in, and receive wages from their working units, as well as persons who have their work posts, but are temporarily absent from work for reasons of study or on sick, injury or maternal leave and still receive wages from their working units.

第四篇

CHAPTER 4

国民经济核算

NATIONAL ECONOMIC ACCOUNTING

表4.1 上海市生产总值(1978～2006)
GROSS DOMESTIC PRODUCT

年份 Year	上海市生产总值(亿元) Gross Domestic Product (100 million yuan)	其中 of which					人均生产总值(元) Per Capita Gross Domestic Product (yuan)
		第一产业 Primary Industry	第二产业 Secondary Industry	其中 of which		第三产业 Tertiary Industry	
				工业 Industry	建筑业 Construction		
1978	272.81	11.00	211.05	207.47	3.58	50.76	2 497
1979	286.43	11.39	221.21	216.62	4.59	53.83	2 568
1980	311.89	10.10	236.10	230.87	5.23	65.69	2 737
1981	324.76	10.58	244.34	237.12	7.22	69.84	2 813
1982	337.07	13.31	249.32	240.75	8.57	74.44	2 877
1983	351.81	13.52	255.32	246.26	9.06	82.97	2 963
1984	390.85	17.26	275.37	263.19	12.18	98.22	3 259
1985	466.75	19.53	325.63	311.12	14.51	121.59	3 855
1986	490.83	19.69	336.02	318.89	17.13	135.12	4 008
1987	545.46	21.60	364.38	336.54	27.84	159.48	4 396
1988	648.30	27.36	433.05	399.53	33.52	187.89	5 162
1989	696.54	29.63	466.18	432.92	33.26	200.73	5 487
1990	781.66	34.24	505.60	469.83	35.77	241.82	6 107
1991	893.77	34.06	550.64	514.79	35.85	309.07	6 954
1992	1 114.32	34.16	677.39	636.68	40.71	402.77	8 650
1993	1 519.23	37.82	902.38	846.71	55.67	579.03	11 758
1994	1 990.86	47.61	1 148.45	1 074.37	74.08	794.80	15 352
1995	2 499.43	59.82	1 419.41	1 308.20	111.21	1 020.20	19 225
1996	2 957.55	68.72	1 596.72	1 452.79	143.93	1 292.11	22 700
1997	3 438.79	72.03	1 774.02	1 598.91	175.11	1 592.74	26 352
1998	3 801.09	73.84	1 871.89	1 670.19	201.70	1 855.36	29 104
1999	4 188.73	74.49	1 984.64	1 787.98	196.66	2 129.60	31 979
2000	4 771.17	76.68	2 207.63	1 998.96	208.67	2 486.86	36 217
2001	5 210.12	78.00	2 403.18	2 166.74	236.44	2 728.94	39 340
2002	5 741.03	79.68	2 622.45	2 368.02	254.43	3 038.90	43 143
2003	6 694.23	81.02	3 209.02	2 941.24	267.78	3 404.19	50 032
2004	8 072.83	83.45	3 892.12	3 593.25	298.87	4 097.26	59 928
2005	9 164.10	90.26	4 452.92	4 129.52	323.40	4 620.92	67 565
2006	10 366.37	93.80	5 028.37	4 670.11	358.26	5 244.20	75 990

注：人均生产总值按户籍人口计算。
Note: Per Capita Gross Domestic Product is calculated according to the number of Shanghai's towners.

表 4.2 上海市生产总值指数(以 1978 年为 100,1978～2006)
INDEX OF GROSS DOMESTIC PRODUCT (1978 = 100)

年 份 Year	上海市 生产总值 Gross Domestic Product	其 中 of which					人均生产 总 值 Per Capita Gross Domestic Product
		第一产业 Primary Industry	第二产业 Secondary Industry	其 中 of which		第三产业 Tertiary Industry	
				工 业 Industry	建筑业 Construction		
1978	100	100	100	100	100	100	100
1979	107.4	99.3	108.6	108.8	97.8	103.1	105.2
1980	116.4	98.7	115.1	115.4	99.4	126.0	111.7
1981	122.9	99.0	120.7	120.1	138.4	137.2	116.4
1982	131.7	124.9	126.3	125.1	164.3	155.6	122.9
1983	142.0	124.9	135.8	134.5	178.9	170.8	130.8
1984	158.5	156.4	149.4	147.5	213.4	195.9	144.5
1985	179.7	121.7	171.7	169.6	237.1	224.7	162.4
1986	187.6	121.5	178.6	175.9	264.8	238.2	167.5
1987	201.7	118.2	191.8	187.9	323.9	259.4	177.7
1988	222.1	123.6	209.8	205.4	363.1	292.1	193.4
1989	228.8	124.0	213.2	209.3	347.1	312.8	197.1
1990	236.8	129.3	219.2	215.0	364.8	329.4	202.3
1991	253.6	129.8	234.3	233.9	296.6	357.7	215.8
1992	291.1	130.3	274.6	275.3	319.4	400.6	247.3
1993	335.1	126.8	320.5	321.8	363.5	455.5	283.8
1994	383.7	130.5	366.0	367.5	414.8	529.3	323.6
1995	438.6	138.9	420.2	420.1	518.5	601.8	368.9
1996	496.1	145.8	466.8	463.8	647.6	710.7	416.2
1997	559.6	151.9	516.3	511.1	757.0	837.9	468.6
1998	617.2	155.2	558.6	551.0	869.0	961.9	516.4
1999	681.4	158.5	608.9	603.9	863.8	1 090.8	568.3
2000	756.4	163.9	668.6	665.5	889.7	1 238.1	627.2
2001	835.8	168.8	748.8	746.0	986.7	1 354.5	689.7
2002	930.2	173.9	839.4	840.7	1 049.8	1 502.1	763.8
2003	1 044.6	177.9	974.5	988.7	1 063.4	1 637.3	851.6
2004	1 192.9	169.0	1 119.7	1 147.9	1 071.9	1 868.2	966.3
2005	1 325.3	154.0	1 248.5	1 283.4	1 149.1	2 075.6	1 065.8
2006	1 484.3	155.2	1 402.1	1 442.5	1 270.9	2 324.7	1 187.3

表4.3 上海市生产总值比上年增长(1978～2006)
GROWTH RATE OF GROSS DOMESTIC PRODUCT RAISED PRECEDING YEAR

单位:%

年份 Year	上海市生产总值 Gross Domestic Product	其中 of which					人均生产总值 Per Capita Gross Domestic Product
		第一产业 Primary Industry	第二产业 Secondary Industry	其中 of which		第三产业 Tertiary Industry	
				工业 Industry	建筑业 Construction		
1978	15.8	27.0	16.6	15.8	89.8	10.6	14.9
1979	7.4	-0.7	8.6	8.8	-2.2	3.1	5.2
1980	8.4	-0.6	6.0	6.1	1.6	22.2	6.1
1981	5.6	0.3	4.9	4.1	39.2	8.9	4.2
1982	7.2	26.2	4.6	4.2	18.7	13.4	5.6
1983	7.8	平	7.5	7.5	8.9	9.8	6.4
1984	11.6	25.2	10.0	9.7	19.3	14.7	10.5
1985	13.4	-22.2	14.9	15.0	11.1	14.7	12.3
1986	4.4	-0.2	4.0	3.7	11.7	6.0	3.2
1987	7.5	-2.7	7.4	6.8	22.3	8.9	6.1
1988	10.1	4.6	9.4	9.3	12.1	12.6	8.8
1989	3.0	0.3	1.6	1.9	-4.4	7.1	1.9
1990	3.5	4.3	2.8	2.7	5.1	5.3	2.7
1991	7.1	0.4	6.9	8.8	-18.7	8.6	6.7
1992	14.8	0.4	17.2	17.7	7.7	12.0	14.6
1993	15.1	-2.7	16.7	16.9	13.8	13.7	14.8
1994	14.5	2.9	14.2	14.2	14.1	16.2	14.0
1995	14.3	6.4	14.8	14.3	25.0	13.7	14.0
1996	13.1	5.0	11.1	10.4	24.9	18.1	12.8
1997	12.8	4.2	10.6	10.2	16.9	17.9	12.6
1998	10.3	2.2	8.2	7.8	14.8	14.8	10.2
1999	10.4	2.1	9.0	9.6	-0.6	13.4	10.0
2000	11.0	3.4	9.8	10.2	3.0	13.5	10.4
2001	10.5	3.0	12.0	12.1	10.9	9.4	9.9
2002	11.3	3.0	12.1	12.7	6.4	10.9	10.8
2003	12.3	2.3	16.1	17.6	1.3	9.0	11.6
2004	14.2	-5.0	14.9	16.1	0.8	14.1	13.5
2005	11.1	-8.9	11.5	11.8	7.2	11.1	10.3
2006	12.0	0.8	12.3	12.4	10.6	12.0	11.4

表 4.4 上海市生产总值结构(1978~2006)
STRUCTURE ON GROSS DOMESTIC PRODUCT

单位:%

年 份 Year	上海市 生产总值 Gross Domestic Product	其中 of which				
		第一产业 Primary Industry	第二产业 Secondary Industry	其中 of which		第三产业 Tertiary Industry
				工 业 Industry	建筑业 Construction	
1978	100	4.0	77.4	76.1	1.3	18.6
1979	100	4.0	77.2	75.6	1.6	18.8
1980	100	3.2	75.7	74.0	1.7	21.1
1981	100	3.3	75.2	73.0	2.2	21.5
1982	100	3.9	74.0	71.4	2.6	22.1
1983	100	3.8	72.6	70.0	2.6	23.6
1984	100	4.4	70.5	67.4	3.1	25.1
1985	100	4.2	69.8	66.7	3.1	26.0
1986	100	4.0	68.5	65.0	3.5	27.5
1987	100	4.0	66.8	61.7	5.1	29.2
1988	100	4.2	66.8	61.6	5.2	29.0
1989	100	4.3	66.9	62.1	4.8	28.8
1990	100	4.4	64.7	60.1	4.6	30.9
1991	100	3.8	61.6	57.6	4.0	34.6
1992	100	3.1	60.8	57.1	3.7	36.1
1993	100	2.5	59.4	55.7	3.7	38.1
1994	100	2.4	57.7	54.0	3.7	39.9
1995	100	2.4	56.8	52.3	4.5	40.8
1996	100	2.3	54.0	49.1	4.9	43.7
1997	100	2.1	51.6	46.5	5.1	46.3
1998	100	1.9	49.3	44.0	5.3	48.8
1999	100	1.8	47.4	42.7	4.7	50.8
2000	100	1.6	46.3	41.9	4.4	52.1
2001	100	1.5	46.1	41.6	4.5	52.4
2002	100	1.4	45.7	41.3	4.4	52.9
2003	100	1.2	47.9	43.9	4.0	50.9
2004	100	1.0	48.2	44.5	3.7	50.8
2005	100	1.0	48.6	45.1	3.5	50.4
2006	100	0.9	48.5	45.0	3.5	50.6

表4.5 主要年份上海市生产总值(按三次产业分)
GROSS DOMESTIC PRODUCT (CLASSIFIED BY THREE INDUSTRIES) IN MAIN YEARS

单位:亿元(100 million yuan)

指 标	Indicators	2001	2005	2006
上海市生产总值	**Gross Domestic Product**	**5 210.12**	**9 164.10**	**10 366.37**
第一产业	Primary Industry	78.00	90.26	93.80
第二产业	Secondary Industry	2 403.18	4 452.92	5 028.37
工 业	Industry	2 166.74	4 129.52	4 670.11
建筑业	Construction	236.44	323.40	358.26
第三产业	Tertiary Industry	2 728.94	4 620.92	5 244.20
交通运输、仓储和邮政业	Transportation, Warehousing and Post	345.99	582.60	669.01
#交通运输业	Transportation	305.25	516.18	595.19
仓储业	Warehousing	21.43	44.21	50.20
信息传输、计算机服务和软件业	Information Transmission, Computer Servcie and Software Industries	176.72	359.21	421.31
批发和零售业	Retail and Wholesale Industries	555.06	840.89	929.16
住宿和餐饮业	Hoteling and Catering	104.30	168.31	194.08
金融业	Financial Industry	529.26	675.12	825.20
房地产业	Real Estate Industry	328.59	676.12	688.10
租赁和商务服务业	Leasehold and Business in Services	136.97	292.19	332.98
科学研究、技术服务和地质勘查业	Scientific Research, Technology Service and Geological Prospecting	114.91	212.91	234.12
水利、环境和公共设施管理业	Water Conservancy, Environment and Public Facility Management Industries	32.59	53.38	56.45
居民服务和其他服务业	Community Service and Other Service Industries	46.16	82.81	113.81
教 育	Education	136.53	269.64	312.62
卫生、社会保障和社会福利业	Health, Social Security and Welfare Industries	72.27	144.63	162.16
文化、体育和娱乐	Culture, Sports and Entertainment	43.96	77.60	88.31
公共管理和社会组织	Public Administration and Social Organizations	105.63	185.51	216.89

表4.6 主要年份上海市生产总值指数(按三次产业分,以上年为100)
INDEX OF GROSS DOMESTIC PRODUCT IN MAIN YEARS(CLASSIFIED BY THREE INDUSTRIES, PRECEDING YEAR = 100)

指 标	Indicators	2001	2005	2006
上海市生产总值	**Gross Domestic Product**	**110.5**	**111.1**	**112.0**
第一产业	Primary Industry	103.0	91.1	100.8
第二产业	Secondary Industry	112.0	111.5	112.3
工 业	Industry	112.1	111.8	112.4
建筑业	Construction	110.9	107.2	110.6
第三产业	Tertiary Industry	109.4	111.1	112.0
交通运输、仓储和邮政业	Transportation, Warehousing and Post	108.9	114.3	111.3
#交通运输业	Transportation	109.0	112.9	111.7
信息传输、计算机服务和软件业	Information Transmission, Computer Servcie and Software Industries	118.1	117.5	117.3
批发和零售业	Retail and Wholesale Industries	115.7	112.7	110.2
住宿和餐饮业	Hoteling and Catering	107.8	111.2	115.4
金融业	Financial Industry	90.9	109.2	121.3
房地产业	Real Estate Industry	120.4	97.1	100.8
租赁和商务服务业	Leasehold and Business in Services	129.5	113.3	112.2
科学研究、技术服务和地质勘查业	Scientific Research, Technological Service and Geological Prospecting	109.9	122.1	107.3
水利、环境和公共设施管理业	Water Conservancy, Environment and Public Facility Management Industries	123.9	108.5	103.2
居民服务和其他服务业	Community Service and Other Services Industries	118.8	110.9	135.3
教 育	Education	114.4	115.0	113.1
卫生、社会保障和社会福利业	Health, Social Security and Welfare Industries	114.0	114.7	109.4
文化、体育和娱乐	Culture, Sports and Entertainment	113.8	117.1	112.0
公共管理和社会组织	Public Administration and Social Organizations	114.5	113.9	114.1

表 4.7 上海市生产总值项目结构(1978～2006)
STRUCTURE OF GROSS DOMESTIC PRODUCT

单位:亿元(100 million yuan)

年 份 Year	上海市生产总值 Gross Domestic Product	劳动者报酬 Compensation of Employees	固定资产折旧 Depreciation of Fixed Assets	生产税净额 Net Taxes on Production	营业盈余 Operating Surplus
1978	272.81	62.03	10.60	45.53	154.65
1979	286.43	68.15	11.13	45.61	161.54
1980	311.89	74.47	13.05	49.49	174.88
1981	324.76	78.99	14.70	54.52	176.55
1982	337.07	85.00	16.30	57.09	178.68
1983	351.81	90.36	18.73	57.51	185.21
1984	390.85	108.79	20.81	68.74	192.51
1985	466.75	125.99	26.16	87.36	227.24
1986	490.83	141.95	33.42	86.31	229.15
1987	545.46	163.88	40.73	98.61	242.24
1988	648.30	197.69	71.85	126.95	251.81
1989	696.54	223.35	79.79	136.01	257.39
1990	781.66	244.03	92.93	149.35	295.35
1991	893.77	302.94	126.62	170.42	293.79
1992	1 114.32	397.72	160.36	207.40	348.84
1993	1 519.23	563.59	159.93	257.30	538.41
1994	1 990.86	692.40	245.26	356.32	696.88
1995	2 499.43	901.83	339.77	430.67	827.16
1996	2 957.55	1 065.85	376.70	576.01	938.99
1997	3 438.79	1 195.63	425.04	716.02	1 102.10
1998	3 801.09	1 341.22	514.85	809.04	1 135.98
1999	4 188.73	1 518.26	615.28	902.10	1 153.09
2000	4 771.17	1 724.29	679.43	1 124.30	1 243.15
2001	5 210.12	1 934.27	769.59	1 184.62	1 321.64
2002	5 741.03	2 205.79	850.69	1 219.35	1 465.20
2003	6 694.23	2 452.32	975.24	1 265.89	2 000.78
2004	8 072.83	2 771.77	1 265.16	1 313.83	2 722.07
2005	9 164.10	3 279.30	1 501.79	1 418.96	2 964.05
2006	10 366.37	3 756.56	1 730.51	1 623.36	3 255.94

表4.8 主要年份上海市生产总值(按所有制分)
GROSS DOMESTIC PRODUCT IN MAIN YEARS (BY OWNERSHIP)

年 份 Year	上海市生产总值 Gross Domestic Product	其 中 of which				
		公有制经济 Public-owned	其 中 of which		非公有制经济 Non-public-owned	其 中 of which
			国有经济 State-owned	集体经济 Collective-owned		#私营和个体 Private
绝对值(亿元)	**Absolute Volume (100 million yuan)**					
1978	272.81	270.10	235.22	34.88	2.71	2.71
1990	781.66	746.03	556.87	189.16	35.63	13.69
1995	2 499.43	2 047.57	1 489.06	558.51	451.86	98.88
1996	2 957.55	2 302.16	1 677.56	624.60	655.39	123.70
1997	3 438.79	2 648.19	1 953.84	694.35	790.60	187.12
1998	3 801.09	2 860.45	2 118.64	741.81	940.64	244.97
1999	4 188.73	3 063.77	2 297.74	766.03	1 124.96	322.96
2000	4 771.17	3 409.97	2 626.33	783.64	1 361.20	453.26
2001	5 210.12	3 554.56	2 773.76	780.80	1 655.56	658.45
2002	5 741.03	3 703.46	2 888.57	814.89	2 037.57	840.34
2003	6 694.23	4 171.16	3 360.21	810.95	2 523.07	1 010.57
2004	8 072.83	4 810.32	4 069.95	740.37	3 262.51	1 270.73
2005	9 164.10	5 277.62	4 488.60	789.02	3 886.48	1 501.73
2006	10 366.37	5 791.89	4 967.55	824.34	4 574.48	1 750.67
构 成(%)	**Composition(%)**					
1978	100	99.0	86.2	12.8	1.0	1.0
1990	100	95.4	71.2	24.2	4.6	1.7
1995	100	81.9	59.6	22.3	18.1	5.2
1996	100	77.8	56.7	21.1	22.2	6.6
1997	100	77.0	56.8	20.2	23.0	7.2
1998	100	75.2	55.7	19.5	24.8	7.3
1999	100	73.2	54.9	18.3	26.8	8.9
2000	100	71.4	55.0	16.4	28.6	9.1
2001	100	68.2	53.2	15.0	31.8	11.7
2002	100	64.5	50.3	14.2	35.5	13.1
2003	100	62.3	50.2	12.1	37.7	13.3
2004	100	59.6	50.4	9.2	40.4	15.8
2005	100	57.6	49.0	8.6	42.4	16.4
2006	100	55.9	47.9	8.0	44.1	16.9

表4.9 主要年份非公有制经济增加值(按产业分)
VALUE ADDED OF NON-PUBLIC-OWNED IN MAIN YEARS (GROWPED BY INDUSTRY)

单位:亿元(100 million yuan)

年 份 Year	非公经济增加值 Value Added	其中 of which			
		第一产业 Primary Industry	第二产业 Secondary Industry	其中 of which 工业 Industry	第三产业 Tertiary Industry
1978	2.71	1.64	0.67	0.40	0.40
1990	35.63	9.01	15.22	13.74	11.40
1995	451.86	13.29	285.73	274.64	152.84
1996	655.39	14.31	424.30	407.69	216.78
1997	790.60	13.42	503.69	470.23	273.49
1998	940.64	13.25	561.66	518.25	365.72
1999	1 124.96	13.56	635.83	585.76	475.57
2000	1 361.20	14.25	773.50	715.18	573.45
2001	1 655.56	14.77	924.21	857.62	716.58
2002	2 037.57	14.34	1 085.12	1 004.78	938.11
2003	2 523.07	13.04	1 459.67	1 378.21	1 050.36
2004	3 262.51	10.44	1 921.74	1 757.96	1 330.33
2005	3 886.48	11.12	2 305.75	2 137.26	1 569.61
2006	4 574.48	11.41	2 723.54	2 541.34	1 839.53

表4.10 上海市生产总值分配(1990~2006)
STRUCTURE OF GROSS DOMESTIC PRODUCT BY DISTRIBUTION

单位:亿元(100 million yuan)

年 份 Year	上海市生产总值 Gross Domestic Product	国家所得 State Owned Product	集体所得 Collective Owned	个人所得 Personal Owned
1990	781.66	252.74	201.99	326.93
1991	893.77	283.08	240.30	370.39
1992	1 114.32	296.98	352.54	464.80
1993	1 519.23	360.66	537.82	620.75
1994	1 990.86	505.14	657.24	828.48
1995	2 499.43	590.96	872.16	1 036.31
1996	2 957.55	725.27	980.04	1 252.24
1997	3 438.79	1 000.07	1 059.09	1 379.63
1998	3 801.09	1 100.75	1 175.22	1 525.12
1999	4 188.73	1 217.92	1 286.23	1 684.58
2000	4 771.17	1 483.36	1 448.83	1 838.98
2001	5 210.12	1 625.56	1 587.93	1 996.63
2002	5 741.03	1 798.64	1 739.11	2 203.28
2003	6 694.23	2 195.62	2 008.80	2 489.81
2004	8 072.83	2 659.12	2 423.58	2 990.13
2005	9 164.10	3 018.63	2 672.07	3 473.40
2006	10 366.37	3 447.83	3 013.79	3 904.75

表 4.11 主要年份上海市生产总值(支出法)
GROSS DOMESTIC PRODUCT IN MAIN YEARS(BY EXPENDITURE APPROACH)

年 份 Year	上海市生产总 值 (亿元) Gross Domestic Product (100 million yuan)	其中 of which 货物和服务净流出 Net Outflows of Goods and Services	本市使用的生产总值 Gross Domestic Product Used	其中 of which 最终消费 Final Consumption	资本形成总额 Gross Capital Formation	上海市生产总值构成(%) Composition of GDP(%) #最终消费 Final Consumption	#资本形成总额 Gross Capital Formation	可供投资率(%) Available Investment Rate(%)
1978	272.81	165.79	107.02	59.06	47.96	21.6	17.6	78.4
1980	311.89	164.13	147.76	81.24	66.52	26.0	21.3	74.0
1981	324.76	158.35	166.41	89.73	76.68	27.6	23.6	72.4
1982	337.07	153.90	187.17	96.90	90.27	27.6	26.8	72.4
1983	351.81	178.76	173.05	101.19	71.86	28.8	20.4	71.2
1984	390.85	171.97	218.88	117.25	101.63	30.0	26.0	70.0
1985	466.75	122.47	344.28	155.15	189.13	33.2	40.5	66.8
1986	490.83	80.97	409.86	181.74	228.12	37.0	46.5	63.0
1987	545.46	103.70	441.76	200.74	241.02	36.8	44.2	63.2
1988	648.30	57.32	590.98	255.42	335.56	39.4	51.8	60.6
1989	696.54	46.24	650.30	298.62	351.68	42.9	50.5	57.1
1990	781.66	91.87	689.79	358.45	331.34	45.9	42.4	54.1
1991	893.77	167.68	726.09	386.06	340.03	43.2	38.0	56.8
1992	1 114.32	150.12	964.20	476.57	487.63	42.8	43.8	57.2
1993	1 519.23	75.60	1 443.63	699.52	744.11	46.0	49.0	54.0
1994	1 990.86	-90.46	2 081.32	919.83	1 161.49	46.2	58.3	53.8
1995	2 499.43	-218.64	2 718.07	1 150.35	1 567.72	46.0	62.7	54.0
1996	2 957.55	-348.05	3 305.60	1 348.76	1 956.84	45.6	66.2	54.4
1997	3 438.79	-210.99	3 649.78	1 600.83	2 048.95	46.6	59.6	53.4
1998	3 801.09	32.25	3 768.84	1 758.09	2 010.75	46.3	52.9	53.7
1999	4 188.73	259.37	3 929.36	1 959.12	1 970.24	46.8	47.0	53.2
2000	4 771.17	356.93	4 414.24	2 244.52	2 169.72	47.0	45.5	53.0
2001	5 210.12	377.21	4 832.91	2 476.20	2 356.71	47.5	45.2	52.5
2002	5 741.03	418.68	5 322.35	2 791.06	2 531.29	48.6	44.1	51.4
2003	6 694.23	399.96	6 294.27	3 217.59	3 076.68	48.1	46.0	51.9
2004	8 072.83	457.99	7 614.84	3 832.59	3 782.25	47.5	46.9	52.5
2005	9 164.10	558.25	8 605.85	4 418.99	4 186.86	48.2	45.7	51.8
2006	10 366.37	523.75	9 842.62	5 079.76	4 762.86	49.0	45.9	51.0

表4.12 主要年份六大支柱产业增加值
VALUE ADDED OF SIX PILLAR INDUSTRIES IN MAIN YEARS

	指　标 Indicators	2000	2005	2006
增加值(亿元)	**Value Added (100 million yuan)**	**1 919.10**	**3 980.88**	**4 691.05**
信息产业	Information Industry	338.18	1 097.91	1 337.89
金融业	Financial Industry	602.95	675.12	825.20
商贸流通业	Trading and Circulation Industry	431.43	840.89	929.16
汽车制造业	Auto Manufacturing	166.05	311.20	359.52
成套设备制造业	Whole-set Equipment Manufacturing Industry	129.73	399.38	572.76
房地产业	Real Estate Industry	263.35	676.12	688.10
增加值占上海市生产总值比重(%)	**Ratio of Value Added to GDP (%)**	**40.2**	**43.4**	**45.3**
信息产业	Information Industry	7.1	12.0	12.9
金融业	Financial Industry	12.6	7.4	8.0
商贸流通业	Trading and Circulation Industry	9.0	9.2	9.0
汽车制造业	Auto Manufacturing	3.5	3.4	3.5
成套设备制造业	Whole-set Equipment Manufacturing Industry	2.7	4.4	5.5
房地产业	Real Estate Industry	5.5	7.4	6.6

①信息产业增加值含有与其他行业的交叉重复因素，本表中"六大支柱产业增加值占上海市生产总值的比重"已经扣除重复计算因素。
②商贸流通业中不包括餐饮业增加值。
❶The ratio of value added from six pillar industries to GDP has excluded some overlapping factors.
❷Trading and circulation industry does not include the catering industry.

表4.13 主要年份信息产业增加值
VALUE ADDED OF INFORMATION INDUSTRY IN MAIN YEARS

	指　标 Indicators	2000	2005	2006
增加值(亿元)	**Value Added (100 million yuan)**	**338.18**	**1 097.91**	**1 337.89**
信息产品制造业	Information Products Manufacturing	195.82	653.75	813.43
信息产品销售业	Information Products Distribution	12.59	21.66	24.91
信息服务业	Information Services	129.77	422.50	499.55
增加值指数(以1998年为100)	**Index of Value Added (1998 = 100)**	**163.2**	**462.0**	**580.7**
信息产品制造业	Information Products Manufacturing	201.1	593.4	746.5
信息产品销售业	Information Products Distribution	126.8	238.0	268.2
信息服务业	Information Services	128.1	350.0	442.4
结　构(%)	**Composition(%)**	**100**	**100**	**100**
信息产品制造业	Information Products Manufacturing	57.9	59.5	60.8
信息产品销售业	Information Products Distribution	3.7	2.0	1.9
信息服务业	Information Services	38.4	38.5	37.3
信息产业增加值占上海市生产总值比重(%)	**Ratio of Value Added of Information Industry to GDP(%)**	**7.1**	**12.0**	**12.9**

表 4.14 旅游产业增加值(2004～2006)
VALUE ADDED OF TOURISM INDUSTRY

指标	Indicators	2004	2005	2006
增加值(亿元)	**Value Added (100 million yuan)**	**498.09**	**584.26**	**695.06**
一、按行业分	Grouped by Sectors			
旅行社服务业	Travel Agency	8.34	9.02	10.43
旅游宾(旅)馆业	Hotel	79.68	91.78	122.47
旅游运输业	Travel Transportation	103.36	120.86	136.88
邮电通信业	Post and Telecommunication	18.95	25.21	27.80
旅游商业	Tourism Commerce	73.63	96.17	107.17
餐饮业	Catering	58.59	68.92	83.93
城市交通业	Urban Traffic	39.43	45.96	59.39
园林文化业	Gardening	76.54	92.42	103.84
金融保险业	Finance Banking and Insurance	6.80	7.61	8.07
其他服务业	Other Services	32.77	26.31	35.08
二、按境内、外分	Grouped by Domestic and Overseas			
境　内	Domestic	405.07	469.94	555.05
境　外	Overseas	93.02	114.32	140.01
旅游产业增加值占上海市生产总值比重(%)	**Ratio of Value Added of Tourism Industry to GDP (%)**	**5.9**	**6.4**	**6.7**

表 4.15 文化产业增加值(2004～2006)
VALUE ADDED OF CULTURE INDUSTRY

指标	Indicators	2004	2005	2006
总　计(亿元)	**Total (100 million yuan)**	**441.40**	**509.23**	**581.38**
文化服务业	**Culture Service**	**268.83**	**307.82**	**358.08**
新闻服务业	News Service	0.08	0.08	0.09
出版发行和版权服务	Issue & Copyright Service	38.69	42.08	49.07
广播、电视、电影服务	Broadcasting, Television & Film Service	19.05	24.17	29.31
文化艺术服务	Art Service	13.83	17.71	19.31
网络文化服务	Net Culture Service	47.25	58.19	69.33
文化休闲娱乐服务	Entertainment Service	74.09	82.26	99.33
其他文化服务	Other Culture Service	75.84	83.33	91.64
文化相关产业	**Culture Relative Service**	**172.57**	**201.41**	**223.30**
文化用品、设备及相关文化产品生产	Production of Stationery, Equipment & Relative Product	124.71	148.48	164.17
文化用品、设备及相关文化产品销售	Sales of Stationery, Equipment & Relative Product	47.86	52.93	59.13
文化产业增加值占上海市生产总值比重(%)	**Ratio of Value Added of Culture Industry to GDP (%)**	**5.47**	**5.56**	**5.61**

表 4.16　主要年份最终消费及构成
FINAL CONSUMPTION AND COMPOSITION IN MAIN YEARS

年份 Year	最终消费(亿元) Final Consumption(100 million yuan)					最终消费构成(%) Composition of Final Consumption (%)	
	合计 Total	居民消费 Household Consumption	其中 of which 农村居民 Rural Households	城镇居民 Urban Households	政府消费 Government Consumption	居民消费 Household Consumption	政府消费 Government Consumption
1978	59.06	48.25	12.82	35.43	10.81	81.7	18.3
1980	81.24	66.31	19.43	46.88	14.93	81.6	18.4
1985	155.15	124.78	38.35	86.43	30.37	80.4	19.6
1990	358.45	284.79	66.15	218.64	73.66	79.5	20.5
1995	1 150.35	926.54	152.90	773.64	223.81	80.5	19.5
1996	1 348.76	1 080.79	168.13	912.66	267.97	80.1	19.9
1997	1 600.83	1 262.12	176.50	1 085.62	338.71	78.8	21.2
1998	1 758.09	1 379.41	178.52	1 200.89	378.68	78.5	21.5
1999	1 959.12	1 528.95	176.73	1 352.22	430.17	78.0	22.0
2000	2 244.52	1 756.27	176.79	1 579.48	488.25	78.2	21.8
2001	2 476.20	1 910.44	181.22	1 729.22	565.76	77.2	22.8
2002	2 791.06	2 134.79	185.58	1 949.21	656.27	76.5	23.5
2003	3 217.59	2 437.44	187.78	2 249.66	780.15	75.8	24.2
2004	3 832.59	2 869.26	186.78	2 682.48	963.33	74.9	25.1
2005	4 418.99	3 271.64	184.02	3 087.62	1 147.35	74.0	26.0
2006	5 079.76	3 763.15	202.19	3 560.96	1 316.61	74.1	25.9

表 4.17　主要年份居民消费水平及指数
HOUSEHOLD CONSUMPTION LEVEL AND INDEX IN MAIN YEARS

年份 Year	居民消费水平(元/人) Household Consumption Level (yuan/person)			指数(以1978年为100) Index(1978=100)		
	全市 Total	其中 of which 农村居民 Rural Households	城镇居民 Urban Households	全市 Total	其中 of which 农村居民 Rural Households	城镇居民 Urban Households
1978	442	283	555	100	100	100
1980	582	437	675	123.1	141.9	114.2
1985	1 031	938	1 078	182.0	252.2	153.1
1990	2 225	1 576	2 542	216.1	249.5	193.7
1995	6 310	4 120	7 050	379.3	402.7	333.3
1996	7 228	4 680	8 033	416.5	438.1	364.0
1997	8 289	5 086	9 234	449.0	462.2	391.3
1998	8 896	5 344	9 871	480.4	480.7	417.5
1999	9 683	5 497	10 753	515.9	495.1	448.0
2000	10 922	5 705	12 168	557.7	509.0	484.3
2001	11 807	6 052	13 114	604.5	543.6	523.0
2002	13 137	6 464	14 569	673.4	580.6	582.1
2003	14 247	6 914	15 631	721.9	616.0	617.0
2004	16 470	7 715	17 883	815.0	671.4	689.8
2005	18 396	9 157	19 573	896.5	778.8	743.6
2006	20 944	10 136	22 294	1 021.1	862.1	847.0

表 4.18 主要年份资本形成总额和指数
GROSS CAPITAL FORMATION AND INDEX IN MAIN YEARS

年份 Year	资本形成总额(亿元) Gross Capital Formation (100 million yuan)			资本形成总额指数(以 1978 年为 100) Index of Gross Capital Formation (1978 = 100)		
	合计 Total	固定资本形成总额 Fixed Capital Formation	存货增加 Inventory Change	总指数 Indices	固定资本形成总额 Fixed Capital Formation	存货增加 Inventory Change
1978	47.96	31.69	16.27	100	100	100
1980	66.52	45.57	20.95	134.6	133.5	136.7
1985	189.13	116.70	72.43	387.6	308.1	564.0
1990	331.34	248.46	82.88	338.1	430.5	131.1
1995	1 567.72	1 380.85	186.87	950.6	1 373.7	218.8
1996	1 956.84	1 711.46	245.38	1 158.8	1 660.8	279.5
1997	2 048.95	1 795.83	253.12	1 175.0	1 700.6	268.3
1998	2 010.75	1 804.81	205.94	1 129.2	1 695.5	201.2
1999	1 970.24	1 801.59	168.65	1 098.7	1 683.7	164.0
2000	2 169.72	1 933.01	236.71	1 152.5	1 746.0	191.0
2001	2 356.71	2 099.99	256.72	1 263.2	1 906.6	216.1
2002	2 531.29	2 366.10	165.19	1 387.0	2 192.6	148.9
2003	3 076.68	2 643.07	433.61	1 588.1	2 365.8	299.4
2004	3 782.25	3 239.04	543.21	1 804.1	2 680.5	347.3
2005	4 186.86	3 743.42	443.44	1 962.8	3 023.6	282.0
2006	4 762.86	4 272.85	490.01	2 186.6	3 383.4	302.6

表 4.19 主要年份经营性固定资产原价年末数
ORIGINAL VALUE OF OPERATING FIXED ASSETS (YEAR-END) IN MAIN YEARS

单位:亿元(100 million yuan)

年份 Year	合计 Total	其中 of which				
		第一产业 Primary Industry	第二产业 Secondary Industry	其中 of which		第三产业 Tertiary Industry
				工业 Industry	建筑业 Construction	
1978	298.53	8.03	205.17	197.68	7.49	85.33
1980	355.16	11.81	225.55	216.16	9.39	117.80
1985	569.97	12.09	377.06	355.61	21.45	180.82
1990	1 263.17	22.80	866.64	827.01	39.63	373.73
1995	4 756.42	59.48	2 915.53	2 810.27	105.26	1 781.41
1996	5 827.13	69.64	3 393.66	3 263.77	129.89	2 363.83
1997	6 915.42	80.87	3 879.13	3 721.96	157.17	2 955.42
1998	8 392.45	82.93	4 573.10	4 406.50	166.60	3 736.42
1999	9 991.27	91.22	5 311.01	5 137.11	173.90	4 589.04
2000	11 684.90	104.25	5 940.30	5 749.23	191.07	5 640.35
2001	12 667.45	112.71	6 451.78	6 249.24	202.54	6 102.96
2002	13 839.09	118.78	6 937.81	6 596.13	341.68	6 782.50
2003	15 639.55	127.33	7 614.96	7 197.71	417.25	7 897.26
2004	18 896.30	152.61	9 183.79	8 717.45	466.34	9 559.90
2005	21 843.13	162.19	10 963.19	10 445.07	518.12	10 717.75
2006	24 226.30	175.30	12 108.99	11 539.16	569.83	11 942.01

表 4.20 主要年份存货年末数
YEAR-END INVENTORY IN MAIN YEARS

单位:亿元(100 million yuan)

年份 Year	合计 Total	其中 of which				
		第一产业 Primary Industry	第二产业 Secondary Industry	其中 of which		第三产业 Tertiary Industry
				工业 Industry	建筑业 Construction	
1978	264.20	3.00	108.10	106.69	1.41	153.10
1980	288.41	1.99	117.84	112.92	4.92	168.58
1985	412.20	2.87	206.32	194.62	11.70	203.01
1990	908.98	7.70	522.20	490.51	31.69	379.08
1995	1 528.21	21.74	1 066.51	1 029.50	37.01	439.96
1996	1 726.41	25.48	1 196.31	1 153.02	43.29	504.62
1997	1 874.05	31.98	1 276.86	1 227.71	49.15	565.21
1998	1 876.73	32.81	1 231.86	1 189.80	42.06	612.06
1999	1 965.43	33.46	1 290.14	1 244.17	45.97	641.83
2000	2 093.40	34.20	1 392.88	1 343.70	49.18	666.32
2001	2 156.65	34.53	1 425.91	1 374.52	51.39	696.21
2002	2 201.73	35.22	1 440.11	1 386.15	53.96	726.40
2003	2 512.05	35.06	1 711.72	1 654.75	56.97	765.27
2004	3 719.86	35.81	2 278.35	2 218.54	59.81	1 405.70
2005	4 032.85	36.53	2 501.82	2 441.09	60.73	1 494.50
2006	4 361.72	37.26	2 713.94	2 652.00	61.94	1 610.52

表 4.21 主要年份每百元增加值占用的资产总额
TOTAL ASSETS PER 100 YUAN WORTH OF VALUE ADDED IN MAIN YEARS

单位:元(yuan)

年份 Year	合计 Total	其中 of which				
		第一产业 Primary Industry	第二产业 Secondary Industry	其中 of which		第三产业 Tertiary Industry
				工业 Industry	建筑业 Construction	
1978	196.80	99.59	141.67	140.09	233.24	447.09
1980	197.59	130.74	141.80	139.17	257.93	408.38
1985	193.69	72.99	163.09	161.39	199.62	295.01
1990	263.14	83.79	256.64	262.37	181.34	302.11
1995	224.82	120.07	254.46	267.18	104.91	189.73
1996	233.95	128.30	268.43	284.16	109.58	196.96
1997	237.63	144.36	274.69	292.90	108.36	200.57
1998	250.70	154.79	292.78	315.71	102.87	212.06
1999	265.31	161.38	312.55	334.95	108.95	224.91
2000	269.69	171.58	315.60	337.03	110.25	231.97
2001	274.49	183.14	316.48	339.61	104.51	240.12
2002	268.81	189.03	309.93	329.52	127.65	235.42
2003	255.39	195.25	275.86	286.18	162.42	237.52
2004	252.50	210.19	267.06	275.36	167.36	239.52
2005	264.58	214.46	279.89	288.44	170.84	250.79
2006	262.70	219.23	281.28	289.90	168.96	245.65

表 4.22 主要年份每百元增加值占用的存货
INVENTORY PER 100 YUAN WORTH OF VALUE ADDED IN MAIN YEARS

单位:元(yuan)

年 份 Year	合 计 Total	其 中 of which				
		第一产业 Primary Industry	第二产业 Secondary Industry	其 中 of which		第三产业 Tertiary Industry
				工 业 Industry	建筑业 Construction	
1978	93.85	27.18	50.70	51.04	30.73	287.71
1980	89.11	20.00	48.73	47.76	91.68	244.87
1985	79.74	12.67	54.96	54.55	63.75	156.88
1990	111.55	21.23	96.27	97.42	81.21	156.29
1995	58.92	30.58	69.68	72.95	31.17	45.61
1996	55.02	34.36	70.86	75.11	27.90	36.55
1997	52.35	39.89	69.71	74.45	26.39	33.58
1998	49.34	43.87	67.01	72.37	22.61	31.73
1999	45.86	44.48	63.54	68.06	22.38	29.44
2000	42.53	44.12	60.77	64.73	22.80	26.30
2001	40.79	44.06	58.65	62.73	21.27	24.96
2002	37.96	43.77	54.64	58.29	20.70	23.41
2003	35.21	43.37	49.11	51.69	20.71	21.91
2004	38.60	42.46	51.26	53.90	19.54	26.49
2005	42.30	40.07	53.67	56.42	18.64	31.38
2006	40.49	39.33	51.86	54.53	17.12	29.60

表 4.23 主要年份每百元增加值占用的固定资产
FIXED ASSETS PER 100 YUAN WORTH OF VALUE ADDED IN MAIN YEARS

单位:元(yuan)

年 份 Year	合 计 Total	其 中 of which				
		第一产业 Primary Industry	第二产业 Secondary Industry	其 中 of which		第三产业 Tertiary Industry
				工 业 Industry	建筑业 Construction	
1978	102.95	72.41	90.97	89.05	202.51	159.39
1980	108.48	110.74	93.07	91.42	166.25	163.51
1985	113.95	60.32	108.14	106.84	135.87	138.13
1990	151.59	62.56	160.37	164.96	100.13	145.83
1995	165.90	89.49	184.78	194.22	73.74	144.11
1996	178.92	93.95	197.57	209.05	81.69	160.41
1997	185.28	104.48	204.98	218.45	81.97	166.98
1998	201.36	110.92	225.77	243.34	80.26	180.34
1999	219.44	116.89	249.02	266.88	86.57	195.47
2000	227.16	127.46	254.83	272.30	87.45	205.67
2001	233.70	139.08	257.83	276.88	83.24	215.16
2002	230.85	145.26	255.29	271.23	106.95	212.01
2003	220.18	151.88	226.75	234.49	141.71	215.61
2004	213.90	167.73	215.80	221.46	147.82	213.03
2005	222.28	174.39	226.22	232.02	152.20	219.41
2006	222.21	179.90	229.42	235.37	151.84	216.05

表 4.24　主要年份全员劳动生产率
OVERALL LABOUR PRODUCTIVITY IN MAIN YEARS

单位:元/人(yuan/person)

年　份 Year	合　计 Total	第一产业 Primary Industry	第二产业 Secondary Industry	第三产业 Tertiary Industry
1978	3 960	455	7 001	3 488
1980	4 322	462	6 886	4 096
1985	6 041	1 408	7 493	6 098
1990	9 940	3 892	10 863	10 382
1995	31 634	7 791	32 503	36 878
1996	37 269	8 717	37 813	44 181
1997	43 497	8 895	44 461	51 279
1998	47 816	9 071	49 227	55 670
1999	52 130	9 191	52 397	61 961
2000	58 443	9 754	59 909	67 345
2001	62 876	10 003	64 470	72 215
2002	67 818	10 297	69 207	77 877
2003	75 665	10 523	81 186	82 534
2004	88 893	12 409	100 507	90 326
2005	98 655	13 123	114 500	96 716
2006	108 623	16 897	126 978	104 295

表 4.25　主要年份固定资产产出率
OUTPUT RATE OF FIXED ASSETS IN MAIN YEARS

单位:%

年　份 Year	合　计 Total	其　中　of which			
		第一产业 Primary Industry	第二产业 Secondary Industry	其　中　of which 工　业 Industry	第三产业 Tertiary Industry
1978	97.1	138.1	109.9	112.3	62.7
1980	92.2	90.3	107.4	109.4	61.2
1985	87.8	165.8	92.5	93.6	72.4
1990	66.0	159.9	62.4	60.6	68.6
1995	60.3	111.8	54.1	51.5	69.4
1996	55.9	106.4	50.6	47.8	62.3
1997	54.0	95.7	48.8	45.8	59.9
1998	49.7	90.2	44.3	41.1	55.5
1999	45.6	85.6	40.2	37.5	51.2
2000	44.0	78.5	39.2	36.7	48.6
2001	42.8	71.9	38.8	36.1	46.5
2002	43.3	68.8	39.2	36.9	47.2
2003	45.4	65.8	44.1	42.6	46.4
2004	46.8	59.6	46.3	45.2	46.9
2005	45.0	57.3	44.2	43.1	45.6
2006	45.0	55.6	43.6	42.5	46.3

上 / 海 / 统 / 计 / 年 / 鉴

主要统计指标解释

■ 生产总值(原国内生产总值)

指按市场价格计算的一个地区所有常住(驻)单位在一定时期内生产活动的最终成果。生产总值有三种表现形态,即价值形态、收入形态和产品形态。从价值形态看,它是所有常住单位在一定时期内所生产的全部货物和服务价值超过同期投入的全部非固定资产货物和服务价值的差额,即所有常住(驻)单位的增加值之和;从收入形态看,它是所有常住(驻)单位在一定时期内所创造并分配给常住(驻)单位和非常住(驻)单位的初次(分配)收入之和;从产品形态看,它是所有常住单位在一定时期内最终使用的货物和服务减去进口货物和服务。在实际核算中,生产总值有三种计算方法,(其三种表现形态体现为三种计算方法,)即生产法、收入法和支出法。三种方法分别从不同的方面反映生产总值及其构成。根据国务院和国家统计局有关我国GDP核算和数据发布制度的规定,上海国内生产总值自2004年起更名为“上海市生产总值”,简称“上海市GDP”。

■ 三次产业

根据社会生产活动历史发展的顺序对产业结构的划分,产品直接取自自然界的部门称为第一产业,对初级产品进行再加工的部门称为第二产业,为生产和消费提供各种服务的部门称为第三产业。

第一产业:农林牧渔业(包括农业、林业、畜牧业、渔业和农林牧渔服务业)。

第二产业:包括采矿业、制造业、电力、燃气及水的生产和供应业、建筑业。

第三产业:除第一、第二产业以外的其他各业。

■ 劳动者报酬

指劳动者因从事生产活动所获得的全部报酬。包括劳动者获得的各种形式的工资、奖金和津贴,既包括货币形式的,也包括实物形式的,还包括劳动者所享受的公费医疗和医药卫生费、上下班交通补贴、单位支付的社会保险费、住房公积金等。对于个体经济来说,其所有者所获得的劳动报酬和经营利润不易区分,这两部分统一作为劳动者报酬处理。

■ 生产税净额

指生产税减生产补贴后的余额。生产税指政府对生产单位从事生产、销售和经营活动以及因从事生产活动使用某些生产要素(如固定资产、土地、劳动力)所征收的各种税、附加费和规费。生产补贴与生产税相反,指政府对生产单位的单方面转移支出,因此视为负生产税,包括政策亏损补贴、价格补贴等。

■ 固定资料折旧

指一定时期内为弥补固定资产损耗按照规定的固定资产折旧率提取的固定资产折旧,或按国民经济核算统一规定的折旧率虚拟计算的固定资产折旧。它反映了固定资产在当期生产中的转移价值。各类企业和企业化管理的事业单位的固定资产折旧是指实际计提的折旧费;不计提折旧的政府机关、非企业化管理的事业单位和居民住房的固定资产折旧是按照统一规定的折旧率和固定资产原值计算的虚拟折旧。原则上,固定资产折旧应按固定资产当期的重置价值计算,但是目前我国尚不具备对全社会固定资产进行重估价的基础,所以暂时只能采用上述办法。

■ 营业盈余

指常住单位创造的增加值扣除劳动者报酬、生产税净额和固定资产折旧后的余额。它相当于企业的营业利润加上生产补贴,但要扣除从利润中开支的工资和福利等。

■ 支出法生产总值

是从最终使用的角度反映一个国家(或地区)一定时期内生产活动最终成果的一种方法,包括最终消费、资本形成总额及货物和服务净出口三部分。计算公式为:

支出法生产总值 = 最终消费 + 资本形成总额 + 货物和服务净出口

■ 最终消费

指常住单位在一定时期内对于货物和服务的全部最终消费支出,也就是常住单位为满足物质、文化和精神生活的需要,从本国经济领土和国外购买的货物和服务的支出;不包括非常住单位在本国经济领土内的消费支出。最终消费分为居民消费和政府消费。

主要统计指标解释

■ 居民消费

指常住住户在一定时期内对货物和服务的全部最终消费支出。居民消费按市场价格计算，即按居民支付的购买者价格计算。购买者价格是购买者取得货物所支付的价格，包括购买者支付的运输和商业费用。居民消费除了直接以货币形式购买货物和服务的消费之外，还包括以其他方式获得的货物和服务的消费支出，即所谓的虚拟消费支出。居民虚拟消费支出包括以下几种类型：单位以实物报酬及实物转移的形式提供给劳动者的货物和服务；住户生产并由本住户消费了的货物和服务，其中的服务仅指住户的自有住房服务；金融机构提供的金融媒介服务；保险公司提供的保险服务。

■ 政府消费

指一定时期内政府部门为全社会提供公共服务的消费支出和免费或以较低价格向住户提供的货物和服务的净支出。前者等于政府服务的产出价值减去政府单位所获得的经营收入的价值，政府服务的产出价值等于它的经常性业务支出加上固定资产折旧；后者等于政府部门免费或以较低价格向住户提供的货物和服务的市场价值减去向住户收取的价值。

■ 资本形成总额

指常住单位在一定时期内获得的，并减去处置的固定资产，加上存货的变动，包括固定资本形成总额和存货增加。

■ 固定资本形成总额

指生产者在一定时期内获得的固定资产减处置的固定资产的价值总额。固定资产是通过生产活动生产出来的，且其使用年限在一年以上、单位价值在规定标准以上的资产，不包括自然资产。可分为有形固定资本形成总额和无形固定资本形成总额。有形固定资本形成总额包括一定时期内完成的建筑工程、安装工程和设备工器具购置（减处置）价值，以及土地改良、新增役、种、奶、毛、娱乐用牲畜和新增经济林木价值。无形固定资本形成总额包括矿藏的勘探、计算机软件等获得减处置。

■ 存货增加

指常住单位在一定时期内存货实物量变动的市场价值，即期末价值减期初价值的差额，再扣除当期由于价格变动而产生的持有收益。存货增加可以是正值，也可以是负值，正值表示存货上升，负值表示存货下降。存货包括生产单位购进的原材料、燃料和储备物资等存货，以及生产单位生产的产成品、在制品和半成品等存货。

■ 货物和服务净流出

指货物和服务流出减货物和服务流入的差额。流出包括常住单位向非常住单位出售或无偿转让的各种货物和服务的价值；流入包括常住单位从非常住单位购买或无偿得到的各种货物和服务的价值。地区核算净流出，除包括本地区对外贸易及国外非贸易往来的净出口额，还包括地区间货物和服务流出减流入后的净额。

■ 信息产业

是指与电子信息相关联的各种活动的集合，包括信息产品的制造、销售和信息服务等活动。由于信息产业增加值是依据若干行业的有关资料进行跨行业核算的，因此不宜将其与上海市生产总值中其他行业的增加值进行加总，否则会造成重复计算。

■ 旅游产业

指本市与旅游相关的各行业，为境内外旅游者提供旅游服务的产业。这些服务包括：旅行社服务、交通运输服务、住宿服务、电讯服务、娱乐服务、餐饮服务、商品零售服务等。由于旅游产业增加值是依据相关行业的有关资料进行跨行业核算的，因此不宜将其与上海市生产总值中其他行业的增加值进行加总，否则会造成重复计算。

■ 全社会劳动生产率

表示全社会从业人员在一定时期内平均每人创造的生产总值（增加值），这是衡量现有劳动力资源生产效率的重要指标。其中平均从业人数包括非正式登记的从业人员。

全社会劳动生产率 = 全市生产总值 / 年均从业人数

■ 固定资本产出率

在一定时期内生产总值（增加值）与经营性固定资产原价的比例，即单位经营性固定资产原价所提供的生产总值（增加值），表示经营性固定资产的投资效益，是反映固定资产产出效率的重要指标。

固定资产产出率 = 全市生产总值 / 经营性固定资产原价年均数

SHANGHAI STATISTICAL YEARBOOK

EXPLANATORY NOTES TO MAJOR STATISTICAL INDICATORS

□ Gross Regional Product(former Gross Domestic Product)

Gross Regional Product refers to the final products at market prices by (of) all resident units of a region during a certain period of time. Gross product is expressed in three different forms, i.e value, income, and products respectively. The form of value added refers to the total value of all products and services produced by all resident units during a certain period of time minus the total value of inputs of non-fixed-assets products and services or the summation of the value added of all resident units; the form of income includes all the income items produced by all resident units and distributed primarily to all resident and non-resident units; the form of product refers to all final goods and services minus imports of goods and services. In the practice of national accounting, it is calculated by three approaches, i.e. product approach, income approach, and expenditure approach, respectively, to reflect Gross Product and its composition of different aspects. According to the regulations of GDP national accounting and data release issued by the State Council and National Bureau of Statistics, since 2004 Shanghai Gross Domestic Product has been renamed as Shanghai Gross Product Value, for short Shanghai GDP.

□ Three Industries

Three Industries have been classified according to the historical sequence of development. Primary industry refers to extraction of natural resources; secondary industry involves processing of primary products; and tertiary industry provides services of various kinds for production and consumption.

Primary industry: Agriculture, forestry, animal husbandry and fishery.(including farming, forestry, animal husbandry, fishery industry and service industry for farming, forestry, animal husbandry and fishery).

Secondary industry: Mining, manufacturing, power, steam and water production and supply and construction.

Tertiary industry: All other industries not included in primary or secondary industries.

□ Compensation of Employees

Compensation of Employees refers to the whole payment of various forms earned by the labourers from the productive activities they are engaged in. It includes wages, bonuses and allowances the labourers earned in monetary form and in kind. It also includes the free medical services provided to the labourers and the medicine expenses, traffic subsidies and social insurance, housing fund paid by the employers. As the individual economy is concerned, since the compensation of employees is not easily distinguished from the operating profit, both are treated as compensation of employees.

□ Net Taxes on Production

Net Taxes on Production refers to the difference of the taxes on production minus the subsidies on production. The taxes on production refers to the various taxes, extra charges and fees levied on the production units on their production, sale and business activities as well as on the use of some factors of production, such as fixed assets, land and labour force in the production activities they are engaged in. In contrast to the taxes on production, the subsidies on production refer to the unilateral government transfer to the production units and are therefore regarded as negative taxes on production. They include subsidies on the loss due to implementation of government policies, price subsidies, etc.

□ Depreciation of Fixed Assets

Depreciation of Fixed Assets refers to the depreciation of fixed assets of a given period, drawn in accordance with the stipulated depreciation rate for the purpose of compensating the wear loss of the fixed assets or the depreciation of fixed assets calculated in a fictitious way in accordance with the stipulated unified depreciation rate in the national economic accounting system. It reflects the value of transfer of the fixed assets in the production of the current period. The depreciation of fixed assets in various enterprises and institutions managed as enterprises refers to the depreciation expenses actually drawn. In government agencies and institutions not managed as enterprises which do not draw the depreciation expenses, as well as for the houses of residents, the depreciation of fixed assets is the imputed depreciation, which is calculated in accordance with the stipulated unified depreciation rate. In principle, the depreciation of fixed assets should be calculated on the basis of the re-purchased value of the fixed assets. However, there is no actual condition to re-evaluate all the fixed assets in China. Therefore, the above-mentioned methods are

EXPLANATORY NOTES TO MAJOR STATISTICAL INDICATORS

temporarily adopted at present.

□ Operating Surplus

Operating Surplus refers to the balance of the value added created by the resident units deducting the labourers remuneration, net taxes on production and the depreciation of fixed assets. It is equivalent to the business profit of the enterprises plus subsidies on production, but the wages and welfare expenses paid from the profits should be deducted.

□ GDP by Expenditure Approach

GDP by Expenditure Approach refers to the method of measuring the final results of production activities of a country (region) during a given period from the perspective of final use. It includes final consumption, total capital formation and net export of goods and services, i.e.:

GDP by expenditure approach = final consumption + total capital formation + net export of goods and services

□ Final Consumption

Final Consumption refers to the total expenditure of resident units on final consumption of goods and services in a certain period, namely the expenditure of the resident units for purchases of goods and services from domestic economic territory and abroad to meet the requirements of material, cultural and spiritual life. It excludes the expenditure of non-resident units on consumption in the economic territory of the country. The final consumption is classified into household consumption and government consumption.

□ Household Consumption

Household Consumption refers to the total expenditure of resident households on the final consumption of goods and services in a certain period of time. The households consumption is calculated at market prices, namely the purchasers prices which the households pay; the purchasers prices of goods are the prices the households pay when they obtain the goods, including the transport and commercial expenses paid by the households. In addition to the consumption of goods and services bought by the households directly with money, the expenditure on goods and services obtained by the households in other ways, i.e. the so-called imputed expenditure on consumption, is also included in the households consumption. The imputation expenditure of the households on consumption includes the following types: (a) the goods and services provided to the households by the units in the form of payment in kind and transfer in kind; (b) the goods and services produced and consumed by the households themselves, in which the services refer only to the services provided by the residential buildings owned by the households; (c) the services of financial intermediary provided by the financial institutions; (d) the insurance services provided by the insurance companies.

□ Government Consumption

Government Consumption refers to the expenditure on the consumption of the public services provided by the government to the whole society and the net expenditure on the goods and services provided by the government to the households at free charge or lower prices in a certain period of time. The former equals to the output value of the government services minus the value of operating income obtained by the government departments. (The output value of the government services equals to its current operating expenditure plus depreciation of fixed assets). The latter equals to the market value of the goods and services provided by the government free of charge or at low prices to the households minus the value received by the government from the households.

□ Gross Capital Formation

Gross Capital Formation refers to the fixed assets acquired minus those disposed and the change in inventory, including the total fixed capital assets formation and the increase in inventory.

□ Gross Fixed Capital Formation

Gross Fixed Capital Formation refers to the value of fixed assets acquired minus those disposed of during a given period. Fixed assets are the assets produced through production activities with specified unit value which could be used for over one year, excluding natural assets. Total fixed capital formation can be categorized into total tangible capital formation and total intangible capital formation. The total tangible capital formation include the value of the construction projects, installation projects completed and the equipment, apparatus and instruments purchased as well as the value of land improved, the value of draught animals, breeding stock, animals for milk, wool and for recreational purpose, and the newly increased forest with economic value during a given period. The total intangible capital formation includes the prospecting of minerals, the acquisition of computer software minus the disposal of them.

EXPLANATORY NOTES TO MAJOR STATISTICAL INDICATORS

□ Increase in Inventory

Increase in Inventory refers to the market value of the change in inventory of resident units during a given period, i.e. the difference of value between the beginning and the end of the period minus the current gains due to the change in prices. The increase in inventory can be positive or negative. A positive value indicates the increase in inventory while a negative value indicates the decrease in stock. The inventory includes the raw materials, fuels and reserve materials purchased by the production units as well as the inventory of finished products, semi–finished products, work–in–progress, etc.

□ Net Outflow of Goods and Services

Net Outflow of Goods and Service refers to difference of outflow of goods and service minus inflow of goods and service. The outflow includes the value of various goods and service sold or gratuitously transferred by resident unit to non–resident unit, and the inflow includes the value of various goods and service sold or gratuitously transferred by non–resident unit to resident unit. The net outflow of district, include the net outflow of foreign trade or non–trade of local district, and also the difference of outflow minus inflow of goods and service between domestic districts.

□ Information Industry

Information Industry refers to the aggregation of all kinds of activities related to electronic information, including manufactory and distribution of information–related products and information service. As accounted by referring to relevant documents of several industries, the value added of the information industry shall not be counted together with that of other industries in the Shanghai GDP to avoid repetitive computation.

□ Tourism Industry

Tourism Industry refers to those tourism–related industries that provide tourism services to domestic and overseas tourists, including: travel agency service, transportation service, hostelling service, telecommunication service, entertainment service, catering service and retailing service, etc.. As accounted by referring to relevant cross–industry data of several industries, the value added of the tourism industry shall not be counted together with that of other industries in the Shanghai GDP to avoid repetitive computation.

□ Whole–society Labor Productivity

Whole–society Labor Productivity refers to the output value (or added value) per capita created by whole–society labors during a certain period. It's an important indicator to evaluate the production efficiency of labors in existence. Of which, the Average Quantity of Employees includes the informality registered employees.

Whole–society Labor Productivity = GDP / Yearly Average Quantity of Employees

□ Fixed Assets Output Rate

Fixed Assets Output Rate refers to the ratio between output value (or added value) and original value of operating fixed assets, viz. output value (or added value) provided by operating fixed assets per unit. It shows the invest benefit of operating fixed assets, and is an important indicator to reflect the output efficiency of fixed assets.

Fixed Assets Output Rate = GDP / Yearly Average Original Value of Operating Fixed Assets

第五篇

CHAPTER 5

财政收支

FISCAL REVENUE AND EXPENDITURE

表5.1 财政收入(1978～2006)
FISCAL REVENUES

单位:亿元(100 million yuan)

年 份 Year	全市财政收入 Fiscal Revenue	其 中 of which		在地方财政收入中 of Local Fiscal Revenue			
		#中央收入 Central Fiscal Revenue	#地方财政收入 Local Fiscal Revenue	税收收入 Taxes	亏损补贴 Loss Subsidies	地方附加收入 Local Additional Revenue	其他收入 Other Revenue
1978	190.67	21.45	169.22			2.38	
1979	192.75	20.06	172.69			2.53	
1980	198.85	24.12	174.73			2.68	
1981	204.52	30.17	174.35			2.82	
1982	200.69	32.70	167.99			2.91	
1983	204.34	47.95	156.39			2.69	
1984	215.79	51.83	163.96			2.86	
1985	263.86	79.63	184.23			2.64	
1986	257.72	78.26	179.46			3.36	
1987	241.36	72.39	168.97			3.84	
1988	261.69	100.07	161.62			4.15	
1989	297.25	130.37	166.88			3.87	
1990	284.36	114.33	166.99	183.31	-28.74	4.26	8.16
1991	324.66	149.13	175.53	182.88	-25.26	4.54	13.37
1992	340.10	154.54	185.56	188.61	-24.81	6.71	15.05
1993	439.53	197.19	242.34	252.99	-33.59	6.09	16.85
1994	615.91	440.58	175.33	196.60	-42.07	5.71	15.09
1995	702.46	475.16	227.30	240.06	-44.95	7.69	24.50
1996	873.76	585.26	288.49	308.26	-45.50	8.03	17.70
1997	1 070.95	718.62	352.33	369.23	-45.88	9.95	19.03
1998	1 146.00	751.49	392.22	406.73	-45.94	11.53	19.90
1999	1 390.58	952.36	431.85	427.23	-44.85	11.90	37.57
2000	1 752.69	1 246.47	497.96	484.00	-37.23	12.73	38.46
2001	1 995.62	1 371.49	620.24	589.91	-36.23	10.79	55.77
2002	2 202.25	1 479.06	719.79	657.70	-35.52	10.84	86.77
2003	2 828.87	1 926.51	899.29	796.87	-36.19	13.06	125.55
2004	3 591.73	2 400.46	1 119.72	1 036.23	-27.51	13.52	97.48
2005	4 095.81	2 651.81	1 433.90	1 238.40	-17.99	16.50	196.99
2006	4 798.93	3 157.02	1 600.37	1 393.97	-4.84	24.29	186.95

① 全市财政收入包括机场建设费、文教部门基金等。
② 本表中的"其他收入"为地方财政收入减税收入、亏损补贴及地方附加收入。
③ 本表至表5.8的数据由市财政局提供.
❶Fiscal Revenue includes airport construction fee, culture and education department fund etc.
❷Other revenue in this table refers to the Local fiscal Revenue substracting Taxes, Loss Subsidies and Local Additional Revenue.
❸ Data in tables 5.1to 5.8 are provided by Shanghai Municipal Financical Bureau.

表5.2 财政支出（1978～2006）
FISCAL EXPENDITURES

单位：亿元（100 million yuan）

年 份 Year	地方财政支出 Local Fiscal Expenditure	其 中 of which					
		#基本建设支出 Capital Construction	#企业挖潜改造支出 Technical Updates and Transformation of Enterprises	#科技三项费用 Science and Technology Promotion	#城市维护费 City Maintenance	#科教文卫事业费 Science, Education Culture and Health Care	#行政管理费 Administration
1978	26.01	11.75	2.41	1.85	0.53	3.06	0.83
1979	27.06	12.73	3.45	0.95	0.75	3.61	0.90
1980	19.18	6.16	2.07	0.67	0.96	4.23	1.14
1981	19.06	5.42	2.93	0.52	1.20	4.62	1.15
1982	20.68	4.96	3.67	0.51	1.57	5.19	1.24
1983	22.39	4.80	4.68	0.82	1.83	5.62	1.41
1984	30.32	7.97	7.02	1.21	2.09	6.43	1.73
1985	46.07	14.23	8.48	0.93	2.75	9.08	1.84
1986	59.08	14.19	12.68	0.86	3.87	10.87	2.08
1987	53.85	10.03	6.95	0.49	4.55	11.98	2.28
1988	65.88	5.65	17.87	0.45	4.63	14.31	1.65
1989	73.31	5.49	16.93	0.49	5.83	16.51	1.89
1990	75.56	13.97	6.88	0.38	6.72	18.45	2.30
1991	86.05	12.77	7.95	0.35	7.34	20.63	2.71
1992	94.99	18.69	3.55	0.23	9.39	24.50	3.59
1993	129.26	22.21	12.44	0.07	11.97	32.82	5.57
1994	196.92	34.42	14.22	0.29	13.22	45.77	7.64
1995	267.89	42.26	28.60	0.15	17.52	61.02	9.62
1996	342.66	58.80	38.08	0.31	19.70	77.87	11.06
1997	428.92	82.78	59.80	0.51	23.81	95.42	13.66
1998	480.70	97.77	51.11	0.88	27.39	108.14	16.35
1999	546.38	119.56	56.21	1.01	29.36	121.45	18.87
2000	622.84	132.39	77.59	1.35	35.52	135.68	22.52
2001	726.38	144.58	100.93	1.29	40.41	156.03	27.46
2002	877.84	184.14	121.20	1.92	47.70	170.73	35.92
2003	1 102.64	244.74	156.77	1.54	55.81	196.11	44.79
2004	1 395.69	310.67	193.91	1.63	79.38	233.82	56.24
2005	1 660.32	369.21	237.92	2.91	98.51	277.45	68.99
2006	1 813.80	395.58	251.99	4.26	120.85	316.12	80.75

表5.3 主要年份地方财政收入
LOCAL FISCAL REVENUE IN MAIN YEARS

	指 标 Indicators	1995	2000	2005	2006
地方财政收入(亿元)	**Local Fiscal Revenue (100 million yuan)**	**227.30**	**497.96**	**1 433.90**	**1 600.37**
#增值税	Value-added Tax	53.10	93.55	226.12	270.21
营业税	Business Tax	88.30	153.81	512.93	558.67
企业所得税	Enterprise Income Tax	42.90	103.03	249.15	270.63
证券交易印花税	Stamp Tax of Stock Transaction	8.84	28.04	1.22	3.46
城市维护建设税	City Maintenance Tax	16.03	22.01	49.79	52.97
个人所得税	Personal Income Tax	15.10	60.24	111.92	131.07
房产税	Real Estate Tax		13.24	34.10	42.68
#市级财政收入	Fiscal Revenue at Municipal Level	105.90	215.81	553.33	782.65
区县级财政收入	Fiscal Revenue at District (County) Level	121.40	282.15	880.57	817.71
地方财政收入构成(%)	**Compostion of Local Fiscal Revenue (%)**	**100**	**100**	**100**	**100**
#增值税	Value-added Tax	23.4	18.8	15.8	16.9
营业税	Business Tax	38.8	30.9	35.8	34.9
企业所得税	Enterprise Income Tax	18.9	20.7	17.4	16.9
证券交易印花税	Stamp Tax of Stock Transaction	3.9	5.6	0.1	0.2
城市维护建设税	City Maintenance Tax	7.1	4.4	3.5	3.3
个人所得税	Personal Income Tax	6.6	12.1	7.8	8.2
房产税	Real Estate Tax		2.7	2.4	2.7
#市级财政收入	Fiscal Revenue at Municipal Level	46.6	43.3	38.6	48.9
区县级财政收入	Fiscal Revenue at District (County) Level	53.4	56.7	61.4	51.1

表5.4 主要年份地方财政支出
LOCAL FISCAL EXPENDITURES IN MAIN YEARS

指　标	Indicators	1995	2000	2005	2006
地方财政支出（亿元）	**Local Fiscal Expenditure (100 million yuan)**	**267.89**	**622.84**	**1 660.32**	**1 813.80**
#基本建设支出	Capital Construction Expenditures	42.12	132.39	369.21	395.58
企业挖潜改造支出	Technical Updates and Transformation of Enterprises	28.46	77.59	237.92	251.99
城市维护费	Maintenance of City	16.18	34.03	98.51	120.85
文体广播卫生事业费	Culture, Sports, Broadcasting and Health Care Expenditures	20.09	44.36	78.59	90.40
教育事业费	Education Expenditures	37.05	84.00	182.94	205.46
科学支出	Scientific Expenditures	3.08	7.32	15.92	20.27
行政管理费	Administrative Expenditures	9.21	22.52	68.99	80.75
#市级财政支出	Fiscal Expenditure at Municipal Level	123.13	291.67	542.18	608.64
区县级财政支出	Fiscal Expenditure at District (County) Level	144.76	331.15	1 118.14	1 205.16
地方财政支出（%）	**Local Fiscal Expenditure (%)**	**100**	**100**	**100**	**100**
#基建拨款	Capital Construction Expenditures	15.7	21.3	22.2	23.8
企业挖潜改造支出	Technical Updates and Transformation of Enterprises	10.6	12.5	14.3	15.2
城市维护费	Maintenance of City	6.0	5.5	5.9	7.3
文体广播卫生事业费	Culture, Sports, Broadcasting and Health Care Expenditures	7.5	7.1	4.7	5.4
教育事业费	Education Expenditures	13.8	13.5	11.0	12.4
科学支出	Scientific Expenditures	1.1	1.2	1.0	1.2
行政管理费	Administrative Expenditures	3.4	3.6	4.2	4.9
#市级财政支出	Fiscal Expenditure at Municipal Level	46.0	46.8	32.7	36.7
区县级财政支出	Fiscal Expenditure at District (County) Level	54.0	53.2	67.3	72.6

表5.5 主要年份各区、县级财政收支
FISICAL REVENUE AND EXPENDITURES OF DISTRICTS AND COUNTIES IN MAIN YEARS

单位:亿元 (100 million yuan)

地 区	District	财政收入 Fiscal Revenue			财政支出 Fiscal Expenditure		
		2000	2005	2006	2000	2005	2006
总 计	**Total**	**282.15**	**880.57**	**817.71**	**331.15**	**1 118.14**	**1 205.16**
黄 浦 区	Huangpu	21.91	38.68	42.55	22.80	54.76	59.78
卢 湾 区	Luwan	11.37	23.58	26.84	11.32	31.94	35.04
徐 汇 区	Xuhui	15.40	43.90	48.30	19.10	55.58	61.32
长 宁 区	Changning	13.74	36.16	39.78	14.80	47.59	51.62
普 陀 区	Putuo	12.70	45.02	35.02	14.56	52.24	51.94
静 安 区	Jing'an	11.00	30.85	34.62	11.27	39.12	43.29
闸 北 区	Zhabei	11.89	30.52	26.67	13.95	36.91	42.15
虹 口 区	Hongkou	14.20	30.01	33.63	16.35	44.04	48.79
杨 浦 区	Yangpu	11.52	35.55	29.80	14.70	43.93	49.85
宝 山 区	Baoshan	16.17	63.60	45.10	17.60	71.47	70.80
闵 行 区	Minhang	18.98	61.96	68.30	20.65	82.08	85.75
嘉 定 区	Jiading	13.33	57.82	42.68	16.12	69.77	72.66
浦东新区	Pudong New Area	56.41	155.31	178.31	69.70	198.79	222.58
金 山 区	Jinshan	8.16	29.30	21.64	13.61	40.39	44.77
松 江 区	Songjiang	12.12	59.21	39.22	13.34	66.18	65.53
青 浦 区	Qingpu	13.24	51.87	34.19	15.36	63.76	59.90
南 汇 区	Nanhui	8.12	37.89	33.53	9.75	46.96	57.02
奉 贤 区	Fengxian	6.53	31.16	22.56	8.04	39.75	42.79
崇 明 县	Chongming	5.36	18.19	14.97	8.13	32.88	39.56

表5.6 主要年份用于教育、卫生、科学部门等的财政支出
FISCAL EXPENDITURE ON CULTURE, EDUCATION, HEALTH CARE AND SCIENCE IN MAIN YEARS

单位:亿元 (100 million yuan)

年份 Year	合计 Total	其中 of which #教育 Education	#卫生 Health Care	#公费医疗 Free Medical Service	#科学 Science	#通信广播 Communication and Broadcasting	#计划生育 Family Planning
1978	3.43	2.05	0.67	0.18	0.11	0.07	0.01
1980	4.77	2.89	0.95	0.20	0.19	0.10	0.02
1985	11.14	6.58	2.35	0.43	0.39	0.30	0.08
1990	21.81	11.35	4.53	1.53	1.76	0.36	0.18
1995	70.97	39.44	9.62	7.35	4.99	0.53	0.34
1996	87.44	49.89	11.19	9.47	5.68	0.61	0.38
1997	105.40	63.59	14.90	11.74	5.58	0.66	0.44
1998	117.48	76.01	12.42	13.53	5.48	0.64	0.49
1999	121.25	84.27	13.51	16.10	6.18	0.62	0.57
2000	133.93	93.79	13.67	17.93	7.32	0.61	0.61
2001	167.37	111.06	17.11	17.46	8.47	0.69	0.72
2002	170.73	116.07	20.65	9.80	9.61	0.58	0.87
2003	196.11	131.37	25.66	10.78	11.34	0.84	1.13
2004	233.82	155.35	31.76	10.50	13.51	0.94	1.62
2005	249.10	182.94	35.41	11.25	15.92	1.09	2.49
2006	285.22	205.46	42.23	13.22	20.27	1.06	2.98

注：2004年起公费医疗支出改为行政事业单位医疗费用支出。
Note: The free Medical Service Expenditure has been changed into Expenditures of Administration and Enterprise Units since 2004.

表5.7 主要年份税收收入(税务口径)
TAXATION IN MAIN YEARS(TAX SCOPE)

单位:亿元 (100 million yuan)

指标	Indicators	2000	2005	2006
税收收入	**Taxation**	**1 479.21**	**3 523.44**	**4 141.85**
#国内增值税	Domestic Value Added Tax	380.21	906.49	1 082.94
国内消费税	Domestic Excise	69.71	126.96	154.60
海关代征	Custom Taxation	313.04	859.30	986.79
营业税	Business Tax	171.42	512.91	558.71
企业所得税	Enterprise Income Tax	142.47	467.95	511.79
涉外企业所得税	Foreign Enterprise Income Tax	43.89	164.96	214.04
个人所得税	Personal Income Tax	67.79	279.81	327.54
证券交易印花税	Stamp Tax of Stock Transaction	245.49	41.12	115.71

上/海/统/计/年/鉴

主要统计指标解释

■ 财政收入

指国家财政参与社会产品分配所取得的收入，是实现国家职能的财力保证。财政收入所包括的内容几经变化，目前主要包括：

（1）各项税收：包括增值税、营业税、消费税、土地增值税、城市维护建设税、资源税、城市土地使用税、企业所得税、个人所得税、关税、证券交易印花税、车辆购置税、农牧业税和耕地占用税等。

（2）专项收入：包括排污费收入、城市水资源费收入、矿产资源补偿费收入、教育费附加收入等。

（3）其他收入：包括利息收入、基本建设贷款归还收入、基本建设收入、捐赠收入等。

（4）国有企业亏损补贴：此项为负收入，冲减财政收入。主要包括对工业企业、商业企业、粮食企业的补贴。

■ 中央财政收入和地方财政收入

指按现行分税制财政体制划分的中央本级收入和地方本级收入。1994 年实行分税制财政体制以后，属于中央财政的收入包括关税、海关代征消费税和增值税，消费税，中央企业所得税，地方银行和外资银行及非银行金融企业所得税，铁道部门、各银行总行、各保险总公司等集中缴纳的营业税、利润和城市维护建设税，车辆购置税，船舶吨税，增值税的 75%部分，证券交易税（印花税）94%部分，个人所得税中的利息所得税，利息所得税之外的个人所得税中央分享的部分，海洋石油资源税。属于地方财政的收入包括营业税，地方企业所得税，利息所得税之外的个人所得税地方分享的部分，城镇土地使用税，固定资产投资方向调节税，城镇维护建设税，房产税，车船使用税，印花税，屠宰税，农牧业税，农业特产税，耕地占用税，契税，土地增值税、国有土地有偿使用收入，增值税 25%部分，证券交易税（印花税）6%部分和除海洋石油资源税以外的其他资源税。

■ 地方财政支出

中央财政支出和地方财政支出 指根据政府在经济和社会活动中的不同职责，划分中央和地方政府的责权，按照政府的责权划分确定的支出。中央财政支出包括国防支出，武装警察部队支出，中央级行政管理费和各项事业费，重点建设支出以及中央政府调整国民经济结构、协调地区发展、实施宏观调控的支出。地方财政支出主要包括地方行政管理和各项事业费，地方统筹的基本建设、技术改造支出，支援农村生产支出，城市维护和建设经费，价格补贴支出等。

SHANGHAI STATISTICAL YEARBOOK

EXPLANATORY NOTES TO MAJOR STATISTICAL INDICATORS

□ Fiscal Revenue

Government Revenue refers to the revenue of the government finance by means of participating in the distribution of the social products, which is the financial resources for ensuring the government to function. The contents of government revenue have been changed several times. Now it includes the following main items:

(1)Various tax revenues, including value added tax, business tax, consumption tax, land value added tax, tax on city maintenance and construction, resources tax, tax on use of urban land, enterprise income tax, personal income tax, tariff, stamp tax on security transactions, tax on purchase of motor vehicles, tax on agriculture and animal husbandry and tax on occupancy of cultivated land, etc.

(2)Special revenues, including revenues from the fee on sewage treatment, fee on urban water resources, fee for the compensation of mineral resources and extra-charges for education, etc.

(3) Other revenues, including revenue from interest, revenue from the repayment of capital construction loan, revenue from capital construction projects, and donations and grants.

(4)Subsidies for the losses of the state-owned enterprises. This is an item of negative revenue, consisting of subsidies to industrial, commercial and grain purchasing and supply enterprises.

□ Central Fiscal Revenue and Local Fiscal Revenue

Central Fiscal Revenue and Local Fiscal Revenue refers to the revenue of the central government and that of the local government as defined by the decentralized taxation system starting from 1994. In accordance with this system, the revenue of the central government includes tariff, consumption tax and value added tax levied by the customs, consumption tax, income tax of the enterprises subordinate to the central government, income taxes of the local banks, foreign-funded banks and non-bank financial institutions, business tax and profits of railways, head offices of banks, head office of insurance company , which are handed over to the government in a centralized way, tax on city maintenance and construction, tax on purchasing motor vehicles, tonnage tax of ships, 75% of the value added tax, 94% of the tax on stock dealing (stamp tax), interest income tax in the personal income tax, proportion of the personal income tax (other that interest income tax) to be shared by the central government, and tax on ocean petroleum resources, The revenue of the local government includes business tax, income tax of the enterprises subordinate to the local government, proportion of the personal income tax (other that interest income tax) to be shared by the central government, tax on the use of urban land, tax on the adjustment of the investment in fixed assets, tax on town maintenance and construction, tax on real estates, tax on the use of vehicles and ships, stamp tax, slaughter tax, tax on agriculture and animal husbandry, tax on special agricultural products, tax on the occupancy of cultivated land, contract tax, value-added tax on land, income from charges on use of state-owned land, 25% of the value added tax, 6% of the tax on stock dealing (stamp tax) and tax on resources other than the ocean petroleum resources.

□ Local Fiscal Expenditure

Local Fiscal Expenditure includes mainly the administrative expenses and various operating expenses at the level of local government, the expenditure for capital construction and technological innovation with the funds raised by the local government, expenditure for supporting rural production, expenditure for city maintenance and construction and expenditure for price subsidies, etc.

第六篇
CHAPTER 6

固定资产投资
INVESTMENT
IN FIXED ASSETS

表6.1 全社会固定资产投资总额(按管理渠道分)(1978～2006)
TOTAL INVESTMENT IN FIXED ASSETS(GROUPED BY ADMINISTRATIVE CHANNELS)

单位:亿元(100 million yuan)

年份 Year	合计 Total	其中 of which						
		基本建设 Capital Construction	更新改造 Technical Updates and Transformation	其他投资 Other Investment	房地产开发 Investment in Real Estate	农村集体 Rural Collective	城镇私人建房 Urban Private Home Construction	农村私人建房 Rural Private Home Construction
1978	27.91	14.46	5.60	3.77		2.96	0.09	0.79
1979	35.58	21.13	7.69	3.26		2.17	0.14	0.94
1980	45.43	25.73	11.30	3.24		3.01	0.17	1.41
1981	54.60	30.80	11.18	3.02		4.65	0.20	3.97
1982	71.34	43.63	14.41	3.58		4.06	0.29	4.32
1983	75.94	43.01	17.44	4.56		4.95	0.25	4.48
1984	92.30	47.42	22.56	5.82		7.07	0.24	7.28
1985	118.56	57.05	35.61	3.26		7.04	0.20	12.00
1986	146.93	71.37	46.83	4.26		9.80	0.18	10.30
1987	186.30	92.10	57.39	4.02	0.97	13.84	0.53	12.66
1988	245.27	115.55	76.95	4.55	1.68	22.19	0.66	16.90
1989	214.76	111.76	61.88	3.42	1.85	16.94	0.64	14.32
1990	227.08	108.54	71.77	3.77	8.16	14.38	0.59	15.96
1991	258.30	108.90	95.21	3.91	7.59	23.62	0.70	14.17
1992	357.38	129.60	126.84	6.52	12.71	55.42	0.55	17.00
1993	653.91	273.64	220.30	9.91	22.04	104.82	2.13	5.33
1994	1 123.29	511.24	304.01	13.99	117.43	141.23	1.21	10.40
1995	1 601.79	551.86	389.20	16.33	466.20	139.57	0.72	13.10
1996	1 952.05	651.28	415.73	12.43	657.79	158.32	1.09	20.00
1997	1 977.59	762.00	386.24	7.43	614.23	166.16	1.09	16.80
1998	1 964.83	844.15	365.01	13.44	577.12	137.40	1.41	12.76
1999	1 856.72	786.81	393.59	9.88	514.83	134.33	1.23	5.54
2000	1 869.67	703.50	396.26	21.21	566.17	161.61	1.50	10.36
2001	1 994.73	712.49	436.84	30.70	630.73	173.13	1.06	9.28
2002	2 187.06	784.13	422.58	54.93	748.89	167.92	1.13	6.87
2003	2 452.11	927.29	388.01	57.01	901.24	170.00	2.07	6.49
2004	3 084.66	1 721.56			1 175.46	180.82	0.95	5.86
2005	3 542.55	1 984.61			1 246.86	304.00		7.08
2006	3 925.09	2 246.93			1 275.59	396.60		5.96

注：2004年起，全社会投资由城镇投资和农村投资两部分组成。其中城镇投资包括建设改造投资和房地产开发投资，农村投资包括农村集体和农村私人建房。

Note: Since 2004, total investment in fix assets was composed of urban investment and rural investment. Urban investment includes construction rebuild investment and real estate investment, and rural investment includes rural collective investment and rural private home construction.

表6.2 全社会固定资产投资总额(按经济类型分)(1978~2006)
TOTAL INVESTMENT IN FIXED ASSETS (GROUPED BY ECONOMIC TYPES)

单位:亿元(100 million yuan)

年 份 Year	合 计 Total	其 中 of which			
		#国 有 经 济 State-owned	#集 体 经 济 Collective-owned	#股份制 经 济 Shareholding	#外商、港澳台 经 济 Hong Kong, Macao, Taiwan and Foreign Funded
1978	27.91	23.83	3.20		
1979	35.58	32.08	2.42		
1980	45.43	40.27	3.58		
1981	54.60	45.00	5.43		
1982	71.34	61.62	5.11		
1983	75.94	65.01	6.20		
1984	92.30	75.80	8.98		
1985	118.56	95.92	10.44		
1986	146.93	122.46	13.99		
1987	186.30	154.45	18.65		
1988	245.27	198.68	29.03		
1989	214.76	178.81	21.00		
1990	227.08	192.24	18.29		
1991	258.30	215.61	27.82		
1992	357.38	275.67	64.16		
1993	653.91	419.22	124.18	32.83	61.61
1994	1 123.29	721.37	189.75	76.99	101.78
1995	1 601.79	935.92	247.11	150.17	208.30
1996	1 952.05	1 048.27	239.47	165.57	340.18
1997	1 977.59	1 148.69	257.10	118.80	367.50
1998	1 964.83	1 087.94	208.84	203.81	405.17
1999	1 856.72	986.82	227.19	268.68	325.58
2000	1 869.67	829.98	156.34	421.53	319.05
2001	1 994.73	760.58	136.81	580.75	362.25
2002	2 187.06	742.72	101.33	631.70	369.96
2003	2 452.11	811.85	116.63	647.27	468.20
2004	3 084.66	955.12	146.58	667.52	851.39
2005	3 542.55	1 240.27	131.07	916.27	640.31
2006	3 925.09	1 460.09	159.31	910.31	725.85

表6.3 主要年份全社会固定资产投资主要指标
MAJOR INDICATORS OF TOTAL INVESTMENT IN FIXED ASSETS IN MAIN YEARS

单位:亿元(100 million yuan)

指标	Indicators	1990	2000	2005	2006
投资总额	**Total Investment**	**227.08**	**1 869.67**	**3 542.55**	**3 925.09**
按隶属关系分	**Grouped by Administrative Relationship**				
中央项目	Central Government Projects	75.49	257.67	420.42	532.93
地方项目	Local Projects	151.59	1 612.00	3 122.13	3 392.16
按构成分	**Grouped by Use of Funds**				
建筑安装工程	Construction and Installation	127.63	882.91	2 079.04	2 114.01
设备、工具、器具购置	Purchase of Equipment and Instruments	79.51	482.47	610.38	762.24
其他费用	Others	19.94	504.29	853.13	1 048.84
按建设性质分	**Grouped by Type of Construction**				
#新　建	New Construction	78.01	730.76	1604.58	1801.45
改　建	Reconstruction	70.48	216.40	231.15	261.04
扩　建	Expansion	47.50	216.71	306.00	415.33
单纯建造生活设施	Construction of Living Facilities	24.00	39.02	9.85	13.03
按产业分	**Grouped by Type of Industry**				
第一产业	Primary Industry	3.20	7.87	5.58	14.29
第二产业	Secondary Industry	133.00	615.94	1 082.10	1 212.71
第三产业	Tertiary Industry	90.88	1 245.86	2 454.87	2 698.09
#住　宅	Residential Housing	42.94	443.90	936.36	854.15
按经济类型分	**Grouped by Economic Types**				
国有经济	State-owned		829.98	1 240.27	1 460.09
非国有经济	Non-state-owned		1 039.69	2 302.28	2 465.00
集体经济	Collective-owned		156.34	131.07	159.31
私营经济	Private		83.29	565.24	626.93
联营经济	Joint Owned		41.20	21.53	21.36
股份制经济	Shareholding		421.53	916.27	910.31
外商经济	Foreign Funded		222.86	504.16	547.48
港澳台经济	Hong Kong, Macao and Taiwan Funded		96.19	136.15	178.37
其他经济	Others		18.28	27.86	21.24
新增固定资产	**Newly Increased Fixed Assets**	**222.99**	**1 493.35**	**2 547.02**	**2 680.85**
固定资产交付使用率(%)	Rate of Fixed Assets Transfered and in Use(%)	98.2	79.9	71.9	68.3
房屋建筑面积(万平方米)	**Floor Space of Buildings (10 000 sq·m)**				
施工面积	Floor Space Under Construction	3 801.46	8 636.31	14 477.85	14 596.49
#住　宅	Residential Housing	2 269.06	4 804.12	8 267.24	8 085.28
竣工面积	Floor Space Completed	2 138.44	3 266.52	4 873.82	4 901.46
#住　宅	Residential Housing	1 339.02	1 724.02	2 819.35	2 746.80

注：从2000年起，固定资产投资统计起点为50万元以上(含50万元)项目，按建设性质分中不包括房地产开发投资(以下同)。
Note: Since 2000, the statistics that have been collected are about projects of fixed assets investment each involving 500,000 yuan and more. In "Type of Construction" the investment in real estate development is excluded(same as follows).

表 6.4 建设改造投资主要指标(2006)
MAJOR INDICATORS OF CONSTRUCTION TRANSFORMATION

单位:亿元(100 million yuan)

指 标	Indicators	全 市 Total	#地 方 Local Projects
投资总额	**Total Investment**	**2 246.93**	**1 725.25**
按建设性质分	**Grouped by Type of Construction**		
#新 建	New Construction	1 508.00	1 297.91
改 建	Reconstruction	230.11	133.64
扩 建	Expansion	370.94	194.88
单纯建造生活设施	Construction of Living Facilities	4.73	4.73
按产业分	**Grouped by Type of Industry**		
第一产业	Primary Industry	5.77	5.77
第二产业	Secondary Industry	924.82	619.31
第三产业	Tertiary Industry	1 316.34	1 100.16
#住 宅	Residential Housing	9.65	6.68
按行业分	**Grouped by Economic Sectors**		
#工 业	Industry	917.93	617.78
交通运输、仓储和邮政业	Transportation, Storage and Post Industries	602.66	552.39
信息传输、计算机服务和软件业	Information Transmission, Computer Servcie and Software Industries	126.90	13.79
批发和零售业	Retail and Wholesale	29.08	28.29
住宿和餐饮业	Hotel and Eateries	27.73	21.68
金融业	Financial Industry	6.28	5.80
房地产业	Real Estate Industry	113.05	112.96
租赁和商务服务业	Leasing and Business Service	5.66	5.58
科学研究、技术服务和地质勘查业	Scientific Research, Technology Service and Geological Prospecting	24.61	18.42
水利、环境和公共设施管理业	Water Conservancy, Environment and Public Facility Management	260.98	259.95
居民服务和其他服务业	Residents Service and Other Service	1.66	1.40
教 育	Education	61.96	25.34
卫生、社会保障和社会福利业	Health, Social Security and Welfare	21.53	20.88
文化、体育和娱乐业	Culture, Sports and Entertainment	9.79	9.66
公共管理和社会组织	Public Administration and Social Organizations	24.45	24.01
新增固定资产	**Newly Increased Fixed Assets**	**1 306.93**	**1 011.67**
固定资产交付使用率(%)	Rate of Fixed Assets Transfered and in Use(%)	58.2	58.6
房屋建筑面积(万平方米)	**Floor Space of Buildings (10 000 sq · m)**		
施工面积	Floor Space Under Construction	2 034.79	1 739.15
#住 宅	Residential Housing	42.14	18.35
竣工面积	Floor Space Completed	782.66	690.35
#住 宅	Residential Housing	10.80	3.15

注：本表不包括农村投资。
Note: Data of this table exclude rural investment.

表6.5 地方固定资产投资主要指标(2005～2006)
MAJOR INDICATORS OF LOCAL INVESTMENT IN FIXED ASSETS

单位:亿元(100 million yuan)

指标	Indicators	2005	2006
投资总额	**Total Investment**	**3 122.13**	**3 392.16**
按构成分	**Grouped by Use of Funds**		
建筑安装工程	Construction and Installation	1 912.76	1 885.98
设备、工具、器具购置	Purchase of Equipment and Instruments	412.84	500.43
其他费用	Others	796.53	1 005.75
按建设性质分	**Grouped by Type of Construction**		
#新　建	New Construction	1 412.19	1 589.97
改　建	Reconstruction	165.23	164.56
扩　建	Expansion	199.12	238.86
单纯建造生活设施	Construction of Living Facilities	9.85	13.03
按产业分	**Grouped by Type of Industry**		
第一产业	Primary Industry	5.50	14.25
第二产业	Secondary Industry	800.47	906.15
第三产业	Tertiary Industry	2 316.16	2 471.76
#住　宅	Residential Housing	932.36	846.59
按行业分	**Grouped by Sectors**		
#工　业	Industry	797.70	903.72
交通运输、仓储和邮政业	Transportation, Storage, Postal and Telecommunications	381.35	575.26
信息传输、计算机服务和软件业	Information Transmission,Computer Servcie and Software Industries	10.82	13.92
批发和零售业	Wholesale and Retail	38.57	46.98
住宿和餐饮业	Hotel and Eateries	33.67	26.52
金融业	Finance	0.99	5.81
房地产业	Real Estate	1 370.42	1 387.94
租赁和商务服务业	Leasing and Business Service	18.03	9.88
科学研究、技术服务和地质勘查业	Scientific Research,Technology Service and Geological Prospecting	12.76	20.18
水利、环境和公共设施管理业	Water Conservancy,Environment and Public Facility Management	318.06	288.35
居民服务和其他服务业	Residents Service and Other Service	1.99	2.48
教　育	Education	33.22	30.45
卫生、社会保障和社会福利业	Health,Social Security and Welfare	18.26	25.31
文化、体育和娱乐业	Culture,Sports and Entertainment	61.69	11.81
公共管理和社会组织	Public Administration and Social Organizations	16.33	26.86
新增固定资产	**Newly Increased Fixed Assets**	**2 033.39**	**2 378.04**
固定资产交付使用率(%)	Rate of Fixed Assets Transfered and in Use(%)	65.1	70.1
房屋建筑面积（万平方米）	**Floor Space of Buildings(10 000 sq·m)**		
施工面积	Floor Space Under Construction	14 087.25	14 139.18
#住　宅	Residential Housing	8 205.07	8 033.03
竣工面积	Floor Space Completed	4 697.36	4 796.34
#住　宅	Residential Housing	2 803.00	2 739.15

表 6.6 工业各行业建设改造投资主要指标(2006)
MAIN INDICATORS OF CONSTRUCTION TRANSFORMATION BY INDUSTRIAL SECTORS

行业	Sectors	施工项目(个) Projects Under Construction (unit)	全部建成投产项目(个) Projects Completed and Put into Production (unit)	建成投产率(%) Rate of Projects Completed and Put into Use	建设改造投资额(万元) Construction Transformation Investment (10 000 yuan)
总　计	**Total**	**3 961**	**2 382**	**66.3**	**12 048 669**
采矿业	**Excavation**	**18**	**9**	**100.0**	**28 559**
石油和天然气开采业	Petroleum and Natural Gas Exploiting	1			21 397
非金属矿采选业	Nonmetal Minerals Mining	17	9	88.9	7 162
制造业	**Manufacturing**	**3 100**	**1 672**	**85.4**	**10 293 275**
农副食品加工业	Farm and Sideline Products Processing	19	7	171.4	54 099
食品制造业	Food Manufacturing	35	17	105.9	84 548
饮料制造业	Beverage Manufacturing	21	12	75.0	13 494
烟草制品业	Tabacco Manufacturing	33	22	50.0	28 574
纺织业	Textile	95	53	79.2	123 142
纺织服装、鞋、帽制造业	Garments, Shoes and Accessories Manufacturing	128	74	73.0	164 463
皮革、毛皮、羽毛(绒)及其他制品业	Leather, Fur, and Wool Products Manufacturing	28	13	115.4	37 365
木材加工及木、竹、藤、棕、草制品业	Timber Processing and Timber, Bamboo, Rattan, Coir and Straw Products Manufacturing	64	51	25.5	37 427
家具制造业	Furniture Manufacturing	29	20	45.0	35 679
造纸及纸制品业	Paper-making and Paper Products Manufacturing	32	23	39.1	77 440
印刷业和记录媒介的复制	Printing and Record Duplicating	35	19	84.2	110 314
文教体育用品制造业	Stationary, Education and Sports Goods Manufacturing	33	19	73.7	42 448
石油加工、炼焦及核燃料加工业	Oil Processing, Coking and Nuclear Fuel Processing	18	5	260.0	73 083
化学原料及化学制品制造业	Raw Chemical Materials and Chemical Products Manufacturing	240	131	83.2	1 150 774
医药制造业	Medicine Manufacturing	59	27	118.5	100 723
化学纤维制造业	Chemical Fiber Manufacturing	10	5	100.0	16 306
橡胶制品业	Rubber Products Manufacturing	42	26	61.5	53 081
塑料制品业	Plastic Products Manufacturing	92	65	41.5	155 360
非金属矿物制品业	Nonmetal Mineral Products	62	38	63.2	106 663
黑色金属冶炼及压延加工业	Smelting and Pressing of Ferrous Metals	419	214	95.8	1 965 626
有色金属冶炼及压延加工业	Smelting and Pressing of Nonferrous Metals	41	31	32.3	114 259
金属制品业	Metal Products Manufacturing	210	129	62.8	432 522
通用设备制造业	General Equipment Manufacturing	297	151	96.7	726 918
专用设备制造业	Special Purpose Equipment Manufacturing	185	101	83.2	488 443
交通运输设备制造业	Transportation Equipment Manufacturing	249	91	173.6	1 317 638
电气机械及器材制造业	Electric Machinery Equipments and Manufacturing	212	112	89.3	486 579
通信设备、计算机及其他电子设备制造业	Communications Equipment, Computer and Other Electronic Equipment Manufacturing	122	64	90.6	1 659 390
仪器仪表及文化、办公用机械制造业	Instruments, Meters, Culture and Office Equipments Manufacturing	29	20	45.0	49 863
工艺品及其他制造业	Artworks and Other Manufacturing	259	131	97.7	584 672
废弃资源和废旧材料回收加工业	Waste Resources and Materials Recycling and Processing	2	1	100.0	2 382
电力、燃气及水的生产和供应业	**Power, Gas, Water Production and Supply**	**843**	**701**	**20.3**	**1 726 835**
电力、热力的生产和供应业	Power and Heat Production and Supply	661	571	15.8	1 164 566
燃气生产和供应业	Gas Production and Supply	53	43	23.3	124 419
水的生产和供应业	Water Production and Supply	129	87	48.3	437 850

表6.7 主要年份新增固定资产
NEWLY INCREASED FIXED ASSETS IN MAIN YEARS

年 份 Year	新增固定资产 (亿元) Newly Increased Fixed Assets (100 million yuan)	其 中 of which #房地产开发 Investment in Real Estate Development	固定资产交付 使用率(%) Rate of Fixed Assets Transferred and in Use(%)
1978	17.46		62.6
1980	23.71		52.2
1985	75.64		63.8
1990	222.99	4.97	98.2
1995	826.94	127.08	51.6
1996	1 199.10	318.58	61.4
1997	1 316.43	427.19	66.6
1998	1 534.90	508.32	78.1
1999	1 858.70	427.66	100.1
2000	1 493.35	477.39	79.9
2001	1 178.24	519.20	59.1
2002	1 207.33	536.22	55.2
2003	1 618.45	812.56	66.0
2004	2 122.14	825.23	68.8
2005	2 547.02	1 054.02	71.9
2006	2 680.85	1 058.94	68.3

表6.8 主要年份固定资产投资资金来源
CAPITAL SOURCES OF INVESTMENT IN FIXED ASSETS IN MAIN YEARS

单位:亿元(100 million yuan)

指 标	Indicators	1990	2000	2005	2006
资金来源合计	**Total Capital Sources**	**261.46**	**2 061.66**	**5 108.34**	**5 746.69**
上年末结余资金	Balance at End of Previous Year	28.85	241.05	860.75	794.67
本年资金来源小计	Sub-total Capital Source of this Year	232.61	1 820.61	4 247.59	4 952.02
国家预算内资金	State Budgetary Funds	14.39	48.30	46.42	74.33
国内贷款	Domestic Loans	62.52	379.21	955.29	1 162.17
债 券	Bonds		4.85	2.00	
利用外资	Foreign Investment	35.46	161.83	235.61	271.20
#外商直接投资	Foreign Direct Investment		73.71	181.47	210.46
自筹资金	Self-Financed Capital	94.13	905.46	1 976.72	2 265.02
#市自筹	Self-Financed by Municipal Government	32.12	72.63	108.91	102.39
企、事业单位自筹	Self-Financed by Enterprises and Institutions	57.13	509.93	1 682.97	1 964.70
其他资金	Other Capital	26.11	320.96	1 031.55	1 179.30
#集 资	Raised Funds		6.29	4.39	0.81
本年各项应付投资款	Investment Due to Pay of this Year		310.42	651.89	785.85
#工程款	Project Funds		76.52	316.36	348.98

表 6.9 市重大项目完成情况(2006)
PROGRESS OF CITY'S MAJOR PROJECTS

单位:万元(10 000 yuan)

项 目	Item	本年完成投资额 Investment in 2006
洋山深水港二期工程	Yangshan Deep-water Port, second phase	259 729
罗泾港区二期工程	Luojing Port Area,second phase	238 711
上海长江桥隧工程	Shanghai Yangtze River Bridge and Tunnel Project	213 855
上海港国际客运中心工程	Shanghai Port, International Passenger Transport Center Project	84 366
浦东国际机场扩建工程	Pudong International Airport Extension Project	505 065
A5 嘉金高速公路	A5 Jiajin Expressway	155 665
A9 沪青平高速公路西段 16 公里	A9 Huqingping Expressway, west section(16 km)	31 471
A30 郊环(东段)	A30 Suburb Ring Road(east sectio)	66 709
A15(浦东机场高速公路)	A15(Pudong Airport Expressway)	35 260
大芦线航道整治一期工程	Dalu Channel Regulation Project, first phase	67 679
赵家沟航道整治工程	Zhaojiagou Channel Regulation Project	7 017
轨道交通 2 号线西延伸工程	Rail Transport No. 2,West Extension Project	196 710
轨道交通 3 号线北延伸	Rail Transport No. 3, North Extension Project	71 000
轨道交通 6 号线	Rail Transport No. 6	185 082
轨道交通 7 号线工程	Rail Transport No. 7	233 295
轨道交通 8 号线杨浦一期工程	Rail Transport No. 8, Yangpu First Phase Project	191 050
轨道交通 9 号线申松线	Rail Transport No. 9,Shensong Line	157 038
中环路(浦西)工程	Middle Ring Road (Puxi)	131 719
河南路改建工程	Henan Road Rebuild Project	103 851
上中路越江工程(双向八车道)	Shangzhong Road Tunnel Project(Eight Lanes)	54 095
军工路越江工程	Jungong Road Tunnel Project	1 000
西藏南路越江工程	South Xizang Road Tunnel Project	21 192
污水治理三期工程	Sewage Treatment Third Phase Project	96 161
长江引水三期陆域水库工程	Yangtze River Diversion Third Phase, Land Reservior Project	652

表 6.9 续表 continued

单位:万元(10 000 yuan)

项 目	Item	本年完成投资额 Investment in 2006
液化天然气(LNG)项目	LNG Item	15 745
外高桥电厂三期工程	Waigaoqiao Electric Power Plant, Third Phase Project	199 768
500KV 静安输电变电	500KV Jingan Transmission Project	30 000
世博会居民动迁安置基础	Resident Movement Allocation Base for World Expo	274 662
浦钢搬迁(世博前期)	Pu Steel 's Movement (Prophase of World Expo)	445 650
聚碳酸酯(PC)	PC	110 260
上海联合异氰酸酯	Shanghai MDI	136 965
上海通用汽车公司南部建设项目	Shanghai GM South Construction Project	126 310
上海汽车工程研究院自主品牌研发	Shanghai Automotive Engineering Academy, R&D of Own Brands	11 267
长兴造船基地(世博前期)	Changxing Ship Building Base(Prophase of World Expo)	406 786
上海电气集团临港重型装备基地	SEC Lingang Heavy Machine Manufacture Base	124 018
外高桥粮食储备库及码头设施	Waigaoiao Foodstuff Storage and Dock Establishment	45 890
上海光源工程	SSRF	36 822
纳米技术及应用国家工程研究中心	National Engineering Research Center for Nanotechnology	1 552
上海组织工程国家工程研究中心	National Engineering Research Center for Shanghai Organic Project	3 040
同济大学上海地面交通工具风洞	Tongji University, Shanghai Ground Vehicle Wind Tunnel	17 004
交通大学闵行校区二期工程	Jiaotong University, Minhang Campus Second Phase Project	105 505
上海海事大学临港校区一期工程	Shanghai Maritime University, Lingang Campus First Phase Project	78 082
上海音乐学院扩建工程	Shanghai Conservatory of Music, Extension Project	6 264
残疾人综合设施暨特奥赛训练基地	Synthetical Establishment for Handicapped and Training Base for Special Olympic Games	25 813
轨道交通 10 号线	Rail Transport No. 10	242 000
轨道交通 11 号线(北段)	Rail Transport No. 11(North Section)	235 802
虹桥综合交通枢纽规划土地前期	Hongqiao Synthetical Traffic Hinge Layout, Land Prophase	600 620

上 / 海 / 统 / 计 / 年 / 鉴

主要统计指标解释

■ 全社会固定资产投资

固定资产投资是国民经济再生产活动的一个重要部分。固定资产投资额是以货币形式表现的在一定时期内建造和购置固定资产的工作量以及与此有关的费用总称。它是反映固定资产投资规模、结构和发展速度的综合性指标。按照现行国家统计制度,全社会固定资产投资包括建设改造、房地产开发、城乡集体经济单位、城乡私人建房和其他经济单位投资。

从 1997 年起,固定资产投资统计起点为 50 万元(含 50 万元)以上项目。

■ 房地产开发投资

指各种登记注册类型的房地产开发公司、商品房建设公司及其他房地产开发法人单位和附属于其他法人单位实际从事房地产开发或经营活动的单位统一开发的包括统代建、拆迁还建的住宅、厂房、仓库、饭店、宾馆、度假村、写字楼、办公楼等房屋建筑物和配套的服务设施,土地开发工程(如道路、给水、排水、供电、供热、通讯、平整场地等基础设施工程)的投资;不包括单纯的土地交易活动。

■ 固定资产投资按国民经济行业分

固定资产投资按国民经济行业分是根据建设项目建成投产后的主要产品或主要用途及社会经济活动性质来确定国民经济行业。一般情况下,一个建设项目或一个企业、事业单位只能属于一种国民经济行业。

■ 固定资产投资按隶属关系分

固定资产投资按隶属关系分是按建设单位或企业、事业、行政单位的主管上级机关确定的。

(1)中央:是指中共中央、人大常委会和国务院各部、委、局、总公司以及直属机构直接领导的建设项目和企业、事业、行政单位。这些单位的固定资产投资计划由国务院各部门直接编制和下达,建设中所需物资、主要设备以及建设中的问题都由中央有关部门安排和解决。

(2)地方:是由省(自治区、直辖市)、地区(州、盟、省辖市)、县(旗、县级市)三级政府及业务主管部门直接领导和管理的建设项目、企业、事业、行政单位。地方项目还包括不隶属以上各级政府及主管部门的建设项目和企业、事业单位,如外商投资企业和无主管部门的企业等。

■ 固定资产投资按构成分

固定资产投资按构成分是按其工作内容和实现方式来划分的,主要分为建筑安装工程,设备、工具、器具购置,其他费用三个部分。

(1)建筑安装工程(建筑安装工作量):指各种房屋、建筑物的建造工程和各种设备、装置的安装工程。包括各种房屋建造工程;各种用途设备基础和各种工业窑炉的砌筑工程及金属结构工程;为施工而进行的各种准备工作和临时工程以及完工后的清理工作等;铁路、道路的铺设,矿井的开凿及石油管道的架设等;水利工程;防空地下建筑等特殊工程;列入房屋工程预算内的暖气、卫生、通风、照明、煤气等设备的价值及装设油饰工程;列入建筑工程预算内的各种管道(蒸汽、压缩空气、石油、给排水等管道)、电力、电讯电缆导线等的敷设工程;以及各种机械设备的安装工程;为测定安装工程质量,对设备进行的试运工作;房地产开发单位进行的商品房屋开发建设工程、土地开发工程。

在安装工程中,不包括被安装设备本身的价值。

(2)设备、工具、器具购置:指建设单位或企、事业单位购置或自制的,达到固定资产标准的设备、工具、器具的价值。新建单位及扩建单位的新建车间,按照设计或计划要求购置或自制的全部设备、工具、器具,不论是否达到固定资产标准均计入“设备、工具、器具购置”中。

(3)其他费用:指在固定资产建造和购置过程中发生的,除上述几项内容以外的各种应分摊计入固定资产的费用。

■ 固定资产投资的资金来源

固定资产投资的资金来源是根据固定资产投资的资金来源不同,分为国家预算内资金、国内贷款、债券、利用外资、自筹资金和其他资金来源。

(1)国家预算内资金:指中央财政和地方财政中由国家统筹安排的基本建设拨款和更新改造拨款,以及中央财政安排的专项拨款中用于基本建设的资金和基本建设拨款改贷款的资金等。

(2)国内贷款:指报告期内企、事业单位向银行及非银行金融机构借入的用于固定资产投资的各种国内借

主要统计指标解释

款。包括银行利用自有资金及吸收的存款发放的贷款、上级主管部门拨入的国内贷款、国家专项贷款(包括煤代油贷款、劳改煤矿专项贷款等)、地方财政专项资金安排的贷款、国内储备贷款、周转贷款等。

(3)债券:

(4)利用外资: 指报告期内收到的用于固定资产投资的国外资金,包括统借统还、自借自还的国外贷款,中外合资项目中的外资,以及对外发行债券和股票等。国家统借统还的外资指由我国政府出面同外国政府、团体或金融组织签订贷款协议、并负责偿还本息的国外贷款。

(5)自筹资金: 指建设单位报告期内收到的,用于进行固定资产投资的上级主管部门、地方和企、事业单位自筹资金。

(6)其他资金来源: 指报告期内收到的除以上各种拨款、借款、自筹资金以外其他用于固定资产投资的资金。

■ 固定资产投资按建设性质分

建设项目的性质一般分为新建、改建、扩建和单纯建造生活设施。

(1)新建:一般指从无到有"平地起家"开始建设的企业、事业和行政单位或独立的工程。现有企业、事业、行政单位一般不属于新建。但如有的单位原有基础很小,经过建设后新增的固定资产价值超过该企、事业、行政单位原有固定资产价值(原值)三倍以上的也应作为新建。

(2) 改建:指现有企业、事业单位,对原有设施进行技术改造或更新(包括相应配套的辅助性生产、生活福利设施)的建设项目。现有企业、事业单位为适应市场变化的需要,而改变企业的主要产品种类(如军工企业转产民用品等) 的建设项目,应作为改建。原有产品生产作业线由于各工序(车间)之间能力不平衡,为填平补齐充分发挥原有生产能力而增建不增加本企业主要产品设计能力的车间,也应作为改建。

(3)扩建:指在厂内或其他地点,为扩大原有产品的生产能力(或效益)或增加新的产品生产能力,而增建主要的生产车间(或主要工程)、分厂、独立的生产线。行政、事业单位在原单位增建业务用房(如学校增建教学用房、医院增建门诊部、病房等)也作为扩建。

现有企、事业单位为扩大原有主要产品生产能力或增加新的产品生产能力,增建一个或几个主要生产车间(或主要工程)、分厂,同时进行一些更新改造工程的,也应作为扩建。

(4)单纯建造生活设施。

■ 新增固定资产

新增固定资产又称交付使用的固定资产,是指已经完成建造和购置过程,并已交付生产或使用单位的固定资产价值。新增固定资产是表示固定资产投资成果的价值量指标,也是反映建设进度、计算固定资产投资效果的必要数据。

■ 固定资产交付使用率

指一定时期新增固定资产与同期完成投资额的比率。该指标是反映固定资产动用速度,衡量建设过程中宏观投资效果的综合指标。由于新增固定资产是较长时期内形成的结果,而投资额则是当年完成的,因此,该指标一般适宜于反映较长时期内固定资产的动用情况。

■ 施工项目

指报告期内进行过建筑或安装施工活动的项目。凡是报告期内施过工的建设项目,不论施工时间长短,均作为施工项目统计。施工项目个数可以反映一定时期固定资产投资的实际规模,与同期建成投产的建设项目个数相比,可以从建设速度的角度反映固定资产投资的效果。根据建设项目施工活动的不同性质,施工项目又分为:本年正式施工项目、本年收尾项目和以前年度全部停缓建项目。

■ 全部建成投产项目

工业项目指设计文件规定形成生产能力的主体工程及其相应配套的辅助设施全部建成,经负荷试运转,证明具备生产设计规定合格产品的条件,并经过验收鉴定合格或达到竣工验收标准,与生产性工程配套的生活福利设施可以满足近期正常生产的需要,正式移交生产的建设项目。非工业项目指设计文件规定的主体工程和相应的配套工程全部建成,能够发挥设计规定的全部效益,经验收鉴定合格或达到竣工验收标准,正式移交使用的建设项目。

■ 建成投产率

指一定时期内全部建成投产项目个数与同期施工项目个数的比率。该指标是从建设单位建设速度的角度反映投资效果的指标。

SHANGHAI STATISTICAL YEARBOOK

EXPLANATORY NOTES TO MAJOR STATISTICAL INDICATORS

□ Total Investment in Fixed Assets

Investment in Fixed Assets constitutes an important portion of the national economic reproduction. Fixed assets investment is a general term for both the work volume of production and purchase of fixed assets and relevant expenditure, in the form of currency, during a certain period. It is a comprehensive indicator of scale, structure and development speed of fixed assets investment. As stipulated in the current national statistics regulations, the social fixed assets investment includes the investment into infrastructure and reformation, real estate development, urban and rural collective economic bodies, private house construction in urban and rural areas and other economic bodies.

From 1997, the fixed assets items only include those with investment of 0.5 million yuan and above.

□ Investment in Real Estate Development

Investment in Real Estate Development refers to the investment by the real estate development companies, commercial buildings construction companies and other real estate development units of various types of ownership in the construction of house buildings, such as residential buildings, factory buildings, warehouses, hotels, guesthouses, holiday villages, office buildings, and the complementary service facilities and land development projects, such as roads, water supply, water drainage, power supply, heating, telecommunications, land leveling and other projects of infrastructure. It excludes the activities in pure land transactions.

□ Investment in Fixed Assets by Sector

Investment in Fixed Assets by Sector refers to determining the classification of construction projects by the major products or the purpose of the projects when they are put into production or use, and by the nature of their social economic activities. In general, one project or one enterprise or institution can only be classified into one sector.

□ Investment in Fixed Assets by Administrative Relationship

Investment in Fixed Assets by Administrative Relationship refers to the classification of investment by the competent authorities under which investment is made by construction units, enterprises, institutions or administrative units.

(1)Central investment refers to the investment in projects or by enterprises, institutions or administrative units which are under the direct leadership and management of the CPC Central Committee, the NPC Standing Committee, the State Council and of the national commissions, ministries, agencies and state-owned large corporations. Various ministries and departments of the State Council prepare and implement plans for investment in fixed assets by those departments, and arrange and ensure the supply of materials and key equipment required for the projects.

(2)Local investment refers to the investment in projects or by enterprises, institutions or administrative units which are under the direct leadership and management of departments under the provincial, prefecture and county governments. Also included are projects by foreign-invested enterprises and enterprises without competent managing authorities.

□ Investment in Fixed Assets by Use of Funds

Investment in Fixed Assets by Use of Funds is classified by their contents. It is mainly classified into 3 categories, i.e. construction and installation, purchase of equipment and instrument, and other expenses.

(1) Construction and installation (work volume of construction and installation) refers to the construction of various houses and buildings and installation of various kinds of equipment and instruments. They include construction of various houses; equipment foundations, industrial kilns and stoves, and metal structure work; preparation works for project construction, and clearing up works post project construction; pavement of railways and roads, drilling of mines and putting up of oil pipes; construction of projects of water conservancy; construction of underground air-raid shelters and construction of other special projects; value of equipment for heating, sanitation, ventilation, lighting, gas, painting, etc. that are covered by the budget of housing projects; laying out of various pipelines (for steam, compressed air, petroleum, tap water and sewage) and lines for electric power and for communications; installation of various machinery equipment, testing operation for pre-testing the quality of installation projects, and land and other development work conducted by real estate developers

EXPLANATORY NOTES TO
MAJOR STATISTICAL INDICATORS

for commercial housing. The value of equipment installed is not included in the value of installation projects.

(2)Purchase of equipment and instruments refers to the total value of equipment, tools, and instruments purchased or self-produced which come up to standards for fixed assets by the construction units or investing enterprises or institutions. Equipment, tools and instruments purchased or self-produced for new workshops by newly established or expanded units are categorized as "purchase of equipment and instruments" no matter whether they come up to the standards for fixed assets.

(3)Other expenses refer to expenses occurring during the construction or purchase of fixed assets other than those mentioned above.

□ Sources of Capital for Investment in Fixed Assets

Sources of Capital for Investment in Fixed Assets include state budgetary appropriation, domestic loans, foreign investment, self-raised funds, and others.

(1)State budgetary appropriation refers to appropriation in the budget of the central and local governments earmarked for capital construction and for innovation projects, and the special appropriation from the budget of the central government for capital construction and for the transfer fund to banks to be issued as loans for capital construction projects.

(2)Domestic loans refer to various funds borrowed by enterprises and institutions from banks and non-bank financial institutions during the reference period for the purpose of investment in fixed assets, including loans issued by banks from their self-owned funds and deposit, loans appropriated by higher responsible authorities, special loans by government (including loan for replacing petroleum with coal, special loan for reform-through-labour coal mines), loans arranged by local government from special funds, domestic reserve loan, and working loan, etc..

(3)Bond

(4)Foreign Investment refers to foreign funds received during the reference period for the purpose of investment in fixed assets, including foreign funds borrowed and managed by the government, by individual units, foreign fund in joint venture program, and issue of bonds and stocks at the international financial markets. The foreign funds borrowed and managed by the government refer to foreign loans borrowed by the government from foreign governments, organizations, or financial institutions under official agreements signed by both parties, under which government is responsible for the repayment of both the principal and interests of the foreign loans.

(5)Self-raised funds refer to funds received by construction enterprises from their higher responsible authorities, local governments, or raised by enterprises or institutions themselves for the purpose of investment in fixed assets during the reference period.

(6)Others refer to funds received during the reference period which are not included in the above-mentioned sources.

□ Investment in Fixed Assets by Type of Construction

The construction projects in general can be classified, by the type of construction, into new construction, expansion, reconstruction and construction of living facilities.

(1)New construction in general refers to newly constructed enterprises, institutions, administrative agencies or independent projects from scratch. Construction in the existing enterprises, institutions or agencies is not considered as new construction. In case the assets of the existing unit is quite small, and the value of newly added fixed assets exceeds the original value of assets by three times, the expansion will be considered as new construction.

(2)Reconstruction refers to construction projects by existing enterprises or institutions in innovation or technical transformation of the old facilities (including auxiliary production equipment and welfare facilities). Also considered as reconstruction is the construction of new workshops by the existing enterprises or institutions to change the variety of products to meet the market demand (such as the production of civil products by defence industries), or to bring the designed production capacity into full play through a more balanced production process on production lines.

(3)Expansion refers to construction of new major production workshop, branch factory or independent production line within a factory or in other locations, for the purpose of increasing the production capacity (or improving efficiency) of the original products. Newly constructed houses for the operation of institutions and administrative organizations (such as the newly constructed buildings for teaching in schools, buildings for clinics or wards in hospitals, etc.) are also classified as expansion.

Also included in the expansion are investments by existing enterprises or institutions in building major production line (s) or branch factory (ies) along with some work on innovation, for the purpose of expending the production capacity of original products or producing new products.

EXPLANATORY NOTES TO MAJOR STATISTICAL INDICATORS

□ Newly Increased Fixed Assets

Newly Increased Fixed Assets, also called fixed assets put into operation, refers to the value of fixed assets that has been put into production or handed over to the production units after the completion of the process of construction and purchase. The newly increased fixed asset is an value indicator of the result of investment. It is also the necessary data for reflecting the construction process and the result of investment in fixed assets.

□ Rate of Fixed Assets Transferred and in Use

Rate of Fixed Assets Transferred and in Use refers to the ratio of the newly increased fixed assets to the total investment made in the same period. This is a comprehensive indicator reflecting the speed of the employment of fixed assets and the investment efficiency at the macro-level. As the newly increase fixed assets is the result of a long period while the investment is completed in the current year, this indicator is expected to be used to reflect the employment of fixed assets over a long period of time.

□ Projects under Construction

Projects under Construction refer to projects with construction and installation activities undertaken in the reference period. All projects that have construction activities undertaken during the reference period are reported as projects under construction irrespective of the length of construction work. The number of projects under construction can reflect the actual size of investment in fixed assets during a given period, and when compared with the number of projects completed and put into use during the same period, it demonstrates the results of investment in fixed assets. Depending on the nature of construction activities, projects under construction can also be classified into projects under construction in current year, winding-up projects in current year and stopped or suspended projects in previous years (with preservation work in current year).

□ Projects Completed and Put into Use

Industrial projects refer to the major projects and accessory facilities completed which result in forming production capacity and have been checked and accepted while the living and welfare facilities have been completed and can ensure normal production and formally put into production. Non-industrial projects refer to the major projects and accessory facilities completed which possess the designed capacity and have been checked, accepted and formally put into production.

□ Rate of Projects Completed and Put into Use

Rate of Projects Completed and Put into Use refers to the ratio of the number of construction projects completed and put into use in certain period of time to the number of projects under construction in the same period. This reflects the investment efficiency from the perspective of the speed of projects construction.

第七篇

CHAPTER 7

对外经济贸易和旅游

FOREIGN ECONOMIC RELATIONS, TRADE AND TOURISM

表7.1 主要年份口岸出口商品总额
TOTAL VALUE OF PORT EXPORTS IN MAIN YEARS

单位:亿美元（100 million USD）

年 份 Year	出口商品总额 Total Value of Port Exports	其中 of which #一般贸易 Ordinary Trade	#来料加工装配贸易 Processing and Assembly Trade with Customers' Materials	#进料加工贸易 Processing Trade with Imported Materials	#对外承包工程货物 Construction Projects in Foreign Countries	#出料加工贸易 Outward Processing Trade
1985	49.08	47.04	0.73	1.05		
1990	86.62	51.39	3.20	30.67	0.41	0.45
1995	256.07	149.16	14.31	90.12	0.63	0.06
1996	272.13	146.05	25.42	97.69	1.01	
1997	334.51	178.93	37.17	115.17	0.71	
1998	374.58	199.24	44.13	127.55	0.79	
1999	442.88	234.43	55.08	149.68	0.59	
2000	615.72	341.02	64.21	205.13	1.25	
2001	680.07	380.43	61.09	228.43	1.26	0.13
2002	818.03	473.13	66.88	266.72	1.44	0.13
2003	1 123.06	618.90	78.81	408.79	1.18	0.12
2004	1 612.68	824.92	126.99	623.27	3.18	0.14
2005	2 124.30	1 057.68	195.83	813.26	6.37	0.16
2006	2 665.65	1 319.56	212.77	1 058.07	9.45	0.14

注：本表至表7.10的数据由上海海关提供。
Note: Data in table7.1 to 7.10 are prorided by Shanghai Custom.

表7.2 主要年份口岸进口商品总额
TOTAL VALUE OF PORT IMPORTS IN MAIN YEARS

单位:亿美元（100 million USD）

年 份 Year	进口商品总额 Total Value of Port Imports	其中 of which #一般贸易 Oridinary Trade	#来料加工装配贸易 Processing and Assembly Trade with Customers' Materials	#进料加工贸易 Processing Trade with Imported Materials	#外商投资企业进口设备 Imported Equipment of Foreign Funded Enterprise	#租赁贸易 Leasing Trade
1985	99.65	93.45	0.43	5.03		
1990	86.27	51.79	2.40	19.70	6.11	
1995	225.30	93.79	13.49	65.96	45.16	0.11
1996	256.57	85.64	20.48	69.33	70.09	3.10
1997	252.32	83.02	27.64	79.79	45.86	3.65
1998	261.80	93.24	29.63	80.37	40.52	2.63
1999	318.63	137.56	35.72	82.84	30.36	4.55
2000	477.39	212.65	44.87	125.13	40.26	2.47
2001	524.81	245.94	47.38	123.39	47.46	2.45
2002	606.98	267.66	48.12	160.91	54.95	1.89
2003	888.95	377.21	54.47	243.24	66.32	2.36
2004	1 213.07	472.16	89.47	338.57	99.72	4.7
2005	1 382.48	502.49	133.69	409.30	74.76	7.85
2006	1 621.89	574.40	122.52	497.41	73.72	23.74

表7.3 按国别(地区)分的口岸出口商品总额(2003～2006)
TOTAL VALUE OF PORT EXPORTS BY COUNTRIES AND REGIONS

单位:亿美元(100 million USD)

国别(地区)	Country (Region)	2003	2004	2005	2006
总　计	**Total**	**1 123.06**	**1 612.68**	**2 124.30**	**2 665.65**
亚　洲	**Asia**	**498.54**	**708.74**	**898.90**	**1 086.64**
#中国香港	Hong Kong, China	78.26	119.92	160.72	184.74
中国台湾	Taiwan, China	28.68	46.96	59.81	77.40
日　本	Japan	194.47	253.42	298.78	334.85
韩　国	Republic of Korea	38.90	57.78	78.66	103.98
新加坡	Singapore	25.50	38.46	48.69	65.67
马来西亚	Malaysia	18.36	28.63	38.27	46.73
泰　国	Thailand	10.29	16.48	22.39	28.24
菲律宾	Philippines	11.44	16.64	16.58	19.67
巴基斯坦	Pakistan	5.53	7.08	8.07	10.21
科威特	Kuwait	1.08	1.24	1.40	1.81
沙特阿拉伯	Saudi Arabia	4.77	7.06	8.84	11.45
阿拉伯联合酋长国	United Arab Emirates	12.95	17.43	23.24	27.96
非　洲	**Africa**	**32.61**	**42.08**	**53.42**	**73.16**
#埃　及	Egypt	3.29	4.64	5.89	8.23
苏　丹	Sudan	0.88	1.11	2.35	3.09
欧　洲	**Europe**	**252.54**	**369.86**	**505.52**	**632.46**
#德　国	Germany	50.15	74.97	99.69	122.30
法　国	France	31.22	41.29	44.84	53.57
意大利	Italy	23.89	30.71	42.81	55.87
荷　兰	Netherlands	29.78	47.65	75.62	91.16
英　国	United Kingdoms	30.15	45.13	59.10	75.54
瑞　典	Sweden	5.09	7.16	9.42	10.78
俄罗斯	Russia	7.86	14.01	18.6	22.95
美　洲	**America**	**313.18**	**454.84**	**618.05**	**812.55**
#美　国	United States	251.04	361.53	501.11	646.99
加拿大	Canada	18.72	29.48	42.58	54.39
巴　西	Brazil	6.62	11.33	14.61	23.94
智　利	Chile	4.45	5.81	7.26	10.18
大洋洲及太平洋岛屿	**Oceanic and PacificIsland**	**26.19**	**37.15**	**48.41**	**60.84**
#澳大利亚	Australia	22.71	32.55	41.94	52.71
新西兰	New Zealand	2.99	4.12	5.50	6.40
其　他	**Others**		**0.01**		

注：其他为无国别数(以下同)。
Note: Others refer to regions without sovereignty(Same as follows).

表 7.4 按国别(地区)分的口岸进口商品总额(2003～2006)
TOTAL VALUE OF PORT IMPORTS BY COUNTRIES AND REGIONS

单位:亿美元 (100 million USD)

国别(地区)	Country (Region)	2003	2004	2005	2006
总　计	**Total**	**888.95**	**1 213.07**	**1 382.48**	**1 621.89**
亚　洲	**Asia**	**525.25**	**742.55**	**873.45**	**1 020.51**
#中国香港	Hong Kong, China	23.86	17.67	17.41	14.23
中国台湾	Taiwan, China	92.02	132.90	155.56	181.37
日　本	Japan	189.00	254.70	267.91	311.91
韩　国	Republic of Korea	83.31	130.02	163.95	176.27
新加坡	Singapore	25.62	34.00	44.30	39.77
马来西亚	Malaysia	26.65	37.22	43.88	52.00
泰　国	Thailand	20.22	29.78	36.53	41.99
菲律宾	Philippines	16.25	25.43	36.08	53.29
巴基斯坦	Pakistan	0.90	1.11	2.15	1.48
科威特	Kuwait	0.21	0.16	0.23	0.27
沙特阿拉伯	Saudi Arabia	2.37	2.97	4.01	3.72
阿拉伯联合酋长国	United Arab Emirates	0.68	0.80	0.95	0.99
非　洲	**Africa**	**7.06**	**11.60**	**13.76**	**16.30**
#埃　及	Egypt	0.33	0.40	0.44	0.40
南　非	South Africa	4.13	5.71	6.62	8.09
欧　洲	**Europe**	**205.93**	**253.55**	**264.89**	**320.15**
#德　国	Germany	88.43	103.97	103.93	125.93
法　国	France	24.99	29.13	28.81	40.31
意大利	Italy	16.53	20.55	23.91	29.56
荷　兰	Netherlands	6.22	8.94	8.17	9.12
英　国	United Kingdoms	10.18	13.71	15.62	20.30
瑞　典	Sweden	10.04	13.67	11.94	13.08
俄罗斯	Russia	4.68	5.53	8.3	8.55
美　洲	**America**	**137.91**	**186.14**	**202.70**	**234.63**
#美　国	United States	93.33	128.21	139.52	170.62
加拿大	Canada	12.69	15.70	14.89	16.57
巴　西	Brazil	10.18	10.69	13.08	12.34
智　利	Chile	12.00	18.63	18.42	16.70
大洋洲及太平洋岛屿	**Oceanic and Pacific Island**	**12.69**	**18.86**	**27.50**	**30.13**
#澳大利亚	Australia	10.31	16.03	23.79	25.15
新西兰	New Zealand	2.37	2.46	3.04	3.70
其　他	**Others**	**0.11**	**0.37**	**0.18**	**0.17**

表 7.5　主要年份外贸进出口商品总额
TOTAL VALUE OF FOREIGN TRADE IMPORTS AND EXPORTS IN MAIN YEARS

年 份 Year	外贸进出口商品总额（亿美元） Total Value of Foreign Trade Imports and Exports (100 million USD)	外贸进口商品总额（亿美元） Total Value of Foreign Trade Imports (100 million USD)	外贸出口商品总额（亿美元） Total Value of Foreign Trade Exports (100 million USD)	外贸进出口差 额（亿美元） Balance (100 million USD)	外贸进出口相当于生产总值的比例(%) Foreign Trade Imports and Export as Percentage of Gross Domestic Product(%)	外贸出口相当于生产总值的比例(%) Foreign Trade Export as Percentage of Gross Domestic Product(%)
1978	30.26	1.33	28.93	27.60	19.1	18.2
1980	45.06	2.40	42.66	40.26	21.5	20.4
1985	51.74	18.13	33.61	15.48	35.5	23.0
1990	74.31	21.10	53.21	32.11	47.0	33.6
1995	190.25	74.48	115.77	41.29	63.6	38.7
1996	222.63	90.25	132.38	42.13	62.6	37.2
1997	247.64	100.40	147.24	46.84	59.7	35.5
1998	313.44	153.88	159.56	5.68	68.3	34.8
1999	386.04	198.19	187.85	-10.34	76.3	37.1
2000	547.10	293.56	253.54	-40.02	94.9	44.0
2001	608.98	332.70	276.28	-56.42	96.7	43.9
2002	726.64	406.09	320.55	-85.54	104.8	46.2
2003	1 123.97	639.15	484.82	-154.33	139.0	59.9
2004	1 600.26	865.06	735.20	-129.86	164.1	75.4
2005	1 863.65	956.23	907.42	-48.81	166.6	81.1
2006	2 274.89	1 139.16	1 135.73	-3.43	174.9	87.3

注：1999 年以前外贸进口、出口商品总额为外经贸委统计口径，1999 年以后为海关统计的上海企业进口、出口总额(以下同)。

Note: Before 1999, the figures of Shanghai's foreign trade imports and exports were based on statistics from Shanghai Foreign Trade and Economic Cooperation Commission. Since 1999, the figures representing imports and exports are made by Shanghai enterprises through Shanghai Custom. Same as follows.

表 7.6　主要年份外贸出口商品总额
TOTAL VALUE OF FOREIGN TRADE EXPORTS IN MAIN YEARS

单位:亿美元 (100 million USD)

指 标	Indicators	1990	2000	2005	2006
出口总额	**Total Value of Exports**	**53.21**	**253.54**	**907.42**	**1 135.73**
按企业性质分	**Grouped by Different Enterprises**				
#国有企业	State-owned Enterprises	50.21	106.78	206.85	248.74
外商投资企业	Foreign-funded Enterprises	2.99	142.61	615.93	759.35
按贸易方式分	**Grouped by Trade**				
#一般贸易	Original Trade	29.03	101.72	339.11	433.04
加工贸易	Processing Trade	24.07	147.83	518.84	637.69
按产品类别分	**Grouped by Different Products**				
#机电产品	Electrical and Mechanical Products	12.68	121.43	602.47	754.15
#高新技术产品	High-tech Products			362.53	442.81

表7.7 主要年份按国别(地区)分的外贸出口商品总额
TOTAL VALUE OF FOREIGN TRADE EXPORTS BY COUNTRIES AND REGIONS IN MAIN YEARS

单位:亿美元 (100 million USD)

国别(地区)	Country (Region)	1978	1990	2000	2005	2006
总 计	**Total**	**28.93**	**53.21**	**253.54**	**907.42**	**1 135.73**
亚 洲	**Asia**	**13.63**	**25.57**	**129.10**	**383.99**	**469.15**
#中国香港	Hong Kong, China	5.78	10.64	23.02	85.66	102.02
中国台湾	Taiwan, China		0.24	5.67	25.71	35.56
日 本	Japan	2.69	7.59	60.81	133.56	151.71
韩 国	Republic of Korea			10.59	30.38	38.67
新加坡	Singapore	0.98	1.82	7.88	22.32	29.88
马来西亚	Malaysia	0.38	0.39	2.59	20.54	22.95
泰 国	Thailand	0.11	0.78	2.48	9.11	11.50
巴基斯坦	Pakistan	0.21	0.33	0.55	2.30	2.92
科威特	Kuwait	0.58	0.58	0.20	0.73	0.90
沙特阿拉伯	Saudi Arabia	0.21	0.66	1.14	2.86	3.72
阿拉伯联合酋长国	United Arab Emirates	0.37	0.90	1.79	7.83	9.14
非 洲	**Africa**	**2.89**	**1.38**	**5.63**	**13.92**	**19.48**
#埃 及	Egypt	0.25	0.13	0.44	1.67	2.53
苏 丹	Sudan	0.20	0.01	0.22	0.74	0.57
阿尔及利亚	Algeria			0.09	0.45	0.70
摩洛哥	Morocco	0.27	0.13	0.20	0.56	0.70
欧 洲	**Europe**	**9.37**	**15.52**	**45.62**	**216.28**	**278.10**
#德 国	Germany	1.93	2.54	9.48	42.48	55.90
法 国	France	0.80	0.85	4.50	20.91	26.09
意大利	Italy	0.73	1.27	4.98	12.71	19.11
荷 兰	Netherlands	0.25	0.74	6.16	35.07	40.26
比利时	Belgium	0.11	0.30	2.95	11.75	14.65
英 国	United Kingdoms	1.19	1.15	7.07	24.70	32.35
俄罗斯	Russia	0.69	1.74	0.37	4.64	7.18
美 洲	**America**	**2.24**	**9.57**	**67.82**	**272.00**	**340.61**
#美 国	United States	1.03	7.45	56.25	227.39	282.74
加拿大	Canada	0.46	0.92	4.04	18.74	22.04
巴 西	Brazil		0.03	1.06	5.41	7.05
古 巴	Cuba			0.07	0.48	0.53
大洋洲及太平洋岛屿	**Oceanic and Pacific Island**	**0.80**	**1.17**	**5.37**	**21.23**	**28.39**
#澳大利亚	Australia	0.67	1.02	4.74	18.43	24.73

表7.8 主要年份按国别(地区)分的外贸进口商品总额

TOTAL VALUE OF FOREIGN TRADE IMPORTS BY COUNTRIES AND REGIONS IN MAIN YEARS

单位:亿美元 (100 million USD)

国别(地区)	Country (Region)	1978	1990	2000	2005	2006
总　计	**Total**	**1.33**	**21.10**	**293.56**	**956.23**	**1 139.16**
亚　洲	**Asia**	**0.75**	**11.15**	**161.59**	**585.84**	**699.01**
#中国香港	Hong Kong, China	0.02	5.30	16.68	11.33	8.63
中国台湾	Taiwan, China		0.21	19.44	98.74	117.33
日　本	Japan	0.69	4.59	70.43	168.87	192.31
韩　国	Republic of Korea			20.63	81.79	97.40
新加坡	Singapore	0.02	0.37	9.39	31.84	30.32
马来西亚	Malaysia	0.01	0.28	6.49	40.13	46.68
泰　国	Thailand		0.10	4.35	25.02	31.49
菲律宾	Philippines			1.83	35.15	52.10
科威特	Kuwait		0.03	0.22	0.44	0.43
沙特阿拉伯	Saudi Arabia			0.78	4.19	3.99
阿拉伯联合酋长国	United Arab Emirates			0.40	1.00	1.31
非　洲	**Africa**		**0.26**	**1.89**	**8.52**	**11.00**
欧　洲	**Europe**	**0.41**	**5.33**	**63.36**	**177.30**	**214.53**
#德　国	Germany	0.13	3.46	26.59	67.27	76.21
法　国	France	0.02	0.11	7.95	22.67	33.85
意大利	Italy	0.05	0.30	4.81	15.25	18.99
荷　兰	Netherlands	0.03	0.09	2.43	6.26	7.02
比利时	Belgium	0.02	0.21	2.83	7.90	8.74
英　国	United Kingdoms	0.04	0.48	3.76	11.83	15.45
瑞　士	Switzerland	0.05	0.22	2.22	9.79	11.21
瑞　典	Sweden	0.02	0.09	4.53	5.24	6.79
美　洲	**America**	**0.07**	**3.14**	**58.60**	**160.13**	**187.24**
#美　国	United States	0.01	2.81	40.11	110.04	131.64
加拿大	Canada	0.02	0.14	7.03	10.43	11.40
巴　西	Brazil			4.11	13.03	17.08
大洋洲及太平洋岛屿	**Oceanic and Pacific Island**	**0.10**	**1.22**	**8.07**	**24.33**	**27.26**
#澳大利亚	Australia	0.07	1.08	6.68	20.84	22.56
新西兰	New Zealand	0.03	0.13	1.25	2.27	2.32
其　他	**Others**			**0.05**	**0.11**	**0.12**

表7.9 外贸出口商品总额(2003~2006)
TOTAL VALUE OF FOREIGN TRADE EXPORTS OF MAJOR COMMODITIES

单位:亿美元(100 million USD)

类别	Types	2003	2004	2005	2006
总计	**Total**	**484.82**	**735.20**	**907.42**	**1 135.73**
初级产品	**Primary Products**	**12.32**	**21.38**	**24.79**	**27.53**
食品及活动物	Food and Livestock	4.22	4.93	5.60	6.62
# 肉及肉制品	Meat and Meat Products	0.69	0.55	0.65	0.70
蔬菜及水果	Vegetable and Fruits	0.96	1.18	1.43	1.93
饮料及烟类	Beverage and Tobacco	1.03	1.04	1.20	1.47
# 烟草及其制品	Tobacco and Tobacco Products	0.92	0.90	1.01	1.13
非食用原料	Non-edible Raw Materials	2.61	2.93	4.34	5.21
矿物燃料、润滑油及其有关原料	Mineral Fuel, Lubricant and Related Raw Materials	4.43	12.44	13.62	14.05
动植物油、脂及蜡	Animal and Plant Oil, Fat and Wax	0.03	0.04	0.03	0.18
工业制成品	**Industrial Products**	**472.50**	**713.82**	**882.63**	**1 108.20**
化学成品及有关产品	Chemicals and Related Products	20.51	28.52	39.20	52.71
# 医药品	Medical Products	3.17	3.56	4.09	4.81
原料制成品	Raw Material Products	68.29	101.94	126.83	177.52
# 橡胶制品	Rubber Products	2.44	3.13	3.74	4.75
纺纱、织物、制成品及有关产品	Spinning, Textile and Related Products	25.49	32.00	36.76	41.48
钢 铁	Steel	7.21	16.36	20.90	37.31
机械及运输设备	Machinery and Transportation Equipments	256.71	421.31	526.32	656.61
# 通用工业机械设备及零件	General-purpose Industrial Machinery Equipments and Parts	24.37	35.67	46.21	57.64
电力机械、器具及电气零件	Electrical Equipments, Tools and Parts	68.71	109.48	124.69	163.80
杂项制品	Assorted Products	126.58	161.38	189.05	220.18
# 服装及衣着附件	Clothing and Dresses	72.17	82.40	89.71	99.75
未分类的商品	Other Commodities	0.41	0.67	1.23	1.18

表 7.10 外贸进口商品总额(2003~2006)
TOTAL VALUE OF FOREIGN TRADE IMPORTS OF MAJOR COMMODITIES

单位:亿美元 (100 million USD)

类 别	Types	2003	2004	2005	2006
总 计	**Total**	**639.15**	**865.06**	**956.23**	**1 139.16**
初级产品	**Primary Products**	**60.64**	**83.36**	**99.46**	**121.33**
食品及活动物	Food and Livestock	4.88	6.26	7.63	9.44
#肉及肉制品	Meat and Meat Products	1.01	0.98	1.59	1.17
蔬菜及水果	Vegetable and Fruits	0.57	0.88	1.28	1.76
饮料及烟类	Beverage and Tobacco	1.03	1.84	3.21	4.32
#烟草及其制品	Tobacco and Tobacco Products	0.08	0.17	0.31	0.20
非食用原料	Non-edible Raw Materials	38.80	51.80	63.19	74.67
矿物燃料、润滑油及其有关原料	Mineral Fuel, Lubricant and Related Raw Materials	10.92	17.97	20.33	27.97
动植物油、脂及蜡	Animal and Plant Oil, Fat and Wax	5.01	5.49	5.10	4.93
工业制成品	**Industrial Products**	**578.51**	**781.70**	**856.77**	**1 017.83**
化学成品及有关产品	Chemicals and Related Products	89.16	110.75	121.65	142.58
#医药品	Medical Products	4.77	6.12	7.35	9.76
原料制成品	Raw Material Products	95.33	115.46	120.93	141.31
#橡胶制品	Rubber Products	3.02	3.65	3.71	5.91
纺纱、织物、制成品及有关产品	Spinning, Textile and Related Products	17.87	20.42	19.80	19.53
钢 铁	Steel	30.52	34.61	32.52	28.15
机械及运输设备	Machinery and Transportation Equipments	332.20	461.84	514.51	628.08
#通用工业机械设备及零件	General-purpose Industrial Machinery Equipments and Parts	37.52	50.56	48.79	55.25
电力机械、器具及电气零件	Electrical Equipments, Tools and Parts	129.61	200.39	244.15	321.51
杂项制品	Assorted Products	61.20	93.32	99.10	104.96
#服装及衣着附件	Clothing and Dresses	2.05	2.13	2.94	3.36
未分类的商品	Other Commodities	0.62	0.33	0.58	0.90

表 7.11 主要年份进出口商品检验情况
IMPORTS AND EXPORTS INSPECTION IN MAIN YEARS

指 标	Indicators	1990	2000	2005	2006
进口商品检验	**Imports Inspection**				
检验批数(批)	Groups of Inspection(group)	7 991	51 940	462 325	633 858
检验金额(亿美元)	Values of Inspection(100 million USD)	32.26	76.16	423.49	595.26
不合格批数(批)	Unqualified Groups (group)	1 327	1 539	18 359	8 706
占检验批数比重(%)	Percentage in Total (%)	16.6	3.0	4.0	1.4
不合格金额(亿美元)	Unqualified Values (100 million USD)	10.75	0.99	16.05	14.58
占检验金额比重(%)	Percentage in Total (%)	33.3	1.3	3.8	2.5
出口商品检验	**Exports Inspection**				
检验批数(批)	Groups of Inspection(group)	101 301	344 138	506 873	637 453
检验金额(亿美元)	Values of Inspection(100 million USD)	95.53	100.86	166.77	226.60
不合格批数(批)	Unqualified Groups (group)	1 854	564	312	327
占检验批数比重(%)	Percentage in Total (%)	1.8	0.2	0.1	0.1
不合格金额(亿美元)	Unqualified Values (100 million USD)	1.82	0.11	0.25	0.07
占检验金额比重(%)	Percentage in Total (%)	1.9	0.1	0.2	…

注：本表数据由市出入境检验检疫局提供。
Note: Data in this table are provided by Shanghai Entry-Exit Inspection and Quarantine Bureau.

表 7.12 主要年份直接吸收外资情况
FOREIGN DIRECT INVESTMENT IN MAIN YEARS

指 标	Indicators	1990	2000	2005	2006
签订合同项目(个)	**Number of Signed Contracts (item)**	**203**	**1 814**	**4 091**	**4 061**
#合资经营	Joint Ventures	161	441	601	540
合作经营	Cooperative Ventures	12	226	44	27
独资经营	Sole-foreign Funded Enterprises	30	1 146	3 442	3 486
签订合同金额(亿美元)	**Contracted Foreign Capital (100 million USD)**	**2.14**	**63.90**	**138.33**	**145.74**
#合资经营	Joint Ventures	1.10	13.86	19.62	24.27
合作经营	Cooperative Ventures	0.38	5.86	2.66	2.86
独资经营	Sole-foreign Funded Enterprises	0.66	44.14	109.47	117.37
实际吸收外资金额(亿美元)	**Foreign Investment Actually Absorbed (100 million USD)**	**1.77**	**31.60**	**68.50**	**71.07**
#合资经营	Joint Ventures	1.08	12.94	14.25	15.84
合作经营	Cooperative Ventures	0.67	2.99	1.62	1.86
独资经营	Sole-foreign Funded Enterprises	0.02	15.67	45.87	53.30

注：本表部分数据由市外国投资工作委员会提供(下表同)。
Note: Data in this table are provided by Shanghai Foreign Investment Commission. (same as follows).

表 7.13 外商直接投资合同项目和金额（2006） NUMBER OF CONTRACTS SIGNED AND VALUES OF FOREIGN DIRECT INVESTMENT PROJECTS

类别	Types	签订合同项目(个) Number of Contracts Signed(item)		签订合同金额(亿美元) Contracted Foreign Capital (100 million USD)		实际吸收外资金额(亿美元) Foreign Investment Actually Absorbed (100 million USD)	
		2006	至2006年底累计 Total by the End of 2006	2006	至2006年底累计 Total by the End of 2006	2006	至2006年底累计 Total by the End of 2006
总 计	**Total**	**4 061**	**44 547**	**145.74**	**1 145.35**	**71.07**	**667.63**
#1 000万美元以上项目	Projects of Over 10 Million USD	348	3751	105.36	831.94		
#工 业	Industry	164	1 988	29.59	225.09		
按投资方式分	**Grouped by Investment Mode**						
#合资经营	Joint Ventures	540	14 906	24.27	330.42	15.84	245.14
合作经营	Cooperative Ventures	27	5 023	2.86	123.93	1.86	84.31
独资经营	Sole-foreign Funded Enterprises	3 486	24 548	117.37	659.18	53.30	310.65
按产业分	**Grouped by Industry**						
第一产业	Primary Industry	6	253	0.24	3.55	0.08	1.47
第二产业	Secondary Industry	1 093	23 650	47.88	650.51	26.83	336.50
#工 业	Industry	1 071	22 824	46.91	635.51	26.54	331.80
第三产业	Tertiary Industry	2 962	20 644	97.62	491.29	44.16	329.66
按主要国别(地区)分	**Grouped by Country and Region**						
#中国香港	Hong Kong, China	919	12 869	35.39	273.53	13.53	174.54
中国澳门	Macao, China	9	219	0.32	3.69	0.09	1.30
中国台湾	Taiwan, China	315	5 239	3.27	45.15	3.15	33.18
日 本	Japan	577	6376	15.82	130.79	8.32	95.20
韩 国	Republic of Korea	231	1 090	2.80	12.47	1.15	7.67
新加坡	Singapore	225	2 321	4.63	59.95	2.99	28.43
泰 国	Thailand	9	366	0.31	4.18	0.10	2.39
德 国	Germany	136	933	4.00	50.68	7.37	33.64
英 国	United Kingdoms	79	681	1.33	21.84	1.36	16.66
法 国	France	45	398	1.05	14.39	0.47	6.68
意大利	Italy	71	371	1.02	4.54	0.31	1.17
美 国	United States	441	5 288	8.17	105.68	3.63	70.79
加拿大	Canada	65	790	0.74	7.71	0.19	3.07
澳大利亚	Australia	65	863	0.56	10.36	0.98	4.74

表 7.14　主要年份外商投资企业生产经营情况
PRODUCTION AND OPERATION OF OVERSEAS-FUNDED ENTERPRISES IN MAIN YEARS

指　标	Indicators	1990	2000	2005	2006
销售（经营）收入（亿元）	Sales (Operation) Revenues (100 million yuan)	111.02	3 977.90	13 974.87	15 618.76
利润总额（亿元）	Total Pre-tax Profits (100 million yuan)	11.04	217.79	667.88	837.19
交纳税金总额（亿元）	Total Tax Payment (100 million yuan)	3.90	158.93	389.04	455.36
外汇总收入（亿美元）	Total Foreign Exchange Inflow (100 million USD)		209.58	817.00	907.23
#经常项目外汇收入	Foreign Exchange Inflow of Current Accounts	11.92	126.39	633.98	743.68
外汇总支出(亿美元)	Total Foreign Exchange Outflow(100 million USD)		205.24	812.90	876.18
#经常项目外汇支出	Foreign Exchange Outflow of Current Accounts	10.81	140.43	665.41	720.50
年末外汇结存(亿美元)	Foreign Exchange Balance at Year End(100 million USD)	5.46	29.55	43.64	48.99
从业人员薪金总额（亿元）	Total Wages and Salaries for Employees (100 million yuan)		180.37	578.81	587.39

表 7.15　主要年份引进技术设备实际到货金额
ARRIVED CAPITAL THROUGH IMPORTED TECHNOLOGY IN MAIN YEARS

单位:万美元(10 000 USD)

国　别(地区)	Country(Region)	1990	2000	2005	2006
总　计	**Total**	**15 063**	**104 558**	**1 863 287**	**2 062 857**
#中国香港	Hong Kong, China	1 688	10 746	21 913	16 986
日　本	Japan	2 868	10 069	410 738	438 295
德　国	Germany	2 925	16 314	365 638	371 729
意大利	Italy	1 755	622	50 878	73 693
美　国	United States	2 226	49 431	247 114	284 945
瑞　士	Switzerland	1 060	1 862	33 207	37 118
英　国	United Kingdoms	667	712	35 810	46 172
瑞　典	Sweden	576	639	17 945	28 803
奥地利	Austria	603	1 162	10 985	11 751
法　国	France	70	1 926	87 576	82 374

注：本表数据由上海海关提供。
Note: Data in this table are provided by Shanghai Custom.

表7.16 主要年份对外经济合作情况
ECONOMIC COOPERATION WITH FOREIGN COUNTRIES OR REGIONS IN MAIN YEARS

	指 标 Indicators	1990	2000	2005	2006
签订合同项目（个）	**Number of Contracted Projects (item)**	**78**	**1 076**	**1 249**	**7 346**
#对外承包工程	Overseas Contracted Projects	12	143	277	2 724
对外劳务合作	Overseas Labor Services Cooperation	66	836	937	4 599
签订合同金额(万美元)	**Value of Contract (10 000 USD)**	**6 010**	**98 050**	**245 962**	**545 723**
#对外承包工程	Overseas Contracted Projects	3 929	76 058	225 308	508 953
对外劳务合作	Overseas Labor Services Cooperation	2 081	20 837	19 500	34 960
实际营业额(万美元)	**Actual Business Volume(10 000 USD)**	**5 131**	**83 790**	**194 050**	**470 179**
#对外承包工程	Overseas Contracted Projects	4 083	61 906	117 214	429 336
对外劳务合作	Overseas Labor Services Cooperation	1 048	21 049	76 266	40 170
年末在外人员(人)	**Persons Abroad(year-end)(person)**	**2 041**	**30 052**	**25 717**	**27 561**
#对外承包工程	Overseas Contracted Projects	121	1 327	2 694	3 531
对外劳务合作	Overseas Labor Services Cooperation	1 920	28 710	23 002	24 002

注：本表至表7.17由市对外经济贸易委员会提供。
Note: Data in table 7.16 to 7.17 are provided by Shanghai Foreign Economic Relation & Trade Commission.

表7.17 海外企业情况(2005～2006)
ENTERPRISES ABROAD

	指 标 Indicators	2005年新增 Established in 2005	至2005年底累计 Total by the end of 2005	2006年新增 Established in 2006	至2006年底累计 Total by the end of 2006
企业数(个)	Number of Enterprises (unit)	59	906	75	981
投资额(万美元)	Investment Value (10 000 USD)	68 775	183 898	52 977	236 875

表7.18 国际会展(2005～2006)
INTERNATIONAL CONFERENCE AND EXHIBITION

	指 标 Indicators	2005	2006
举办国际会展次数(次)	International Exhibit(time)	276	295
国际会展展出总面积(万平方米)	Total Square of International Exhibit(10 000 sq·m)	376	434

表7.19 旅行社接待经营情况（2003～2006）
TOURISTS RECEIVED BY TOUR AGENCIES

指标	Indicators	2003	2004	2005	2006
接待境内外来沪旅游者(万人次)	**Overseas and Domestic Tourists (10 000 person-times)**	**431.84**	**633.47**	**750.89**	**880.24**
境外旅游者	Overseas Tourists	51.48	78.40	95.01	107.34
#外国人	Foreigners	47.17	74.92	90.01	101.67
中国香港	Tourists from Hong Kong, China	2.75	1.83	1.48	2.28
中国澳门	Tourists from Macao, China	0.01	0.01	0.01	0.03
中国台湾	Tourists from Taiwan,China	1.55	1.64	3.51	3.36
境内旅游者	Domestic Tourists	380.36	555.07	655.88	772.90
出境旅游者(万人次)	Tourists Going Abroad (10 000 person-times)	28.77	49.86	51.71	58.54
经营和财务状况	Operation and Financial Status				
营业收入(亿元)	Operational Revenues(100 million yuan)	68.54	108.22	132.43	169.49
利润总额(亿元)	Total Profits(100 million yuan)	-0.28	1.81	1.61	1.71

注：本表至表7.22的数据由市旅游事业管理委员会提供。
Note: Data in table 7.19 to table 7.22 are provided by Shanghai Municipal Tourism Administrative Commission.

表7.20 住宿业接待经营情况（2003～2006）
OPERATION OF HOTELS

指标	Indicators	2003	2004	2005	2006
年末客房数（万间）	**Year-end Guest Rooms(10 000 rooms)**	**11.54**	**11.49**	**12.57**	**13.71**
年末客房床位数（万张）	Year-end Guest Beds(10 000 beds)	21.90	21.72	24.05	25.95
客房平均出租率（%）	**Average Room Occupancy Rate (%)**	**57.2**	**62.9**	**67.3**	**64.8**
#星级宾馆	Star-rated Hotels	61.1	69.0	65.6	63.9
实际住宿人次数（万人次）	**Actual Number of Guests (10 000 person-times)**	**1 824.12**	**2 070.13**	**2 378.86**	**2 422.34**
#境外来沪	Overseas Visitors	247.87	345.04	558.51	570.90
实际住宿人天数（万人天）	**Actual Number of Guests and Days of Stay (10 000 person-day)**	**3 060.52**	**3 595.18**	**4 036.98**	**4 110.44**
#境外来沪	Overseas Visitors	847.17	863.49	1 150.65	1 212.11
营业收入（亿元）	**Operational Revenues (100 million yuan)**	**130.41**	**165.59**	**194.47**	**212.03**
#客房收入	Room Rate Revenues	69.33	89.99	110.19	121.95
餐饮收入	Catering Revenues	39.27	49.80	55.36	59.99
商品收入	Commodity Sales Revenues	3.54	3.68	4.04	4.14
利润总额（亿元）	**Total Profits (100 million yuan)**	**4.66**	**22.67**	**23.97**	**27.93**

表 7.21　旅游星级饭店基本情况(2006)
BASIC STATISTICS OF STAR-RATED TOURISM HOTELS

	指 标 Indicators	合 计 Total	五星级 Five-Star	四星级 Four-Star	三星级 Three-Star	二星级 Two-Star	一星级 One-Star
饭店数(个)	Number of Hotels(unit)	317	26	43	126	114	8
客房数(万间)	Number of Rooms (10 000 rooms)	5.89	1.20	1.52	2.19	0.95	0.03
床位数(万张)	Number of Beds (10 000 beds)	9.71	1.66	2.33	3.91	1.74	0.07
客房平均出租率(%)	Average Occupancy Rate (%)	63.9	72.6	66.7	60.0	57.7	64.9
营业收入(亿元)	Business Revenues (100 million yuan)	154.11	75.39	40.46	30.02	8.03	0.21
平均房价 (元/间天)	Average Room Rates (yuan/room. day)	645	1 406.43	658.49	333.92	221.63	174.89

表 7.22　国内旅游者来沪人数和人均消费支出 (2002～2006)
NUMBER OF DOMESTIC TOURISTS VISITING SHANGHAI AND PER CAPITA CONSUMPTION EXPENDITURES

	指 标 Indicators	2002	2003	2004	2005	2006
国内旅游者来沪人数(万人次)	**Number of Domestic Tourists Visiting Shanghai(10 000 person-times)**	**8 761**	**7 603**	**8 505**	**9 012**	**9 684**
外省市来沪旅游人数(万人次)	Number of Tourists from other Provinces Visiting Shanghai (10 000 person-times)	6 797	5 630	6 346	6 805	7 327
本市市民在本地旅游人数(万人次)	Number of Local Tourists (10 000 person-times)	1 964	1 973	2 159	2 207	2 357
国内旅游者人均消费支出 (元)	**Consumption Expenditure Per Person (yuan)**	**1 134**	**1 465**	**1 430**	**1 452**	**1 466**
#长途交通费	Long-distance Traffic Expenditure	194	170	194	176	174
住宿费	Accommodation Expenditure	165	233	220	219	211
餐饮费	Food Expenditure	175	249	232	220	217
购物费	Shopping Expenditure	357	521	420	553	536
门票费	Ticket Expenditure	40	44	119	96	112
娱乐费	Entertainment Expenditure	48	52	33	30	47
市内交通费	Local Traffic Expenditure	70	79	87	88	94
邮电通信费	Post and Telecommunications Expenditure	20	19	27	37	35

注：本表为抽样调查资料。
Note: Data in this table are from the sampling survey.

表 7.23 主要年份国际旅游入境人数
NUMBER OF OVERSEAS TOURISTS THROUGH SHANGHAI CUSTOM IN MAIN YEARS

指　标	Indicators	1978	1990	2000	2005	2006
国际旅游入境人数（万人次）	**Number of Overseas Tourists Through Shanghai Custom(10 000 person-times)**	**24.02**	**89.30**	**181.40**	**571.35**	**605.67**
#外国人	Foreigner	17.07	46.06	139.14	452.27	485.40
#日　本	Japanese	5.73	22.60	53.76	119.76	136.93
新加坡	Singaporean	0.34	1.02	5.29	13.69	15.23
德　国	German	0.73	1.60	7.11	20.33	21.79
法　国	French	0.70	1.19	5.39	13.44	15.68
英　国	Briton	0.44	1.11	1.69	13.89	16.69
意大利	Italian	0.39	0.99	1.88	7.65	8.52
加拿大	Canadian	0.34	0.81	2.25	8.06	10.13
美　国	American	3.87	4.67	13.78	44.51	54.60
澳大利亚	Australian	0.42	0.53	3.23	10.99	13.08
港澳同胞	Hong Kong and Macao Chinese		10.33	17.62	48.59	47.74
台湾同胞	Taiwanese	6.29	31.03	19.88	70.49	72.53
平均每天来沪旅游人数（人次/天）	**Average Number of Tourists Visiting Shanghai Everyday (person-time/day)**	**658**	**2 447**	**4 970**	**15 654**	**16 594**
来沪旅游者平均逗留天数（天/人）	**Average Time Tourists Staying in Shanghai (day/person)**	**3.87**	**2.83**	**3.92**	**3.50**	**3.60**
国际旅游(外汇)收入（亿美元）	**Foreign Exchange Earnings from International Tourism(100 million USD)**	**0.56**	**2.31**	**16.13**	**36.08**	**39.61**

①本表数据由市旅游事业委员会、市出入境边防检查总站等提供。
②自 2003 年起，国际旅游入境人数包括由上海入境的(剔除在上海空港中转的游客)外国人、华侨、港澳台旅客以及经外省市入境后来沪的外国人、华侨、港澳台游客两部分。
③自 2005 年起，华侨旅游人数归并外国旅游人数，不再单列。
❶Data in this table are provided by Shanghai Municipal Tourism Administrative Commission ,Shanghai Entry-Exit Inspection and Quarantine Bureau and ect.
❷Since 2003,the number of overseas tourists through Shanghai Custom has been from two troops of foreigners,overseas Chinese and tourists from HongKong, Macao and Taiwan. One troop comes to China through Shanghai Custom,the other troop comes to Shanghai through other Custom in China. (The transferring passengers in Shanghai airport are not included).
❸Since 2005, the number of overseas Chinese incorporate into foreigner tourists.

表 7.24 上海国际友好城市、与上海建立国际友好交流关系的城市一览 (2006 年末) FOREIGN CITIES WITH SISTER-CITY RELATIONSHIP OR FRIENDLY EXCHANGE RELATIONSHIP WITH SHANGHAI (BY THE END OF YEAR 2006)

城市	Cities	国家	Countries	缔结日期	Relationship Eastablished Date
上海国际友好城市	**Cities with Sister-city Relationship**				
横滨市	Yokohama	日　本	Japan	1973 年 11 月 30 日	Nov. 30, 1973
大阪市	Osaka	日　本	Japan	1974 年 4 月 18 日	Apr. 18, 1974
米兰市	Milan	意大利	Italy	1979 年 6 月 25 日	Jun. 25, 1979
鹿特丹市	Rotterdam	荷　兰	Netherlands	1979 年 11 月 23 日	Nov. 23, 1979
旧金山市	San Francisco	美　国	United States	1980 年 1 月 28 日	Jan. 28, 1980
萨格勒布市	Zagreb	克罗地亚	Croatia	1980 年 6 月 18 日	Jun. 18, 1980
大阪府	Osaka	日　本	Japan	1980 年 11 月 21 日	Nov. 21, 1980
咸兴市	Hamhung	朝　鲜	D. P. R. Korea	1982 年 6 月 18 日	Jun. 18, 1982
大马尼拉市	Manila	菲律宾	Philippines	1983 年 6 月 15 日	Jun. 15, 1983
卡拉奇市	Karachi	巴基斯坦	Pakistan	1984 年 2 月 15 日	Feb. 15, 1984
安特卫普市	Antwerp	比利时	Belgium	1984 年 5 月 27 日	May. 27, 1984
蒙特利尔市	Montreal	加拿大	Canada	1985 年 5 月 14 日	May. 14, 1985
比雷埃夫斯市	Piraiev	希　腊	Greece	1985 年 6 月 24 日	Jun. 24, 1985
滨海省	Binhai City	波　兰	Poland	1985 年 7 月 4 日	Jul. 4, 1985
汉堡市	Hamburg	德　国	Germany	1985 年 6 月 29 日	Jun. 29, 1985
卡萨布兰卡市	Casablanca	摩洛哥	Morocco	1986 年 9 月 8 日	Sep. 8, 1986
马赛市	Marseilles	法　国	France	1987 年 10 月 26 日	Oct. 26, 1987
圣堡罗市	Sao Paul	巴　西	Brazil	1988 年 7 月 7 日	Jul. 7, 1988
圣彼得堡市	St Petersburg	俄罗斯	Russia	1988 年 12 月 15 日	Dec. 15, 1988
昆士兰州	Queensland	澳大利亚	Australia	1989 年 5 月 24 日	May. 24, 1989
伊斯坦布尔市	Istanbul	土耳其	Turkey	1989 年 10 月 23 日	Oct. 23, 1989
亚历山大省	Alexandria	埃　及	Egypt	1992 年 5 月 12 日	May. 12, 1992
海法市	Haifa	以色列	Israel	1993 年 6 月 22 日	Jun. 22, 1993
釜山市	Pusan	韩　国	Republic of Korea	1993 年 8 月 24 日	Aug. 24, 1993
胡志明市	Ho Chi Minh City	越　南	Viet Nam	1994 年 5 月 14 日	May. 14, 1994
维拉港	Port-Vila	瓦努阿图	Vanuatu	1994 年 6 月 8 日	Jun. 8, 1994
达尼丁市	Dunedin	新西兰	New Zealand	1994 年 10 月 21 日	Oct. 21, 1994

注：本表至表 7.25 的资料由市外事办公室提供。
Note: Data in table 7.24 to 7.25 are provided by Shanghai Municipal Foreign Affairs Office.

表 7.24 续表 1 continued

城市	Cities	国家	Countries	缔结日期	Relationship Eastablished Date
市级国际友好城市	**Shanghai's International Sister Cities**				
塔什干市	Tashkent	乌兹别克	Uzbekistan	1994 年 12 月 15 日	Dec. 15,1994
波尔图市	Oporto	葡萄牙	Portugal	1995 年 4 月 15 日	Apr. 15,1995
亚丁省	Aden	也　门	Yemen	1995 年 9 月 14 日	Sep. 14,1995
温得和克市	Windhoek	纳米比亚	Namibia	1995 年 11 月 1 日	Nov. 1,1995
圣地亚哥省	Santiago	古　巴	Cuba	1996 年 7 月 30 日	Jul. 30,1996
罗萨里奥市	Rosario	阿根廷	Argentina	1997 年 6 月 17 日	Jun. 17,1997
埃斯波市	Espoo	芬　兰	Finland	1998 年 9 月 4 日	Sep. 4,1998
哈利斯科州	Jalisco Estado	墨西哥	Mexico	1998 年 11 月 18 日	Nov. 18,1998
利物浦市	Liverpool City	英　国	United Kingdom	1999 年 10 月 18 日	Oct. 18,1999
马普托市	Maputo	莫桑比克	Mozambique	1999 年 10 月 25 日	Oct. 25,1999
清迈府	Chiengmai	泰　国	Thailand	2000 年 4 月 2 日	Apr. 2,2000
迪拜市	Dubai	阿联酋	United Arab Emirates	2000 年 5 月 30 日	May. 30,2000
夸祖鲁 - 纳塔尔省	KwaZulu-Natal	南　非	South Africa	2001 年 5 月 16 日	May. 16,2001
瓜亚基尔市	Guayaquil	厄瓜多尔	Ecuador	2001 年 7 月 6 日	Jul. 6,2001
瓦尔帕莱索	Valparaiso	智　利	Chile	2001 年 7 月 10 日	Jul. 10,2001
巴塞罗那	Barcelona	西班牙	Spain	2001 年 10 月 31 日	Oct. 31,2001
奥斯陆市	Oslo	挪　威	Norway	2001 年 11 月 10 日	Nov. 10,2001
康斯坦察县	Constanta	罗马尼亚	Romania	2002 年 4 月 15 日	Apr. 15,2002
科伦坡市	Colombo	斯里兰卡	Srilanka	2003 年 8 月 11 日	Aug. 11,2003
哥德堡市	Gothenburg	瑞　典	Sweden	2003 年 10 月 23 日	Oct. 23,2003
布拉迪斯拉发州	Bratislara	斯洛伐克	Slovak	2003 年 11 月 10 日	Nov. 10,2003
奥胡斯州	Arhus	丹　麦	Danmark	2003 年 11 月 10 日	Nov. 10,2003
科　克	Cork	爱尔兰	Ireland	2005 年 5 月 19 日	May. 19,2005
东爪哇省	East Jawa Province	印　尼	Indonesia	2006 年 8 月 30 日	Aug 30,2006
区镇级国际友好城市	**Shanghai Districts' International Friendship Cities**				
日本枚方市 - 长宁区	Hirakata-Changning	日　本	Japan	1987 年 12 月 16 日	Dec. 16,1987
日本八尾市 - 嘉定区	Yao-Jiading	日　本	Japan	1986 年 9 月 13 日	Sep. 13,1986
日本寝屋川市 - 卢湾区	Neyagawa-Luwan	日　本	Japan	1994 年 5 月 12 日	May. 12,1994
日本泉佐野市 - 徐汇区	Yizumisano-Xuhui	日　本	Japan	1994 年 10 月 21 日	Oct. 21,1994
纳米比亚奥卡汉贾市 - 马桥镇	Okahandja-Maqiao Town	纳米比亚	Namibia	1998 年 12 月 16 日	Dec. 16,1998
菲律宾大马尼拉署马卡蒂市 - 黄浦区	City of Makati-Huangpu	菲律宾	Philippines	2002 年 9 月 26 日	Sep. 26,2002

表 7.24 续表 2　continued

城　市 Cities		国　家 Countries		缔结日期 Relationship Eastablished Date	
上海与国外建立友好交流关系的城市	**Cities with Friendly Exchange Relations**				
芝加哥市	Chicago	美　国	United States	1985 年 9 月 5 日	Sep. 5, 1985
罗纳 - 阿尔卑斯大区	Rhone-Aples	法　国	France	1986 年 1 月 20 日	Nov. 20, 1986
符拉迪沃斯托克市	Vladivostok	俄罗斯	Russia	1993 年 4 月 27 日	Apr. 27, 1993
全罗南道	Cholla-Namdo	韩　国	Republic of Korea	1996 年 4 月 19 日	Apr. 19, 1996
伦敦城	London City	英　国	United Kingdom	1996 年 9 月 4 日	Sep. 4, 1996
长崎县	Nagasaki	日　本	Japan	1996 年 10 月 14 日	Oct. 14, 1996
伦巴底大区	Lombardy Region	意大利	Italy	2002 年 11 月 19 日	Nov. 19, 2002
全罗北道	Jeollabukdo Trade	韩　国	Korea	2003 年 4 月 16 日	Apr. 16, 2003
尼科西亚市	Nicosia	塞浦路斯	Cyprus	2004 年 9 月 4 日	Sep. 4, 2004
萨尔茨堡	Salzburg	奥地利	Austria	2004 年 11 月 3 日	Nov. 3, 2004

表 7.25　各国驻沪总领事馆一览 (2006 年底)
LIST OF GENERAL CONSULATES OF FOREIGN COUNTRIES IN SHANGHAI (BY THE END OF YEAR 2006)

馆　名 Consulates		领区地域 Consular Region	
俄罗斯	Russia	上海、浙江、江苏、安徽	Shanghai, Zhejiang, Jiangsu and Anhui
波　兰	Poland	上海、浙江、江苏、安徽、福建	Shanghai, Zhejiang, Jiangsu, Anhui and Fujian
印　度	India	上海、浙江、江苏	Shanghai, Zhejiang and Jiangsu
韩　国	Republic of Korea	上海、浙江、江苏、安徽	Shanghai, Zhejiang, Jiangsu and Anhui
日　本	Japan	上海、浙江、江苏、安徽	Shanghai, Zhejiang, Jiangsu and Anhui
澳大利亚	Australia	上海、浙江、江苏、安徽	Shanghai, Zhejiang, Jiangsu and Anhui
古　巴	Cuba	上海、浙江、江苏、安徽	Shanghai, Zhejiang, Jiangsu and Anhui
法　国	France	上海、浙江、江苏	Shanghai, Zhejiang and Jiangsu
以色列	Israel	上海、浙江、江苏	Shanghai, Zhejiang and Jiangsu
美　国	United States	上海、浙江、江苏、安徽	Shanghai, Zhejiang, Jiangsu and Anhui
荷　兰	Netherlands	上海、浙江、江苏、安徽	Shanghai, Zhejiang, Jiangsu and Anhui
英　国	United Kingdom	上海、浙江、江苏	Shanghai, Zhejiang and Jiangsu
捷　克	Czech	上海、浙江、江苏、安徽	Shanghai, Zhejiang, Jiangsu and Anhui
德　国	Germany	上海、浙江、江苏、安徽	Shanghai, Zhejiang, Jiangsu and Anhui

表 7.25 续表 1 continued

馆 名	Consulates	领区地域	Consular Region
瑞 士	Switzerland	上海、浙江、江苏、安徽	Shanghai, Zhejiang, Jiangsu and Anhui
加拿大	Canada	上海、浙江、江苏、安徽	Shanghai, Zhejiang, Jiangsu and Anhui
新西兰	New Zealand	上海、浙江、江苏、安徽	Shanghai, Zhejiang, Jiangsu and Anhui
墨西哥	Mexico	上海、浙江、江苏、福建、湖南、江西	Shanghai, Zhejiang ,Jiangsu,Fujian,Hunan and Jiangxi
丹 麦	Denmark	上海、浙江、江苏、安徽	Shanghai, Zhejiang, Jiangsu and Anhui
意大利	Italy	上海、浙江、江苏、安徽	Shanghai, Zhejiang, Jiangsu and Anhui
伊 朗	Iran	上海、浙江、江苏、安徽	Shanghai, Zhejiang, Jiangsu and Anhui
新加坡	Singapore	上海、浙江、江苏	Shanghai, Zhejiang and Jiangsu
奥地利	Austria	上海、浙江、江苏、安徽	Shanghai, Zhejiang, Jiangsu and Anhui
芬 兰	Finland	上海、浙江、江苏、安徽	Shanghai, Zhejiang, Jiangsu and Anhui
智 利	Chile	上海、浙江、江苏、安徽	Shanghai, Zhejiang, Jiangsu and Anhui
瑞 典	Sweden	上海、浙江、江苏、安徽	Shanghai, Zhejiang, Jiangsu and Anhui
挪 威	Norway	上海、浙江、江苏、安徽	Shanghai, Zhejiang, Jiangsu and Anhui
比利时	Belgium	上海、浙江、江苏、安徽	Shanghai, Zhejiang, Jiangsu and Anhui
泰 国	Thailand	上海、浙江、江苏、安徽	Shanghai, Zhejiang, Jiangsu and Anhui
土耳其	Turkey	上海、浙江、江苏、安徽	Shanghai, Zhejiang, Jiangsu and Anhui
埃 及	Egypt	上海、浙江、江苏、安徽	Shanghai, Zhejiang, Jiangsu and Anhui
西班牙	Spain	上海、浙江、江苏	Shanghai, Zhejiang and Jiangsu
柬埔寨	Camboclia	上海、浙江、江苏、安徽	Shanghai, Zhejiang, Jiangsu and Anhui
马来西亚	Malaysia	上海、浙江、江苏	Shanghai, Zhejiang and Jiangsu
罗马尼亚	Romania	上海、浙江、江苏	Shanghai, Zhejiang and Jiangsu

表 7.25 续表 2 continued

馆 名	Consulates	领区地域	Consular Region
阿根廷	Argentina	上海、浙江、江苏、安徽	Shanghai, Zhejiang, Jiangsu and Anhui
爱尔兰	Ireland	上海、浙江、江苏、安徽、江西	Shanghai, Zhejiang, Jiangsu ,Anhui, and Jiangxi
乌克兰	Ukraine	上海、浙江、江苏、安徽、福建、江西	Shanghai, Zhejiang, Jiangsu ,Anhui,Fujian and Jiangxi
巴 西	Brazil	上海、浙江、江苏、安徽	Shanghai, Zhejiang, Jiangsu and Anhui
秘 鲁	Peru	上海、浙江、江苏、安徽、福建、江西	Shanghai, Zhejiang, Jiangsu , Anhui,Fujian and Jiangxi
菲律宾	The Philippines	上海、江苏、安徽、湖北	Shanghai, Jiangsu ,Anhui and Hubai
南 非	South Africa	上海、浙江、江苏、安徽、山东、福建、广东	Shanghai, Zhejiang, Jiangsu ,Anhui,Shantong,Fujian and Guangdong
乌拉圭	Uruguay	上海、浙江、江苏、安徽	Shanghai, Zhejiang, Jiangsu and Anhui
巴基斯坦	Pakistan	浙江、江苏、安徽	Zhejiang, Jiangsu and Anhui
摩纳哥	Monaco	浙江、江苏、安徽	Zhejiang, Jiangsu and Anhui
尼泊尔	Nepal	上海	Shanghai
斯洛伐克	Slovakia	浙江、江苏、安徽、福建、江西	Zhejiang, Jiangsu and Anhui,Fujian and Jiangxi
希 腊	Greece	浙江、江苏、安徽、山东、福建、江西	Zhejiang, Jiangsu and Anhui,Shantong, Fujian and Jiangxi
匈牙利	Hungary	浙江、江苏、安徽	Zhejiang, Jiangsu and Anhui
牙买加	Jamaice	浙江、江苏、安徽	Zhejiang, Jiangsu and Anhui
哈萨克斯坦	Kazakhstan	浙江、江苏、安徽、福建、江西	Zhejiang, Jiangsu and Anhui,Fujian and Jiangxi
保加利亚	Bulgaria	浙江、江苏、安徽、福建、江西	Zhejiang, Jiangsu and Anhui,Fujian and Jiangxi
葡萄牙	Portugal	浙江、江苏、安徽、江西	Zhejiang, Jiangsu ,Anhui and Jiangxi
斯里兰卡	Sri Lanka	浙江、江苏、安徽、湖南、福建	Zhejiang, Jiangsu and Anhui, Hunan and Fujian
塞尔维亚	Serbia	浙江、江苏、安徽	Zhejiang, Jiangsu and Anhui
委内瑞拉	Venezuela	浙江、江苏	Zhejiang and Jiangsu
卢森堡	Luxembourg	浙江、江苏、安徽、福建	Zhejiang, Jiangsu, Anhui and Fujian
乌兹别克	Uzbekistan	浙江、江苏、安徽、福建、江西	Zhejiang, Jiangsu and Anhui,Fujian and Jiangxi
巴布亚新几内亚	Papua New Guinea	上 海	Shanghai
马尔代夫	Maldives	上 海	Shanghai

①波兰领馆原设天津,1954 年 10 月 22 日迁来上海,当时系领事馆,1955 年 6 月 17 日升格为总领事馆。
②1990 年 10 月 3 日德国统一后原民主德国驻上海领事馆被联邦德国驻上海总领事馆合并。
③原苏联驻上海总领事馆于 1991 年 12 月更名为俄罗斯驻上海总领事馆。
❶ Poland consulate was in Tianjin formerly and moved to Shanghai in Oct. 22, 1954. In Jun. 17, 1955, it was upgraded as Consulate General.
❷ In Oct. 3, 1990, former Democratic Germany consulate was combined by the Consulate General of United Germany after Germany unified.
❸ In Dec. 1991, former U. S. S. R. Consulate General renamed as Russian Consulate General.

上 / 海 / 统 / 计 / 年 / 鉴

主要统计指标解释

口岸进出口总额

指由海关统计的进出口商品总额。统计方法依据联合国的国际贸易统计原则，反映进出上海而引起物质资源储备增加或减少的商品运动。按上述原则应具备条件：实际进出上海(海关关境)，不仅包括经商业交易行为的进出口货品，也包括援助、捐赠等未发生买卖关系的货品价值。出口按离岸价(FOB)统计，进口按到岸价(CIF)统计。

外贸进出口总额

指海关统计中按经营单位即进出口企业在海关注册地的行政区域口径统计的数据，它反映的是上海行政辖区内各类具有进出口经营权企业（外贸企业）的进出口。它不包含外省市外贸企业途经上海口岸由上海海关结关放行及统计的进出口商品，但包含上海外贸企业经由非上海口岸进出口结关放行及统计的商品。

外商直接投资

指外国企业和经济组织或个人(包括华侨、港澳台胞以及我国在境外注册的企业)按我国有关政策、法规，用现汇、实物、技术等在我国境内开办外商独资企业、与我国境内的企业或经济组织共同举办中外合资经营企业、合作经营企业或合作开发资源的投资（包括外商投资收益的再投资）以及企业投资总额内直接投资者对企业的贷款，即外方股东贷款(需在报告期内将相应合同及贷款协议报商务部备案核查)。

引进技术设备

指通过贸易途径从国外获得发展我国国民经济和提高技术水平所需要的技术装备。引进方式有：许可证贸易(技术贸易)、生产线(包括成套设备)、单机(包括关键设备)、软硬件结合(同时引进技术和设备)和其他。

引对外承包工程

对外承包工程包括各对外承包公司以招标议标承包方式承揽的下列业务：(1)承包国外工程建设项目。(2)承包我国对外经济援助项目。(3)承包我国驻外机构的工程建设项目。(4)承包我国境内利用外资进行建设的工程项目。(5)与外国承包公司合营或联合承包工程项目时我国公司分包部分。(6)以服务成果向业主收费的技术服务项目(包括承担地形地貌测绘；地质资源勘探与普查；建设区域规划；提供设计文件、图纸、生产工艺技术资料和工程技术经济咨询；工程项目的可行性考察、研究和评估；进行技术指导和培训人员等)。(7)对外承包兼营的房屋开发业务。对外承包工程的营业额是以货币表现的本期内完成的对外承包工程的工作量，包括以前年度签订的合同和本年度新签订的合同在报告期完成的工作量。

对外劳务合作

指以收取工资的形式向业主或承包商提供技术和劳动服务的活动。上海对外承包公司在境外开办的合营企业，上海公司同时又提供劳务的，其劳务部分也纳入劳务合作统计。劳务合作营业额按报告期内向雇主提交的结算数(包括工资、加班费和奖金等)统计。

国际旅游入境人数

指来上海参观、访问、旅行、探亲、访友、休养、考察、参加会议和从事经济、科技、文化、教育、体育、宗教等活动的外国人、华侨、港澳和台湾同胞的人数。不包括来上海常住1年以上的外国专家、留学生等。上海入境的境外旅游人数包括从上海口岸入境的境外旅游人数和从我国其他口岸入境的境外旅游人数。

国际旅游(外汇)收入

指入境旅游的外国人、华侨、港澳台同胞在上海旅游过程中发生的一切旅游支出。

SHANGHAI STATISTICAL YEARBOOK

EXPLANATORY NOTES TO MAJOR STATISTICAL INDICATORS

□ Total Value of Port Imports and Exports

Total Value of Imports and Exports refers to the aggregate volume of commodities that are imported or exported through Shanghai's ports. The statistics method follows the international trade statistics principles set by the United Nations. It reflects the fluctuation of Shanghai's material reserves caused by export or import. Requirements involved in the principle is: the commodities refer to those enter or leave Shanghai's ports, including not only the business trading activities but also the commodities value of the aid and donations that haven't been involved in sales . Exports are calculated according to FOB price, and imports are calculated according to CIF.

□ Total Value of Foreign Trade Imports and Exports

Total Value of Foreign Trade Imports and Exports is offered by Customs authorities, covering the operation units, or the enterprises involved in import and export, that have registered in the administrative regions where the Customs operate. It reflects the import and export of all the enterprises with import and export rights (foreign trade enterprises) under the administration of Shanghai Municipality. It excludes those commodities of foreign trade enterprises from out of town that underwent customs clearance at Shanghai ports but includes commodities of foreign trade enterprises of Shanghai that underwent customs clearance in non-Shanghai ports.

□ Foreign Direct Investment

Foreign Direct Investment refers to the investments made inside China by foreign enterprises and economic organizations or individuals (including overseas Chinese, compatriots in Hong Kong, Macao and Chinese enterprises registered abroad), in line with the relevant policies and laws of China, for the establishment of wholly foreign-owned enterprises, and joint ventures or development projects launched in China (including re-investment of profits from foreign businesses), and the funds that enterprises borrow from abroad in the total investment of projects which are approved by the relevant departments of the governments and the loans from the direct investors within the total investment of the projects, i.e., foreign shareholders' loans. (The related contracts and loans agreements in the report period should be filed with the Ministry of Commerce)

□ Import of Technology and Equipment

Import of Technology and Equipment refers to technology and equipments obtained through the trade channel from other countries which are needed for advancing China's national economy and improving its technological level. The import form includes: licensing (technological trade), production lines (including complete plant), single machine (including key equipments), combination of hardware and software (importing technology and equipments simultaneously) and others.

□ Overseas Contracted Projects

Overseas Contracted Projects refer to projects undertaken by Chinese contractors (project contracting companies) through bidding process. They include: (1) overseas civil engineering construction projects financed by foreign investors. (2)overseas projects financed by the Chinese government through its foreign-aid programs. (3)construction projects of Chinese diplomatic missions, trade offices and other institutions stationed abroad. (4) construction projects in China financed by foreign investment. (5) sub-contracted projects to be taken by Chinese contractors through a joint umbrella project with foreign contractor (s). (6)technical assistance projects in the form of service results and chargeable to the owners (such as topographic surveying, geological prospecting, development zone programming, provision of documents, blueprint, materials on production process, technical consultation, project feasibility studies and evaluation, personnel training, etc.). and (7)housing development projects. The business turnover from international contracting is the work of contracted projects completed during the reporting period, expressed in monetary terms, including completed work on project contracts signed in previous years.

□ Overseas Labor Service Cooperation

Overseas Labor Service Cooperation refers to activities of providing technology and labor services to employers or contractors by collecting salaries and wages. Labor services provid-

EXPLANATORY NOTES TO MAJOR STATISTICAL INDICATORS

ed by Shanghai's international contrasting corporations to their overseas joint ventures shall be included into the statistics of overseas services. The business turn over of overseas labor services is the settlement price (including salaries, overtime pay and bonuses) submitted to the employers during the reporting period.

□ Foreign Exchange Earnings from International Tourism

Foreign Exchange Earnings from International Tourism refer to the total expenditures of foreigners, overseas Chinese, Chinese compatriots from Hong, Macao and Taiwan during their stay in Shanghai.

第八篇

CHAPTER 8

价格水平

PRICES

表8.1 居民消费价格和商品零售价格指数(1978～2006)
OVERALL RESIDENTS CONSUMER PRICE INDEX AND RETAIL PRICE INDEX

年 份 Year	居民消费价格指数 Overall Residents Consumer Price Index		年 份 Year	商品零售价格指数 Retail Price Index	
	以上年价格为100 preceding year = 100	以1978年价格为100 1978 = 100		以上年价格为100 preceding year = 100	以1978年价格为100 1978 = 100
1978	100.5	100.0	1978	100.1	100.0
1979	100.9	100.9	1979	101.0	101.0
1980	105.9	106.9	1980	106.5	107.6
1981	101.4	108.3	1981	101.5	109.2
1982	100.3	108.7	1982	100.3	109.5
1983	100.2	108.9	1983	100.1	109.6
1984	102.2	111.3	1984	102.2	112.0
1985	115.2	128.2	1985	116.4	130.4
1986	106.3	136.3	1986	106.7	139.1
1987	108.1	147.3	1987	108.8	151.4
1988	120.1	176.9	1988	121.3	183.6
1989	115.9	205.1	1989	116.7	214.3
1990	106.3	218.0	1990	104.8	224.6
1991	110.5	240.9	1991	109.5	245.9
1992	110.0	265.0	1992	109.7	269.8
1993	120.2	318.5	1993	117.5	317.0
1994	123.9	394.6	1994	117.5	372.4
1995	118.7	468.4	1995	113.0	420.9
1996	109.2	511.5	1996	105.0	441.9
1997	102.8	525.8	1997	98.8	436.6
1998	100.0	525.8	1998	95.1	415.2
1999	101.5	533.7	1999	97.3	404.0
2000	102.5	547.0	2000	96.4	389.5
2001	100.0	547.0	2001	98.6	384.0
2002	100.5	549.8	2002	98.7	379.0
2003	100.1	550.3	2003	99.0	375.4
2004	102.2	562.2	2004	100.9	378.8
2005	101.0	567.6	2005	99.4	376.7
2006	101.2	574.5	2006	100.2	377.4

注：本表至表8.13由国家统计局上海调查总队提供资料。
Note: Data in this table to table 8.13 are provided by Survey Office of the National Bureau of Statistics in Shanghai.

表 8.2 居民消费价格指数(1991~2006, 以 1990 年价格为 100)
OVERALL RESIDENTS CONSUMER PRICE INDEX (1990 = 100)

年 份 Year	居民消费价格指数 Overall Residents Consumer Price Index	食 品 Food	烟酒及用品 Cigarettes, Liquors and Related Items	衣 着 Clothing
1991	110.5	113.5	103.0	105.7
1992	121.6	128.7	113.0	115.7
1993	146.1	157.2	124.5	137.3
1994	181.0	207.1	139.5	158.8
1995	214.9	261.2	149.1	172.8
1996	234.6	288.6	149.1	187.8
1997	241.2	288.6	134.6	189.9
1998	241.2	282.3	129.2	178.5
1999	244.8	274.9	129.8	175.5
2000	250.9	270.0	126.1	167.2
2001	250.9	270.8	124.7	165.4
2002	252.2	278.6	123.4	161.2
2003	252.5	282.3	123.1	157.2
2004	257.8	305.6	121.0	148.1
2005	260.3	319.4	120.6	136.4
2006	263.4	327.5	120.9	145.2

表 8.2 续表 continued

年 份 Year	家庭设备用品及维修服务 Home Appliances and Repair Service	医疗保健和个人用品 Medicine, Medical Services and Personal Aricles	交通和通信 Means of Transportation and Communication	娱乐教育文化用品及服务 Recreation, Education and Culture Articles	居 住 Residence
1991	112.5	113.1	108.5	96.9	129.3
1992	115.4	132.7	108.9	93.8	153.9
1993	126.4	151.8	127.5	115.7	206.8
1994	140.2	180.9	149.5	136.1	249.4
1995	145.5	199.0	171.5	158.2	300.0
1996	144.2	210.9	181.9	187.6	329.1
1997	131.8	215.4	210.3	205.6	396.9
1998	121.9	219.5	218.1	218.6	450.9
1999	117.5	223.6	245.1	244.1	477.5
2000	112.5	223.4	271.9	296.6	493.3
2001	109.3	217.6	266.7	302.8	504.6
2002	106.8	212.4	258.4	305.3	504.6
2003	105.1	212.4	248.9	306.2	510.2
2004	102.8	212.2	240.4	306.0	518.5
2005	103.6	212.9	234.3	300.8	533.7
2006	106.4	215.2	227.8	295.5	549.2

表8.3 居民消费价格指数(1991～2006，以上年价格为100)
OVERALL RESIDENTS CONSUMER PRICE INDEX (PRECEDING YEAR = 100)

年 份 Year	居民消费价格指数 Overall Residents Consumer Price Index	食 品 Food	烟酒及用品 Cigarettes, Liquors and Related Items	衣 着 Clothing
1991	110.5	113.5	103.0	105.7
1992	110.0	113.4	109.7	109.5
1993	120.2	122.1	110.2	118.6
1994	123.9	131.8	112.0	115.7
1995	118.7	126.1	106.9	108.8
1996	109.2	110.5	100.0	108.7
1997	102.8	100.0	90.3	101.1
1998	100.0	97.8	96.0	94.0
1999	101.5	97.4	100.4	98.3
2000	102.5	98.2	97.2	95.3
2001	100.0	100.3	98.9	98.9
2002	100.5	102.9	98.9	97.5
2003	100.1	101.3	99.8	97.5
2004	102.2	108.3	98.3	94.2
2005	101.0	104.5	99.7	92.1
2006	101.2	102.5	100.2	106.4

表8.3 续表 continued

年 份 Year	家庭设备用品及维修服务 Home Appliances and Repair Service	医疗保健和个人用品 Medicine, Medical Services and Personal Aricles	交通和通信 Means of Transportation and Communication	娱乐教育文化用品及服务 Recreation, Education and Culture Articles	居 住 Residence
1991	112.5	113.1	108.5	96.9	129.3
1992	102.6	117.3	100.4	96.8	119.0
1993	109.5	114.4	117.0	123.4	134.4
1994	110.9	119.2	117.3	117.6	120.6
1995	103.8	110.0	114.7	116.2	120.3
1996	99.1	106.0	106.1	118.6	109.7
1997	91.4	102.1	115.6	109.6	120.6
1998	92.5	101.9	103.7	106.3	113.6
1999	96.4	101.9	112.4	111.7	105.9
2000	95.7	99.9	110.9	121.5	103.3
2001	97.2	97.4	98.1	102.1	102.3
2002	97.7	97.6	96.9	100.8	100.0
2003	98.4	100.0	96.3	100.3	101.1
2004	97.8	100.0	96.5	99.9	101.6
2005	100.8	100.3	97.5	98.3	102.9
2006	102.7	101.1	97.3	98.2	102.9

表8.4　主要年份居民消费价格指数（以上年价格为100）
CLASSIFIED RESIDENTS CONSUMER PRICE INDEX IN MAIN YEARS (PRECEDING YEAR = 100)

类　别	Types	2001	2005	2006
居民消费价格指数	**Overall Residents Consumer Price Index**	**100.0**	**101.0**	**101.2**
#服务项目价格	Services Items Price	105.4	102.7	101.2
食　品	**Food**	**100.3**	**104.5**	**102.5**
粮　食	Grain	102.9	103.0	101.9
淀粉及薯类	Starch and Potatoes	103.6	105.2	95.6
干豆类及豆制品	Dry Beans and Bean Products	95.6	103.0	99.0
油　脂	Oil or Fat	84.5	91.2	97.6
肉禽及其制品	Meat Poultry and Their Products	99.3	105.7	100.6
蛋	Eggs	102.4	105.8	95.4
水产品	Aquatic Products	100.1	114.2	102.0
菜	Vegetables	108.9	103.3	105.2
#鲜　菜	Fresh Vegetables	110.2	103.5	104.8
调味品	Flavoring	99.2	102.1	104.4
糖	Sugars	101.4	103.2	102.1
茶及饮料	Tea and Beverages	98.4	99.3	100.5
干鲜瓜果	Dried and Fresh Fruits	104.3	99.4	111.5
#鲜　果	Fresh Fruits	105.8	98.0	114.8
糕点饼干面包	Cakes, Biscuits and Bread	100.5	98.1	98.9
奶及奶制品	Milk and Its Products	100.8	100.8	102.3
在外用膳食品	Out-of-home Food	98.0	104.5	102.5
其他食品及食品加工服务	Other Food and Food Processing Service	99.2	101.1	102.8
烟酒及用品	**Cigarettes, Liquors and Related Items**	**98.9**	**99.7**	**100.2**
烟　草	Tobacco	99.2	99.5	99.8
酒	Liquors	98.2	99.8	100.2
吸烟饮酒用品	Cigarettes and Spirits Related Items	100.0	100.9	104.8
衣　着	**Clothing**	**98.9**	**92.1**	**106.4**
服　装	Garments	96.4	90.8	106.3
男式服装	Men' Wear	99.0	92.0	101.6
女式服装	Women's Wear	94.7	91.5	109.6
儿童服装	Children's Wear	95.4	76.0	109.3
衣着材料	Clothing Materials	98.7	105.1	97.8
鞋袜帽	Shoes, Socks and Hats	106.2	94.5	107.9
#鞋	Shoes	106.6	94.4	109.1
衣着加工服务	Garment Processing Service	100.0	103.4	100.0

表 8.4 续表 continued

类 别	Types	2001	2005	2006
家庭设备用品及维修服务	**Home Appliances and Repair Service**	**97.2**	**100.8**	**102.7**
耐用消费品	Durable Consumer Goods	94.7	98.6	101.2
室内装饰品	Interior Decorations	101.0	99.3	100.0
床上用品	Bed Articles	100.5	96.9	100.6
家庭日用杂品	Daily Use Household Articles	98.6	103.4	102.8
家庭服务及加工维修服务	Other Daily Use Articles	100.0	109.8	112.0
医疗保健和个人用品	**Medicine, Medical Services and Personal Aricles**	**97.4**	**100.3**	**101.1**
医疗保健	Medicine and Medical Services	96.5	100.4	98.1
#中药材及中成药	Herbs and Ready-made Traditional Chinese Medicine	105.5	99.2	100.9
西 药	Western Medicine	92.0	95.6	95.1
保健器具及用品	Healthcare Equipment	95.4	100.0	99.7
医疗保健服务	Medical and Healthcare Service	100.0	106.5	98.8
个人用品及服务	Personal Aricles and Service	99.8	100.2	107.1
交通和通信	**Means of Transportation and Communication**	**98.1**	**97.5**	**97.3**
交 通	Transport	102.3	99.9	98.9
#交通工具	Transport Tools	97.9	92.9	91.3
通 信	Communications	94.4	94.9	94.9
通信工具	Communications Tools	69.7	66.1	70.4
通信服务	Communications Service	103.1	100.0	100.0
娱乐教育文化用品及服务	**Recreation, Education andCulture Articles**	**102.1**	**98.3**	**98.2**
文娱用耐用消费品及服务	Durable Consumer Goods for Recreational Use	91.2	85.8	87.8
教 育	Education	109.6	99.5	100.0
文化娱乐用品	Recreation and Culture Articles	105.2	102.6	101.6
旅 游	Tourism	96.2	107.0	103.0
居 住	**Residence**	**102.3**	**102.9**	**102.9**
建房及装修材料	Construction and Decoration Materials	97.5	103.9	107.0
租 房	House Leasing	111.0	100.0	99.5
自有住房	Self-owned House	99.8	106.9	102.3
水电燃料	Water, Electricity and Fuels	101.7	101.0	100.4
#水	Water	109.3	105.1	100.0
电	Electricity	100.0	100.0	100.6
液化石油气	LPG	118.4	115.8	104.3
管道煤气	Gas	100.0	100.0	100.0

表8.5 商品零售价格指数（2001～2006，以上年价格为100)）
COMMODITY RETAIL PRICE INDEX (PRECEDING YEAR =100)

类别	Types	2001	2002
商品零售价格指数	**Overall Retail Price Index**	**98.6**	**98.7**
食品类	Food	98.4	100.3
粮　食	Grain	100.1	96.7
淀粉及薯类	Starch and Potatoes	100.4	101.3
干豆类及豆制品	Dry Beans and Bean Products	111.3	94.3
油　脂	Oil or Fat	81.4	97.9
肉禽及其制品	Meat Poultry and Their Products	100.4	99.0
蛋	Eggs	110.7	100.5
水产品	Aquatic Products	90.1	101.1
菜	Vegetables	107.1	106.4
调味品	Flavoring	99.5	100.8
糖	Sugars	104.4	98.5
干鲜瓜果	Dried and Fresh Fruits	107.3	104.6
糕点饼干面包	Cakes, Biscuits and Bread	99.8	98.9
奶及奶制品	Milk and Its Products	99.8	99.9
在外用膳食品	Out-of-home Food	100.7	98.9
其它食品	Other Food	99.5	99.9
饮料、烟酒	Beverages, Tobacco and Liquor	98.4	97.7
服装、鞋帽类	Garments, Shoes and Hats	107.7	95.0
纺织品类	Textiles	98.8	99.4
家用电器及音像器材	Household Appliances and Audio-video Appliances	95.0	93.5
文化办公用品	Cultural Office Articles	98.7	92.7
日用品	Daily Use Articles	99.0	99.8
体育娱乐用品	Sports and Recreation Goods	99.1	97.9
交通、通信用品	Transportation and Communication Goods	97.4	96.6
家　具	Furniture	90.4	100.1
化妆品	Cosmetics	100.7	97.4
金银珠宝	Jewelry	87.2	100.0
中西药品及医疗保健用品	Traditional Chinese and Western Medicines	98.7	99.5
书报杂志及电子出版物	Newspapers and Magazines and Electronic Publications	99.5	98.9
燃　料	Fuels	111.4	106.8
建筑材料及五金电料	Building Materials and Hardwares	101.8	103.8

表 8.5 续表 continued

	类别 Types	2003	2004	2005	2006
商品零售价格指数	**Overall Retail Price Index**	**99.0**	**100.9**	**99.4**	**100.2**
食品类	Food	101.5	108.6	104.7	102.7
粮　食	Grain	100.5	128.8	102.1	102.4
淀粉及薯类	Starch and Potatoes	109.2	107.2	105.2	95.6
干豆类及豆制品	Dry Beans and Bean Products	102.7	124.8	103.6	99.5
油　脂	Oil or Fat	106.8	114.4	91.2	97.6
肉禽及其制品	Meat Poultry and Their Products	101.7	117.6	105.5	100.6
蛋	Eggs	101.0	118.6	105.8	95.4
水产品	Aquatic Products	103.9	107.7	114.4	102.0
菜	Vegetables	101.5	95.5	103.4	105.2
调味品	Flavoring	98.4	103.0	102.1	104.4
糖	Sugars	98.9	103.1	103.8	103.8
干鲜瓜果	Dried and Fresh Fruits	97.6	118.3	99.4	111.5
糕点饼干面包	Cakes, Biscuits and Bread	101.4	100.9	98.4	98.9
奶及奶制品	Milk and Its Products	101.4	99.6	100.8	102.3
在外用膳食品	Out-of-home Food	100.7	103.1	104.4	102.5
其它食品	Other Food	101.5	96.9	101.1	102.8
饮料、烟酒	Beverages, Tobacco and Liquor	99.5	98.8	99.6	100.1
服装、鞋帽类	Garments, Shoes and Hats	96.7	93.9	92.6	106.6
纺织品类	Textiles	99.8	102.2	99.4	100.1
家用电器及音像器材	Household Appliances and Audio-video Appliances	95.8	93.4	93.1	92.6
文化办公用品	Cultural Office Articles	93.7	91.9	91.6	95.2
日用品	Daily Use Articles	99.1	98.4	100.5	102.5
体育娱乐用品	Sports and Recreation Goods	97.4	96.8	94.7	95.6
交通、通信用品	Transportation and Communication Goods	91.2	90.2	88.5	87.5
家　具	Furniture	99.5	98.2	100.1	101.2
化妆品	Cosmetics	100.4	99.0	96.1	98.0
金银珠宝	Jewelry	106.5	107.9	107.3	114.7
中西药品及医疗保健用品	Traditional Chinese and Western Medicines	98.3	95.6	97.7	97.6
书报杂志及电子出版物	Newspapers and Magazines and Electronic Publications	98.3	99.6	98.0	100.8
燃　料	Fuels	108.6	107.0	109.1	110.0
建筑材料及五金电料	Building Materials and Hardwares	100.8	104.7	104.0	106.1

表8.6 主要年份工业品出厂价格指数（以1995年价格为100）
PRODUCER PRICE INDEX OF INDUSTRIAL PRODUCTS IN MAIN YEARS(1995 = 100)

类别	Types	1996	2000	2001	2002
工业品出厂价格指数	**Producer Price Index of Industrial Products**	**97.6**	**89.6**	**86.7**	**83.6**
按轻重工业分	**Grouped by Light or Heavy Industries**				
轻工业	Light Industry	96.3	86.6	84.7	82.1
以农产品为原料	Using Farm Products as Raw Materials	101.7	94.5	94.4	93.4
以非农产品为原料	Using Non-farm Products as Raw Materials	90.5	78.7	75.1	71.3
重工业	Heavy Industry	98.6	91.8	88.2	84.8
采　掘	Mining and Guarrying			100.0	100.4
原　料	Raw Material	95.8	93.4	92.1	90.3
加　工	Manufacturing	104.1	93.5	88.5	84.1
按用途分	**Grouped by Use**				
生产资料	Means of Production	95.8	87.7	84.4	80.9
生活资料	Consumer Goods	100.3	92.4	90.0	87.6
#食　品	Food	106.2	109.6	112.5	115.3
衣　着	Clothing	98.3	88.7	88.3	88.1
一般日用品	Non-Durable Consumer Goods	102.0	93.5	90.9	88.3
耐用消费品	Durable Consumer Goods	95.9	86.0	81.7	77.4
按工业部门分	**Grouped by Sector**				
冶金工业	Metallurgy Industry	97.5	84.6	83.3	80.5
电力工业	Electric Power Industry	97.7	103.0	103.2	102.8
煤碳及炼焦工业	Coal and Coling Industry	112.9	151.3	157.0	164.4
石油工业	Petroleum Industry	100.3	143.7	143.4	140.0
化学工业	Chemical Industry	92.6	91.7	88.2	84.9
机械工业	Machinery Industry	100.6	85.2	79.7	75.1
建筑材料工业	Building Material Industry	98.8	95.6	97.8	94.2
森林工业	Forest Industry	70.9	49.3	48.1	46.3
食品工业	Food Industry	106.1	106.7	109.7	112.2
纺织工业	Textile Industry	89.6	85.6	82.3	78.0
缝纫工业	Sewing Industry	91.8	77.6	77.0	76.8
皮革工业	Leather Industry	96.9	95.3	96.0	94.8
造纸工业	Paper Making Industry	101.3	80.9	79.1	74.9
文教艺术用品工业	Cultural Educational and Art Goods	105.0	96.5	93.5	92.6
其他工业	Others Industry	102.5	113.0	113.6	119.2

注：采掘业工业品出厂价格指数以2001年价格为100计算。
Note: The prices of mining and quarrying industry in 2001 are set at 100.

表8.6 续表 continued

	类 别 Types	2003	2004	2005	2006
工业品出厂价格指数	**Producer Price Index of Industrial Products**	**84.8**	**87.8**	**89.4**	**89.9**
按轻重工业分	**Grouped by Light or Heavy Industries**				
轻工业	Light Industry	81.4	82.2	82.7	81.7
以农产品为原料	Using Farm Products as Raw Materials	94.3	97.3	97.7	98.3
以非农产品为原料	Using Non-farm Products as Raw Materials	70.1	69.9	70.4	69.2
重工业	Heavy Industry	87.2	91.5	93.6	95.9
采 掘	Mining and Guarrying	113.0	134.8	167.8	192.4
原 料	Raw Material	97.5	110.3	120.9	130.8
加 工	Manufacturing	84.9	86.8	86.8	87.0
按用途分	**Grouped by Use**				
生产资料	Means of Production	83.4	88.5	91.3	92.4
生活资料	Consumer Goods	85.9	84.8	83.7	82.8
#食 品	Food	115.4	116.9	117.7	118.2
衣 着	Clothing	87.9	90.0	91.3	91.6
一般日用品	Non-Durable Consumer Goods	87.7	88.8	89.4	90.2
耐用消费品	Durable Consumer Goods	74.4	70.3	67.3	64.2
按工业部门分	**Grouped by Sector**				
冶金工业	Metallurgy Industry	90.6	107.3	117.3	122.1
电力工业	Electric Power Industry	102.1	104.1	105.5	106.3
煤碳及炼焦工业	Coal and Coking Industry	191.3	214.9	216.9	219.1
石油工业	Petroleum Industry	162.9	189.5	228.7	261.9
化学工业	Chemical Industry	87.8	95.1	101.6	103.7
机械工业	Machinery Industry	72.6	70.6	68.6	67.2
建筑材料工业	Building Material Industry	94.4	100.0	94.8	91.3
森林工业	Forest Industry	45.4	44.8	45.2	45.7
食品工业	Food Industry	114.1	118.8	120.5	121.7
纺织工业	Textile Industry	80.5	83.4	83.1	83.5
缝纫工业	Sewing Industry	76.7	78.7	79.9	80.0
皮革工业	Leather Industry	94.2	94.4	94.4	95.1
造纸工业	Paper Making Industry	73.5	72.9	71.8	71.5
文教艺术用品工业	Cultural Educational and Art Goods	91.8	90.9	90.6	89.0
其他工业	Others Industry	121.0	127.2	129.2	135.8

表8.7 工业品出厂价格指数（2000～2006，以上年价格为100）
PRODUCER PRICE INDEX OF INDUSTRIAL PRODUCTS IN MAIN YEARS (PRECEDING YEAR =100)

类别	Types	2000	2001	2002
工业品出厂价格指数	**Producer Price Index of Industrial Products**	**102.5**	**96.7**	**96.4**
按轻重工业分	**Grouped by Light or Heavy Industries**			
轻工业	Light Industry	99.9	97.8	97.0
以农产品为原料	Using Farm Products as Raw Materials	99.4	99.8	98.9
以非农产品为原料	Using Non-farm Products as Raw Materials	100.2	95.4	94.9
重工业	Heavy Industry	104.3	96.1	96.1
采掘	Mining and Guarrying		100.0	100.4
原料	Raw Material	110.9	98.7	98.1
加工	Manufacturing	99.0	94.7	95.0
按用途分	**Grouped by Use**			
生产资料	Means of Production	105.4	96.3	95.8
生活资料	Consumer Goods	98.0	97.3	97.3
#食品	Food	98.2	102.6	102.6
衣着	Clothing	99.9	99.6	99.8
一般日用品	Non-Durable Consumer Goods	97.4	97.2	97.1
耐用消费品	Durable Consumer Goods	97.3	95.1	94.7
按工业部门分	**Grouped by Sector**			
冶金工业	Metallurgy Industry	104.6	98.4	96.7
电力工业	Electric Power Industry	98.3	100.2	99.6
煤碳及炼焦工业	Coal and Coking Industry	102.7	103.8	104.7
石油工业	Petroleum Industry	135.9	99.8	97.7
化学工业	Chemical Industry	108.7	96.2	96.3
机械工业	Machinery Industry	96.9	93.6	94.2
建筑材料工业	Building Material Industry	108.4	102.2	96.4
森林工业	Forest Industry	97.4	97.6	96.3
食品工业	Food Industry	98.2	102.8	102.3
纺织工业	Textile Industry	105.5	96.2	94.8
缝纫工业	Sewing Industry	97.4	99.1	99.8
皮革工业	Leather Industry	97.6	100.7	98.8
造纸工业	Paper Making Industry	110.0	97.8	94.7
文教艺术用品工业	Cultural Educational and Art Goods	99.4	96.9	99.0
其他工业	Other Industry	98.2	100.5	105.0

表 8.7 续表 continued

	类 别 Types	2003	2004	2005	2006
工业品出厂价格指数	**Producer Price Index of Industrial Products**	**101.4**	**103.6**	**101.7**	**100.6**
按轻重工业分	**Grouped by Light or Heavy Industries**				
轻工业	Light Industry	99.2	101.0	100.6	98.8
以农产品为原料	Using Farm Products as Raw Materials	101.0	103.2	100.4	100.6
以非农产品为原料	Using Non-farm Products as Raw Materials	98.3	99.8	100.7	98.2
重工业	Heavy Industry	102.9	105.0	102.3	102.4
采 掘	Mining and Guarrying	112.6	119.3	124.5	114.7
原 料	Raw Material	108.0	113.1	109.7	108.2
加 工	Manufacturing	100.9	102.3	99.9	100.3
按用途分	**Grouped by Use**				
生产资料	Means of Production	103.1	106.1	103.2	101.2
生活资料	Consumer Goods	98.1	98.7	98.7	98.9
#食 品	Food	100.1	101.3	100.6	100.5
衣 着	Clothing	99.7	102.5	101.4	100.4
一般日用品	Non-Durable Consumer Goods	99.3	101.3	100.7	100.9
耐用消费品	Durable Consumer Goods	96.1	94.6	95.7	95.4
按工业部门分	**Grouped by Sector**				
冶金工业	Metallurgy Industry	112.5	118.4	109.3	104.1
电力工业	ElectricPowerIndustry	99.3	101.9	101.3	100.8
煤碳及炼焦工业	CoalandCokingIndustry	116.4	112.3	100.9	101.0
石油工业	PetroleumIndustry	116.3	116.3	120.7	114.5
化学工业	ChemicalIndustry	103.4	108.2	106.9	102.0
机械工业	MachineryIndustry	96.6	97.3	97.1	98.1
建筑材料工业	BuildingMaterialIndustry	100.2	105.9	94.8	96.4
森林工业	ForestIndustry	98.2	98.5	101.1	101.0
食品工业	FoodIndustry	101.7	104.1	101.5	101.0
纺织工业	TextileIndustry	103.2	103.7	99.6	100.6
缝纫工业	SewingIndustry	99.8	102.6	101.5	100.2
皮革工业	LeatherIndustry	99.4	100.3	99.9	100.8
造纸工业	PaperMakingIndustry	98.1	99.2	98.5	99.6
文教艺术用品工业	CulturalEducationalandArtGoods	99.2	99.0	99.7	98.2
其他工业	OtherIndustry	101.5	105.1	101.6	105.1

表8.8 主要年份原材料燃料动力购进价格指数(以 1995 年价格为 100)
PURCHASING PRICE INDEX OF RAW MATERIALS, FUELS AND POWER IN MAIN YEARS (1995 = 100)

	类 别 Types	1996	2000	2001	2002
原材料燃料动力购进价格指数	**Purchasing Price Index of Raw Materials, Fuels and Power**	**97.6**	**94.2**	**92.9**	**90.8**
燃料动力	Fuel and Power	109.9	131.6	131.4	133.5
黑色金属材料	Ferrous Metals	96.0	86.7	90.6	90.6
#钢 材	Rolled-steel	98.5	88.6	88.4	85.6
有色金属材料和电线	Nonferrous Metals and Electric Wire	87.3	76.9	71.7	68.2
化工原料	Chemical Raw Materials	93.7	96.7	87.4	81.1
木材及纸浆	Wood and Paper Pulps	102.8	76.8	72.9	71.1
建筑材料及非金属矿	Building Materials and Nonmetal Minerals	123.9	105.1	106.8	102.8
其他工业原材料及半成品	Other Industrial Raw and Processed Materials		93.3	94.2	92.1
农副产品	Farm and Sideline Products	100.6	101.1	100.4	99.9
纺织原料	Textile Raw Material	90.0	73.1	70.8	66.9

注：其它工业原材料及半成品以 1996 年为 100。
Note: The Prices of Other Industrial Raw and Processed Materials in 1996 are set at 100.

表8.8 续表 continued

	类 别 Types	2003	2004	2005	2006
原材料燃料动力购进价格指数	**Purchasing Price Index of Raw Materials, Fuels and Power**	**96.6**	**112.5**	**120.2**	**125.9**
燃料动力	Fuel and Power	143.7	179.4	222.6	246.9
黑色金属材料	Ferrous Metals	103.0	138.7	143.0	132.5
#钢 材	Rolled-steel	93.3	114.9	126.3	121.2
有色金属材料和电线	Nonferrous Metals and Electric Wire	69.9	83.8	94.0	130.8
化工原料	Chemical Raw Materials	86.9	99.4	110.4	114.0
木材及纸浆	Wood and Paper Pulps	70.7	71.3	72.3	72.6
建筑材料及非金属矿	Building Materials and Nonmetal Minerals	105.9	121.8	108.3	108.1
其他工业原材料及半成品	Other Industrial Raw and Processed Materials	91.0	93.7	93.1	96.2
农副产品	Farm and Sideline Products	109.1	120.4	118.2	124.1
纺织原料	Textile Raw Material	68.2	71.6	72.8	73.2

表8.9 主要年份原材料燃料动力购进价格指数（以上年价格为100）
PURCHASING PRICE INDEX OF RAW MATERIALS, FUELS AND POWER IN MAIN YEARS (PRECEDING YEAR =100)

类 别	Types	1995	2000	2001	2002
原材料燃料动力购进价格指数	**Purchasing Price Index of Raw Materials, Fuels and Power**	**113.3**	**107.1**	**98.7**	**97.7**
燃料动力	Fuels and Power	107.6	116.7	99.9	101.6
黑色金属材料	Ferrous Metals	99.1	96.7	104.5	100.1
#钢 材	Rolled-steel	98.8	102.6	99.7	96.9
有色金属材料和电线	Nonferrous Metals and Electric Wire	131.7	111.4	93.2	95.1
化工原料	Chemical Raw Materials	124.1	123.5	90.4	92.7
木材及纸浆	Wood and Paper Pulps	121.3	101.6	94.9	97.6
建筑材料及非金属矿	Building Materials and Nonmetal Minerals	92.1	99.5	101.6	96.3
其他工业原材料及半成品	Other Industrial Raw and Processed Materials		104.6	100.9	97.7
农副产品	Farm and Sideline Products	123.3	97.2	99.3	99.5
纺织原料	Textile Raw Material	114.8	96.9	96.8	94.5

表8.9 续表 continued

类 别	Types	2003	2004	2005	2006
原材料燃料动力购进价格指数	**Purchasing Price Index of Raw Materials, Fuels and Power**	**106.4**	**116.4**	**106.8**	**104.8**
燃料动力	Fuels and Power	107.7	124.8	124.1	110.9
黑色金属材料	Ferrous Metals	113.7	134.6	103.2	92.7
#钢 材	Rolled-steel	108.9	123.2	109.9	95.9
有色金属材料和电线	Nonferrous Metals and Electric Wire	102.5	119.9	112.2	139.1
化工原料	Chemical Raw Materials	107.3	114.3	111.1	103.2
木材及纸浆	Wood and Paper Pulps	99.3	100.9	101.5	100.3
建筑材料及非金属矿	Building Materials and Nonmetal Minerals	103.0	115.1	88.9	99.8
其他工业原材料及半成品	Other Industrial Raw and Processed Materials	98.9	103.0	99.3	103.3
农副产品	Farm and Sideline Products	109.2	110.4	98.1	105.1
纺织原料	Textile Raw Material	102.0	104.9	101.8	100.5

表8.10 固定资产投资价格指数（1996～2006，以1995年价格为100）
PRICE INDEX OF INVESTMENT IN FIXED ASSETS (1995 = 100)

年 份 Year	固定资产投资价格指数 Price Index of Fixed Asset Investment	建筑安装工程 Building Project Price Index	# 人工费 Manpower Cost Price Index	# 材料费 Material Price Index	# 机械费 Machinery Price Index	设备工器具购置 Equipment and Instrument Price Index	其他费用投资 Other Investment Price Index
1996	107.0	108.9	114.2	97.4	118.5	101.7	107.7
1997	107.5	110.4	124.5	96.1	123.8	99.5	108.6
1998	105.8	109.2	119.5	94.5	123.5	95.6	108.1
1999	103.8	106.8	123.6	90.8	124.1	92.6	107.9
2000	103.8	108.4	124.3	92.4	123.8	89.8	107.8
2001	104.5	111.0	135.5	93.6	123.5	86.7	109.2
2002	104.8	113.1	149.7	93.4	126.9	83.8	109.5
2003	107.4	119.0	156.5	98.5	133.1	81.7	111.1
2004	114.6	131.6	165.4	110.3	144.7	81.3	116.3
2005	115.5	132.8	173.3	109.7	152.8	79.1	120.0
2006	115.6	132.9	181.6	108.1	157.3	77.0	122.4

表8.11 固定资产投资价格指数（1995～2006，以上年价格为100）
PRICE INDEX OF INVESTMENT IN FIXED ASSETS (PRECEDING YEAR = 100)

年 份 Year	固定资产投资价格指数 Price Index of Fixed Asset Investment	建筑安装工程 Building Project Price Index	# 人工费 Manpower Cost Price Index	# 材料费 Material Price Index	# 机械费 Machinery Price Index	设备工器具购置 Equipment and Instrument Price Index	其他费用投资 Other Investment Price Index
1995	103.1	101.9	108.7	99.5		104.8	107.0
1996	107.0	108.9	114.2	97.4	118.5	101.7	107.7
1997	100.5	101.4	109.0	98.7	104.5	97.8	100.8
1998	98.4	98.9	96.0	98.3	99.7	96.1	99.6
1999	98.1	97.8	103.4	96.1	100.5	96.9	99.8
2000	100.0	101.5	100.6	101.8	99.8	97.0	99.9
2001	100.7	102.4	109.0	101.2	99.7	96.5	101.3
2002	100.3	101.9	110.5	99.8	102.8	96.7	100.3
2003	102.4	105.2	104.5	105.5	104.9	97.5	101.4
2004	106.7	110.6	105.7	112.0	108.7	99.4	104.7
2005	100.8	100.9	104.8	99.4	105.6	97.4	103.2
2006	100.1	100.1	104.8	98.6	102.9	97.3	102.0

表8.12 房地产价格指数（2001～2006，以2000年价格为100）
REAL ESTATE PRICE INDEX (2000 = 100)

	类 别 Types	2001	2002	2003
房屋销售价格指数	**Price Index of Real Estate Sales**	**104.4**	**112.0**	**134.5**
商品房	Commodity Housing	101.8	110.1	132.7
住 宅	Residence	102.1	111.0	134.7
非住宅	Non-residence	98.3	102.0	114.0
公 房	Public Housing	107.4	108.2	108.2
二手房	Second-hand Housing	110.8	117.1	142.4
房屋租赁价格指数	**Price Index of Real Estate Leasing**	**104.9**	**103.9**	**106.0**
住 宅	Residence	107.4	107.4	108.7
#公 房	Public Housing	115.2	115.2	115.2
办公楼	Offices	98.6	97.9	103.0
商业娱乐用房	Commercial and Entertainment Housing	107.2	104.0	102.8
厂业仓储用房	Workshops and Warehouses	118.8	121.2	125.5
土地交易价格指数	**Price Index of Land Exchange**	**97.2**	**103.3**	**118.9**
#居住用地	Residential	92.2	102.3	125.1
工业仓储用地	Workshops and Warehouses	91.6	82.7	84.0

表8.12 续表 continued

	类 别 Types	2004	2005	2006
房屋销售价格指数	**Price Index of Real Estate Sales**	**155.9**	**171.1**	**168.9**
商品房	Commodity Housing	153.7	167.8	162.8
住 宅	Residence	156.0	170.4	165.0
非住宅	Non-residence	132.3	143.6	141.6
公 房	Public Housing	108.2		
二手房	Second-hand Housing	167.3	185.1	188.4
房屋租赁价格指数	**Price Index of Real Estate Leasing**	**111.9**	**115.9**	**120.6**
住 宅	Residence	110.1	113.7	116.4
#公 房	Public Housing	115.2		
办公楼	Offices	110.1	117.2	121.6
商业娱乐用房	Commercial and Entertainment Housing	110.4	111.4	118.2
厂业仓储用房	Workshops and Warehouses	131.8	133.7	135.1
土地交易价格指数	**Price Index of Land Exchange**	**143.1**	**153.0**	**154.8**
#居住用地	Residential	161.8	170.6	169.7
工业仓储用地	Workshops and Warehouses	85.1	88.3	90.8

①按照国家统计局新的调查制度规定，取消房屋价格统计中原“私房”调查指标，改为“二手房”统计指标。
②二手房是指进入房屋市场进行交易，第二次以上进行产权登记的商品房。 表中2005年以前二手房为私房数据。
③自2005年起，按照国家统计局新的调查制度规定，取消房屋价格统计中“公房”价格统计指标。
❶According to the new investigation system regulation of National Bureau of Statistics, the investigate indicator of Private Housing was canceled and instead of Second-hand Housing.
❷Second-hand Housing refers to the houses traded in the housing market, and property right registered for more than once. Data of 2005 and year before refer to Private Housing.
❸Since 2005, according to the new investigation system regulation of National Bureau of Statistics, the indicator of Public Housing has been canceled.

表 8.13 房地产价格指数(2000～2006,以上年价格为 100)
REAL ESTATE PRICE INDEX (PRECEDING YEAR =100)

	类 别 Types	2000	2001	2002
房屋销售价格指数	**Price Index of Real Estate Sales**	**98.6**	**104.4**	**107.3**
商品房	Commodity Housing	98.5	101.8	108.2
住 宅	Residence	98.5	102.1	108.7
非住宅	Non-residence	98.2	98.3	103.8
公 房	Public Housing	100.0	107.4	100.7
二手房	Second-hand Housing	99.1	110.8	105.7
房屋租赁价格指数	**Price Index of Real Estate Leasing**	**95.8**	**104.9**	**99.0**
住 宅	Residence	104.1	107.4	100.0
#公 房	Public Housing	104.1	115.2	100.0
办公楼	Offices	87.6	98.6	99.3
商业娱乐用房	Commercial and Entertainment Housing	103.6	107.2	97.0
厂业仓储用房	Workshops and Warehouses	92.3	118.8	102.0
土地交易价格指数	**Price Index of Land Exchange**	**91.9**	**97.2**	**106.3**
#居住用地	Residential	86.3	92.2	111.0
工业仓储用地	Workshops and Warehouses	93.3	91.6	90.3

表 8.13 续表 continued

	类 别 Types	2003	2004	2005	2006
房屋销售价格指数	**Price Index of Real Estate Sales**	**120.1**	**115.9**	**109.7**	**98.7**
商品房	Commodity Housing	120.5	115.8	109.2	97.0
住 宅	Residence	121.4	115.8	109.2	96.8
非住宅	Non-residence	111.7	116.1	108.5	98.6
公 房	Public Housing	100.0	100.0		
二手房	Second-hand Housing	121.6	117.5	110.6	101.8
房屋租赁价格指数	**Price Index of Real Estate Leasing**	**102.1**	**105.5**	**103.6**	**104.0**
住 宅	Residence	101.2	101.3	103.3	102.3
#公 房	Public Housing	100.0	100.0		
办公楼	Offices	105.2	106.9	106.4	103.8
商业娱乐用房	Commercial and Entertainment Housing	98.9	107.3	101.0	106.1
厂业仓储用房	Workshops and Warehouses	103.6	105.0	101.4	101.1
土地交易价格指数	**Price Index of Land Exchange**	**115.1**	**120.3**	**106.9**	**101.2**
#居住用地	Residential	122.2	129.4	105.4	99.5
工业仓储用地	Workshops and Warehouses	101.5	101.4	103.7	102.9

上/海/统/计/年/鉴

主要统计指标解释

■ 居民消费价格指数

居民消费价格指数是度量一组代表性消费商品及服务项目价格水平随着时间而变动的相对数，反映居民家庭购买的消费品及服务价格水平的变动情况。它是宏观经济分析和决策、价格总水平监测和调控以及国民经济核算的重要指标。其按年度计算的变动率通常被用来作为反映通货膨胀或紧缩程度的指标。

现行的居民消费价格指数按用途分为八个大类，包括食品、烟酒及用品、衣着、家庭设备用品及维修服务、医疗保健和个人用品、交通和通信、娱乐教育文化用品及服务、居住。

■ 商品零售价格指数

商品零售价格指数是反映一定时期内城乡商品零售价格变动趋势和程度的相对数。商品零售价格的变动直接影响城乡居民的生活支出和国家的财政收入，影响居民购买力和市场供需的平衡，影响消费与积累的比例关系。因此，该指数可以从一个侧面对上述经济活动进行观察和分析。

■ 工业品出厂价格指数

工业品出厂价格指数是反映一定时期内全部工业产品出厂价格总水平的变动趋势和程度的相对数，包括工业企业售给本企业以外所有单位的各种产品和直接售给居民用于生活消费的产品。该指数可以观察出厂价格变动对工业总产值及增加值的影响。

■ 原材料燃料动力购进价格指数

原材料燃料和动力购进价格指数是反映工业企业作为生产投入，从物资交易市场和能源、原材料生产企业购买原材料、燃料和动力产品时，所支付的价格水平变动趋势和程度的统计指标，是扣除工业企业物质消耗成本中的价格变动影响的重要依据。

目前，我国编制的原材料燃料和动力购进价格指数所调查的产品包括燃料动力、黑色金属、有色金属、化工、建材等九大类的近1800种产品。

■ 固定资产投资价格指数

固定资产投资价格指数是反映一定时期内固定资产投资品及项目的价格变动趋势和程度的相对数。固定资产投资额是由建筑安装工程投资完成额、设备工器具购置投资完成额和其他费用投资完成额三部分组成的。编制固定资产投资价格指数应首先分别编制上述三部分投资的价格指数，然后采用加权算术平均法求出固定资产投资价格总指数。

该指数可以准确地反映固定资产投资中涉及的各类投资品和收费项目价格变动趋势和变动幅度，消除按现价计算的固定资产投资指标中的价格变动因素，真实地反映固定资产投资的规模、速度、结构和效益，为国家科学地制定、检查固定资产投资计划并提高宏观调控水平，为完善国民经济核算体系提供科学的、可靠的依据。

■ 房屋销售价格指数

房屋销售指以买卖方式转移房地产的所有权。它包括商品房销售、公房和私房出售三部分。房屋销售价格指数是指房屋销售价格总水平变动趋势的相对数。

■ 房屋租赁价格指数

房屋租赁指以支付租金形式取得房屋使用权。它包括住宅租赁、办公用房租赁 、商业用房租赁和厂房仓库租赁部分。房屋租赁价格指数是指房屋租赁价格总水平变动趋势和程度的相对数。

■ 土地交易价格指数

指房地产开发商或其他建设单位在进行商品房开发之前，为取得土地使用权而实际支付的价格的变动趋势和程度的相对数。

SHANGHAI STATISTICAL YEARBOOK

EXPLANATORY NOTES TO MAJOR STATISTICAL INDICATORS

□ Consumer Price Index

The Consumer Price Index is an index that reflects the time-based change of prices of a group of representative consumption commodities and services. It is an important reference factor for macro-economic analysis and strategy, monitoring and adjustment of overall price level and the national economic budgeting. The year-on-year change of the index is often a norm reflecting the inflation or deflation.

The current CPI covers eight categories of goods and services: food; tobacco, liquor and related articles; garments; household facilities, articles and repair services; medical and health care and personal items; traffic and telecommunications; education, culture and recreation articles and services and residence.

□ Retail Price Index

Retail Price Index reflect the trend and degree of change in retail prices of commodities during a given period. The change in retail prices of commodities directly affect the living expenditure of urban and rural residents, government revenue, purchasing power of residents and the equilibrium of market supply and demand, and the ratio of consumption to accumulation. Therefore, the retail price indices are useful to analyze the changes of the above economic activities.

□ Producer Price Index of Industrial Products

Producer Price Index of Industrial Products reflect the trend and degree of changes in general ex-factory prices of all industrial products during a given period, including sales of industrial products by an industrial enterprise to all units outside the enterprise, as well as sales of consumer goods to residents. It can be used to analyze the impact of ex-factory prices on gross output value and value-added of the industrial sector.

□ Purchasing Price Index of Raw Materials, Fuels and Power

Purchasing Price Index of Raw Materials, Fuels and Power reflect changes in the level and degree of prices paid by industrial enterprises when they purchase production input such as raw materials, fuels and power from the market or from other energy or raw materials producing enterprises. These indices provide important basis for measuring the material consumption of industrial enterprises after removing influence of price changes.

At present, close to 1,800 products in 9 categories, including fuels and power, ferrous metals, non-ferrous metals, chemicals, building materials, are covered in China for the survey to produce indices of purchasing prices of raw materials, fuels and power.

□ Price Index of Investment in Fixed Assets

Price Indices of Investment in Fixed Assets reflect the trend and degree of changes in prices of investment goods and projects in fixed assets during a given period. The investment in fixed assets consists of three components, namely the investment in construction and installation, the investment in purchases of equipment and instrument, and the investment in other items. Price indices of investment in fixed assets are calculated as the weighted arithmetic mean of the price indices of the three components of investment in fixed assets.

Removing the factor of price change in the aggregates of investment at current prices, this indicator shows the changes in the prices of commodities and fees involved in the investment of fixed assets, and can be used to observe the actual size, growth, structure, and efficiency of investment in fixed assets and provides reliable and scientific data for government planning, management, decision-making, and further improving the current national accounting system.

□ Price Index of Real Estate Sales

Real estate sales refer to the transference of ownership of real estate through selling and buying. Included are the sales of commodity housings, public housings and private housings. The Price Index of Real Estate Sales is an indicator of the general trend and variation degrees of the sales price of the real estate.

□ Price Index of Real Estate Leasing

Real estate leasing refers to the acquisition of the real estate ownership by means of paying rent. Included are the leasing of residential houses, office building, workshop and warehouse, and hotel and restaurant. The Price Index of Real Estate leasing is an indica-

EXPLANATORY NOTES TO MAJOR STATISTICAL INDICATORS

tor of general trend and variation of the leasing price of real estate.

□ Price Index of Land Exchange

Price Index of Land Exchange is an indicator of the general trend and variation of the paid price in order to obtain the ownership of the land by the real estate developer or other construction organizations before the development.

第九篇
CHAPTER 9

人民生活
LIVING STANDARDS

表 9.1 从业人员报酬(1978 ~ 2006) COMPENSATION OF EMPLOYEES

年 份 Year	从业人员报酬 (亿元) Compensation of Employees (100 million yuan)	按产业分 Grouped by Industry			按登记注册类型分 Classified According to the Categories of registration		
		第一产业 Primary Industry	第二产业 Secondary Industr	第三产业 Tertiary Industry	国有单位 State-owned Units	集体单位 Collective-owned Units	其他单位 Other Ownership Units
1978	28.18	1.31	17.18	9.69	23.88	4.30	
1979	32.90	1.44	20.43	11.03	27.77	5.13	
1980	38.26	1.66	23.42	13.18	31.71	6.55	
1981	39.76	1.61	24.40	13.75	32.55	7.21	
1982	41.55	1.59	25.15	14.81	33.83	7.72	
1983	43.21	1.48	26.07	15.66	35.07	8.14	
1984	54.13	1.63	33.29	19.21	43.39	10.29	0.45
1985	69.63	2.10	42.86	24.67	55.96	13.18	0.49
1986	84.89	2.45	51.70	30.74	68.32	15.84	0.73
1987	96.36	2.64	58.18	35.54	78.15	17.46	0.75
1988	117.04	3.18	70.35	43.51	94.78	20.91	1.35
1989	134.04	3.60	81.41	49.03	106.57	25.17	2.30
1990	150.48	4.02	89.48	56.98	121.56	25.64	3.28
1991	177.55	4.64	105.25	67.66	142.00	30.24	5.31
1992	223.36	2.47	135.49	85.40	179.43	35.40	8.53
1993	290.42	2.57	157.10	130.75	212.10	39.56	38.76
1994	374.44	3.11	186.81	184.52	268.19	48.59	57.66
1995	465.67	3.53	232.10	230.04	324.72	56.99	83.96
1996	521.63	3.72	250.94	266.97	359.56	60.18	101.89
1997	547.87	3.69	245.59	298.59	366.61	60.11	121.15
1998	554.86	3.47	255.43	276.61	342.88	49.65	162.33
1999	635.84	3.35	277.11	332.39	380.58	48.36	206.90
2000	647.55	3.32	283.20	361.03	369.65	38.88	239.02
2001	716.95	3.25	301.93	411.77	389.26	36.91	290.78
2002	788.55	3.76	333.64	451.15	404.89	34.18	349.48
2003	873.06	2.53	373.19	497.34	434.93	32.43	405.70
2004	925.33	2.69	383.84	538.80	435.30	31.00	459.03
2005	1 245.44	3.21	478.97	763.26	474.39	30.28	740.77
2006	1 598.09	3.92	646.41	937.76	559.02	31.15	1 007.92

①本表至表 9.3，2006 年从业人员报酬包括 120 人以上私营企业从业人员报酬。
②本表"其他单位"包括港澳台及外商投资企业。
❶Compensation of Employees of 2006 include those of private enterprises above 120 persons in this table to table 9.3.
❷"Other" in this table includes foreign invested and HongKong, Macau and Taiwan funded enterprises.

表9.2 从业人员报酬(2006)
COMPENSATION OF EMPLOYEES

单位:亿元 (100 million yuan)

行 业	Sectors	合 计 Total	国有单位 State-owned Unit	集体单位 Collective-owned Unit	港澳台及外商投资单位 Units with Investment from Hong Kong, Macao, Taiwan and Foreign Countries	其他单位 Other Unit
全 市	**Total**	**1 598.09**	**559.02**	**31.15**	**372.79**	**635.13**
一、按产业分	**Grouped by Industry**					
第一产业	Primary Industry	3.92	1.57	0.38	0.05	1.92
第二产业	Secondary Industry	656.41	104.21	5.20	281.17	265.82
第三产业	Tertiary Industry	937.76	453.24	25.57	91.57	367.38
二、按行业分	**Grouped by Sector**					
农、林、牧、渔业	Farming, Forestry, Animal Husbandry and Fishery	3.92	1.57	0.38	0.05	1.92
工 业	Industry	586.45	85.30	4.34	278.41	218.40
采矿业	Mining	0.34	0.31			0.03
制造业	Manufacturing	558.56	67.15	4.03	275.79	211.58
电力、燃气及水的生产和供应业	Power, Gas and Water Production and Supply	27.56	17.85	0.30	2.62	6.79
建筑业	Construction	69.96	18.91	0.86	2.77	47.42
交通运输、仓储和邮政业	Transportation, Warehousing and Post	130.01	42.93	1.24	18.31	67.53
#交通运输	Transportation	116.42	32.61	1.09	17.43	65.29
邮政业	Postal	9.42	9.22			0.20
信息传输、计算机服务和软件业	Information Transmission, Computer Servcies and Software Industries	51.69	12.30	0.13	15.01	24.24
#信息传输	Information Transmission	23.89	11.36	0.12	8.09	4.32
批发和零售业	Wholesale and Retail	113.21	16.40	4.31	8.71	83.79
批发业	Wholesale	80.55	10.04	2.37	5.48	62.67
零售业	Retail	32.66	6.37	1.94	3.23	21.12
住宿和餐饮业	Hoteling and Catering	26.79	8.30	0.34	6.09	12.06
#餐饮业	Catering	13.55	0.90	0.22	3.37	9.07
金融业	Financial Industries	117.59	37.93		18.36	61.30
房地产业	Real Estate	34.70	9.53	0.65	4.46	20.05
租赁和商务服务业	Leasing and Business Services	90.51	19.17	6.83	13.97	50.54
科学研究、技术服务和地质勘查业	Scientific Research, Technological Service and Geological Prospecting	66.92	53.16	0.55	4.30	8.90
水利、环境和公共设施管理业	Water Conservancies, Environment and Public Facilities Management	15.45	12.34	0.79	0.44	1.88
居民服务和其他服务业	Resident Service and Other Services	30.97	2.94	0.86	0.72	26.45
教 育	Education	97.65	94.65	0.46	0.09	2.54
卫生、社会保障和社会福利业	Healthcare, Social Security and Social Welfare	66.61	56.53	8.02	0.15	1.92
卫 生	Healthcare	62.21	53.54	7.68	0.15	0.85
社会保障	Social Security	2.90	1.57	0.27		1.05
社会福利业	Social Welfare	1.49	1.42	0.06		0.01
文化、体育和娱乐业	Culture, Sports and Entertainment	24.59	17.01	0.36	0.96	6.26
文 化	Culture	21.07	14.17	0.35	0.35	6.20
体 育	Sports	2.58	2.54	0.01	0.03	
娱乐业	Entertainment	0.94	0.30		0.58	0.06
公共管理和社会组织	Public Administration and Social Organizations	71.09	70.07	1.02		

表9.3 从业人员平均报酬(2006)
AVERAGE ANNUAL COMPENSATION OF EMPLOYEES

单位:元 (yuan)

行业	Sectors	合计 Total	国有单位 State-owned Unit	集体单位 Collective-owned Unit	港澳台及外商投资单位 Units with Investment from Hong Kong, Macao,Taiwan and Foreign Countries	其他单位 Other Unit
全 市	**Total**	**31 371**	**40 141**	**22 959**	**40 964**	**23 915**
一、按产业分	**Grouped by Industry**					
第一产业	Primary Industry	19 459	22 610	26 644	16 719	16 724
第二产业	Secondary Industry	29 079	37 128	17 972	36 330	22 646
第三产业	Tertiary Industry	33 294	41 017	24 278	67 409	24 984
二、按行业分	**Grouped by Sector**					
农、林、牧、渔业	Farming, Forestry, Animal Husbandry and Fishery	19 459	22 610	26 644	16 719	16 724
工 业	Industry	29 225	37 697	18 077	36 171	22 135
采矿业	Mining	56 531	75 392			15 538
制造业	Manufacturing	28 606	35 871	17 303	35 966	21 696
电力、燃气及水的生产和供应业	Power, Gas and Water Production and Supply	51 501	46 133	44 621	90 961	60 293
建筑业	Construction	27 908	34 765	17 455	65 087	25 344
交通运输、仓储和邮政业	Transportation, Warehousing and Post	34 813	36 883	14 640	67 341	30 501
#交通运输	Transportation	34 624	36 700	14 427	67 703	30 496
邮政业	Postal	37 544	38 307			19 391
信息传输、计算机服务和软件业	Information Transmission, Computer Servcies and Software Industries	65 704	71 398	26 450	84 230	56 231
#信息传输	Information Transmission	82 867	73 890	28 929	98 742	89 238
批发和零售业	Retail and Wholesale	20 468	38 856	19 899	49 599	17 764
批发业	Wholesale	19 143	47 706	24 432	66 729	16 412
零售业	Retail	24 681	30 061	16 225	34 560	23 510
住宿和餐饮业	Hoteling and Catering	22 402	28 115	16 468	22 701	19 713
#餐饮业	Catering	18 368	28 602	15 477	17 482	18 149
金融业	Financial Industries	70 546	89 394		134 177	55 438
房地产业	Real Estate	30 308	33 147	21 122	36 943	28 420
租赁和商务服务业	Leasing and Business Services	23 896	26 194	22 216	163 152	18 980
科学研究、技术服务和地质勘查业	Scientific Research, Technological Service and Geological Prospecting	47 822	43 299	36 534	158 175	68 888
水利、环境和公共设施管理业	Water Conservancies,Environment and Public Facilities Management	29 508	30 687	17 718	31 467	29 929
居民服务和其他服务业	Resident Service and Other Services	17 121	23 895	15 554	15 942	16 684
教 育	Education	37 819	38 577	25 830	71 577	22 416
卫生、社会保障和社会福利业	Healthcare, Social Security and Social Welfare	40 892	44 112	38 811	65 345	13 831
卫 生	Healthcare	43 191	45 128	39 474	65 345	14 805
社会保障	Social Security	21 790	35 591	31 271		13 145
社会福利业	Social Welfare	27 031	27 836	19 003		13 152
文化、体育和娱乐业	Culture, Sports and Entertainment	38 230	46 218	28 323	30 333	27 113
文 化	Culture	39 598	49 959	28 245	44 068	27 173
体 育	Sports	34 065	34 350	37 133	18 350	
娱乐业	Entertainment	26 541	28 669		26 150	21 830
公共管理和社会组织	Public Administration and Social Organizations	41 018	41 277	28 656		

表 9.4 职工工资总额和平均工资(1978～2006)
TOTAL WAGES AND AVERAGE ANNUAL WAGES OF STAFF AND WORKERS

年 份 Year	职工工资总额(亿元) Total Wages of Staff and Workers (100 million yuan)	其中 of which			职工平均工资(元) Average Annual Wages of Staff and Workers (yuan)	其中 of which		
		国有单位 State-owned Units	集体单位 Collective-owned Units	其他单位 Other Ownership Units		国有单位 State-owned Units	集体单位 Collective-owned Units	其他单位 Other Units
1978	28.12	23.82	4.30		672	716	500	
1979	32.73	27.63	5.10		784	834	590	
1980	38.10	31.59	6.51		873	918	702	
1981	39.59	32.42	7.17		870	910	727	
1982	41.34	33.71	7.63		883	920	750	
1983	42.91	34.93	7.98		897	935	763	
1984	53.72	43.19	10.08	0.45	1 110	1 160	938	1 149
1985	68.99	55.50	13.00	0.49	1 416	1 467	1 227	1 628
1986	83.35	67.49	15.15	0.71	1 689	1 752	1 443	2 029
1987	94.78	77.19	16.87	0.72	1 893	1 960	1 623	2 510
1988	114.47	93.62	19.55	1.30	2 277	2 354	1 951	2 715
1989	131.10	105.08	23.77	2.25	2 608	2 691	2 259	3 235
1990	146.78	119.26	24.30	3.22	2 917	3 037	2 394	3 611
1991	172.84	139.12	28.51	5.21	3 375	3 487	2 817	4 363
1992	217.21	175.95	32.89	8.37	4 273	4 451	3 363	5 486
1993	279.33	206.12	36.60	36.61	5 650	5 784	4 253	7 043
1994	357.89	259.78	44.73	53.38	7 401	7 529	5 389	9 617
1995	440.75	314.69	51.61	74.45	9 279	9 578	6 309	11 518
1996	492.70	348.96	54.92	88.82	10 663	11 015	7 051	13 186
1997	510.10	353.69	53.69	102.72	11 425	11 733	7 329	14 313
1998	510.35	330.10	44.13	136.12	12 059	12 361	7 138	14 430
1999	583.54	366.21	43.22	174.11	14 147	14 419	7 935	16 736
2000	614.53	371.39	39.35	203.79	15 420	15 737	8 041	17 942
2001	678.29	389.91	35.79	252.59	17 764	17 820	8 525	20 865
2002	733.31	404.44	31.54	297.33	19 473	19 777	8 707	21 886
2003	803.84	430.92	30.52	342.40	22 160	22 541	9 844	24 359
2004	837.39	428.49	29.36	379.53	24 398	24 726	11 539	26 270
2005	1 146.97	463.24	28.44	655.29	26 823	28 803	12 819	26 792
2006	1 475.93	539.88	28.41	907.64	29 569	36 010	15 209	27 459

①本表至表 9.6，2006 年职工工资总额和平均工资包括 120 人以上的私营企业职工工资。
②本表"其他单位"包括港澳台及外商投资企业。
❶Total Wages and Average Wages of Workers of 2006 include those of privare enterprises above 120 persons in this table to table 9.6.
❷"Other" in this table includes foreign invested and HongKong, Macau and Taiwan funded enterprises.

表 9.5　职工工资总额（2006）
TOTAL WAGES OF STAFF AND WORKERS

行业 Sectors		职工工资总额（亿元） Total Wages of Staff Workers (100 million yuan)				
		合计 Total	国有单位 State -owned Units	集体单位 Collective-owned Units	港澳台及外商投资单位 Units with Investment from Hong Kong, Macao, Taiwan and Foreign Countries	其他单位 Other Ownership Units
全　市	**Total**	**1 475.93**	**539.88**	**28.41**	**304.27**	**603.37**
一、按产业分	**Grouped by Industry**					
第一产业	Primary Industry	3.42	1.33	0.40	0.04	1.65
第二产业	Secondary Industry	598.33	105.09	4.50	231.74	257.00
第三产业	Tertiary Industry	874.18	433.46	23.51	72.49	344.72
二、按行业分	**GroupedbySector**					
农、林、牧、渔业	Farming, Forestry, Animal-Husbandry and Fishery	3.42	1.33	0.40	0.04	1.65
工　业	Industry	533.55	87.63	4.00	229.95	211.97
采矿业	Mining	0.33	0.30			0.03
制造业	Manufacturing	505.80	69.53	3.67	227.37	205.22
电力、燃气及水的生产和供应业	Power, Gas and Water Production and Supply	27.42	17.80	0.32	2.58	6.72
建筑业	Construction	64.78	17.46	0.50	1.79	45.03
交通运输、仓储和邮政业	Transportation, Warehousing and Post	122.62	40.39	1.07	17.34	63.83
#交通运输	Transportation	112.40	32.90	0.97	16.66	61.87
邮政业	Postal	6.42	6.38			0.04
信息传输、计算机服务和软件业	Information Transmission, Computer Servcies and Software Industries	48.75	11.83	0.13	12.87	23.91
#信息传输	Information Transmission	21.75	10.91	0.13	6.57	4.14
批发和零售业	Retail and Wholesale	103.47	17.07	3.95	6.94	75.51
批发业	Wholesale	76.12	9.90	2.09	4.16	59.98
零售业	Retail	27.35	7.17	1.86	2.78	15.54
住宿和餐饮业	Hoteling and Catering	22.30	7.12	0.32	3.76	11.10
#餐饮业	Catering	11.36	0.83	0.21	1.65	8.67
金融业	Financial Industries	108.51	36.58		13.14	58.79
房地产业	Real Estate	29.16	7.96	0.48	2.86	17.86
租赁和商务服务业	Leasingand Business Services	84.85	17.60	6.78	11.24	49.23
科学研究、技术服务和地质勘查业	Scientific Research, Technological Service and Geological Prospecting	61.32	50.57	0.48	2.65	7.62
水利、环境和公共设施管理业	Water Conservancies Environmentand Public Facilities Management	14.67	11.85	0.68	0.39	1.75
居民服务和其他服务业	Resident Serviceand Other Services	30.06	2.63	0.69	0.61	26.13
教　育	Education	93.97	92.52	0.30	0.05	1.10
卫生、社会保障和社会福利业	Healthcare, Social Security and Social Welfare	62.67	53.31	7.42	0.06	1.88
卫　生	Healthcare	58.54	50.57	7.09		0.82
社会保障	Social Security	2.87	1.53	0.28		1.05
社会福利业	Social Welfare	1.26	1.21	0.05		0.01
文化、体育和娱乐业	Culture, Sports and Entertainment	22.21	15.29	0.32	0.59	6.01
文　化	Culture	19.29	12.70	0.31	0.30	5.97
体　育	Sports	2.36	2.32	0.01	0.02	
娱乐业	Entertainment	0.57	0.26		0.26	0.04
公共管理和社会组织	Public Administrationand Social Organizations	69.63	68.74	0.89		

表9.6 职工平均工资(2006)
AVERAGE ANNUAL WAGES OF STAFF AND WORKERS

行业 Sectors		职工平均工资（元） Average Annual Wages of Staff and Workers (yuan)				
		合计 Total	国有单位 State-owned Units	集体单位 Collective-owned Units	港澳台及外商投资单位 Units with Investment from Hong Kong, Macao, Taiwan and Foreign Countries	其他单位 Other Ownership Units
全市	**Total**	**29 569**	**36 010**	**15 209**	**40 683**	**23 592**
一、按产业分	**Grouped by Industry**					
第一产业	Primary Industry	19 398	24 645	27 162	18 717	15 654
第二产业	Secondary Industry	25 917	24 190	8 298	35 512	22 015
第三产业	Tertiary Industry	32 800	40 915	17 937	76 188	24 988
二、按行业分	**GroupedbySector**					
农、林、牧、渔业	Farming, Forestry, Animal-Husbandry and Fishery	19 398	24 645	27 162	18 717	15 654
工业	Industry	25 743	22 966	7 895	35 385	21 400
采矿业	Mining	53 855	76 854			15 574
制造业	Manufacturing	25 055	20 285	7 383	35 144	20 956
电力、燃气及水的生产和供应业	Power, Gas and Water Production and Supply	51 546	46 338	37 944	89 073	60 883
建筑业	Construction	27 440	33 025	13 949	65 978	25 456
交通运输、仓储和邮政业	Transportation, Warehousing and Post	35 158	36 507	10 538	68 780	31 474
#交通运输	Transportation	34 916	35 752	10 213	69 420	31 504
邮政业	Postal	40 728	43 108			3 893
信息传输、计算机服务和软件业	Information Transmission, Computer Servcies and Software Industries	68 688	77 700	26 940	95 336	57 275
#信息传输	Information Transmission	95 816	80 926	28 287	144 773	97 919
批发和零售业	Retail and Wholesale	18 761	23 154	10 551	54 063	17 662
批发业	Wholesale	18 289	35 645	14 433	65 883	16 312
零售业	Retail	20 213	15 608	8 111	42 618	25 954
住宿和餐饮业	Hoteling and Catering	22 679	26 397	11 240	35 683	19 158
#餐饮业	Catering	18 896	22 912	9 776	35 668	17 431
金融业	Financial Industries	72 959	94 278		134 351	58 701
房地产业	Real Estate	34 075	40 355	30 325	49 147	30 555
租赁和商务服务业	Leasing and Business Services	21 553	26 603	15 319	145 796	17 867
科学研究、技术服务和地质勘查业	Scientific Research, Technological Service and Geological Prospecting	46 502	43 030	28 084	106 102	75 189
水利、环境和公共设施管理业	Water Conservancies Environmentand Public Facilities Management	33 028	35 007	19 615	30 608	30 056
居民服务和其他服务业	Resident Serviceand Other Services	16 178	13 823	12 846	15 287	16 598
教育	Education	39 501	40 309	15 981	52 021	17 157
卫生、社会保障和社会福利业	Healthcare, Social Security and Social Welfare	42 853	46 585	41 391	30 242	13 754
卫生	Healthcare	45 585	47 782	42 265	30 242	14 605
社会保障	SocialSecurity	20 492	30 376	30 228		13 145
社会福利业	SocialWelfare	32 978	33 932	22 046		15 431
文化、体育和娱乐业	Culture, Sportsand Entertainment	38 079	45 858	23 527	33 936	27 469
文化	Culture	39 165	49 255	29 357	45 859	27 463
体育	Sports	34 289	34 623	35 563	17 657	
娱乐业	Entertainment	25 699	31 293		27 873	28 371
公共管理和社会组织	Public Administrationand Social Organizations	42 703	42 834	34 466		

表9.7 主要年份离退休、退职人员养老金
LABOUR INSURANCE AND WELFARE FUNDS FOR RETIRED STAFF IN MAIN YEARS

指 标	Indicators	1990	2000	2005	2006
离退休、退职人员养老金(亿元)	**Labour Insurance and Welfare Funds for Nonworking Staff and Workers (100 million yuan)**	**19.47**	**205.14**	**346.60**	**394.20**
离休职工的离休费	Pensions for Retired Veteran Cadres	0.97	7.32	11.52	13.23
退休职工的退休费	Pensions for Retired	18.25	195.90	331.85	375.65
退职人员的退职生活费	Living Expenses for the Resigned	0.25	1.92	3.23	5.32

注：本表至表9.10由市劳动和社会保障局提供。
Note: This table to table 9.10 are provided by Shanghai Municipal Labour and Social Security Bureau.

表9.8 按登记注册类型分的离退休、退职人员养老金(2006)
WORKERS CLASSIFIED ACCORDING TO THE CATEGORIES OF REGISTRATION

指 标	Indicators	劳保福利费用 Labour Insurance and Welfare Funds	国有单位 State-owned Units	集体单位 Collective-owned Units	其他单位 Other Units
离退休、退职人员养老金(亿元)	**Labour Insurance and Welfare Funds for Nonworking Staff and Workers (100 million yuan)**	**394.20**	**245.16**	**52.90**	**96.14**
离休职工的离休费	Pensions for Retired Veteran Cadres	13.23	10.75	0.26	2.22
退休职工的退休费	Pensions for Retired	375.65	231.86	51.46	92.33
退职人员的退职生活费	Living Expenses for Resigned	5.32	2.55	1.18	1.59

注：本表"其他单位"包括港澳台及外商投资企业。
Note: "Other" in this table includes foreign invested and HongKong, Macau and Taiwan funded enterprises.

表9.9 主要年份职工福利费用
LABOUR INSURANCE AND WELFARE FUNDS FOR STAFF AND WORKERS IN MAIN YEARS

指 标	Indicators	1990	2000	2005	2006
职工劳保福利费(亿元)	**Labour Insurance and Welfare Funds for Working Staff and Workers (100 million yuan)**	**30.78**	**96.93**	**102.04**	**135.07**
集体福利事业补贴费和设施费	Subsidies for Collective Welfare Funds	5.49	8.54	14.10	31.31
文体宣传费	Expenses for Cultural Activities, Sports and Propaganda	0.44	1.34	1.54	9.44
其 他	Other	24.85	87.05	86.40	94.32

注：本表为在职职工口径(下表同)。
Note: The scope of data in this table refere to working staff and workers. (same as follow)

表9.10 按登记注册类型分的职工福利费用（2006）
WORKERS CLASSIFIED ACCORDING TO THE CATEGORIES OF REGISTRATION

指　标	Indicators	劳保福利费用 Labour Insurance and Welfare Funds	国有单位 State-owned Units	集体单位 Collective-owned Units	其他单位 Other Units
在职职工福利费(亿元)	**Welfare Funds for Working Staff and Workers (100 million yuan)**	**135.07**	**42.24**	**3.13**	**89.70**
集体福利事业补贴费和设施费	Subsidies for Collective Welfare Funds	31.31	7.63	0.95	22.73
文体宣传费	Expenses for Cultural Activities, Sports and Propaganda	9.44	0.72	0.08	8.64
其　他	Other	94.32	33.89	2.10	58.33

注：本表“其他单位”包括港澳台及外商投资企业。
Note: "Other" in this table includes foreign invested and HongKong, Macau and Taiwan funded enterprises.

表9.11 居民储蓄存款(1997～2006)
DEPOSITS OF RESIDENTS

年　份 Year	居民储蓄存款(亿元) Deposits of Residents (100 million yuan)	其中 of which: 定期储蓄 Time Account	其中 of which: 活期储蓄 Current Account	人均储蓄存款(元) Average Deposits
1997	2 109.18	1 843.25	265.93	13 851
1998	2 372.94	2 017.16	355.78	15 303
1999	2 597.12	2 119.82	477.30	16 447
2000	2 627.07	2 084.21	542.86	16 338
2001	3 109.50	2 301.33	808.17	19 218
2002	4 915.54	3 603.05	1 312.49	30 249
2003	6 054.60	4 260.87	1 793.73	35 390
2004	6 960.99	4 904.93	2 056.06	39 956
2005	8 432.49	6 071.83	2 360.66	47 416
2006	9 480.28	6 701.97	2 778.31	48 080

注：本表数据由中国人民银行上海总部提供。 2000 年起居民储蓄存款为中外资本外币存款余额。
Note: Data in this table are provided by Shanghai Headquarters of the People's Bank of China. Since 2000, the deposits of residents refered to all deposits in foreign and domestic currrency of foreign and domestic capital.

表9.12 城市居民家庭生活基本情况(1980～2006)
BASIC STATISTICS OF URBAN HOUSEHOLDS

年 份 Year	调查户数 (户) Number of Households Surveyed (household)	平均每户家庭人口 (人) Average Number Persons per Household (person)	平均每户就业人口 (人) Average Number of Employees per Household (person)	平均每户就业面 (%) Percentage of Emplyment per Household (%)	平均每一就业者负担人数 (人) Persons Supported by Each Employee (person)	平均每人可支配收入 (元) Average Per Capita Disposable Income (yuan)
1980	500	4.06	2.41	59.4	1.69	637
1981	500	4.06	2.47	60.8	1.65	637
1982	500	4.03	2.48	61.5	1.62	659
1983	500	4.00	2.52	63.0	1.58	691
1984	500	3.94	2.53	64.2	1.56	834
1985	500	3.72	2.27	61.0	1.64	1 075
1986	500	3.66	2.30	62.8	1.60	1 293
1987	500	3.55	2.20	62.0	1.61	1 437
1988	500	3.38	2.08	61.5	1.62	1 723
1989	500	3.27	2.00	61.2	1.63	1 975
1990	500	3.25	1.98	60.9	1.64	2 182
1991	500	3.18	1.91	60.1	1.67	2 486
1992	500	3.11	1.86	59.8	1.68	3 009
1993	500	3.03	1.77	58.4	1.71	4 277
1994	500	3.07	1.69	55.0	1.82	5 868
1995	500	3.11	1.65	53.1	1.88	7 172
1996	500	3.07	1.58	51.5	1.95	8 159
1997	500	3.08	1.58	51.3	1.94	8 439
1998	500	3.09	1.58	51.1	1.95	8 773
1999	500	3.08	1.74	56.5	1.78	10 932
2000	500	3.04	1.64	53.9	1.85	11 718
2001	500	3.00	1.55	51.7	1.94	12 883
2002	500	2.91	1.52	52.2	1.91	13 250
2003	500	2.99	1.55	51.8	1.93	14 867
2004	1 000	3.04	1.53	50.3	1.99	16 683
2005	1 000	3.01	1.55	51.5	1.94	18 645
2006	1 000	3.02	1.60	53.0	1.89	20 668

注：本表至表9.31为居民家庭收支抽样调查资料，由国家统计局上海调查总队提供。
Note: Data in this table to table 9.31 are obtained from the sample survey of households and provided by Survey Office of the National Bureau of Statistics in Shanghai.

表 9.12 续表 continued

年 份 Year	平均每人消费支出（元） Average Per Capita Consumption Expenditures (yuan)	其 中 of Which 服务性消费支出 Service Consumption Expenditures	服务性消费支出占消费支出比重(%) Percentage of Service Consumption Expenditures to the Total Expenditure (%)	平均每人可支配收入指数（以 1980 价格年为 100） Index of Per Capita Disposable Income (1980 = 100)	平均每人消费支出指数（以 1980 年价格为 100） Index of per Capita consumption Expenditures (1980 = 100)	恩格尔系数 Engel Coefficient
1980	553	75	13.6	100	100	56.0
1981	585	78	13.4	98.6	104.2	56.8
1982	576	82	14.3	101.8	102.4	58.8
1983	615	87	14.2	106.5	109.2	58.6
1984	726	101	13.9	125.8	126.1	56.5
1985	992	121	12.2	140.7	149.5	52.1
1986	1 170	136	11.7	159.2	166.0	52.7
1987	1 282	161	12.6	163.7	168.2	54.5
1988	1 648	170	10.3	163.4	180.1	52.6
1989	1 812	190	10.5	161.6	170.8	55.8
1990	1 937	233	12.0	167.9	171.7	56.5
1991	2 167	294	13.6	173.1	173.9	56.9
1992	2 509	376	15.0	190.6	183.1	55.9
1993	3 530	583	16.5	225.4	214.2	53.1
1994	4 669	762	16.3	249.5	228.7	53.5
1995	5 868	924	15.7	256.9	242.2	53.4
1996	6 763	1 263	18.7	267.6	255.6	50.7
1997	6 820	1 241	18.2	269.3	250.7	51.7
1998	6 866	1 371	20.0	280.0	252.4	50.6
1999	8 248	1 849	22.4	343.7	298.7	45.2
2000	8 868	2 231	25.2	359.4	313.3	44.5
2001	9 336	2 482	26.6	395.2	329.9	43.4
2002	10 464	3 033	29.0	438.4	365.7	39.4
2003	11 040	3 369	30.5	491.4	385.4	37.2
2004	12 631	4 084	32.3	539.6	431.5	36.4
2005	13 773	4 447	32.3	597.1	465.8	35.9
2006	14 762	4 841	32.8	654.0	493.3	35.6

注：平均每人可支配收入指数和平均每人消费支出指数是扣除价格因素后按同口径计算的。

Note: Index of per Caspita Disposable Income and Index of per Capita Consumption Expenditures are calculated by deducting prices according to the same caliber.

表9.13 城市居民家庭生活基本情况（2006，按收入水平分组）
BASIC STATISTICS OF URBAN HOUSEHOLD INCOME AND EXPENDITURES (2006, GROUPED BY INCOME LEVEL)

指标	Indicators	总平均 Total Average	低收入户 Low Income	中等偏下户 Medium-low Income
调查户数（户）	Number of Households Surveyed (household)	1 000	200	200
平均每户家庭人口（人）	Average Number of Persons Per Household (person)	3.02	3.10	3.10
平均每户就业人口（人）	Average Number of Employees Per Household (person)	1.60	1.37	1.59
平均每户就业面（%）	Percentage of Employment Per Household (%)	53.0	44.2	51.3
平均每一就业者负担人数（人）	Persons Supported by Each Employee (person)	1.89	2.26	1.95
可支配收入(元)	Average per Capita Disposable Income(yuan)	20 668	8 973	13 045
工薪收入	Salaries	13 962	5 554	8 197
经营净收入	Net Income from Household Business	959	273	432
财产性收入	Property Income	300	27	86
转移性收入	Transferred Income	5 447	3 119	4 330
#养老金或离退休金	Pensions and Retirement Pay	4 189	2 436	3 631
出售财物收入(元)	Income from Selling Properties(yuan)	1 027	2	1
借贷收入(元)	Averageper Capita Borrowing(yuan)	5 147	1 018	1 212
#住房借贷	Housing Loan	785		
提取储蓄存款	Pick up Savings Deposits	4 062	987	1 212
消费支出(元)	Average Per Capita Consumption Expenditures(yuan)	14 762	8 004	11 233
#服务性消费支出	Service Consumption Expenditure	4 841	2 515	3 495
购房与建房支出(元)	Buying and Building House Expenditure(yuan)	2 953	6	20
转移性支出(元)	Transferred Expenditure(yuan)	1 504	386	953
社会保障支出(元)	Social Security Expenditure(yuan)	1 771	746	1 050
借贷支出(元)	Lending Expenditure(yuan)	7 847	1 247	3 341

表9.13 续表 continued

指 标	Indicators	中等收入户 Medium Income	中等偏上户 Medium-high Income	高收入户 High Income
调查户数（户）	Number of Households Surveyed (household)	200	200	200
平均每户家庭人口（人）	Average Number of Persons Per Household (person)	2.95	3.03	2.91
平均每户就业人口（人）	Average Number of Employees Per Household (person)	1.49	1.70	1.87
平均每户就业面（%）	Percentage of Employment Per Household (%)	50.5	56.1	64.3
平均每一就业者负担人数（人）	Persons Supported by Each Employee (person)	1.98	1.78	1.56
可支配收入（元）	Averageper Capita Disposable Income(yuan)	16 774	22 994	42 884
工薪收入	Salaries	10 213	14 908	31 974
经营净收入	NetIncome from Household Business	564	738	2 893
财产性收入	Property Income	201	439	777
转移性收入	Transferred Income	5 796	6 909	7 240
#养老金或离退休金	Pensions and Retirement Pay	5 066	5 624	4 260
出售财物收入(元)	Income from Selling Properties(yuan)	1	1 602	3 660
借贷收入(元)	Averageper Capita Borrowing(yuan)	3 645	4 347	16 178
#住房借贷	Housing Loan	253	1 028	2 752
提取储蓄存款	Pickup Savings Deposits	3 210	3 279	12 118
消费支出(元)	Averageper Capita Consumption Expenditures(yuan)	13 142	15 815	26 325
#服务性消费支出	Service Consumption Expenditure	4 158	4 980	9 325
购房与建房支出(元)	Buyingand Building House Expenditure(yuan)	1 993	2 086	11 161
转移性支出(元)	Transferred Expenditure(yuan)	1 055	1 809	3 424
社会保障支出(元)	Social Security Expenditure(yuan)	1 457	1 814	3 920
借贷支出(元)	Lending Expenditure(yuan)	4 472	9 034	21 933

表9.14 主要年份城市居民家庭人均可支配收入
PER CAPITA DISPOSABLE INCOME OF URBAN HOUSEHOLDS IN MAIN YEARS

单位:元(yuan)

年 份 Year	人均可支配收入 Average per Capita Disposable Income	工薪收入 Salaries	经营性收入 Net Income from Household Business	财产性收入 Property Income	转移性收入 Transferred Income
1980	637	551			86
1985	1 075	795			280
1990	2 182	1 548	1	21	612
1991	2 486	1 780		29	677
1992	3 009	2 138	3	44	824
1993	4 277	3 099	4	37	1 137
1994	5 868	4 224	28	54	1 562
1995	7 172	5 002	69	92	2 009
1996	8 159	5 889	87	61	2 122
1997	8 439	5 969	150	69	2 251
1998	8 773	6 004	98	57	2 614
1999	10 932	7 326	156	68	3 382
2000	11 718	7 832	120	65	3 701
2001	12 883	7 975	119	39	4 750
2002	13 250	7 915	436	94	4 805
2003	14 867	10 097	377	130	4 263
2004	16 683	11 422	507	215	4 539
2005	18 645	12 409	798	292	5 146
2006	20 668	13 962	959	300	5 447

注：2002 年起，人均可支配收入不包括出售财物收入和个人交纳的社会保障支出。 其他年份按原口径计算。
Note： Per Capita Disposable exclude income from selling properties and social security expenditure from 2002.

表9.15 主要年份城市居民家庭人均可支配收入与消费支出
PER CAPITA ANNUAL DISPOSABLE INCOME AND CONSUMPTION EXPENDITURES OF URBAN HOUSEHOLDS IN MAIN YEARS

单位:元(yuan)

指 标	Indicators	2000	2005	2006
人均可支配收入	**Average per Capita Disposable Income**	**11 718**	**18 645**	**20 668**
低收入户	Low Income	6 840	7 851	8 973
中等偏下户	Medium-low Income	8 815	11 800	13 045
中等收入户	Medium Income	10 529	15 668	16 774
中等偏上户	Medium-high Income	12 892	21 313	22 994
高收入户	High Income	19 959	37 722	42 884
人均消费支出	**Average per Capita Consumption Expenditures**	**8 868**	**13 773**	**14 762**
低收入户	Low Income	6 272	7 698	8 004
中等偏下户	Medium-low Income	7 516	9 807	11 233
中等收入户	Medium Income	8 555	11 524	13 142
中等偏上户	Medium-high Income	9 445	15 024	15 815
高收入户	High Income	12 763	25 470	26 325

表 9.16 主要年份城市居民家庭人均消费支出
PER CAPITA CONSUMPTION EXPENDITURES OF URBAN HOUSEHOLDS IN MAIN YEARS

单位:元(yuan)

年 份 Year	消费支出 Total Consumption Expenditures	食 品 Food	衣 着 Clothing	家庭设备用品及服务 Household Facilities, Articles and Services	医 疗 保 健 Medicines and Medical Services	交通和通 信 Traffic and Communi-cations	教育文化娱乐服务 Education, Culture and Recreation Services	居 住 Residence	杂项商品和服务 Miscellanecus Commodities and Services
1980	553	310	79	50	7	20	49	26	12
1985	992	517	151	118	5	30	91	43	37
1990	1 937	1 095	208	196	11	58	231	90	48
1995	5 868	3 131	561	637	113	321	508	401	196
1996	6 763	3 429	590	614	148	496	827	416	243
1997	6 820	3 526	552	525	197	397	828	605	190
1998	6 866	3 477	472	453	261	406	893	674	230
1999	8 248	3 731	551	772	347	583	1 094	842	328
2000	8 868	3 947	567	683	501	759	1 287	794	330
2001	9 336	4 056	577	579	558	958	1 422	796	390
2002	10 464	4 120	613	653	734	1 115	1 668	1 189	372
2003	11 040	4 102	751	792	603	1 259	1 834	1 280	419
2004	12 631	4 593	797	780	762	1 703	2 195	1 327	474
2005	13 773	4 940	940	800	797	1 984	2 273	1 412	627
2006	14 762	5 249	1 027	877	763	2 333	2 432	1 436	645

表 9.17 主要年份城市居民家庭人均消费支出构成
COMPOSITION OF PER CAPITA CONSUMER EXPENDITURES OF URBAN HOUSEHOLDS IN MAIN YEARS

单位:%

年 份 Year	消费支出 Total Consumption Expenditures	食 品 Food	衣 着 Clothing	家庭设备用品及服务 Household Facilities Articles and Services	医 疗 保 健 Medicine and Medical Services	交通和通 信 Traffic and Communi-cations	教育文化娱乐服务 Education, Cultural and Recreation Services	居 住 Residence	杂项商品和服务 Miscellanecus Commodities and Services
1980	100	56.0	14.3	9.0	1.3	3.6	8.9	4.8	2.1
1985	100	52.1	15.3	11.9	0.5	3.0	9.2	4.3	3.7
1990	100	56.5	10.8	10.1	0.6	3.0	11.9	4.6	2.5
1995	100	53.4	9.6	10.9	1.9	5.5	8.6	6.8	3.3
1996	100	50.7	8.7	9.1	2.2	7.3	12.2	6.2	3.6
1997	100	51.7	8.1	7.7	2.9	5.8	12.1	8.9	2.8
1998	100	50.6	6.9	6.6	3.8	5.9	13.0	9.8	3.4
1999	100	45.2	6.7	9.3	4.2	7.1	13.3	10.2	4.0
2000	100	44.5	6.4	7.7	5.6	8.6	14.5	9.0	3.7
2001	100	43.4	6.2	6.2	6.0	10.3	15.2	8.5	4.2
2002	100	39.4	5.9	6.2	7.0	10.7	15.9	11.4	3.5
2003	100	37.2	6.8	7.2	5.4	11.4	16.6	11.6	3.8
2004	100	36.4	6.3	6.2	6.0	13.4	17.4	10.5	3.8
2005	100	35.9	6.8	5.8	5.8	14.4	16.5	10.2	4.6
2006	100	35.6	6.9	5.9	5.2	15.8	16.5	9.7	4.4

表9.18 主要年份城市居民家庭人均消费支出
PER CAPITA CONSUMPTION EXPENDITURES OF URBAN HOUSEHOLD IN MAIN YEARS

单位:元(yuan)

类别	Types	1990	2000	2005	2006
消费支出	**Total Consumption Expenditures**	**1 937**	**8 868**	**13 773**	**14 762**
食　品	Food	1 095	3 947	4 940	5 249
#粮　油	Grain and Oil	73	396	432	452
肉禽蛋水产品	Meat, Poultry, Eggs and Aquatic Products	426	1 324	1 345	1 352
蔬　菜	Vegetables	109	305	383	402
干鲜瓜果	Dry and Fresh Fruits	89	293	334	378
糕点、奶及奶制品	Cake, Milk and Dairy Products	65	315	379	410
在外饮食	Dining Out	135	710	1 331	1 482
衣　着	Clothing	208	567	940	1 027
#服　装	Garments	93	387	694	753
家庭设备用品及服务	Household Facilities, Articles and Services	196	683	800	877
#耐用消费品	Durable Consumer Goods	74	340	410	458
医疗保健	Medicines and Medical Services	11	501	797	763
#药品费	Medicines	7	244	334	327
滋补保健品	Medical Prouducts		169	235	194
交通和通信	Traffic and Communications	58	759	1 984	2 333
交　通	Traffic	53	375	1 161	1 396
#交通费	Traffic Fees	46	335	521	581
通　信	Communications	5	384	822	937
#电信费	Telecommunication Fees		272	654	743
教育文化娱乐服务	Education, Culture and Recreation Articles and Services	231	1 287	2 273	2 432
教　育	Education	23	585	1 136	1 225
#非义务学杂费	Tuition for Non-compulsory Education			564	574
义务学杂费	Tuition for Compulsory Education			27	24
成人教育费	Adult Education Fee		78	137	197
文化娱乐服务	Culture and Recreation Services	10	147	490	504
文化娱乐用品	Culture and Recreation Articles	198	555	647	703
#家用电脑	Computers		197	206	243
书报杂志	Books, Newspapers and Magazines	22	73	72	67
居　住	Residence	90	794	1 412	1 436
#水　费	Water	6	72	94	93
电　费	Electricity	31	258	341	354
燃料费	Fuels	17	157	173	169
租赁房房租	Rent	17	142	112	120
物业管理费	Estate Management Fee		20	123	122
杂项商品和服务	Miscellanecus Commodities and Services	48	330	627	645

表9.19 城市居民家庭人均消费支出（2006，按收入水平分组）
PER CAPITA CONSUMPTION EXPENDITURES OF URBAN HOUSEHOLD (2006, GROUPED BY INCOME LEVEL)

单位:元(yuan)

类别	Types	总平均 Total Average	低收入户 Low Income	中等偏下户 Medium-low Income
消费支出	**Total Consumer Expenditures**	**14 762**	**8 004**	**11 233**
食　品	Food	5 249	3 569	4 743
#粮　油	Grain and Oil	452	431	459
肉禽蛋水产品	Meat, Poultry, Eggs and Aquatic Products	1 352	1 115	1 353
蔬　菜	Vegetables	402	370	424
干鲜瓜果	Dry and Fresh Fruit	378	245	323
糕点、奶及奶制品	Cake, Milk and Dairy Products	410	275	342
在外饮食	Dining Out	1 482	625	1 088
衣　着	Clothing	1 027	406	707
#服　装	Garments	753	285	504
家庭设备用品及服务	Household Facilities Articles and Services	877	299	587
#耐用消费品	Durable Consumer Goods	458	143	324
医疗保健	Medicine and Medical Services	763	410	506
#药品费	Medicines	327	232	240
滋补保健品	Medical Prouducts	194	62	139
交通和通信	Traffic and Communications	2 333	838	1 245
交　通	Traffic	1 396	325	503
#交通费	Traffic Fees	581	262	406
通　信	Telecommunications	937	513	742
#电信费	Communication Fees	743	412	611
教育文化娱乐服务	Education, Culture and Recreation Articles and Services	2 432	1 570	1 892
教　育	Education	1 225	1 183	1 163
#非义务学杂费	Tuition for Non-compulsory Education	574	747	692
义务学杂费	Tuition for Compulsory Education	24	35	20
成人教育费	Adult Education Fee	197	35	104
文化娱乐服务	Culture and Recreation Services	504	135	234
文化娱乐用品	Culture and Recreation Articles	703	252	495
#家用电脑	Computers	243	126	215
书报杂志	Books, Newspapers and Magazines	67	31	42
居　住	Residence	1 436	720	1 176
#水　费	Water	93	79	91
电　费	Electricity	354	277	319
燃料费	Fuels	169	142	158
租赁房房租	Rent	120	69	125
物业管理费	Estate Management Fee	122	42	55
杂项商品和服务	Miscellanecus Commodities and Services	645	192	377

表 9.19 续表 continued

单位:元(yuan)

类别	Types	中等收入户 Medium Income	中等偏上户 Medium-high Income	高收入户 High Income
消费支出	**Total Consumer Expenditures**	**13 142**	**15 815**	**26 325**
食 品	Food	5 064	5 710	7 292
#粮 油	Grain and Oil	468	466	437
肉禽蛋水产品	Meat, Poultry, Eggs and Aquatic Products	1 406	1 466	1 429
蔬 菜	Vegetables	410	427	380
干鲜瓜果	Dry and Fresh Fruit	386	445	501
糕点、奶及奶制品	Cake, Milk and Dairy Products	424	450	571
在外饮食	Dining Out	1 187	1 611	2 985
衣 着	Clothing	901	1 159	2 023
#服 装	Garments	643	848	1 533
家庭设备用品及服务	Household Facilities Articles and Services	740	1 001	1 819
#耐用消费品	Durable Consumer Goods	362	534	957
医疗保健	Medicine and Medical Services	700	888	1 348
#药品费	Medicines	339	354	480
滋补保健品	Medical Prouducts	192	293	292
交通和通信	Traffic and Communications	1 651	2 190	5 948
交 通	Traffic	723	1 175	4 419
#交通费	Traffic Fees	589	621	1 063
通 信	Telecommunications	928	1 015	1 529
#电信费	Communication Fees	751	776	1 194
教育文化娱乐服务	Education, Culture and Recreation Articles and Services	2 269	2 503	4 026
教 育	Education	1 130	961	1 714
#非义务学杂费	Tuition for Non-compulsory Education	553	342	532
义务学杂费	Tuition for Compulsory Education	18	18	28
成人教育费	Adult Education Fee	160	196	510
文化娱乐服务	Culture and Recreation Services	427	642	1 121
文化娱乐用品	Culture and Recreation Articles	712	900	1 191
#家用电脑	Computers	212	302	366
书报杂志	Books, Newspapers and Magazines	67	93	103
居 住	Residence	1 331	1 582	2 433
#水 费	Water	93	99	104
电 费	Electricity	352	374	453
燃料费	Fuels	176	181	190
租赁房房租	Rent	127	162	119
物业管理费	Estate Management Fee	90	165	269
杂项商品和服务	Miscellanecus Commodities and Services	486	782	1 436

表 9.20 主要年份城市居民家庭平均每人主要消费品消费量
PER CAPITA CONSUMPTION OF MAJOR CONSUMER GOODS OF URBAN HOUSEHOLDS IN MAIN YEARS

商品名称	Name of Commodities	1990	2000	2005	2006
粮　食(千克)	Grain(kg)	82.7	68.8	59.5	60.7
食用植物油(千克)	Edible Vegetable Oil(kg)	9.3	11.0	9.5	9.5
猪　肉(千克)	Pork(kg)	20.3	17.3	18.7	19.0
牛羊肉(千克)	Beef and Mutton(kg)	2.1	2.2	2.6	2.8
家禽类(千克)	Poultry(kg)	8.4	15.1	12.4	11.4
蛋　类(千克)	Eggs(kg)	11.5	12.7	10.5	10.5
水产品类(千克)	Aquatic Products(kg)	22.8	27.6	26.0	26.0
鲜　菜(千克)	Vegetables(kg)	113.4	104.7	98.9	98.8
酒　类(千克)	Liquor(kg)	15.2	14.5	12.1	12.3
水果类(千克)	Fruits(kg)	55.9	74.3	66.2	68.2
鲜乳品和酸奶(千克)	Fresh Milk and Yogurt (kg)	22.5	29.4	29.6	29.7
服　装(件)	Clothing (unit)	6.1	7.3	8.9	9.3
生活用水(立方米)	Household Water Consumption (cubic meters)		53.3	53.0	51.7
生活用电(千瓦/时)	Household Power Consumption (kwh)		421.3	573.5	593.4
液化石油气(千卡)	Liquified Petroleum Gas (kc)	2.6	3.3	1.0	0.7
管道煤气(立方米)	Pipeline Gas (cubic meters)		155.7	141.5	139.6

表 9.21 主要年份平均每百户城市居民家庭年末耐用消费品拥有量
PER 100 URBAN HOUSEHOLDS YEAR-END POSSESSION OF DURABLE CONSUMER GOODS IN MAIN YEARS

商品名称	Name of Commodities	1990	2000	2005	2006
彩色电视机（台）	Color TV Set (unit)	77	147	177	179
照相机（架）	Camera (unit)	44	71	85	86
摄像机（架）	Video Camera (unit)		3	10	11
家用电脑（台）	Personal Computer (unit)		26	81	91
健身器材（台）	Gymnasfic Equipment (unit)		6	10	11
移动电话（部）	Mobile Phone (unit)		29	181	200
影碟机（台）	VCD Player (unit)		50	93	99
钢　琴（架）	Piano (unit)		3	4	5
组合音响（台）	Music Center (unit)	1	32	48	48
家用空调器（台）	Household Air Conditioner (unit)		96	168	175
洗衣机（台）	Washing Machine (unit)	72	93	97	98
电冰箱（台）	Household Refrigerator (unit)	88	102	104	104
热水淋浴器（台）	Water Heater (unit)		64	90	93
微波炉（台）	Microwave Oven (unit)		78	96	96
消毒碗柜(台)	Dish-sterilization Boxes(unit)			14	13

表 9.22 农村居民家庭生活基本情况(1990～2006) BASIC STATISTICS OF RURAL HOUSEHOLDS

年 份 Year	调查户数(户) Number of Households Surveyed (household)	平均每户人口(人) Average Number of Person per Household (person)	平均每户劳动力(人) Average Number of Labours per Household (person)	平均每一劳动力负担人数(人) Persons Supported by Each Person (person)	平均每人总收入(元) Average Gross Income Per Capita (yuan)	平均每人可支配收入(元) Average Disposable Income Per Capita (yuan)	平均每人总支出(元) Average Expenditures Per Capita (yuan)
1990	1000	3.68	2.46	1.49	1 990	1 665	1 592
1991	600	3.49	2.36	1.48	2 376	2 003	1 893
1992	600	3.43	2.36	1.46	2 581	2 226	2 322
1993	600	3.41	2.45	1.39	3 149	2 727	2 660
1994	600	3.41	2.51	1.36	3 940	3 437	3 320
1995	600	3.47	2.54	1.37	4 861	4 246	4 041
1996	600	3.40	2.54	1.34	5 506	4 846	4 581
1997	600	3.35	2.48	1.35	5 933	5 277	4 953
1998	600	3.33	2.50	1.33	5 965	5 407	4 924
1999	600	3.31	2.54	1.30	5 924	5 481	4 431
2000	600	3.31	2.53	1.31	6 400	5 565	5 578
2001	600	3.29	2.48	1.33	6 827	5 850	6 353
2002	600	3.33	2.52	1.32	7 080	6 212	6 988
2003	600	3.34	2.59	1.29	7 260	6 658	6 931
2004	600	3.33	2.54	1.31	7 994	7 337	7 580
2005	600	3.21	2.19	1.47	9 234	8 342	8 663
2006	600	3.20	2.24	1.43	10 225	9 213	9 344

表 9.22 续表 continued

年 份 Year	平均每人生活消费支出（元） per Capita Consumpition Expenditures (yuan)	平均每人可支配收入指数（以1990年为100） Index of per Capita Disposable Income (1990 = 100)	平均每人生活消费支出指数（以1990年为100） Index of Per Capita Consumption Expenditures (1990 = 100)	平均每人年底居住房屋面积（平方米） Average per Capita Living Space Year-end (sq. m)	平均每百户购买商品房面积（平方米） Commodity Housing Floor Space Purchased by Every 100 Households(sq. m)	平均每百户购买商品房金额（万元） Commodity Housing Value Purchased by Every 100 Households (10 000 yuan)
1990	1 262	100.0	100.0	37.08		
1991	1 540	120.3	122.0	39.60		
1992	1 967	133.7	155.7	42.07		
1993	2 200	163.8	174.3	44.22		
1994	2 715	206.4	215.1	44.15		
1995	3 368	255.0	266.9	43.08		
1996	3 868	291.1	306.5	45.47	159.20	8.27
1997	4 228	316.9	335.0	46.44	147.80	12.10
1998	4 207	324.7	333.4	47.24	128.70	12.10
1999	3 867	329.2	306.4	49.00	53.00	6.55
2000	4 138	336.1	327.9	53.58	48.30	5.30
2001	4 753	351.3	376.6	54.70	75.80	6.40
2002	5 311	373.1	420.8	57.08	196.80	20.90
2003	5 670	399.9	449.3	59.03	121.78	20.63
2004	6 329	440.7	502.0	59.84	126.50	23.84
2005	7 265	501.0	575.7	56.56	67.20	10.13
2006	8 006	553.3	634.4	59.99	57.80	17.64

①2000 年前平均每人可支配收入按纯收入口径计算，平均每人总收入不包括内部亲友赠送。

②根据国家统计局抽样调查方案规定，2005 年起，本市农村居民家庭抽样调查样本 600 户中，包括了由“农转居”进入郊区小城镇的 150 户居民家庭。

❶The per Capita Disposable Income before 2000 refers to the Net Income. The Gross Income excludes the donations from relatives and friends.

❷According to sample survey project of National Bureau of statistics, since 2005, there are one hundred and fifty households that move into small town in suburb among the six hundred sample of rural households.

表9.23 农村居民家庭人均可支配收入分组占全部户数比重（1990～2006）
PERCENTAGE OF RURAL HOUSEHOLDS IN TOTAL GROUPED BY DISPOSABLE INCOME

单位:%

年 份 Year	2 000 元以下 Below 2 000 yuan	2 000～3 000 元 2 000～3 000 yuan	3 000～4 000 元 3 000～4 000 yuan	4 000～5 000 元 4 000～5 000 yuan	5 000～6 000 元 5 000～6 000 yuan	6 000～7 000 元 6 000～7 000 yuan
1990	69.9	24.5	4.1	1.5		
1991	55.3	33.3	8.0	2.2	1.2	
1992	44.0	35.3	14.7	4.0	2.0	
1993	27.0	37.3	22.5	8.5	4.7	
1994	16.0	29.8	23.0	14.8	8.3	4.2
1995	9.5	19.5	23.2	17.2	13.0	7.5
1996	6.3	13.7	20.8	20.3	16.8	7.0
1997	5.0	11.5	18.8	17.5	14.8	12.3
1998	5.6	9.3	18.0	17.7	13.7	13.7
1999	6.5	11.3	17.7	17.5	11.2	10.0
2000	5.2	10.5	15.7	13.7	16.2	11.2
2001	5.0	11.2	12.5	12.8	13.3	14.3
2002	4.5	10.2	12.0	14.3	13.2	11.8
2003	2.8	7.8	11.8	12.5	12.5	13.3
2004	2.7	5.0	7.8	11.0	11.2	12.2
2005	3.5	4.3	8.8	9.8	10.7	9.0
2006	1.0	3.3	4.2	7.5	11.8	9.0

表9.23 续表1 continued

单位:%

年 份 Year	7 000～8 000 元 7 000～8 000 yuan	8 000～9 000 元 8 000～9 000 yuan	9 000～10 000 元 9 000～10 000 yuan	10 000～11 000 元 10 000～11 000 yuan	11 000 元以上 11 000 yuan Over
1994	1.3	1.2	0.7	0.7	
1995	4.0	1.8	1.8	2.5	
1996	5.7	4.0	2.5	2.9	
1997	5.5	6.2	2.0	6.4	
1998	7.3	4.7	3.2	6.8	
1999	8.0	5.7	4.0	2.7	5.4
2000	10.3	6.2	2.8	2.5	5.7
2001	9.0	6.7	4.3	3.0	7.9
2002	8.3	6.5	6.5	3.8	8.9
2003	8.8	8.9	6.7	3.9	11.0
2004	13.3	10.0	5.8	5.5	15.5
2005	11.5	6.7	6.2	6.7	22.8
2006	8.8	11.2	8.0	6.5	28.7

表 9.24 农村居民家庭人均可支配收入情况（1990～2006）
PER CAPITA DISPOSABLE INCOME OF RURAL HOUSEHOLDS

年 份 Year	人均可支配收入(元) Average Disposable Income per Capita (yuan)	工资性收入 Wages	家庭经营纯收入 Household Business Income	转移性和财产性收入 Property and Transferred Income	比重(以人均可支配收入为100) Proportion(Average Disposable Income Per Capita = 100)		
					工资性收入 Wages	家庭经营纯收入 Household Business Income	转移性和财产性收入 Property and Transferred Income
1990	1 665	1 066	539	60	64.0	32.4	3.6
1991	2 003	1 235	681	87	61.7	34.0	4.3
1992	2 226	1 454	685	87	65.3	30.8	3.9
1993	2 727	1 662	949	116	60.9	34.8	4.3
1994	3 437	2 112	1 084	241	61.5	31.5	7.0
1995	4 246	2 734	1 183	329	64.4	27.9	7.7
1996	4 846	3 240	1 278	328	66.9	26.4	6.7
1997	5 277	3 736	1 226	315	70.8	23.2	6.0
1998	5 407	3 869	1 185	353	71.6	21.9	6.5
1999	5 481	4 192	929	360	76.5	16.9	6.6
2000	5 565	4 310	934	321	77.4	16.8	5.8
2001	5 850	4 491	967	392	76.8	16.5	6.7
2002	6 212	4 920	774	518	79.2	12.5	8.3
2003	6 658	5 284	813	561	79.4	12.2	8.4
2004	7 337	5 757	886	694	78.5	12.1	9.4
2005	8 342	6 364	811	1 167	76.3	9.7	14.0
2006	9 213	6 892	766	1 555	74.8	8.4	16.8

注：2000 年前平均每人可支配收入按纯收入口径计算。
Note: The per Capita Annual Disposable Income before 2000 refers to the Net Income.

表 9.25 农村居民家庭人均可支配收入和人均生活消费支出（1995～2006）
PER CAPITA DISPOSABLE INCOME AND LIVING EXPENDITURES FOR CONSUMPTION OF RURAL HOUSEHOLDS

单位：元(yuan)

年 份 Year	总平均 Average	低收入户 Low Income	中等偏下户 Medium-low Income	中等收入户 Medium Income	中等偏上户 Medium-high Income	高收入户 High Income
人均可支配收入	**Average per Capita Disposable Income**					
1995	4 246	1 951	3 071	3 899	5 044	7 593
1996	4 846	2 228	3 504	4 399	5 546	8 760
1997	5 277	2 361	3 727	4 854	6 222	9 461
1998	5 407	2 385	3 849	4 965	6 392	9 738
1999	5 481	2 212	3 692	4 883	6 528	10 266
2000	5 565	2 330	3 906	5 264	6 725	10 405
2001	5 850	2 351	4 078	5 649	7 122	10 930
2002	6 212	2 429	4 266	5 701	7 513	11 989
2003	6 658	2 761	4 621	6 213	7 972	12 777
2004	7 337	3 122	5 148	7 006	8 775	13 652
2005	8 342	3 347	5 594	7 612	9 755	15 309
2006	9 213	3 830	6 194	8 412	10 714	16 843
人均生活消费支出	**Average per Capita Consumption Expenditures**					
1995	3 368	1 813	2 680	2 704	3 408	6 546
1996	3 868	2 229	2 860	3 182	4 221	6 995
1997	4 228	2 558	3 334	3 986	4 866	6 532
1998	4 207	2 468	3 163	3 347	4 871	7 362
1999	3 867	2 275	2 940	4 181	4 279	5 909
2000	4 138	2 390	3 387	3 887	5 487	5 880
2001	4 753	2 921	3 250	4 334	5 356	8 449
2002	5 311	2 350	4 341	4 834	5 873	9 683
2003	5 670	2 886	3 681	5 363	6 286	10 769
2004	6 329	4 076	4 914	5 309	6 992	10 971
2005	7 265	4 618	5 690	6 317	7 059	12 975
2006	8 006	4 788	6 001	6 951	8 015	15 058

表9.26 农村居民家庭人均生活消费支出(1990～2006)
PER CAPITA CONSUMPTION EXPENDITURES OF RURAL HOUSEHOLDS

单位:元(yuan)

年份 Year	生活消费支出 Total Consumption Expenditures	食品 Food	衣着 Clothing	居住 Residence	家庭设备用品及服务 Household Facilities, Articles and Services	交通和通信 Traffic and Communi-cations	文教娱乐用品及服务 Education, Culture and Recreation Articles and Services	医疗保健 Medicines and Medical Services	其他商品和服务 Other Commodities and Services
1990	1 262	586	107	272	129	6	59	33	70
1991	1 540	739	134	324	151	15	85	35	57
1992	1 967	853	148	451	232	31	121	45	86
1993	2 200	1 022	157	357	259	65	220	50	70
1994	2 715	1 315	213	454	267	79	222	75	90
1995	3 368	1 491	233	761	284	159	256	73	111
1996	3 868	1 657	256	816	363	200	347	108	121
1997	4 228	1 756	267	921	338	240	414	174	118
1998	4 207	1 775	239	876	369	226	463	170	89
1999	3 867	1 669	202	681	389	197	474	160	95
2000	4 138	1 823	201	724	225	279	559	209	118
2001	4 753	1 915	226	890	294	340	673	265	150
2002	5 311	1 872	226	1 392	281	462	661	280	137
2003	5 670	2 004	250	1 437	297	587	676	333	86
2004	6 329	2 191	280	1 446	344	720	806	425	117
2005	7 265	2 676	367	1 323	458	739	936	562	204
2006	8 006	3 024	418	1 658	481	780	920	549	176

表9.27 农村居民家庭人均生活消费支出构成(1990～2006)
COMPOSITION OF PER CAPITA CONSUMER EXPENDITURES OF RURAL HOUSEHOLDS

单位:%

年份 Year	生活消费支出 Total Consumption Expenditures	食品 Food	衣着 Clothing	居住 Residence	家庭设备用品及服务 Household Facilities, Articles and Services	交通和通信 Traffic and Communi-cations	文教娱乐用品及服务 Education, Culture and Recreation Articles and Services	医疗保健 Medicines and Medical Services	其他商品和服务 Other Commodities and Services
1990	100	46.4	8.5	21.6	10.2	0.5	4.7	2.6	5.5
1991	100	48.0	8.7	21.0	9.8	1.0	5.5	2.3	3.7
1992	100	43.4	7.5	22.9	11.8	1.6	6.1	2.3	4.4
1993	100	46.4	7.1	16.2	11.8	3.0	10.0	2.3	3.2
1994	100	48.4	7.9	16.7	9.8	2.9	8.2	2.8	3.3
1995	100	44.3	6.9	22.6	8.4	4.7	7.6	2.2	3.3
1996	100	42.8	6.6	21.1	9.4	5.2	9.0	2.8	3.1
1997	100	41.5	6.3	21.8	8.0	5.7	9.8	4.1	2.8
1998	100	42.2	5.7	20.8	8.8	5.4	11.0	4.0	2.1
1999	100	43.1	5.2	17.6	10.1	5.1	12.3	4.1	2.5
2000	100	44.0	4.9	17.5	5.4	6.7	13.5	5.1	2.9
2001	100	40.3	4.7	18.7	6.2	7.1	14.2	5.6	3.2
2002	100	35.2	4.3	26.2	5.3	8.7	12.4	5.3	2.6
2003	100	35.4	4.4	25.3	5.2	10.4	11.9	5.9	1.5
2004	100	34.6	4.4	22.9	5.4	11.4	12.7	6.7	1.9
2005	100	36.8	5.1	18.2	6.3	10.2	12.9	7.7	2.8
2006	100	37.8	5.2	20.7	6.0	9.7	11.5	6.9	2.2

表 9.28 农村居民家庭人均可支配收入（2006，按收入水平分组）
AVERAGE PER CAPITA DISPOSABLE INCOME OF RURAL HOUSEHOLDS (2006,GROUPED BY INCOME LEVEL)

单位:元(yuan)

指 标	Indicators	总平均 Total Average	4 000 元以下 Below 4 000 yuan	4 000 ~5 000 元 4 000 ~5 000 yuan	5 000 ~6 000 元 5 000 ~6 000 yuan
平均每人可支配收入	**Average per Capita Disposable Income**	**9 213**	**2 828**	**4 513**	**5 519**
工资性收入	Wage	6 892	1 817	3 463	4 085
在非企业组织中劳动得到	Gained from Non-enterprise Organizations	1 095	32	186	487
在本乡地域内劳动得到	Gained from Local Enterpreses	4 490	1 301	2 922	2 934
#在本地乡镇企业劳动得到	Gained from Local Township Enterprises	2 423	1 008	1 729	1 617
常住人口外出从业得到	Gained from Outgoing Employment by Resident	1 307	484	355	664
家庭经营纯收入	Household Business Income	766	469	520	444
#农业纯收入	Agricultural Income	510	518	474	368
财产性收入	Property Income	556	174	96	236
#利息收入	Interest Income	24	1		23
租金收入	Rental Income	343	150	77	123
土地征用补偿	Compensation for Land Requisition	87	7	5	35
转移性收入	Transferred Income	999	368	434	754
#离退休金、养老金	Pension	879	349	331	750

表 9.28 续表 continued

单位:元(yuan)

指 标	Indicators	6 000 ~7 000 元 6 000 ~7 000 yuan	7 000 ~8 000 元 7 000 ~8 000 yuan	8 000 ~10 000 元 8 000 ~10 000 yuan	10 000 元以上 Over 10 000 yuan
平均每人可支配收入	**Average per Capita Disposable Income**	**6 488**	**7 493**	**8 973**	**14 786**
工资性收入	Wage	4 198	5 734	6 639	11 331
在非企业组织中劳动得到	Gained from Non-enterprise Organizations	523	417	964	2 250
在本乡地域内劳动得到	Gained from Local Enterpreses	2 756	4 197	4 208	7 028
#在本地乡镇企业劳动得到	Gained from Local Township Enterprises	1 664	2 465	2 745	3 271
常住人口外出从业得到	Gained from Outgoing Employment by Resident	919	1 120	1 467	2 053
家庭经营纯收入	Household Business Income	559	786	713	1 106
#农业纯收入	Agricultural Income	496	512	622	505
财产性收入	Property Income	313	250	609	1 008
#利息收入	Interest Income	18	7	19	45
租金收入	Rental Income	225	157	354	618
土地征用补偿	Compensation for Land Requisition	34	7	85	186
转移性收入	Transferred Income	1 418	723	1 012	1 341
#离退休金、养老金	Pension	1 309	585	1 005	1 072

注：常住人口外出是以乡镇为界线。
Note: The criterion which differentiates local and outgoing employment of permanent residents is the geographical border of towns.

表 9.29 农村居民家庭人均总支出（2006，按可支配收入水平分组）
PER CAPITA EXPENDITURES OF RURAL HOUSEHOLDS (2006,GROUPED BY INCOME LEVEL)

单位：元(yuan)

指标	Indicators	总平均 Total Average	4 000 元以下 Below 4 000 yuan	4 000～5 000 元 4 000～5 000 yuan	5 000～6 000 元 5 000～6 000 yuan
平均每人总支出	**Per Capita Expenditures**	**9 344**	**4 444**	**6 634**	**5 916**
#生活消费支出	Consumption Expenditures	8 006	3 626	5 925	5 069
食品	Food	3 024	1 983	2 201	2 466
衣着	Clothing	418	163	197	298
居住	Residence	1658	337	1 560	457
家庭设备用品及服务	Household Faclities, Articles and Services	481	161	378	210
交通通信	Traffic and Communications	780	304	645	506
文教娱乐用品及服务	Education,Culture and Recreation Articles and Services	920	384	649	682
医疗保健	Medicine and Medical Services	549	241	213	357
其他	Others	176	53	82	93
家庭经营支出	Household Business Expenditures	528	388	313	298
#种植业生产费用	Farming Costs	128	175	179	139
牧业生产费用	Animal Husbandry Costs	62	93	121	76
购置生产性固定资产	Buying Productive Fixed Assets	23	18		5
财产性支出	Property Expenditures	2	1		
转移性支出	Transferred Expenditures	780	409	393	543

表 9.29 续表 continued

单位：元(yuan)

指标	Indicators	6 000～7 000 元 6 000～7 000 yuan	7 000～8 000 元 7 000～8 000 yuan	8 000～10 000 元 8 000～10 000 yuan	10 000 元以上 Over 10 000 yuan
平均每人总支出	**Per Capita Expenditures**	**8 058**	**8 377**	**8 726**	**13 555**
#生活消费支出	Consumption Expenditures	6 845	5 729	7 647	11 935
食品	Food	2 596	2 694	2 975	3 944
衣着	Clothing	339	241	409	659
居住	Residence	1 527	634	1 266	3 037
家庭设备用品及服务	Household Faclities, Articles and Services	377	372	623	666
交通通信	Traffic and Communications	563	670	779	1 132
文教娱乐用品及服务	Education,Culture and Recreation Articles and Services	885	748	840	1 321
医疗保健	Medicine and Medical Services	437	246	553	898
其他	Others	121	124	202	278
家庭经营支出	Household Business Expenditures	456	1 871	201	530
#种植业生产费用	Farming Costs	106	176	104	108
牧业生产费用	Animal Husbandry Costs	236	15	32	15
购置生产性固定资产	Buying Productive Fixed Assets	17	184	8	
财产性支出	Property Expenditures			6	2
转移性支出	Transferred Expenditures	717	590	863	1 080

表9.30 主要年份农村居民家庭平均每人主要消费品消费量
PER CAPITA CONSUMPTION OF MAJOR CONSUMER GOODS OF RURAL HOUSEHOLDS IN MAIN YEARS

商品名称	Name of Commodities	1990	2000	2005	2006
粮　食（千克）	Grain (kg)	236.49	222.27	146.16	160.58
#稻　谷	Rice	229.92	205.25	134.33	152.14
豆类及豆制品(千克)	Beans and Their Products(kg)		5.71	8.05	7.19
油脂类（千克）	Edible Oil (kg)	7.92	7.99	8.62	8.17
蔬菜及菜制品(千克)	Vegetables and Their Products(kg)	119.89	92.41	70.59	66.84
肉禽及其制品（千克）	Meat, Poultry and Their Products (kg)	21.88	29.68	36.48	35.92
蛋类及蛋制品（千克）	Eggs and Their Products (kg)	8.38	10.71	7.66	7.68
奶及奶制品（千克）	Milk and Dairy Products(kg)		2.07	9.12	9.68
水产品（千克）	Aquatic Products (kg)	9.82	14.51	19.12	20.64
#鱼　类	Fish		10.11	12.14	12.90
虾、贝、蟹类	Shrimp,Testacean,Crab		2.61	4.70	5.39
水果及水果制品(千克)	Fruits and Their Products(kg)	21.00	36.94	29.52	33.21
食　糖（千克）	Suger (kg)	3.59	2.47	1.92	1.86
卷　烟（盒）	Cigarette (case)	58.59	44.49	49.46	50.66
酒（千克）	Liquor (kg)	12.71	16.58	18.23	18.31

表9.31 主要年份平均每百户农村居民家庭年末耐用消费品拥有量
PER 100 RURAL HOUSEHOLD YEAR-END POSSESSION OF DURABLE CONSUMER GOODS IN MAIN YEARS

商品名称	Name of Commodities	1990	2000	2005	2006
黑白电视机（台）	Black/ White TV Set (unit)	74	61	21	19
彩色电视机（台）	Color TV Set (unit)	25	97	157	167
电风扇（台）	Electric Fans (unit)	204	326	306	299
电冰箱（台）	Household Refrigerator (unit)	29	74	89	94
洗衣机（台）	Washing Machine (unit)	45	69	86	89
录音机（台）	Recorder (unit)	27	38	26	25
影碟机（台）	VCD Player (unit)		27	33	31
轻骑、摩托车（辆）	Moped and Motorcycle (vehicle)	1	73	72	74
家用空调器（台）	Household Air Conditioner (unit)		14	84	99
抽油烟机（台）	Cooking Soat Inducer (unit)		35	60	65
微波炉（台）	Microwave Oven (unit)		14	66	71
吸尘器（台）	Vacuam Cleaner (unit)		9	21	24
热水淋浴器（台）	Water Heater (unit)		44	78	83
移动电话（部）	Mobile Phone (unit)		19	130	148
家用电脑（台）	Personal Computer (unit)		5	32	38

上 / 海 / 统 / 计 / 年 / 鉴

主要统计指标解释

■ 从业人员报酬

指各单位在一定时期内直接支付给本单位全部从业人员的劳动报酬总额。包括在岗职工工资总额和本单位其他从业人员劳动报酬两部分。

■ 职工工资总额

指在报告期内直接支付给本单位职工的劳动报酬或生活费。职工工资总额包括在岗职工工资和离岗职工生活费两部分。

在岗职工工资是指单位在报告期内直接支付给本单位在岗职工的劳动报酬。包括计时工资、计件工资、计件标准工资、奖金和计件超额工资、津贴和补贴、加班加点工资和其他工资。

(1)计时工资是指按计时工资标准和工作时间支付给个人的劳动报酬。

(2)计件工资是指对已做工作按计件单价支付的劳动报酬。

(3)计件标准工资是指实行计件工资制的单位,按照批准的计件单价和规定的劳动定额或工作量支付给计件工人的劳动报酬。

(4)奖金和计件超额工资.奖金是指支付给在岗职工的超额劳动报酬和增收节支的劳动报酬。计件超额工资是计件工资的一部分，按计件工人超额完成定额任务后所得的工资。

(5)津贴和补贴:是指为了补偿职工特殊或额外的劳动消耗和因其他特殊原因支付给职工的津贴，以及为了保证职工工资水平不受物价影响支付给职工的物价补贴。津贴包括补偿职工特殊或额外劳动消耗的津贴及岗位性津贴、保健性津贴、技术性津贴、年功性津贴,地区津贴、其他津贴。补贴包括:为保证职工工资水平不受物价上涨或变动影响而支付的各种补贴，如副食品价格补贴(含肉类等价格补贴)、粮、油、蔬菜等价格补贴、煤价补贴、房贴、水电贴、房改补贴以及提高煤炭价格后,部分地区实行的民用燃料和照明电价格补贴等。

(6)加班加点工资是指对法定节假日和公休假日工作的职工，以及在正常工作日以外延长工作时间的职工按规定支付的加班工资和加点工资。

(7)其他工资是指其他根据国家规定支付的工资。如附加工资、保留工资以及调整工资补发的上年工资等。

离岗职工生活费是离岗职工已不在本单位从事其他工作但仍保留劳动关系期间从本单位领取的生活费。

■ 职工平均工资

指企业、事业、机关单位的职工在一定时期内平均每人所得的货币工资额。它表明一定时期职工工资收入的高低程度，是反映职工工资水平的主要指标。计算公式为:

职工平均工资 = 报告期实际支付的全部职工工资总额 / 报告期全部职工平均人数

■ 城市居民可支配收入

指居民可用于最终消费支出和其他非义务性支出以及储蓄的总和,即居民家庭可以用来自由支配的收入。它是家庭总收入扣除交纳的所得税、个人交纳的社会保障费以及调查户的记账补贴后的收入。不包括出售财物和借贷收入。

■ 城市居民家庭消费支出

指城市居民家庭用于日常生活的全部支出。包括食品、衣着、家庭设备用品及服务、医疗保健、交通和通信、教育文化娱乐服务、居住、杂项商品和服务等八大类。

■ 城市居民家庭人均服务性消费支出

指调查户用于本家庭支付社会提供的各种文化和生活方面的非商品性服务费用。服务性消费的特点在于其劳动过程和消费过程在时间与空间上的统一。在居民家庭八大类消费中,服务性消费支出包括:1、食品类中加工服务费和部分在外饮食费用; 2、衣着类中衣着加工服务费;3、家庭设备用品及服务类中家庭服务(如家政服务费用);4、医疗保健类中医疗费(如诊疗费、上门出诊费、护工费用);5、交通和通信类中交通工具服务费(如汽车使用、维修费用)、交通费中使用飞机、轮船、火车等交通工具费用、通信服务费(如电信费、邮费);6、教育文化娱乐服务类中文化娱乐服务费(如参观、游览费用、健身活动费、团体旅游、其他文娱活动费)、文娱用品修理服务费、教育费(如义务、非义务教育支出)、成人教育支出、家教费、培训班费用、择校费;7、居住类中租赁费用、部分房屋装潢费用(人工费用)、居住服务费(如物业管理、维修费

主要统计指标解释

用);8、杂项商品和服务(如美容、洗澡、理发费用,旅馆住宿等费用)。

■ 城乡居民储蓄存款余额

指某一时点城乡居民存入银行及农村信用社的储蓄金额,包括城镇居民储蓄存款和农民个人储蓄存款,不包括居民的手存现金和工矿企业、部队、机关、团体等单位存款。

■ 农村居民可支配收入

指一定时期内农村居民总收入中，扣除家庭经营费用支出、生产性固定资产折旧、交纳税金和上交承包金、公益性及转移支付后的(包括养老、失业、合作医疗、保险基金及罚款等支付),可用于生活消费、生产投资和储蓄的收入。它与纯收入的主要区别是扣除了转移性支付,加上实际得到的公益性及转移性收入后的余额。农村居民可支配收入包括:工资性收入、家庭经营净收入、财产性收入、转移性净收入。

■ 农村居民家庭生活消费支出

指农村住户用于物质生活和精神生活方面的支出。包括食品,衣着,居住,家庭设备用品及服务,医疗保健,交通和通信,文化教育娱乐用品及服务,其他商品和服务等消费支出。

■ 财产性收入

指金融资产或有形非生产性资产的所有者向其他机构单位提供资金或将有形非生产性资产供其支配，作为回报而从中获得的收入。

■ 转移性收入

指农村住户和住户成员无须付出任何对应物而获得的货物、服务、资金或资产所有权等,不包括无偿提供的用于固定资本形成的资金。一般情况下,是指农村住户在二次分配中的所有收入。

SHANGHAI STATISTICAL YEARBOOK

EXPLANATORY NOTES TO MAJOR STATISTICAL INDICATORS

□ Compensation of Employees

Compensation of Employees refers to total payment by various units to their employees during a certain period of time, including wages to permanent staff and workers and payment to other employees.

□ Total Wages of Staff and Workers

Total Wages of Staff and Workers refers to the compensation for services or living cost a unit pays to its employees on the payroll, including the living cost paid to those not on duty.

Wages of working staff and workers refers to the compensation for services paid to its employees who are on duty, including time wages, piece rate wage, standard piece-rate wage, bonuses and extra piece-rate wages, allowances and subsidies, overtime payment and other remunerations.

(1)Time wages refer to the payment for services rated on the hourly system.

(2)Piece rate wages refer to payment for work rated on the piece system.

(3)Standard piece-rate wages refer to payment a unit pays to a worker according to a rate approved by an authority.

(4)Bonus and extra piece-rate wages. Bonus refers to the payment to an on-duty employee for his or her work above their quota and for their work in increasing production and savings for the unit. Extra piece-rate wages are part of the piece-rate wages and paid for the work an employee finishes above his or her quota.

(5)Allowances and subsidies refer to the compensation paid for special or extra services, the loss the price factors cost an employee, or for other reasons. Allowances refer to payment for special or extra services or special fund for post, healthcare, professional skills, yearly achievement, regional economic gap and other reasons. Subsidies are paid to secure an employee's salary against the fluctuating prices, including price compensation for non-staple food (such as meat products), grain, oil, vegetable, coal, housing, tap water, housing reforms, as well as price compensation paid during a coal price hike for consumption of fuel and power in some regions.

(6) Overtime payment is paid to employees for work he or she does during state holidays amd other holidays or outside the working hours.

(7) Other remunerations refer to the payment stipulated by the state, such as extra salary, reserve salary and money paid for the previous year arising from a salary raise.

Living cost for off-duty employees refer to the payment for living cost to an employee who keeps his or her labor relationship with a unit though they are not working for it.

□ Average Wages of Staff and Workers

Average Wages of Staff and Workers refers to the average wage in money terms per person during a certain period of time for staff and workers in enterprises, institutions, and government agencies, which reflects the general level of wage income during a certain period of time and is calculated as follows:

Average Wages of Staff and Workers = Total Wages of Staff and Workers at Reference Time /Average Number of Staff and Workers at Reference Time.

□ Disposable Income of Urban Households

Disposable Income of Urban Households refers to the actual income at the disposal of members of the households which can be used for final consumption, other non-compulsory expenditure and savings, which is part of the urban households' income that can be disposed by the urban households themselves. It is the income after deducting personal income tax, social insurance paid by individuals and investigation allowance from the total income of the households. The income from selling properties and borrowing are not included.

□ Consumption Expenditures of Urban Households

Consumption Expenditures of Urban Households refer to all the expenditures paid by urban households for consumption in daily life, including 8 categories as follows: food; clothing; household facilities, articles and services; medical care; traffic and telecommunication; education, culture and recreation services; housing; miscellaneous commodities and services.

□ Urbanities' Per-capita Spending on Srvices

Urbanities' Per-capita Spending on Services refers to urbanites pay for services rather than commodities. Services are of-

EXPLANATORY NOTES TO MAJOR STATISTICAL INDICATORS

fered and consumed at the same time and place. The service spending for an urban family falls into the following eight types: 1. Money paid for food processing and money spent while eating out; 2. Money paid for clothing processing; 3. Domestic services and services for home amenities; 4. Medical cost (including medical diagnosis and treatment, in-home medical services and nursing cost); 5. Transport tool service fees (such as for the use of a car and maintenance fee thereby arising), transport tools (plane, ship, train) fees, post and telecommunications fees; 6. Fees for culture and entertainment services (such as tour and fitness building), fees for repair of sports and entertainment items, education cost (spending on obligatory and non-obligatory education), adult education cost, tutor fees, training courses fees and extra money paid as sponsorship fee to a school a student outside his or her education community; 7. Housing rents, some interior decoration cost (for labor), residence service fees (such as for property management and repairs); 8. Fees for other services (such as at a beauty salon, bathhouse, hairdresser's and hotels).

□ Deposits of Residents

Deposits of Residents refer to the total value of saving deposits of urban and rural households in banks and rural credit cooperatives at a given point of time, including the saving deposit of urban households and the savings deposit of rural households. The cash in hand by households and the deposits of organizations such as enterprises, military units, government agencies, institutions, etc. are not included.

□ Disposable Income of Rural Households

Disposable Income of Rural Households refers to the part of the rural households' income in a certain period after deducting family business expenditure, depreciation of productive fixed assets, taxes, contract expenditure, welfare funds and transferred expenditure, (including pensions, unemployment relief, cooperative medical funds, premiums and fines), which can be used for personal consumption, production investment and deposit. It differs from the net income in that it is the balance of the actual welfare and transferred income after deducting transferred expenditure. The disposable income includes: wages and salaries, net income from household business, property income, net transferred income.

□ Living Expenditures for Consumption of Rural Households

Living Expenditures for Consumption of Rural Households refer to expenditures of material and culture life of rural household, including expenses on food, clothing, housing, household appliances and service, medical and health care, traffic and communication items, cultural, education and recreation items and service and other commodities and service.

□ Property Income

Property Income refers to the income received as returns by owners of financial assets or tangible non-productive assets by providing capitals or tangible non-productive assets to other institutional units.

□ Transferred Income

Transferred Income refers to the receipt by rural households and their members of goods, services, capitals or rights of assets without giving or repaying accordingly, excluding capitals provided to them for the formation of fixed assets. In general, it refers to all income received by rural households through redistribution.

第十篇

CHAPTER 10

城市建设

URBAN CONSTRUCTION

表 10.1 主要年份城市基础设施投资额
URBAN INFRASTRUCTURE INVESTMENT IN MAIN YEARS

单位:亿元(100 million yuan)

年份 Year	合计 Total	其中 of which						
		电力建设 Electric Power	运输邮电 Transportation, Postal and Telecommunications	其中 of which		公用设施 Facilities for Public Use	其中 of which	
				交通运输 Transportation	邮电通信 Postal and Telecommunications		公用事业 Public Utilities	市政建设 Civil Construction
1950～1978	60.08	19.71	23.25	19.41	3.84	17.12	6.85	10.27
1980	9.55	5.31	2.91	2.31	0.60	1.33	0.64	0.69
1985	23.49	3.97	6.75	5.52	1.23	12.77	7.88	4.89
1986	24.78	5.68	8.40	6.56	1.84	10.70	5.67	5.03
1987	32.64	9.31	12.39	10.02	2.37	10.94	5.36	5.58
1988	37.08	14.18	12.35	8.80	3.55	10.55	4.01	6.54
1989	36.09	11.69	9.96	6.16	3.80	14.44	6.84	7.60
1990	47.22	17.53	10.06	7.17	2.90	19.63	10.83	8.80
1991	61.38	19.79	19.07	14.49	4.58	22.52	9.15	13.37
1992	84.35	19.70	21.44	15.01	6.43	43.21	12.58	30.63
1993	167.94	25.77	46.44	31.75	14.69	95.73	37.91	57.82
1994	238.16	41.57	72.68	36.83	35.85	123.91	26.77	97.14
1995	273.78	57.33	79.36	25.94	53.42	137.09	35.03	102.06
1996	378.78	77.61	147.21	69.66	77.55	153.96	48.31	105.65
1997	412.85	80.24	146.10	85.06	61.04	186.51	52.24	134.27
1998	531.38	89.58	181.46	108.79	72.67	260.34	58.37	201.97
1999	501.39	83.05	166.16	102.24	63.92	252.18	64.20	187.98
2000	449.90	64.61	117.52	48.83	68.69	267.77	104.43	163.34
2001	510.78	72.22	168.42	60.72	107.70	270.14	92.25	177.89
2002	583.49	62.14	171.24	63.01	108.23	350.11	148.42	201.69
2003	604.62	66.00	350.35	273.77	76.58	188.28	36.91	151.36
2004	672.58	89.52	371.35	316.96	54.39	211.71	26.92	184.80
2005	885.74	124.22	443.90	385.58	58.32	317.62	41.33	276.28
2006	1 125.54	116.23	703.24	589.52	113.72	306.07	56.23	249.84

注：本表各项投资额均不包括住宅建设投资。从2003年起，交通运输投资包括公用设施中市内公共交通投资(下表同)。

Note: All items in this table exclude Investment in Residential Housing. Since 2003, Public Traffic Investment, which is belong to Facilities for Public Use has been included in Transportation Investment(same as follows).

表 10.2 用于公用事业和市政建设的投资额（1985～2006）
INVESTMENT IN PUBLIC UTILITIES AND CIVIL CONSTRUCTION

单位：亿元（100 million yuan）

年份 Year	公用事业 Public Utilities	其中 of which		市政建设 Civil Construction	其中 of which			
		自来水 Tap Water	煤气 Gas		园林绿化 Parks and Green Areas	环境卫生 Environmental Sanitation	市政工程管理 Administration of Civil Utilities	其他 Others
1985	7.88			4.89				
1986	5.67	2.74	1.78	5.03	0.43	0.71	3.84	0.05
1987	5.36	2.53	1.79	5.58	0.30	0.34	4.94	…
1988	4.01	0.72	1.25	6.54	0.24	0.58	5.72	…
1989	6.84	0.90	1.03	7.60	0.01	0.52	7.02	0.05
1990	10.83	1.06	1.81	8.80	0.11	0.37	8.31	0.01
1991	9.15	2.35	4.46	13.37	0.15	0.45	12.77	…
1992	12.58	3.24	6.14	30.63	0.32	0.79	28.45	1.07
1993	37.91	6.90	16.72	57.82	0.52	1.06	56.24	…
1994	26.77	11.49	7.80	97.14	2.42	1.01	93.47	0.24
1995	35.03	13.12	12.97	102.06	4.27	1.26	96.21	0.32
1996	48.31	22.12	14.61	105.65	2.66	1.14	101.80	0.05
1997	52.24	27.08	10.03	134.27	5.11	1.62	127.41	0.13
1998	58.37	14.59	13.15	201.97	9.10	3.35	189.41	0.11
1999	64.20	6.41	9.89	187.98	28.62	2.97	155.73	0.66
2000	104.43	5.35	6.88	163.34	38.76	19.34	102.36	2.88
2001	92.25	5.97	5.83	177.89	32.92	2.97	140.63	1.37
2002	148.42	8.62	6.83	201.69	38.83	1.47	160.64	0.75
2003	36.91	22.89	14.02	151.36	33.85	9.25	107.73	0.53
2004	26.92	16.66	10.26	184.80	16.69	7.01	160.22	0.88
2005	41.33	29.66	11.67	276.28	13.88	15.36	246.58	0.46
2006	56.23	43.79	12.44	249.84	26.41	10.17	213.26	…

表 10.3 主要年份各类房屋构成情况
COMPOSITION OF BUILDINGS IN MAIN YEARS

单位：万平方米（10 000 sq. m）

指标	Indicators	1978	1990	2000	2005	2006
总计	**Total**	**8 653**	**17 256**	**34 206**	**64 198**	**70 282**
居住房屋	**Residential Buildings**	**4 117**	**8 901**	**20 865**	**37 997**	**40 857**
花园住宅	Villas	128	158	250	1 380	1 464
公寓	Apartments	90	118	206	491	528
职工住宅	Staff Dwellings	1 140	4 884	17 939	33 610	36 504
新式里弄	Improved Residential Blocks	433	474	428	541	534
旧式里弄	Old Residential Blocks	1 777	3 067	1 896	1 836	1 689
简屋	Simple Housings	464	123	84	37	36
其他	Others	85	77	62	104	101
非居住房屋	**Non-Residential Buildings**	**4 536**	**8 355**	**13 341**	**26 201**	**29 425**
工厂	Plants	2 543	4 822	5 739	11 521	13 276
学校	Schools	504	927	1 417	2 326	2 456
仓库堆栈	Warehouses	354	472	650	1 182	1 305
办公楼	Offices	228	599	2 416	4 334	4 674
商场店铺	Stores	228	403	1 191	3 241	3 788
医院	Hospitals	123	203	367	564	591
旅馆	Hotels	55	237	376	620	651
影剧院	Theatres and Cinemas	20	34	47	69	72
其他	Others	481	658	1 138	2 345	2 612

①本表至表 10.7 的数据由市房屋土地资源管理局提供。
②本表按建筑面积计算(下表同)。
❶Data in table 10.3 to 10.7 are provided by Shanghai Municipal Building and Land Administration Bureau.
❷Data in table is calculated according to floor space of builings (the same follow).

表 10.4 主要年份八层以上房屋情况
BUILDINGS OVER EIGHT STOREYS IN MAIN YEARS

指标	Indicators	单位 Unit	1980	1990	2000	2005	2006
总计	**Total**	**幢（building）**	**121**	**748**	**3 529**	**10 045**	**11 989**
		万平方米（10 000 sq. m）	**127**	**914**	**6 180**	**13 100**	**14 821**
8～10 层	8～10 Storeys	幢（building）	78	207	536	1 394	1 556
		万平方米（10 000 sq. m）	68	170	451	871	939
11～15 层	11～15 Storeys	幢（building）	33	244	684	3 889	4 897
		万平方米（10 000 sq. m）	42	242	875	2 936	3 597
16～19 层	16～19 Storeys	幢（building）	7	145	831	2 020	2 486
		万平方米（10 000 sq. m）	12	182	1 100	2 553	2 966
20～29 层	20～29 Storeys	幢（building）	3	137	1 266	2 090	2 316
		万平方米（10 000 sq. m）	4	229	2 695	4 343	4 695
30 层以上	Over 30 Storeys	幢（building）		15	212	652	734
		万平方米（10 000 sq. m）		92	1 059	2 401	2 594

表 10.5 各区县房屋建筑分布情况（2006）
DISTRIBUTION OF BUILDINGS IN DIFFERENT DISTRICTS ANO COUNTIES

单位：万平方米（10 000 sq. m）

地 区 District		建筑面积合 计 Total	其 中 of which #年内新增 Newly Constructed	居住房屋 Residential	其 中 of which #年内新增 Newly Constructed	非居住房屋 Non-Residential	其 中 of which #年内新增 Newly Constructed
总 计	**Total**	**70 282**	**6 084**	**40 857**	**2 860**	**29 425**	**3 224**
浦东新区	Pudong New Area	11 157	727	6 890	459	4 267	268
黄 浦 区	Huangpu	1 908	41	830	9	1 078	32
卢 湾 区	Luwan	1 275	32	744	28	531	4
徐 汇 区	Xuhui	4 272	85	2 960	59	1 311	26
长 宁 区	Changning	2 965	65	1 893	65	1 072	
静 安 区	Jing'an	1 513	22	820	12	693	10
普 陀 区	Putuo	4 571	310	3 069	183	1 502	127
闸 北 区	Zhabei	2 618	48	1 475	30	1 143	18
虹 口 区	Hongkou	2 946	72	1 826	47	1 121	25
杨 浦 区	Yangpu	4 289	134	2 693	82	1 597	53
宝 山 区	Baoshan	5 394	601	3 418	363	1 976	238
闵 行 区	Minhang	7 228	838	4 832	406	2 396	432
嘉 定 区	Jiading	4 482	502	1 911	257	2 571	245
金 山 区	Jinshan	1 629	190	922	96	706	94
松 江 区	Songjiang	6 459	141	2 476	-135	3 982	276
青 浦 区	Qingpu	3 161	1 750	1 294	585	1 867	1 165
南 汇 区	Nanhui	2 128	244	1 472	207	656	37
奉 贤 区	Fengxian	1 570	211	906	54	664	157
崇 明 县	Chongming	717	71	426	53	292	18

注：由于本年统计范围为国有土地上的房屋，松江区本年居住房屋统计范围有所调整，所以房屋面积减少。
Note: This year, the statistical scale refers to the buildings on state-owned land. There are some reduce of building areas since the statistical scale of Songjiang District has been adjusted.

表 10.6　各区县各类房屋分布情况 (2006)
DISTRIBUTION OF BUILDINGS IN DIFFERENT DISTRICTS AND COUNTIES

单位：万平方米（10 000 sq. m）

地　区 District		居住房屋 Residential Buildings	其　中　of which				
			花园住宅 Villas	公　寓 Apartments	一类职工住宅 Staff Dwellings of 1st Class	二类职工住宅 Staff Dwellings of 2nd Class	三类职工住宅 Staff Dwellings of 3rd Class
总　计	**Total**	**40 856.50**	**1 464.00**	**528.40**	**11 422.80**	**24 027.30**	**1 054.40**
浦东新区	Pudong New Area	6 890.00	306.70	19.60	2 580.10	3 881.70	54.80
黄 浦 区	Huangpu	830.20	1.30	2.70	478.90	127.60	7.30
卢 湾 区	Luwan	744.00	14.70	263.40	155.90	140.10	7.00
徐 汇 区	Xuhui	2 960.30	78.40	114.30	1 017.20	1 540.30	28.70
长 宁 区	Changning	1 892.70	54.90	17.60	751.50	993.10	8.10
静 安 区	Jing'an	819.60	21.40	35.80	476.90	134.30	3.40
普 陀 区	Putuo	3 069.50	29.60	17.50	1 292.40	1 611.70	24.30
闸 北 区	Zhabei	1 474.50	0.50	0.20	578.60	710.50	27.30
虹 口 区	Hongkou	1 825.50	9.60	15.70	798.70	756.60	15.30
杨 浦 区	Yangpu	2 692.50	3.70	2.10	890.10	1 636.10	13.40
宝 山 区	Baoshan	3 418.30	4.70		326.30	2 988.90	2.10
闵 行 区	Minhang	4 832.00	203.80	3.20	1 085.70	2 981.70	465.30
嘉 定 区	Jiading	1 911.40	37.60		31.20	1 604.30	200.90
金 山 区	Jinshan	922.40			90.50	737.50	58.90
松 江 区	Songjiang	2 476.10	468.90		502.70	1 379.30	
青 浦 区	Qingpu	1 293.70	185.40	36.10	143.20	773.40	102.90
南 汇 区	Nanhui	1 471.80	10.60		126.70	889.60	26.30
奉 贤 区	Fengxian	906.20	32.20		78.20	773.90	2.10
崇 明 县	Chongming	425.70			17.70	366.50	6.30

表 10.6 续表 1 continued

单位：万平方米（10 000 sq. m）

地　区 District		新式里弄 Improved Residential Blocks	其中 of Which 旧式里弄 Old Residential Blocks 一等 1st Class	二等 2 nd Class	简屋 Simple Housings	其他 Others
总　计	**Total**	**534.00**	**529.80**	**1 159.30**	**35.80**	**100.90**
浦东新区	Pudong New Area	2.30	23.30	14.10	7.40	0.10
黄 浦 区	Huangpu	29.40	109.60	37.40	0.50	35.50
卢 湾 区	Luwan	73.20	78.00	8.50	0.50	2.70
徐 汇 区	Xuhui	75.50	15.80	49.80	2.70	37.60
长 宁 区	Changning	21.60	1.20	42.40	0.50	1.80
静 安 区	Jing'an	97.10	27.40	18.40	0.00	4.90
普 陀 区	Putuo	5.10	11.10	68.80	2.60	6.40
闸 北 区	Zhabei	0.80	65.70	87.80	2.20	0.80
虹 口 区	Hongkou	65.30	96.20	56.40	4.60	7.00
杨 浦 区	Yangpu	4.90	28.00	103.10	10.20	1.00
宝 山 区	Baoshan		17.40	78.70		
闵 行 区	Minhang			90.10	0.10	
嘉 定 区	Jiading	0.70	1.00	34.40	2.10	1.10
金 山 区	Jinshan		2.30	33.20	0.10	
松 江 区	Songjiang			125.10		
青 浦 区	Qingpu		7.50	43.70		0.30
南 汇 区	Nanhui	155.40	42.00	218.60	1.30	1.60
奉 贤 区	Fengxian	2.80	0.70	16.30	0.90	
崇 明 县	Chongming		2.50	32.50	0.10	

表 10.6 续表 2 continued

单位：万平方米（10 000 sq. m）

地 区	District	非居住房屋 Non-Residential Buildings	其中 of Which 工厂 Plants	学校 Schools	仓库堆栈 Warehouses	办公楼 Offices
总 计	**Total**	**29 425.50**	**13 276.10**	**2 455.60**	**1 305.40**	**4 673.70**
浦东新区	Pudong New Area	4 266.90	695.10	272.30	92.80	1 486.70
黄 浦 区	Huangpu	1 077.70	88.80	51.50	33.40	542.20
卢 湾 区	Luwan	531.20	87.10	41.40	7.80	213.40
徐 汇 区	Xuhui	1 311.20	256.40	196.10	44.40	319.80
长 宁 区	Changning	1 072.40	260.50	139.70	28.60	316.80
静 安 区	Jing'an	693.10	130.70	43.10	4.50	275.60
普 陀 区	Putuo	1 502.00	458.80	148.10	205.60	248.30
闸 北 区	Zhabei	1 143.20	460.20	110.80	67.50	133.40
虹 口 区	Hongkou	1 120.70	366.40	147.40	74.90	156.70
杨 浦 区	Yangpu	1 596.50	906.60	218.50	78.30	101.90
宝 山 区	Baoshan	1 976.00	890.00	140.00	205.90	195.20
闵 行 区	Minhang	2 395.80	1 412.70	117.20	125.40	120.20
嘉 定 区	Jiading	2 570.90	1 875.80	157.20	30.70	107.70
金 山 区	Jinshan	706.10	411.20	51.10	25.10	51.30
松 江 区	Songjiang	3 982.50	2 958.70	288.60	157.70	120.30
青 浦 区	Qingpu	1 867.50	1 289.50	117.60	70.10	131.50
南 汇 区	Nanhui	656.40	282.40	130.40	15.70	45.40
奉 贤 区	Fengxian	663.80	323.00	41.80	18.10	71.40
崇 明 县	Chongming	291.60	122.00	42.80	18.80	36.00

表10.6 续表3 continued

单位：万平方米（10 000 sq. m）

地 区 District		其 中 of Which				
		商场店铺 Stores	医 院 Hospitals	旅 馆 Hotels	影剧院 Theatres and Cinemas	其 他 Others
总 计	**Total**	**3 788.00**	**590.60**	**650.90**	**71.50**	**2 613.70**
浦东新区	Pudong New Area	1 201.20	73.30	141.00	12.80	291.60
黄 浦 区	Huangpu	181.60	33.70	61.80	9.40	75.20
卢 湾 区	Luwan	98.50	20.00	28.80	2.10	32.10
徐 汇 区	Xuhui	97.60	45.20	54.90	1.90	295.00
长 宁 区	Changning	94.40	31.20	75.30	2.40	123.50
静 安 区	Jing'an	94.60	31.60	68.10	3.30	41.60
普 陀 区	Putuo	225.90	26.30	25.10	2.40	161.60
闸 北 区	Zhabei	224.90	38.80	19.20	1.10	87.30
虹 口 区	Hongkou	159.00	37.40	38.30	2.40	138.00
杨 浦 区	Yangpu	120.80	56.20	13.10	3.70	97.30
宝 山 区	Baoshan	185.40	21.50	25.60	4.50	308.00
闵 行 区	Minhang	148.60	13.10	14.60	3.60	440.40
嘉 定 区	Jiading	219.90	19.20	8.20	1.40	150.80
金 山 区	Jinshan	89.50	18.00	10.10	2.70	47.10
松 江 区	Songjiang	252.80	25.30	35.40	7.10	136.60
青 浦 区	Qingpu	137.60	21.10	13.10	3.30	83.60
南 汇 区	Nanhui	106.80	16.60	3.80	5.40	49.90
奉 贤 区	Fengxian	124.30	45.00	8.70	1.40	30.10
崇 明 县	Chongming	24.50	17.10	5.90	0.80	24.00

表 10.7 各区县八层以上房屋分布(2006)
DISTRIBUTION OF BUILDINGS OVER EIGHT STOREYS BY DISTRICTS AND COUNTIES

单位：万平方米 (10 000 sq. m)

地区 District		合计 Total		8～10层 8～10 Storeys		11～15层 11～15 Storeys	
		幢 Building	面积 Floor Space	幢 Building	面积 Floor Space	幢 Building	面积 Floor Space
总计	**Total**	**11 989**	**14 821**	**1 556**	**939**	**4 897**	**3 597**
浦东新区	Pudong New Area	2 079	2 724	232	145	891	669
黄浦区	Huangpu	429	965	87	95	57	76
卢湾区	Luwan	313	649	27	19	50	58
徐汇区	Xuhui	1 026	1 427	123	76	271	208
长宁区	Changning	741	1 368	121	77	179	209
静安区	Jing'an	429	909	43	40	40	40
普陀区	Putuo	1 348	1 582	120	68	406	292
闸北区	Zhabei	507	764	53	35	207	178
虹口区	Hongkou	635	1 059	72	67	138	137
杨浦区	Yangpu	1 490	1 052	196	59	734	310
宝山区	Baoshan	401	354	52	32	277	233
闵行区	Minhang	1 664	1 119	322	191	1 005	638
嘉定区	Jiading	64	78	7	3	43	51
金山区	Jinshan	106	79	12	6	52	36
松江区	Songjiang	391	359	27	22	296	237
青浦区	Qingpu	99	138	14	8	71	100
南汇区	Nanhui	152	85	26	14	104	55
奉贤区	Fengxian	80	89	4	4	60	60
崇明县	Chongming	35	21	18	8	16	10

表 10.7 续表 continued

单位：万平方米（10 000 sq. m）

地区 District		16～19 层 16～19 Storeys		20～29 层 20～29 Storeys		30 层以上 Over 30 Storeys	
		幢 Building	面积 Floor Space	幢 Building	面积 Floor Space	幢 Building	面积 Floor Space
总　计	**Total**	**2 486**	**2 966**	**2 316**	**4 695**	**734**	**2 594**
浦东新区	Pudong New Area	443	533	402	817	111	560
黄 浦 区	Huangpu	77	142	132	342	76	310
卢 湾 区	Luwan	51	80	119	274	66	218
徐 汇 区	Xuhui	271	315	275	560	86	268
长 宁 区	Changning	153	217	221	545	67	320
静 安 区	Jing'an	66	91	203	451	77	287
普 陀 区	Putuo	326	325	358	606	138	291
闸 北 区	Zhabei	109	291	118	211	20	49
虹 口 区	Hongkou	193	269	178	372	54	214
杨 浦 区	Yangpu	344	294	186	325	30	64
宝 山 区	Baoshan	63	66	9	23		
闵 行 区	Minhang	253	191	76	90	8	9
嘉 定 区	Jiading	9	11	4	9	1	4
金 山 区	Jinshan	34	21	8	16		
松 江 区	Songjiang	48	66	20	34		
青 浦 区	Qingpu	10	18	4	12		
南 汇 区	Nanhui	22	16				
奉 贤 区	Fengxian	14	20	2	5		
崇 明 县	Chongming			1	3		

表 10.8 主要年份市政工程设施情况
CIVIL FACILITIES IN MAIN YEARS

	指 标 Indicators	1990	2000	2005	2006
道路长度(公里)	Length of Roads(km)	1 631	6 641	12 227	14 619
#高级、次高级	High-grade, Mid-grade		6 136	12 121	14 365
道路面积(万平方米)	Area of Roads(10 000 sq. m)	1 787	8 147	20 942	21 490
城市桥梁(座)	Bridges(bridge)	553	4 432	8 070	10 199
防洪堤长度(公里)	Length of Floodwalls(km)		335	1 070	1 070
城市排水管道长度(公里)	Length of Sewage Pipelines(km)	1 892	3 920	6 933	7 430
污水处理厂污水处理能力(万吨/日)	Capacity of Sewage Treatment(10 000 tons/day)	41	463	471	488
防汛泵站(座)	Pumping Stations of Flood Prevention (bridge)	134	160	159	159

① 本表数据由市水务局、市政工程管理局提供。
②2005、2006 年,防洪堤包括海塘。
③2006 年起,道路中包括公路中的村道。
❶Data in this table are provided by Shanghai Water Authority and Shanghai Municipal Administration Bureau.
❷The Floodwall includes the Seawall in 2005 and 2006.
❸Data of village road has been included in that of roads since 2006.

表 10.9 主要年份自来水情况
TAP WATER SUPPLY IN MAIN YEARS

	指 标 Indicators	1990	2000	2005	2006
水厂个数(个)	Number of Water Works(unit)	8	218	179	146
水厂生产能力(万立方米/日)	Production Capacity (10 000 cu. m/day)	462	1 048	1 096	1 138
供水管道长度(公里)	Length of Water Supply Pipelines(km)	3 483	15 943	23 718	26 619
供水总量(亿立方米)	Volume of Water Supply(100 million cu. m)	13.32	24.00	28.65	29.19
售水总量(亿立方米)	Sales Volume of Tap Water(100 million cu. m)	12.25	19.75	22.81	23.30
#工业用水	Industrial Use	5.90	5.49	6.42	6.43
生活用水	Living Use	6.36	14.26	16.39	16.88
#居民生活用水	Living Use for Residents	3.29	6.82	8.12	8.52
日用水量(万立方米)	Daily Average Water Consumed(10 000 cu. m)	335.60	541.20	624.80	638.50

注：本表数据由市水务局提供。
Note: Data in this table are provided by Shanghai Water Authority.

表 10.10 主要年份用电量
ELECTRICITY POWER CONSUMPTION IN MAIN YEARS

	指 标 Indicators	1990	2000	2005	2006
用电量(亿千瓦·时)	Power Consumption(100 million kwh)	264.74	559.42	921.97	990.15
#工业用电	Industrial Consumption	220.97	393.13	617.59	656.10
农业用电	Agricultural Consumption	7.22	8.92	5.76	5.34
城市居民生活用电	Urban Residential Consumption	14.44	53.20	109.2	122.37

注：本表数据由市电力公司提供。
Note: Data in this table are provided by Shanghai Electric Power Corporation.

表 10.11 主要年份煤气、液化石油气、天然气情况
GAS,LIQUEFIED PETROLEUM GAS AND NATURAL GAS IN MAIN YEARS

指 标	Indicators	1990	2000	2005	2006
煤 气	**Gas**				
煤气生产能力(万立方米/日)	Production Capacity(10 000 cu. m/day)	488	984	1 134	1 013
煤气管线长度(公里)	Length of Gas Pipelines(km)	2 700	6 606	8 468	8 778
煤气供气总量(亿立方米)	Total Gas Supply(100 million cu. m)	12.72	21.31	22.86	21.76
煤气销售总量(亿立方米)	Total Sales Volume(100 million cu. m)	12.15	18.40	19.97	19.22
#生产用气	Production Use	4.50	2.53	1.91	1.75
生活用气	Residential Use	7.63	15.77	17.88	17.19
家庭煤气用户数(万户)	Households Users(10 000 households)	113.19	255.89	236.54	230.22
液化石油气	**Liquefied Petroleum Gas(LPG)**				
液化石油气销售总量(万吨)	Sales of LPG(10 000 tons)	5.97	45.94	45.26	45.86
#家庭用量	Household Consumption	4.27	20.47	23.97	26.70
液化石油气用户数(万户)	LPG Users(10 000 households)	30.23	242.73	257.41	265.73
#家庭用户数	Household Users	29.64	239.30	253.89	260.10
天然气	**Natural Gas**				
天然气销售总量(亿立方米)	Sales of Natural Gas(100 million cu. m)		2.16	17.50	22.58
天然气管线长度(公里)	Length of Natural Gas Pipelines(km)		1 742.40	6 370.43	8 349.20
家庭天然气用户数(万户)	Household Users of Natural Gas(10 000 households)		38.10	186.37	216.93

注：本表数据由市市政工程管理局提供。
Note: Data in this table are provided by Shanghai Municipal Administration Bureau.

表 10.12 主要年份公共交通和轮渡情况
PUBLIC TRANSPORTATION AND FERRY IN MAIN YEARS

指 标	Indicators	1990	2000	2005	2006
公共汽电车	**Buses and Trolley Buses**				
公交线路长度(公里)	Length of Public Bus Lines(km)	18 593	23 260	21 794	21 776
公交线路条数(条)	Number of Public Bus Lines(line)	390	978	940	944
运营公交车辆数(辆)	Operating Public Transportation Vehicles(vehicle)	6 264	17 939	17 985	17 284
#公共汽车	Buses	5 341	17 358	17 509	16 899
客运总量(亿人次)	Passenger Volume (100 million person-times)	54.37	26.49	27.81	27.40
出租汽车	**Taxi**				
运营车辆(辆)	Operating Vehicles(vehicle)	11 298	42 943	47 794	48 022
#小客车	Small Passenger Car	8 095	40 806	45 900	45 959
载客车次(万次)	Number of Carryings(10 000 times)	2 129	37 599	56 401	58 920
运营里程(亿公里)	Operation Length(100 million km)	3.76	46.48	58.12	61.05
#营业里程	Operation Lengths	2.97	24.35	34.75	36.72
运营收入(亿元)	Operation Revenues(100 million yuan)	5.76	76.68	115.41	124.97
运营单位(个)	Operation Unit(unit)	1 666	1 178	3 600	3 646
轮 渡	**Ferry**				
年末轮渡船数(艘)	Year-end Number of Ferry Boats(ship)	111	95	54	53
乘客人数(亿人次)	Passenger Volume(100 million person-times)	3.74	1.85	1.25	1.19

注：本表数据由市城市交通管理局、市航务管理处提供。
Note: Data in this table are provided by Shanghai Urban Traffic Management Bureau and Shanghai Municipal Navigation Management Department.

表 10.13 轨道交通、高架道路、黄浦江大桥和隧道基本情况 (2002 ~ 2006)
BASIC FACTS OF URBAN RAILWAY COMMUNICATION, ELEVATED ROADS, BRIDGES ACROSS HUANGPU RIVER AND TUNNELS

指　标	Indicators	2002	2003	2004	2005	2006
轨道交通	**Urban Metro**					
运营车辆(节)	Operating Vehicles(car)	330	445	611	695	829
运营线路长度(公里)	Length of Operation Lines(km)	62.92	108.65	121.23	147.80	169.40
行驶里程(万列・公里)	Mileage(10 000 vehicle-km)	633.29	813.18	957.04	1 205	1 457.32
客运总量(万人次)	Volume of Passenger Traffic(10 000 person-times)	35 739	40 604	48 007	59 406	65 569
利润总额(万元)	Total Pre-tax Profits(10 000 yuan)	3 863	2 658	1 720	2 300	1 692
年末从业人数(人)	Year-end Number of Staff and Workers(person)	4 321	7 703	8 290	7 411	8 458
高架、大桥和隧道	**Elevated Roads, Bridges and Tunnels**					
高架道路长度(公里)	Length of Elevated Roads(km)	71	76	77	77	77
越江大桥数(座)	Number of Bridges Across Huangpu River(bridge)	5	6	6	6	6
越江隧道数(条)	Tunnels Across Huangpu River (tunnel)	2	4	5	6	6

注：本表数据由市市政工程管理局、城市交通管理局提供。
Note: Data in this table are provided by Shanghai Municipal Administration Bureau and Shanghai Municipal Traffic Management Bureau.

表 10.14 主要年份城市设施水平
LEVEL OF URBAN FACILITIES IN MAIN YEARS

指　标	Indicators	1990	2000	2005	2006
人均年自来水生活用水(立方米)	Per Capita Water Consumption for Residential Use(cu. m)	78.4	86.9	92.2	93.0
自来水普及率(%)	Percentage of Population with Access to Tap Water(%)	100.00	99.97	99.99	99.99
人均拥有道路长度(公里)	Per Capita Length of Roads(km)	2.08	5.84	8.99	10.69
人均拥有道路面积(平方米)	Per Capita Area of Roads(sq. m)	2.28	7.17	15.4	15.7
每万人拥有城市排水管道长度(公里)	Length of Sewage Pipelines Per 10 000 Persons(km)	1.47	2.86	5.10	5.43
每万人拥有公共车辆(辆)	Number of Public Transportation Vehicles Per 10 000 Persons(vehicle)	7.43	14.30	13.22	12.63
每万人拥有出租汽车(辆)	Number of Taxi Per 10 000 Persons(vehicle)	8.80	32.49	35.14	35.10
人均拥有公共绿地面积(平方米)	Per Capita Public Green Areas (sq. m)	1.02	4.60	11.01	11.50
每万人拥有公共厕所(座)	Number of Public Lavatories Per 10 000 Persons(unit)	0.79	1.67	2.67	2.74

① 本表数据由市水务局、市政工程管理局、市绿化局等单位提供。
②1990 年平均每人生活用水、自来水普及率为中心城区数据。
③自 2005 年起人均年自来水生活用水口径调整。
❶Data in this table are provided by Shanghai Water Authority, Shanghai Municipal Administration Bureau, Shanghai Municipal Virescence Bureau, and etc.
❷ Per Captita Water Consumption for Residential Use and Percentage of Population with Access to Tap Water only cover the downtown areas for 1990.
❸ Since 2005, the scope of per Capita Water Consumption for Residential Use has been adjusted.

表 10.15　主要年份城市园林绿化情况
PARKS, GARDENS AND GREEN AREAS IN MAIN YEARS

单位:公顷(hectare)

年　份 Year	城市园林绿地面积 Total Area of Urban Parks, Gardens and Green Areas	其　中　of which				
		#公共绿地 Public Green Area	其　中　of which		#专用绿地 Special-Purpose Green Area	#园林苗圃 Gardens and Nurseries
			公园面积 Area of Parks	街道绿地 Roadside Green Area		
1978	761	383	309	75		308
1980	1738	390	319	71	970	303
1985	2 339	522	412	110	1 551	143
1990	3 570	983	712	271	2 255	294
1995	6 561	1 793	920	873	4 429	309
1996	7 231	2 008	933	1 076	4 889	305
1997	7 849	2 484	961	1 523	5 083	253
1998	8 855	3 117	976	2 141	5 456	253
1999	11 117	3 856	993	2 863	6 888	318
2000	12 601	4 812	1 153	3 658	7 346	388
2001	14 771	5 820	1 291	4 529	8 624	248
2002	18 758	7 810	1 411	6 399	9 591	267
2003	24 426	9 450	1 473	7 977	10 218	335
2004	26 689	10 979	1 481	9 498	10 921	335
2005	28 865	12 038	1 521	10 516	11 591	335
2006	30 609	13 307	1 529	11 782	12 202	331

注：本表至表 10.17 由市绿化管理局提供。
Note: Data in table 10.15 to 11.17 are provided by Shanghai Landscape Bureau.

表 10.15 续表 continued

年　份 Year	公园数 (个) Parks (unit)	游园人数 (万人次) Visitors to Parks and Zooes (10 000 person-times)	植树数 (万株) Trees Planted (10 000 trees)	行道树实有数 (万株) Roadside Trees (10 000 trees)	新辟绿地面积(公顷) Greenlands Newly Created (hectare)	绿化覆盖率 (%) Coverage Rate of Urban Green Areas(%)
1978	42	3 876	35	13		8.2
1980	45	6 404	60	13	44	8.2
1985	52	8 372	208	15	226	9.7
1990	83	8 474	130	23	186	12.4
1995	100	9 064	279	33	516	16.0
1996	105	9 797	355	41	587	17.0
1997	108	9 757	383	43	728	17.8
1998	111	9 285	773	48	1 077	19.1
1999	115	9 601	845	54	1 315	20.3
2000	122	8 184	827	57	1 458	22.2
2001	125	8 561	1 384	65	1 374	23.8
2002	133	8 796	2 729	68	2 600	30.0
2003	136	9 629	2 540	74	4 904	35.2
2004	136	13 381	2 037	80	2 434	36.0
2005	144	13 656	2 117	83	2 116	37.0
2006	144	16 652	2 187	86	1 691	37.3

表 10.16 各区县绿化情况(2006)
BASIC FACTS OF URBAN VIRESCENCE IN DIFFERENT DISTRICTS AND COUNTIES

地 区 District		园林绿地面积 (公顷) Total Area of Parks, Gardens and Green Areas (hectare)	其 中 of which #公共绿地面积 Public Green Areas	公园数 (个) Number of Parks (unit)	公园游园人数 (万人次) Visitors to Parks and Zooes (10 000 person-times)
总 计	**Total**	**30 608.97**	**13 306.81**	**144**	**16 651.69**
浦东新区	Pudong New Area	8 739.40	4 242.47	17	1 379.42
黄浦区	Huangpu	118.99	83.95	7	2 124.68
卢湾区	Luwan	98.75	48.89	5	821.29
徐汇区	Xuhui	1 107.36	410.78	11	1 377.78
长宁区	Changning	1 052.94	392.35	13	1 704.14
静安区	Jing'an	77.49	29.22	2	202.91
普陀区	Putuo	1 005.95	442.51	16	1 365.01
闸北区	Zhabei	488.78	196.18	7	829.04
虹口区	Hongkou	376.24	142.85	9	2 087.27
杨浦区	Yangpu	970.25	403.68	14	1 558.99
宝山区	Baoshan	3 745.05	1 380.44	10	1 641.75
闵行区	Minhang	3 227.47	1 821.50	9	578.82
嘉定区	Jiading	1 894.92	990.59	5	214.31
金山区	Jinshan	1 083.85	464.87	7	125.85
松江区	Songjiang	1 317.19	437.98	4	250.94
青浦区	Qingpu	1 808.37	814.10	3	54.88
南汇区	Nanhui	1 523.30	523.73	2	144.80
奉贤区	Fengxian	1 807.84	414.78	1	168.40
崇明县	Chongming	164.83	65.94	2	21.41

表 10.16 续表 continued

地 区 District		绿化覆盖面积（公顷）Green Area Coverage Areas (hectare)	绿化覆盖率（%）Coverage Rate of Urban Green Areas (%)	绿化种植数（万株）Trees Planted (10 000 trees)	行道树实有数（万株）Roadside Trees (10 000 trees)	人均公共绿地面积（平方米）Per Capita Public Green Areas (sq. m)
总 计	**Total**	**32 304.30**	**44.77**	**2 186.63**	**86.02**	**11.50**
浦东新区	Pudong New Area	8 998.49	44.77	196.19	37.19	24.20
黄浦区	Huangpu	152.61	12.36	11.38	0.93	1.37
卢湾区	Luwan	134.43	16.70	12.19	0.97	1.56
徐汇区	Xuhui	1 364.50	24.92	12.08	3.63	4.63
长宁区	Changning	1 153.49	30.12	18.62	2.56	6.37
静安区	Jing'an	123.76	16.24	9.77	1.17	0.94
普陀区	Putuo	1 140.77	20.81	75.63	4.56	5.15
闸北区	Zhabei	548.98	18.76	55.94	1.76	2.81
虹口区	Hongkou	438.81	18.69	63.99	2.26	1.81
杨浦区	Yangpu	1 136.59	18.72	53.53	3.05	3.74
宝山区	Baoshan	3 848.93	40.09	468.78	4.48	18.90
闵行区	Minhang	3 379.05	49.82	310.34	7.03	24.71
嘉定区	Jiading	1 966.80	46.64	0.97	4.88	23.59
金山区	Jinshan	1 143.96	37.84	156.36	2.77	15.48
松江区	Songjiang	1 347.92	42.49	…	1.85	11.31
青浦区	Qingpu	1 852.47	46.99	251.76	2.76	29.42
南汇区	Nanhui	1 544.86	52.05	212.21	0.89	11.57
奉贤区	Fengxian	1 831.61	54.95	208.69	1.67	13.46
崇明县	Chongming	196.27		68.20	1.61	

注：绿化覆盖率、人均公共绿地面积不包括崇明县在内。
Note: Data of total Coverage Rate of Urban Green Areas and Per Capita Public Green Areas include all the other districts except Chongming.

上/海/统/计/年/鉴

主要统计指标解释

■ 城市基础设施

城市基础设施包括电力建设、交通运输、邮电通信、公用事业和市政建设等。

■ 道路长度

指道路长度和与道路相通的桥梁、隧道的长度，按车行道中心线计算。

■ 城市园林绿地面积

指报告期末用作园林和绿化的各种绿地面积。包括公共绿地、居住区绿地、单位附属绿地、防护绿地、生产绿地、道路绿地和风景林地面积。

不包括:

(1)屋顶绿化、垂直绿化、阳台绿化和室内绿化。

(2)以物质生产为主的林地、耕地、牧草地、果园和竹园等。

(3)城市总体规划中不列入绿地的水域。

■ 公共绿地

指向公众开放的市级、区级、居住区级各类公园、街旁游园，包括其范围内的水域。其中居住区级公园应不小于1万平方米，街旁游园的宽度不小于8米，面积不小于400平方米。

■ 供水管道长度

指从送水泵至用户水表之间所有管道的长度。不包括新安装尚未使用的管道。

■ 供水总量

指报告期供水企业(单位)供出的全部水量。包括有效供水量和漏损水量。

■ 生活用水

生活用水包括公共服务用水和居民家庭用水。公共服务用水指为城市社会公共生活服务的用水。包括行政事业单位、部队营区和公共设施服务、社会服务业、批发零售贸易业、旅馆饮食业以及其他公共服务业等单位的用水。居民家庭用水指城市范围内所有居民家庭的日常生活用水。包括城市居民、农民家庭、公共供水站用水。

■ 煤气生产能力

指报告期末煤气生产厂制气、净化、输送等环节的综合生产能力，不包括备用设备能力。一般按设计能力计算，如果实际生产能力大于设计能力时，应按实际测定的生产能力计算。测定时应以制气、净化、输送三个环节中最薄弱的环节为主。

■ 供气总量

指全年燃气企业(单位)向用户供应的燃气数量。包括销售量和损失量。

■ 排水管道长度

指所有排水总管、干管、支管、检查井及连接井进出口等长度之和。

■ 运营公交车辆数

指年末公交企业(单位)用于运营业务的全部车辆数。以企业(单位)固定资产台帐中已投入运营的车辆数为准。

■ 污水日处理能力

指污水处理厂(或处理装置)每昼夜处理污水量的设计能力。

SHANGHAI STATISTICAL YEARBOOK

EXPLANATORY NOTES TO MAJOR STATISTICAL INDICATORS

□ Urban Infrastructure Facilities

Urban Infrastructure Facilities include facilities for power generating, transportation, post and telecommunication, public utilities, development of municipal engineering.

□ Length of Roads

The length of roads refers to the length of roads and of the bridges and tunnels connected to the roads, calculated by the center line of the roads.

□ Area of Urban Parks Gardens and Green Areas

Area of Urban Parks, Gardens and Green Areas refers to the total area occupied for green projects at the end of the reference period, including public green land, green land in residential quarters, green land attached to institutions, protection green land, production green land, roadside green land and forest in scenic spots. It does not include the following:

(1) Greenery and plants on roofs, balconies, indoors and vertical green areas;

(2) Forest, cultivated land grassland, orchards and bamboo grooves that are for production purpose and etc.;

(3) Water areas that are not included in urban master plan as green land.

□ Public Green Area

Public Green Area refers to green areas open to the public such as municipal, community and neighborhood parks and roadside parks, including waters within parks. Neighborhood parks should occupy an area larger than 10,000 square meters, and the width of roadside parks should occupy an area larger than 400 square meters, with a width of more that 8 meters.

□ Length of Water Supply Pipelines

Length of Water Supply Pipelines refers to the total length of all the pipelines between the water pumps and the user's water meters, excluding pipelines newly installed but not used yet.

□ Volume of Water Supply

Volume of Water Supply refers to the total volume of water supplied by water-works (units) during the reference period, including both the effective water supply and loss during the water supply.

□ Consumption of Water for Living Use

Consumption of Water for Living Use refers to the water consumption of households for daily life and the water consumption of public service facilities. The latter refers to water consumption for urban public services, including the consumption of government agencies and public institutions, military barracks, public facilities, wholesale and retail outlets, restaurants, hotels, and other units providing public services. Household water consumption refers to consumption of water for daily life of all households in the boundary of cities, including households of urban residents and farmers, and public water supply stations.

□ Production Capacity of Gaswork Gas

Production Capacity of Gaswork Gas refers to the comprehensive production capacity of the urban gasworks in gas generation, purification and delivery at the end of the reference period, excluding capacity of the reserved facilities. In general, it is determined by the designed capacity, and when actual production capacity is larger than the designed capacity, the capacity is determined by the actual measurement on the weakest link in the production, purification and delivery.

□ Total Gas Supply

Total of Gas Supply refers to the total volume of gas provided to users by gas-producing enterprises (units) in a year, including the volume sold and the volume lost.

□ Length of Sewage Pipes

Length of Sewage Pipes refers to the total length of general drainage, trunks, branch and inspection wells, connection wells, inlets and outlets, etc.

□ Number of Operating Public Transportation Vehicles

Number of Operating Public Transportation Vehicles refers

EXPLANATORY NOTES TO MAJOR STATISTICAL INDICATORS

to the total number of vehicles under operation by public transport enterprises (units) at the end of the year, based on the records of operational vehicles by the enterprises (units).

□ Daily Capacity of Sewage Treatment

Daily Capacity of Sewage Treatment refers to the designed 24 hour capacity of sewage disposal by the sewage treatment works or facilities.

第十一篇

CHAPTER 11

AGRICULTURE

表 11.1 农业总产值(1978～2006)
GROSS OUTPUT VALUE OF AGRICULTURE

单位:亿元(100 million yuan)

年 份 Year	农业总产值 Gross Output Value of Agriculture	其中 of which				
		种植业 Planting	林 业 Forestry	牧 业 Animal Husbandry	副 业 Sideline	渔 业 Fishery
1978	18.26	13.49	0.06	3.67	0.18	0.86
1979	20.41	15.10	0.04	4.22	0.15	0.90
1980	18.90	11.40	0.06	6.27	0.20	0.97
1981	20.33	11.91	0.21	6.38	0.60	1.23
1982	23.97	13.80	0.23	7.81	0.57	1.56
1983	22.68	12.59	0.20	7.80	0.80	1.29
1984	26.59	16.41	0.21	8.06	0.51	1.40
1985	31.38	15.63	0.21	12.25	0.47	2.82
1986	33.76	16.83	0.24	12.75	0.49	3.45
1987	38.84	17.69	0.34	15.48	0.54	4.79
1988	53.07	22.47	0.45	22.18	0.54	7.43
1989	60.63	25.53	0.39	26.41	0.42	7.88
1990	68.16	29.09	0.37	30.25	0.41	8.04
1991	73.65	30.51	0.39	33.38	0.40	8.97
1992	80.01	32.80	0.43	37.19	0.41	9.18
1993	96.20	40.52	0.41	42.95		12.31
1994	140.24	60.19	0.49	62.04		17.52
1995	182.47	77.71	0.45	81.48		22.83
1996	200.95	87.64	0.67	85.46		27.18
1997	204.41	85.20	0.47	88.37		30.37
1998	206.75	89.10	0.84	87.27		29.54
1999	206.90	87.86	0.98	86.35		31.71
2000	216.50	89.81	1.41	87.35		37.92
2001	227.61	95.53	3.52	88.43		40.13
2002	233.57	97.21	7.75	83.48		45.13
2003	247.29	98.17	13.05	81.13		49.21
2004	248.89	109.32	13.14	70.77		49.90
2005	233.39	111.25	11.11	54.34		51.64
2006	237.01	119.99	10.43	46.29		55.25

注：从 2003 年起，农业总产值包括农林牧渔服务业产值。
Note: Since 2003, the gross output value of agriculture has included the output value of service industry for planting, forestry, animal husbandry and fishery.

表 11.2 农业总产值指数(以 1978 年为 100,1978 ~ 2006)
INDEX OF GROSS OUTPUT VALUE OF AGRICULTURE(1978 = 100)

年 份 Year	农业总产值指数 Gross Output Value Index of Agriculture	其 中 of which				
		种植业 Planting	林 业 Forestry	牧 业 Animal Husbandry	副 业 Sideline	渔 业 Fishery
1978	100	100	100	100	100	100
1979	101.4	92.9	121.9	128.1	432.2	101.6
1980	92.1	78.6	152.9	115.8	1 958.3	104.1
1981	100.0	83.9	144.0	140.2	1 747.2	97.3
1982	117.4	97.4	161.1	170.1	2 163.3	107.3
1983	109.9	86.0	116.1	167.3	2 335.7	123.6
1984	124.5	109.0	98.4	167.5	1 486.4	114.7
1985	113.0	88.2	107.2	181.4	1 377.9	127.6
1986	119.7	89.5	134.5	201.2	1 406.5	149.5
1987	122.5	90.6	138.9	206.7	1 557.3	158.1
1988	130.3	95.3	166.0	227.0	1 546.2	160.0
1989	132.0	92.3	134.9	245.6	1 211.6	171.8
1990	139.5	96.3	139.7	271.2	1 192.0	164.3
1991	146.2	95.6	153.7	299.0	1 161.3	172.7
1992	154.7	101.3	144.0	322.9	1 185.4	168.8
1993	147.9	94.1	129.4	313.8		166.8
1994	159.4	96.0	130.5	336.7		215.0
1995	177.0	104.0	125.2	363.0		252.4
1996	191.6	114.5	168.6	389.1		269.6
1997	202.5	123.1	133.0	404.3		288.4
1998	207.3	129.4	185.2	412.1		278.6
1999	212.6	133.2	258.3	418.0		289.2
2000	220.9	141.2	414.9	414.6		321.9
2001	236.5	145.2	629.7	433.7		392.0
2002	243.6	145.7	1 546.0	416.4		442.6
2003	246.3	135.3	2 062.4	395.5		544.4
2004	229.6	144.0	2 070.6	306.5		526.4
2005	205.5	136.7	1 613.0	221.6		555.4
2006	206.9	141.1	1 514.6	205.0		587.6

表 11.3 主要年份农副产品产量
OUTPUT OF MAJOR FARM AND SIDELINE PRODUCTS IN MAIN YEARS

指 标	Indicators	1980	1990	2000	2005	2006
农副产品	**Farm and Sideline Products**					
粮 食(万吨)(包括大豆)	Grain(10 000 tons)(Including Soybean)	186.85	244.36	174.00	105.36	111.30
棉 花(万吨)	Cotton(10 000 tons)	7.62	1.22	0.12	0.18	0.20
油 料(万吨)	Oil Plants(10 000 tons)	9.60	18.20	16.37	6.94	5.31
# 油菜籽	Rapeseed	9.58	18.17	15.71	6.51	4.91
蔬 菜(万吨)	Vegetables(10 000 tons)	112.55	186.79	377.00	409.03	418.76
西甜瓜(万吨)	Watermelons and Muskmelons(10 000 tons)	10.28	30.77	49.88	64.75	66.99
蚕 茧(吨)	Pod(ton)	104	311	79	28	3
水 果(万吨)	Fruits(10 000 tons)	3.70	9.42	22.54	33.63	38.93
# 生 梨	Pear	2.32	1.15	1.74	1.88	3.16
柑 桔	Citrus Fruits	0.03	2.58	10.18	17.99	19.66
畜禽产品	**Livestock and Poultry**					
生猪出栏量(万头)	Quantity of Sold Hogs(10 000 heads)	350.66	411.80	471.46	280.00	252.70
生猪年末圈存量(万头)	Hogs In Pens By Year-end(10 000 heads)	260.93	237.53	241.60	153.16	127.74
奶牛年末头数(万头)	Cows In Pens By Year-end(10 000 heads)	2.65	7.09	5.83	5.33	5.46
羊年末头数(万头)	Sheep In Pens By Year-end(10 000 heads)	41.15	37.19	55.44	30.08	28.26
兔年末圈存量(万头)	Rabbits In Pens By Year-end(10 000 heads)	108.23	130.62	88.90	31.5	29.08
猪 肉(万吨)	Pork(10 000 tons)	16.76	23.32	25.96	18.02	16.18
牛羊肉(万吨)	Beef and Mutton(10 000 tons)	0.17	0.30	0.79	0.65	0.60
家禽出栏量(万羽)	Quantity of Poultry Sold Birds(10 000 fowls)	2 577	7 357	17 213	7 461	5 065
牛 奶(万吨)	Milk(10 000 tons)	7.33	22.68	25.95	23.76	22.09
鲜 蛋(万吨)	Fresh Egg(10 000 tons)	4.59	15.07	16.64	8.40	6.76
水产品	**Aquatic Products**					
海水产品(万吨)	Seawater Aquatic Products(10 000 tons)	18.56	17.04	12.23	15.03	19.44
淡水产品(万吨)	Freshwater Aquatic Products(10 000 tons)	1.89	10.32	16.64	20.32	19.31

表 11.4 主要农副产品产量与建国以来最高年产量的比较(2006)
OUTPUT OF MAJOR FARM AND SIDELINE PRODUCTS IN COMPARISON WITH THE PEAK YEAR SINCE 1949

指 标	Indicators	2006	建国以来最高年 Peak Year Since 1949		2006 年为建国以来最高年份(%) 2006/Peak Year Since 1949(%)
			年 份 Year	产 量 Output	
农产品	**Farm products**				
粮 食(万吨)	Grain(10 000 tons)	111.3	1 978	260.88	42.7
#小 麦	Wheat	11.34	1 999	38.44	29.5
大 麦	Barley	3.48	1 984	34.79	10.0
后季稻	Late Season Rice	2.93	1 978	104.21	2.8
晚 稻	Late Rice	86.77	1 991	164.27	52.8
棉 花(万吨)	Cotton(10 000 tons)	0.20	1 978	12.10	1.7
油菜籽(万吨)	Rapeseed(10 000 tons)	4.91	1 992	21.84	22.5
蔬 菜(万吨)	Vegetables(10 000 tons)	418.76	2 002	476.60	87.9
西甜瓜(万吨)	Watermelons and Muskmelons(10 000 tons)	66.99	2 003	76.50	87.6
水 果(万吨)	Fruits(10 000 tons)	38.93	2 006	38.93	100.0
畜产品	**Animal Husbandry Products**				
猪年末圈存数(万头)	Quantity of Hogs in Pens(year-end) (10 000 heads)	127.74	1 978	365.74	34.9
猪 肉(万吨)	Pork(10 000 tons)	16.18	2 001	26.40	61.3
奶牛年末头数(万头)	Quantity of Milk Cow(year-end)(10 000 heads)	5.46	1 991	7.31	74.7
牛 奶(万吨)	Milk(10 000 tons)	22.09	2 002	27.98	78.9
家禽出栏量(万羽)	Quantity of Poultry Sold(10 000 fowls)	5 065	1 997	17 851	28.4
鲜 蛋(万吨)	Fresh Eggs(10 000 tons)	6.76	2 001	16.87	40.1
水产品	**Aquatic Products**				
海水产品(万吨)	Seawater Aquatic Products(10 000 tons)	19.44	2 006	19.44	100.0
淡水产品(万吨)	Freshwater Aquatic Products(10 000 tons)	19.31	2 003	22.13	87.3

注：建国以来最高年年份和产量均是指 2005 年及以前的年份和产量，不包括 2006 年在内。
Note: Peak year and output of peak year since 1949 refer to the years before 2005, excluding 2006.

表 11.5 主要年份农作物总播种面积
TOTAL SOWN AREA OF PLANTING IN MAIN YEARS

年 份 Year	总播种面积（万公顷） Total Sown Area (10 000 hectare)	粮食作物 Grain Crops		经济作物 Cash Crops		其他作物 Others	
		播种面积 Sown Area	占总播种面积(%) Percentage of the Total(%)	播种面积 Sown Area	占总播种面积(%) Percentage of the Total(%)	播种面积 Sown Area	占总播种面积(%) Percentage of the Total(%)
1990	63.11	41.71	66.1	11.16	17.7	10.24	16.2
1995	54.22	34.40	63.5	8.88	16.4	10.94	20.1
1996	57.01	35.38	62.1	8.33	14.6	13.30	23.3
1997	55.23	36.58	66.2	6.91	12.5	11.74	21.3
1998	55.64	35.25	63.4	7.42	13.3	12.97	23.3
1999	55.17	33.50	60.7	7.97	14.5	13.70	24.8
2000	52.15	25.88	49.6	8.84	17.0	17.43	33.4
2001	49.09	21.12	43.0	8.08	16.5	19.89	40.5
2002	47.67	18.77	39.4	8.07	16.9	20.83	43.7
2003	41.92	14.83	35.4	6.07	14.5	21.02	50.1
2004	40.44	15.47	38.3	4.90	12.1	20.07	49.6
2005	40.36	16.61	41.1	4.75	11.8	19.00	47.1
2006	40.14	16.55	41.2	3.73	9.3	19.86	49.5

表 11.6 农牧业特色种养产品产量(2005～2006)
OUTPUT OF SPECIAL PRODUCTS IN FARMING AND ANIMAL HUSBANDRY

指 标	Indicators	2005	2006	指 标	Indicators	2005	2006
桃 子(万吨)	Peach(10 000 tons)	10.28	11.32	鸵 鸟(只)	Ostrich(fowl)	578	804
葡 萄(万吨)	Grape(10 000 tons)	2.67	3.39	肉 鸽(万只)	Meat Dove(10 000 fowls)	467	496
草 莓(万吨)	Strawberry(10 000 tons)	2.66	2.33	甲 鱼(吨)	Soft-shelled Turtle(ton)	1 481	1 038
无花果(吨)	Fig(ton)	56	36	牛 蛙(吨)	Bullforg(ton)	98	16
弥猴桃(吨)	Kiwi(ton)	178	312	河 蟹(万吨)	Hairy Crab(10 000 tons)	1.40	1.61

表 11.7　主要年份农业商品产值和商品率
OUTPUT VALUE OF AGRICULTURAL COMMODITY AND COMMODITY RATE IN MAIN YEARS

指　标	Indicators	1990	2000	2005	2006
农业商品产值(亿元)	**Output Value of Agricultural Commodity (100 million yuan)**	**52.21**	**179.79**	**187.49**	**188.90**
#种植业	Planting	16.08	61.84	83.42	89.46
#粮食作物	Grain Crops	5.47	10.15	9.20	9.53
牧　业	Animal Husbandry	27.84	80.75	50.74	42.85
#猪	Hogs	11.85	29.82	23.56	21.05
禽	Poultry	8.17	33.41	13.95	9.20
蛋	Eggs	4.99	7.94	4.68	3.89
渔　业	Fishery	7.71	36.53	50.30	53.98
#淡水产品	Freshwater Aquatic Products	4.35	25.14	36.88	38.33
农业商品率(%)	**Agricultural Commodity Rate(%)**	**76.6**	**83.0**	**80.3**	**79.7**
#种植业	Planting	55.3	68.8	75.0	74.6
#粮食作物	Grain Crops	33.5	45.4	46.1	46.6
牧　业	Animal Husbandry	92.0	92.4	93.4	92.6
#猪	Hogs	97.6	95.8	96.1	97.3
禽	Poultry	92.0	91.9	90.7	89.2
蛋	Eggs	90.5	82.3	90.6	88.1
渔　业	Fishery	96.0	96.3	97.4	97.7
#淡水产品	Freshwater Aquatic Products	93.9	95.9	96.9	97.0

表 11.8　主要年份农产品出口情况
EXPORTS OF AGRICULTURAL PRODUCTS IN MAIN YEARS

单位:亿元(100 million yuan)

指　标	Indicators	2000	2005	2006
农产品出口总额	**Output Value of Exports of Agricultural Products**	**7.88**	**14.55**	**17.63**
#农业产品	Farm Products	0.63	2.98	2.93
牧业产品	Animal Husbardry Products	1.71	0.38	0.25
渔业产品	Fishery Products	5.55	11.19	14.45
农产品直接出口总额	**Output Value of Direct Exports of Agricultural Products**	**6.82**	**10.79**	**13.34**
#农业产品	Farm Products	0.47	2.38	2.35
牧业产品	Animal Husbardry Products	0.99	0.37	0.19
渔业产品	Fishery Products	5.37	8.04	10.80
主要出口产品	**Main Products of Exports**			
蔬　菜	Vegetables	0.19	1.66	1.75
白　蒜	Garlics	0.03	0.24	0.15
活　猪	Hogs	0.63	0.31	0.22
水产品	Aquatic Products	5.55	11.19	14.45
海水产品	Seawater Aquatic Products	5.29	8.26	11.83
淡水产品	Freshwater Aquatic Products	0.26	2.93	2.62

表 11.9 主要年份农田水利工程投资
INVESTMENT IN FARM WATER CONSERVANCY PROJECTS IN MAIN YEARS

单位:万元(10 000 yuan)

年 份 Year	合 计 Total	国家投资 State Investment	其 中 of which 海 塘 Seadike	农田水利 Farm Water Conservancy	基本建设 Capital Construction	乡、镇自筹 Funds Raised by Township and Town	企事业和区县自筹 Funds Raised by Enterprises and Public Affairs Departments
1978	17 431	13 542	719	8 512	4 134	3 889	
1980	13 172	8 080	623	4 519	2 765	5 092	
1990	26 143	15 959	907	10 877	1 506	10 184	
1995	62 474	44 651	6 103	10 583	21 800	17 823	
1996	76 467	56 421	6 470	16 159	20 693	20 046	
1997	83 097	60 497	14 467	27 153	22 447	22 600	
1998	108 565	83 596	9 660	25 712	37 780	24 969	
1999	150 324	119 193	18 580	32 882	53 660	31 131	
2000	184 102	151 539	22 063	31 282	53 532	32 563	
2001	244 337	188 477	10 598	42 406	120 575	32 178	23 682
2002	382 935	264 370	23 548	59 869	140 875	28 140	90 425
2003	516 075	375 688	13 083	78 515	199 341	27 568	112 819
2004	576 050	219 506	7 317	71 920	97 328	57 676	298 868
2005	543 780	176 215	7 010	34 973	55 290	66 421	301 145
2006	467 449	202 815	2 603	85 161	30 423	37 330	227 304

表 11.10 主要年份农村用电量
RURAL ELECTRICITY POWER CONSUMPTION IN MAIN YEARS

年 份 Year	农村用电量 (亿千瓦·时) Rural Electricity Power Consumption (100 million kwh)	其 中 of which 机电排灌 Motorized Drainage and Irrigation	农、副业加工 Farming and Sideline Products Processing	乡村办工业 Rural Enterprises
1978	8.93	1.51	2.78	3.36
1980	12.23	1.24	3.10	6.28
1985	21.87	1.44	3.01	14.73
1990	32.16	1.75	4.00	22.85
1995	58.19	2.00	7.26	41.24
1996	62.07	2.01	7.79	44.16
1997	64.98	1.94	6.92	47.55
1998	67.91	2.09	6.79	49.55
1999	70.89	2.09	6.34	52.67
2000	73.19	2.34	6.12	49.71
2001	79.66	1.51	3.57	62.51
2002	81.79	1.24	3.62	57.56
2003	89.70	1.12	3.24	61.53
2004	114.35	1.17	2.41	79.01
2005	124.53	0.99	2.70	99.72
2006	143.54	1.03	2.84	97.98

表11.11 主要年份农业机械拥有量
POSSESSION OF AGRICULTURAL MACHINERY IN MAIN YEARS

	机械名称 Name of Machinery	1990	2000	2005	2006
农业机械总动力(万千瓦)	**Total Power of Agricultural Machinery(10 000 kw)**	**276.50**	**142.50**	**96.46**	**97.23**
耕作机械动力合计(万千瓦)	Total Power of Farming Machinery(10 000 kw)	65.09	37.60	23.25	23.46
#大、中型拖拉机(台)	Large and Medium Tractors(set)	11 600	7 844	4 210	4 262
(万千瓦)	(10 000 kw)	42.73	29.30	15.84	16.28
小型拖拉机(台)	Small Tractors(set)	26 335	9 253	8 152	7 904
(万千瓦)	(10 000 kw)	22.35	8.30	7.41	7.18
排灌机械动力合计(万千瓦)	**Total Power of Drainage and Irrigation Machinery (10 000 kw)**	**30.13**	**25.92**	**21.89**	**21.32**
收获机械动力合计 (万千瓦)	Total Power of Harvest Machinery(10 000 kw)	56.04	33.30	16.08	13.58
#联合收割机(台)	Combined Harvesters(set)	3 033	4 991	2 251	2 030
(万千瓦)	(10 000 kw)	0.91	2.70	3.18	3.40
机动收割机(台)	Swathers(set)	380	87	61	10
机动脱粒机(万台)	Motorized Threshers(10 000 sets)	14.35	11.34	4.78	3.91
(万千瓦)	(10 000 kw)	44.56	30.05	12.23	9.94
植物保护机械动力合计(万千瓦)	Total Power of Plant Protecting Machine(10 000 kw)	3.88	3.07	1.92	2.36
#机动喷雾器(万台)	Motorized Nebulizers(10 000 sets)	2.45	2.07	1.2	1.39
(万千瓦)	(10 000 kw)	3.88	3.07	1.92	2.35
渔业机械动力合计(万千瓦)	Total Power of Fishery Machinery(10 000 kw)	17.83	23.40	21.39	24.16
#机动渔船(艘)	Motorized Fishing Boats(ship)	2 683	2 905	1 248	1 420
(万千瓦)	(10 000 kw)	17.83	20.50	15.26	18.15
运输机械动力合计(万千瓦)	Total Power of Transport Machinery(10 000 kw)	83.34	8.11	4.06	4.08
#农用载重汽车(万千瓦)	Agricultural Camions(10 000 kw)	39.32	5.89	2.90	2.93
(辆)	(automobile)	6 413	953	507	519
机动运输船(万千瓦)	Motorized Transport Vessels(10 000 kw)	8.77	2.22	1.16	1.15
(艘)	(ship)	6 623	1 545	441	403
其他农业机械动力合计(万千瓦)	Total Power of Other Agricultural Machine(10 000 kw)	20.07	11.13	7.76	8.27
#推土机(万千瓦)	Bulldozers(10 000 kw)	0.01	0.25	0.34	0.29
(辆)	(automobile)	2	45	57	47

表 11.12 主要年份农业技术应用和综合开发情况
TECHNOLOGY APPLICATIONS AND INTEGRATIVE EXPLOITATION IN AGRICULTURE IN MAIN YEARS

指 标	Indicators	1990	2000	2005	2006
机耕面积(万公顷)	Areas of Motorized Cultivation(10 000 hectares)	29.14	23.46	17.21	17.18
机电排灌总控制面积(万公顷)	Total Area with Motorized Drainage and Irrigation Facilities (10 000 hectares)	31.97	28.59	20.56	19.30
机种面积(万公顷)	Areas of Motorized Planting(10 000 hectares)	2.05	6.08	3.38	4.14
占粮食播种面积(%)	Percentage in Total Planting Area of Grain(%)	4.9	23.5	20.3	25.0
机收面积(万公顷)	Areas of Motorized Harvesting(10 000 hectares)	7.78	16.42	14.57	14.74
占粮食收获面积(%)	Percentage in Total Harvesting Area of Grain(%)	18.6	63.4	87.7	89.0
喷、滴管灌面积(万公顷)	Areas of Irrigating by Insufflantion and Dripping Pipeline (10 000 hectares)	1.07	0.43	0.20	0.22
机械植保面积(万公顷)	Areas of Mechancial Protecting(10 000 hectares)	1.87	41.10	19.87	27.01
化肥施用面积(万公顷)	Areas of Chemical Fertilizing(10 000 hectares)		32.10	25.78	23.72
化肥施用量(实物量)(万吨)	Chemical Fertilizer Consumption(real)(10 000 tons)	100.63	82.54	62.01	59.19
化肥施用量(折纯量)(万吨)	Chemical Fertilizer Consumption (convert to pure amount)(10 000 tons)	19.62	19.33	14.44	14.53
农药施用面积(万公顷)	Areas of Farm Pesticides(10 000 hectares)		31.02	26.75	25.81
农药施用量(万吨)	Farm Pesticides Consumption(10 000 tons)	1.88	1.10	0.84	0.83
农用塑料薄膜使用量(万吨)	Agricultural Plastic Film Consumption(10 000 tons)		2.13	2.44	2.21
地膜覆盖面积(万公顷)	Areas Covered by Plastic Film(10 000 hectares)		2.05	3.17	3.12
蔬菜大棚面积(万公顷)	Areas of Trellis of Vegetables(10 000 hectares)	0.08	0.15	0.67	0.59
温室面积(公顷)	Areas of Greenhouse(hectares)	12.61	88.15	253.00	362.80
科技攻关重点项目数(个)	Number of Key Science and Technology Projects(unit)		103	59	20
科技攻关重点项目投资额(亿元)	Investment of Key Science and Techndogy Projects (100 million yuan)		1.00	0.38	0.30
常年菜田面积(万公顷)	Areas of Perennial Vegetable Farmland(10 000 hectares)	1.11	1.25	3.26	3.23
#设施菜田	Established Vegetable Farmland		0.27	0.26	0.37
精养渔塘面积(万公顷)	Areas of Find-breed Ponds(10 000 hectares)	1.10	1.05	0.69	0.65
粮食良种使用面积(万公顷)	Areas of Well-bred Provision Farmland(10 000 hectares)		23.56	15.28	15.32

上 / 海 / 统 / 计 / 年 / 鉴

主要统计指标解释

■ 农业总产值

农业总产值是以货币表现的农、林、牧、渔业全部产品的总量和对农林牧渔生产活动进行的各种支持性服务活动的价值。它反映一定时期内农业生产的总规模和总成果。

农、林、牧、渔业的统计范围是:

(1) 农业　包括农作物种植业和其他农业。

农作物种植业包括谷物、豆类、薯类、棉、油料、糖料、麻类、烟叶、蔬菜、药材、瓜类和其他农作物的种植,以及茶园、桑园、果园的生产经营。

其他农业包括采集野生植物的果实、纤维、树胶、树脂、油料以及柴草、野生药材、菌类等及农民家庭兼营的商品性工业。

(2) 林业　包括林木的栽培(不包括茶园、桑园和果园的栽培、管理和收获等活动)、林产品的采集和村及村以下合作经济组织和农户的竹木采伐。

(3) 牧业　包括除渔业养殖以外的一切动物饲养和放牧,以及野生动物的捕猎和饲养。

(4) 渔业　包括水生动物和海藻类植物的养殖和捕捞。

(5) 农林牧渔服务业　包括农林牧渔业生产活动进行的各种支持性服务活动。但不包括各种科学技术和专业技术服务活动。

从所有制看,包括国有经济的各种专业农(农、林、牧、渔)场以及国家各级机关团体学校、科研机构、部队经营的农业;集体所有制的乡镇村各级办农场;农村各种经济组织经营的农、林、牧、渔业以及工矿企业家属集体经营的农业;农民家庭自营的农林牧渔业及兼营商品性工业等。

农业总产值的计算方法通常是按农林牧渔业产品及其副产品的产量分别乘以各自单位产品价格求得,少数生产周期较长、当年没有产品或产品产量不易统计的,则采用间接方法匡算其产值,然后将四业产品产值和服务业产值相加即为农业总产值。

1957 年以前的农业总产值中包括了厩肥和农民自给性手工业(如农民自制衣服、鞋、袜,自己从事粮食初步加工等)。1958 年及以后的农业总产值,林业中增加了村及村以下竹木采伐产值;牧业中取消了厩肥产值;副业中取消了农民自给性手工业产值,增加了村及村以下办的工业产值;渔业中增加了海洋捕捞水产品产值。1980 年及以后的农业总产值,在副业中增加了农民家庭兼营工业商品部分的产值。从 1984 年起村及村以下办工业产值划归工业。从 1993 年起,取消副业。将野生动物的捕猎划入牧业,野生植物采集和农民家庭兼营商品性工业划归农业。从 2003 年起,农业总产值中包括了农林牧渔服务业产值。

■ 农业机械总动力

指用于农、林、牧、渔业生产的各种动力机械的动力总和。动力机械包括耕作、排灌、种植、植物保护、收获、农产品加工、运输、畜牧、渔业、农田水利等各种机械。不包括专门用于乡办工业、基本建设、非农业运输、科学试验和教学等非农业生产方面用的动力机械与作业机械的数量。

■ 农作物播种面积

指报告期内收获农产品的作物的实际播种或移植有农作物的面积。凡是实际种植农作物的面积,不论种植在耕地上还是种植在非耕地上,均包括在农作物播种面积中。在播种季节基本结束后,因遭灾而重新改种和补种的农作物面积,也包括在内。

■ 粮食产量

指全社会的产量。包括国有经济经营的、集体统一经营的和农民家庭经营的粮食产量,还包括工矿企业办的农场和其他生产单位的产量。粮食除包括稻谷、小麦、玉米、高粱、谷子及其他杂粮外,还包括薯类和豆类。其产量计算方法,豆类按去豆荚后的干豆计算;薯类(包括甘薯和马铃薯,不包括芋头和木薯)1963 年以前按每 4 公斤鲜薯折 1 公斤粮食计算,从 1964 年开始改为按 5 公斤鲜薯折 1 公斤粮食计算。城市郊区作为蔬菜的薯类(如马铃薯等)按鲜品计算,并且不作粮食统计。其他粮食一律按脱粒后的原粮计算。1989 年以前粮食产量数据主要靠全面报表取得,1989 年开始使用抽样调查数据。

■ 棉花产量

指全社会的产量。包括春播棉和夏播棉。产量按皮棉计算。3 公斤籽棉折 1 公斤皮棉,不包括木棉。

主要统计指标解释

■ 油料产量

指全部油料作物的生产量。包括花生、油菜籽、芝麻、向日葵籽、胡麻籽(亚麻籽)和其他油料。不包括大豆、木本油料和野生油料。花生以带壳干花生计算。

■ 水产品产量

指人工养殖的水产品和天然生长的水产品的捕捞量。包括海水的鱼类、虾蟹类、贝类和藻类以及内陆水域的鱼类、虾蟹类和贝类,不包括淡水生植物。水产品产量是通过各级水产和统计部门逐级上报取得数据。1995 年及以前,贝类中牡蛎按鲜肉计算;蚶、蛤、蛙按 5 斤鲜品折 1 斤计算。1996 年以后则统一按鲜品计算。

■ 猪、牛、羊肉产量

指当年出栏并已屠宰、除去头蹄下水后带骨肉(即胴体重)的重量。包括全社会范围内的产量。1996 年前为各级逐级上报数据。1996 年第一次农业普查以后,由于畜牧业产品年报数据与普查数据之间存在一定的差距,国家统计局农调总队对畜牧业年报数据与普查数据进行衔接。1999 年以后,国家统计局开展了猪、牛、羊、禽等主要畜禽品种的抽样调查, 并用抽样数据作为国家定案数据使用。未开展抽样调查的品种,仍使用各级统计部门逐级上报数据。

SHANGHAI STATISTICAL YEARBOOK

EXPLANATORY NOTES TO MAJOR STATISTICAL INDICATORS

□ Gross Output Value of Agriculture

Gross Output Value of Agriculture refers to the total volume of products of farming, forestry, animal husbandry and fishery expressed in the monetary terms and output value of all kinds of service activities that support farming, forestry, animal husbandry and fishery production. It reflects the overall scale and achievements of agricultural production during a given period of time.

The scope of statistics on farming, forestry, animal husbandry, and fishery are as follows:

(1)Farming includes cultivation of farm crops and other agricultural activities.

Cultivation of farm crops include cultivation of grain crops, legume crops, tuber-crops, cotton, oil-bearing crops, sugar crops, bastfiber plants, tobacco, vegetables, medicinal herbs, melon crops, and cultivation and management of tea plantations, mulberry fields and orchards.

Other agricultural activities include harvesting wild fruits, fiber, tree gum, resin, oil-bearing plants, firewood, wild medicinal herbs, fungus, and rural-household commodity industries.

(2)Forestry refers to planting trees of various kinds (excluding tea plantations, mulberry fields and orchards), collection of forestry products and cutting and felling of bamboo and trees by villages and other cooperative organizations under village level.

(3)Animal husbandry refers to raising and grazing of all kinds of farm animals except fishing and aquatic cultivating, and hunting and rising of wild animals.

(4)Fishery refers to cultivation and catching of fish and other aquatic products and cultivation and collection of seaweed and other aquatic plants.

(5)Service Industry for Farming, Forestry, Animal Husbandry and Fishery refers to all kinds of service activities that support farming, forestry, animal husbandry and fishery production, whereas activities of science, technology and professional service are not included.

In terms of ownership, China's agriculture includes specialized state farms (for farming, forestry, animal husbandry, fishery), farms managed by various government agencies, organizations, schools, research institutions, and army; farms managed by rural collective organizations at levels of the township, town, and village; farming, forestry, animal husbandry, fishery run by various rural collective organizations and farming run by collective family members' organizations of mining and industrial enterprises; farming, forestry, animal husbandry and fishery and some commodity industries run by individual farmers.

Gross output value of agriculture is obtained by first multiplying the output of products or by-products by their unit price. For a small number of products, annual output of which is not available or difficult to get due to the long production/growing process involved, the output value will be estimated through an indirect approach. The sum of output value of all products of farming, forestry, animal husbandry and fishery and output value of service activities will then and together to form gross output value of agriculture.

Before 1957, China's gross agricultural output value included the value of barnyard manure and handicraft products for self-consumption (clothes, shoes, stockings, and initial grain processing under-taken by peasants). After 1958, the output value of cutting and felling of bamboo and trees by villages and other cooperative organizations under villages have been included in forestry; value of barnyard manure has been excluded from animal husbandry; the value of self-consumed handicrafts has been excluded from sideline occupations, while output value of industries run by villages and cooperative organizations under village level has been included in sideline occupations and output value of fish catches by motor fishing boats has been added to fishery. Since 1980, the output value of handicraft products made for sale by farmer households has been added to sideline occupations, From 1984, industries run by villages and cooperative organizations under village level have been included in the sector of industry. After 1993, the category of sideline occupations has been canceled and hunting of wild animals has been classified into husbandry, and harvesting of wild vegetation and commodity industry run by rural households have been grouped into the category of agriculture. Since 2003, the output value of service industry for farming, forestry, animal husbandry and fishery is included in the gross output value of agriculture.

□ Total Power of Agricultural Machinery

Total Power of Agricultural Machinery refers to the total mechanical power of machinery used in farming, forestry animal

EXPLANATORY NOTES TO MAJOR STATISTICAL INDICATORS

husbandry and fishery, including machines used for ploughing, irrigation and drainage, crop growing, plant protection, harvesting, farm product processing, transport, stock breeding, fishery and water conservancy. Machinery employed for non-agricultural purposes such as township industry, capital construction, non-agricultural transport, scientific experiments and for teaching is excluded.

□ Sown Area of Planting

Sown Area of Planting refers to area of land sown or transplanted with crops that have been harvested during report period, regardless of being in cultivated area or non-cultivated area. Area of land re-sown due to natural disasters is also included.

□ Grain Output

Grain Output refers to the total output in the whole country including grains produced by state farms, collective units, rural households, as well as by farms affiliated to industrial and mining enterprises and other production units. Grain includes rice, wheat, corn, sorghum, millet and other miscellaneous grains as well as tubers and bean. Output of beans refers to dry beans without pods. The output of tubers (sweet potatoes and potatoes, not including taros and cassava) was converted into that of grain at the ratio 4:1, i.e. 4 kilograms of fresh tubers was equivalent to 1 kilogram of grain up to 1963. Since 1964 the ratio for conversion has been 5: 1. Tubers supplied as vegetables (such as potatoes) in cities and suburbs are calculated as fresh vegetables and their output is not included in the output of grain. Output of all other grains refers to husked grain. Data on grain production before 1989 were obtained through Comprehensive Statistical Reporting System. Since 1989, data from sample surveys are used.

□ Cotton Output

Cotton Output refers to the cotton production in the whole country including cotton sown in spring and in autumn. Output is measured as the weight of ginned cotton. Three kilograms of seed-cotton are equivalent to 1 kilogram of ginned cotton, excluding ceiba.

□ Output of Oil Plants

Output of Oil Plants refers to the total production of oil-bearing crops of various kinds, including peanuts, (dry, in shell) rapeseeds, sesame, sunflower seeds, flax seeds, and other oil-bearing crops. Soybeans, oil-bearing woody plants, and wild oil-bearing crops are not included.

□ Output of Aquatic Products

Output of Aquatic Products refers to catches of both artificially cultured and naturally grown aquatic products, including fish, shrimps, crabs and shellfish in sea and inland water as well as seaweed. Freshwater plants are not included. Data on output of aquatic products are reported by aquatic product and statistical agencies level by level. Before 1995, among the shellfish, the oyster was counted as fresh meat; 5 kilograms of ark shell, clams and frogs are equivalent to 1 kilogram of fresh aquatic products; they are all counted as fresh aquatic products since 1996.

□ Output of Pork, Beef, and Mutton

Output of Pork, Beef, and Mutton refers to the meat of slaughtered hogs, cattle, sheep and goats with head, feet, and offal taken away. Data refers to the production of the whole country. The first agriculture census of China in 1996 revealed some discrepancy between the production of animal products from the annual reports and that from the census. Efforts were made by the Rural Socio-economic Survey Organization of NBS to adjust the output value of animal husbandry to make the figures from the annual reports consistent with the census data. Since 1999, NBS conducted sample survey for the major animal husbandry products, such as hogs, cattle, sheep and goats and fowls, and the data from sample surveys are used as national finalized data. Those products, which are not covered by the sample survey, are still reported by statistical agencies level by level.

第十二篇

CHAPTER 12

工 业

INDUSTRY

表 12.1 工业总产值及指数(1978～2006)
GROSS OUTPUT VALUE AND INDEX OF INDUSTRY

年 份 Year	工业总产值（亿元） Gross Output Value of Industry(100 million yuan)			工业总产值指数（以 1978 年为 100） Indices of Gross Output Value of Industry (1978 = 100)		
	合 计 Total	轻工业 Light Industry	重工业 Heavy Industry	总指数 Index	轻工业 Light Industry	重工业 Heavy Industry
1978	514.01	266.02	247.99	100.0	100.0	100.0
1979	556.30	290.78	265.52	108.6	109.7	107.6
1980	598.75	331.13	267.62	115.7	123.4	108.3
1981	620.12	360.12	260.00	120.0	135.9	104.6
1982	634.65	359.62	275.03	125.6	139.9	111.9
1983	663.53	363.92	299.61	134.4	147.6	121.8
1984	728.12	395.60	332.52	147.7	163.3	132.7
1985	862.73	456.59	406.14	167.7	184.3	151.9
1986	952.21	493.09	459.12	177.0	192.2	162.6
1987	1 073.84	556.96	516.88	188.9	206.3	172.4
1988	1 304.66	679.17	625.49	208.8	227.2	191.4
1989	1 524.67	789.57	735.10	215.0	233.6	197.3
1990	1 642.75	846.63	796.12	223.6	241.8	206.7
1991	1 947.18	976.34	970.84	255.2	269.2	241.9
1992	2 429.96	1 132.75	1 297.21	306.7	306.4	306.6
1993	3 327.04	1 401.33	1 925.71	368.2	352.7	380.1
1994	4 255.19	1 890.12	2 365.06	435.3	429.9	437.6
1995	5 349.53	2 432.67	2 916.86	510.9	504.2	513.9
(1995)	(4 547.47)	(2 092.89)	(2 454.57)			
1996	5 126.22	2 334.29	2 791.73	590.1	568.7	606.4
1997	5 649.93	2 528.19	3 121.74	675.7	640.4	704.1
1998	5 763.67	2 527.56	3 236.11	728.5	657.7	788.7
1999	6 213.24	2 679.71	3 533.53	805.1	709.1	887.5
2000	7 022.98	2 903.40	4 119.59	913.7	782.2	1 027.7
2001	7 806.18	2 986.59	4 819.59	1 063.8	865.2	1 234.8
2002	8 730.00	3 169.30	5 560.70	1 219.1	934.7	1 463.2
2003	11 708.49	3 550.80	8 157.68	1 601.9	1 064.0	2 061.3
2004	14 595.29	3 871.33	10 723.97	1 927.1	1 268.2	2 492.2
2005	16 876.78	4 299.31	12 577.48	2 195.0	1 395.0	2 873.5
2006	19 631.23	4 747.28	14 883.94	2 500.1	1 494.0	3 341.9

注：从 1996 年开始，工业总产值按新规定计算，括号内数为 1995 年新规定数。（以下同。）

Note: Since 1996, new regulations have been adopted in calculating total industrial gross output value of industry. The figures of 1995 in brackets are calculated in line with the new regulations. Same as follows.

表 12.2 各区县工业企业主要指标（2006）
MAJOR INDICATIORS OF INDUSTRIAL ENTERPRISES IN DISTRICTS AND COUNTIES

地 区 District		单位数(个) Number of Enterprises (unit)	从业人员 (万人) Employees (10 000 persons)	工业总产值 (亿元) Gross Output Value of Industry (100 million yuan)	年末资产总计 (亿元) Total Assets (year-end) (100 million yuan)	主营业务收入 (亿元) Prime Operating Revenue (100 million yuan)	利润总额 (亿元) Total Pre-tax Profits (100 million yuan)
总 计	**Total**	**14 404**	**269.67**	**18 573.13**	**17 926.10**	**19 266.93**	**1 096.92**
浦东新区	Pudong New Area	2 378	47.45	4 306.13	4 432.93	4 623.49	267.80
黄 浦 区	Huangpu	81	2.39	127.26	178.71	164.91	4.65
卢 湾 区	Luwan	48	1.06	39.66	55.79	45.53	0.25
徐 汇 区	Xuhui	417	8.47	513.14	460.59	569.60	28.65
长 宁 区	Changning	118	2.12	91.45	112.77	93.92	4.89
静 安 区	Jing'an	38	0.61	29.25	67.89	32.77	12.21
普 陀 区	Putuo	348	5.39	216.89	215.42	217.41	15.39
闸 北 区	Zhabei	184	3.61	149.12	157.47	154.84	5.88
虹 口 区	Hongkou	111	2.11	61.17	85.08	64.55	2.91
杨 浦 区	Yangpu	265	6.17	506.89	782.87	537.97	85.30
宝 山 区	Baoshan	798	37.49	1 763.73	2 053.75	1 946.55	213.90
闵 行 区	Minhang	1 915	15.11	2 617.95	2 173.59	2 636.17	135.74
嘉 定 区	Jiading	1 789	31.62	1 729.76	1 339.79	1 735.38	103.24
金 山 区	Jinshan	714	12.72	966.52	645.62	929.74	28.30
松 江 区	Songjiang	1 546	15.72	2 442.05	1 474.71	2 507.78	67.48
青 浦 区	Qingpu	1 181	14.69	802.13	712.03	787.38	39.63
南 汇 区	Nanhui	1 043	33.00	645.20	562.66	643.50	39.99
奉 贤 区	Fengxian	1 119	22.41	632.66	577.36	616.96	21.03
崇 明 县	Chongming	276	4.55	125.78	117.32	129.61	7.36

注：本表至表 12.19 为国有企业及销售收入在 500 万元以上的非国有企业。
Note: Data in this table to table 12.19 is collected from state-owned enterprises and non-state-owned enterprises with revenue of sales more than 5 million yuan.

表 12.3 规模以上工业企业主要指标（2006）
MAJOR INDICATORS OF THE CITY'S INDUSTRIAL ENTERPRISES ABOVE THE SET SCALE

类 别	Types	单位数（个）Number of Enterprises (unit)	从业人员（万人）Employees (10 000 persons)
总 计	**Total**	**14 404**	**269.67**
按隶属关系分	**Grouped by Subordination**		
#中央工业	Central Government	192	17.11
市(局)属工业	Municipality	1 202	46.89
区属工业	District	771	12.20
县属工业	County	24	0.49
街道属工业	Subdistrict	115	1.71
镇属工业	Town	2 001	36.87
乡属工业	Township	195	3.14
村属工业	Village	1 270	15.48
按登记注册类型分	**Grouped by Registration Categories**		
内 资	Domestic	8 857	120.88
国 有	State-owned	407	14.17
集 体	Collective-owned	911	8.62
股份合作	Share-holding Coorperation	497	5.24
联 营	Joint Owned	198	3.16
有限责任公司	Companies with Limited Liabilities	1 142	24.75
股份有限公司	Share-holding Companies with Limited Liabilities	90	7.84
私 营	Private	5 579	56.70
其 他	Others	33	0.39
港澳台商投资	Hong Kong, Macao and Taiwan Funded	1 782	41.02
外商投资	Foreign Funded	3 765	107.76
按轻、重工业分	**Grouped by Light and Heavy Industry**		
轻工业	Light Industry	6 060	112.18
重工业	Heavy Industry	8 344	157.49
按企业规模分	**Grouped by Size of Enterprises**		
大型企业	Large	93	39.74
中型企业	Medium	1 444	96.27
小型企业	Small	12 867	133.66
按工业行业分	**Grouped by Sectors**		
采矿业	Mining Industry	2	0.03
石油和天然气开采业	Petroleum and Natural Gas Exploiting	1	0.02
非金属矿采选业	Nonmetal Minerals Mining	1	0.01
制造业	Manufacture Industry	14 322	265.64
农副食品加工业	Farm and Sideline Products Processing	171	2.17
食品制造业	Food Manufacturing	255	5.71

工业总产值（亿元）Gross Output Value of Industry (100 million yuan)	年末资产总计（亿元）Total Assets (year-end) (100 million yuan)	固定资产净值年平均余额（亿元）Average Net Value of Fixed Assets (100 million yuan)	流动资产年平均余额（亿元）Average Current Assets (100 million yuan)
18 573.13	**17 926.10**	**5 880.38**	**8 712.15**
3 749.43	4 888.35	2 029.95	1 697.26
4 339.54	5 101.32	1 606.96	2 375.68
645.57	581.07	148.97	330.28
8.81	8.63	2.58	5.27
75.03	67.98	13.11	39.28
1326.71	1 155.52	306.82	681.42
175.24	111.33	26.68	71.60
589.70	421.78	88.64	291.11
6 879.44	8 462.55	2 817.88	3 544.90
1 116.74	2 223.91	1 003.98	646.24
287.54	223.98	47.45	151.76
175.53	128.34	26.52	84.88
106.67	86.39	23.53	51.80
1 596.76	2 027.43	576.00	1 109.16
1 735.76	2 306.96	794.49	635.23
1826.45	1 433.31	335.03	848.69
34.00	32.22	10.87	17.13
2 475.41	2 051.98	623.79	1 071.58
9 218.29	7 411.57	2 438.71	4 095.67
4 202.39	4 084.71	1 084.94	2 219.12
14 370.74	13 841.39	4 795.44	6 493.03
7 072.00	6 810.39	2 497.02	2 681.40
5 858.98	5 878.73	1 855.79	3 045.04
5 642.15	5 236.99	1 527.57	2 985.71
19.65	40.97	11.40	20.54
19.56	40.88	11.38	20.49
0.09	0.09	0.03	0.06
17 820.92	16 263.20	4 664.53	8 532.83
152.54	110.55	25.03	67.16
237.75	255.01	64.08	128.49

表 12.3 续表 1 continued

类 别	Types	单位数（个）Number of Enterprises (unit)	从业人员（万人）Employees (10 000 persons)
饮料制造业	Beverage Manufacturing	64	1.33
烟草制品业	Tabacco Manufacturing	2	0.41
纺织业	Textile	930	15.84
纺织服装、鞋、帽制造业	Garments, Shoes and Accessories Manufacturing	1 036	22.01
皮革、毛皮、羽毛(绒)及其制品业	Leather, Fur, and Wool Products Manufacturing	223	5.48
木材加工及木、竹、藤、棕、草制品业	Timber Processing and Timber, Bamboo, Rattan, Coir and Straw Products Manufacturing	162	2.27
家具制造业	Furniture Manufacturing	253	5.10
造纸及纸制品业	Paper-making and Paper Products Manufacturing	318	3.42
印刷业和记录媒介的复制	Printing and Record Duplicating	355	4.35
文教体育用品制造业	Stationary, Education and Sports Goods Manufacturing	275	6.51
石油加工、炼焦及核燃料加工业	Oil Processing, Coking and Nuclear Fuel Processing	48	2.45
化学原料及化学制品制造业	Raw Chemical Materials and Chemical Products Manufacturing	1 008	11.39
医药制造业	Medicine Manufacturing	208	5.22
化学纤维制造业	Chemical Fiber Manufacturing	55	0.73
橡胶制品业	Rubber Products Manufacturing	241	4.86
塑料制品业	Plastic Products Manufacturing	931	12.07
非金属矿物制品业	Nonmetal Mineral Products	622	8.79
黑色金属冶炼及压延加工业	Smelting and Pressing of Ferrous Metals	173	5.31
有色金属冶炼及压延加工业	Smelting and Pressing of Nonferrous Metals	243	4.25
金属制品业	Metal Products Manufacturing	1 271	16.63
通用设备制造业	General Equipment Manufacturing	1 605	25.43
专用设备制造业	Special Purpose Equipment Manufacturing	838	11.73
交通运输设备制造业	Transportation Equipment Manufacturing	716	20.18
电气机械及器材制造业	Electric Machinery Equipments and Manufacturing	1 148	21.98
通信设备、计算机及其他电子设备制造业	Communications Equipment, Computer and Other Electronic Equipment Manufacturing	656	31.65
仪器仪表及文化、办公用机械制造业	Instruments, Meters, Culture and Office Equipments Manufacturing	315	5.46
工艺品及其他制造业	Artworks and Other Manufacturing	163	2.64
废弃资源和废旧材料回收加工业	Waste Resources and Materials Recycling and Processing	37	0.25
电力、燃气及水的生产和供应业	**Production and Supply of Power, Gas and Water**	**80**	**4.00**
电力、热力的生产和供应业	Production and Supply of Electricity and Thermal Power	28	2.12
燃气生产和供应业	Production and Supply of Gas	11	0.88
水的生产和供应业	Production and Supply of Water	41	1.00

工业总产值(亿元) Gross Output Value of Industry (100 million yuan)	年末资产总计(亿元) Total Assets (year-end) (100 million yuan)	固定资产净值年平均余额(亿元) Average Net Value of Fixed Assets (100 million yuan)	流动资产年平均余额(亿元) Average Current Assets (100 million yuan)
116.31	108.79	43.51	51.94
229.77	456.57	29.74	245.60
358.92	350.79	99.01	194.04
405.72	269.23	58.43	173.39
119.30	94.17	20.31	65.39
76.95	66.35	17.96	40.23
175.19	114.82	27.50	70.92
157.80	159.19	65.33	77.99
139.95	177.21	71.31	82.93
151.53	118.00	28.88	71.01
919.04	444.58	214.55	141.99
1 333.15	1 435.47	540.81	581.99
236.50	316.24	96.49	158.33
48.58	54.77	24.98	22.42
155.58	165.31	54.94	87.54
398.16	409.50	139.24	206.48
391.95	500.78	153.29	278.98
1 445.74	1 914.39	761.43	657.34
415.97	205.58	54.90	120.92
670.43	570.80	140.05	348.47
1 530.60	1 503.31	293.49	1 020.17
457.57	535.09	128.29	323.59
1 894.69	2 157.88	484.85	1 034.54
1 275.76	988.74	199.84	623.57
3 919.32	2 435.87	757.41	1 422.41
300.12	242.72	39.59	178.65
85.94	79.78	23.92	44.52
20.07	21.69	5.36	11.84
732.56	**1 621.93**	**1 204.45**	**158.78**
638.84	1 325.30	1 028.99	91.78
64.93	102.15	50.45	39.31
28.80	194.48	125.01	27.68

表 12.3 续表2 continued

类别	Types	年末负债合计 Total Liabilities (year-end)	年末所有者权益 Owners'Equity (year-end)
总 计	**Total**	**9 014.05**	**8 912.05**
按隶属关系分	**Grouped by Subordination**		
#中央工业	Central Government	1 897.24	2 991.11
市(局)属工业	Municipality	2 561.19	2 540.14
区属工业	District	319.09	261.98
县属工业	County	4.93	3.70
街道属工业	Subdistrict	33.52	34.46
镇属工业	Town	623.57	531.96
乡属工业	Township	67.53	43.80
村属工业	Village	218.41	203.38
按登记注册类型分	**Grouped by Registration Categories**		
内 资	Domestic	3 826.23	4 636.32
国 有	State-owned	699.44	1 524.47
集 体	Collective-owned	123.57	100.41
股份合作	Share-holding Coorperation	67.64	60.69
联 营	Joint Owned	51.08	35.31
有限责任公司	Companies with Limited Liabilities	1 138.00	889.43
股份有限公司	Share-holding Companies with Limited Liabilities	855.95	1 451.02
私 营	Private	878.86	554.45
其 他	Others	11.69	20.54
港澳台商投资	Hong Kong, Macao and Taiwan Funded	1 072.84	979.14
外商投资	Foreign Funded	4 114.98	3 296.59
按轻、重工业分	**Grouped by Light and Heavy Industry**		
轻工业	Light Industry	1 948.24	2 136.46
重工业	Heavy Industry	7 065.81	6 775.59
按企业规模分	**Grouped by Size of Enterprises**		
大型企业	Large	2 961.49	3 848.90
中型企业	Medium	3 169.61	2 709.11
小型企业	Small	2 882.95	2 354.04
按工业行业分	**Grouped by Sectors**		
采矿业	Mining Industry	9.24	31.73
石油和天然气开采业	Petroleum and Natural Gas Exploiting	9.17	31.71
非金属矿采选业	Nonmetal Minerals Mining	0.07	0.02
制造业	Manufacture Industry	8 537.07	7 726.13
农副食品加工业	Farm and Sideline Products Processing	60.78	49.78
食品制造业	Food Manufacturing	147.50	107.51

单位:亿元(100 million yuan)

主营业务收入 Prime Operating Revenue	利润总额 Total After-tax Profits	税金总额 Total Tax and Duties	成本费用总额 Total Cost and Expenses
19 266.93	**1 096.92**	**681.54**	**18 184.28**
3 927.59	353.93	274.12	3 518.17
4 692.24	254.74	199.05	4 445.70
694.38	26.93	16.83	677.04
8.84	0.29	0.31	8.63
74.15	4.93	2.14	70.78
1 308.13	76.65	33.66	1 238.55
174.79	5.45	3.41	170.75
597.82	44.32	17.95	560.65
7 189.91	535.12	390.86	6 666.97
1 161.96	112.41	178.89	986.99
277.59	16.20	11.42	268.12
173.81	12.19	6.80	165.68
107.53	4.83	3.68	104.04
1 720.82	113.51	57.59	1 633.40
1 920.43	179.77	79.87	1 772.59
1 790.93	94.05	51.91	1 701.76
36.83	2.17	0.69	34.38
2 480.41	98.08	52.77	2 398.99
9 596.60	463.71	237.92	9 118.32
4 297.25	282.52	259.13	3 963.79
14 969.68	814.40	422.42	14 220.50
7 600.71	452.23	364.66	7 083.39
5 950.20	356.60	153.03	5 648.91
5 716.02	288.08	163.86	5 451.99
20.07	11.46	1.88	7.80
19.97	11.46	1.86	7.71
0.10		0.03	0.09
18 479.78	1 035.55	629.92	17 439.75
170.44	6.42	3.15	165.30
271.90	11.10	14.07	264.55

表 12.3 续表 3 continued

	类 别 Types	年末负债合计 Total Liabilities (Year-end)	年末所有者权益 Owners Equity (Year-end)
饮料制造业	Beverage Manufacturing	55.92	52.88
烟草制品业	Tabacco Manufacturing	17.63	438.94
纺织业	Textile	185.21	165.58
纺织服装、鞋、帽制造业	Garments, Shoes and Accessories Manufacturing	151.13	118.10
皮革、毛皮、羽毛(绒)及其制品业	Leather, Fur, and Wool Products Manufacturing	59.56	34.61
木材加工及木、竹、藤、棕、草制品业	Timber Processing and Timber, Bamboo, Rattan, Coir and Straw Products Manufacturing	38.44	27.91
家具制造业	Furniture Manufacturing	64.68	50.14
造纸及纸制品业	Paper-making and Paper Products Manufacturing	91.04	68.14
印刷业和记录媒介的复制	Printing and Record Duplicating	77.62	99.59
文教体育用品制造业	Stationary, Education and Sports Goods Manufacturing	67.11	50.90
石油加工、炼焦及核燃料加工业	Oil Processing, Coking and Nuclear Fuel Processing	159.60	284.98
化学原料及化学制品制造业	Raw Chemical Materials and Chemical Products Manufacturing	804.42	631.05
医药制造业	Medicine Manufacturing	160.78	155.46
化学纤维制造业	Chemical Fiber Manufacturing	21.76	33.01
橡胶制品业	Rubber Products Manufacturing	97.49	67.81
塑料制品业	Plastic Products Manufacturing	215.14	194.36
非金属矿物制品业	Nonmetal Mineral Products	280.61	220.17
黑色金属冶炼及压延加工业	Smelting and Pressing of Ferrous Metals	809.71	1 104.68
有色金属冶炼及压延加工业	Smelting and Pressing of Nonferrous Metals	125.49	80.09
金属制品业	Metal Products Manufacturing	311.41	259.39
通用设备制造业	General Equipment Manufacturing	923.97	579.34
专用设备制造业	Special Purpose Equipment Manufacturing	298.44	236.65
交通运输设备制造业	Transportation Equipment Manufacturing	1 080.69	1 077.19
电气机械及器材制造业	Electric Machinery Equipments and Manufacturing	552.30	436.45
通信设备、计算机及其他电子设备制造业	Communications Equipment, Computer and Other Electronic Equipment Manufacturing	1 512.50	923.37
仪器仪表及文化、办公用机械制造业	Instruments, Meters, Culture and Office Equipments Manufacturing	113.30	129.42
工艺品及其他制造业	Artworks and Other Manufacturing	38.06	41.72
废弃资源和废旧材料回收加工业	Waste Resources and Materials Recycling and Processing	14.79	6.90
电力、燃气及水的生产和供应业	**Production and Supply of Power, Gas and Water**	**467.74**	**1 154.19**
电力、热力的生产和供应业	Production and Supply of Electricity and Thermal Power	327.42	997.89
燃气生产和供应业	Production and Supply of Gas	51.76	50.39
水的生产和供应业	Production and Supply of Water	88.57	105.91

单位:亿元(100 million yuan)

主营业务收入 Prime Operating Revenue	利润总额 Total After-tax Profits	税金总额 Total Tax and Duties	成本费用总额 Total Cost and Expenses
117.37	6.27	11.56	107.64
230.21	79.07	133.88	65.98
358.27	11.42	9.65	349.93
389.23	19.78	10.00	370.17
116.07	6.94	2.46	109.55
79.17	3.17	1.57	76.06
173.96	12.57	3.61	162.34
158.42	5.24	5.45	154.66
141.54	11.99	6.79	130.92
154.74	5.71	2.54	151.00
922.74	-11.65	29.12	935.32
1 317.39	45.94	40.18	1 260.73
246.60	18.38	14.64	234.38
47.83	2.61	1.62	45.74
171.22	7.06	3.62	165.71
402.36	16.23	10.37	388.32
406.77	19.45	14.30	393.01
1 639.00	188.36	66.24	1 467.43
415.81	9.38	5.56	408.74
680.89	41.18	15.53	644.95
1 484.16	118.35	39.23	1 373.13
462.57	30.93	16.46	437.25
2 124.68	165.45	111.43	1 948.56
1 291.74	94.14	26.67	1 207.74
4 043.42	70.06	18.83	3 996.10
308.93	31.67	7.94	280.10
113.19	7.35	2.79	106.11
39.16	0.98	0.65	38.31
767.08	**49.91**	**49.74**	**736.74**
643.61	49.19	48.22	602.64
95.59	-2.09	0.97	99.44
27.88	2.81	0.56	34.65

表 12.4 工业企业销售产值和新产品产值(2006)
SALES VALUE AND NEW PRODUCTS VALUE OF INDUSTRIAL ENTERPRISES

单位:亿元(100 million yuan)

类 别	Types	工业销售产值 Sales Value of Industry	其中 of which: #出口交货值 Delivery Value of Industry Export	新产品产值 New Products Value
总 计	**Total**	**18 392.60**	**5 853.58**	**3 063.08**
按隶属关系分	**Grouped by Subordination**			
#中央工业	Central Government	3 735.78	574.00	661.71
市(局)属工业	Municipality	4 308.74	768.85	1 689.40
区属工业	District	647.58	109.42	22.62
县属工业	County	8.79	1.86	0.50
街道属工业	Subdistrict	74.87	17.90	1.05
镇属工业	Town	1 299.21	355.38	42.34
乡属工业	Township	173.23	46.59	0.91
村属工业	Village	591.45	101.19	1.50
按登记注册类型分	**Grouped by Registration Categories**			
内 资	Domestic	6 816.10	704.15	682.80
国 有	State-owned	1 111.57	63.32	96.69
集 体	Collective-owned	283.15	13.66	3.69
股份合作	Share-holding Coorperation	172.08	12.50	1.21
联 营	Joint Owned	106.03	8.45	5.53
有限责任公司	Companies with Limited Liabilities	1 599.71	231.96	298.36
股份有限公司	Share-holding Companies with Limited Liabilities	1 723.78	176.37	247.51
私 营	Private	1 786.96	189.04	28.17
其 他	Others	32.82	8.85	1.63
港澳台商投资	Hong Kong, Macao and Taiwan Funded	2 449.84	883.45	310.75
外商投资	Foreign Funded	9 126.66	4 265.98	2 069.53
按轻、重工业分	**Grouped by Light and Heavy Industry**			
轻工业	Light Industry	4 161.13	1 321.24	382.05
重工业	Heavy Industry	14 231.46	4 532.33	2 681.03
按企业规模分	**Grouped by Size of Enterprises**			
大型企业	Large	7 041.54	2 838.78	1 921.44
中型企业	Medium	5 772.21	1 932.58	939.51
小型企业	Small	5 578.85	1 082.22	202.13
按工业行业分	**Grouped by Sectors**			
采矿业	**Mining Industry**	**20.08**		
石油和天然气开采业	Petroleum and Natural Gas Exploiting	19.97		
非金属矿采选业	Nonmetal Minerals Mining	0.11		
制造业	**Manufacture Industry**	**17 640.88**	**5 853.24**	**3 063.08**
农副食品加工业	Farm and Sideline Products Processing	152.30	17.34	0.07
食品制造业	Food Manufacturing	234.67	18.39	2.41

注：新产品产值是指国家级或市经委认证并颁发给新产品证书，且在新产品证书规定的有效期内生产的产品产值。

Note: New Products Value refers to the value of the products which have been awarded the new products certificate by the relevant state or city authorities and are manufactured during the time limit as specified in the new product certificate.

表 12.4 续表 continued

单位:亿元(100 million yuan)

类别	Types	工业销售产值 Sales Value of Industry	其中 of which #出口交货值 Delivery Value of Industry Export	新产品产值 New Products Value
饮料制造业	Beverage Manufacturing	119.03	4.06	0.51
烟草制品业	Tabacco Manufacturing	230.56	6.40	
纺织业	Textile	357.97	125.87	14.62
纺织服装、鞋、帽制造业	Garments, Shoes and Accessories Manufacturing	388.37	179.79	15.80
皮革、毛皮、羽毛(绒)及其制品业	Leather, Fur, and Wool Products Manufacturing	117.28	66.04	1.26
木材加工及木、竹、藤、棕、草制品业	Timber Processing and Timber, Bamboo, Rattan, Coir and Straw Products Manufacturing	75.85	24.12	0.34
家具制造业	Furniture Manufacturing	173.99	78.24	1.06
造纸及纸制品业	Paper-making and Paper Products Manufacturing	157.23	13.40	0.48
印刷业和记录媒介的复制	Printing and Record Duplicating	139.08	9.73	0.37
文教体育用品制造业	Stationary, Education and Sports Goods Manufacturing	152.07	94.71	20.26
石油加工、炼焦及核燃料加工业	Oil Processing, Coking and Nuclear Fuel Processing	917.97	5.22	41.75
化学原料及化学制品制造业	Raw Chemical Materials and Chemical Products Manufacturing	1 307.40	163.39	86.03
医药制造业	Medicine Manufacturing	228.19	34.38	45.25
化学纤维制造业	Chemical Fiber Manufacturing	46.72	9.10	0.40
橡胶制品业	Rubber Products Manufacturing	153.55	50.89	15.52
塑料制品业	Plastic Products Manufacturing	394.01	89.94	7.79
非金属矿物制品业	Nonmetal Mineral Products	385.72	62.71	7.92
黑色金属冶炼及压延加工业	Smelting and Pressing of Ferrous Metals	1 439.61	188.40	162.23
有色金属冶炼及压延加工业	Smelting and Pressing of Nonferrous Metals	410.56	60.56	24.67
金属制品业	Metal Products Manufacturing	664.44	181.23	13.94
通用设备制造业	General Equipment Manufacturing	1 516.73	351.27	478.49
专用设备制造业	Special Purpose Equipment Manufacturing	446.05	95.51	58.02
交通运输设备制造业	Transportation Equipment Manufacturing	1 875.58	350.19	888.11
电气机械及器材制造业	Electric Machinery Equipments and Manufacturing	1 270.38	381.87	141.33
通信设备、计算机及其他电子设备制造业	Communcations Equipment, Computer and Other Electronic Equipment Manufacturing	3 884.73	3 036.63	973.77
仪器仪表及文化、办公用机械制造业	Instruments, Meters, Culture and Office Equipments Manufacturing	294.47	137.76	60.21
工艺品及其他制造业	Artworks and Other Manufacturing	86.56	16.07	0.46
废弃资源和废旧材料回收加工业	Waste Resources and Materials Recycling and Processing	19.83	0.01	
电力、燃气及水的生产和供应业	**Production and Supply of Power, Gas and Water**	**731.64**	**0.34**	
电力、热力的生产和供应业	Production and Supply of Electricity and Thermal Power	638.80		
燃气生产和供应业	Production and Supply of Gas	64.91	0.18	
水的生产和供应业	Production and Supply of Water	27.93	0.16	

表 12.5 工业企业经济效益指标(2006) ECONOMIC EFFICIENCY INDICATORS OF INDUSTRIAL ENTERPRISES

类别	Types	工业经济效益综合指数 Industrial Economic Benefit Synthetic Index	总资产贡献率(%) Total Assets Contribution Ratio (%)	资产保值增值率(%) Ratio of Capital Hold and Rise (%)	资产负债率(%) Asset-debt Ratio (%)
总计	**Total**	**207.34**	**11.2**	**115.0**	**50.3**
#国有及国有控股企业	Enterprises Owned by the State or with the State Holding Major Shares	286.57	12.9	113.8	43.6
#大中型企业	Large and Medium Enterprises	314.38	13.4	114.2	42.6
按隶属关系分	**Grouped by Subordination**				
中央工业	Central Government	448.30	14.2	111.5	38.8
地方工业	Municipality	186.02	10.1	116.8	54.6
按轻、重工业分	**Grouped by Light and Heavy Industry**				
轻工业	Light Industry	182.84	14.4	109.8	47.7
重工业	Heavy Industry	227.83	10.3	116.7	51.1
按企业规模分	**Grouped by Size of Enterprise**				
大型企业	Large	338.91	13.3	118.2	43.5
中型企业	Medium	194.37	10.1	112.4	53.9
小型企业	Small	169.38	10.0	113.0	55.1

表 12.5 续表 continued

类别	Types	工业全员劳动生产率(元/人) Overall Industrial Labor Productivity (yuan/person)	流动资产周转次数(次) Turnover of Current Assets (time)	成本费用利润率(%) Ratio of pre-tax Profits to Cost and Expenses(%)	工业产品销售率(%) Sales Rate of Industrial Products (%)
总计	**Total**	**166 662.9**	**2.2**	**6.0**	**99.0**
#国有及国有控股企业	Enterprises Owned by the State or with the State Holding Major Shares	279 083.4	2.19	8.26	99.79
#大中型企业	Large and Medium Enterprises	320 134.9	2.3	8.6	99.8
按隶属关系分	**Grouped by Subordination**				
中央工业	Central Government	528 888.0	2.3	10.1	99.6
地方工业	Municipality	140 996.5	2.2	5.1	98.9
按轻、重工业分	**Grouped by Light and Heavy Industry**				
轻工业	Light Industry	115 226.5	1.9	7.1	99.0
重工业	Heavy Industry	203 431.6	2.3	5.7	99.0
按企业规模分	**Grouped by Size of Enterprise**				
大型企业	Large	364 384.6	2.8	6.4	99.6
中型企业	Medium	152 049.9	2.0	6.3	98.5
小型企业	Small	117 941.2	1.9	5.3	98.9

表 12.6 国有及国有控股企业主要指标占全市比重（2006）
PROPORTION OF THE MAJOR INDICATORS OF ENTERPRISES OWNED BY THE STATE OR WITH THE STATE HOLDING MAJOR SHARES

指　标	Indicators	合　计 Total	国有及国有控股企业 Enterprises Owned by the State or with the State Holding Major Shares	占全市比重(%) Proportion(%)
企业单位数（个）	Number of Enterprises (unit)	14 404	1 348	9.4
从业人员（万人）	Year-end Employees (10 000 persons)	269.67	56.13	20.8
工业总产值(亿元)	Gross Output Value of Industry (100 million yuan)	18 573.13	6 929.42	37.3
年末资产总计(亿元)	Total Assets (year-end) (100 million yuan)	17 926.1	8 781.05	49.0
流动资产年平均余额(亿元)	Average Current Assets(100 million yuan)	8 712.15	3 426.82	39.3
固定资产净值年平均余额(亿元)	Average Net Value of Fixed Assets (100 million yuan)	5 880.38	3 272.72	55.7
年末负债合计(亿元)	Total Liabilities (year-end) (100 million yuan)	9 014.05	3 824.89	42.4
年末所有者权益(亿元)	Owners Equity (year-end) (100 million yuan)	8 912.05	4 956.16	55.6
主营业务收入(亿元)	Prime Operating Revenue(100 million yuan)	19 266.93	7 489.72	38.9
产品销售税金及附加(亿元)	Product Sales Tax and Addition (100 million yuan)	191.08	178.32	93.3
利润总额(亿元)	Total Pre-Tax Profits (100 million yuan)	1 096.92	568.99	51.9
税金总额(亿元)	Total Tax and Duty (100 million yuan)	681.54	445.64	65.4
亏损企业数（个）	Number of Loss-making Enterprises (unit)	2 591	306	11.8
亏损企业亏损额(亿元)	Total Losses Made by Enterprises-in-red (100 million yuan)	217.83	65.99	30.3

表 12.7 六个重点发展工业行业主要指标（2006）
MAJOR INDICATORS OF SIX KEY INDUSTRIES ABOVE THE SET SCALE

行 业	Sectors	单位数（个）Number of Enterprises (unit)	从业人员（万人）Year-end Employees (10 000 persons)	工业总产值（亿元）Gross Output Value of Industry (100 million yuan)
总 计	**Total**	**4 876**	**112.85**	**11 917.35**
电子信息产品制造业	Electronic Information Product Manufacturing	1 467	46.16	4 560.53
汽车制造业	Automobile Manufacturing	407	11.73	1 462.34
石油化工及精细化工制造业	Petrochemical and Fine Chemical Products Manufacturing	890	12.51	2 158.11
精品钢材制造业	Fine Steel Manufacturing	169	5.26	1 445.03
成套设备制造业	Equipment Complex Manufacturing	1 601	29.73	1 979.31
生物医药制造业	Bio-medicine Manufacturing	342	7.46	312.03
六个重点发展工业行业占全市比重(%)	**Percentage of the Six Key Industries in Shanghai (%)**	**34.0**	**41.9**	**64.2**

表 12.7 续表 1 continued

行 业	Sectors	工业增加值（亿元）Value Added of Industry (100 million yuan)	工业销售产值（亿元）Sales Value of Industry (100 million yuan)	年末资产总计（亿元）Total Property (year-end) (100 million yuan)
总 计	**Total**	**2 504.97**	**11 790.74**	**10 763.59**
电子信息产品制造业	Electronic Information Product Manufacturing	856.75	4 526.63	2 959.48
汽车制造业	Automobile Manufacturing	356.93	1 446.35	1 512.73
石油化工及精细化工制造业	Petrochemical and Fine Chemical Products Manufacturing	333.48	2 131.99	1 751.74
精品钢材制造业	Fine Steel Manufacturing	360.21	1 438.95	1 913.70
成套设备制造业	Equipment Complex Manufacturing	496.11	1 945.13	2 227.31
生物医药制造业	Bio-medicine Manufacturing	101.49	301.69	398.63
六个重点发展工业行业占全市比重(%)	**Percentage of the Six Key Industries in Shanghai (%)**	**51.9**	**64.1**	**60.0**

表 12.7 续表 2 continued

行 业	Sectors	主营业务收入（亿元）Prime Operating Revenue (100 million yuan)	利润总额（亿元）Total Pre-tax Profits (100 million yuan)	税金总额（亿元）Total Tax and Duties (100 million yuan)
总 计	**Total**	**12 426.42**	**659.36**	**335.11**
电子信息产品制造业	Electronic Information Product Manufacturing	4 704.77	118.21	32.14
汽车制造业	Automobile Manufacturing	1 666.42	133.11	106.76
石油化工及精细化工制造业	Petrochemical and Fine Chemical Products Manufacturing	2 141.44	29.44	66.04
精品钢材制造业	Fine Steel Manufacturing	1 638.35	188.32	66.21
成套设备制造业	Equipment Complex Manufacturing	1 954.11	167.39	47.10
生物医药制造业	Bio-medicine Manufacturing	321.33	22.89	16.86
六个重点发展工业行业占全市比重(%)	**Percentage of the Six Key Industries in Shanghai (%)**	**64.5**	**60.1**	**49.3**

表 12.8 信息产品制造业主要指标（2006）
MAJOR INDICATORS OF INFORMATION PRODUCTS MANUFACTURING INDUSTRY

单位:亿元(100 million yuan)

指 标	Indicators	工业总产值 Gross Output Value of Industry	工业销售产值 Sales Value of Industry	年末资产总计 Total Assets (year-end)
总 计	**Total**	**4 560.54**	**4 526.63**	**2 959.48**
通信设备制造	Communications Equipment	342.07	336.12	351.58
雷达及配套产品制造	Radar ane Supported Product	0.39	0.42	0.37
广播电视设备制造	Broadcast and Television Equipment	17.19	16.57	12.46
电子计算机制造	Computer	2 372.44	2 366.23	710.18
家用视听设备制造	Household Seeing and Hearing Equipment	218.92	217.78	116.48
电子测量仪器制造	Geodesic Equipment of Electron	98.53	95.39	87.20
电子专用设备制造	Special Equipment of Electron	116.62	114.24	112.24
电子元件制造	Electronic Component	383.48	380.82	391.99
电子器件制造	Electronic Equipment	611.20	595.07	891.66
#集成电路制造	Integrated Circuit	331.14	317.50	568.95
电子机电产品制造	Machinery and Electronic Products of Electron	389.04	393.79	274.06
电子专用材料制造	Special Materials of Electron	10.66	10.20	11.26

表 12.8 续表 continued

单位:亿元(100 million yuan)

指 标	Indicators	主营业务收入 Prime Operating Revenue	利润总额 Total Pre-tax Profits	税金总额 Total Tax and Duty
总 计	**Total**	**4 704.77**	**118.20**	**32.13**
通信设备制造	Communications Equipment	343.24	18.08	2.64
雷达及配套产品制造	Radar ane Supported Product	0.54	0.02	0.04
广播电视设备制造	Broadcast and Television Equipment	16.19	0.54	0.19
电子计算机制造	Computer	2 501.14	11.18	4.52
家用视听设备制造	Household Seeing and Hearing Equipment	224.98	0.78	1.62
电子测量仪器制造	Geodesic Equipment of Electron	100.33	14.59	2.77
电子专用设备制造	Special Equipment of Electron	117.17	9.53	3.39
电子元件制造	Electronic Component	390.19	28.85	5.55
电子器件制造	Electronic Equipment	597.73	10.83	5.51
#集成电路制造	Integrated Circuit	323.56	27.36	2.20
电子机电产品制造	Machinery and Electronic Products of Electron	402.10	22.67	5.61
电子专用材料制造	Special Materials of Electron	11.16	1.13	0.29

表 12.9 高技术产业主要指标(2005～2006)
MAIN FACT ABOUT HIGH TECHNOLOGY INDUSTRY

类 别	Types	工业总产值(亿元) Gross Output Value of Industry (100 million yuan) 2005	2006
总 计	**Total**	**4 002.53**	**4 460.97**
占全市比重(%)	**Proportion (%)**	**25.1**	**24.4**
按登记注册类型分	**Grouped by Registration Categories**		
#国 有	State-owned	36.92	38.39
集 体	Collective-owned	6.41	5.65
股份制企业	Share Holding	233.09	265.9
外商投资企业	Foreign Funded	370.32	4 122.71
按技术领域分	**Grouped by Technology Areas**		
信息化学品制造	Information Chemical Product	6.74	9.23
医药制造业	Medical and Pharmaceutical Product	219.03	234.03
航空航天器制造	Aviation and Aircraft Manufaturing	16.51	22.01
电子及通信设备制造业	Electron and Communicate Equipments	1 325.89	1 534.92
电子计算机及办公设备制造业	Electronic Computers and Office Equipments	2 242.16	2 429.43
医疗设备及仪器仪表制造业	Medical Treatment Instrument and Meter	192.2	231.35

表 12.9 续表 1 continued

类 别	Types	工业销售产值(亿元) Sales Value of Industry (100 million yuan) 2005	2006	年末资产总计(亿元) Total Property(year-end) (100 million yuan) 2005	2006
总 计	**Total**	**3 888.56**	**4 410.8**	**2 907.29**	**3 014.34**
占全市比重(%)	**Proportion(%)**	**24.8**	**24.3**	**20.0**	**17.1**
按登记注册类型分	**Grouped by Registration Categories**				
#国 有	State-owned	35.63	38.27	66.92	65.25
集 体	Collective-owned	6.09	5.23	6.05	5.12
股份制企业	Share Holding	226.99	261.47	339.82	369.83
外商投资企业	Foreign Funded	3 596.16	4 078.57	2 469.77	2 547.93
按技术领域分	**Grouped by Technology Areas**				
信息化学品制造	Information Chemical Product	6.36	8.93	7.47	9.01
医药制造业	Medical and Pharmaceutical Product	209.42	226.04	301.87	309.5
航空航天器制造	Aviation and Aircraft Manufaturing	15.51	21.35	29.11	31.89
电子及通信设备制造业	Electron and Communicate Equipments	1 290.2	1 506.41	1 631.71	1 708.57
电子计算机及办公设备制造业	Electronic Computers and Office Equipments	2 176.16	2 422.91	754.77	753.25
医疗设备及仪器仪表制造业	Medical Treatment Instrument and Meter	190.91	225.16	182.37	202.12

表 12.9 续表 2　continued

类　别	Types	主营业务收入(亿元) Prime Operating Revenue (100 million yuan)		利润总额(亿元) Total Pre-tax Profits (100 million yuan)	
		2005	2006	2005	2006
总　计	**Total**	**4 065.56**	**4 601.42**	**96.44**	**119.26**
占全市比重 (%)	**Proportion (%)**	**24.8**	**24.2**	**10.3**	**11**
按登记注册类型分	**Grouped by Registration Categories**				
#国　有	State-owned	36.07	37.83	3.09	2.78
集　体	Collective-owned	5.86	4.93	0.18	0.3
股份制企业	Share Holding	252.3	293.34	15.57	16.49
外商投资企业	Foreign Funded	3 747.28	4 235.78	76.27	98.04
按技术领域分	**Grouped by Technology Areas**				
信息化学品制造	Information Chemical Product	6.94	9.92	0.64	1.09
医药制造业	Medical and Pharmaceutical Product	230.84	244.22	16.26	18.51
航空航天器制造	Aviation and Aircraft Manufaturing	15.47	19.86	0.77	1.23
电子及通信设备制造业	Electron and Communicate Equipments	1 302.3	1 530.06	29.92	55.88
电子计算机及办公设备制造业	Electronic Computers and Office Equipments	2 309.2	2 562.99	27.95	15.35
医疗设备及仪器仪表制造业	Medical Treatment Instrument and Meter	200.82	234.37	20.89	27.2

表 12.9 续表 3　continued

类　别	Types	税金总额(亿元) Total Tax and Duties (100 million yuan)		产品销售率(%) Sales Rate of Industrial Products(%)	
		2005	2006	2005	2006
总　计	**Total**	**42.27**	**42.14**	**97.2**	**98.9**
占全市比重 (%)	**Proportion (%)**	**7.1**	**6.2**		
按登记注册类型分	**Grouped by Registration Categories**				
#国　有	State-owned	1.81	1.73	96.5	99.7
集　体	Collective-owned	0.25	0.25	95.0	92.6
股份制企业	Share Holding	9.37	10.85	97.4	98.3
外商投资企业	Foreign Funded	29.91	28.37	97.1	98.9
按技术领域分	**Grouped by Technology Areas**				
信息化学品制造	Information Chemical Product	0.15	0.23	94.3	96.7
医药制造业	Medical and Pharmaceutical Product	14.44	14.61	95.6	96.6
航空航天器制造	Aviation and Aircraft Manufaturing	0.13	0.18	93.9	97.0
电子及通信设备制造业	Electron and Communicate Equipments	15.26	13.93	97.3	98.1
电子计算机及办公设备制造业	Electronic Computers and Office Equipments	4.93	5.03	97.1	99.7
医疗设备及仪器仪表制造业	Medical Treatment Instrument and Meter	7.36	8.17	99.3	97.3

表 12.10 都市型工业主要指标(2005 ~ 2006)
MAIN STATISTICS OF URBAN INDUSTRIES

类别	Types	单位数(个) Number of Enterprises (unit)		从业人员(万人) Employees (10 000 persons)		工业总产值(亿元) Gross Output Value of Industry (100 million yuan)	
		2005	2006	2005	2006	2005	2006
总计	**Total**	**3 866**	**3 643**	**72.43**	**71.19**	**2 109.95**	**2 271.47**
按企业规模分	**Grouped by Size of Enterprises**						
大型	Large	17	16	4.57	4.92	206.36	202.01
中型	Medium	310	380	20.97	25.16	861.91	1 043.75
小型	Small	3 539	3 247	46.89	41.1	1 041.68	1 025.71
按登记注册类型分	**Grouped by Registration Categories**						
内资	Domestic Investment	2 206	2 051	29.78	28.39	617.68	700.97
国有	State-owned	83	76	1.45	0.93	30.15	30.19
集体	Collective-owned	207	163	2.22	2	43.09	38.67
股份合作	Share-holding Coorperative	103	81	1.29	1.07	24.33	22.2
联营	Joint Owned	50	37	0.9	0.69	15.23	16.23
有限责任公司	Companies with Limited Liabilities	279	244	5.69	4.77	159	181.16
股份有限公司	Sharek-holding Companies with Limited Liabilities	24	18	1.23	0.95	41.72	39.25
私营	Private	1 450	1 422	16.93	17.79	302.76	370.44
其他	Others	10	10	0.07	0.18	1.40	2.83
港澳台商投资	Hong Kong, Macao and Taiwan Funded	567	538	13.11	13.76	341.62	378.25
外商投资	Foreign Funded	1 093	1 054	29.54	29.04	1 150.65	1 192.25
按行业分	**Grouped by Sectors**						
服装服饰业	Garment and Trappings	1 350	1 282	28.78	27.46	459.12	517.67
食品加工制造业	Food Processing	470	449	8.40	8.78	454.19	489.61
包装、印刷业	Packaging and Printing	514	490	5.7	5.66	183.19	198.75
室内装饰用品制造业	Indoor Decoration Materials and Equipments Manufacturing	646	615	10.67	10.95	321.57	369.17
化妆品及清洁洗涤用品制造业	Cosmetics and Cleaning Manufacturing	177	171	1.96	2.25	128.58	165.55
工艺美术品、旅游用品制造业	Art Crafts and Tourism Equipments Manufacturing	491	435	10.12	9.49	294.05	275.1
小型电子信息产品制造业	Small Electronic Information Products Manufacturing	218	201	6.80	6.61	269.26	255.61

表 12.10 续表 1　continued

单位:亿元 (100 million yuan)

类　别	Types	工业销售产值 Sales Value of Industry		年末资产总计 Total Assets (year-end)		主营业务收入 Prime Operating Revenue	
		2005	2006	2005	2006	2005	2006
总　计	**Total**	**2 091.92**	**2 248.61**	**1 863.03**	**1 961.93**	**2 184.03**	**2 351.2**
按企业规模分	**Grouped by Size of Enterprises**						
大　型	Large	202.55	201.44	163.18	168.85	228.53	223.77
中　型	Medium	856.21	1 025.94	758.18	889.19	892.97	1 070.22
小　型	Small	1 033.16	1 021.23	941.67	903.89	1 062.53	1 057.21
按登记注册类型分	**Grouped by Registration Categories**						
内　资	Domestic Investment	606.47	694.7	618.97	658.21	646.25	738.52
国　有	State-owned	30.11	29.88	48.66	43.78	30.81	32.66
集　体	Collective-owned	41.97	37.5	42.63	37.58	41.56	37.67
股份合作	Share-holding Coorperative	23.84	22.12	21.11	21.3	23.69	22.11
联　营	Joint Owned	15.09	16.02	12.89	10.05	16.08	16.27
有限责任公司	Companies with Limited Liabilities	155.21	182.21	174.59	173.89	184.71	209.06
股份有限公司	Share-holding Companies with Limited Liabilities	40.91	39.22	96.45	92.77	51.53	55.51
私　营	Private	297.96	364.93	221.34	276.75	296.57	362.44
其　他	Others	1.37	2.83	1.3	2.1	1.30	2.8
港澳台商投资	Hong Kong, Macao and Taiwan Funded	337.54	379.24	322.1	358.88	364.33	411.95
外商投资	Foreign Funded	1 147.91	1 174.67	921.96	944.84	1 173.45	1 200.74
按行业分	**Grouped by Sectors**						
服装服饰业	Garment and Trappings	450.79	496.89	322.48	347.74	455.68	497.07
食品加工制造业	Food Processing	454.66	489.4	429.53	454.59	498.67	540.77
包装、印刷业	Packaging and Printing	181.74	197.54	241.29	243.28	182.99	201.89
室内装饰用品制造业	Indoor Decoration Materials and Equipments Manufacturing	319.19	369.25	269.54	279.67	322.60	374.57
化妆品及清洁洗涤用品制造业	Cosmetics and Cleaning Manufacturing	129.58	166.79	129.17	166.03	140.26	172.85
工艺美术品、旅游用品制造业	Art Crafts and Tourism Equipments Manufacturing	292.17	275.05	209.59	217.97	314.96	306.62
小型电子信息产品制造业	Small Electronic Information Products Manufacturing	263.79	253.69	261.42	252.64	268.87	257.42

表 12.10 续表 2 continued

单位:亿元 (100 million yuan)

类 别	Types	利润总额 Total Pre-tax Profits 2005	2006	税金总额 Total Tax and Duties 2005	2006
总 计	**Total**	**111.97**	**133.04**	**72.26**	**77.01**
按企业规模分	**Grouped by Size of Enterprises**				
大 型	Large	12.56	13.13	3.62	5.43
中 型	Medium	51.80	71.62	35.86	41.80
小 型	Small	47.62	48.29	32.78	29.78
按登记注册类型分	**Grouped by Registration Categories**				
内 资	Domestic Investment	29.35	35.86	21.51	25.41
国 有	State-owned	1.39	1.97	1.89	1.86
集 体	Collective-owned	2.67	2.06	1.88	1.36
股份合作	Share-holding Coorperative	1.78	1.72	1.20	1.05
联 营	Joint Owned	0.23	0.72	0.80	0.58
有限责任公司	Companies with Limited Liabilities	8.15	9.01	5.11	7.63
股份有限公司	Share-holding Companies with Limited Liabilities	4.35	3.89	1.64	1.87
私 营	Private	10.68	16.22	8.96	10.90
其 他	Others	0.10	0.26	0.03	0.16
港澳台商投资	Hong Kong, Macao and Taiwan Funded	12.43	18.35	7.77	11.76
外商投资	Foreign Funded	70.19	78.84	42.99	39.84
按行业分	**Grouped by Sectors**				
服装服饰业	Garment and Trappings	19.10	23.08	10.26	11.58
食品加工制造业	Food Processing	18.48	23.07	24.94	28.14
包装、印刷业	Packaging and Printing	11.73	15.20	8.55	8.98
室内装饰用品制造业	Indoor Decoration Materials and Equipments Manufacturing	19.29	22.25	7.37	7.96
化妆品及清洁洗涤用品制造业	Cosmetics and Cleaning Manufacturing	6.64	11.85	10.23	10.74
工艺美术品、旅游用品制造业	Art Crafts and Tourism Equipments Manufacturing	11.30	16.87	5.62	6.10
小型电子信息产品制造业	Small Electronic Information Products Manufacturing	25.43	20.72	5.28	3.51

表 12.11　主要年份工业产品产量
OUTPUT OF INDUSTRIAL PRODUCTS IN MAIN YEARS

年　份 Year	化学纤维 (万吨) Chemical Fibers (10 000 tons)	食用植物油 (万吨) Vegetatble Oil (10 000 tons)	啤　酒 (亿升) Beer (100 million litres)	照相机 (万台) Cameras (10 000 units)	彩色电视机 (万部) Color TV Set (10 000 units)
1978	11.59	7.32	0.5	10.57	0.24
1980	15.15	6.77	0.66	20.69	0.55
1985	22.49	11.13	0.83	53.51	71.75
1990	25.74	13.42	1.66	20.62	81.48
1995	37.83	39.94	2.16	153.23	111.77
1996	38.61	17.38	2.0	198.99	42.59
1997	39.26	12.35	2.61	373.95	70.42
1998	40.93	19.46	2.69	428.58	107.80
1999	37.38	8.03	2.65	517.75	152.05
2000	47.15	11.55	3.04	1 116.94	147.97
2001	45.46	10.32	3.33	630.13	108.30
2002	51.67	9.65	3.62	723.81	137.02
2003	54.17	8.64	3.99	1 212.88	158.15
2004	48.45	3.51	5.92	1 514.39	135.08
2005	49.78	45.11	7.05	1 164.73	145.46
2006	50.6	72.86	7.17	760.73	251.67

表 12.11 续表 1　continued

年　份 Year	家用洗衣机 (万台) Household Washing Machines (10 000 units)	家用电冰箱 (万台) Household Refrigerators (10 000 units)	房间空调器 (万台) Household Airconditioners (10 000 units)	燃气热水器 (万台) Water Heaters (10 000 units)	传真机 (万部) Facsimile Printers (10 000 units)
1980	0.81	0.42	0.10		
1985	113.85	20.49	0.74		
1990	101.29	53.36	1.83		
1995	144.80	128.72	62.46		
1996	141.52	93.12	86.75	37.90	3.03
1997	124.81	30.72	88.20	36.25	11.89
1998	72.55	38.61	113.98	36.52	10.67
1999	57.03	43.03	180.70	35.07	23.89
2000	62.11	43.12	186.08	32.27	23.60
2001	70.79	43.44	223.57	27.86	22.45
2002	95.92	35.97	217.57	36.32	28.17
2003	134.27	34.46	239.72	37.24	22.97
2004	165.67	33.14	399.16	51.86	22.68
2005	183.26	42.68	358.57	65.64	22.40
2006	288.74	101.08	410.60	69.89	27.22

表 12.11 续表 2 continued

年 份 Year	机制纸及纸板(万吨) Machine-Made Paper and Paperboards (10 000 tons)	钢(万吨) Steel (10 000 tons)	成品钢材(万吨) Rolled-Steel Products (10 000 tons)	生 铁(万吨) Pig Iron (10 000 tons)	塑 料(万吨) Plastic (10 000 tons)	轮胎外胎(万条) Tires (10 000 tires)
1978	27.34	476.52	360.08	149.86	12.86	149.59
1980	29.57	521.61	412.63	171.12	14.57	174.85
1985	41.29	570.16	451.18	215.37	17.46	219.00
1990	46.49	914. 62	609.59	526.90	25.35	318.78
1995	47.08	1 006.92	738.08	664.04	33.91	375.31
1996	38.85	1 441.92	1 175.74	964.03	65.46	942.69
1997	40.00	1 532.42	1 296.48	1 054.56	64.56	829.57
1998	45.46	1 603.75	1 417.58	1 208.57	77.42	957.75
1999	45.42	1 668.62	1 486.08	1 337.75	89.67	804.43
2000	43.54	1 778.70	1 544.46	1 473.00	95.47	830.66
2001	41.35	1 874.71	1 641.11	1 468.91	104.19	545.97
2002	42.61	1 719.42	1 626.98	1 276.12	129.57	704.80
2003	44.40	1 726.65	1 710.80	1 300.24	158.26	846.92
2004	35.96	1 823.65	1 818.41	1 356.47	163.44	927.17
2005	35.73	1 927.96	1 964.16	1 582.89	61.93	932.27
2006	85.87	1 902.82	2 129.78	1 639.13	66.21	1 055.47

表 12.11 续表 3 continued

年 份 Year	水 泥(万吨) Cement (10 000 tons)	平板玻璃(万重量箱) Plate Glass (10 000wt. cases)	发电设备(万千瓦) Power Generating Equipments (10 000 kw)	金属切削机床(台) Metal-cutting Machines (unit)	发电量(亿千瓦·时) Electric Power Generation (100 million kwh)	硫 酸(万吨) Sulfuric (10 000 tons)
1978	139.47	111.87	109.80	17 384	199.32	34.49
1980	161.28	132.79	58.20	16 949	206.41	38.76
1985	219.31	160.08	133.00	19 408	256.25	35.22
1990	230.30	503.05	210.20	13 796	284.10	40.04
1995	433.22	634.63	496.50	15 833	403.42	31.03
1996	443.77	687.63	494.30	15 379	428.64	36.24
1997	338.47	691.08	541.60	18 700	458.48	36.79
1998	330.95	701.45	403.85	11 916	482.16	32.59
1999	251.14	641.81	314.55	17 822	498.01	38.38
2000	311.69	751.88	179.00	22 346	553.09	34.22
2001	334.75	755.80	336.20	21 839	572.86	36.15
2002	351.58	718.42	461.90	27 252	608.92	30.41
2003	568.24	789.21	1 013.70	33 497	684.99	31.41
2004	665.01	845.81	1 520.3	13 975	766.15	33.67
2005	719.97	830.61	2 138.05	13 158	728.74	33.32
2006	818.28	762.75	2 944.71	13 372	710.96	30.37

表 12.11 续表 4　continued

年　份 Year	程控交换机 (万线) Program Controlled Exchanges (10 000 lines)	微型电子计算机(万部) Personal Computers (10 000 units)	彩色显像管 (万只) Color Tubes (10 000 units)	移动通信基站设备(万信道) Mobile Communication Facilities (10 000 channels)
1990	95.23	0.77	74.83	
1995	476.60	4.07	244.31	
1996	580.93	6.20	255.22	
1997	631.62	40.39	298.69	
1998	794.96	21.16	422.16	
1999	915.46	40.09	457.17	
2000	1 091.64	42.04	515.08	1.60
2001	1 752.90	47. 13	519.23	39.49
2002	1 227.25	75.25	631.55	24.82
2003	1 883.47	734.68	713.53	28.20
2004	2 054.28	996.09	745.73	57.67
2005	796.59	2 176.17	533.18	115.03
2006	553.53	2 670.09	507.57	174.16

表 12.11 续表 5　continued

年　份 Year	集　成 电路(万块) Semi-conduct IC (10 000 units)	汽　车 (万辆) Motor Vehicles (10 000 vehicles)	其　中 of which #轿　车 Cars	民用钢质船舶 (万总吨) Civil Steel Ships (10 000 syn-tons)
1978		1.04	0.26	25.18
1980		1.47	0.53	17.26
1985		1.22	0.86	40.13
1990	1 167	2.81	2.46	39.07
1995	15 290	16.27	16.07	83.33
1996	11 624	20.17	20.02	77.54
1997	88 098	23.30	23.15	85.29
1998	92 908	23.64	23.50	79.93
1999	170 001	25.58	25.42	62.47
2000	239 330	25.29	25.15	118.81
2001	225 315	29.00	28.88	177.59
2002	339 494	39.19	39.05	87.08
2003	397 313	59.58	58.84	109.77
2004	548 727	55.96	54.99	296.17
2005	677 003	48.45	48.09	235.59
2006	640 483	65.28	64.47	295.48

注：2000 年开始移动通信设备不包括手机。
Note： The figure of mobile communication facilities has excluded mobile phones since 2000.

表 12.12 主要工业产品生产、销售总量(2006)
OUTPUT AND SALES OF MAIN INDUSTRIAL PRODUCTS

产品名称	Product	单 位 Unit	生产量 Output	销售量 Sales
发电量	Electric Power Generation	亿千瓦・时(100 million kwh)	710.96	561.83
啤 酒	Beer	亿升(100 million litres)	7.17	7.19
无酒精饮料(软饮料)	Non-alcoholic Beverage	万吨(10 000 tons)	229.31	226.46
卷 烟	Cigarettes	亿支(100 million pieces)	829.31	831.04
化学纤维	Chemical Fibers	万吨(10 000 tons)	50.60	46.63
纱	Yarn	万吨(10 000 tons)	10.74	9.15
布	Cloth	亿米(100 million m)	1.03	1.03
丝织品	Silk Products	万米(10 000 m)	463.50	367.73
呢 绒	Wool Fabric	万米(10 000 m)	1 699.28	1 692.05
毛 线	Knitting Wool	吨(ton)	3 997	3 713
服 装	Garments	亿件(100 million cases)	6.73	6.59
皮 鞋	Leather Shoes	万双(10 000 pairs)	2 431.91	2 460.54
机制纸及纸版	Paperboard	万吨(10 000 tons)	85.87	86.12
汽 油	Gasoline	万吨(10 000 tons)	248.16	220.36
柴 油	Diesel Oil	万吨(10 000 tons)	639.32	638.45
焦 炭	Coke	万吨(10 000 tons)	735.57	173.28
硫 酸	Sulphuric Acid	万吨(10 000 tons)	30.37	26.71
烧 碱	Caustic Soda	万吨(10 000 tons)	39.53	36.47
合成氨	Synthetic Ammonia	万吨(10 000 tons)	14.37	8.89
农用化肥	Ag-fertilizer	万吨(10 000 tons)	3.00	2.87
#氮 肥	Nitrogen	万吨(10 000 tons)	2.11	2.08
磷 肥	Phophate	万吨(10 000 tons)	0.90	0.80
化学农药	Chemical Pesticides	万吨(10 000 tons)	1.58	1.53
乙 烯	Ethylene	万吨(10 000 tons)	193.83	43.55
合成橡胶	Synthetic Rubber	万吨(10 000 tons)	18.92	18.28
合成洗涤剂	Synthetic Detergents	万吨(10 000 tons)	23.95	23.83
中成药	Chinese Patent Medicines	万吨(10 000 tons)	1.01	1.03
轮胎外胎	Tires	万条(10 000 tires)	1 055.47	1 016.37
水 泥	Cement	万吨(10 000 tons)	818.28	811.49
平板玻璃	Plate Glass	万重量箱(10 000 wt. cases)	762.75	689.98
生 铁	Pig Iron	万吨(10 000 tons)	1 639.13	6.60
钢	Steel	万吨(10 000 tons)	1 902.82	104.12
金属切削机床	Metal-cutting Machines	台(unit)	13 372	12 685
#数控机床	Digital Machine Tools	台(unit)	1 147	1 099

表 12.12 续表 continued

	产品名称 Product	单　位 Unit	生产量 Output	销售量 Sales
成品钢材	Rolled-steel Products	万吨(10 000 tons)	2 129.78	2 125.13
内燃机	Internal Combustion Engines	万千瓦(10 000 kw)	7 399.57	4 241.63
缝纫机	Sewing Machines	万架(10 000 units)	87.78	89.90
大中型拖拉机	Large and Medium Size Tractors	万台(10 000 units)	1.22	1.13
汽　车	Motor Vehicles	万辆(10 000 vehicles)	65.28	65.08
#轿　车	Cars	万辆(10 000 vehicles)	64.47	64.22
摩托车	Motorcycles	万辆(10 000 vehicles)	53.90	53.88
自行车	Bicycles	万辆(10 000 vehicles)	694.73	692.58
民用钢质船舶	Civil Steel Ships	万总吨(10 000 syn-tons)	295.48	295.48
发电设备	Power Generating Equipments	万千瓦(10 000 kw)	2 944.71	2 900.47
电力电缆	Electric Cable	万公里(10 000 km)	9.73	9.45
家用洗衣机	Household Washing Machines	万台(10 000 units)	288.74	287.44
家用电冰箱	Household Refrigerators	万台(10 000 units)	101.08	101.24
电风扇	Electric Fans	万台(10 000 units)	303.10	307.57
房间空调器	Household Air-conditioners	万台(10 000 units)	410.60	418.72
排油烟机	Range Hoods	万台(10 000 units)	3.55	3.38
微波炉	Microware Oven	万台(10 000 units)	332.16	332.20
电饭锅	Electric Rice Cookers	万个(10 000 units)	136.75	128.82
吸尘器	Vacuum Cleaners	万台(10 000 units)	21.38	21.09
燃气热水器	Water Heaters	万台(10 000 units)	69.89	70.70
程控交换机	Program-controlled Exchanges	万线(10 000 lines)	553.53	553.44
传真机	Facsimile Printers	万部(10 000 units)	27.22	26.79
微型电子计算机	Personal Computers	万部(10 000 units)	2 670.09	2 667.70
彩色显像管	Color Tubes	万只(10 000 units)	507.57	483.05
电视机	Television Sets	万部(10 000 units)	251.67	247.54
#彩色电视机	Color TV Sets	万部(10 000 units)	251.67	247.54
组合音响	Stereo System	万部(10 000 units)	26.52	26.72
照相机	Cameras	万台(10 000 units)	760.73	761.30
表	Watches	万只(10 000 units)	145.17	150.30
移动通信基站设备	Mobile Communication Base Station Facilities	万信道(10 000 channels)	174.16	174.05
光学仪器	Optical Instruments	万台(10 000 units)	13.78	13.80

表 12.13 国有工业企业主要指标(2006)
MAJOR INDICATORS OF STATE-OWNED INDUSTRIAL ENTERPRISES

类别	Types	单位数(个) Number of Enterprises (unit)	从业人员(万人) Employees (10 000 persons)
总计	**Total**	**407**	**14.17**
按隶属关系分	**Grouped by Subordination**		
#中央工业	Central Government	67	5.84
市(局)属工业	Municipality	244	7.26
区属工业	District	75	0.66
县属工业	County	1	0.17
按轻、重工业分	**Grouped by Light and Heavy Industry**		
轻工业	Light Industry	137	4.24
重工业	Heavy Industry	270	9.93
按企业规模分	**Grouped by Size of Enterprises**		
大型企业	Large	11	4.56
中型企业	Medium	87	6.09
小型企业	Small	309	3.52
按工业行业分	**Grouped by Sectors**		
采矿业	**Mining Industry**	**1**	**0.01**
非金属矿采选业	Nonmetal Minerals Mining	1	0.01
制造业	**Manufacture Industry**	**387**	**11.97**
农副食品加工业	Farm and Sideline Products Processing	7	0.04
食品制造业	Food Manufacturing	4	0.05
饮料制造业	Beverage Manufacturing	2	0.01
烟草制品业	Tabacco Manufacture	1	0.37
纺织业	Textile	17	1.05
纺织服装、鞋、帽制造业	Garments, Shoes and Accessories Manufacturing	8	0.01
皮革、毛皮、羽毛(绒)及其制品业	Leather, Fur, and Wool Products Manufacturing	5	0.09
木材加工及木、竹、藤、棕、草制品业	Timber Processing and Timber, Bamboo, Rattan,Coir and Straw Products Manufacturing	2	0.01

工业总产值 (亿元) Gross Output Value of Industry (100 million yuan)	年末资产总计 (亿元) Total Assets (year-end) (100 million yuan)	固定资产净值年平均余额 (亿元) Average Net Value of Fixed Assets (100 million yuan)	流动资产年平均余额 (亿元) Average Current Assets (100 million yuan)
1 116.74	**2 223.91**	**1 003.98**	**646.24**
863.80	1 788.48	860.63	452.01
218.78	403.90	131.73	176.73
21.69	23.01	8.91	11.89
2.00	2.06	0.94	0.93
337.97	673.65	121.23	320.36
778.77	1 550.26	882.74	325.89
762.55	1 714.20	844.54	405.21
244.79	343.80	101.91	167.93
109.40	165.90	57.53	73.10
0.09	**0.09**	**0.03**	**0.06**
0.09	0.09	0.03	0.06
656.97	**1 191.02**	**195.61**	**580.60**
1.01	1.46	0.26	0.60
1.11	1.13	0.20	0.72
0.21	0.29	0.08	0.21
228.03	452.56	28.20	244.02
13.21	29.35	8.57	14.40
1.36	0.96	0.18	0.69
1.27	1.80	0.86	0.69
0.16	0.19	0.07	0.06

表 12.13 续表 1 continued

类别	Types	单位数（个）Number of Enterprises (unit)	从业人员（万人）Employees (10 000 persons)
家具制造业	Furniture Manufacturing	6	0.05
造纸及纸制品业	Paper-making and Paper Products Manufacturing	2	0.01
印刷业和记录媒介的复制	Printing and Record Duplicating	30	0.57
文教体育用品制造业	Stationary, Education and Sports Goods Manufacturing	3	0.01
化学原料及化学制品制造业	Raw Chemical Materials and Chemical Products Manufacturing	37	1.00
医药制造业	Medicine Manufacturing	15	0.82
化学纤维制造业	Chemical Fiber Manufacturing	2	0.04
橡胶制品业	Rubber Products Manufacturing	6	0.20
塑料制品业	Plastic Products Manufacturing	17	0.19
非金属矿物制品业	Nonmetal Mineral Products	17	0.56
黑色金属冶炼及压延加工业	Smelting and Pressing of Ferrous Metals	8	0.58
有色金属冶炼及压延加工业	Smelting and Pressing of Nonferrous Metals	7	0.13
金属制品业	Metal Products Manufacturing	15	0.33
通用设备制造业	General Equipment Manufacturing	58	1.79
专用设备制造业	Special Purpose Equipment Manufacturing	39	0.89
交通运输设备制造业	Transportation Equipment Manufacturing	36	2.66
电气机械及器材制造业	Electric Machinery Equipments and Manufacturing	15	0.13
通信设备、计算机及其他电子设备制造业	Communcations Equipment, Computer and Other Electronic Equipment Manufacturing	13	0.15
仪器仪表及文化、办公用机械制造业	Instruments, Meters, Culture and Office Equipments Manufacturing	13	0.22
工艺品及其他制造业	Artworks and Other Manufacturing	2	0.02
电力、燃气及水的生产和供应业	**Production and Supply of Power, Gas and Water**	**19**	**2.20**
电力、热力的生产和供应业	Production and Supply of Electricity and Thermal Power	7	1.41
燃气生产和供应业	Production and Supply of Gas	5	0.45
水的生产和供应业	Production and Supply of Water	7	0.33

工业总产值（亿元）Gross Output Value of Industry (100 million yuan)	年末资产总计（亿元）Total Assets (year-end) (100 million yuan)	固定资产净值年平均余额（亿元）Average Net Value of Fixed Assets (100 million yuan)	流动资产年平均余额（亿元）Average Current Assets (100 million yuan)
1.24	0.96	0.25	0.68
0.53	0.50	0.13	0.39
22.23	35.29	18.19	11.32
0.37	0.40	0.12	0.26
75.37	91.93	27.91	28.89
27.64	48.37	14.32	22.38
0.79	2.72	1.53	0.64
2.33	4.81	0.86	2.66
6.68	6.79	3.35	2.98
18.58	29.42	5.32	16.10
41.55	147.48	15.43	45.95
3.93	3.76	0.91	2.35
17.19	21.55	8.55	7.70
53.45	59.90	9.16	38.16
25.44	39.88	7.30	23.39
97.35	188.93	40.15	102.22
2.44	3.60	0.77	2.51
7.87	6.28	1.48	3.89
5.47	10.52	1.40	6.65
0.17	0.16	0.03	0.11
459.68	**1 032.80**	**808.35**	**65.59**
432.07	911.96	740.76	34.95
18.56	47.40	23.55	21.63
9.05	73.44	44.04	9.02

表 12.13 续表 2 continued

	类 别 Types	年末负债合计 Total Liabilities (year-end)	年末所有者权益 Owner's Equity (year-end)
总 计	**Total**	**699.44**	**1 524.47**
按隶属关系分	**Grouped by Subordination**		
#中央工业	Central Government	455.93	1 332.55
市(局)属工业	Municipality	226.25	177.65
区属工业	District	11.19	11.81
县属工业	County	1.40	0.66
按轻、重工业分	**Grouped by Light and Heavy Industry**		
轻工业	Light Industry	126.43	547.22
重工业	Heavy Industry	573.01	977.25
按企业规模分	**Grouped by Size of Enterprises**		
大型企业	Large	428.74	1 285.46
中型企业	Medium	169.02	174.79
小型企业	Small	101.68	64.22
按工业行业分	**Grouped by Sectors**		
采矿业	**Mining Industry**	**0.07**	**0.02**
非金属矿采选业	Nonmetal Minerals Mining	0.07	0.02
制造业	**Manufacture Industry**	**489.46**	**701.56**
农副食品加工业	Farm and Sideline Products Processing	1.16	0.30
食品制造业	Food Manufacturing	0.41	0.73
饮料制造业	Beverage Manufacturing	0.38	-0.09
烟草制品业	Tabacco Manufacture	17.57	435.00
纺织业	Textile	17.55	11.81
纺织服装、鞋、帽制造业	Garments, Shoes and Accessories Manufacturing	0.35	0.61
皮革、毛皮、羽毛(绒)及其制品业	Leather, Fur, and Wool Products Manufacturing	2.49	-0.69
木材加工及木、竹、藤、棕、草制品业	Timber Processing and Timber, Bamboo, Rattan, Coir and Straw Products Manufacturing	0.1	0.09

单位:亿元(100 million yuan)

主营业务收入 Prime Operating Revenue	利　润 总　额 Total Pre-tax Profits	税　金 总　额 Total Tax and Duties	成本费用 总　额 Total Cost and Expenses
1 161.96	**112.41**	**178.89**	**986.99**
886.28	109.75	168.63	699.22
242.39	2.74	9.30	253.78
20.75	0.06	0.65	21.19
2.07		0.13	2.11
342.86	85.2	138.79	180.75
819.10	27.21	40.11	806.24
785.51	100.22	164.78	607.25
266.54	10.92	10.13	265.39
109.91	1.26	3.99	114.35
0.10		**0.03**	**0.09**
0.10		0.03	0.09
680.46	**94.53**	**148.02**	**515.49**
0.89	-0.12	0.01	1.01
1.14	0.11	0.07	1.17
0.25	0.26		0.32
228.46	78.75	133.63	64.56
16.66	0.14	0.94	17.47
1.33	0.01	0.15	1.35
1.19	-0.11	0.02	1.41
0.16		0.01	0.18

表 12.13 续表 3 continued

类别	Types	年末负债合计 Total Liabilities (year-end)	年末所有者权益 Owners'Equity (year-end)
家具制造业	Furniture Manufacturing	0.48	0.48
造纸及纸制品业	Paper-making and Paper Products Manufacturing	0.30	0.20
印刷业和记录媒介的复制	Printing and Record Duplicating	12.43	22.87
文教体育用品制造业	Stationary, Education and Sports Goods Manufacturing	0.22	0.18
化学原料及化学制品制造业	Raw Chemical Materials and Chemical Products Manufacturing	44.59	47.34
医药制造业	Medicine Manufacturing	21.78	26.59
化学纤维制造业	Chemical Fiber Manufacturing	2.52	0.20
橡胶制品业	Rubber Products Manufacturing	3.69	1.12
塑料制品业	Plastic Products Manufacturing	3.66	3.14
非金属矿物制品业	Nonmetal Mineral Products	18.74	10.68
黑色金属冶炼及压延加工业	Smelting and Pressing of Ferrous Metals	103.53	43.95
有色金属冶炼及压延加工业	Smelting and Pressing of Nonferrous Metals	3.26	0.50
金属制品业	Metal Products Manufacturing	10.85	10.70
通用设备制造业	General Equipment Manufacturing	44.72	15.18
专用设备制造业	Special Purpose Equipment Manufacturing	21.88	17.99
交通运输设备制造业	Transportation Equipment Manufacturing	142.81	46.12
电气机械及器材制造业	Electric Machinery Equipments and Manufacturing	2.88	0.72
通信设备、计算机及其他电子设备制造业	Communcations Equipment, Computer and Other Electronic Equipment Manufacturing	4.72	1.57
仪器仪表及文化、办公用机械制造业	Instruments, Meters, Culture and Office Equipments Manufacturing	6.27	4.26
工艺品及其他制造业	Artworks and Other Manufacturing	0.14	0.02
电力、燃气及水的生产和供应业	**Production and Supply of Power, Gas and Water**	**209.92**	**822.89**
电力、热力的生产和供应业	Production and Supply of Electricity and Thermal Power	160.32	751.64
燃气生产和供应业	Production and Supply of Gas	18.24	29.16
水的生产和供应业	Production and Supply of Water	31.35	42.09

单位:亿元(100 million yuan)

主营业务收入 Prime Operating Revenue	利　润 总　额 Total Pre-tax Profits	税　金 总　额 Total Tax and Duties	成本费用 总　额 Total Cost and Expenses
1.14	0.01	0.05	1.14
0.53	-0.02	0.02	0.57
24.81	1.74	1.46	23.27
0.37		0.05	0.38
73.05	4.15	1.79	70.77
26.89	2.29	1.41	25.82
0.86	-0.32	0.01	1.20
2.36	-0.08	0.06	2.51
6.29	0.57	0.36	5.80
19.67	0.40	0.77	20.25
40.93	0.91	0.80	42.32
4.00	-0.22	0.06	4.29
18.87	1.69	1.01	17.32
51.31	0.83	2.09	51.67
26.58	1.11	1.35	26.50
114.43	2.27	1.26	115.51
2.46	-0.07	0.13	2.56
8.43	-0.34	0.07	9
7.21	0.54	0.42	6.97
0.17	0.03	0.02	0.16
481.40	17.87	30.85	471.41
436.17	17.52	30.51	421.45
36.18	-1.41	0.27	38.08
9.04	1.76	0.06	11.87

表 12.14 股份制、港澳台商和外商投资企业主要指标(2006)
MAJOR INDICATORS OF SHARE-HOLDING ENTERPRISES AND ENTERPRISES WITH INVESTMENT FROM OTHER COUNTRIES OR FROM HONG KONG, MACAO AND TAIWAN

指 标	Indicators	股份有限公司 Stock-holding Companies with Limited Liabilities	港澳台商投资企业 Enterprises with Investment from Hong kong, Macao and Taiwan
单位数(个)	Number of Enterprises (unit)	90	1 782
从业人员(万人)	Employees(10 000 persons)	7.84	41.02
工业总产值(亿元)	Gross Output Value of Industry(100 million yuan)	1 735.76	2 475.41
出口交货值(亿元)	Delivery Value of Exports(100 million yuan)	176.37	883.45
实收资本(股本)(亿元)	Paid-up Capital(Stock Capital)(100 million yuan)	417.42	688.86
#国家资本(国家股)	State Capital(State Stock)	215.81	35.86
年末资产总计(亿元)	Total Assets(year-end)(100 million yuan)	2 306.96	2 051.98
流动资产合计(亿元)	Total Current Assets(100 million yuan)	699.90	1 121.04
流动资产年平均余额(亿元)	Average Current Assets(100 million yuan)	635.23	1 071.58
固定资产合计(亿元)	Total Fixed Assets(100 million yuan)	975.85	689.25
固定资产原价(亿元)	Original Value of Fixed Assets(100 million yuan)	1 895.30	1 181.32
固定资产净值(亿元)	Net Value of Fixed Assets(100 million yuan)	832.23	631.94
固定资产净值年平均余额(亿元)	Average Net Value of Fixed Assets(100 million yuan)	794.49	623.79
年末负债合计(亿元)	Total Liabilities(year-end)(100 million yuan)	855.95	1 072.84
流动负债合计(亿元)	Total Current Liabilities(100 million yuan)	616.67	931.03
长期负债合计(亿元)	Long-Term Liabilities(100 million yuan)	183.84	135.71
年末所有者权益(亿元)	Owners' Equity(year-end)(100 million yuan)	1 451.02	979.14
主营业务收入(亿元)	Prime Operating Revenue(100 million yuan)	1 920.43	2 480.41
利润总额(亿元)	Total Pre-tax Profits(100 million yuan)	179.77	98.08
税金总额(亿元)	Total Tax and Duties(100 million yuan)	79.87	52.77

其中 of which				其　中 of which		
#与港澳台商合资合作经营 Joint and Cooperation Enterprises with Investment from Hong Kong, Macao and Taiwan	#港澳台商独　资 Ventures Solely Invested by Business from Hong kong, Macao and Taiwan	#港澳台商投资股份有限公司 Stock-holding Companies with Limited Liabilities with Investment from Hong Kong, Macao and Taiwan	外商投资企　业 Foreign-invested Enterprises	#中外合资合作企业 Sino-foreign Joint and Cooperation Enterprises	#外商独资 Solely Foreign-invested Ventures	#外商投资股份有限公司 Stock-holding Companies with Limited Liabilities with Foreign Investment
810	958	14	3 765	1 577	2 166	22
17.55	19.45	4.03	107.76	43.36	61.67	2.74
859.55	930.36	685.50	9 218.29	4 069.69	4 863.86	284.73
213.33	503.02	167.11	4 265.98	942.66	3 250.98	72.34
256.69	275.29	156.88	2 641.71	1 285.23	1 193.47	163.01
7.61		28.26	83.96	41.29	0.43	42.25
763.64	692.15	596.20	7 411.57	3 599.39	3 388.78	423.40
457.45	414.91	248.68	4 334.77	2 024.49	2 049.16	261.12
432.68	395.23	243.67	4 095.67	1 930.34	1 920.35	244.99
230.03	243.01	216.20	2 655.68	1 375.69	1 185.43	94.57
366.77	400.84	413.71	4 093.30	2 095.33	1 793.61	204.36
213.34	223.82	194.77	2 476.35	1 276.71	1 113.16	86.48
210.04	213.17	200.58	2 438.71	1 245.49	1 102.05	91.17
418.80	387.12	266.92	4 114.98	1 898.73	2 021.03	195.22
376.36	320.59	234.07	3 512.40	1 562.31	1 759.63	190.46
38.67	64.19	32.85	581.88	329.17	248.00	4.71
344.83	305.03	329.28	3 296.59	1 700.66	1 367.75	228.18
871.08	913.71	695.62	9 596.60	4 277.53	5 025.26	293.81
35.41	38.89	23.77	463.71	285.07	159.30	19.35
20.19	13.74	18.83	237.92	168.31	62.76	6.84

表 12.15 大中型工业企业主要指标(2006)
MAJOR INDICATORS OF LARGE AND MEDIUM SIZED INDUSTRIAL ENTERPRISES

类 别	Types	单位数（个）Number of Enterprises (unit)	从业人员（万人）Employees (10 000 persons)	工业总产值（亿元）Gross Output Value of Industry (100 million yuan)
总　计	**Total**	**1 537**	**136.01**	**12 930.98**
按轻、重工业分	**Grouped by Light and Heavy Industry**			
大型企业	Large Enterprises	93	39.74	7 072.00
轻工业	Light Industry	25	7.89	554.47
重工业	Heavy Industry	68	31.85	6 517.52
中型企业	Medium Enterprises	1 444	96.27	5 858.98
轻工业	Light Industry	613	40.04	1 824.77
重工业	Heavy Industry	831	56.23	4 034.21
按隶属关系分	**Grouped by Subordination**			
大型企业	Large Enterprises	93	39.74	7 072.00
中央工业	Central Government	15	10.17	2 856.99
地方工业	Local Government	78	29.58	4 215.01
中型企业	Medium Enterprises	1 444	96.27	5 858.98
中央工业	Central Government	50	5.29	666.06
地方工业	Local Government	1 394	90.98	5 192.92
按从业人员分	**Grouped by Number of Employees**			
1 万人及以上	10 000 persons and above	7	10.27	2 927.31
5 000 ~ 9 999 人	5 000 ~ 9 999 persons	16	9.83	1 680.44
3 000 ~ 4 999 人	3 000 ~ 4 999 persons	40	12.59	1 970.44
1 000 ~ 2 999 人	1 000 ~ 2 999 persons	241	38.47	2 506.55
1 000 人以下	Below 1 000 persons	1 233	64.86	3 846.25
按工业总产值分	**Grouped by Gross Output Value of Industry**			
10 亿元及以上	1 000 million yuan and above	182	45.60	9 634.84
5 ~ 9.99 亿元	500 ~ 999 million yuan	181	19.21	1 256.82
1 ~ 4.99 亿元	100 ~ 499 million yuan	775	52.15	1 773.18
5 000 ~ 9 999 万元	50 ~ 99.99 million yuan	312	15.03	232.30
1 000 ~ 4 999 万元	10 ~ 49.99 million yuan	84	3.88	33.79
1 000 万元以下	Below 10 million yuan	3	0.13	0.05
按固定资产原价分	**Grouped by Original Value of Fixed Assets**			
10 亿元及以上	1 000 million yuan and above	90	31.73	7 272.38
1 ~ 9.99 亿元	100 ~ 999 million yuan	594	56.74	3 878.66
5 000 ~ 9 999 万元	50 ~ 99.99 million yuan	317	19.50	753.25
1 000 ~ 4 999 万元	10 ~ 49.99 million yuan	474	25.10	917.44
1 000 万元以下	Below 10 million yuan	62	2.94	109.25

工业销售产值（亿元）Sales Value of Industry Products (100 million yuan)	实收资本（股本）（亿元）Paid-in Capital (fixed capital stock) (100 million yuan)	年末资产总计（亿元）Total Assets (year-end) (100 million yuan)	年末负债合计（亿元）Total Liabilities (year-end) (100 million yuan)	主营业务收入（亿元）Prime Operation Revenue (100 million yuan)	利润总额（亿元）Total Pre-tax Profits (100 million yuan)	税金总额（亿元）Total Tax and Duties (100 million yuan)	成本费用总额（亿元）Total Costs and Expenses (100 million yuan)
12 813.75	**3 388.91**	**12 689.11**	**6 131.10**	**13 550.91**	**808.83**	**517.69**	**12 732.29**
7 041.54	1 345.47	6 810.39	2 961.49	7 600.71	452.23	364.66	7 083.39
558.93	127.15	792.44	210.34	593.69	92.57	140.50	425.27
6 482.61	1 218.32	6 017.95	2 751.15	7 007.02	359.66	224.16	6 658.12
5 772.21	2 043.44	5 878.73	3 169.61	5 950.20	356.60	153.03	5 648.91
1 794.51	567.00	1 672.45	843.38	1 858.33	109.64	66.16	1 759.82
3 977.70	1 476.44	4 206.28	2 326.23	4 091.87	246.97	86.87	3 889.09
7 041.54	1 345.47	6 810.39	2 961.49	7 600.71	452.23	364.66	7 083.39
2 841.81	532.03	3 807.64	1 342.23	3 019.98	280.34	251.47	2 678.77
4 199.73	813.44	3 002.74	1 619.26	4 580.73	171.89	113.19	4 404.61
5 772.21	2 043.44	5 878.73	3 169.61	5 950.20	356.60	153.03	5 648.91
667.19	264.01	836.19	441.37	674.19	66.10	14.98	612.53
5 105.01	1 779.43	5 042.54	2 728.24	5 276.00	290.51	138.05	5 036.38
2 918.35	448.33	3 084.76	1 072.45	3 087.58	243.51	141.29	2 840.88
1 670.03	346.85	1 291.71	805.71	1 941.83	81.45	50.52	1 851.25
1 975.43	386.64	1 899.27	753.22	2 059.81	95.80	158.29	1 900.41
2 450.71	896.85	2 749.68	1 595.59	2 557.08	181.57	65.54	2 415.13
3 799.22	1 310.23	3 663.69	1 904.13	3 904.62	206.50	102.05	3 724.63
9 560.03	2 013.93	8 798.31	4 060.79	10 116.54	639.28	426.53	9 421.13
1 239.19	527.68	1 492.60	813.36	1 312.09	65.26	34.57	1 263.60
1 746.04	689.81	1 962.05	1 011.47	1 825.68	100.95	47.58	1 749.89
233.82	117.40	317.38	170.95	245.34	5.50	6.96	242.26
34.61	37.69	109.44	68.62	43.99	-2.25	1.73	48.24
0.05	2.39	9.33	5.92	7.27	0.10	0.32	7.18
7 237.49	1 891.41	7 825.97	3 446.92	7 717.59	494.22	384.29	7 167.43
3 822.95	1 195.96	3 568.69	1 913.46	4 032.71	209.36	99.56	3 856.55
751.25	167.95	645.56	372.47	773.72	48.57	16.91	732.78
895.74	120.22	579.03	355.36	923.63	50.41	15.08	876.96
106.32	13.38	69.86	42.88	103.25	6.28	1.85	98.58

表 12.15 续表 continued

类　别	Types	单位数（个）Number of Enterprises (unit)	从业人员（万人）Employees (10 000 persons)	工业总产值（亿元）Gross Output Value of Industry (100 million yuan)
按工业行业分	**Grouped by Sectors**			
制造业	**Manufacture Industry**	**1 515**	**132.51**	**12 300.84**
农副食品加工业	Farm and Sideline Products Processing	14	0.77	59.42
食品制造业	Food Manufacturing	42	3.30	149.20
饮料制造业	Beverage Manufacturing	16	0.87	93.19
烟草制品业	Tabacco Manufacturing	16	0.87	93.19
纺织业	Textile	84	5.69	125.96
纺织服装、鞋、帽制造业	Garments, Shoes and Accessories Manufacturing	89	5.76	179.85
皮革、毛皮、羽毛(绒)及其制品业	Leather, Fur, and Wool Products Manufacturing	22	2.30	53.81
木材加工及木、竹、藤、棕、草制品业	Timber Processing and Timber, Bamboo, Rattan, Coir and Straw Products Manufacturing	13	0.70	20.61
家具制造业	Furniture Manufacturing	26	2.65	111.73
造纸及纸制品业	Paper-making and Paper Products Manufacturing	21	0.98	58.64
印刷业和记录媒介的复制	Printing and Record Duplicating	25	1.38	54.62
文教体育用品制造业	Stationary, Education and Sports Goods Manufacturing	42	3.14	81.67
石油加工、炼焦及核燃料加工业	Oil Processing, Coking and Nuclear Fuel Processing	4	2.25	895.75
化学原料及化学制品制造业	Raw Chemical Materials and Chemical Products Manufacturing	65	4.45	692.57
医药制造业	Medicine Manufacturing	43	3.13	155.48
化学纤维制造业	Chemical Fiber Manufacturing	3	0.14	8.61
橡胶制品业	Rubber Products Manufacturing	30	2.59	96.52
塑料制品业	Plastic Products Manufacturing	78	4.49	120.50
非金属矿物制品业	Nonmetal Mineral Products	52	3.59	143.08
黑色金属冶炼及压延加工业	Smelting and Pressing of Ferrous Metals	18	3.88	1 252.75
有色金属冶炼及压延加工业	Smelting and Pressing of Nonferrous Metals	28	2.39	171.72
金属制品业	Metal Products Manufacturing	89	5.68	261.17
通用设备制造业	General Equipment Manufacturing	125	11.48	929.32
专用设备制造业	Special Purpose Equipment Manufacturing	82	4.91	194.02
交通运输设备制造业	Transportation Equipment Manufacturing	113	13.24	1 599.56
电气机械及器材制造业	Electric Machinery Equipments and Manufacturing	143	12.42	773.74
通信设备、计算机及其他电子设备制造业	Communications Equipment, Computer and Other Electronic Equipment Manufacturing	189	25.80	3 546.82
仪器仪表及文化、办公用机械制造业	Instruments, Meters, Culture and Office Equipments Manufacturing	40	2.96	192.37
工艺品及其他制造业	Artworks and Other Manufacturing	16	1.12	47.20
废弃资源和废旧材料回收加工业	Reclaim and Processing of Abandoned Resources and Materials	1	0.05	1.20
电力、燃气及水的生产和供应业	**Production and Supply of Power, Gas and Water**	**22**	**3.50**	**630.14**
电力、热力的生产和供应业	Production and Supply of Electricity and Thermal Power	9	1.97	570.70
燃气生产和供应业	Production and Supply of Gas	7	0.84	40.78
水的生产和供应业	Production and Supply of Water	6	0.69	18.65

工业销售产值（亿元）Sales Value of Industry Products(100 million yuan)	实收资本（股本）（亿元）Paid-in Capital (fixed capital stock)(100 million yuan)	年末资产总计（亿元）Total Assets (year-end)(100 million yuan)	年末负债合计（亿元）Total Liabilities (year-end)(100 million yuan)	主营业务收入（亿元）Prime Operation Revenue (100 million yuan)	利润总额（亿元）Total Pre-tax Profits (100 million yuan)	税金总额（亿元）Total Tax and Duties (100 million yuan)	成本费用总额（亿元）Total Costs and Expenses (100 million yuan)
12 184.43	**3 108.89**	**11 331.12**	**5 801.75**	**12 886.94**	**771.61**	**474.82**	**12 089.22**
58.34	11.36	35.88	19.83	72.68	2.51	1.60	70.30
146.18	49.82	149.16	71.56	177.75	11.29	10.79	169.64
96.70	34.31	79.32	40.56	94.32	5.18	9.94	86.35
230.56	20.30	456.57	17.63	230.21	79.07	133.88	65.98
127.44	61.67	168.10	82.24	128.86	3.49	3.45	127.19
168.54	34.37	126.49	69.31	170.95	13.49	4.53	157.68
52.66	7.38	51.42	28.01	51.93	5.37	1.33	46.72
19.61	5.21	17.62	9.82	19.64	0.95	0.23	18.70
110.35	15.08	64.60	35.67	110.04	9.92	2.04	100.90
58.34	28.48	71.61	43.69	58.74	2.03	2.18	57.15
54.08	27.75	69.28	28.40	56.51	4.60	2.90	52.17
82.06	15.65	59.54	37.25	82.89	2.15	1.22	81.76
895.08	168.59	432.81	154.01	899.35	-12.98	28.68	913.21
681.01	287.80	793.00	419.46	679.12	37.72	21.39	646.45
148.37	63.11	208.14	113.08	164.45	13.26	10.32	156.55
8.29	7.12	11.96	4.94	8.61	-0.02	0.11	8.69
94.84	35.28	109.83	68.81	111.20	1.35	1.57	111.04
118.61	53.87	156.75	78.59	120.69	4.72	3.31	116.76
141.46	65.66	216.09	125.90	154.62	5.17	5.38	151.14
1 242.19	363.51	1 742.84	734.04	1 428.35	181.98	60.56	1 262.48
171.51	30.90	90.84	57.54	174.60	2.67	1.26	172.50
260.71	57.75	221.41	111.18	273.12	20.83	4.70	254.81
924.19	196.03	950.21	624.43	878.39	70.95	20.30	810.89
186.33	91.48	265.65	143.46	195.95	12.57	7.19	186.57
1 582.77	435.68	1 867.42	927.41	1 832.85	150.24	102.49	1 669.41
770.67	155.00	597.35	333.49	792.47	63.03	14.51	737.10
3 514.63	734.51	2 129.57	1 334.94	3 661.96	56.73	12.75	3 621.93
189.82	37.90	145.09	68.89	198.82	18.02	4.41	182.67
47.90	13.13	40.27	16.20	56.91	5.24	1.73	51.58
1.20	0.20	2.29	1.41	0.97	0.07	0.07	0.88
629.32	**280.02**	**1 357.99**	**329.36**	**663.97**	**37.22**	**42.87**	**643.07**
570.70	164.06	1 127.54	211.34	574.24	39.58	41.72	542.56
40.76	55.45	94.12	50.09	71.52	-2.58	0.91	75.85
17.85	60.51	136.34	67.93	18.21	0.22	0.24	24.66

表 12.16 国有大中型工业企业主要指标(2006)
MAJOR INDICATORS OF STATE-OWNED LARGE AND MEDIUM-SIZED INDUSTRIAL ENTERPRISES

类 别	Types	单位数(个) Number of Enterprises (unit)	从业人员(万人) Employees (10 000 persons)	工业总产值(亿元) Gross Output Value of Industry (100 million yuan)
总 计	**Total**	**98**	**10.65**	**1 007.34**
按轻、重工业分	**Grouped by Light and Heavy Industry**			
大型企业	Large Enterprises	11	4.56	762.55
轻工业	Light Industry	5	1.34	260.15
重工业	Heavy Industry	6	3.22	502.40
中型企业	Medium Enterprises	87	6.09	244.79
轻工业	Light Industry	19	1.64	44.55
重工业	Heavy Industry	68	4.45	200.24
按隶属关系分	**Grouped by Subordination**			
大型企业	Large Enterprises	11	4.56	762.55
中央工业	Central Government	8	3.80	741.25
地方工业	Local Government	3	0.76	21.30
中型企业	Medium Enterprises	87	6.09	244.79
中央工业	Central Government	21	1.61	109.06
地方工业	Local Government	66	4.48	135.72
按从业人员分	**Grouped by Number of Employees**			
1 万人及以上	10 000 persons and above	1	1.22	422.23
5 000 ~9 999 人	5 000 ~9 999 persons	1	0.90	45.84
3 000 ~4 999 人	3 000 ~4 999 persons	4	0.74	255.13
1 000 ~2 999 人	1 000 ~2 999 persons	22	3.97	135.24
1 000 人以下	Below 1 000 persons	70	3.81	148.90
按工业总产值分	**Grouped by Gross Output Value of Industry**			
10 亿元及以上	10 00 million yuan and above	7	3.32	770.34
5 ~9.99 亿元	500 ~999 million yuan	13	1.80	91.74
1 ~4.99 亿元	100 ~499 million yuan	54	4.56	130.08
5 000 ~9 999 万元	50 ~99.99 million yuan	17	0.72	12.10
1 000 ~4 999 万元	10 ~49.99 million yuan	7	0.25	3.08
按固定资产原价分	**Grouped by Original Value of Fixed Assets**			
10 亿元及以上	1 000 million yuan and above	11	4.10	792.25
1 ~9.99 亿元	100 ~999 million yuan	42	4.27	148.50
5 000 ~9999 万元	50 ~99.99 million yuan	23	1.35	41.78
1 000 ~4999 万元	10 ~49.99 million yuan	21	0.90	23.75
1 000 万元以下	Below 10 million yuan	1	0.03	1.06

工业销售产值（亿元） Sales Value of Industry Products(100 million yuan)	实收资本（股本）（亿元） Paid-in Capital (fixed capital stock) (100 million yuan)	年末资产总计（亿元） Total Assets (year-end) (100 million yuan)	年末负债合计（亿元） Total Liabilities (year-end) (100 million yuan)	主营业务收入（亿元） Prime Operation Revenue (100 million yuan)	利润总额（亿元） Total Pre-tax Profits (100 million yuan)	税金总额（亿元） Total Tax and Duties (100 million yuan)	成本费用总额（亿元） Total Costs and Expenses (100 million yuan)
1 004.27	**302.82**	**2 058.01**	**597.76**	**1 052.05**	**111.14**	**174.91**	**872.64**
763.85	175.54	1 714.20	428.74	785.51	100.22	164.78	607.25
263.57	54.30	545.56	65.04	263.34	80.35	135.12	100.73
500.28	121.23	1 168.65	363.70	522.17	19.87	29.66	506.52
240.42	127.29	343.80	169.02	266.54	10.92	10.13	265.39
43.74	20.19	72.77	33.85	46.17	2.67	2.37	45.41
196.68	107.10	271.04	135.17	220.37	8.25	7.75	219.98
763.85	175.54	1 714.20	428.74	785.51	100.22	164.78	607.25
739.92	145.20	1 636.19	386.42	761.45	99.80	164.06	580.64
23.93	30.33	78.02	42.32	24.06	0.42	0.72	26.61
240.42	127.29	343.80	169.02	266.54	10.92	10.13	265.39
107.46	38.30	130.76	55.50	110.31	9.76	4.09	103.39
132.95	88.98	213.04	113.52	156.23	1.17	6.04	162.00
422.23	62.32	902.51	156.91	426.04	17.28	29.21	409.74
44.85	14.45	110.49	96.26	65.43	0.26	0.35	66.11
258.88	56.05	542.64	66.38	256.68	80.54	134.21	94.41
132.49	92.34	314.47	178.68	152.39	8.91	5.44	151.79
145.82	77.66	187.89	99.53	151.51	4.14	5.69	150.59
769.78	132.34	1 559.93	307.70	792.09	103.49	165.27	608.01
91.98	84.84	255.29	154.42	92.27	5.15	3.99	93.77
127.77	75.04	208.70	112.67	149.33	2.71	4.82	151.11
11.60	9.41	27.25	16.02	14.93	0.10	0.67	15.92
3.13	1.20	6.83	6.95	3.43	-0.31	0.16	3.83
791.13	208.14	1 763.43	429.19	832.56	105.76	166.01	650.00
148.50	74.15	217.26	118.68	149.98	3.72	6.61	152.89
40.10	16.65	54.25	31.92	44.45	1.38	1.16	44.82
23.47	3.83	21.73	16.75	24.00	0.26	1.13	23.85
1.07	0.05	1.33	1.21	1.06	0.01		1.08

表 12.16 续表 continued

类　别	Types	单位数（个）Number of Enterprises (unit)	从业人员（万人）Employees (10 000 persons)	工业总产值（亿元）Gross Output Value of Industry (100 million yuan)
按工业行业分	**Grouped by Sectors**			
制造业	**Manufacture Industry**	**91**	**8.59**	**553.60**
烟草制品业	Tabacco Manufacturing	1	0.37	228.03
纺织业	Textile	4	0.76	10.50
印刷业和记录媒介的复制	Printing and Record Duplicating	4	0.35	18.05
化学原料及化学制品制造业	Raw Chemical Materials and Chemical Products Manufacturing	7	0.58	51.78
医药制造业	Medicine Manufacturing	8	0.72	25.55
化学纤维制造业	Chemical Fiber Manufacturing	1	0.04	0.62
橡胶制品业	Rubber Products Manufacturing	1	0.09	1.14
非金属矿物制品业	Nonmetal Mineral Products	6	0.41	11.52
黑色金属冶炼及压延加工业	Smelting and Pressing of Ferrous Metals	4	0.51	34.70
有色金属冶炼及压延加工业	Smelting and Pressing of Nonferrous Metals	1	0.06	1.71
金属制品业	Metal Products Manufacturing	4	0.25	12.14
通用设备制造业	General Equipment Manufacturing	22	1.28	42.84
专用设备制造业	Special Purpose Equipment Manufacturing	10	0.56	18.92
交通运输设备制造业	Transportation Equipment Manufacturing	14	2.43	91.6
通信设备、计算机及其他电子设备制造业	Communications Equipment, Computer and Other Electronic Equipment Manufacturing	1	0.04	0.44
仪器仪表及文化、办公用机械制造业	Instruments, Meters, Culture and Office Equipments Manufacturing	3	0.15	4.07
电力、燃气及水的生产和供应业	**Production and Supply of Power, Gas and Water**	**7**	**2.06**	**453.74**
电力、热力的生产和供应业	Production and Supply of Electricity and Thermal Power	2	1.37	428.94
燃气生产和供应业	Production and Supply of Gas	4	0.44	18.25
水的生产和供应业	Production and Supply of Water	1	0.25	6.55

工业销售产值（亿元）Sales Value of Industry Products (100 million yuan)	实收资本（股本）（亿元）Paid-in Capital (fixed capital stock) (100 million yuan)	年末资产总计（亿元）Total Assets (year-end) (100 million yuan)	年末负债合计（亿元）Total Liabilities (year-end) (100 million yuan)	主营业务收入（亿元）Prime Operation Revenue (100 million yuan)	利润总额（亿元）Total Pre-tax Profits (100 million yuan)	税金总额（亿元）Total Tax and Duties (100 million yuan)	成本费用总额（亿元）Total Costs and Expenses (100 million yuan)
550.66	181.05	1 051.81	393.59	576.77	95.33	144.37	407.63
228.82	17.40	452.56	17.57	228.46	78.75	133.63	64.56
13.53	5.82	22.16	13.16	13.79	0.47	0.84	14.19
17.84	12.04	28.72	10.12	20.59	1.67	1.25	18.95
51.37	15.56	56.67	18.73	52.4	4.68	1.39	49.6
25.42	8.94	44.91	19.67	24.82	2.35	1.27	23.69
0.61	1.11	1.38	1.00	0.61	-0.21		0.84
1.15	0.01	2.34	2.08	1.15	-0.08	0.02	1.23
11.24	3.14	19.80	13.18	12.55	0.13	0.56	12.80
33.33	44.30	140.53	98.36	33.01	0.86	0.64	34.12
1.79	0.88	1.54	1.39	1.79	-0.16	0.02	2.00
12.37	5.54	16.29	7.63	13.70	1.85	0.84	11.94
40.87	11.24	43.82	31.81	40.45	1.24	1.55	40.03
18.09	12.97	30.16	14.54	19.52	1.09	1.11	19.13
89.78	40.26	181.84	137.7	108.07	2.45	0.94	108.81
0.44	0.1	0.57	1.31	0.44	-0.25	0.01	0.64
3.99	1.76	8.52	5.33	5.42	0.5	0.32	5.11
453.60	121.77	1 006.19	204.17	475.28	15.81	30.53	465.01
428.94	63.65	908.62	159.12	432.75	17.28	30.24	418.17
18.12	32.97	45.22	18.02	35.85	-1.41	0.25	37.74
6.55	25.14	52.35	27.03	6.68	-0.06	0.04	9.1

表 12.17　闵行经济技术开发区主要指标(2006)
MAJOR INDICATORS OF MINHANG ECONOMIC AND TECHNICAL DEVELOPMENT ZONE

类　别	Types	单位数(个) Number of Enterprises (unit)	工业总产值(亿元) Gross Output Value of Industry (100 million yuan)
总　计	**Total**	**84**	**348.91**
按登记注册类型分	**Grouped by Registration Categories**		
国　有	State-owned	1	
其他有限责任公司	Other Limited Liability Company	3	1.40
私营有限责任公司	Private Limited Liability Company	1	0.95
与港澳台商合资经营	Joint Ventures with Investment from Hong Kong, Macao and Taiwan	9	5.37
与港澳台商合作经营	Cooperation Ventures with Investment from Hong Kong, Macao and Taiwan		
港澳台商独资	Hong Kong, Macao and Taiwan Enterprises	4	2.53
港澳台商投资股份有限公司	Hong Kong, Macao and Taiwan Funded Share-holding Limited Liability Company	1	1.62
中外合资经营	Joint Ventures	26	166.52
中外合作经营	Cooperation Ventures	1	2.22
外商独资企业	Solely Foreign-funded Enterprise	37	155.27
外商投资股份有限公司	Foreign-funded Joint Venture Company	1	13.03
按轻重工业分	**Grouped by Light and Heavy Industry**		
轻工业	Light Industry	49	178.16
重工业	Heavy Industry	35	170.75
按企业规模分	**Grouped by Size of Enterprises**		
大型企业	Large	2	65.27
中型企业	Medium	33	230.07
小型企业	Small	49	53.57
按行业分	**Grouped by Sectors**		
食品制造业	Food Manufacturing	6	16.56
饮料制造业	Beverage Manufacturing	4	47.70
纺织业	Textile	8	4.09
纺织服装、鞋、帽制造业	Garments, Shoes and Accessories Manufacturing	7	4.66
皮革、毛皮、羽毛(绒)及其制品业	Leather, Fur, and Wool Products Manufacturing	1	0.77
家具制造业	Furniture Manufacturing	2	0.99
印刷业和记录媒介的复制	Printing and Record Duplicating	5	28.23
化学原料及化学制品制造业	Raw Chemical Materials and Chemical Products Manufacturing	5	27.63
医药制造业	Medicine Manufacturing	1	0.48
化学纤维制造业	Chemical Fibre Manufacturing	1	13.03
塑料制品业	Plastic Products Manufacturing	7	9.69
非金属矿物制品业	Nonmetal Mineral Products	3	11.33
有色金属冶炼及压延加工业	Smelting and Pressing of Nonferrous Metals	1	6.80
金属制品业	Metal Products Manufacturing	2	0.65
通用设备制造业	General Equipment Manufacturing	11	82.89
专用设备制造业	Special Prupose Equipment Manufacturing	2	1.49
交通运输设备制造业	Transportation Equipment Manufacturing	2	5.81
电气机械及器材制造业	Electric Machinery Equipments and Manufacturing	7	37.08
通信设备、计算机及其他电子设备制造	Communications Equipment, Computer and Other Electronic Equipment Manufacturing	2	3.61
仪器仪表及文化、办公用机械制造业	Instruments, Meters, Culture and Office Equipments Manufacturing	4	32.51
工艺品及其他制造业	Artworks and Other Manufacturing	3	12.91

工业销售产值（亿元）Sales Value of Industrial Products (100 million yuan)	实收资本（股本）（亿元）Paid-in Capital (fixed capital stock) (100 million yuan)	年末资产总计（亿元）Total Assets (year-end) (100 million yuan)	年末负债合计（亿元）Total Liabilities (year-end) (100 million yuan)	主营业务收入（亿元）Prime Operating Revenue (100 million yuan)	利润总额（亿元）Total Pre-tax Profits (100 million yuan)	税金总额（亿元）Total Tax and Duties (100 million yuan)
351.86	**94.05**	**294.79**	**148.96**	**353.79**	**34.38**	**19.57**
0.40	0.48	1.20	1.80	0.33	-0.23	0.06
1.41	0.54	1.47	1.56	1.46	-0.27	0.05
0.92	0.05	0.62	0.57	0.51		
7.35	1.63	5.49	1.77	8.46	0.80	0.38
2.96	2.24	4.09	1.39	3.01	0.26	0.06
2.46	0.09	2.06	0.34	2.45	0.31	0.27
165.12	35.46	136.67	65.06	164.89	19.09	7.06
2.04	1.30	2.46	3.42	2.04	-0.40	0.12
156.73	42.62	120.84	55.96	156.47	15.58	11.57
12.48	9.63	19.88	17.10	14.16	-0.75	
181.65	39.31	121.65	54.86	179.82	17.20	13.65
170.21	54.73	173.15	94.11	173.97	17.18	5.93
64.66	21.66	68.84	38.48	65.41	6.10	1.86
235.35	52.11	166.74	80.92	232.31	20.31	14.42
51.84	20.28	59.21	29.56	56.06	7.97	3.30
16.49	2.66	8.73	6.11	19.27	1.08	1.32
51.82	6.02	34.94	18.88	47.43	3.92	5.04
4.66	2.47	5.65	1.88	4.72	0.50	0.12
4.74	0.83	2.33	0.66	3.85	0.09	0.01
0.74	0.06	0.45	0.28	0.74	0.08	0.07
0.96	0.87	1.60	0.47	1.00	0.14	0.12
29.35	10.18	18.11	6.73	29.75	2.64	3.16
25.87	5.72	17.13	7.96	24.65	3.17	2.79
0.48	0.61	0.57	0.45	0.48	-0.04	
12.48	9.63	19.88	17.10	14.16	-0.75	
9.85	2.55	7.33	2.89	9.98	0.79	0.11
11.60	8.18	16.96	12.65	10.71	-1.66	0.06
6.89	2.10	4.14	1.52	6.89	-0.19	0.05
0.63	0.10	0.37	0.04	0.66	0.02	0.01
82.64	21.53	81.26	37.50	84.55	12.99	3.67
1.46	2.14	3.11	0.96	2.05	0.09	0.12
5.32	2.24	9.65	7.36	5.49	0.47	0.09
38.03	6.03	29.80	15.27	38.35	5.39	1.42
3.56	1.13	2.48	0.83	3.57	0.20	0.05
31.38	2.95	14.06	7.40	32.51	2.29	0.42
12.90	6.06	16.24	2.02	12.97	3.14	0.91

表 12.18　漕河泾新兴技术开发区主要指标(2006)
MAJOR INDEXES OF CAOHEJING NEW TECHNICAL DEVELOPMENT ZONE

类　别	Types	单位数（个）Number of Enterprises (unit)	工业总产值（亿元）Gross Output Value of Industry (100 million yuan)	工业销售产值（亿元）Sales Value of Industrial Products (100 million yuan)
总　计	**Total**	**162**	**281.36**	**286.13**
按登记注册类型分	**Grouped by Registration Categories**			
国　有	State-owned	6	2.3	2.14
集　体	Collective-owned	1	0.21	0.2
股份合作	Share-holding Cooperation	3	1.36	1.43
国有独资公司	Solely State Fund Company	1	0.08	0.09
其他有限责任公司	Other Companies with Limited Liabilities	22	10.68	10.81
股份有限公司	Share-holding Companies with Limited Liabilities	6	11.78	11.70
私营合伙	Private Cooperation	1	0.05	0.05
私营有限责任公司	Private Companies with Limited Liabilities	22	6.88	6.74
合资经营(港或澳、台资)	Joint Venture(or Hong Kong, Macao and Taiwan Funded)	4	1.55	1.56
港澳台商独资	Solely Hong Kong, Macao and Taiwan Funded	19	76.36	84.09
中外合资经营	Sino-foreign joint ventures	19	41.94	41.42
中外合作经营	Sino-foreign Cooperation	2	0.24	0.23
外商独资企业	Solely Foreign Funded	52	112.45	110.16
外商投资股份有限公司	Foreign Funded Share-holding Companies with Limited Liabilities	4	15.48	15.49
按轻、重工业分	**Grouped by Light and Heavy Industry**			
轻工业	Light Industry	35	26.68	26.35
重工业	Heavy Industry	127	254.68	259.78
按企业规模分	**Grouped by Size of Enterprises**			
大型企业	Large	3	105.40	113.10
中型企业	Medium	21	110.30	108.09
小型企业	Small	138	65.66	64.94
按工业行业分	**Grouped by Sectors**			
食品制造业	Food Manufacturing	1	0.39	0.33
饮料制造业	Beverage Manufacturing	1	0.05	0.06
纺织业	Textile	1	0.13	0.13
纺织服装、鞋、帽制造业	Garments, Shoes and Accessories Manufacturing	2	0.35	0.22
印刷业和记录媒介的复制	Printing and Record Duplicating	5	2.56	2.46
文教体育用品制造业	Stationary, Education and Sports Goods Manufacturing	1	0.15	0.18
化学原料及化学制品制造业	Raw Chemical Materials and Chemical Products	8	27.98	27.08
医药制造业	Medicine Manufacturing	7	3.01	2.89
金属制品业	Metal Products Manufacturing	3	0.39	0.42
通用设备制造业	General Equipment Manufacturing	13	12.14	11.56
专用设备制造业	Special Purpose Equipment Manufacturing	11	3.30	3.37
交通运输设备制造业	Transportation Equipment Manufacturing	1	0.10	0.15
电气机械及器材制造业	Electric Machinery Equipments Manufacturing	15	13.14	13.46
通信设备、计算机及其他电子设备制造	Communications Equipment, Computer and Other Electric Machinery Equipments and Manufacturing	67	192.32	198.87
仪器仪表及文化、办公用机械制造业	Instruments, Meters, Culture and Office Equipments Manufacturing	26	25.36	24.96

实收资本（股本）（亿元）Paid-in Capital (fixed capital stock) (100 million yuan)	年末资产总计（亿元）Total Assets (year-end) (100 million yuan)	年末负债合计（亿元）Total Liabilities (year-end) (100 million yuan)	主营业务收入（亿元）Prime Operating Revenue (100 million yuan)	利润总额（亿元）Total Pre-tax Profits (100 million yuan)	税金总额（亿元）Total Tax and Duties (100 million yuan)
84.61	**265.42**	**137.38**	**304.11**	**12.46**	**4.18**
0.78	2.79	1.48	2.76	0.24	0.06
0.03	0.16	0.09	0.20	0.02	0.01
0.57	1.37	0.51	1.52	0.03	0.03
0.03	0.04	0.02	0.09		0.01
6.35	22.65	15.56	15.20	-0.39	0.40
2.03	12.12	10.61	13.64	-0.31	0.06
0.01	0.04	0.02	0.05		
0.81	4.21	2.34	6.81	0.75	0.18
1.32	1.95	0.75	1.63	0.11	0.07
9.05	27.25	15.47	84.45	-0.62	0.39
24.05	57.91	22.68	44.44	2.46	0.38
0.28	0.42	0.02	0.23	0.02	0.01
26.11	89.36	50.33	113.66	7.80	1.94
13.19	45.14	17.49	19.44	2.35	0.63
12.69	41.82	30.50	33.65	-1.72	0.22
71.92	223.61	106.88	270.46	14.18	3.96
9.39	41.88	32.22	113.57	0.42	0.46
41.46	126.66	56.31	115.00	7.02	2.03
33.76	96.89	48.85	75.55	5.02	1.70
0.05	0.23	0.14	0.44	0.04	0.02
0.20	0.20	0.19	0.07	-0.11	0.01
0.02	0.09	0.07	0.13	0.01	
0.18	0.24	0.07	0.17	-0.01	0.01
1.84	5.75	1.23	2.94	0.25	0.01
0.16	0.18	0.17	0.23		0.02
6.18	23.93	11.51	26.37	2.71	1.48
2.94	5.40	1.41	3.34	0.54	0.05
0.31	0.56	0.39	0.39	-0.05	0.01
2.16	9.86	3.67	11.92	2.22	0.29
1.19	3.24	2.07	3.40	0.23	0.11
0.02	0.09	0.07	0.14		
4.38	13.50	5.40	14.45	0.28	0.1
54.12	175.60	94.74	211.43	4.84	0.99
10.86	26.54	16.23	28.68	1.51	1.09

表 12.19 国家级、市级工业园区主要经济指标(2006)
MAJOR ECONOMIC INDICATORS OF MUNICIPAL AND NATIONAL INDUSTRIAL ZONES

指标	Indicators	国家级开发区 National Level Develop Zone	其中 of which 外高桥保税区 Waigaoqiao Free Trade Zone	金桥出口加工区 Jinqiao Export Processing Zone
单位数(个)	Number of Enterprises(unit)	842	198	281
从业人员(万人)	Employees(10 000 persons)	33.83	5.40	10.39
工业总产值(亿元)	Gross Output Value of Industry(100 million yuan)	4 698.43	513.00	1 488.06
出口交货值(亿元)	Delivery Value of Industry Exports(100 million yuan)	2 870.61	275.18	421.33
实收资本(股本)(亿元)	Paid-in Capital(Fixed capital stock)(100 million yuan)	1 088.21	92.17	450.84
年末资产总计(亿元)	Total Assets(year-end)(100 million yuan)	3 469.38	358.06	1 248.07
流动资产合计(亿元)	Total Current Assets(100 million yuan)	2 036.83	240.67	806.82
流动资产年平均余额(亿元)	Average Current Assets (100 million yuan)	1 920.42	219.52	766.91
固定资产合计(亿元)	Total Fixed Assets(100 million yuan)	952.41	105.48	304.67
固定资产原价(亿元)	Original Value of Fixed Assets(100 million yuan)	1 640.27	186.08	569.92
固定资产净值年平均余额(亿元)	Average Net Value of Fixed Assets (100 million yuan)	877.11	97.36	277.97
年末负债合计(亿元)	Total Liabilities(year-end)(100 million yuan)	1 813.73	203.07	642.31
年末流动负债合计(亿元)	Total Current Liabilities(year-end)(100 million yuan)	1 611.6	182.78	613.06
长期负债合计(亿元)	Total Long-term Liabilities(100 million yuan)	197.84	19.51	27.48
年末所有者权益(亿元)	Owners' Equity(year-end)(100 million yuan)	1 655.65	154.99	605.76
主营业务收入(亿元)	Prime Operating Revenue(100 million yuan)	5 060.52	527.01	1 749.43
利润总额(亿元)	Total Pre-tax Profits(100 million yuan)	235.8	30.95	116.68
税金总额(亿元)	Total Tax and Duties(100 million yuan)	107.92	6.30	70.13
亏损总额(亿元)	Total Loss(100 million yuan)	32.82	5.27	8.23

张江高科技园区 Zhangjiang Hi-Tec Park	漕河泾新兴技术开发区 Caohejing Hi-tec Park	漕河泾出口加工区 Caohejing Export Processing Zone	闵行经济技术开发区 Minhang Hi-tec Park	上海松江出口加工区 Songjiang Export Processing Zone	市级开发区 Municipal Level Development Zone	其中 of which 上海宝山工业园区 Baoshan Industrial Park	上海月杨工业园区 Yueyang Industrial Park
72	162	2	84	43	2 859	72	73
3.40	3.85	1.35	3.57	5.87	60.33	1.50	1.49
299.38	281.36	507.15	348.91	1 260.57	3 922.06	76.49	102.09
178.73	162.70	507.15	72.48	1 253.05	1 138.74	14.15	44.42
308.80	84.61	8.20	94.05	49.54	1 276.03	20.94	18.54
794.64	265.42	88.79	294.79	419.60	3 671.83	63.97	59.92
223.70	169.93	65.92	204.26	325.52	1 919.07	34.21	36.50
198.55	164.70	85.65	185.66	299.44	1 765.73	31.83	34.99
276.44	72.17	22.28	80.02	91.34	1 528.81	25.17	19.48
468.10	141.28	27.50	141.39	106.00	1 997.63	31.69	24.95
251.40	68.89	20.19	75.15	86.15	1 337.07	21.44	16.67
242.00	137.38	81.53	148.96	358.49	2 082.45	35.16	32.49
122.11	123.70	81.53	145.45	342.98	1 623.99	30.19	29.98
119.42	13.49		2.46	15.48	438.09	4.97	2.19
552.65	128.04	7.27	145.83	61.12	1 589.38	28.81	27.43
290.35	304.11	514.69	353.79	1321.13	3 919.8	77.36	108.32
29.80	12.46	0.79	34.38	10.75	178.58	5.31	6.54
7.71	4.18		19.57	0.02	114.66	1.32	2.19
6.18	5.02		4.50	3.62	90.46	0.32	0.05

表 12.19 续表 1 continued

指标	Indicators	上海富盛经济开发区 Fusheng Economic Development Zone	上海浦东空港工业园区 Pudong Konggang Industrial Park	上海市嘉定区工业园区 Jiading Industrial Park
单位数(个)	Number of Enterprises(unit)	1	124	397
从业人员(万人)	Employees(10 000 persons)	…	1.72	8.74
工业总产值(亿元)	Gross Output Value of Industry(100 million yuan)	1.60	60.03	440.82
出口交货值(亿元)	Delivery Value of Industry Exports(100 million yuan)		15.36	185.97
实收资本(股本)(亿元)	Paid-in Capital(Fixed capital stock)(100 million yuan)	0.01	14.76	119.06
年末资产总计(亿元)	Total Assets(year-end)(100 million yuan)	0.44	55.27	356.1
流动资产合计(亿元)	Total Current Assets(100 million yuan)	0.42	34.29	219.46
流动资产年平均余额(亿元)	Average Current Assets (100 million yuan)	0.42	31.89	206.02
固定资产合计(亿元)	Total Fixed Assets(100 million yuan)	0.01	17.19	117
固定资产原价(亿元)	Original Value of Fixed Assets(100 million yuan)	0.02	20.23	175.47
固定资产净值年平均余额(亿元)	Average Net Value of Fixed Assets (100 million yuan)	0.01	15.08	111.67
年末负债合计(亿元)	Total Liabilities(year-end)(100 million yuan)	0.42	32.35	197.24
年末流动负债合计(亿元)	Total Current Liabilities(year-end)(100 million yuan)	0.42	28.68	178.64
长期负债合计(亿元)	Total Long-term Liabilities(100 million yuan)		2.83	17.94
年末所有者权益(亿元)	Owners' Equity(year-end)(100 million yuan)	0.02	22.93	158.85
主营业务收入(亿元)	Prime Operating Revenue(100 million yuan)	1.60	58.35	447.91
利润总额(亿元)	Total Pre-tax Profits(100 million yuan)	0.01	4.86	22.7
税金总额(亿元)	Total Tax and Duties(100 million yuan)	0.01	1.77	7.82
亏损总额(亿元)	Total Loss(100 million yuan)		0.25	5.46

上海市嘉定区汽车产业园区 Jiading Automobile Industrial Park	上海莘庄工业区 Xinzhuang Industrial Paek	上海青浦工业园区 Qingpu Industrial Park	上海西郊经济开发区 Xijiao Economic Development Zone	上海松江工业园区 Songjiang Industrial Park	上海松江经济开发区 Songjiang Economic Development Zone	上海奉贤经济开发区 Fengxian Economic Development Zone	上海金山工业园区 Jinshan Industrial Park
294	176	332	106	448	122	106	52
5.99	4.03	6.79	2.64	11.77	1.96	2.15	1.02
653.58	329.42	287.78	94.52	639.68	84.56	131.73	43.97
55.91	118.59	106.1	31.22	295.53	27.60	52.53	7.92
162.87	116.21	114.64	45.56	193.16	17.49	42.95	12.61
489.83	352.89	280.99	105.77	550.39	58.67	122.77	37.31
288.53	184.22	155.66	51.33	315.32	35.68	78.09	16.24
279.44	175.9	140.6	43.55	289.45	33.73	73.76	15.66
182.5	151.92	107.99	45.65	201.28	17.62	33.63	18.12
305.56	163.86	149.57	64.52	275.16	24.28	41.23	21.72
165.91	126.09	98.31	37.46	181.29	15.84	28.26	16.26
213.96	214.57	141.77	52.24	324.43	32.94	70.97	20.24
203.92	154.39	125.95	49.38	299.06	30.02	66.67	14.85
9.85	59.96	14.07	1.18	22.7	2.48	3.57	2.9
275.87	138.32	139.22	53.54	225.96	25.73	51.8	17.06
659.5	317.61	274.85	93.7	658.61	78.75	147.01	40.20
45.04	10.64	16.52	4.26	27.78	5.14	4.27	1.82
43.51	6.99	6.63	3.61	12.07	2.5	2.67	1.11
1.47	15.6	4.71	0.66	6.95	0.13	3.38	0.73

表 12.19 续表 2　continued

指标	Indicators	上海枫泾工业园区 Fengjing Industrial Park	上海市北工业园区 Shibei Industrial Park	上海崇明工业园区 Congming Industrial Park
单位数(个)	Number of Enterprises(unit)	79	34	19
从业人员(万人)	Employees(10 000 persons)	1.25	0.59	0.36
工业总产值(亿元)	Gross Output Value of Industry(100 million yuan)	86.81	23.65	7.71
出口交货值(亿元)	Delivery Value of Industry Exports(100 million yuan)	10.38	1.85	3.55
实收资本(股本)(亿元)	Paid-in Capital(Fixed capital stock)(100 million yuan)	21.46	8.52	1.31
年末资产总计(亿元)	Total Assets(year-end)(100 million yuan)	59.59	21	7.73
流动资产合计(亿元)	Total Current Assets(100 million yuan)	29.87	13.81	4.46
流动资产年平均余额(亿元)	Average Current Assets (100 million yuan)	25.95	12.65	4.37
固定资产合计(亿元)	Total Fixed Assets(100 million yuan)	18.77	6.83	2.59
固定资产原价(亿元)	Original Value of Fixed Assets(100 million yuan)	20.18	12.72	3.42
固定资产净值年平均余额(亿元)	Average Net Value of Fixed Assets (100 million yuan)	14.95	6.63	2.42
年末负债合计(亿元)	Total Liabilities(year-end)(100 million yuan)	29.89	9.26	4.64
年末流动负债合计(亿元)	Total Current Liabilities(year-end)(100 million yuan)	27.82	8.25	4.54
长期负债合计(亿元)	Total Long-term Liabilities(100 million yuan)	1.97	0.93	0.08
年末所有者权益(亿元)	Owners' Equity(year-end)(100 million yuan)	29.7	11.74	3.09
主营业务收入(亿元)	Prime Operating Revenue(100 million yuan)	75.39	24.24	7.78
利润总额(亿元)	Total Pre-tax Profits(100 million yuan)	4.29	1.18	0.67
税金总额(亿元)	Total Tax and Duties(100 million yuan)	2.17	0.57	0.27
亏损总额(亿元)	Total Loss(100 million yuan)	0.17	0.12	0.05

上海星火工业园区 Xinghuo Industrial Park	上海浦东康桥工业园区 Pudong Kangqiao Industial Park	上海化学工业园区 Chemical Industrial Park	上海新杨工业园区 Xinyang Industrial Psrk	上海浦东合庆工业园区 Pudong Heqing Industrial Park	上海南汇工业园区 Nanhui Industrial Park	上海奉贤工业园区 Fengxian Industrial Park	上海未来岛物流科技园区 Future Island Logistic Technology Zone
26	188	17	14	72	55	47	5
0.93	4.12	0.35	0.27	1.1	0.72	0.69	0.15
132.12	283.18	311.65	10.7	60.3	25.37	15.71	18.6
26.04	89.12	29.37	0.46	6.23	11.44		5.01
39.75	89.88	200.3	1.38	18.48	10.35	3.49	2.3
126.93	274.87	523.89	9.09	62.7	26.92	12.49	12.3
54.64	157.99	127.25	4.88	43.24	15.47	7.51	10.01
51.65	139.77	98.91	4.34	40.48	13.76	7.16	9.44
67	95.9	366.54	2.85	15.8	9.14	4.13	1.7
91.37	132.97	394.29	3.59	21.48	10.31	5.74	3.29
55.51	87.66	306.42	2.44	13.5	7.23	4.32	1.7
91.41	153.52	357.23	5.44	32.49	14.09	6.85	8.87
61.13	132.53	113.18	5.09	31.47	12.38	6.71	8.72
30.28	20.57	237.34	0.35	0.87	0.85	0.14	0.07
35.52	121.36	166.66	3.65	30.22	12.83	5.65	3.43
129.18	285.6	300.83	10.79	62.74	25.71	14.96	18.81
-0.85	21.3	-11.57	0.99	3.53	1.72	0.57	1.87
1.3	7.4	7.52	0.44	1.44	0.48	0.33	0.56
3.6	3.32	42.16	0.07	1	0.23	0.04	

上/海/统/计/年/鉴

主要统计指标解释

■ 工　业

指从事自然资源的开采，对采掘品和农产品进行加工和再加工的物质生产部门。具体包括:(1)对自然资源的开采，如采矿、晒盐等（但不包括禽兽捕猎和水产捕捞);(2)对农副产品的加工、再加工,如粮油加工、食品加工、缫丝、纺织、制革等;(3)对采掘品的加工、再加工,如炼铁、炼钢、化工生产、石油加工、机器制造、木材加工等,以及电力、自来水、煤气的生产和供应等;(4)对工业品的修理、翻新,如机器设备的修理、交通运输工具(包括小卧车)的修理等。

1984 年以前农村的村及村以下办工业归属农业，1984 年以后划归工业。

工业统计调查单位为独立核算法人工业企业。

独立核算法人工业企业指从事工业生产经营活动的单位。独立核算法人工业企业应同时具备以下条件:①依法成立,有自己的名称、组织机构和场所,能够承担民事责任;②独立拥有和使用资产,承担负债,有权与其他单位签订合同;③独立核算盈亏,并能够编制资产负债表。

■ 轻工业

指主要提供生活消费品和制作手工工具的工业。按其所使用的原料不同,可分为两大类:(1)以农产品为原料的轻工业，是指直接或间接以农产品为基本原料的轻工业。主要包括食品制造、饮料制造、烟草加工、纺织、缝纫、皮革和毛皮制作、造纸以及印刷等工业;(2)以非农产品为原料的轻工业,是指以工业品为原料的轻工业。主要包括文教体育用品、化学药品制造、合成纤维制造、日用化学制品、日用玻璃制品、日用金属制品、手工工具制造、医疗器械制造、文化和办公用机械制造等工业。

■ 重工业

指为国民经济各部门提供物质技术基础的主要生产资料的工业。按其生产性质和产品用途,可以分为下列三类:(1)采掘(伐)工业,是指对自然资源的开采,包括石油开采、煤炭开采、金属矿开采、非金属矿开采等工业;(2) 原材料工业，指向国民经济各部门提供基本材料、动力和燃料的工业。包括金属冶炼及加工、炼焦及焦炭、化学、化工原料、水泥、人造板以及电力、石油和煤炭加工等工业;(3)加工工业,是指对工业原材料进行再加工制造的工业。包括装备国民经济各部门的机械设备制造工业、金属结构、水泥制品等工业,以及为农业提供的生产资料如化肥、农药等工业。

根据上述划分原则，修理业中以重工业产品为修理作业对象的划为重工业,反之划为轻工业。

■ 工业总产值

(1)定义:工业总产值是以货币形式表现的,工业企业在一定时期内生产的工业最终产品或提供工业性劳务活动的总价值量。它反映一定时间内工业生产的总规模和总水平。

(2)计算原则:

工业生产的原则，即凡是企业在报告期生产的经检验合格的产品,不管是否在报告期销售,均包括在内。

最终产品的原则,即凡是计入工业总产值的产品,必须是本企业生产的经检验合格的，不需要再进行任何加工的最终产品。如果企业有中间产品(半成品)对外销售,则对外销售的中间产品应视为企业的最终产品。

工厂法原则，即工业总产值是以工业企业作为基本计算(核算)单位,即按企业的最终产品计算工业总产值。按这种方法计算的工业总产值，不允许同一产品价值在企业内部重复计算,不能把企业内部各个车间(分厂)生产的成果相加,但允许企业间的重复计算。

(3)内容及计算方法:1995 年全国工业普查对工业总产值（原规定）的内容及计算原则和方法做了某些修订,修订后的工业总产值(新规定)包括三项内容:即本期生产成品价值、对外加工费收入、在制品半成品期末期初差额价值三部分。

本期生产成品价值:指企业本期生产,并在报告期内不再进行加工,经检验、包装入库的全部工业成品(半产品)价值合计,包括企业生产的自制设备及提供给本企业在建工程、其他非工业部门和福利部门等单位使用的成品价值。本期生产成品价值为按自备原材料生产的产品的数量乘以本期不含增值税(销项税额)的产品实际销售平均单价计算；会计核算中按成本价格转帐的自制设备和自产自用的成品,按成本价格计算生产成品价值。生产成品价值中不包括用定货者来料加工的成品(半产品)价值。

对外加工费收入：指企业在报告期内完成的对外承

主要统计指标解释

接的工业品加工（包括用定货者来料加工产品）的加工费收入和对外工业修理作业所取得的加工费收入。对外加工费收入按不含增值税（销项税额）的价格计算，可根据会计“产品销售收入”科目的有关资料取得。

对于本企业对内非工业部门提供的加工修理、设备安装的劳务收入，如果企业会计核算基础较好，能取得这部分资料，而且这部分价值所占比重较大，应包括在对外加工费收入中。

自制半成品在制品期末期初差额价值：指企业报告期在制品期末减期初的差额价值，本指标一般可以从会计核算资料中取得。如果会计产品成本核算中不计算半成品、在制品的成本，则总产值中也不包括这部分价值，反之则包括。

（4）工业总产值统计范围变化和计算方法修订情况：

1984 年以前工业总产值不包括村办工业，村办工业总产值划归农业。1984 年以后工业总产值包括村办工业。

1995 年工业普查对工业总产值计算方法做了修订，即从 1995 年始按新修订（新规定）方法计算工业总产值。新规定与原规定的区别如下：

全价与加工费的计算原则不同：新规定为凡自备原材料，不论其生产繁简程度如何，一律按全价计算工业总产值；凡来料加工，允许按加工费计算工业总产值。原规定则视生产加工的繁简程度不同，规定哪些行业按全价，哪些行业按加工费计算工业总产值。

自制半成品、在产品期末期初差额价值的计算原则不同：新规定要求，凡会计产品成本核算时计算了成本的差额价值，总产值中就应包括，否则可不包括；原规定则按生产周期六个月的界限区分，凡生产周期六个月以上的企业，总产值计算中应包括这部分差额价值，否则可不包括。

计算价格不同：新规定按不含增值税（销项税额）的价格计算；原规定则按含增值税（销项税额）的价格计算。

■ 大、中、小型企业

大中小型企业划分标准：自 2003 年年报起，大中小型企业划分标准执行“统计上大中小型企业划分办法（暂行）”（国统字[2003]17 号）。即大型企业必须同时达到从业人员数≥2000 人、销售收入≥30000 万元、资产总额≥40000 万元；中型企业必须同时达到 2000 人＞从业人员数≥300 人、30000 万元＞销售收入≥3000 万元、40000 万元＞资产总额≥4000 万元；其余的均为小型企业。

■ 资产总计

资产是指企业拥有或者控制的能以货币计量的经济资源，包括各种财产、债权和其他权利。资产按其流动性（即资产的变现能力和支付能力）划分为：流动资产、长期投资、固定资产、无形资产、递延资产和其他资产。该指标根据企业会计“资产负债表”中“资产总计”项目的期末数增列。

■ 流动资产合计

指可以在一年或者超过一年的一个营业周期内变现或者耗用的资产，包括现金及各种存款、短期投资、应收及预付货款、存款等。

■ 流动资产平均余额

指企业在报告期内全部流动资产的平均余额。

■ 固定资产净值年平均余额

指固定资产净值在报告期内余额的平均数。计算公式为：

固定资产净值年平均余额 =1 至 12 月各月月初、月末固定资产净值之和 /24

该指标根据“资产负债表”中“固定资产原价”、“累计折旧”指标的期初、期末数计算填列。

固定资产净值指固定资产原价减去历年已提折旧额后的净额。计算公式为：

固定资产净值 = 固定资产原价 − 累计折旧

■ 负债合计

指企业所承担的能以货币计量，将以资产或劳务偿付的债务总计。负债一般按偿还期长短分为流动负债和长期负债。流动负债合计是指企业在一年内或超过一年的一个营业周期内偿还的债务；长期负债合计是指偿还期在一年以上或者超过一年的一个营业周期内偿还债务。

■ 所有者权益

指企业投资人对企业净资产的所有权。企业净资产等于企业全部资产减去全部负债后的余额，包括企业投资人对企业的最初投入的实际到位的资产及资本公积金、盈余公积金和未分配利润。所有者权益合计数小于零，表示企业资不抵债。

■ 利润总额

指企业生产经营活动的最终成果，是企业在一定时期内实现的盈亏相抵后的利润总额（亏损以“–”号表示），

主要统计指标解释

它等于营业利润加上补贴收入加上投资收益加上营业外净收入再加上以前年度损益调整。

■ 总资产贡献率

反映企业全部资产的获利能力，是企业经营业绩和管理水平的集中体现，是评价和考核企业盈利能力的核心指标。计算公式为：

总资产贡献率(%)= 利润总额 + 税金总额 + 利息支出 / 平均资金总额 × 100%

公式中：税金总额为产品销售税金及附加与应缴增值税之和；平均资产总额为期初期末资产之和的算术平均值。

■ 资产负债率

该指标既反映企业经营风险的大小，也反映企业利用债权人提供的资金从事经营活动的能力。计算公式为：

资产负债率(%)= 负债总额 / 资产总额 × 100%

资产与负债均为报告期期末数。

■ 流动资产周转次数

指一定时期内流动资产完成的周转次数，反映投入工业企业流动资金的周转速度。计算公式为：

流动资产周转资转 = 产品销售收入 / 全部流动资产平均余额

公式中：全部流动资产平均余额为期初和期末的流动资产之和的算术平均值。

■ 成本费用利润率

反映企业投入的生产成本及费用的经济效益，同时也反映企业降低成本所取得的经济效益。计算公式为：

成本费用利润(%)= 利润总额 / 成本费用总额 × 100%

公式中：成本费用总额为产品销售成本、销售费用、管理费用、财务费用之和。

■ 产品销售率

该指标反映工业产品已实现销售的程度，是分析工业产销衔接情况、研究工业产品满足社会需求的指标。计算公式为：

产品销售率 (%)= 工业销售产值 / 工业总产值 (现价) × 100%

■ 资产保值增值率

该指标反映企业净资产的变动状况，是企业发展能力的集中体现。计算公式为：

资产保值增值率＝报告期期末所有者权益 / 上年同期期末所有者权益

所有者权益等于资产总计减负债总计。

■ 全员劳动生产率

该指标反映企业的生产效率和劳动投入的经济效益。计算公式为：

$$全员劳动生产率(元/人)=\frac{工业增加值}{全部从业人员平均人数}$$

SHANGHAI STATISTICAL YEARBOOK

EXPLANATORY NOTES TO MAJOR STATISTICAL INDICATORS

□ Industry

Industry refers to the material production sector which is engaged in extraction of natural resources and processing and reprocessing of minerals and agricultural products, including (1) extraction of natural resources, such as mining, salt production (but not including hunting and fishing); (2) processing and reprocessing of farm and sideline produces, such as rice husking, flour milling, wine making, oil pressing, silk reeling, spinning and weaving, and leather making; (3) manufacture of industrial products, such as steel making, iron smelting, chemicals manufacturing, petroleum processing, machine building, timber processing; water and gas production and electricity generation and supply; (4)repairing of industrial products such as the repairing of machinery and means of transport (including cars).

Prior to 1984, the rural industry run by villages and cooperative organizations under village was classified into agriculture. Since 1984, it has been grouped into industry.

Units of industrial statistics survey corporate industrial enterprises with independent accounting system.

Corporate industrial enterprises with independent accounting system refer to enterprises engaging in industrial production activities, which meet the following requirements: ① They are established legally, having their own names, organizations, location, able to take civil liability; ② They possess and use their assets independently, assume liabilities, and are entitled to sign contracts with other units; ③ They are financially independent and compile their own balance sheets.

□ Light Industry

Light Industry refers to the industry that produces consumer goods and hand tools. It consists of two categories, depending on the materials used:

(1) Industries using farm products as raw materials. These are branches of light industry which directly or indirectly use farm products as basic raw materials, including the manufacture of food and beverages, tobacco processing, textile, clothing, fur and leather manufacturing, paper making, printing, etc.

(2) Industries using non farm products as raw materials. These are branches of light industry which use manufactured goods as raw materials, including the manufacture of cultural, educational articles and sports goods, chemicals, synthetic fiber, chemical products for daily use, glass products for daily use, metal products for daily use, hand tools, medical apparatus and instruments, and the manufacture of cultural and clerical machinery.

□ Heavy Industry

Heavy Industry refers to the industry which produces capital goods, and provides various sectors of the national economy with necessary material and technical basis. It consists of the following three branches according to the purpose of production or the use of products:

(1) Mining, quarrying and logging industry refers to the industry that extracts natural resources, including extraction of petroleum, coal, metal and non-metal ores.

(2) Raw materials industry refers to the industry that provides various sectors of the national economy with raw materials, fuels and power. It includes smelting and processing of metals, coking and coke chemistry, chemical materials and building materials such as cement, plywood, and power, petroleum refining and coal dressing.

(3) Manufacturing industry refers to the industry that processes raw materials. It includes machine building industry which equips sectors of the national economy, industries of metal structure and cement products, industries producing means of agricultural production, such as chemical fertilizers and pesticides.

According to the above principle of classification, the repairing trades which are engaged primarily in repairing products of heavy industry are classified into heavy industry while these engaged in repairing products of light industry are classified into light industry.

□ Gross Output Value of Industry

(1) Definition: Gross industrial output value is the total volume of final industrial products produced and industrial services provided during a given period. It reflects the total achievements and overall scale of industrial production during a given period.

(2) Principles for calculation:

Statistics on industrial production follow the principle that all products produced by the enterprises and accepted during the reference period are to be included no matter whether they are

EXPLANATORY NOTES TO MAJOR STATISTICAL INDICATORS

sold or not during the reference period.

Determination of final products follow the principle that all products that are included in the calculation of grow industrial output value are the final products of the enterprise which have been accepted through quality check and require no further processing. If an enterprise has intermediate (semi-finished) products to sell, these intermediate products are considered as the final products of the enterprise.

Gross industrial output value is calculated following the principle of factory approach, i.e. industrial enterprise is used as the basic accounting unit in calculating the gross industrial output value. By this approach, value of the same product is not to be double counted, and the output value of different workshops (branch factories) should not be added. However, this approach does not exclude the possibility of double counting between enterprises.

(3) Content and calculation method: The old definition of gross industrial output value was modified during the national industrial census in 1995. The revised (new) definition of gross industrial output value consists of 3 components: value of the finished products during the reference period, income from external processing, and value of change in semi-finished products at the end and at the beginning of the reference period.

Value of the finished products during the reference period: refers to the value of all finished (semi-finished) industrial products that are produced during the reference period without the need for further processing, checked for acceptance, packed and put into the warehouse of the enterprise, including the value of own-produced equipment and the value of products provided to the projects under construction of the enterprise, and to other non-industrial or welfare units. Value of finished products during the reference period is calculated by the quantity of products produced using own materials multiplied by the average unit prices at which products are sold(excluding value-added tax). Own-produced equipment and products produced for own use are value at cost prices as in the case of enterprise accounting. Value of finished products does not include the value of finished products (semi-finished products) that are produced using the materials from the clients who make the orders.

Income from external processing: refers to income from contracted external processing of industrial products (including processing of industrial products using materials from the clients), and the income from industrial repairing work provided to other units. Income from external processing is calculated using information from the item "products sales income" in the enterprise accounting at the prices excluding value-added tax.

For income from services such as processing, repairing and installation of equipment provided to non-industrial units within the enterprise, if the accounting work of the enterprise is good enough to separate it from other records, and the share of such services is significant, it should also be included in the income from external processing.

Value of change in semi-finished products at the end and at the beginning of the reference period: refers to the value of change in semi-finished products at the end and at the beginning of the reference period, which generally can be obtained from accounting records of enterprises. If the enterprise accounting excludes the cost of semi-finished products, then it should not be included in the gross industrial output value, and vice versa.

(4) Changes in the coverage and method of calculation of gross industrial output value

Prior to 1984, the value of rural industry run by villages was classified into agriculture instead of industry. Since 1984, it has been included in the gross industrial output value.

Method of calculation for the gross industrial output value was modified in the industrial census in 1995. The difference in the new method as compared with the old one is outlined below:

Principle in using full value vs. processing fee: The new method stipulates that all products produced using own materials are to be calculated with full value in reporting the gross industrial output value irrespective of sophistication of production, and for external processing, it allows calculation using processing fee. In the old method, however, the use of full value or processing fee was determined by the degree of sophistication of production in different branches of industries.

Principle in determining the value of change in semi-finished products: The new method requires that value of the change in semi-finished products should be included in the gross industrial output value if it is included in the accounting record of the enterprise, otherwise it should not be included. By the old method, it is determined by the type of enterprises in terms of production cycle. If the production cycle is over 6 months, the value of change in semi-finished products is included in the gross industrial output value, otherwise it is excluded.

Difference in prices: The new method uses prices excluding value-added tax in the calculation of gross industrial output value, while the old method used prices including value-added tax.

EXPLANATORY NOTES TO MAJOR STATISTICAL INDICATORS

□ Large, Medium and Small Enterprises

Since 2003 annual report enforcement, the criteria for classifying large, medium and small enterprises has been based on The Method for Classifying Large, Medium and Small Enterprises (Provisional) (State Statistics Bureau [2003] No.17). That is, an enterprise could be entitled Large Enterprise only when it has more than 2000 employees, its sales revenue exceeds 300 million yuan and total property exceeds 400 million yuan , simultaneously. An enterprise could be entitled Medium Enterprise when its employee number ranges from 300 to 2000, its sales revenue ranges from 30 million to 300 million yuan and its total property ranges from 40 million to 400 million yuan, simultaneously. All other enterprises should be entitled Small Enterprises.

□ Total Assets

Total Assets refer to all economic resources, in monetary terms, that is owned or controlled by enterprises, including properties, creditors equity and other economic rights of all forms. Classified by the degree of equitability, total assets include circulating assets, long-term investment, fixed assets, intangible assets and deferred assets, and other assets. Data on this indicator can be obtained by the year-end figures of total assets in the Assets and Liability Table of accounting records of enterprises.

□ Total Current Assets

Total Current Assets refer to capitals which can be cashed in or spent or consumed in an operating cycle of one year or over one year, including cash, all kinds of deposits, short term investment, receivable and payable payment for goods or deposits.

□ Average Current Assets

Average Current Assets refer to the average value of all working capitals of the enterprise during the reference period.

□ Annual Average Net Value of Fixed Assets

Annual Average Net Value of Fixed Assets refer to average of the net value of fixed assets during the reference period, calculated with the following formula:

Annual Average Net Value of Fixed Assets = sum of net value of fixed assets at the beginning and at the end of each month from January to December / 24.

Information on this indicator can be obtained from the beginning and ending figures of the original value of fixed assets and cumulative depreciation from the Assets and Liability Table of enterprises.

Net value of fixed assets refers to the original value of fixed assets minus depreciation over the years, i.e.:

Net value of fixed assets = original value of fixed assets – cumulative depreciation

□ Total Liabilities

Total liabilities refer to the total debts of an enterprise which can be calculated in monetary term and will be repaid in the forms of assets or service. Usually, the debts are divided into liquid liability and long-term debt according to the length of the payback period. The liquid liability is the debt that an enterprise will pay back during an operation cycle which is either shorter or longer than a year. The long-term debt refers to a debt whose payback period is longer than a year or which will be repaid during an operation cycle that is longer than a year.

□ Owners' Equity

Owners' Equity refers to investors ownership of net assets of the enterprise, which is equal to the total assets of the enterprise minus its total liabilities, including the primary input actually received at the enterprise from investors, capital accumulation fund, surplus accumulation fund and undistributed profit. When the total of owners' equity is less than zero, that indicates the liability of the enterprise is larger that its assets.

□ Total Profits

Total Profits refer to the final achievements of production and operation of the enterprises, represented by the total profits after deducting losses (loss is expressed by the negative figure). It is the sum of profits from operation, income from subsidies, investment earnings, net income from activities other than operation, and adjustment of profits and losses of previous years.

□ Total Assets Contribution Ratio

Total Assets Contribution Ratio reflects the profit-making capability of all assets of the enterprise and is a key indicator manifesting the performance and management and evaluating the profit-making potential of the enterprise. It is calculated as follows:

Total Assets Contribution Ratio (%) = [(total profits + total taxes + interest payment) / average assets] × 100%

In the above formula, total taxes is the sum of tax and extra charges on the sales of products and value-added tax payable;

EXPLANATORY NOTES TO MAJOR STATISTICAL INDICATORS

and average assets is the arithmetic mean of the sum of beginning assets and ending assets.

□ Ratio of Debts to Assets

Ratio of Debts to Assets reflect both the operation risk and the capability of the enterprise in making use of the capital from the creditors. It is calculated as follows:

Ratio of Debts to Assets (%) =(total debts / total assets) × 100%

Both assets and debts are figures at the end of the reference period.

□ Turnover of Current Assets

Turnover of Current Assets refers to the number of times of turnover of working capital in a given period of time, which reflects the speed of the turnover of working capital of industrial enterprises, and is calculated as follows:

Turnover of Current Assets= (sales revenue of products) / (average balance of total working capital)

In the above formula, average balance of total current assets refers to the arithmetic mean of the sum of working capital at the beginning and at the end of the reference period.

□ Ratio of Pre-tax Profits to Cost and Expenses

Ratio of Pre-tax Profits to Cost and Expenses refers to the ratio of profits realized in a given period to the total costs in the same period, which reflects the economic efficiency of input cost and is calculated as follows:

Ratio of Pre-tax Profits to Cost and Expenses (%)=(total profits/ total costs) × 100%

Total costs in the above formula is the sum of cost of products sold, marketing cost, management cost and financial cost.

□ Sales Rate of Industrial Products

Sales Rate of Industrial Products reflects the degree at which industrial products are sold. It helps to analyze the linkage between production and sales and the extent of the needs of the society that has been met by the supply of industrial products. It is calculated as follows:

Sales Rate of Industrial Products= (Industrial sales / Gross industrial output value at current prices) × 100%

□ Ratio of Capital Hold and Rise

Ratio of Capital Hold and Rise reflects the changes of an enterprise's net assets. It epitomizes the growth capability of an enterprise. Its calculating formula is:

Ratio of Capital Hold and Rise= Ownership equity at the end of the reporting period/Ownership equity at the same period of the previous year.

Ownership equity is the result of total assets minus total liabilities.

□ Overall Labour Productivity

Overall Labour Productivity is an indicator reflecting the production efficiency of an enterprise and the economic efficiency of its labour input, calculated by the formula:

Overall Labour Productivity (yuan/person) = industrial value-added/average of all persons engaged.

第十三篇

CHAPTER 13

建筑业

CONSTRUCTION

表 13.1 建筑业主要指标(1978～2006)
MAJOR INDICATORS OF CONSTRUCTION ENTERPRISES

年 份 Year	年末从业人员 (万人) Year-end Employees (10 000 persons)	总产值 (亿元) Output Value (100 million yuan)	房屋竣工面积 (万平方米) Floor Space of Building Completed (10 000 sq. m)	平均每个职工房屋竣工面积 (平方米/人) Area of Completed Building for Every Staff and Worker (sq. m/person)	全员劳动生产率 (按总产值计算) (元/人) Overall Labor Productivity (In Term of Output Value) (yuan/person)
1978	10.07	5.55	234.03	26.32	6 005
1979	23.35	13.98	564.62	26.10	6 226
1980	27.27	17.07	607.91	24.13	6 513
1981	30.21	18.03	649.93	22.28	5 941
1982	30.73	21.56	684.61	22.90	6 928
1983	33.35	24.64	736.34	22.46	7 189
1984	32.94	30.62	799.40	23.10	8 402
1985	33.35	36.73	819.24	23.78	10 070
1986	35.53	49.91	867.08	22.87	12 147
1987	35.83	59.45	872.25	22.66	14 455
1988	36.70	68.83	836.73	21.26	16 251
1989	34.43	74.75	758.34	19.70	18 053
1990	34.01	75.62	747.88	20.01	18 569
1991	34.62	84.30	775.63	20.14	21 022
1992	36.33	117.68	860.49	19.92	26 221
1993	36.90	193.00	1 144.16	26.10	44 020
1994	39.95	309.68	1 557.87	29.33	58 305
1995	41.10	391.42	1 485.87	25.44	67 023
1996	36.19	450.41	1 514.58	26.95	80 161
1997	37.40	564.37	1 777.41	29.60	93 995
1998	40.88	593.11	1 913.55	33.08	102 531
1999	39.01	573.06	1 950.76	33.86	99 473
2000	35.91	631.64	1 909.11	33.02	109 244
2001	35.52	730.33	2 434.73	39.55	118 641
2002	41.97	822.27	2 596.95	42.23	133 698
2003	50.52	1 195.80	3 609.20	71.44	153 910
2004	74.26	1 724.40	4 672.53	62.92	168 719
2005	72.23	1 889.25	5 648.85	78.21	182 299
2006	73.44	2 285.38	6 506.41	88.59	208 368

表 13.2 建筑业主要指标（2006）
MAJOR INDICATORS OF CONSTRUCTION ENTERPRISES

类 别	Types	企业数（个）Number of Enterprises (unit)	年末从业人员（万人）Year-end Employees (10 000 persons)	竣工产值（亿元）Output Value of Construction Completed (100 million yuan)
总 计	**Total**	**2 764**	**73.44**	**1 541.84**
按登记注册类型分	**Grouped By Registration Categories**			
内 资	Domestic Investment	2 607	71.91	1 479.09
#国 有	State-owned	136	10.28	227.02
集 体	Collective Owned	136	4.19	73.64
股份合作	Stock-holding Cooperation	29	0.21	2.04
联 营	Joint Owned	27	0.50	9.15
有限责任公司	Companies with Limited Liabilition	612	18.92	484.89
股份有限公司	Stock-holding Companies Liabilities	49	3.95	182.16
私 营	Private	1 611	33.71	496.04
港澳台商投资	Hong Kong, Macao and Taiwan Funded	88	0.82	24.20
外商投资	Foreign Funded	69	0.71	38.54
按行业分	**By Sectors**			
房屋和土木工程建筑业	Housing Construction and Civil Engineering Industry	1 210	56.34	1 176.41
建筑安装业	Construction and Installation Industry	647	8.89	201.99
建筑装饰业	Construction and Decoration Industry	678	6.00	128.91
其他建筑业	Other Construction Industries	229	2.20	34.53
按资质标准分	**By Qualification Standard**			
#施工总承包	Chief Construction Contract	1 234	58.56	1 256.08
专业承包	Professional Contract	1 530	14.88	285.76

表 13.2 续表 1 continued

类 别	Types	总产值（亿元）Output Value (100 million yuan)	其 中 of which #建筑工程 Construction	#安装工程 Installation
总 计	**Total**	**2 285.38**	**1 802.73**	**365.54**
按登记注册类型分	**Grouped By Registration Categories**			
内 资	Domestic Investment	2 181.66	1 729.95	342.06
#国 有	State-owned	332.51	259.26	56.94
集 体	Collective Owned	93.14	72.48	17.28
股份合作	Stock-holding Cooperation	2.69	1.09	1.52
联 营	Joint Owned	13.96	11.41	0.95
有限责任公司	Companies with Limited Liabilition	803.05	619.17	141.90
股份有限公司	Stock-holding Companies Liabilities	179.97	156.25	20.41
私 营	Private	746.47	600.54	102.98
港澳台商投资	Hong Kong, Macao and Taiwan Funded	42.72	34.78	5.32
外商投资	Foreign Funded	61.00	38.00	18.16
按行业分	**By Sectors**			
房屋和土木工程建筑业	Housing Construction and Civil Engineering Industry	1 766.12	1 556.70	136.15
建筑安装业	Construction and Installation Industry	274.02	59.29	204.67
建筑装饰业	Construction and Decoration Industry	190.24	164.91	15.11
其他建筑业	Other Construction Industries	55.02	21.84	9.62
按资质标准分	**By Qualification Standard**			
#施工总承包	Chief Construction Contract	1 862.77	1 547.16	238.72
专业承包	Professional Contract	422.62	255.57	126.81

表 13.2 续表 2 continued

类别 Types		房屋建筑面积(万平方米) Floor Space of Buildings (10 000 sq. m)		年末自有机械设备 Machinery and Equipment Owned(year-end)	
		施工面积 Under Construction	竣工面积 Completed	总台数(万台) Number (10 000 units)	总功率(万千瓦) Capacity (10 000 kw)
总　计	**Total**	**15 868.22**	**6 506.41**	**15.43**	**297.25**
按登记注册类型分	**Grouped By Registration Categories**				
内　资	Domestic Investment	15 515.85	6 345.94	14.78	292.42
#国　有	State-owned	2 806.05	920.67	1.69	33.96
集　体	Collective Owned	1 021.55	511.56	0.89	9.05
股份合作	Stock-holding Cooperation	5.58	4.09	0.09	0.43
联　营	Joint Owned	52.18	28.94	0.18	3.64
有限责任公司	Companies with Limited Liabilition	3 372.41	1 394.43	4.43	129.60
股份有限公司	Stock-holding Companies Liabilities	2 192.21	779.53	0.55	35.31
私　营	Private	5 903.56	2 674.70	6.92	79.83
港澳台商投资	Hong Kong, Macao and Taiwan Funded	95.66	12.60	0.35	1.56
外商投资	Foreign Funded	256.71	147.86	0.31	3.27
按行业分	**By Sectors**				
房屋和土木工程建筑业	Housing Construction and Civil Engineering Industry	15 632.52	6 395.52	10.18	243.39
建筑安装业	Construction and Installation Industry	162.45	82.14	2.46	33.18
建筑装饰业	Construction and Decoration Industry	32.89	14.39	2.05	10.71
其他建筑业	Other Construction Industries	40.35	14.36	0.74	9.97
按资质标准分	**By Qualification Standard**				
#施工总承包	Chief Construction Contract	15 314.52	6 257.98	10.66	252.41
专业承包	Professional Contract	553.70	248.42	4.78	44.84

表 13.3 建筑业主要财务指标(2006)
MAJOR ACCOUNTING INDICATORS OF CONSTRUCTION ENTERPRISES

指 标	Indicators	合 计 Total	内 资 Domestic Investment
施工企业单位数（个）	Number of Construction Enterprises (unit)	2 764	2 607
固定资产原价（亿元）	Fixed Assets (Original Value) (100 million yuan)	362.25	349.58
固定资产净值（亿元）	Fixed Assets (Net Value) (100 million yuan)	206.06	198.68
自有机械设备台数（万台）	Machinery and Equipment (10 000 units)	15.43	14.78
自有机械设备净值（亿元）	Machinery and Equipment (Net Value) (100 million yuan)	87.92	86.47
自有机械设备总功率（万千瓦）	Capacity of Machinery and Equipment (10 000 kw)	297.25	292.42
总产值（亿元）	Output Value(100 million yuan)	2 285.38	2 181.66
资产合计（亿元）	Assets at Year-end (100 million yuan)	2 553.94	2 415.66
#流动资产	Total Current Assets	2 080.41	1 950.95
固定资产	Total Fixed Assets	269.50	261.89
无形及递延资产	Intangible and Defered Assets	17.10	16.80
负债合计（亿元）	Total Liabilities at Year-end (100 million yuan)	1 872.31	1 765.56
流动负债	Current Liabilities	1 819.66	1 713.03
长期负债	Long-term Liabilities	52.65	52.53
所有者权益（亿元）	Total Owners Equity (100 million yuan)	681.63	650.10
企业总收入（亿元）	Total Revenue of Enterprises (100 million yuan)	2 771.23	2 630.39
工程结算收入	Revenue of Engineering Settlement Accounts	2 718.39	2 579.05
其他业务收入	Other Revenue	52.83	51.33
施工面积（万平方米）	Floor Space of Building Under Construction (10 000 sq·m)	15 868.22	15 515.85
竣工面积（万平方米）	Floor Space of Building Completed (10 000 sq·m)	6 506.41	6 345.94
利润总额（亿元）	Total Profits (100 million yuan)	106.66	99.30
全员劳动生产率（元/人）（按总产值计算）	Overall Labor Productivity(yuan/person) (In Term of Output Value)	208 368	206 245
技术装备率（元/人）	Per Capita Machinery Value (yuan/person)	11 970	12 024
动力装备率（千瓦/人）	Per Capita Machinery Capacity (kw/person)	4.0	4.1
房屋建筑面积竣工率（%）	Rate of Building Completed (%)	41.0	40.9
产值利润率（%）	Ratio of Profit/Gross Output Value (%)	4.7	4.6
产值利税率（%）	Ratio of Profit and Taxes/Gross Output Value (%)	8.2	8.1

其中 of which					
国有 State-owned	集体 Collective-Owned	股份合作 Stock-holding Cooperation	联营 Joint Owned	有限责任公司 Companies With Limited Liabilition	股份有限公司 Stock-holding Companies Liabilities
136	136	29	27	612	49
42.26	7.45	0.62	1.38	172.96	44.56
24.32	4.83	0.40	0.73	93.43	20.79
1.69	0.89	0.09	0.18	4.43	0.55
9.33	1.23	0.07	0.44	36.36	16.16
33.96	9.05	0.43	3.64	129.60	35.31
332.51	93.14	2.69	13.96	803.05	179.97
358.35	95.58	4.44	8.40	921.84	232.00
271.47	85.36	3.79	7.63	718.00	167.43
27.66	7.40	0.49	0.73	133.63	28.81
4.60	0.33	0.02		5.34	2.76
288.06	74.09	2.93	5.47	704.88	161.12
275.87	72.10	2.93	5.46	681.07	153.88
12.19	1.99		0.01	23.82	7.24
70.29	21.49	1.51	2.94	216.96	70.88
445.96	87.76	4.32	14.47	971.66	280.38
438.16	86.42	4.27	14.33	941.30	279.44
7.80	1.34	0.05	0.14	30.36	0.95
2 806.05	1 021.55	5.58	52.18	3 372.41	2 192.21
920.67	511.56	4.09	28.94	1 394.43	779.53
7.86	1.92	0.08	0.16	27.65	5.95
208 962	191 058	113 470	226 331	256 073	180 552
9 082	2 944	3 450	8 799	19 219	40 924
3.3	2.2	2.0	7.2	6.9	8.9
32.8	50.1	73.2	55.5	41.3	35.6
2.4	2.1	3.0	1.1	3.4	3.3
6.0	5.2	7.5	4.2	6.9	8.5

表 13.3 续表 Continued

指标	Indicators	其中 of which 私营 Private	港澳台商投资 Hong Kong, Macao and Taiwan Funded	外商投资 Foreign Funded
施工企业单位数（个）	Number of Construction Enterprises (unit)	1 611	88	69
固定资产原价（亿元）	Fixed Assets (Original Value) (100 million yuan)	79.64	4.00	8.67
固定资产净值（亿元）	Fixed Assets (Net Value) (100 million yuan)	53.86	1.89	5.48
自有机械设备台数（万台）	Machinery and Equipment (10 000 units)	6.92	0.35	0.31
自有机械设备净值（亿元）	Machinery and Equipment (Net Value) (100 million yuan)	22.71	0.81	0.63
自有机械设备总功率（万千瓦）	Capacity of Machinery and Equipment (10 000 kw)	79.83	1.56	3.27
总产值（亿元）	Output Value(100 million yuan)	746.47	42.72	61.00
资产合计（亿元）	Assets at Year-end (100 million yuan)	786.80	42.25	96.03
#流动资产	Total Current Assets	689.72	39.86	89.60
固定资产	Total Fixed Assets	62.83	1.91	5.70
无形及递延资产	Intangible and Defered Assets	3.74	0.08	0.22
负债合计（亿元）	Total Liabilities at Year-end (100 million yuan)	521.57	31.63	75.12
流动负债	Current Liabilities	514.34	31.57	75.06
长期负债	Long-term Liabilities	7.23	0.07	0.05
所有者权益（亿元）	Total Owners Equity (100 million yuan)	265.23	10.62	20.91
企业总收入（亿元）	Total Revenue of Enterprises (100 million yuan)	814.20	45.56	95.28
工程结算收入	Revenue of Engineering Settlement Accounts	803.55	45.39	93.95
其他业务收入	Other Revenue	10.65	0.18	1.33
施工面积（万平方米）	Floor Space of Building Under Construction (10 000 sq·m)	5 903.56	95.66	256.71
竣工面积（万平方米）	Floor Space of Building Completed (10 000 sq·m)	2 674.70	12.60	147.86
利润总额（亿元）	Total Profits (100 million yuan)	55.69	0.82	6.54
全员劳动生产率（元/人）（按总产值计算）	Overall Labor Productivity (yuan/person) (In Term of Output Value)	176 499	238 577	289 197
技术装备率（元/人）	Per Capita Machinery Value (yuan/person)	6 736	9 952	8 833
动力装备率（千瓦/人）	Per Capita Machinery Capacity (kw/person)	2.4	1.9	4.6
房屋建筑面积竣工率（%）	Rate of Buiding Completed (%)	45.3	13.2	57.6
产值利润率（%）	Ratio of Profit/Gross Output Value (%)	7.5	1.9	10.7
产值利税率（%）	Ratio of Profit and Taxes/Gross Output Value (%)	10.7	4.2	13.7

表 13.4 各区、县建筑业主要指标(2006)
MAIN CONSTRUCTION INDUSTRY STATISTICS OF DISTRICTS AND COUNTIES

地 区	District	企业数(个) Number of Enterprises (unit)	年末从业人员(万人) Year-end Employees (10 000 persons)	总产值(亿元) Output Value (100 million yuan)
总 计	**Total**	**2 764**	**73.44**	**2 285.38**
浦东新区	Pudong New Area	377	14.19	343.21
黄 浦 区	Huangpu	130	2.00	106.74
卢 湾 区	Luwan	80	0.80	27.07
徐 汇 区	Xuhui	185	4.77	216.44
长 宁 区	Changning	152	2.67	92.35
静 安 区	Jing'an	109	1.24	50.87
普 陀 区	Putuo	183	4.40	145.29
闸 北 区	Zhabei	93	4.19	174.41
虹 口 区	Hongkou	172	5.95	172.33
杨 浦 区	Yangpu	187	3.37	106.71
宝 山 区	Baoshan	171	7.11	278.45
闵 行 区	Minhang	153	3.62	88.30
嘉 定 区	Jiading	115	2.64	55.94
金 山 区	Jinshan	82	2.55	49.22
松 江 区	Songjiang	139	4.30	96.38
青 浦 区	Qingpu	92	2.86	63.46
南 汇 区	Nanhui	137	1.98	102.51
奉 贤 区	Fengxian	181	3.55	74.89
崇 明 县	Chongming	26	1.25	40.82

表 13.4 续表 Continued

地 区	District	房屋建筑施工面积(万平方米) Floor Space of Buildings Under Construction (10 000 sq. m)	房屋建筑竣工面积(万平方米) Floor Space of Buildings Completed (10 000 sq. m)	其中 of which #住宅 Residence
总 计	**Total**	**15 868.22**	**6 506.41**	**3 074.01**
浦东新区	Pudong New Area	3 107.52	921.52	479.69
黄 浦 区	Huangpu	374.68	127.01	100.46
卢 湾 区	Luwan	115.11	51.79	13.31
徐 汇 区	Xuhui	452.37	147.41	47.76
长 宁 区	Changning	949.67	375.12	82.62
静 安 区	Jing'an	511.54	180.44	106.22
普 陀 区	Putuo	1 317.37	463.65	341.55
闸 北 区	Zhabei	448.88	191.68	92.42
虹 口 区	Hongkou	1 239.99	446.40	229.34
杨 浦 区	Yangpu	515.52	205.35	82.62
宝 山 区	Baoshan	1 472.78	711.84	224.89
闵 行 区	Minhang	860.02	290.45	210.82
嘉 定 区	Jiading	664.33	290.69	136.67
金 山 区	Jinshan	255.60	121.31	60.29
松 江 区	Songjiang	1 113.16	667.05	256.74
青 浦 区	Qingpu	579.83	301.13	116.04
南 汇 区	Nanhui	917.34	472.41	177.74
奉 贤 区	Fengxian	562.31	334.99	156.41
崇 明 县	Chongming	410.18	206.17	158.41

上 / 海 / 统 / 计 / 年 / 鉴

主要统计指标解释

建筑业总产值

建筑业总产值是以货币形式表现的建筑(安装)业企业在一定时期内生产的建筑业产品和提供的服务的总和。建筑业总产值包括:

(1)建筑工程产值:指列入建筑工程预算内的各种工程价值。

(2)(设备)安装工程产值:指设备安装工程价值,不包括被安装设备本身价值。

(3)其他产值:建筑业总产值中除建筑工程、安装工程以外的产值。包括房屋构筑物修理产值、非标准设备制造产值、总包企业向分包企业收取的管理费以及不能明确划分的施工活动所完成的产值。

a. 房屋构筑物修理产值:指房屋和构筑物修理所完成的产值,但不包括被修理房屋、构筑物本身价值和生产设备的修理产值。

b. 非标准设备制造产值:指加工制造没有定型的非标准生产设备的加工费和原材料价值(如化工厂、炼油厂用的各种罐、槽,矿井生产统一使用的各种漏斗、三角槽、阀门等)以及附属加工厂为本企业承建工程制作的非标准设备的价值。

房屋建筑施工面积

指在报告期内施过工的全部房屋建筑面积,包括本期新开工的房屋面积、上期施工跨入本期继续施工的房屋面积、上期停缓建在本期恢复施工的房屋面积、本期竣工的房屋面积及本期施工后又停缓建的房屋面积。

房屋建筑竣工面积

指在报告期内房屋建筑按照设计要求全部完工,达到了(住人和)使用条件,经验收鉴定合格,正式移交使用单位的房屋建筑面积。

年末自有机械设备总台数

指归本企业所有,属于本企业固定资产的生产性机械设备年末总台数。包括施工机械、生产设备、运输设备以及其他设备。

年末自有机械设备总功率

指本企业自有施工机械、生产设备、运输设备以及其他设备等列为在册固定资产的生产性机械设备年末总功率,按设定能力或查定能力计算。包括机械本身的动力和为该机械服务的单独动力设备,如电动机等。计算单位用千瓦,动力换算可按 1 马力=0.735 千瓦折合成千瓦数。电焊机、变压器、锅炉不计算动力。

企业总收入

指与企业生产经营直接有关的各项收入,包括工程结算收入和其他业务收入。计算公式为:

企业总收入 = 工程结算收入 + 其他业务收入

房屋建筑面积

指房屋建筑物勒脚以上外墙外围的水平截面面积,包括房屋建筑物的有效面积和结构面积。该指标是从实物形态上反映建设规模和建设成果的重要指标之一,也是检查工程形象进度、计算工程造价、分析投资效果、研究施工任务和建筑材料之间平衡情况的重要依据。

SHANGHAI STATISTICAL YEARBOOK

EXPLANATORY NOTES TO MAJOR STATISTICAL INDICATORS

□ Gross Output Value of Construction

Gross Output Value of Construction refers to total of construction products and services, expressed in money terms, produced or rendered by (completed by) construction and installation enterprises during a given period of time. It includes:

(1) Output value of construction projects, that is the value of projects covered by the project budgets;

(2) Output value of installation projects, that is the value of the installation of equipment, (excluding the value of the equipment to be installed);

(3) Output value of other projects refers to other output value of gross output value of construction industry besides construction and installation projects. It includes the output value of building repairing, nonstandard equipment manufacturing, the management fees going from subcontractor to original contractor and other construction output value which can not be measured off definitely.

□ Floor Space of Buildings Under Construction

Floor Space of Buildings Under Construction refers to floor space of buildings under construction during the reference period, including newly started buildings, buildings started earlier and continued during the reference period, and buildings suspended earlier but restarted during the reference period, buildings completed during the reference period, and buildings under construction and then suspended during the reference period.

□ Floor Space of Buildings Completed

Floor Space of Buildings Completed refers to the floor space of buildings that are completed in the reference period in accordance with the requirements of the design, up to the standard for putting them into use, and have been checked and accepted by concerned departments as qualified ones.

□ Total Number of Machinery and Equipment Owned by the End of Year

Total Number of Machinery and Equipment Owned by the End of Year refers to the number of machines and equipment owned by the enterprises, and listed as the fixed assets of the enterprises by the end of the year, including machinery and equipment for construction, production and transportation.

□ Total Capacity of Machinery and Equipment Owned by the End of Year

Total Capacity of Machinery and Equipment Owned by the End of Year refers to the total power of machinery and equipment owned by the enterprises, and listed as the fixed assets of the enterprises by the end of the year, including machinery and equipment for construction, production and transportation. The power of the machinery is calculated on basis of the designed or verified capacity, covering the power of the machinery/equipment and the separate power equipment serving the machinery/equipment (such as electric motors), but excluding welders, transformers and boilers. The unit used for the calculation of power is kilowatt, with horsepower converted to kilowatt by 1 horsepower=0.735 kilowatt.

□ Total Revenue of Enterprises

Total Revenue of Enterprises refers to the sum of income from production and operation of enterprises, including income from settlement of projects and other operational income, namely:

Total Revenue of Enterprises=Income from Settlement of Projects + Other Operational Income

□ Floor Space of Buildings

Floor Space of Buildings refers to total floor space of the horizontal section of outer walls above the plinth of the building, including the effective area and the area occupied by the structure. This indicator is one of the important indicators in physical terms to reflect the scale and accomplishment of the construction industry, and important basis for monitoring the progress, calculating the cost, analyzing the efficiency and studying the supply of building materials in relation with the construction projects.

第十四篇

CHAPTER 14

交通运输、邮政和信息传输

TRANSPORTATION, POSTS AND INFORMATION TRANSMISSION

表 14.1　主要年份运输线路长度
LENGTHS OF TRAFFIC LINES IN MAIN YEARS

指标	Indicators	1990	2000	2005	2006
铁路运输	**Railway**				
运营里程(公里)	Operation Mileage (km)	259	257	269	269
正线延展里程(公里)	Mainline Railway Length Extended (km)	356	397	406	412
公路运输	**Highway**				
通车里程(公里)	Operation Mileage(km)	3 050	6 078	8 110	10 392
# 高速公路	High Speed Highways	36	98	560	581
内河航道	**Navigable Inland Waterways**				
航道里程(公里)	Length of Navigable Inland Waterways (km)	2 100	2 100	2 110	2 110

①本表至表 14.8 数据由上海铁路局、市城市交通管理局、市港口管理局、上海机场集团、市航务管理处等单位提供。
②2006 年公路运输通车里程包含村道。
❶Data in this table to table 14.8 are provided by Shanghai Railway Bureau, Shanghai Municipal Traffic Administrative Bureau, Shanghai Port Administrative Bureau ,Shanghai Airport Group and Shanghai Navigation Administrative Department.
❷Highway operation mileage of 2006 includes village roads.

表 14.2　主要年份交通运输主要指标
MAJOR INDICATORS OF TRANSPORTATION IN MAIN YEARS

指标	Indicators	1990	2000	2005	2006
公路运输	**Highway Transportation**				
货运汽车每车吨年产量(万吨·公里)	Annual Tonnage of Each Ton-wagon (10 000 tons · km)	1.72	1.50	1.64	0.85
汽油车耗油 (升/百吨·公里)	Oil Consumption of Gasoline Trucks (litre/100 tons · km)	6.50	6.87	8.85	8.50
柴油车耗油 (升/百吨·公里)	Oil Consumption of Diesel Trucks (litre/100 tons · km)	4.00	4.77	4.51	6.60
水路运输	**Waterway Transportation**				
海运船舶每吨船年产量(万吨·公里)	Annual Tonnage of Each Ton Sea Vessel (10 000 tons · km)	4.64	4.37	4.98	4.85
远洋货轮每吨船年产量(万吨·公里)	Annual Tonnage of Each Ton Ocean Ship (10 000 tons · km)	6.90	9.08	11.29	12.21
港　口	**Harbor**				
船舶平均在港停泊时间 (天)	Average Days of Vessel Berthed at Harbor (day)	1.5	0.9	0.4	0.4

表 14.3　主要年份旅客发送量
PASSENGER DEPARTING IN MAIN YEARS

单位:万人次(10 000 person-times)

年　份 Year	旅客发送量 Passenger Departures	其　中　of Which 铁　路 Railway	公　路 Highway	港　口 Harbor	民用航空 Civil Aviation
1980	2 369	1 692	200	446	31
1985	3 434	2 320	410	622	82
1990	3 835	2 476	605	555	199
1995	5 265	2 929	1 257	512	567
1996	5 822	2 804	1 974	422	622
1997	6 057	2 779	2 277	328	673
1998	6 139	2 760	2 006	678	695
1999	6 406	2 906	2 178	581	741
2000	6 893	2 980	2 482	539	892
2001	6 324	3 231	1 508	543	1 042
2002	7 326	3 518	2 046	526	1 236
2003	7 212	3 391	2 052	528	1 241
2004	8 968	4 076	2 465	621	1 806
2005	9 487	4 313	2 468	626	2 080
2006	10 205	4 458	2 784	654	2 309

①1997 年前港口旅客发送量为港务局公用码头范围，1998 年以后扩大为全港范围。 以下同。
②2000 年前旅客发送量是专业运输部门的数字，2001 年开始改为跨省市旅客运输的行业统计数字。
❶Before 1997, the harbor passenger traffic volume referred to the amount passing through the public ports under the administration of Port Administration Bureau. From 1998, the volume covered all the ports in Shanghai. Same as follows.
❷The passenger departures volume before 2000 is based on the figures for special traffic departments and the volume since 2001 is based on the figures for the inter-provincial passenger transport industries.

表 14.4　主要年份旅客周转量
TURNOVER VOLUME OF PASSENGER TRAFFIC IN MAIN YEARS

单位:亿人·公里 (100 million persons · km)

年　份 Year	旅客周转量 Turnover Volume of Passenger Traffic	其　中　of Which 铁　路 Railway	公　路 Highway	水　运 Waterway	民用航空 Civil Aviation
1980	49.31	15.67	1.24	32.39	
1985	87.20	24.30	4.32	44.63	13.95
1990	113.94	26.85	8.42	40.84	37.84
1995	170.98	34.18	8.23	31.71	96.86
1996	171.81	31.49	8.83	24.13	107.36
1997	181.99	31.44	12.61	16.52	121.42
1998	199.15	30.68	12.07	9.97	146.43
1999	217.95	34.18	15.81	7.94	160.02
2000	234.72	35.40	16.44	6.77	176.11
2001	286.93	37.81	42.31	5.48	201.30
2002	332.12	39.48	50.43	4.41	237.80
2003	353.62	38.10	58.00	4.65	252.88
2004	599.62	46.35	72.09	4.49	476.70
2005	663.93	48.86	75.06	4.52	535.48
2006	742.87	51.23	86.85	4.52	600.28

表 14.5 主要年份货物运输量
FREIGHT TRAFFIC VOLUME IN MAIN YEARS

单位:万吨(10 000 tons)

年份 Year	货物运输量 Freight Traffic Volume	其中 of which				
		铁路 Railway	公路 Highway	水运 Waterway	其中 of which #远洋运输 Ocean Shipping	民用航空 Civil Aviation
1980	20 037	4 484	7 284	8 267	1 098	2
1985	24 243	5 059	9 216	9 965	1 402	3
1990	26 777	5 186	8 714	12 864	2 246	13
1995	27 571	6 416	6 273	14 845	2 778	37
1996	45 821	6 213	25 023	14 544	3 594	41
1997	45 938	5 817	25 991	14 082	4 201	48
1998	46 230	5 292	26 352	14 529	4 844	57
1999	48 398	4 910	27 171	16 241	5 783	76
2000	52 206	5 307	28 369	18 442	7 022	88
2001	54 049	5 584	28 869	19 496	7 129	100
2002	58 901	5 836	29 759	23 174	7 210	132
2003	63 861	6 400	30 678	26 621	7 832	162
2004	65 758	3 862	31 554	30 148	8 603	194
2005	71 304	3 841	32 684	34 557	10 091	222
2006	75 184	3 790	33 799	37 342	11 766	253

①2005 年起铁路数据由上海铁路局提供，2005 年前数据由上海铁路分局提供。
②2005 年起民航货物吞吐量不包括旅客行李。
❶The railway data of 2005 are provided by Shanghai Railway Bureau and the data before 2005 were provided by Shanghai Railway Branch Bureau.
❷The Freight transportation volume of civil aviation in 2005 doesn't include the freight transportation volume.

表 14.6 主要年份货物周转量
TURNOVER VOLUME OF FREIGHT TRAFFIC IN MAIN YEARS

单位:亿吨·公里(100 million tons·km)

年份 Year	货物周转量 Turnover Volume of Freight Traffic	其中 of which				
		铁路 Railway	公路 Highway	水运 Waterway	其中 of which #远洋运输 Ocean Shipping	民用航空 Civil Aviation
1980	1 487	87	8	1 392	778	
1985	2 015	102	11	1 902	1 072	
1990	3 359	111	11	3 236	1 957	1
1995	4 187	143	9	4 030	2 259	5
1996	3 814	133	49	3 627	2 721	5
1997	4 016	123	47	3 840	3 049	6
1998	4 838	117	49	4 665	3 794	7
1999	5 606	113	51	5 432	4 020	10
2000	6 620	122	56	6 430	5 285	12
2001	6 992	113	60	6 808	5 511	11
2002	7 472	100	65	7 295	5 674	12
2003	8 587	118	69	8 385	6 376	15
2004	10 036	42	71	9 899	7 486	24
2005	12 132	47	73	11 986	9 285	27
2006	13 837	55	80	13 683	10 817	19

①2004 年起，上海铁路分局改为上海铁路局，货物周转量数据有所调整。
②2006 年民航货物周转量未包括中国货运航空公司的数据。
❶Since 2004, Shanghai Railway Branch Bureau has been change into Shanghai Railway Bureau ,the turnover volume of freight has been adjusted accordingly.
❷In 2006,the date of China Cargo Airlines didn't included in the turnover volume of fright of aviotion.

表 14.7 主要年份港口码头情况
PORTS IN MAIN YEARS

年份 Year	码头长度(万米) Length of Harbor (10 000 m)	泊位(个) Berths (unit)	其中 of which #万吨级 10 000 Tonnage	其中 of which #集装箱泊位 Container Berths	港口货物吞吐量(万吨) Cargo at Ports Throughput (10 000 tons)	其中 of which 进港 Input	出港 Output
1980	1.28	92	46	2	8 483	5 800	2 683
1985	1.39	98	46	4	11 291	7 972	3 319
1990	1.77	122	64	7	13 959	9 461	4 498
1995	1.90	140	68	12	16 567	12 097	4 470
1996	1.90	138	69	12	16 402	11 947	4 455
1997	1.96	142	71	12	16 397	11 851	4 546
1998	7.58	1 108	109	13	16 388	11 839	4 549
1999	7.69	1 110	113	18	18 641	12 936	5 705
2000	7.64	1 098	111	18	20 440	13 791	6 649
2001	7.67	1 087	112	18	22 099	14 922	7 177
2002	7.92	1 096	115	20	26 384	17 444	8 940
2003	8.76	1 202	125	24	31 621	20 607	11 014
2004	8.90	1 198	123	24	37 896	24 113	13 783
2005	8.95	1 181	124	28	44 317	27 539	16 778
2006	9.16	1 140	131	32	53 748	34 598	19 151

注：1997 年以前，码头长度、泊位为原港务局数据，从 1998 年后，为全港数据。
Note: Before 1997, the figures of length of harbor and berths were from the ports belonged Port Administration Bureau, and after 1998, they have been collected from all types of ports.

表 14.8 主要年份国际集装箱和外贸货物吞吐量
INTERNATIONAL CONTAINERS AND CARGO THROUGHPUT OF FOREIGN TRADE IN MAIN YEARS

年份 Year	国际标准集装箱吞吐量重量(万吨) Weight of International Containers (10 000 tons)	国际标准集装箱吞吐量(万 TEU) International Containers (10 000 TEU)	其中 of which 进港 Input	出港 Output	外贸货物吞吐量(万吨) Cargo Throughput of Foreign Trade (10 000 tons)	其中 of which 进港 Input	出港 Output
1980	23.4	2.99	1.56	1.43	1 791	1 360	431
1985	184.4	20.45	10.80	9.65	2 871	2 411	460
1990	445.5	45.60	22.40	23.20	2 593	1 869	724
1995	1 388.9	152.60	69.30	83.30	4 086	2 605	1 481
1996	1 785.1	197.10	92.40	104.70	4 136	2 681	1 454
1997	2 303.6	252.80	114.70	138.10	4 713	2 931	1 782
1998	2 765.7	306.60	141.10	165.50	4 904	3 024	1 879
1999	3 948.5	421.60	196.70	224.90	6 285	3 899	2 386
2000	5 169.6	561.20	266.10	295.10	7 633	4 549	3 084
2001	5 911.4	634.00	305.40	328.60	8 653	5 216	3 437
2002	7 821.7	861.20	414.10	447.10	10 609	6 349	4 260
2003	10 225.1	1 128.25	544.40	583.80	12 968	7 607	5 361
2004	13 294.0	1 455.40	699.60	755.80	15 836	9 091	6 745
2005	16 250.4	1 808.40	887.20	921.30	18 492	10 098	8 394
2006	19 595.2	2 171.90	1 064.40	1 107.50	21 268	10 987	10 281

注：TEU 是“折合 20 英尺标准箱”英文缩写语。
Note: TEU is the abbreviation, which refers to 20-foot equivalent unit.

表 14.9 民用车辆拥有量（2004～2006）
CIVIL MOTOR VEHICLES

单位：万辆(10 000 vehicles)

指 标	Indicators	2004	2005	2006
总 计	**Total**	**202.85**	**221.74**	**238.13**
#汽 车	Civil Automobile	83.51	95.15	107.04
载客汽车	Passenger Vehicles	64.69	76.00	87.06
#轿 车	Cars	44.60	53.59	62.81
载货汽车	Freight Trucks	18.82	19.16	19.98
摩托车	Motorcycle	113.85	120.42	124.15
农用运输车	Farm Vehicles	0.15	0.17	0.18
拖拉机	Tractors	1.30	1.24	1.22

注：本表数据由上海市公安局车管所提供，拖拉机数据由市农机办提供(下表同)。
Note: Data in this table are provided by Shanghai Land-carriage Administration(same as follows).

表 14.10 个人民用车辆拥有量（2004～2006）
INDIVIDUAL CIVIL MOTOR VEHICLES

单位：万辆(10 000 vehicles)

指 标	Indicators	2004	2005	2006
总 计	**Total**	**142.77**	**157.65**	**172.45**
#汽 车	Civil Automobile	31.77	41.00	50.94
载客汽车	Passenger Vehicles	31.47	41.00	50.91
#轿 车	Cars	24.28	32.21	40.95
载货汽车	Freight Trucks	0.30	0.04	0.03
摩托车	Motorcycle	109.87	116.52	120.13
农用运输车	Farm Vehicles	0.13	0.14	0.16

表 14.11 主要年份邮政电信情况
POST AND TELECOMMUNICATION IN MAIN YEARS

指 标	Indicators	1985	1990	2000	2005	2006
邮电局、所(个)	Post Offic (unit)	481	535	580	631	649
报刊图书销售点(个)	Publications Sales Outlet (unit)	252	346	3 212	2 346	2 330
邮政信筒信箱(个)	Mail Box (unit)	3 770	3 914	4 224	4 022	3 842
集邮品销售点(个)	Stamps Sales Outlet(unit)	183	203	296	349	351
邮政储蓄网点(个)	Postal Savings Office (unit)		271	422	429	440
邮路条数(条)	Number of Mail Route (route)		427	638	738	768
邮路总长度(万公里)	Total Length of Mail Routes (10 000 km)	4.40	16.10	21.17	21.13	8.97
农村投递路线总长度(万公里)	Length of Rural Delivery Routes (10 000 km)	2.74	2.30	2.73	2.68	3.00
长途电话业务电路(2M)	Long Distance Call Line(2M)				46 136	94 818
长途光览线路长度(公里)	Long-distance Cable (km)			1 770	5 141	3 042
数字微波线路长度(公里)	Digital Microwave Line(km)				196	123

注：本表数据由市邮政局、市通信管理局提供。
Note: Data in this table are provided by Shanghai Municipal Post Bureau and Shanghai Communications Administration Bureau.

表 14.12 主要年份邮政业务主要指标
MAJOR INDICATORS OF POSTAL BUSINESS IN MAIN YEARS

指 标	Indicators	1985	1990	2000	2005	2006
邮政业务总量(亿元)	Volume of Postal Business (100 million yuan)			22.40	38.49	43.59
函 件(亿件)	Mails (100 million units)	2.19	2.96	4.61	7.08	10.36
国内特快专递(万件)	Domestic Express Mails (10 000 pieces)	0.23	33.00	709.90	1 541.20	1 930.10
国际特快专递(万件)	International Express Mails (10 000 pieces)	1.97	15.00	52.10	144.30	182.30
邮政储蓄期末余额(亿元)	Postal Saving Deposit Balance (100 million yuan)		10.98	153.50	510.80	522.90
报纸、杂志累计订销数(亿份)	Total Copies of Newspapers and Magazines Subscribed and Sold (100 million pieces)	11.76	8.71	11.30	12.33	12.45
集邮业务(万枚)	Stamp Collection Business (10 000 stamps)		5 132	9 467	4 422	3 560

注：本表数据由市邮政局提供。
Note: Data in this table are provided by Shanghai Municipal Post Bureau.

表 14.13 电信业务主要指标（2003～2006）
MAJOR INDICATORS OF TELECOM BUSINESS

指标	Indicators	2003	2004	2005	2006
电信业务总量(亿元)	Volume of Telecom Business (100 million yuan)	247.40	311.20	375.77	511.41
年末固定电话用户（万户）	Year-end Installed Telephones (10 000 households)	734	868	996.70	1 112.3
#住宅电话	Household Phones Installed	528	542	685	738
移动电话用户（万户）	Mobile Phone Subscribers(10 000 households)	1 099	1 311	1 444	1 610
全年长途通话时长（亿分钟）	Long-distance Call Lasting Time (100 million minutes)	76.8	100.7	110.0	151.4
#固定电话长途通话时长	Installed Telephone Domestic Long-distance Call Lasting Time	25.9	32.8	31.2	32.6
#固定电话国内长途电话通话量	Domestic Trunk Calls	24.6	31.5	30.0	31.2
固定电话国际及港澳台电话通话量	Overseas Calls	1.3	1.3	1.3	1.4
移动电话长途通话时长	Mobile Telephone Long-distance Call Lasting Time	15.7	20.4	19.6	27.2
IP 电话通话时长	IP Telephone Long-distance Call Lasting Time	35.2	47.5	59.2	91.6
移动电话通话量（亿次）	Mobile Calls (100 million times)	102.40	127.50	156.5	221.7
#本地通话量	Local Calls	93.50	116.30	144.8	207.8
长途通话量	Long-distance Calls	8.90	11.20	11.7	13.9
数字数据用户（万户）	Digital and Data Users (10 000 households)	2.61	2.54	2.4	1.8
局用交换机容量（含接入网设备容量）(万门)	Capacity of Office Telephone Exchanges(Including Access Network Capacity) (10 000 units)	873	912	1 357	1 391

①本表数据由市信息化委员会、市通信管理局提供。
②接入网设备容量是指安装在电信企业用于连接用户节点的电话交换机容量。
❶Data in this table are provided by Shanghai Municipal Information Commission and Shanghai Communications Administration Bureau.
❷Access network refers to the capacity of telephone exchanges installed in the office of telecommunication service providers for communication between user nodes.

表 14.14 邮电通信水平（2003～2006）
POSTAL AND TELECOM LEVEL

指标	Indicators	2003	2004	2005	2006
电话主线普及率（%）*	Popularity Rate of Telephone Line（%）	42.9	49.8	56.1	61.3
住宅电话普及率（%）	Popularity Rate of Household Telephone（%）	108.6	110.5	137.9	147.7
平均每一邮政局所服务面积（平方公里）	Average Area Served by One Post Office（sq·km）	11.0	10.3	10.0	9.77
平均每一邮政局所服务人口（万人）	Average Population Served by Every Post Office（10 000 persons）	2.33	2.20	2.10	2.11
人均每年发函件数（件）	Average Number of Letters Mailed（piece）	38	44	52	57
人均每年购报刊数（份）	Average Number of Newspaper and Magazine Purchased（piece）	100	98	91	91
平均每百人拥有移动电话（部）	Number of Mobile Telephone Owned per Hundred Persons（unit）	64.2	75.3	81.0	88.7

注：本表数据由市通信管理局提供。
Note：Data in this table are provided by Shanghai Communications Administration Bureau.

表 14.15 信息化基础设施情况（2003～2006）
INFRASTRUCTURE OF INFORMATIZATION

指标	Indicators	2003	2004	2005	2006
长途光缆线路总长度（公里）	Total Length of Long-distance Optical Cable（k·m.）	2 981	4 603	5 141	3 042
信息通信管线长度（沟公里）	Length of Information Communication Pielines（channel k·m.）	1 010	1 255	1 621	2 451
卫星站点（个）	Satellite Station（unit）	906	917	925	831
国际互联网宽带（兆）	Wide Band of Internet（M）	7 695	18 530	30 000	40
本地信息交互流量（万千兆）	Local Information Exchange Flow（10 000 K·M）	100	133	130	2 113
有线电视双向改造用户数（万户）	Users of CATV Bil-rebuilding（10 000 households）	170.5	172.89	185.66	200.3
国际互联网用户（万户）	Users of Internet（10 000 households）	432	633	803	957
每千人国际互联网用户数（户）	Users of Internet per Thousand People（household）	32.2	46.8	59.0	52.7
家庭宽带接入用户（万户）	Users of Wide Band for Public（10 000 household）	92.49	158.82	247.40	301.68
每百户家庭宽带接入用户（户）	Users of Wide Band for Public per Hundred Household（household）	19.0	32.4	49.8	60.4

①2006 年起，国际互联网宽带计量单位改为 Gbps。
②2006 年起，本地信息交互流量计量单位改为 TB。
③每千人国际互联网用户数按常住人口计算。
④表 14.15 至表 14.18 由市信息化委员会提供。
❶Since 2006, the measure unit of internet has been change to Gbps.
❷Since 2006, the measure unit of local information exchange flow has been change to TB.
❸Users of Internet per Thousand People were calculated by resident population.
❹Data in table 14.15 to 18 are provided by Shanghai Municipal Informution Commissiom.

表 14.16 信息服务业经营情况(2004～2006)
OPERATION OF INFORMATION SERVICE INDUSTRY

指标	Indicators	2004	2005	2006
信息服务业经营收入(亿元)	Operating Revenue of Information Service Industry (100 million yuan)	655.6	916.8	1 221.45
#计算机服务及软件业	Computer Service & Software Industry	302.78	455.17	616.70
#自产软件	Self-program Software	90.83	118.90	104.05
系统集成	System Integration	94.16	100.14	120.58
软件收入超亿元企业(家)	Enterprises of Over 100 million Software Revenue (unit)	35	43	56
信息服务业从业人员(万人)	Employees of Information Service Industry (10 000 persons)	9.90	14.46	18.03
#计算机服务及软件业	Computer Service & Software Industry	7.10	11.83	14.12

注：2006 年计算机服务及软件业为软件产业口径。
Note: In 2006, Computer Service & Software Industry refer to the scale of software industry.

表 14.17 信息技术应用(2005～2006)
APPLICATION OF INFORMATION TECHNOLOGY

指标	Indicators	2005	2006
社会公共服务领域信息化	**Informatization of Public Service**		
"市民信箱"累计注册用户(万户)	Accumulative Registered Users of Citizen Mail Box(10 000 houses)	33.98	124.26
"付费通"业务平台交易量(万笔)	All-year Exchange Volum of FFT(10 000 units)	733.75	1 976.48
"付费通"业务平台交易额(亿元)	All-year Exchange Value of FFT(100 million yuan)	9.27	16.23
社保卡累计发放量(万张)	Accumulative Volum of Social Insurance Card (10 000 pieces)	72.68	1 004.32
交通卡累计销售量(万张)	Accumulative Volum of Traffic Card (10 000 pieces)	504.73	2 568.06
交通卡销售额(亿元)	All-year Sales Value of Traffic Card (100 million yuan)	8.28	10.06
银行卡累计发卡量(万张)	Accumulative Volum of Bank Card (10 000 pieces)	5 729.80	5 610.89
银行卡交易额(亿元)	All-year Exchange Value of Bank Card (100 million yuan)	2 761.18	3 666.19
#持卡消费金额	Consumption Value with Bank Card	1 233.15	1 793.70
社会信用体系	**Social Credit System**		
个人信用信息入库量(万条)	Newly Recorded Individual Credit Information (10 000 pieces)	618	770
个人信用报告累计出具数量(万份)	Accumulative Provided Volum of Individual Credit Information Report (10 000 pieces)	460	643
企业信用信息入库量(万条)	Newly Recorded Enterprise Credit Information (10 000 pieces)	60	60

表 14.18 电子商务(2005～2006)
ELECTRONIC COMMERCE

指标	Indicators	2005	2006
电子商务交易额(亿元)	Trade Value of E-commerce (100 million yuan)	1 623.12	1 899.65
累计发放数字证书(万张)	Accumulative Granted Digital Certificate (10 000 pieces)	56.10	71.63

上 / 海 / 统 / 计 / 年 / 鉴

主要统计指标解释

■ 铁路运营里程

铁路运营里程又称营业长度（包括正式营业和临时营业里程），指办理客货运输业务的铁路正线总长度。凡是全线或部分建成双线及以上的线路，以第一线的实际长度计算；复线、站线、段管线、岔线和特殊用途线以及不计算运费的联络线都不计算营业里程。铁路营业里程是反映铁路运输业基础设施发展水平的重要指标，也是计算客货周转量、运输密度和机车车辆运用效率等指标的基础资料。

■ 内河航道里程

内河航道里程也称内河通航里程，指在一定时期内，能通航运输船舶及排筏的天然河流、湖泊水库、运河及通航渠道的长度。包括全年季节性通航累计三个月以上的航道，不包括仅供零散流放竹、木排的河道。该指标可以反映内河水运网的规模、水平和发展情况。

■ 货物（旅客）周转量

指在一定时期内，由各种运输工具运送的货物（旅客）数量与其相应运输距离的乘积之总和，是反映运输业生产总成果的重要指标，也是编制和检查运输生产计划，计算运输效益、劳动生产率以及核算运输单位成本的主要基础资料。通常以吨公里和人公里为计算单位。计算货物周转量通常按发出站与到达站之间的最短距离，也就是计费距离计算。

■ 货（客）运量

指在一定时期内，各种运输工具实际运送的货物（旅客）数量。它是反映运输业为国民经济和人民生活服务的数量指标，也是制定和检查运输生产计划、研究运输发展规模和速度的重要指标。货运按吨计算，客运按人计算。货物不论运输距离长短、货物类别，均按实际重量统计。旅客不论行程远近或票价多少，均按一人一次客运量统计；半价票、小孩票也按一人统计。

■ 港口货物吞吐量

指经水运进出港区范围，并经过装卸的货物数量，包括邮件及办理托运手续的行李、包裹以及补给运输船舶的燃、物料和淡水。货物吞吐量按货物流向分为进口、出口吞吐量，按货物交流性质分为外贸货物吞吐量和国内贸易货物吞吐量。货物吞吐量的货类构成及其流向，是衡量港口生产能力大小的重要指标。

■ 国际标准集装箱吞吐量

凡经过水运进、出港区范围，并经过装卸的集装箱箱数和重量（含集装箱自重），通常是按进港和出港分别统计。

TEU 是“折合 20 英尺标准箱”的英文缩写。它是指各种尺寸的国际标准集装箱的自然箱数，按各自的换算比例，折算为 20 英尺标准箱的换算箱数。其换算比例为：40 英尺箱 1 ∶ 2；35 英尺箱 1 ∶ 1.75；20 英尺箱 1 ∶ 1；10 英尺箱 1 ∶ 0.5。

■ 民用车辆拥有量

指报告期末，在公安交通管理部门按照《机动车注册登记工作规范》，已注册登记领有民用车辆牌照的全部汽车数量。汽车拥有量统计的主要分类：根据汽车结构分为载客汽车、载货汽车及其他汽车；根据汽车所有者不同分为个人（私人）汽车、单位汽车；根据汽车的使用性质分为营运汽车、非营运汽车和特种汽车；根据汽车大小规格不同载客汽车分为大型、中型、小型和微型，载货汽车分为重型、中型、轻型和微型。

■ 邮政业务总量

指以货币表现的邮政部门用于邮政服务的总数量。它综合反映了一定时期邮政工作的总成果，是研究邮政业务量构成和发展趋势的重要指标。它用各种邮政分类业务量，如函件件数、电报份数、订销报刊累计份数等，分别乘以相应的平均单位（不变价），加总后再加上其他业务收入求得。

■ 住宅电话用户

指安装在居民住宅或农民家里并按照住宅电话用户登记注册和收费的电话用户。包括私人付费、单位付费和按规定免费安装的住宅电话用户。

■ 移动电话用户

指通过移动电话交换机进入移动电话网、占用移动电话号码的电话用户。用户数量以报告期末在移动电话

主要统计指标解释

营业部门实际办理登记手续进入移动电话网的户数进行计算,一部移动电话统计为一户。

■ 数字数据用户 (DDN)

指在 DDN 数据通信网上接通的,在邮电部门办理登记手续的数据传输用户。

■ 局用交换机容量

指安装在电信企业用于接续本地固定电话的电话交换机容量。

■ 电话主线普及率

指按行政区划人口计算的平均每百人拥有电话主线。

SHANGHAI STATISTICAL YEARBOOK

EXPLANATORY NOTES TO MAJOR STATISTICAL INDICATORS

□ Operation Mileage of Railways

Operation Mileage of Railways refers to the total length of the trunk line under passenger and freight transportation (including both full operation and temporary operation). The calculation is based on the actual length of the first line even if this line has a full or partial double track or more tracks, excluding double tracks, station sidings, tracks under the charge of stations, branch lines, special-purpose lines and the non-payable connecting lines. The length of railways in operation is an important indicator to show the development of the infrastructure for the railway transport, and also the essential data to calculate volume of passenger freight transport, traffic density and utilization efficiency of the locomotives and carriages.

□ Length of Navigable Inland Waterways

Length of Navigable Inland Waterways is an indicator reflecting the size and development of inland water network, it refers to the length of the natural rivers, lakes, reservoirs, canals, and ditches open to navigation during a given period, which enables the transport by ships and rafts. It includes the channels open to navigation for over an accumulative 3 months in a year, yet this does not include the river courses, which are only used to float odd logs and bamboo rafts. This indicator can reflect the scale, level and development situation of the inland waterway network.

□ Turnover Volume of Freight (Passenger) Traffic

Turnover Volume of Freight(Passenger) Traffic refers to the total of the product of the physical volume of transported cargo (passengers) by the transport distance, usually using ton/kilometer and person/kilometer as calculating units. Normally, the shortest distance between the departure point and the destination is the basis to calculate the freight turnover volume, that is to say, the payable distance. This is an important indicator to show the total results of the transport industry, to prepare and examine the transport plan and to measure the efficiency, the labor productivity and the unit cost of transport.

□ Freight (Passenger) Traffic Volume

Freight (Passenger) Traffic Volume refers to the volume of freight (passenger) transported with various means. The freight (passenger) traffic provides a quantitative measure to show how the transport industry serves the national economy and people, and is also an important indicator for planning the transport industry and for studying the development scale and speed of the transport industry. Freight transport is calculated in tons and passenger traffic is calculated in the number of persons. Despite the type of freight and travelling distance, the freight transport is calculated in the actual weight of the goods: and despite the travelling distance and ticket price, the passenger traffic is calculated by the principle that one person can be counted only once in one travel. The passenger who travels with a half price ticket or a child ticket is also calculated as one person.

□ Cargo at Ports Throughput

Cargo at Ports Throughput refers to the volume of cargo passing in and out the harbor area of the ports and having been loaded and unloaded. The volume includes that of the postal matters, registered luggage and fuels, materials and fresh water as supplies of the ships. The volume of freight handled may be classified by direction of flow as freight for import and freight for export, or by nature of cargo as freight for domestic trade and freight for foreign trade. As an important indicator, the volume of freight handled by type of cargo and by main flow direction reflects the production capacity of ports.

□ International Container Throughput Capacity

International Container Throughput Capacity refers to number and weight of containers which are loaded or unloaded within port area via water carriage. It is often calculated by entering and leaving port, respectively. TEU was the abbreviation of twenty foot equivalent unit, which refers to converted number of all kinds of containers. The conversion method is based on respective conversion ratio and the number of all kinds of container is converted to the standard number of twenty foot equivalent unit. The conversion ratio is: 40 feet container 1 : 2, 35 feet container 1 : 1.75, 20 feet container 1 : 1, 10 feet container 1 : 0.5.

□ Civil Motor Vehicles

Civil Motor Vehicles refers to the total numbers of vehicles

EXPLANATORY NOTES TO MAJOR STATISTICAL INDICATORS

that are registered and received vehicles' license tags according to the Work Standard for Motor Vehicles Registration formulated by transport management office under department of public security at the end of reference period. They are divided into following categories according to the structure of motor vehicles: passenger vehicles, trucks and others; and private vehicles and vehicles for units use according to ownerships; working vehicles, non-working vehicles and special motor vehicles according to kind of usage; large passenger vehicles, medium passenger vehicles and small passenger vehicles, heavy trucks, light -heavy trucks and light trucks according to sizes of vehicles.

□ Volume of Post Business

Volume of Post Business refers to the total amount of post services provided by the post department, which reflects the total achievements by the post departments during a given period of time in a comprehensive way, and is an important indicator to study the composition and development of the post business. It is arrived by first multiplying the business volume of different types, such as number of letters, telegrams and accumulated number of newspaper and journals subscribed and sold, etc. by their respective average unit price (fixed price) and then adding these products together, plus the income from other business revenues.

□ Household TelePhone Subscribers

Household Telephone Subscribers refer to telephone sets installed in the dwelling units of urban or rural residents, and registered as residence subscribers for payment, including 3 types of payment for the service: private payment, public payment and free service.

□ Mobile Phone Subscribers

Mobile Phone Subscribers refer to the persons who own mobile telephone numbers and are connected with the mobile telephone communication network through the mobile telephone switchboards. The number of subscribers is calculated by the subscribers who have completed registration at mobile communication business centers and entered into the mobile telephone network. One mobile telephone is taken as a user.

□ Digital and Data Users

Digital and Data Users refer to the data transmission users who log to the DDN data telecommunications network and have registered with the post and telecommunications authority.

□ Capacity of Office Telephone Exchanges

Capacity of Office Telephone Exchanges refers to the capacity of telephone exchanges installed in the office of telecommunication service providers for communication between fixed telephones.

□ Popularity Rate of Telephone Lines

Popularity Rate of Telephone Lines is based on the number of telephone lines for every hundred people in terms of population stipulated in the administrative areas.

第十五篇

CHAPTER 15

批发和零售

WHOLESALE AND RETAIL

表 15.1 批发零售贸易业、餐饮业产业活动单位(1978～2006)
BUSINESS UNITS OF WHOLESALES, RETAILERS AND CATERING

年 份 Year	产业活动单位数(万个) Number of Business Units (10 000 units)	其 中 of which			
		批发零售贸易业 Wholesale and Retail	其 中 of which		餐饮业 Catering
			批发业 Wholesale	零售业 Retail	
1978	2.34	1.75	0.13	1.62	0.35
1979	3.38	2.37	0.26	2.11	0.39
1980	3.77	2.50	0.27	2.23	0.39
1981	4.27	2.63	0.27	2.36	0.51
1982	5.48	3.26	0.29	2.97	0.71
1983	6.26	3.75	0.30	3.45	0.76
1984	8.93	5.82	0.26	5.56	1.05
1985	10.85	7.26	0.23	7.03	1.31
1986	10.78	7.10	0.28	6.82	1.31
1987	11.87	7.96	0.29	7.67	1.46
1988	12.89	8.72	0.28	8.44	1.65
1989	13.14	8.78	0.28	8.50	1.86
1990	12.91	8.60	0.27	8.33	1.83
1991	13.50	8.99	0.26	8.73	1.99
1992	14.92	10.18	0.38	9.80	2.12
1993	13.59	11.31	0.78	10.53	2.28
1994	13.82	11.54	0.73	10.81	2.28
1995	16.34	13.69	0.84	12.85	2.65
1996	19.64	17.12	3.32	13.80	2.53
1997	20.29	17.64	3.48	14.16	2.65
1998	20.32	17.67	3.48	14.19	2.65
1999	22.56	19.69	3.66	16.03	2.87
2000	22.75	19.85	3.79	16.06	2.90
2001	24.34	21.31	4.23	17.08	3.03
2002	26.19	23.15	3.88	19.27	3.04
2003	26.09	23.00	3.25	19.75	3.09
2004	29.76	26.68	5.44	21.24	3.08
2005	33.56	30.42	7.79	22.63	3.14
2006	33.95	30.73	7.89	22.84	3.22

①1978～1992 年，产业活动单位数包括服务业，1993 年以后则不包括服务业。
②产业活动单位数含个体户数。
❶The numbers of business units include the service sector for 1978～1992, but not starting from 1993.
❷The number of business units includes the private businesses.

表 15.2 批发零售贸易业、餐饮业从业人员(1978～2006)
EMPLOYEES OF WHOLESALES, RETAILERS AND CATERING

年 份 Year	从业人员 (万人) Employees (10 000 persons)	其 中 of which			
		批发零售 贸易业 Wholesale and Retaile	其 中 of which		餐饮业 Catering
			批发业 Wholesale	零售业 Retail	
1978	39.62	30.70	5.46	25.24	5.57
1979	44.70	32.94	7.87	25.07	5.82
1980	45.78	33.94	7.91	26.03	5.66
1981	48.47	35.31	8.41	26.90	6.25
1982	50.24	36.70	9.05	27.65	6.51
1983	51.30	37.64	8.86	28.78	6.51
1984	55.24	40.57	8.81	31.76	6.86
1985	62.64	45.41	8.99	36.42	7.66
1986	63.76	44.98	8.96	36.02	7.97
1987	66.13	45.98	8.85	37.13	8.18
1988	72.80	50.89	9.42	41.47	8.67
1989	77.31	52.20	9.67	42.53	9.35
1990	74.75	50.48	8.19	42.29	9.33
1991	75.41	52.47	8.53	43.94	10.71
1992	87.27	63.71	13.74	49.97	10.98
1993	109.98	98.44	29.68	68.76	11.54
1994	88.51	77.49	27.58	49.91	11.02
1995	111.24	94.78	34.31	60.47	16.46
1996	145.67	122.21	50.79	71.42	23.46
1997	149.97	125.64	53.68	71.96	24.33
1998	150.96	126.56	53.67	72.89	24.40
1999	153.90	128.18	53.93	74.25	25.72
2000	154.32	128.41	53.79	74.62	25.91
2001	165.68	138.73	56.33	82.40	26.95
2002	179.34	152.19	65.40	86.79	27.15
2003	174.93	147.91	59.31	88.60	27.02
2004	181.25	156.21	74.77	81.44	25.04
2005	195.92	169.60	84.71	84.89	26.32
2006	203.51	174.49	86.32	88.17	29.02

①1978～1992 年，从业人员包括服务业，1993 年以后则不包括服务业。
②从业人员包括离岗从业人员。
❶Employees include the service sector for 1978～1992, but not starting from 1993.
❷Employees includes non-working employees.

表 15.3 限额以上批发贸易业产业活动单位和从业人员（2006）
NUMBER OF BUSINESS UNITS AND EMPLOYEES OF WHOLESALE TRADE ABOVE THE SET SCALE

类 别	Types	法人企业（个）Number of Corporations (unit)	产业活动单位数（个）Number of Business Units (unit)	从业人员（人）Number of Employees (person)
总 计	**Total**	**2 620**	**3 603**	**181 657**
按登记注册类型分	**Grouped by Registration Categories**			
内资企业	Domestic Enterprises	2 147	3 122	135 192
国 有	State-owned	180	244	13 576
集 体	Collective-owned	84	97	5 592
私 营	Private	1 373	1 631	53 802
股份制公司	Share Holding	33	92	12 286
其他内资	Others	477	1 058	49 936
外商投资	Foreign Funded	345	351	36 699
港澳台商投资	Hong Kong, Macao and Taiwan Funded	128	130	9 766
按行业分	**Grouped By Sectors**			
农畜产品批发	Primary and Livestock Products	20	36	870
食品、饮料及烟草制品批发	Food, Beverage and Tabacco	205	674	27 224
#米、面制品及食用油批发	Rice, Flour and Cooking Oil	39	101	3 038
烟草制品批发	Tabacco	22	367	9 327
纺织、服装及日用品批发	Textile Products, Gaments and Commodity	349	354	30 803
#服装批发	Garments	107	108	8 484
文化、体育用品及器材批发	Culture & Sports Articles and Equipments	69	109	8 869
医药及医疗器材批发	Medicines and Special Appliances of Medicines	117	318	21 874
矿产品、建材及化工产品批发	Mineral Products, Materials of Construction and Chemical Products	847	1 034	32 388
#煤炭及制品批发	Coal	36	45	1 816
石油及制品批发	Petroleum	87	94	4 201
金属及金属矿批发	Metal Products and Metal Minerals	370	382	9 483
建材批发	Building Materials	69	70	8 224
机械设备、五金交电及电子产品批发	Mechinery Equipments, Hardwares, Electric Appliances and Eletronic Products	716	745	42 923
#汽车、摩托车及零配件批发	Spare and Component Parts for Automobiles and Motorcycles	78	81	5 524
家用电器批发	Household Electrical Equipment	52	54	5 230
计算机、软件及辅助设备批发	Computers, Softwares and Accessorial Equipments	92	102	6 301
贸易经济与代理	Economic Trade and Agency	47	47	1 510
其他批发	Others	250	286	15 196

表 15.4 限额以上零售贸易业产业活动单位和从业人员(2006)
NUMBER OF BUSINESS UNITS AND EMPLOYEES OF RETAIL TRADE ABOVE THE SET SCALE

类别	Types	法人企业(个) Number of Corporations (unit)	产业活动单位数(个) Number of Business Units (unit)	从业人员(人) Number of Employees (person)
总计	**Total**	**1 203**	**11 398**	**297 308**
按登记注册类型分	**Grouped by Registration Categories**			
内资企业	Domestic Investment Enterprises	1 139	10 743	254 621
国有	State-owned	100	660	10 029
集体	Collective-owned	99	441	7 590
私营	Private	556	982	42 352
股份制公司	Share Holding	44	1 596	69 299
其他内资	Others	340	7 064	125 351
外商投资	Foreign Funded	37	569	31 883
港澳台商投资	Hong Kong, Macao and Taiwan Funded	27	86	10 804
按行业分	**Grouped By Sectors**			
综合零售业	Comprehensive Retail Sale	228	6 365	207 878
#百货零售	Articles For Daily Use	87	144	21 386
超级市场零售	Retail Sale of Supermarket	92	1 701	148 944
食品、饮料及烟草制品专门零售	Food, Beverage and Tabacco	92	481	9 663
纺织、服装及日用品专门零售	Textile, Garments and Articles for Daily Use	94	403	13 420
#服装零售	Garments	40	100	6 702
文化、体育用品及器材专门零售	Culture & Sports Articles and Equipments	87	1 785	8 822
#体育用品零售	Sports Articles	8	43	1 454
图书零售	Books	16	19	1 709
医药及医疗器材专门零售	Medicines and Special Appliances of Medicines	69	1 049	10 260
#药品零售	Medicine	58	989	9 300
汽车、摩托车、燃料及零配件专门零售	Automobiles, Motocycles, Fuels and Their Parts	354	719	22 285
#汽车零售	Automobiles	184	187	11 878
机动车燃料零售	Fuels of Power-Vehicles	128	480	8 560
家用电器及电子产品专门零售	Household Electrical Appliances and Electronic Products	105	297	14 236
#家用电器零售	Household Electrical Appliances and Electronic Products	32	161	9 800
计算机、软件及辅助设备零售	Computers, Softwares and Accessorial Equipments	48	70	2 342
通信设备零售	Telecommunication Appliances	16	54	1 881
五金、家具及室内装修材料专门零售	Hardwares, Furnitures and Materials of Decoration	90	144	7 080
无店铺及其他零售	No-Shop and Others	84	155	3 664
#邮购及电子销售	Mail Orders and Electronic Sales	4	4	928

表 15.5 社会消费品零售总额(1978～2006)
TOTAL RETAIL SALES OF CONSUMER GOODS

单位:亿元(100 million yuan)

年份 Year	社会消费品零售总额 Total Retail Sales of Consumer Goods	按商品用途分 By Use			
		食品类 Foods	衣着类 Clothing	用品类 Articles	燃料类 Fuels
1978	54.10	26.51	11.60	15.16	0.83
1979	68.28	30.05	16.07	21.28	0.88
1980	80.43	34.30	19.75	25.44	0.94
1981	88.73	38.78	21.27	27.73	0.95
1982	89.80	40.72	19.57	28.52	0.99
1983	100.68	44.20	22.31	33.18	0.99
1984	123.72	50.18	27.71	44.81	1.02
1985	173.39	64.08	35.51	72.70	1.10
1986	196.84	76.99	39.38	79.31	1.16
1987	225.25	91.01	42.52	90.41	1.31
1988	295.83	119.36	53.66	121.17	1.64
1989	331.38	140.03	51.95	137.70	1.70
1990	333.86	142.15	52.33	137.23	2.15
1991	382.06	162.82	52.91	163.30	3.03
1992	464.82	190.70	67.04	202.83	4.25
1993	675.92	259.93	101.30	309.26	5.43
1994	834.76	325.44	123.89	378.86	6.57
1995	1 050.96	407.44	153.74	481.96	7.82
1996	1 258.00	490.97	178.80	579.12	9.11
1997	1 435.38	564.62	200.62	659.61	10.53
1998	1 593.27	640.84	212.85	728.22	11.36
1999	1 722.33	694.03	228.18	787.62	12.50
2000	1 865.28	743.31	248.94	858.33	14.70
2001	2 016.37	802.53	266.31	931.02	16.51
2002	2 203.89	874.76	289.43	1 021.84	17.85
2003	2 404.45	939.29	309.70	1 135.27	20.19
2004	2 656.91	1 043.26	341.28	1 247.39	24.98
2005	2 972.97	1 172.05	381.31	1 388.32	31.29
2006	3 360.41	1 328.30	425.70	1 566.55	39.86

表 15.6 社会消费品零售总额(1978 ~ 2006)
RETAIL SALES OF CONSUMER GOODS

单位:亿元(100 million yuan)

年 份 Year	社会消费品零售总额 Total Retail Sales of Consumer Goods	按经济类型分 By Type of Ownership				
		国有经济 State-owned	集体经济 Collective-owned	私营经济 Private-owned	个 体 Individual	其 他 Others
1978	54.10	39.50	14.41		0.19	
1979	68.28	46.47	21.32		0.20	0.29
1980	80.43	54.01	25.31		0.24	0.87
1981	88.73	56.57	30.28	0.04	0.29	1.55
1982	89.80	56.48	31.39	0.03	0.32	1.58
1983	100.68	63.17	34.55	0.02	0.70	2.24
1984	123.72	75.63	43.80	0.02	1.68	2.59
1985	173.39	102.59	59.49	0.18	6.42	4.71
1990	333.86	179.37	115.59	2.05	16.17	20.68
1991	382.06	200.25	135.30	2.72	18.70	25.09
1992	464.82	247.68	157.56	5.75	22.88	30.95
1993	675.92	295.96	202.05	0.51	41.45	180.94
1994	834.76	249.27	198.56	0.64	65.00	321.29
1995	1 050.96	247.10	193.03	0.86	76.44	533.54
1996	1 258.00	238.54	183.50	30.10	92.64	713.22
1997	1 435.38	225.35	173.85	21.83	114.88	899.47
1998	1 593.27	210.92	161.70	59.48	126.94	1 093.71
1999	1 722.33	180.33	141.83	62.77	141.16	1 259.01
2000	1 865.28	150.09	118.26	496.86	153.57	1 443.36
2001	2 016.37	135.69	105.90	596.21	172.66	1 602.12
2002	2 203.89	131.91	102.19	699.75	190.66	1 779.13
2003	2 404.45	133.36	102.68	803.74	208.45	1 959.96
2004	2 656.91	134.44	102.78	935.44	233.01	2 186.68
2005	2 972.97	135.44	103.00	1 117.73	257.74	2 476.79
2006	3 360.41	138.43	104.62	1 342.60	284.46	1 490.30

注：1997 年以前私营经济为合营。
Note：The figures of Private Owned before 1997 refer to these of Joint Owned.

表 15.6 续表 continued

单位:亿元(100 million yuan)

年 份 Year	按销售地区分 By Regions		按行业分 By Sectors			
	区 Districts	县 Counties	批发零售贸易业 Wholesale and Retail Trade	餐饮业 Catering Trade	制造业 Manufacturing	其他行业 Others
1978	41.42	12.68	47.55	2.39	1.65	2.51
1979	51.60	16.68	59.02	2.82	2.54	3.90
1980	61.08	19.35	70.28	3.41	4.24	2.50
1981	66.66	22.07	77.53	3.68	4.61	2.91
1982	67.49	22.31	77.31	3.76	5.44	3.29
1983	75.62	25.06	84.93	4.26	7.72	3.77
1984	93.71	30.01	103.27	4.90	10.60	4.95
1985	133.59	39.80	150.03	7.58	8.41	7.37
1990	265.83	68.03	265.67	17.08	15.15	35.96
1991	302.54	79.52	300.26	20.91	17.70	43.19
1992	361.64	103.18	362.03	25.92	20.25	56.62
1993	530.97	144.95	559.56	35.47	29.24	51.65
1994	666.00	174.76	684.81	42.74	32.75	74.46
1995	832.92	218.04	864.01	52.61	38.05	96.29
1996	1 006.16	251.84	1 032.78	78.50	39.84	106.88
1997	1 156.08	27.30	1 173.94	93.49	44.38	123.57
1998	1 289.03	304.24	1 298.40	96.58	45.41	152.88
1999	1 398.60	323.73	1 391.08	114.93	47.22	169.10
2000	1 521.68	343.60	1 493.13	134.12	49.16	188.87
2001	1 665.46	350.91	1 619.13	148.88	50.78	197.58
2002	1 884.77	319.12	1 756.77	193.68	52.66	200.78
2003	2 063.71	340.74	1 920.20	225.83	53.87	204.55
2004	2 292.63	364.28	2 108.59	279.44	56.29	212.59
2005	2 588.86	384.11	2 340.57	350.32	59.84	222.24
2006	2 938.73	421.68	2 695.62	452.16		212.63

注：县的零售额包括崇明县全部及宝山区、嘉定区、闵行区、浦东新区、松江区、金山区、青浦区、奉贤区和南汇区中镇以下地区零售额。
Note: The retail sales of consumer goods include Chongming County and those at town level and below from Baoshan, Jiading, Pudong New Area, Songjiang, Jinshan, Qingpu, Fengxian and Nanhui Districts.

表 15.7 主要消费品零售量(1990 ~ 2006)
RETAIL SALES OF MAIN CONSUMER GOODS

年 份 Year	皮 鞋 (万双) Leather Shoes (10 000 pairs)	化妆品 (亿元) Cosmetics (100 million yuan)	照相机 (万架) Cameras (10 000 units)	彩色电视机 (万台) Color TV Sets (10 000 units)
1990	1 813		13.43	23.04
1991	1 784		11.19	26.67
1992	1 629	2.16	12.73	26.25
1993	1 678	4.16	16.36	35.58
1994	1 977	5.29	16.55	34.33
1995	1 852	11.67	23.35	37.60
1996	1 501	10.32	21.42	36.12
1997	1 606	10.91	21.52	49.03
1998	1 415	12.46	19.49	60.87
1999	1 842	15.42	20.98	71.65
2000	1 623	21.70	25.12	80.69
2001	1 897	28.53	28.52	88.43
2002	2 097	32.87	30.14	99.78
2003	2 257	36.07	32.21	111.96
2004	2 438	40.74	34.64	117.79
2005	27.33	47.71	37.33	127.49
2006	30.86	54.54	40.75	136.49

表 15.7 续表 1 continued

年 份 Types	洗衣机 (万台) Washing Machines (10 000 units)	家用空调器 (万台) Air-conditioners (10 000 units)	摄像机 (万架) Video Cameras (10 000 units)	电冰箱 (万台) Refrigerators (10 000 units)
1990	13.73	1.12		16.18
1991	15.57	2.34		18.57
1992	15.60	4.59		19.16
1993	19.44	9.68	0.58	22.39
1994	20.73	19.48	0.78	24.06
1995	27.92	33.93	0.95	27.32
1996	24.66	39.11	0.99	26.45
1997	28.81	39.70	1.17	27.48
1998	35.21	40.87	1.63	32.41
1999	34.17	37.27	1.48	30.00
2000	33.75	42.10	1.73	33.75
2001	38.05	43.78	2.36	35.46
2002	44.61	54.97	3.02	41.14
2003	51.17	80.76	4.08	47.48
2004	56.12	108.37	5.11	52.54
2005	64.58	120.00	5.99	58.42
2006	70.84	118.51	6.55	65.16

表 15.7 续表 2 continued

年　份 Types	汽　车 （万辆） Automobiles （10 000 vehicles）	金饰品 （亿元） Gold Ornaments （100 million yuan）	微波炉 （万台） Microwave Ovens （10 000 units）	热水淋浴器 （万台） Water Heaters （10 000 units）
1992		13.60		14.04
1993		21.38	6.47	24.42
1994	3.45	16.17	16.50	24.66
1995	4.62	24.51	23.19	28.38
1996	3.84	23.95	29.63	26.18
1997	5.11	26.45	35.76	26.78
1998	5.11	27.16	34.94	21.72
1999	4.96	22.51	30.50	20.52
2000	4.81	23.09	31.71	21.55
2001	5.10	26.00	33.53	21.81
2002	6.40	28.93	45.93	24.28
2003	7.84	30.52	55.98	31.38
2004	8.91	33.17	60.21	35.21
2005	9.08	39.95	66.25	40.54
2006	9.55	48.23	68.77	45.14

表 15.7 续表 3 continued

年　份 Types	电　脑 （台） Computers （set）	脱排油烟机 （万台） Range Hoods （10 000 units）	钢　琴 （台） Pianoes （set）	移动电话机 （万台） Mobile Telephone （10 000 units）
1992		8.63		
1993		11.96		
1994		11.59		
1995		17.36		
1996	3 903	15.59	1 904	
1997	12 564	15.97	2 207	
1998	37 279	16.85	3 660	
1999	76 529	15.41	3 863	13.67
2000	127 854	17.35	3 999	27.41
2001	158 134	17.76	4 190	40.73
2002	170 344	20.59	4 357	61.66
2003	184 665	23.43	4 539	130.43
2004	199 267	27.62	3 766	165.96
2005	220 551	34.83	5 338	186.47
2006	242 472	39.18	6 203	230.29

表 15.8 主要年份批发零售贸易业购、销、存总额
PURCHASE, SALES AND INVENTORY OF WHOLESALE AND RETAIL TRADE IN MAIN YEARS

单位:亿元(100 million yuan)

指 标	Indicators	1978	1990	2000	2005	2006
商品购进总额	**Purchase of Commodities**	**259.35**	**1 129.49**	**6 615.75**	**11 043.73**	**13 044.42**
#从生产者购进	Purchase from Producers	190.27	597.66	3 498.32	5 001.84	6 142.47
从批发零售贸易业购进	Purchase from Wholesale and Retail	69.08	113.79	3 067.15	4 638.06	5 646.35
商品销售总额	**Sales of Commodities**	**303.43**	**1 305.41**	**7 474.81**	**12 943.25**	**15 504.05**
零 售	Retail	47.55	265.67	1 723.31	2 611.31	2 896.29
批 发	Wholesale	255.88	1 039.74	5 751.50	10 331.94	12 607.76
#售给批发零售贸易	Sales to Retail and Wholesale	110.61	168.14	3 548.54	6 136.97	7 232.73
年末库存总额	**Year-end Inventory**	**47.27**	**230.97**	**262.50**	**383.35**	**419.76**

注：本表为国内批发零售贸易业、物资供销业、对外贸易业统计口径。
Note: The figures in this table are based on wholesale, retail trade, purchase and sales of commodities and foreign trade.

表 15.9 批发零售贸易业商品购、销、存总额(2006)
PURCHASE, SALES AND INVENTORY OF WHOLESALE AND RETAIL TRADE

单位:亿元 (100 million yuan)

类 别	Types	商品购进总额 Purchase of Commodities	商品销售总额 Sales of Commodities	商品库存总额 Year-end Inventory
总 计	**Total**	**13 044.42**	**15 504.05**	**419.76**
限额以上单位	Above the Set Scale	10 538.05	12 329.52	331.75
#国有及国有控股	State-owned and State-controlled	3 619.89	3 998.73	205.29
限额以下单位	Below the Set Scale	2 506.37	3 174.53	98.01

表 15.10 批发零售贸易业商品销售总额(2003~2006)
SALES OF COMMODITIES OF WHOLESALE AND RETAIL

单位:亿元(100 million yuan)

类 别	Types	2003	2004	2005	2006
商品销售总额	**Sales of Commodities**	**10 112.14**	**11 254.81**	**12 943.25**	**15 504.05**
#食 品	Food	699.34	706.17	814.22	960.78
饮 料	Beverage	91.58	103.60	115.20	140.38
烟 酒	Tabacco and Liquor	458.89	462.80	574.33	711.21
服装、鞋帽	Garments, Shoes and Hats	481.51	559.71	659.90	678.30
针、纺织品	Textile Products	261.06	317.25	352.46	405.48
化妆品	Cosmetics	81.29	100.18	120.11	150.14
金银珠宝	Jewelry	59.69	68.56	75.90	94.61
日用品	Articles for Daily Use	211.08	271.30	301.14	435.17
五金、电料	Hardware and Electrical Appliances	100.25	110.93	118.25	121.79
体育、娱乐用品	Recreation and Sports Articles	41.00	52.74	60.34	73.05
书报、杂志	Books and Newspapers	80.86	88.45	97.83	106.21
电子出版物及音像制品	Electronic Publications and Audio-video Products	24.14	29.31	34.56	41.47
家用电器和音响器材	Household Appliances and Audio-video Equipments	264.43	293.95	375.67	459.59
中西药品	Medicines	280.32	308.19	340.55	361.87
文化、办公用品	Culture and Office Articles	95.76	127.02	164.62	217.30
家 具	Furnitures	58.31	80.28	95.78	147.02
通信器材	Telecommunication Appliances	157.51	201.35	265.38	345.00
建筑及装潢材料	Materials for Construction and Decoration	194.56	240.80	280.05	313.92
机电产品及设备	Mechanical and Electrical Equipments	1 644.10	1 905.04	2 044.11	2 217.86

表 15.11 批发零售贸易业主要工业品购进量(2003～2006)
PURCHASE OF MAJOR INDUSTRIAL PRODUCTS OF WHOLESALE AND RETAIL TRADE

商品名称	Name of Commodities	2003	2004	2005	2006
卷 烟(万箱)	Cigarettes (10 000 cases)	272.28	290.11	323.79	352.75
酒(万吨)	Liquor (10 000 tons)	54.74	58.29	61.94	65.07
棉 布(万米)	Cotton Cloth (10 000 m)	1 779	1 801	1 861	2 005
呢 绒(万米)	Wool Fabric (10 000 m)	1 235	1 355	1 331	1 345
绸 缎(万米)	Silk and Statins (10 000 m)	534	601	647	698
各种服装(万件)	Garments (10 000 pieces)	12 001	12 556	12 988	13 450
皮 鞋(万双)	Leather Shoes (10 000 pairs)	1 392	1 451	2 211	2 338
自行车(万辆)	Bicycles (10 000 vehicles)	72.31	80.22	94.41	100.03
电风扇(万台)	Electrical Fans (10 000 units)	87.92	92.11	96.19	98.23
电视机(万台)	TV Sets (10 000 units)	94.79	101.59	126.04	132.99
#彩色电视机	Color TV Sets	94.70	100.05	125.90	130.87
录音机(万台)	Recorders (10 000 units)	52.97	56.13	71.57	81.48
照相机(万架)	Cameras (10 000 units)	31.97	34.52	44.45	62.29
电冰箱(万台)	Refrigerators (10 000 units)	54.42	58.12	66.17	70.39
洗衣机(万台)	Washing Machines (10 000 units)	47.21	49.37	59.86	72.76
家用空调器(万台)	Household Air-conditioners (10 000 units)	89.80	95.22	142.44	159.72
影碟机(万台)	Video Player (10 000 units)	57.17	60.10	86.35	87.41
脱排油烟机(万架)	Range Hoods (10 000 units)	25.06	28.12	30.61	35.56
热水淋浴器(万架)	Water Heaters (1 0000 units)	25.98	29.18	38.71	46.35
微波炉(万台)	Microware Ovens (10 000 units)	52.08	61.34	61.10	69.36
电话机(万只)	Telephones (10 000 units)	109.24	133.58	121.45	130.74
电 脑(万台)	Computers (10 000 units)	10.43	12.22	17.20	23.69
煤 油(万吨)	Kerosene (10 000 tons)	386.15	398.19	488.95	508.58
柴 油(万吨)	Diesel Oil (10 000 tons)	2 428.24	2 627.25	2 889.97	3 095.38

表 15.12 批发零售贸易业主要工业品销售量(2003～2006)
SALES OF MAJOR INDUSTRIAL PRODUCTS OF WHOLESALE AND RETAIL

商品名称	Name of Commodities	2003	2004	2005	2006
卷　烟（万箱）	Cigarettes (10 000 cases)	274.31	295.06	311.77	332.15
酒（万吨）	Liquor (10 000 tons)	54.87	59.19	62.13	68.31
棉　布（万米）	Cotton Cloth (10 000 m)	1 822	1 899	1 957	2 218
呢　绒（万米）	Wool Fabric (10 000 m)	1 189	1 301	1 334	1 434
绸　缎（万米）	Silk and Satins (10 000 m)	523	597	521	701
服　装（万件）	Garments (10 000 pieces)	12 236	12 848	14 183	16 764
皮　鞋（万双）	Leather Shoes (10 000 pairs)	1 252	1 501	1 722	2 464
自行车（万辆）	Bicycles (10 000 vehicles)	72.37	82.31	85.83	110.23
电风扇（万台）	Electrical Fans (10 000 units)	85.39	93.21	85.14	100.63
电视机（万台）	TV Sets (10 000 units)	120.58	125.47	130.14	137.03
#彩色电视机	Color TV Sets	120.48	128.39	130.00	135.03
录音机（万台）	Recorders (10 000 units)	56.21	60.50	70.87	84.51
照相机（万架）	Cameras (10 000 units)	31.42	38.35	42.10	63.61
电冰箱（万台）	Refrigerators (10 000 units)	57.11	60.77	64.96	77.88
洗衣机（万台）	Washing Machines (10 000 units)	57.98	59.44	61.73	76.87
家用空调器（万台）	Household Air-conditioners (10 000 units)	112.61	115.29	135.87	162.66
影碟机（万台）	Video Players (10 000 units)	63.06	65.25	80.28	90.61
脱排油烟机（万架）	Range Hoods (10 000 units)	30.98	32.89	35.08	40.34
热水淋浴器（万架）	Water Heaters (10 000 units)	33.13	35.51	47.91	51.66
微波炉（万台）	Microware Ovens (10 000 units)	58.29	65.12	68.01	78.88
电话机（万只）	Telephones (10 000 units)	112.84	118.84	130.37	139.05
煤　油（万吨）	Kerosene (10 000 tons)	419.61	474.01	487.35	492.13
柴　油（万吨）	Diesel Oil (10 000 tons)	2 498.50	3 440.17	3 501.08	3 611.12

表 15.13 批发零售贸易业主要农副产品纯购进量(2003～2006)
NET PURCHASE OF MAJOR FARM AND SIDELINE PRODUCTS OF WHOLESALE AND RETAIL TRADE

单位:万吨 (10 000 tons)

商品名称	Name of Commodities	从生产者购进 Purchase from Producers			
		2003	2004	2005	2006
粮　食(贸易粮)	Grain (for Trading)	88.67	92.10	95.25	97.80
食用植物油	Edible Vegetable Oil	6.03	6.25	8.01	10.27
猪和猪肉	Hogs and Porks	8.96	9.23	10.54	11.48
牛和牛肉	Oxes and Beef	0.71	0.78	0.75	0.87
家　禽	Poultries	0.90	0.95	0.91	0.90
鲜　蛋	Fresh Eggs	1.62	1.70	1.65	2.25
水产品	Aquatic Products	8.86	9.55	11.46	14.19
鲜　菜	Fresh Vegetable	75.71	79.14	89.75	95.05
棉　花	Cotton	0.50	0.62	0.50	0.84

表 15.13 续表 continued

单位:万吨 (10 000 tons)

商品名称	Name of Commodities	从市外批发零售贸易购进 Purchase from Wholesale and Retail of Outside City			
		2003	2004	2005	2006
粮　食(贸易粮)	Grain (for Trading)	153.48	160.11	170.47	185.93
食用植物油	Edible Vegetable Oil	48.50	53.19	56.14	60.16
猪和猪肉	Hogs and Pork	13.13	14.58	18.33	20.27
牛和牛肉	Oxes and Beef	1.13	1.28	1.35	1.01
家　禽	Poultries	1.46	1.59	0.98	0.73
鲜　蛋	Fresh Eggs	3.97	4.15	4.05	3.98
水产品	Aquatic Products	0.54	0.71	0.86	0.99
鲜　菜	Fresh Vegetable	73.64	75.33	83.45	100.07
棉　花	Cotton	5.32	6.01	6.85	7.67

表 15.14 限额以上批发贸易业商品购、销、存总额(2006)
PURCHASE, SALES AND INVENTORY OF WHOLESALE TRADE ABOVE THE SET SCALE

单位:亿元(100 million yuan)

类　别	Types	商品购进总额 Purchase of Commodities	商品销售总额 Sales of Commodities	商品库存总额 Year-end Inventory
总　计	**Total**	**8 313.49**	**9 676.11**	**146.33**
按登记注册类型分	**Grouped by Type of Registration**			
内资企业	Domestic Fund Enterprises	6 212.32	7 158.91	104.46
国有企业	State-Owned Enterprises	1 701.61	2 125.87	17.58
集体企业	Collective-Owned Enterprises	103.77	112.78	12.09
股份合作企业	Share Holding Cooperative Enterprises	86.49	76.29	4.93
联营企业	Joint-Owned Enterprises	78.25	82.77	5.58
有限责任公司	Companies with Limited Liabilities	2 189.73	2 301.53	22.55
股份有限公司	Share Holding Companies with Limited Liabilities	576.04	672.72	26.97
私营企业	Private Enterprises	1 467.36	1 777.60	13.55
其他企业	Others	9.07	9.35	1.21
港澳台商投资企业	Hong Kong, Macao and Taiwan Funded Enterprises	425.75	480.48	20.11
外商投资企业	Foreign Funded Enterprises	1 675.42	2 036.72	21.76
按行业分	**Grouped by Sector**			
农畜产品批发	Primary and Livestock Products	29.06	38.59	2.86
食品、饮料及烟草制品批发	Food, Beverage and Tabacco	730.99	852.89	20.30
#米、面制品及食用油批发	Rice, Flour and Cooking Oil	72.99	89.27	6.13
烟草制品批发	Tabacco	278.87	321.48	6.92

表 15.14 续表 continued

单位:亿元(100 million yuan)

类别	Types	商品购进总额 Purchase of Commodities	商品销售总额 Sales of Commodities	商品库存总额 Year-end Inventory
纺织、服装及日用品批发	Textile Products, Gaments and Commodity	404.20	472.83	17.42
#服装批发	Garments	104.61	113.07	9.71
文化、体育用品及器材批发	Culture & Sports Articles and Equipments	86.32	130.53	19.01
医药及医疗器材批发	Medicines and Special Appliances of Medicines	300.32	325.04	16.78
矿产品、建材及化工产品批发	Mineral Products, Materials of Construction and Chemical Products	4 688.03	5 574.94	31.71
#煤炭及制品批发	Coal	98.55	107.10	2.88
石油及制品批发	Petroleum	2 310.87	2 437.77	12.07
金属及金属矿批发	Metal Products and Metal Minerals	1 405.76	1 835.17	2.86
建材批发	Building Materials	91.78	95.23	7.87
化肥批发	Chemical Fertilizer	31.82	32.97	6.03
机械设备、五金交电及电子产品批发	Mechinery Equipments, Hardwares, Electric Appliances and Eletronic Products	1 833.82	1 983.36	30.01
#汽车、摩托车及零配件批发	Spare and Component Parts for Automobiles and Motorcycles	248.88	288.54	18.08
家用电器批发	Household Electrical Equipment	114.82	91.52	5.13
计算机、软件及辅助设备批发	Computers, Softwares and Accessorial Equipments	335.00	357.94	3.23
贸易经纪与代理	Economic Trade and Agency	141.88	188.15	4.57
其他批发	Others	98.87	109.78	3.97

表 15.15 限额以上零售贸易业商品购、销、存总额(2006)
PURCHASE, SALES AND INVENTORY OF RETAIL TRADE ABOVE THE SET SCALE

单位:亿元(100 million yuan)

类别	Types	商品购进总额 Purchase of Commodities	商品销售总额 Sales of Commodities	商品库存总额 Year-end Inventory
总计	**Total**	**2 224.56**	**2 653.41**	**185.42**
按登记注册类型分	**Grouped by Type of Registration**			
内资企业	Domestic Enterprises	1 823.35	2 199.89	145.80
国有企业	State-Owned Enterprises	53.92	59.98	8.55
集体企业	Collective-Owned Enterprises	37.80	41.67	4.49
股份合作企业	Share Holding Cooperative Enterprises	9.00	9.77	0.53
联营企业	Joint-Owned Enterprises	30.24	31.56	0.23
有限责任公司	Companies with Limited Liabilities	573.88	758.07	49.65
股份有限公司	Share Holding Companies with Limited Liabilities	536.00	699.13	39.17
私营企业	Private Enterprises	555.55	572.60	38.82
其他企业	Others	26.96	27.11	4.36
港澳台商投资企业	Hong Kong, Macao and Taiwan Funded	113.30	123.97	8.76
外商投资企业	Foreign Funded Enterprises	287.91	329.55	30.86
按行业分	**Grouped by Sector**			
#综合零售业	Comprehensive Retail Sale	1 011.08	1 351.65	92.80
食品、饮料及烟草制品专门零售	Food, Beverage and Tabacco	61.37	77.91	3.61
纺织、服装及日用品专门零售	Textile Products, Gaments and Commodity	60.77	68.75	15.56
文化、体育用品及器材专门零售	Culture & Sports Articles and Equipments	78.88	87.00	15.53
医药及医疗器材专门零售	Medicines and Special Appliances of Medicines	50.72	58.10	6.77
汽车、摩托车、燃料及零配件专门零售	Automobiles, Motocycles, Fuels and Their Parts	683.49	700.02	24.30
家用电器及电子产品专门零售	Household Electrical Appliances and Electronic Products	188.38	196.97	17.31
五金、家具及室内装修材料专门零售	Hardwares, Furnitures and Materials of Decoration	53.25	60.28	7.28

表 15.16 限额以上批发零售贸易业主要生产资料销售量(2003~2006)
SALES OF MAJOR MEANS OF PRODUCTION OF WHOLESALE AND RETAIL SALES TRADE ABOVE THE SET SCALE

单位:万吨(10 000 tons)

生产资料名称	Names of Means of Production	2003	2004	2005	2006
钢材	Steels	606.40	1 168.86	1 807.99	2 656.65
铜	Cuprum	45.45	44.61	57.38	60.06
铝	Aluminium	13.23	15.02	21.34	33.76
煤炭	Coal	2 020.85	1 453.86	3 016.67	3 315.22
汽油	Gasoline	1 354.70	1 390.34	1 213.18	1 186.33
煤油	Coal Oil	419.61	474.01	502.88	309.40
柴油	Diesel Oil	2 055.43	3 440.17	2 961.25	3 085.83
水泥	Concrete	119.80	93.52	118.73	169.20

表 15.17 限额以上批发零售贸易业主要商品销售额(2006)

TOTAL SALES OF ENTERPRISES ABOVE THE SET SCALE IN WHOLESALE AND RETAIL TRADE OF MAIN COMMODITIES

单位:亿元(100 million yuan)

类 别	Types	合 计 Total	批 发 Wholesale Trade	零 售 Retail Trade
食品、饮料、烟酒	Food, Beverages, Tobacco and Liquor	1 835.21	1 173.72	661.49
#肉禽蛋	Meat, Poultry and Eggs	106.39	57.81	48.58
饮 料	Beverages	107.50	55.90	59.60
烟 酒	Tobacco and Liquor	609.47	458.19	151.28
服装鞋帽、针、纺织品	Clothing, Shoes, Hats and Textiles	1 062.11	779.28	282.83
#服 装	Clothing	622.27	425.73	196.54
针、纺织品	Knitwear and Textiles	346.21	301.78	44.43
化妆品	Cosmetics	102.81	55.38	47.43
金银珠宝	Gold, Silver and Jewelry	64.89	29.07	35.82
日用品	Articles for Daily Use	380.37	232.49	147.88
#洗涤用品	Washing Articles	43.48	22.96	20.52
五金、电料	Hardware and Electrical Materials	103.88	68.99	34.89
体育、娱乐用品	Sports and Recreation Articles	57.28	35.02	22.26
书报杂志	Newspapers and Magazines	79.68	45.32	34.36
电子出版物及音像制品	E-journal and Video Products	6.68	3.58	3.10
家用电器和音像器材	Household Appliances and Video Appliances	398.21	227.94	170.27
中西药品	Traditional Chinese and Western Medicines	349.47	200.31	149.16
#西 药	Western Medicines	166.45	86.98	79.47
中草药及中成药	Traditional Chinese Medicines	115.66	62.98	52.68
文化办公用品	Cultural and Official Goods	466.84	405.75	61.09
家 具	Furniture	79.58	42.09	37.49
通讯器材	Communication Appliances	219.30	157.82	61.48
汽 车	Automobile	1 094.11	895.31	198.80
建筑及装潢材料	Building and Decoration Materials	177.01	113.23	63.78
机电产品及设备	Mechanical and Electrical Products	688.78	684.26	4.52
其 他	Others	5 163.31	5 112.89	50.42

表 15.18 限额以上批发零售贸易业商品销售量(2006)

TOTAL SALES NUMBER OF ENTERPRISES ABOVE THE SET SCALE IN WHOLESALE AND RETAIL TRADE BY COMMODITIES

名　称	Name of Commodities	销售合计 Total	批　发 Wholesale Trade	零　售 Retail Trade
粮　食(万吨)	Grain (10 000 tons)	247.61	209.80	37.81
食用植物油(万吨)	Edible Vegetable Oil (10 000 tons)	47.43	30.86	16.57
卷　烟(万箱)	Tobacco (10 000 boxes)	196.80	176.75	20.05
酒(万吨)	Alcohol (10 000 tons)	47.15	30.77	16.38
#白　酒	Distilled spirit	18.17	13.95	4.22
啤　酒	Beer	15.63	11.32	4.31
布(万米)	Colth (10 000 meters)	712.83	700.04	12.79
服　装(万件)	Dress (10 000 units)	485.67	339.90	145.77
鞋(万双)	Shoes (10 000 pairs)	136.34	86.08	50.26
彩色电视机(万台)	Colour TV Sets (10 000 units)	170.26	29.62	140.64
电　脑(微型计算机)(万台)	Personal Computers (10 000 units)	37.53	29.64	7.89
组合音响(万台)	Hi-Fi Stereo Component System (10 000 unit)	30.49	16.93	13.56
电冰箱(万台)	Refrigerators (10 000 units)	102.70	30.62	72.08
洗衣机(万台)	Washing Machines (10 000 units)	100.88	30.79	70.09
摄像机(万台)	Pickup Cameras (10 000 units)	7.80	0.40	7.40
影碟机(万台)	Video Disc Players (10 000 units)	113.61	29.09	84.52
家用空调器(万台)	Household Air Conditioners (10 000 units)	171.81	51.12	120.69
微波炉(万台)	Micro-ovens (10 000 units)	98.88	20.14	78.74
普通电话机(万台)	Telephones (10 000 units)	151.04	80.98	70.06
移动电话(万台)	Hand Telephones (10 000 units)	925.31	688.21	237.10
照相机(万台)	Cameras (10 000 units)	45.61	16.88	28.73
#数码照相机	Numeral Cameras	17.05	8.01	9.04
煤　油(万吨)	Kerosene (10 000 tons)	309.40	308.07	1.33
煤　炭(万吨)	Coal (10 000 tons)	3 315.22	3 309.69	5.53
柴　油(万吨)	Diesel Oil (10 000 tons)	3 085.83	3 072.64	13.19
汽　车(万辆)	Automobiles (10 000 vehicles)	58.02	48.47	9.55
#轿　车	Car	53.07	44.27	8.80
汽　油(万吨)	Gasoline (10 000 tons)	1 186.33	1 174.01	12.32
钢　材(万吨)	Steel Products (10 000 tons)	2 656.65	2 654.63	2.02
水　泥(万吨)	Cement (10 000 tons)	169.20	164.05	5.15
木　材(万立方米)	Wood (10 000 cu. m)	60.55	60.05	0.50

表 15.19 限额以上批发零售贸易业主要财务指标（2004～2006）
MAIN FINANCIAL INDICATORS OF WHOLESALE AND RETAIL SALES ABOVE THE SET SCALE

单位:亿元(100 million yuan)

指 标	Indicators	2004	2005	2006
流动资产	Current Assets	2 369.88	2 929.27	3 229.85
#存 货	Inventory	579.87	722.78	811.94
固定资产原价	Fixed Assets Original Value	527.89	546.78	632.69
累计折旧	Accumulative Depreciation	146.30	169.94	201.05
#本年折旧	Depreciation	27.15	31.20	38.47
资产总计	Total Assets	3 330.24	3 926.22	4 317.05
负债合计	Total Liabilities	2501.02	2 727.25	2 961.32
所有者权益合计	Total Owner's Equities	1 029.23	1 198.97	1 355.73
实收资本	Paid-up Capital	795.74	862.49	858.18
#国家资本	State Capital	138.83	132.19	123.22
港澳台资本	Hongkong Maiwan Capital	23.76	38.17	40.74
外商资本	Foreign Capital	163.29	242.71	222.50
主营业务收入	Prime Operating Revenues	9 459.53	11 236.19	13 065.98
主营业务成本	Operating Costs	8 304.33	9 874.12	12 065.15
营业费用	Operating Expenses	474.95	501.98	553.29
主营业务税金及附加	Sales Taxes and Extra Charges	8.68	10.10	14.81
主营业务利润	Profits of Major Management	664.62	737.71	952.92
管理费用	Management Expenses	215.38	243.12	256.52
财务费用	Financial Expenses	20.46	24.09	23.52
营业利润	Operating Profits	183.79	248.71	283.07
利润总额	Total Profits	164.00	223.35	325.83
主营业务应付工资总额	Total Payable Salaries Involved in Major Business	112.88	130.25	137.49
主营业务应付福利费总额	Total Payable Welfare Involved in Major Business	15.06	21.89	20.44

表 15.20 限额以上批发零售贸易业主要财务指标(2006)
MAIN FINANCIAL INDICATORS OF WHOLESALE AND RETAIL ENTERPRISES ABOVE THE SET SCALE

类别	Types	流动资产 Current Assets	固定资产原价 Fixed Assets Original Value	资产总计 Total Assets
总　计	**Total**	**3 229.85**	**632.69**	**4 317.05**
一、按登记注册类型分	**Grouped by Type of Registration**			
批发贸易业	Wholesale Trade	2 609.60	251.74	3 225.34
内资企业	Domestic Enterprises	1 795.82	204.21	2 295.65
国有企业	State-Owned Enterprises	358.79	39.16	442.32
集体企业	Collective-Owned Enterprises	30.80	7.68	43.18
股份合作企业	Share Holding Cooperative Enterprises	18.48	0.76	20.10
联营企业	Joint-Owned Enterprises	17.64	2.53	23.31
有限责任公司	Companies with Limited Liabilities	514.04	82.17	675.08
股份有限公司	Share Holding Companies with Limited Liabilities	162.79	26.65	271.87
私营企业	Private Enterprises	683.18	43.66	803.51
其他企业	Others	10.10	1.60	16.28
港澳台商投资企业	Hong Kong, Macao and Taiwan Funded	135.13	5.69	154.80
外商投资企业	Foreign Funded Enterprises	678.65	41.83	774.89
零售贸易业	Retail Trade	620.24	380.95	1 091.71
内资企业	Inner Enterprises	480.70	281.47	863.91
国有企业	State-Owned Enterprises	23.41	12.88	37.83
集体企业	Collective-Owned Enterprises	11.06	9.46	21.85
股份合作企业	Share Holding Cooperative Enterprises	3.90	0.64	5.33
联营企业	Joint-Owned Enterprises	7.11	7.06	14.21
有限责任公司	Responsibility Co. Ltd.	167.97	67.59	246.66
股份有限公司	Share Holding Co. Ltd.	115.13	152.44	326.99
私营企业	Private Enterprises	143.97	29.01	200.15
其他企业	Others	8.16	2.38	10.89
港澳台商投资企业	Hong Kong, Macao and Taiwan Funded	39.14	36.17	67.89
外商投资企业	Foreign Invested Enterprises	100.41	63.31	159.91

单位:亿元(100 million yuan)

负债合计 Total Liabilities	所有者权益合计 Total Owner's	实收资本 Paid-up Capital	主营业务收入 Prime Operating Revenues	主营业务成本 Operating Costs	主营业务利润 Profits from Major Business	利润总额 Total Profits
2 961.32	**1 355.73**	**858.18**	**13 065.98**	**12 065.15**	**952.92**	**325.83**
2 223.44	1 001.9	609.26	10 672.33	9 951.17	688.48	264.89
1 582.20	713.45	397.92	8 416.37	8 006.25	384.41	181.46
329.79	112.53	59.07	3 059.98	2 930.73	125.61	93.63
28.22	14.96	6.14	105.01	98.97	5.08	1.98
17.65	2.45	0.99	74.50	72.75	1.69	0.68
14.98	8.32	4.04	83.61	78.22	4.56	2.04
446.07	229.01	127.52	2 037.77	1 918.43	112.26	42.05
149.20	122.67	48.33	636.55	605.79	30.13	9.96
584.46	219.05	147.60	2 408.62	2 291.65	104.70	31.11
11.83	4.46	4.23	10.33	9.71	0.38	0.01
115.46	39.35	22.45	388.24	350.09	36.14	11.18
525.78	249.10	188.89	1 867.72	1 594.83	267.93	72.25
737.88	353.83	248.92	2 393.65	2 113.98	264.44	60.94
551.74	312.16	164.58	1 916.95	1 697.08	206.05	47.35
23.36	14.47	7.94	57.25	48.13	8.67	2.30
10.81	11.04	6.10	36.87	32.65	3.94	1.91
2.58	2.76	2.35	9.69	8.51	1.05	0.34
10.22	3.99	1.30	28.37	26.80	1.48	0.52
176.40	70.27	35.92	664.54	581.45	77.24	16.49
164.22	162.77	74.15	555.91	481.04	72.60	22.57
155.33	44.81	36.14	543.47	500.46	38.33	2.51
8.82	2.05	0.68	20.85	18.04	2.74	0.71
43.92	23.97	20.52	109.60	87.67	20.98	7.97
142.22	17.70	63.82	367.10	329.23	37.41	5.62

表 15.20 续表 continued

类 别	Types	流动资产 Current Assets	固定资产原价 Fixed Assets Original Value	资产总计 Total Assets
二、按行业分	**Grouped by Sector**			
批发贸易业	Wholesale Trade	2 609.60	251.74	3 225.34
农畜产品批发	Primary and Livestock Products	8.82	1.90	10.63
食品、饮料及烟草制品批发	Food, Beverage and Tabacco	180.31	44.68	251.92
纺织、服装及日用品批发	Textile Products, Gaments and Commodity	332.91	30.34	448.34
文化、体育用品及器材批发	Culture & Sports Articles and Equipments	49.64	8.15	65.26
医药及医疗器材批发	Medicines and Special Appliances of Medicines	184.63	33.93	243.30
矿产品、建材及化工产品批发	Mineral Products, Materials of Construction and Chemical Products	905.93	57.29	1 077.36
机械设备、五金交电及电子产品批发	Mechinery Equipments, Hardwares, Electric Appliances and Eletronic Products	611.48	46.15	745.63
贸易经济与代理	Economy on Trade and Agency	46.38	1.82	49.82
其他批发	Others	289.50	27.50	333.08
零售贸易业	Retail Trade	620.24	380.95	1 091.71
综合零售业	Comprehensive Retail Sale	338.35	277.88	638.13
食品、饮料及烟草制品专门零售	Food, Beverage and Tabacco	18.44	7.42	36.62
纺织、服装及日用品专门零售	Textile Products, Gaments and Commodity	30.29	8.83	40.96
文化、体育用品及器材专门零售	Culture & Sports Articles and Equipments	29.39	5.12	40.35
医药及医疗器材专门零售	Medicines and Special Appliances of Medicines	13.05	4.28	26.86
汽车、摩托车、燃料及零配件专门零售	Automobiles, Motocycles, Fuels and Their Parts	109.24	57.03	184.31
家用电器及电子产品专门零售	Household Electrical Appliances and Electronic Products	38.27	2.30	45.82
五金、家具及室内装修材料专门零售	Hardwares, Furnitures and Materials of Decoration	19.12	7.58	35.93
无店铺及其他零售	No-Shop and Others	24.10	10.51	42.73

单位:亿元(100 million yuan)

负债合计 Total Liabilities	所有者权益合计 Total Owner's	实收资本 Paid-up Capital	主营业务收入 Prime Operating Revenues	主营业务成本 Operating Costs	主营业务利润 Profits from Major Business	利润总额 Total Profits
2 223.44	1 001.9	609.26	10 672.33	9 951.17	688.48	264.89
7.61	3.02	2.64	26.46	25.72	0.70	0.02
148.95	102.97	55.17	632.04	554.85	72.74	42.87
306.04	142.29	99.21	1 055.76	910.32	139.17	23.11
42.89	22.78	12.10	119.08	108.22	10.29	1.67
173.53	69.77	33.10	478.52	427.94	49.11	10.51
781.96	295.40	180.08	5 294.44	5 085.18	200.90	109.07
494.03	251.60	119.23	1 892.40	1 757.04	126.09	45.38
36.60	13.22	8.45	175.50	165.38	9.31	1.60
231.83	100.85	99.28	998.13	916.52	80.17	30.66
737.88	353.83	248.92	2 393.65	2 113.98	264.44	60.94
463.50	174.62	127.59	1 195.00	1 024.87	161.49	31.11
15.96	20.66	9.05	61.72	49.29	11.98	4.70
26.57	14.39	10.13	59.71	43.79	15.23	1.98
27.67	12.67	8.59	71.93	60.25	10.43	3.92
12.38	14.49	9.26	44.11	35.80	7.66	0.98
106.03	78.28	56.57	670.50	633.89	34.60	11.96
34.05	11.77	6.62	188.96	177.02	11.35	1.35
22.41	13.52	12.68	51.85	43.89	7.36	3.53
29.31	13.43	8.43	49.87	45.18	4.34	1.41

表 15.21 限额以上餐饮业主要财务指标（2004~2006）
MAIN FINANCIAL INDICATORS OF CATERING SECTOR ABOVE THE SET SCALE

单位:亿元(100 million yuan)

	指 标 Indicators	2004	2005	2005
流动资产	Current Assets	41.89	43.60	64.37
#存 货	Inventory	4.64	5.10	6.32
固定资产原价	Fixed Assets Original Value	39.12	44.76	56.92
累计折旧	Accumulative Depreciation	12.39	15.65	20.56
#本年折旧	Depreciation	3.08	3.83	4.54
资产总计	Total Assets	100.03	94.49	124.56
负债合计	Total Liabilities	71.40	64.13	87.84
所有者权益合计	Total Owner's Equities	28.63	30.36	36.73
实收资本	Paid-up Capital	35.41	31.05	39.57
#国家资本	State Capital	3.16	0.78	1.42
港澳台资本	Hongkong Macao, Taiwan Capital	6.59	6.95	8.33
外商资本	Foreign Capital	9.74	6.66	9.67
主营业务收入	Prime Operating Revenues	155.55	157.66	195.49
主营业务成本	Operating Costs	72.50	72.03	88.55
营业费用	Operating Expenses	49.92	53.86	67.17
主营业务税金及附加	Sales Taxes and Extra Charges	8.16	8.14	9.87
主营业务利润	Profits of Major Management	68.92	65.75	84.83
管理费用	Management Expenses	18.97	19.42	23.06
财务费用	Financial Expenses	1.36	1.15	1.90
营业利润	Operating Profits	3.00	5.49	6.41
利润总额	Total Profits	4.06	5.49	6.16
主营业务应付工资总额	Total Payable Salaries Involved in Major Business	17.08	17.54	21.44
主营业务应付福利费总额	Total Payable Welfare Involved in Major Business	0.83	2.26	2.24

表 15.22 限额以上连锁零售业、住宿和餐饮业经营情况(2005~2006)
THE BASIC STATISTICS OF CHAIN RETAIL, ACCOMMODATION AND CATERING ABOVE SET SCALE

	指 标 Indicators	2005	2006
门店总数(个)	Number of Stores(unit)	15 775	16 547
营业面积(万平方米)	Operational Area(10 000 sq. m)	809.16	865.81
从业人数(万人)	Number of Persons Employed(10 000 person)	24.47	26.01
商品购进总额(亿元)	Purchase of Commodities(100 million yuan)	1 222.94	1 460.66
商品销售总额(亿元)	Sales of Commodities (100 million yuan)	1 815.32	2 048.13
#零售额	Retail Sales	1 201.03	1 321.55
餐饮业营业收入(亿元)	Total Operating Revenue (100 million yuan)	35.69	40.89

表 15.23 商品交易市场成交情况(2006)
DEALS IN MERCHANDISE EXCHANGE MARKET

分 类	Types	摊位数量(个) Quantitye of Stalls (unit)	成交额(亿元) Transaction Volume (100 million yuan)
总 计	**Total**	**139 257**	**3 377.04**
#食品、饮料、烟酒类	Foodstuff, Beverage, Tobacco and Liquor	69 441	478.48
服装、鞋帽、针纺织品类	Garments, Shoes and Hats, Textile Products	18 408	40.11
化妆品类	Cosmetics	216	0.42
金银珠宝类	Jewelry	162	0.18
日用品类	Articles for Daily Use	6 534	13.39
五金、电料类	Hardware and Electrical Appliances	1 175	4.12
体育、娱乐用品类	Recreation and Sports Articles	106	0.36
书报杂志类	Books, Newspapers and Magazines	246	5.30
电子出版物及音像制品类	Electronic Publications and Audio-video Products	138	0.31
家用电器和音像器材类	Household Appliances and Audio-video Equipments	1 414	14.32
中西药品类	Medicines	212	0.34
文化办公用品类	Culture and Office Articles	2 777	18.57
家具类	Furnitures	3 285	25.14
通讯器材类	Telecommunication Appliances	1 844	6.65

表 15.24 汽车销售情况(2004 ~ 2006)
DISTRIBUTION OF AUTOMOBILE

指 标	Indicators	2004	2005	2006
汽车销售量(万辆)	Sales Number of Cars(10 000 vehicles)	51.94	55.32	58.02
#零售量	Retail Sales Number	8.91	9.08	9.55
汽车销售总额(亿元)	Total Sale of Cars(100 million yuan)	1 163.58	1 179.98	1 192.89
#零售额	Retail Sale	200.53	207.76	213.27
轿车销售量(万辆)	Sales Number of Saloon Cars(10 000 vehicles)	48.01	49.65	53.07
#零售量	Retail Sales Number	8.30	8.32	8.80
#私人轿车	Personal Saloon Car	6.37	6.49	6.95
轿车销售额(亿元)	Sales of Saloon Cars (100 million yuan)	1 109.03	1 117.86	1 166.48
#零售额	Retail Sale	196.85	200.03	209.31
二手车交易量(万辆)	Dealing Number of Secondhand Cars(10 000 vehicles)	15.44	16.55	22.23
#轿 车	Saloon Car	6.80	7.50	11.77

表 15.25 主要超市公司基本情况(2006)
BASIC STATISTICS OF MAJOR SUPERMARKET COMPANIES

名 称	Name	网 点(个) Outlets (unit)	其中 of which 本 市 Directly -operated Stores in the City	市 外 Directly-operated Stores Outside the City	销售额(亿元) Sales Volume (100 million yuan)
联华超市公司	Lianhua Supermarket Company	3 928	2 178	1 750	440.27
#上海联家超市有限公司	Shanghai Lianjia Supermarket Co., Ltd.	11	11		45.11
大润发超市公司	RT-Mart Supermarket Company	36	8	28	229.75
农工商超市有限公司	Nonggongshang Supermarket Company	1 872	1 551	321	196.20
上海华联超市公司	Shanghai Hualian Supermarket Company	1 955	765	1 190	150.05
麦德龙现购自运有限公司	Metro Cash & Carry Co Ltd	33	4	29	93.67
上海易初莲花连锁超市有限公司	Shanghai Lotus ChainSupermarket Co.,Ltd	23	20	3	96.08
华联集团吉买盛购物中心有限公司	Hualian GSM Shopping Center Co Ltd	21	17	4	39.02
上海家得利超市有限公司	Shanghai Homegain Supermarket Co., Ltd.	135	112	23	26.62
上海捷强烟草糖酒(集团)连锁有限公司	Shanghai Jieqiang Tobacco, Sugar & Wine (Group) Chain Co., Ltd.	245	208	37	16.78
上海欧尚超市有限公司	Shanghai Auchan Supermarket Company	4	4		20.22
上海屈臣氏日用品有限公司	Shanghai Watsons Daily Articles Co.,Ltd	39	39		6.90
上海商务世界百货有限公司	Shanghai Commercial World Department Store Co. Ltd	4	4		11.30
上海家家乐商业发展有限公司	Jiajiale Supermarket Company	35	35		2.73
上海顶顶鲜超市有限公司	Shanghai Tops Supermarket Co., Ltd.	27	27		0.57
上海城市超市有限公司	Shanghai City Supermarket Co Ltd	4	4		1.27
上海新亚厨房食品有限公司	Shanghai New Asia Kitchen Food Co Ltd	6	6		0.06

表 15.26 成交额前 30 位的商品交易市场一览(2006)
BASIC STATISTICS OF 30 COMMODITY EXCHANGE MARKETS WITH TRANSACTION VOLUME BEFORE NO.30

名称	Name	摊位数量(个) Number of Stalls (unit)	成交额(亿元) Transaction Volume (100 million yuan)
上海市物贸中心有色金属交易市场	Shanghai Commodity Center Non-ferreous Metal Exchange Market	300	768.44
上海逸仙钢材市场经营管理(集团)有限公司	Shanghai Yixian Steel Market Management Ltd.	720	430.59
上海中油石油交易中心有限公司	Shanghai Zhongyou Oil Exchange Center	275	299.00
上海宝山钢材交易市场	Baoshan Steel Material Exchange Market	592	210.00
上海石化物资交易中心有限公司	Shanghai Petrochemical Commodity Exchange Center	126	129.71
长江有色金属现货市场	Changjiang Non-ferreous Metal on Hand Market	32	111.12
上海诚通香山金属交易有限公司	Xiangshan Steel Material Exchange Market	291	85.76
上海柏树钢铁交易市场管理有限公司	Shanghai Baishu Steel Exchange Market	42	84.00
上海中昊化工网上交易中心有限公司	Shanghai Zhonghao Network Exchange Center	300	80.20
新沪办钢材交易市场经营管理有限公司	New Huban Steel Exchange Market	35	60.00
上海联合汽车市场经营管理有限公司	Shanghai Lianhe Automobile Group	41	53.04
上海华东钢材市场	Shanghai East China Steel Market	160	51.49
上海铁闵钢材市场经营管理有限公司	Shanghai Tiemin Steel Exchange Market	308	51.40
沪西水产市场	Shanghai Huxi Aquatic Product Market	510	50.00
上海危险化学品交易市场经营管理有限公司	Shanghai Dangerous Chemical Products Exchange Market	510	50.00
上海金桥原产地商品交易市场	Shanghai Jinqiao Exchange Market of Original Commodities	90	45.50
上海市旧机动车交易市场	Shanghai Secondhand Automobile Exchange Market	47	39.79
铜川水产市场	Tongchuan Aquatic Product Market	900	39.48
上海中山化工市场	Shanghai Zhongshan Chemical Products Market	399	36.10
上海农产品中心批发市场有限公司	Shanghai Agriculture Center Distribution Market	553	34.15
上海曹安路市场	Shanghai Caoan Road Market	1 749	31.65
上海康健建材市场	Shanghai Kangjian Construction Material Market	304	29.60
上海安亭汽车市场经营管理有限公司	Shanghai Anting Motor Vehicles Market	29	28.54
上海江杨农产品批发市场经营管理有限公司	Shanghai Jiangyang Agriculture Products Distribution Market	800	27.33
上海砖贸综合市场经营管理有限公司	Shanghai Zhuanmao Integrative Market	3 130	24.74
上海毛家塘南北货批发市场经营管理有限公司	Maojiatang Local Products Wholesale Market	450	24.08
上海金山市场有限公司	Shanghai Jinshan Market	3 337	23.71
上海市江桥批发市场经营管理有限公司	Shanghai Jiangqiao Wholesale Market	1 300	21.73
上海东方汽配城	Shanghai Orient Automobile Parts Market	615	20.94
上海二手车交易市场有限公司	Shanghai Secondhand Aotumobile Exchange Market	17	20.69

上/海/统/计/年/鉴

主要统计指标解释

社会消费品零售总额

指批发和零售业、餐饮业、新闻出版业、邮政业和其他服务业等，售予城乡居民用于生活消费的商品和社会集团用于公共消费的商品之总量。社会消费品零售总额包括：

一、批发和零售业企业(单位)：

1. 售予城乡居民的各种生活消费品；

2. 售予入境旅游的外国人、华侨、港澳台同胞的各类商品；

3. 售予行政事业单位、社会团体、军队和武警等机构的商品，以及以零售方式售予各类企业的商品。具体包括：用于非生产和社会交往的办公用品，如通讯设备、计算器具和设备、电讯网络设备、文印设备、音像视听器材和设备、纸张、本册、文具及装订文印材料、家具、日用电器、针纺织品、清洁卫生用品、文体用品、奖品、纪念品、礼品等；供内部人员乘坐的交通工具和燃料；用于办公设施修缮的各类配件、材料、工具等；用于取暖和防暑降温的设备、燃料、材料及食品等；专用于教学的用品和设备；非营利医疗机构的中、西药品、中药材和医疗设备器材；非专用的劳动保护用品；不对外营业的内部食堂用的餐具、炊具、设备、清洁卫生工具和食品、燃料等；军队、武警用于其人员生活的衣着品和个人用品；其他各类非生产性设备和用品。

二、餐饮业出售的主食、菜肴、烟酒饮料和其他商品。

三、新闻出版业、邮政业售予城乡居民、企事业单位、军队和武警等机构的书报杂志、音像制品、邮品等。

四、其他服务业出售的食品、烟酒饮料、服装鞋帽、日常生活用品、医药保健用品、艺术品、工艺美术品、玩具、殡葬用品以及其他消费品。

商品购进总额

指从本企业(单位)以外的单位和个人购进(包括从境外直接进口)作为转卖或加工后转卖的商品总额。它反映批发零售贸易业从国内、国外市场上购进商品的总量。商品购进总额包括：(1) 从工农业生产者购进的商品；(2) 从出版社、报社的出版发行部门购进的图书、杂志和报纸；(3)从各种登记注册类型的批发零售贸易企业(单位)购进的商品；(4)从其他单位购进的商品，如从机关、团体、企业等单位购进的剩余物资，从餐饮业、服务业购进的商品，从海关、市场管理部门购进的缉私和没收的商品，从居民手中收购的废旧商品等；(5)从国(境)外直接进口的商品。不包括企业(单位)为自身经营用和未通过买卖行为而收入的商品以及销售退回、商品升溢等。

商品销售总额

指对本企业以外的单位和个人出售(包括对国(境)外直接出口)的商品。这个指标反映批发零售贸易业在上海市场以及上海以外市场上销售商品的总量。商品销售总额包括：(1) 售给城乡居民和社会集团消费用的商品；(2) 售给工业、农业、建筑业、运输邮电业、批发零售贸易业、餐饮业、服务业等作为生产、经营使用的商品；(3) 售给批发零售贸易业作为转卖或加工后转卖的商品；(4) 对国(境)外直接出口的商品。不包括：出售本企业自用的废旧包装用品，未通过买卖行为付出的商品，经本单位介绍，由买卖双方直接结算，本单位只收取手续费的业务，购货退出的商品以及商品损耗和损失等。

主营业务收入

指企业在销售商品、提供劳务等日常活动中所产生的收入总额。

主营业务成本

指企业已销商品应负担的进货原价和商品进价成本。

营业费用

指批发零售贸易企业在购、销、存过程中发生的各项经营费用。包括运输费、装卸费、包装费、保险费、展览费、差旅费、广告费、商品损耗、进出口商品累计佣金、经营人员的工资及福利费等。

EXPLANATORY NOTES TO MAJOR STATISTICAL INDICATORS

□ Total Retail Sales of Consumer Goods

Total Retail Sales of Consumer Goods refer to the sum of retail sales of commodities sold by wholesale, retail, catering, publishing, post and telecommunications and other service industries to urban and rural households for private consumption and to social institutions for public consumption. Retail sales of consumer goods include:

Sales by wholesale and retail units:

of consumer goods sold to urban and rural households

of commodities sold to foreigners, overseas Chinese and Chinese compatriots from Hong Kong, Macau and Taiwan visiting in China

of commodities sold to government agencies, institutions, social organizations, military and armed police units, and commodities sold to enterprises in the form of retail sales. More specifically, they include: office facilities and articles for non-production purposes such as communications equipment, computing equipment and instruments, TV and network equipment, printing and copying equipment, audio-visual equipment and instruments, paper, notebooks, stationeries, furniture, electric appliances, knitwear, sanitation and cleaning articles, cultural and sport articles, articles for prizes, souvenirs, etc.; transport vehicles and fuels for employees; materials, spare parts and tools for the maintenance of office facilities; equipment, fuels, materials and food for winter heating or summer cooling purposes; articles and equipment for teaching purpose; Chinese and western medicines and medical equipment and facilities purchased by non profit-making medical institutes; non-specialized work safety articles; cooking utensils, tableware, equipment, cleaning articles, food and fuels purchased by internal cafeterias; clothes and personal articles purchased by military or armed police units for their officials and soldiers; and other equipment and articles for non-production purposes.

Sales of stable food, cooked dishes, beverages, tobaccos and other articles by catering units.

Sales of books, newspapers, magazines, audio-visual products and post products by publishing, post and telecommunications departments to urban and rural households and to enterprises, institutions, military and armed police units.

Sales of food, beverages, tobaccos, clothing, hats, footwear, articles for daily use, medicines, medical and health articles, work of art, handicrafts, toys, funeral articles and other articles by other service industries.

□ Total Purchase of Commodities

Purchase, Sales and Stock of Commodities by Wholesale and Retail Trades refer to the total volume of commodities purchased, total volume of sales and exports, and the stock of commodities by wholesale and retail enterprises (establishments) of different status of registration from domestic and overseas markets. This indictor reflects the relationship among purchase, sales and stock of commodities in the circulation of goods and reveals the existing problems.

□ Total Sales of Commodities

Total Sales of Commodities refer to the selling of commodities to other establishments and individuals (including direct export). Reflecting the total value of sales of commodities at Shanghai markets and out-of-Shanghai markets, this indicator includes: (1) commodities sold to urban and rural households and institutions for their consumption; (2) commodities sold to establishments in industry, agriculture, construction, transportation, post and telecommunications, wholesale and retail trade, catering and service trade and public utility for their production and operation; (3) commodities sold to wholesale and retail establishments for re-selling, with or without further processing; and (4) commodities for direct export to other countries. Excluded are selling of waste packaging materials used by enterprises themselves commodities transferred without buying or selling procedures, commission income from brokerage in transactions whose settlement is directly handled by buyers and sellers, rejected commodities in the purchase, loss in commodities, etc.

□ Prime Operating Revenue

Prime Operating Revenue refers to the earnings a corporation receives in daily activity such as selling goods and offering labor service.

□ Operating Cost

Operating Cost refers to the cost a corporation paid to buy and deliver the commodities.

EXPLANATORY NOTES TO MAJOR STATISTICAL INDICATORS

□ Operating Expenses

Operating Expenses refer to the spendings that a wholesaler or retailer pays in buying, selling or stocking goods. It includes fees incurred in transport, loading and unloading, packaging, insurance, exhibition, business trip, advertisement, commodity wastage, commissions in import and export, salaries and bonus paid to workers involved.

第十六篇

CHAPTER 16

金融业

FINANCE

表 16.1 主要年份金融机构存贷款余额
SAVING DEPOSIT AND LOAN BALANCE OF FINANCIAL INSTITUTIONS IN MAIN YEARS

单位:亿元(100 million yuan)

指 标	Indicators	1995	2000	2005	2006
金融机构存款余额	**Saving Deposit Balance of Financial Institutions**	**4 675.09**	**9 349.83**	**23 320.86**	**26 454.88**
中资金融机构	Chinese Financial Institutions	4 565.56	9 088.66	22 219.53	24 924.65
人民币	RMB	3 783.51	7 771.50	20 779.87	23 535.24
外汇(折人民币)	Foreign Currencies(Converting into RMB)	782.05	1 317.16	1 439.66	1 389.41
外资金融机构	Foreign-funded Financial Institutions	109.53	261.17	1 101.33	1 530.23
外汇(折人民币)	Foreign Currencies (Converting into RMB)	109.53	196.41	485.34	636.86
人民币	RMB		64.76	615.99	893.37
金融机构贷款余额	**Loan Balance of Financial Institutions**	**3 832.04**	**7 254.26**	**16 798.12**	**18 603.92**
中资金融机构	Chinese Financial Institutions	3 332.53	6 427.84	14 801.05	15 968.94
人民币	RMB	2 822.71	5 959.51	13 709.78	14 826.93
外汇(折人民币)	Foreign Currencies (Converting into RMB)	509.82	468.33	1 091.27	1 142.01
外资金融机构	Foreign-funded Financial Institutions	499.51	826.42	1 997.07	2 634.99
外汇(折人民币)	Foreign Currencies (Converting into RMB)	499.51	635.50	1 326.46	1 479.64
人民币	RMB		190.92	670.61	1 155.35

注：本表至表 16.5 的数据由中国人民银行上海分行提供。
Note: Data in this table to table 16.5 are provided by Shanghai Branch of People's Bank of China.

表 16.2 主要年份中资金融机构人民币存款余额
RMB SAVING DEPOSIT OF CHINESE FINANCIAL INSTITUTIONS IN MAIN YEARS

单位:亿元(100 million yuan)

指 标	Indicators	2000	2005	2006
各项存款余额	**All Deposits**	**7 771.50**	**20 779.87**	**23 535.24**
企业存款	Enterprise Deposits	4 424.97	10 270.29	11 565.63
活期存款	Current Deposits	3 433.00	7 280.87	8 349.92
定期存款	Time Deposits	991.97	2 989.42	3 215.71
财政存款	Fiscal Deposits	179.68	237.55	396.74
机关团体存款	Deposits of Institutions and Organizations	91.12	770.99	956.05
储蓄存款	Savings Deposits	2 524.05	7 665.60	8 726.99
活期储蓄	Current Deposits	536.96	2 179.02	2 566.39
定期储蓄	Time Deposits	1 987.09	5 486.58	6 160.6
农业存款	Agricultural Deposits	171.29	490.8	502.58
委托存款	Entrusted Deposits	133.55	319.55	244.77
其他存款	Other Deposits	186.71	1 025.09	1 142.48

表 16.3 主要年份中资金融机构人民币贷款余额
RMB LOAN BALANCE OF CHINESE FINANCIAL INSTITUTIONS IN MAIN YEARS

单位：亿元(100 million yuan)

指 标	Indicators	2000	2005	2006
各项贷款余额	**All Loans**	**5 959.51**	**13 709.78**	**14 826.93**
#短期贷款	Short-term Loans	4 343.10	4 728.63	4 674.67
工业贷款	Industrial Loans	1 159.99	1 357.03	1 460.69
商业贷款	Commercial Loans	685.41	473.75	692.85
建筑业贷款	Construction Industry Loans	179.52	283.77	376.42
农业贷款	Agricultural Loans	31.59	23.80	9.98
乡镇企业贷款	Township Enterprise Loans	291.11	354.13	92.82
三资企业贷款	Overseas-funded Enterprise	439.39	219.14	138.9
私营企业及个体贷款	Private Business Loans	21.39	77.42	112.19
其他短期贷款	Other Short-term Loans	1 534.71	1 939.59	1 790.82
#个人短期消费贷款	Personal Short-term Consumption Loans		30.38	42.97
中长期贷款	Mid and Long-term Loans	1 071.39	7 640.02	8 963.1
基本建设贷款	Capital Construction Loans	523.79	2 750.76	3 271.3
技术改造贷款	Loans For Technical Updates and Transformation	404.71	154.89	155.83
其他中长期贷款	Other Mid and Long-term Loans	142.89	4 734.37	5 535.97
#个人中长期消费贷款	Personal Mid and Long-term Consumption Loans		2 783.78	2 610.19
融资租赁	Financing Leasing	2.79	7.14	6.98
委托贷款	Entrnsted Loans	124.01	294.41	203.35
票据融资	Bill Financing		1 007.36	964.02
各项垫款	All Advanced Money		12.83	14.81

表 16.4 个人贷款总额(2003～2006)
TOTAL AMOUNT OF PERSONAL LOANS

单位：亿元(100 million yuan)

指 标	Indicators	2003	2004	2005	2006
个人贷款总额	**Total Amount of Personal Loans**	**2 276.42**	**3 019.07**	**3 149.01**	**3 069.15**
个人消费贷款	Personal Consumption Loans	1 930.03	2 672.65	2 814.16	2 653.16
#个人住房贷款	Housing Mortgage Loans	1 709.13	2 445.53	2 644.94	2 483.73
汽车消费贷款	Car Consumption Loans	84.68	79.28	47.85	28.04
公积金贷款	Accumulation Fund Loans	346.39	346.42	334.85	415.99
个人住房贷款占个人消费贷款额比重(%)	**Percentage of Housing Mortgage Loans in Personal Consumption Loans**	**88.6**	**91.5**	**94.0**	**93.6**

表 16.5 主要年份银行现金收入和支出
CASH INCOME AND PAYOUT IN MAIN YEARS

单位:亿元(100 million yuan)

年 份 Year	现金收入 Cash Income	其 中 of which #商品销售收入 Commodity Sales Income	#储蓄存款收入 Savings Income	#服务事业收入 Service Income	现金支出 Cash Payout	其 中 of which #工资及对个人支出 Wage and Personal Payout	#储蓄存款支出 Savings Payout	#行政管理支出 Administrative Payout
1985	229.63	138.28	53.03	16.18	197.55	87.08	44.84	12.45
1990	554.62	267.02	166.78	45.30	523.97	213.50	126.17	52.04
1991	697.34	312.02	220.87	59.38	667.14	256.55	178.78	64.94
1992	1 107.00	407.75	369.79	85.01	1 089.77	344.11	342.68	103.08
1993	1 766.29	594.21	647.16	126.20	1 776.11	495.36	585.66	208.33
1994	2 218.79	690.47	893.00	181.97	2 300.72	680.32	703.91	285.53
1995	3 017.36	828.25	1 398.83	208.13	3 102.50	913.91	1 201.86	342.88
1996	3 469.05	938.91	1 596.81	241.53	3 650.54	932.22	1 734.95	518.44
1997	4 026.57	998.75	1 877.66	279.41	4 219.72	779.27	2 404.84	606.30
1998	5 681.56	1 384.74	2 866.31	439.09	5 856.38	1 023.70	3 117.37	744.89
1999	6 430.00	1 506.02	3 370.06	493.27	6 612.87	949.15	3 749.12	856.16
2000	7 946.79	1 827.34	4 042.11	552.84	8 041.05	897.47	4 738.28	1 085.23
2001	10 102.34	2 085.64	5 937.10	574.42	10 305.35	977.28	6 268.39	1 426.58
2002	11 698.86	2 428.06	7 155.32	616.39	11 947.35	1 079.77	7 196.26	1 789.68
2003	15 378.63	2 918.36	10 064.82	693.09	15 730.94	1 407.72	9 836.08	2 274.99
2004	19 969.87	3 195.19	13 704.06	775.16	20 358.79	1 734.34	13 487.46	2 478.33
2005	21 195.88	3 152.31	14 838.14	745.68	21 701.53	1 919.32	14 417.49	2 615.49
2006	24 114.40	3 232.63	16 842.89	974.62	24 708.35	2 135.47	16 533.01	2 808.89

表 16.6 主要年份主要要素市场交易情况和资金拆借情况
TRANSACTIONS OF MAIN MATERIAL MARKETS AND INTERBANK FUNDING IN MAIN YEARS

指 标	Indicators	2000	2005	2006
银行间资金拆借(亿元)	**National Interbank Funding (100 million yuan)**	**23 191.99**	**232 104.37**	**390 643.62**
资金拆借总额	Total Funding	6 728.07	12 783.09	21 503.11
债券市场成交额	Total Bond Turnover	16 463.92	219 321.28	369 140.51
债券回购	Bonds Repurchase	15 781.24	159 007.15	265 912.71
现券交易	Currency Transaction	682.68	60 133.14	102 563.93
远期交易	Forward Transaction		180.99	663.87
年末资金拆借余额	Year-end Total Funding Balance	289.00	431.12	500.35
黄金交易所成交金额(亿元)	**Total Gold Turnover (100 million yuan)**		**1 168.43**	**2 245.5**
钻石交易所成交金额(亿美元)	**Total Diamond Tumover (100 million USD)**		**4.10**	**5.73**
产权交易市场	**Property Right Market**			
交易项目(项)	Trade Volume (item)		3 395	2 866
交易金额(亿元)	Trade Turnover (100 million yuan)		823.15	844.12

注：本表数据由中国银行间同业拆借中心、上海黄金交易所、上海钻石交易所、上海市产权交易管理办公室等提供。
Note: Data in this table are provided by National Intertank Funding Center, Shanghai Gold Exchange, Shanghai Diamond Exchang and Shanghai Property Right Exchange Administration Office ect .

表 16.7 主要存款项目利率表 INTEREST RATES FOR MAJOR DEPOSITS

单位:%

类别 Types		1991 年 4 月 21 日 Apr. 21, 1991	1993 年 5 月 15 日 May. 15, 1993	1993 年 7 月 11 日 Jul. 11, 1993	1996 年 5 月 1 日 May. 1, 1996
城乡居民和单位存款	**Deposits of Residents and Corporations**				
活　期	Current Account	1.80	2.16	3.15	2.97
定　期	Time Account				
整存整取	Whole-deposit, Whole-withdrawal				
三个月	3 Months	3.24	4.86	6.66	4.86
半　年	6 Months	5.40	7.20	9.00	7.20
一　年	1 Year	7.56	9.18	10.98	9.18
二　年	2 Years	7.92	9.90	11.70	9.90
三　年	3 Years	8.28	10.80	12.24	10.80
五　年	5 Years	9.00	12.06	13.86	12.06
八年及八年以上	8 Years and above	10.08	14.58	17.10	
零存整取、整存零取、存本取息	Odd-deposit but Whole-withdrawal, Whole-deposit but Odd-withdrawal Deposit-Principal but Withdrawal-interets				
一　年	1 Year	6.12	7.20	9.00	7.20
三　年	3 Years	6.84	9.18	10.98	9.18
五　年	5 Years	7.56	10.80	12.24	10.80
定活两便	Time-current Deposit Integrated	*	*	*	*

①本表数据由中国人民银行提供(下表同)。
②2000 年、2001 年、2003 年、2005 年的存款利率没有变动。
③"*"按一年期以内定期整存整取同档次利率打六折执行。
❶Data in this table are provided by the People's Bank of China (same as follows).
❷The interest rates for deposits in 2000、2001、2003 、2005 remained unchanged.
❸A 60 percent discount in interest rates.

表 16.7 续表 1 continued

单位:%

类别 Types		1996 年 8 月 23 日 Aug. 23, 1996	1997 年 10 月 23 日 Oct. 23, 1997	1998 年 3 月 25 日 Mar. 25, 1998	1998 年 7 月 1 日 Jul. 1, 1998
城乡居民和单位存款	**Deposits of Residents and Corporations**				
活　期	Current Account	1.98	1.71	1.71	1.44
定　期	Time Account				
整存整取	Whole-deposit, Whole-withdrawal				
三个月	3 Months	3.33	2.88	2.88	2.79
半　年	6 Months	5.40	4.14	4.14	3.96
一　年	1 Year	7.47	5.67	5.22	4.77
二　年	2 Years	7.92	5.94	5.58	4.86
三　年	3 Years	8.28	6.21	6.21	4.95
五　年	5 Years	9.00	6.66	6.66	5.22
八年及八年以上	8 Years and above				
零存整取、整存零取、存本取息	Odd-deposit but Whole-withdrawal, Whole-deposit but Odd-withdrawal Deposit-Principal but Withdrawal-interets				
一　年	1 Year	5.40	4.14	4.14	3.96
三　年	3 Years	7.47	5.67	5.22	4.77
五　年	5 Years	8.28	6.21	6.21	4.95
定活两便	Time-current Deposit Integrated	*	*	*	*

表 16.7 续表 2 continued

单位:%

类 别	Types	1998 年 12 月 7 日 Dec. 7, 1998	1999 年 6 月 10 日 Jun. 10, 1999	2002 年 2 月 21 日 Feb. 21, 2002	2004 10 月 29 日 Oct. 29, 2004 年	2006 8 月 19 日 Aug. 19, 2006
城乡居民和单位存款	**Deposits Of Residents And Corporations**					
活 期	Current Account	1.44	0.99	0.72	0.72	0.72
定 期	Time Account					
整存整取	Whole-deposit, Whole-withdrawal					
三个月	3 Months	2.79	1.98	1.71	1.71	1.80
半 年	6 Months	3.33	2.16	1.89	2.07	2.25
一 年	1 Year	3.78	2.25	1.98	2.25	2.25
二 年	2 Years	3.96	2.43	2.25	2.70	3.06
三 年	3 Years	4.14	2.70	2.52	3.24	3.69
五 年	5 Years	4.50	2.88	2.79	3.60	4.14
八年及八年以上	8 Years and Above					
零存整取、整存零取、存本取息	Odd-deposit but Whole-withdrawal, Whole-deposit but Odd-withdrawal Deposit-Principal but Withdrawal-interets					
一 年	1 Year	3.33	1.98	1.71	1.71	1.80
三 年	3 Years	3.78	2.16	1.89	2.07	2.25
五 年	5 Years	4.14	2.25	1.98	2.25	2.52
定活两便	Time-current Deposit Integrated	*	*	*		

表 16.8 主要贷款项目利率表
INTEREST RATES FOR MAJOR LOANS

单位:%

类 别	Types	1991 年 4 月 21 日 Apr. 21, 1991	1993 年 5 月 15 日 May. 15, 1993	1993 年 7 月 11 日 Jul. 11, 1993	1996 年 5 月 1 日 May. 1, 1996	1996 年 8 月 23 日 Aug. 23, 1996
短期贷款	**Short-term Loans**					
六个月	6 Months	8.10	8.82	9.00	9.72	9.18
一 年	1 Year	8.64	9.36	10.98	10.98	10.08
中长期贷款	**Mid And Long-term Loans**					
一至三年(含三年)	1 ~ 3 Years(including 3 years)	9.00	10.80	12.24	13.14	10.98
三至五年(含五年)	3 ~ 5 Years(including 5 years)	9.54	12.06	13.86	14.94	11.70
五年以上	Above 5 Years	9.72	12.24	14.04	15.12	12.42

注: 2000 年、2001 年、2003 年、2005 年的贷款利率没有变动。
Note: The interest for loans in 2000, 2001, 2003 and 2005 remained unchanged.

表 16.8 续表 1 continued

单位:%

	类别 Types	1997 年 10 月 23 日 Oct. 23, 1997	1998 年 3 月 25 日 May. 25, 1998	1998 年 7 月 1 日 Jul. 1, 1998	1998 年 12 月 7 日 Dec. 7, 1998
短期贷款	**Short-term Loans**				
六个月	6 Months	7.65	7.02	6.57	6.12
一 年	1 Year	8.64	7.92	6.93	6.39
中长期贷款	**Mid and Long-term Loans**				
一至三年(含三年)	1 ~ 3 Years (including 3 years)	9.36	9.00	7.11	6.66
三至五年(含五年)	3 ~ 5 Years(including 5 years)	9.90	9.72	7.65	7.20
五年以上	Above 5 Years	10.53	10.35	8.01	7.56

表 16.8 续表 2 continued

单位:%

	类别 Types	1999 年 6 月 10 日 Jun. 10, 1999	2002 年 2 月 21 日 Feb. 21, 2002	2004 年 10 月 29 日 Oct. 29, 2004	2006 年 4 月 28 日 Apr28, 2006	2006 年 8 月 19 日 Aug. 19, 2006
短期贷款	**Short-term Loans**					
六个月	6 Months	5.58	5.04	5.22	5.40	5.58
一 年	1 Year	5.85	5.31	5.58	5.85	6.12
中长期贷款	**Mid and Long-term Loans**					
一至三年(含三年)	1 ~ 3 Years(including 3 years)	5.94	5.49	5.76	6.03	6.30
三至五年(含五年)	3 ~ 5 Years(including 5 years)	6.03	5.58	5.85	6.12	6.48
五年以上	Above 5 Years	6.21	5.76	6.12	6.39	6.84

表 16.9 主要年份上海证券交易所上市公司股本结构
CAPITAL STOCK STRUCTURES OF PUBLIC COMPANIES IN SHANGHAI STOCK EXCHANGE IN MAIN YEARS

单位:亿元(100 million yuan)

指标	Indicators	1995	2000	2005	2006
总 计	**Total**	**557.76**	**2 127.93**	**5 408.06**	**12 366.62**
非流通股份	Non-circulation Shares	365.48	1 383.43	3 461.84	8 025.07
国家股	State Shares	245.38	926.68	2 749.89	4 466.65
境内发起法人股	Domestic Sponsoring Corporate Shares	74.31	278.17	404.53	523.98
外资法人股	Foreign Corporate Shares	5.59	21.76	46.53	60.12
募集法人股	Raised Corporate shares	34.87	119.22	227.80	62.21
内部职工股	Employees Shares	1.29	13.11	1.91	2.09
转配遗留及其他	Transferred, Left and Others	4.04	24.49	31.18	2 910.02
可流通股份	Circulation Shares	192.28	744.50	1 946.22	4 341.55
A 股	A Shares	95.21	563.92	1 457.70	2 144.31
B 股	B Shares	34.65	85.07	103.51	110.17
H 股	H Shares	62.42	95.51	385.01	2 087.07

注：本表至表 16.16 的数据由上海证券交易所提供。
Note: Data in table 16.9 to 16.16 are provided by Shanghai Stock Exchange.

表 16.10 上海证券交易所有价证券成交总额(1991~2006)
TOTAL VOLUME OF PRICED SECURITIES TRADING IN SHANGHAI STOCK EXCHANGE

单位:亿元(100 million yuan)

年份 Year	合计 Total	股票 Shocks	其中 of which A股 A Shares	B股 B Shares	基金 Funds	债券 Bonds	国债 State Treasury Bond	回购 Repo
1991	46	8					32	
1992	324	247	233	14			70	
1993	2 607	2 468	2 302	79	12	87	87	
1994	25 546	5 735	5 627	108	117	19 575	19 575	63
1995	55 154	3 103	3 403	61	306	51 628	51 628	1 172
1996	27 661	9 115	9 020	95	497	17 403	17 402	12 439
1997	29 843	13 763	13 550	213	220	15 396	15 381	11 912
1998	34 336	12 386	12 304	82	605	21 267	21 235	15 188
1999	35 992	16 966	16 826	140	1 366	17 447	17 401	12 124
2000	49 901	31 374	31 030	344	1 334	16 896	16 804	13 147
2001	44 144	22 709	19 877	2 833	1 349	19 794	19 726	15 343
2002	48 528	16 959	16 442	517	557	30 877	30 800	24 419
2003	82 783	20 824	20 541	283	362	61 596	58 482	52 982
2004	76 717	26 470	26 229	241	249	49 998	47 048	44 086
2005	49 718	19 240	19 061	179	156	28 138	26 394	23 621
2006	91 912	57 817	57 245	572	777	18 130	17 025	15 487

表 16.11 上证综合指数(1990～2006)
SHANGHAI COMPOSITE INDEX

年 份 Year	开 盘 Open	最 高 High	日 期 Date		最 低 Low	日 期 Date		收 盘 Close
1990	96.05	127.61	12 月 31 日	31, Dec	95.79	12 月 19 日	19, Dec	127.61
1991	127.61	292.75	12 月 31 日	31, Dec	104.96	5 月 17 日	17, May	292.75
1992	293.74	1 429.01	5 月 26 日	26, May	292.76	1 月 2 日	2, Jan	780.39
1993	773.89	1 558.98	2 月 16 日	16, Feb	750.46	12 月 20 日	20, Dec	833.80
1994	837.70	1 052.94	9 月 13 日	13, Sep	325.89	7 月 29 日	29, July	647.87
1995	637.72	926.41	5 月 22 日	22, May	524.43	2 月 7 日	7, Feb	555.29
1996	550.26	1 258.69	12 月 11 日	11, Dec	512.83	1 月 19 日	19, Jan	917.02
1997	914.06	1 510.18	5 月 12 日	12, May	870.80	2 月 20 日	20, Feb	1 194.10
1998	1 200.95	1 422.95	6 月 4 日	4, June	1 043.02	8 月 18 日	18, Aug	1 146.70
1999	1 144.89	1 756.18	6 月 30 日	30, June	1 047.83	5 月 17 日	17, May	1 366.58
2000	1 368.69	2 125.72	11 月 23 日	23, Nov	1 361.21	1 月 4 日	4, Jan	2 073.48
2001	2 077.08	2 245.44	6 月 14 日	14, June	1 514.86	10 月 22 日	22, Oct	1 645.97
2002	1 643.49	1 748.89	6 月 25 日	25, June	1 339.2	1 月 29 日	29, Jan	1 357.65
2003	1 347.43	1 649.60	4 月 16 日	16, Apr	1 307.40	11 月 13 日	13, Nov	1 497.04
2004	1 492.72	1 777.52	4 月 6 日	6, Apr	1 260.32	9 月 13 日	13, Sep	1 266.50
2005	1 260.78	1 318.27	3 月 8 日	8, Mar	1 011.5	7 月 11 日	11, July	1 161.06
2006	1 163.88	2 698.90	12 月 29 日	29, Dec	1 161.91	1 月 4 日	4, Jan	2 675.47

表 16.12 主要年份上海证券交易所市场概况
SHANGHAI STOCK EXCHANGE MARKET IN MAIN YEARS

指 标	Indicators	2000	2005	2006
上市公司数(个)	Quantity of Public Company (unit)	572	834	842
上市股票数(个)	Quantity of Listed Stock(unit)	614	878	886
上市证券数(个)	Quantity of Negotiable Securities(unit)	657	1 069	1 126
股票发行股数(亿股)	Shares of Stocks Issued (100 million shares)	2 032.42	5 023.05	10 279.54
A 股	A Shares	1 947.35	4 919.54	10 169.37
B 股	B Shares	85.07	103.51	110.17
股票市价总值(亿元)	Aggregate Value of Stocks in Market Price (100 million yuan)	26 930.86	23 096.13	71 612.38
A 股	A Shares	26 596.32	22 856.07	71 117.95
B 股	B Shares	334.54	240.06	494.43
流通股数(亿股)	Shares in Circulation (100 million shares)	648.99	1 561.21	2 254.48
A 股	A Shares	563.92	1 457.70	2 144.31
B 股	B Shares	85.07	103.51	110.17
流通市值(亿元)	Value in circulation (100 million yuan)	8 481.33	6 754.61	16 428.33
A 股	A Shares	8 146.79	6 514.55	15 933.90
B 股	B Shares	334.54	240.06	494.43
市场筹资额(亿元)	Funds Raised from Market (100 million yuan)	919.95	299.77	1 743.18
首次发行 A 股	IPO of A Shares	591.18	28.55	1 180.23
再次发行 A 股	Additional A Shares Issued	325.13	271.22	534.18
首次发行 B 股	IPO of B Shares	3.64		
可转换债券	Convertible Loan Stock			28.77

注：2005、2006 年未发行 B 股。
Note: There were no IPO of B shares in 2005 and 2006.

表 16.13 主要年份上海证券交易所投资者开户情况
ACCOUNT-OPENING BY INVESTORS IN SHANGHAI STOCK EXCHANGE IN MAIN YEARS

单位：万户（10 000 households）

指　标	Indicators	1995	2000	2005	2006
年末开户总数	**Total Accounts Year-end**				
总　数	Total	685.20	2 957.84	3 747.91	3 901.53
个　人	Private	682.32	2 944.89	3 726.63	3 878.76
机　构	Institution	2.88	12.95	21.28	22.77
A 股开户数	**A Shares Accounts**				
总　数	Total	682.50	2 943.32	3 648.06	3 799.94
个　人	Private	680.00	2 931.20	3 628.00	3 778.51
机　构	Institution	2.50	12.12	20.06	21.43
B 股开户数	**B Shares Accounts**				
总　数	Total	2.70	14.52	99.86	101.59
个　人	Private	2.32	13.69	98.63	100.25
机　构	Institution	0.38	0.83	1.23	1.34
当年新开户总数	**Newly Opened Accounts During the Year**				
总　数	Total	110.31	676.72	44.83	153.62
个　人	Private	109.75	672.09	44.22	152.13
机　构	Institution	0.56	4.64	0.61	1.49
A 股新开户数	**Newly Opened Accounts of A Shares**				
总　数	Total	109.50	671.08	44.34	151.88
个　人	Private	109.00	666.52	43.81	150.51
机　构	Institution	0.50	4.56	0.53	1.37
B 股新开户数	**Newly Opened Accounts of B Shares**				
总　数	Total	0.81	5.64	0.50	1.74
个　人	Private	0.75	5.56	0.41	1.62
机　构	Institution	0.06	0.08	0.09	0.12

注：本表数据不含基金帐户。
Note: The data in this table don't include fund account.

表 16.14 上海股份制企业首次发行 A 股一览表
LIST OF IPO OF A SHARES OF SHANGHAI ENTERPRISES

名 称	Name	股票面值 Par Value of Stocks (元) (yuan)	发行价 Issued Price (元) (yuan)	总股本 Aggregate of Capital Stock (万股) (10 000 shares)	发行量 Issued Volume (万股) (10 000 shares)	筹资额 Capital Raised (万元) (10 000 yuan)
1984 年	**Year of 1984**			**50**	**50**	**50**
飞乐音响	Feile Accoustics	1.00	1.00	50	50	50
1985 年	**Year of 1985**			**530**	**530**	**530**
延中实业	Yan Zhong	1.00	1.00	500	500	500
爱 使	AiShi	1.00	1.00	30	30	30
1987 年	**Year of 1987**			**17 895**	**2 410**	**2 410**
真空电子	Vacuum Electron	1.00	1.00	15 694	1 450	1 450
申华实业	Shenhua	1.00	1.00	100	100	100
飞乐股份	Feile	1.00	1.00	2 101	860	860
1988 年	**Year of 1988**			**650**	**485**	**485**
豫园商城	Yuyuan Bazar	1.00	1.00	650	485	485
1991 年	**Year of 1991**			**3 400**	**2 703**	**12 961**
兴业房产	Xingye Real Estate	1.00	3.50	2 000	1 303	4 561
浦东大众	Pudong Dazhong	1.00	6.00	1 400	1 400	8 400
1992 年	**Year of 1992**			**1 036 691**	**184 676**	**823 737**
二纺机	ErfangJi	1.00	3.80	17 954	3 820	14 516
轻工机械	Light Ind Mach	1.00	2.40	16 516	1 000	2 400
嘉 丰	Jiafeng	1.00	3.50	7 063	1 150	4 025
联合实业	United Holding	1.00	4.30	9 293	1 100	4 730
异型钢管	Special Steel Tube	1.00	2.80	3 610	1 275	3 570
中纺机	China Textile Mach	1.00	3.80	13 810	2 800	10 640
大众出租	DaZhong Taxi	1.00	4.90	6 090	1 000	4 900
第一铅笔	First Pencil	1.00	4.00	3 900	1 008	4 032
永生制笔	Wing Sung	1.00	7.20	5 604	1 200	8 640
胶带股份	Rubber Belt	1.00	3.50	4 395	1 000	3 500
丰华圆珠	Fenghua Ballpen	1.00	5.50	5 672	1 800	9 900
第一食品	1st Provision Store	1.00	5.80	2 839	1 300	7 540
联华合纤	Lian Hua Fibre	1.00	5.58	7 289	2 000	11 160
氯碱化工	Chlor Alkali	1.00	5.40	59 181	8 643	46 672
冰箱压缩	Refrige Compressor	1.00	4.80	11 991	4 000	19 200
联 农	United Agriculture	1.00	5.00	2 500	1 700	8 500
金 陵	Jinling	1.00	4.20	5 099	1 817	7 631
嘉宝实业	Jiabao	1.00	5.00	10 626	2 500	12 500

① 每股面值为 1 元人民币，对历史曾出现的大于 1 元面额的股票，均被换算到当前 1 元面额。
② “＊”表示在深圳交易所中小板上市。
③ 未列入的年份是因为该年未发行 A 股。
❶ Par value of each share is one yuan. The par value of the stocks used to be above one yuan have all been converted to one yuan.
❷ The mark ＊ refers to the stocks came into market in Shenzhen Stock Exchange.
❸ There are some years unlisted because there were no IPO of A shares in those years.

表 16.14 续表 1 continued

名称	Name	股票面值 Par Value of Stocks (元) (yuan)	发行价 Issued Price (元) (yuan)	总股本 Aggregate of Capital Stock (万股) (10 000 shares)	发行量 Issued Volume (万股) (10 000 shares)	筹资额 Capital Raised (万元) (10 000 yuan)
轮胎橡胶	Tyre and Rubber	1.00	6.80	45 201	2 000	13 600
复华实业	Forward	1.00	5.20	4 339	1 500	7 800
水仙电器	Narcissus Electric	1.00	4.60	8 578	2 500	11 500
申达实业	Shenda	1.00	3.00	13 655	3 500	10 500
电　器	Electric	1.00	4.40	40 651	4 500	19 800
新世界	New World	1.00	8.80	1 500	641	5 641
棱光实业	Lengguang	1.00	2.20	3 380	1 500	3 300
龙头股份	Dragon Head	1.00	3.80	17 447	4 500	17 100
中百一店	No. 1 Store	1.00	8.90	12 108	5 300	47 170
华联商厦	Shanghai Hualian	1.00	9.28	8 153	4 500	41 760
双鹿电器	Shuanglu Elec	1.00	5.66	9 217	3 500	19 810
海鸟电子	Albatronics	1.00	4.00	1 529	600	2 400
三爱富	3F New Material	1.00	3.40	5 000	2 000	6 800
广电股份	Radio and Audio	1.00	4.80	45 922	6 538	31 382
黄浦房产	Huangpu Real Estate	1.00	6.08	8 024	2 893	17 589
浦东金桥	Jin Qiao	1.00	2.50	30 000	3 000	7 500
国脉实业	Guo Mai	1.00	5.18	7 000	2 879	14 913
众城实业	Zhongcheng	1.00	1.20	6 180	1 000	1 200
申　能	Shenergy	1.00	2.80	240 274	27 988	78 366
爱　建	Aijian	1.00	7.00	15 000	4 500	31 500
望春花	Wang Chun Hua	1.00	5.00	3 022	1 200	6 000
国嘉实业	Citic-Jiading	1.00	3.60	2 998	1 000	3 600
新亚快餐	New Asia Fast Food	1.00	3.28	1 700	700	2 296
外高桥	Outer Gaoqiao	1.00	2.80	28 000	1 000	2 800
原　水	Raw Water	1.00	3.80	66 242	17 249	65 546
新锦江	Jinjiang Tower	1.00	5.20	16 630	8 000	41 600
豫圆商城	Yuyuan Bazar	1.00	8.00	11 290	5 350	42 800
南洋实业	Nanyang Int'l	1.00	5.58	6 600	2 574	14 363
浦东强生	Qiang Sheng Taxi	1.00	2.85	1 800	720	2 052
陆家嘴	Lujiazui	1.00	2.80	71 500	1 500	4 200
沪昌特钢	Huchang Sp Steel	1.00	2.80	40 000	8 931	25 007
良华实业	Liang Hua	1.00	2.45	6 269	2 300	5 636
东方明珠	Oriential Pearl	1.00	5.10	41 000	4 000	20 400
商业网点	Commerial Re	1.00	4.10	4 850	2 000	8 200
凌　桥	Lingqiao Tapwater	1.00	1.50	18 200	3 700	5 550
1993 年	**Year of 1993**			**802 423**	**117 441**	**470 986**
中华企业	China Enterprise	1.00	6.50	7 863	2 000	13 001
钢　运	Steel Trans	1.00	4.00	5 084	1 500	6 000

表 16.14 续表2　continued

名　称	Name	股票面值 Par Value of Stocks (元) (yuan)	发行价 Issued Price (元) (yuan)	总股本 Aggregate of Capital Stock (万股) (10 000 shares)	发行量 Issued Volume (万股) (10 000 shares)	筹资额 Capital Raised (万元) (10 000 yuan)
上海凤凰	Phoenix Bicycle	1.00	6.00	25 176	3 000	18 000
邮通设备	Posts and Telecoms	1.00	5.00	6 661	1 900	9 500
上海石化	Shanghai Petrochem	1.00	3.00	455 000	55 000	165 000
上海三毛	Sanmao Textile	1.00	4.00	6 659	1 750	7 000
亚　通	Ya Tong	1.00	2.80	5 016	1 800	5 040
大　江	Dajiang (Group)	1.00	4.00	45 935	2 500	10 000
上海永久	Forever Bicycle	1.00	5.50	17 101	2 300	12 650
耀皮玻璃	Yaohua Pilkington	1.00	6.30	28 999	2 952	18 598
隧　道	Tunnel Engineering	1.00	3.40	8 433	2 900	9 860
物贸中心	Goods and Materials	1.00	3.70	13 987	1 900	7 030
万象集团	Wan Xiang	1.00	5.00	5 000	2 000	10 000
益民集团	Yimin	1.00	6.60	5 033	1 270	8 382
时　装	Fashion Clothing	1.00	5.40	5 000	2 000	10 800
兰　生	Lansheng	1.00	5.50	14 163	3 550	19 525
友谊华侨	Friendship	1.00	5.20	4 500	1 500	7 800
上菱电器	Shangling Electric	1.00	5.50	20 365	2 700	14 850
界龙实业	Jielong	1.00	4.00	5 000	1 859	7 436
农垦商社	Saic Trading	1.00	5.00	5 019	1 260	6 300
第九百货	No.9 Store	1.00	5.00	5 000	2 000	10 000
上　柴	Diesel Engine	1.00	5.20	22 942	2 800	14 560
中西药业	Zhongxi Pharm	1.00	5.00	5 000	1 920	9 600
工业缝纫	Industrial Sewing	1.00	5.80	11 920	2 200	12 760
英　雄	Hero	1.00	5.80	7 501	1 680	9 744
钢　管	Steel Tube	1.00	4.00	15 840	2 200	8 800
同济科技	Tongji Science	1.00	6.00	5 009	1 300	7 800
自　仪	Auto Instrument	1.00	3.50	19 086	3 200	11 200
四　药	No.4 Pharm	1.00	4.50	5 797	1 500	6 750
华东电脑	East-china Computer	1.00	3.00	5 000	2 000	6 000
海　欣	Haixin	1.00	7.00	9 334	1 000	7 000
1996 年	**Year of 1996**			**122 255**	**23 810**	**128 078**
东海股份	Shanghai Donghai	1.00	5.80	12 392	2 710	15 718
民丰实业	Minfeng	1.00	4.90	8 689	1 950	9 555
上海港机	Shanghai Port Ma	1.00	5.18	11 960	4 000	20 720
浦东不锈	Pudong Stainless	1.00	5.40	24 000	6 000	32 400
新亚股份	New Asia	1.00	4.90	35 464	1 900	9 310
巴士股份	Shanghai Bus	1.00	5.80	5 200	2 200	12 760
张江高科	Zhangjiang Hi-te	1.00	6.15	10 000	2 500	15 375
中国高科	China High Tech	1.00	4.80	14 550	2 550	12 240

表 16.14 续表 3 continued

	名 称 Name	股票面值 Par Value of Stocks (元) (yuan)	发行价 Issued Price (元) (yuan)	总股本 Aggregate of Capital Stock (万股) (10 000 shares)	发行量 Issued Volume (万股) (10 000 shares)	筹资额 Capital Raised (万元) (10 000 yuan)
1997 年	**Year of 1997**			**679 249**	**88 250**	**431 558**
江南重工	Jiangnan Heavy Industry	1.00	5.37	13 201	6 000	32 220
中纺投资	China Textile Investment	1.00	6.20	11 000	3 000	18 600
上海梅林	Shanghai Meilin	1.00	4.00	27 000	10 000	40 000
华源股份	China Energy	1.00	7.04	23 853	4 000	28 160
东方航空	Eastern Airline	1.00	2.45	486 695	30 000	73 500
上海汽车	Shanghai Auto	1.00	7.02	100 000	30 000	210 600
东风电仪	Dongfeng Elec Instruments	1.00	7.55	5 000	1 250	9 438
长江投资	Changjiang Investment	1.00	4.76	12 500	4 000	19 040
1998 年	**Year of 1998**			**241 343**	**75 800**	**472 438**
沪东重机	Hudong Heavy Machine	1.00	3.83	21 954	7 000	26 810
航天机电	Hangtian Elec	1.00	5.76	27 200	6 800	39 168
上海贝岭	Shanghai Belling	1.00	6.53	33 419	12 000	78 360
上海建工	Shanghai Construction	1.00	6.67	53 700	15 000	100 050
虹桥机场	Hongqiao Airport	1.00	6.41	90 000	30 000	192 300
复星实业	Shanghai Fuxing	1.00	7.15	15 070	5 000	35 750
1999 年	**Year of 1999**			**273 340**	**48 500**	**466 640**
浦发银行	Pudong Development Bank	1.00	10.00	241 000	40 000	400 000
紫江实业	Zijiang	1.00	7.84	32 340	8 500	66 640
2000 年	**Year of 2000**			**1 373 420**	**216 700**	**1 086 166**
上港集箱	Shanggang Containers	1.00	11.98	90 220	21 000	251 580
宝钢股份	Baosteel	1.00	4.18	1 251 200	187 700	784 586
东方创业	Dongfang	1.00	6.25	32 000	8 000	50 000
2001 年	**Year of 2001**			**87 151**	**24 000**	**241 290**
上海家化	Shanghai Jahwa	1.00	9.18	27 000	8 000	73 440
上海能源	Shanghai Energy	1.00	9.00	40 151	11 000	99 000
交大昂立	Jiao Tong University	1.00	13.77	20 000	5 000	68 850
2002 年	**Year of 2002**			**340 218**	**70 000**	**286 700**
中海发展	Zhonghai Development	1.00	2.36	203 000	35 000	82 600
上海航空	Shanghai Airlines	1.00	5.33	72 100	20 000	106 600
光明乳业	Brightness Milk	1.00	6.50	65 118	15 000	97 500
2003 年	**Year of 2003**			**171 934**	**29 500**	**175 950**
上海电力	Shanghai Power	1.00	5.80	156 351	24 000	139 200
中科合臣	Synica	1.00	7.00	7 600	3 000	21 000
置信电气	Zhixin Electric	1.00	6.30	7 983	2 500	15 750
2004 年	**Year of 2004**			**43 494**	**14 440**	**107 523**
浦东建设	Pudong Construction	1.00	4.85	22 600	8 000	38 800
现代制药	Modern Oharmacy	1.00	8.08	8 719	3 300	26 664
科华生物 *	Kehua Bio-engineering	1.00	11.12	6 875	1 800	20 016
思源电器 *	Sieyuan Electric	1.00	16.45	5 300	1 340	22 043
2006 年	**Year of 2006**			**349 577**	**121 800**	**456 144**
招商轮船	CMES	1.00	3.71	343 340	120 000	445 200
威尔泰	Welltech	1.00	6.08	6 237	1 800	10 944

表 16.15 上海股份制企业首次发行 B 股一览
LIST OF IPO OF B SHARES OF SHANGHAI ENTERPRISES

名 称	Name	股票面值（元）Face Value (yuan)	发行价 Issued Price 美 元 USD	折人民币(元) Converting into RMB (yuan)	发行量(万股) Issual Volume (10 000 shares)	筹资额 Capital Raised 万美元 10 000 USD	折人民币(万元) Converting into RMB (10 000 yuan)
1992 年	**Year of 1992**				**85 500**	**65 558**	**426 891**
真 空	Vacuum	1.00	0.712	4.20	10 000	7 120	42 000
二 纺	Erfang Ji	1.00	0.610	3.88	12 500	7 625	48 500
大 众	Dazhong	1.00	0.650	4.30	2 500	1 625	10 750
永 生	Wing Sung	1.00	0.836	5.30	2 500	2 090	13 250
中 铅	First Pencil	1.00	0.520	3.47	2 500	1 300	8 675
中 纺	China Textile	1.00	0.610	4.00	7 000	4 270	28 000
胶 带	Bubber Belt	1.00	0.531	3.50	2 500	1 328	8 750
氯 碱	Chlor Alkali	1.00	0.800	5.25	24 000	19 200	126 000
轮 胎	Tyre and Rubber	1.00	1.100	7.30	17 000	18 700	124 066
冰 箱	Refrigerator	1.00	0.460	3.38	5 000	2 300	16 900
1993 年	**Year of 1993**				**85 300**	**38 464**	**339 100**
金 桥	Jinqiao	1.00	0.344	2.80	11 000	3 784	30 800
外高桥	Outer Gaoqiao	1.00	0.380	4.07	8 500	3 230	34 595
联 华	Lian Hua	1.00	0.380	3.34	3 000	1 140	10 020
新锦江	Jinjiang Tower	1.00	0.379	3.30	9 000	3 411	29 700
永 久	Forever Bicycle	1.00	0.355	3.09	6 000	2 130	18 540
凤 凰	Phoenix Bicycle	1.00	0.405	3.52	10 000	4 050	35 200
海 欣	HaiXin	1.00	0.700	6.09	3 500	2 450	21 315
耀 皮	Yaohua Pilkinton	1.00	0.720	6.27	10 000	7 200	62 664
大 江	Dajiang (Group)	1.00	0.402	3.50	3 500	1 407	12 250
上 柴	Diesel Engine	1.00	0.523	4.55	10 000	5 230	45 500
英 雄	Hero	1.00	0.439	3.82	3 500	1 537	13 370
三 毛	Sanmao	1.00	0.344	2.98	3 300	1 135	9 834
友 谊	Friendship	1.00	0.440	3.83	4 000	1 760	15 312

①每股面值为 1 元人民币，对历史曾出现的大于 1 元面额的股票，均被换算到当前 1 元面额。
②未列出的年份是因为该年未发行 B 股。
❶ Par value of each share is one yuan. The par value of the stocks used to be above one yuan have all been converted to one yuan.
❷There are some years unlisted because there were no IPO of B shares in those years.

表 16.15 续表 1 continued

	名 称 Name	股票面值（元）Face Value (yuan)	发行价 Issued Price 美 元 USD	折人民币(元) Converting into RMB (yuan)	发行量（万股）Issued Volume (10 000 shares)	筹资额 Capital Raised 万美元 10 000 USD	折人民币(万元) Converting into RMB (10 000 yuan)
1994 年	**Year of 1994**				**86 500**	**39 400**	**349 970**
工 缝	Industrial Sewing	1.00	0.420	3.65	7 500	3 150	27 405
上 菱	Shangling	1.00	0.750	6.52	7 000	5 250	45 654
钢 管	Steel Tube	1.00	0.398	4.00	8 000	3 184	32 000
物 贸	Goods and Materials	1.00	0.258	3.70	5 000	1 290	18 500
自 仪	Auto Instrument	1.00	0.248	2.16	7 000	1 736	15 103
国 旅	Int'L Travel	1.00	0.360	3.08	6 000	2 160	18 461
邮 通	Posts and Telecoms	1.00	0.520	4.44	6 000	3 120	26 614
水 仙	Narcissus	1.00	0.265	2.26	10 000	2 650	22 602
陆家嘴	Lujiazui	1.00	0.668	5.69	20 000	13 360	113 850
新 亚	New Asia	1.00	0.350	2.98	10 000	3 500	29 781
1995 年	**Year of 1995**				**8 000**	**2 216**	**18 400**
金 泰	Jintai	1.00	0.277	2.30	8 000	2 216	18 400
1996 年	**Year of 1996**				**26 000**	**6 344**	**52 577**
汇 丽	Huili	1.00	0.187	1.54	8 000	1 496	12 320
华源股份	Huayuan Stocks	1.00	0.280	2.33	10 000	2 800	23 300
开 开	Kai Kai	1.00	0.256	2.12	8 000	2 048	16 957
1997 年	**Year of 1997**				**10 000**	**4 330**	**35 900**
振 华	Zhenghua	1.00	0.433	3.59	10 000	4 330	35 900
1998 年	**Year of 1998**				**35 000**	**9 704**	**80 408**
凯 马	Kaima B	1.00	0.276	2.29	24 000	6 624	54 888
茉织华	Mozhihua	1.00	0.280	2.32	11 000	3 080	25 520
2000 年	**Year of 2000**				**18 400**	**4 379**	**36 248**
凌 云	Lingyun	1.00	0.238	1.97	18 400	4 379	36 248

表 16.16 上海股份制企业在境外首次发行股票一览表
LIST OF OVERSEAS IPO OF SHANGHAI ENTERPRISES

	股票名称 Stock Title	上市日期 Date of IPO	上市地点 Place of IPO		发行价(元) 港币/美元 Issued Price (yuan) HKD/USD	发行量(万股) Issued Volume (10 000 shares)	筹资额(万元) Capital Raised (10 000 yuan)	
							港币/美元 HKD/USD	折人民币 Convert into RMB
1993 年	**Year of 1993**							
上海石化	SPC	1993.11.08	香　港	Hong Kong	1.58	168 000	265 440	198 240
1994 年	**Year of 1994**							
海兴轮船	Haixing Shipping	1994.11.11	香　港	Hong Kong	1.46	108 000	157 680	171 870
1997 年	**Year of 1997**							
东方航空	China Eastern	1997.02.05	香　港	Hong Kong	1.38	156 695	216 239	231 909
2000 年	**Year of 2000**							
复旦微电子	Fudan Microelectronics	2000.08.04	香　港	Hong Kong	0.80	12 500	10 000	10 700
2002 年	**Year of 2002**							
交大慧谷	Jiaoda Withub Information	2002.07.31	香　港	Hong Kong	0.66	13 200	8 712	9 322
复旦张江	Fudan-Zhangjiang	2002.08.13	香　港	Hong Kong	0.80	19 800	15 840	16 949
2003 年	**Year of 2003**							
联华超市	Lianhua Super Market	2003.06.27	香　港	Hong Kong	3.88	15 000	58 125	62 194
携程网	Ctrip	2003.12.09	美　国	USA	18.00	420	7 560	8 089
2004 年	**Year of 2004**							
复地集团	Forte Land	2004.02.06	香　港	Hong Kong	2.35	73 300	172 258	184 316
灵通网	Linktone	2004.03.04	美　国	USA	14.00	614	8 596	71 175
中芯国际	SMIC	2004.03.17	美　国	USA	17.50	9 788	171 290	1418 281
中芯国际	SMIC	2004.03.18	香　港	Hong Kong	2.69	25 758	69 289	74 139
盛大网	Shanda	2004.05.13	美　国	USA	11.00	1 380	15 180	125 690
中海集装箱	CSCL	2004.06.16	香　港	Hong Kong	3.18	242 000	768 350	822 135
青浦消防	Qingpu Fire	2004.06.24	香　港	Hong Kong	0.54	5 556	3 000	3 210
前程无忧	51job	2004.09.28	美　国	USA	14.00	525	7 350	60 858
第九城市	The 9 Limited	2004.12.15	美　国	USA	17.00	607	10 319	85 441
2005 年	**Year of 2005**							
上海电气	Shanghai Electric	2005.04.28	香　港	Hong Kong	1.70	297 291	505 395	540 773
交通银行	Communication Bank	2005.06.23	香　港	Hong Kong	2.50	585 600	1 464 000	1 566 480
上海栋华	Shanghai Donghua	2005.07.13	香　港	Hong Kong	0.53	10 300	5 459	5 841
分众传媒	Focus Media	2005.07.13	美　国	USA	17.00	1 010	17 170	142 168
新宇亨得利	Xinyu Hendry	2005.09.27	香　港	Hong Kong	1.32	28 750	37 950	40 607

① 香港上市的货币币种为港元，美国上市的货币币种为美元。
② 外资股折算汇率：2005 年前为年末汇率，2005 年为股票发行月的月末汇率。
❶ The Currency of stock issued in Hong Kong refers to HK Dollar, while the counterpart refers to US dollar.
❷Foreign fund share's converting exchange rate: it's year-end exchange rate before 2005, while it's month-end exchange rate of IPO month after 2005.

表 16.17 主要年份保险及保险中介机构
INSURERS AND INSURANCE AGENTS IN MAIN YEARS

单位：个(unit)

指 标	Indicators	2000	2004	2005	2006
保险机构	**Insurers**	**21**	**58**	**70**	**76**
外 资	Foreign-funded	12	19	24	24
中 资	Domestic-funded	9	39	46	52
财产险公司	Property Insurance Company		25	28	31
人寿险公司	Life Insurance Company		26	35	36
再保险公司	Reinsurance Company		3	3	3
保险中介机构	**Insurance Agents**	**1**	**110**	**157**	**205**

注：本表至表 16.19 的数据由中国保监委上海保监局提供。
Note: Data in table 16.17 to 16.19 are prorided by Shanghai Insurance Rrgulatory Bureau.

表 16.18 保险公司主要业务指标(2006)
MAJOR BUSINESS INDICATORS OF INSURANCE COMPANIES

单位：亿元(100 million yuan)

指 标	Indicators	保险金额 Sum Insured	保 费 Premium	赔款及给付 Compensation and Claims
总 计	**Total**		**407.04**	**91.31**
财产保险	**Property Insurance**	**194 849**	**101.33**	**45.17**
#企业财产险	Enterprise Property Insurance		13.74	4.18
家庭财产险	Household Property Insurance		0.62	0.23
机动车辆险	Motor Vehicles Insurance		52.33	29.31
责任险	Liability Insurance		10.47	4.00
人寿保险	**Liability Insurance**	**106 807**	**264.92**	**36.15**
健康险	Health Insurance		31.09	8.06
人身意外伤害险	Accidents Insurance		9.71	1.93

表 16.19 保险费收入和赔款及给付(2000~2006)
PREMIUM INCOME, COMPENSATION AND PAYMENT

年 份 Year	保险费收入(亿元) Premium Income (100 million yuan)	其 中 of which		赔款及给付支出(亿元) Compensation and Payment (100 millon yuan)	其 中 of which		赔付率(%) Compensation Ratio (%)
		#人寿保险 Liability Insurance	#财产保险 Property Insurance		#人寿保险 Liability Insurance	#财产保险 Property Insurance	
2000	127.23	92.14	35.09	36.44	20.56	15.88	28.5
2001	180.25	140.3	39.95	38.82	19.61	19.21	21.5
2002	237.61	193.3	44.31	49.97	28.38	21.59	21.0
2003	289.93	232.5	57.43	61.97	34.87	27.1	21.4
2004	307.11	231.3	75.81	70.86	36.79	34.07	23.1
2005	333.62	245.76	87.86	87.46	40.20	47.26	26.2
2006	407.04	305.72	101.33	91.31	46.14	45.17	22.4

上 / 海 / 统 / 计 / 年 / 鉴

主要统计指标解释

■ 存　款

是企业、机关、团体或居民等根据资金必须收回的原则，把货币资金存入银行或其他信用机构保管并取得一定利息的一种信用活动形式。根据存款对象的不同可划分为企业存款、财政存款、机关团体存款、储蓄存款等科目。它是银行信贷资金的主要来源。

■ 贷　款

是银行或其他信用机构根据资金必须归还的原则，按一定利率，为企业、个人等提供资金的一种信用活动形式。我国银行贷款分为短期贷款、中期流动资金贷款、中长期贷款、信托贷款以及工业贷款、商业贷款等科目。

■ 综合指数

以全部上市公司作为样本计算的股票价格指数。

■ 股票筹资额

上市公司发行股票所筹集的资金数量，等于股票发行量乘以发行价。

■ 保险公司

在中国境内的、经过保险监督管理部门批准设立，并依法登记注册的各类商业保险公司。

■ 保险金额

指保险人承担赔偿或者给付保险金责任的最高限额。

■ 保险费

是指投保人根据保险合同的有关规定，为保险受益人取得因保险事故发生所造成的经济损失予以补偿（或给付）权利，付给保险人的代价。包括财产险和人身险储金类支出。

■ 保险赔款及给付

指保险事故发生后，经查证确属保险责任范围以内的保险标的损失，保险人根据保险合同的规定履行赔偿义务，给予被保险人（或投保人指定的受益人）的款项。

SHANGHAI STATISTICAL YEARBOOK

EXPLANATORY NOTES TO MAJOR STATISTICAL INDICATORS

□ Deposits

Deposits are a form of credit by which enterprises, institutions, organizations or residents put money into banks and other credit institutions for safekeeping and earn interests under the principle of free withdrawal. According to different depositors, deposits are divided into enterprise deposits, treasury deposits, deposits of institutions and organizations, urban savings deposits and other deposits. Deposits constitute a major source of bank credit funds.

□ Loans

Loans are a form of credit by which banks and other credit institutions provide funds with a specified interest to enterprises and individuals under the principle of free repayment. Loans from Chinese banks include short term loans, medium term circulating capital loans, long term loans, trust loans, industrial loans and commercial loans.

□ Composite Index

Composite Index refers to stock price index taking all the listed companies as samples.

□ Raised Capital

Raised Capital refers to money raised by listed companies, i.e., volume of issued shares times the issue prices.

□ Insurance Companies

Insurance Companies refer to commercial insurance companies of various forms registered by law and established in China with the approval of insurance regulatory agencies.

□ Sum Insured

Sum Insured refers to the maximum that the insurant will get for the claim of the case insured.

□ Premium

Premium is the fee paid by the insurant to the insurer to obtain the obligation of compensation from the insurance within the agreed terms. It includes saving payment for property and life insurance.

□ Insurance Indemnity

Insurance Indemnity is the compensation paid by the insurer to the insurant or the beneficiary, when an accident has happened to the insured property or life and the loss has been investigated and verified to be within the insurance obligation.

第十七篇

CHAPTER 17

房地产业

REAL ESTATE

表 17.1 全社会房屋施工面积、竣工面积(1985～2006)
TOTAL FLOOR SPACE OF CONSTRUCTION AND COMPLETED BUILDINGS

年 份 Year	施工面积（万平方米） Floor Area of Construction (10 000 sq. m.)	其中 of which #住宅 Residential Housing	竣工面积（万平方米） Floor Area Completed (10 000 sq. m.)	其中 of which #住宅 Residential Housing	房屋建筑面积竣工率（%） Construction Completion Rate (%)	其中 of which #住宅 Residential Housing
1985	4 162.15	2 651.52	2 909.58	2 112.04	69.9	79.7
1986	4 874.44	2 469.27	2 493.93	1 790.01	51.2	72.5
1987	4 382.40	2 658.05	2 700.96	1 874.90	61.6	70.5
1988	4 369.20	2 667.00	2 457.34	1 758.29	56.2	65.9
1989	3 683.77	2 048.20	1 941.80	1 246.58	52.7	60.9
1990	3 801.46	2 269.06	2 138.44	1 339.02	56.3	59.0
1991	3 611.53	2 157.46	1 923.92	1 160.61	53.3	53.8
1992	4 709.52	2 463.79	2 608.20	1 379.18	55.4	56.0
1993	4 724.30	2 142.39	2 031.76	1 017.54	43.0	47.5
1994	6 720.70	3 520.27	2 519.09	1 349.24	37.5	38.3
1995	10 566.42	6 195.12	3 093.93	1 746.82	29.3	28.2
1996	10 730.85	5 874.26	3 254.57	1 872.65	30.3	31.9
1997	9 955.21	5 450.13	3 614.19	2 179.68	36.3	40.0
1998	9 364.36	5 113.52	3 364.43	1 963.51	35.9	38.4
1999	8 364.48	4 608.49	3 257.57	1 731.55	38.9	37.6
2000	8 636.31	4 804.12	3 266.52	1 724.02	37.8	35.9
2001	8 588.49	5 236.93	3 215.12	1 743.90	37.4	33.3
2002	9 425.42	5 994.70	3 102.54	1 880.50	32.9	31.4
2003	11 023.24	6 974.27	3 582.34	2 280.79	32.5	32.7
2004	12 291.81	7 873.44	4 932.57	3 270.43	40.1	41.5
2005	14 477.85	8 267.24	4 873.82	2 819.35	33.7	34.1
2006	14 596.49	8 085.28	4 901.46	2 746.80	33.6	34.0

表 17.2 住宅投资和竣工建筑面积(1978～2006)
INVESTMENT IN RESIDENTIAL HOUSING AND FLOOR SPACE OF BUILDINGS COMPLETED

年 份 Year	住宅投资额 (亿元) Investment in Residential Housing (100 million yuan)	占全社会固定资产投资总额比重(%) As Percentage of Total Investment in Fixed Asset	住宅竣工建筑面积 (万平方米) Floor Area of Residence Building Completed (10 000 sq. m.)	市区人均居住面积 (平方米) Dwelling Area per Capita (sq. m.)	市区人均使用面积 (平方米) Housing Area per Capita (sq. m.)
1978	1.79	7.4	199.61	4.5	
1979	2.23	6.9	215.99	4.3	
1980	4.24	10.4	304.32	4.4	
1981	9.87	18.1	1 380.70	4.5	
1982	10.95	15.3	1 363.63	4.7	
1983	11.16	14.7	1 347.79	4.9	
1984	15.72	17.0	1 788.44	5.0	
1985	25.18	21.2	2 112.04	5.4	7.5
1986	28.03	19.1	1 790.01	6.0	8.3
1987	35.79	19.2	1 874.90	6.2	8.6
1988	44.73	18.2	1 758.29	6.3	8.7
1989	34.67	16.1	1 246.58	6.4	8.9
1990	42.94	18.9	1 339.02	6.6	9.1
1991	48.92	18.9	1 160.61	6.7	9.3
1992	61.23	17.1	1 379.18	6.9	9.6
1993	77.14	11.8	1 017.54	7.3	10.1
1994	300.65	26.8	1 349.24	7.5	10.4
1995	433.76	27.1	1 746.82	8.0	11.1
1996	466.99	23.9	1 872.65	8.7	12.0
1997	458.22	23.2	2 179.68	9.3	12.9
1998	404.96	20.6	1 963.51	9.7	13.4
1999	378.82	20.4	1 731.55	10.9	15.1
2000	443.90	23.7	1 724.02	11.8	16.3
2001	466.71	23.4	1 743.90	12.5	17.3
2002	584.51	26.7	1 880.50	13.1	18.1
2003	694.30	28.3	2 280.79	13.8	19.0
2004	922.61	29.9	3 270.43	14.8	20.4
2005	936.36	26.4	2 819.35	15.5	21.3
2006	854.15	21.8	2 746.80	16.0	22.0

注：1981 年以前住宅投资额和住宅竣工建筑面积数据不包括城乡私人建房和农村投资，从 1981 年开始为全社会口径。
Note: Before 1981, investments and floor area of residential housing completed in this table don't cover private-built houses in urban and rural areas and rural investment, the whole society is covered since 1981.

表 17.3 主要年份房地产开发投资情况
INVESTMENT IN REAL ESTATE DEVELOPMENT IN MAIN YEARS

单位:亿元 (100 million yuan)

指 标	Indicators	1995	2000	2005	2006
投资总额	**Total Investment**	**466.20**	**566.17**	**1 246.86**	**1 275.59**
#商品房屋建设投资	Investment in Commodity Housing	286.45	476.32	1 094.42	1 153.71
土地开发投资	Investment in Land Development	53.19	25.91	65.66	63.36
在投资总额中	**Of Total Investment**				
住 宅	Residence	280.38	408.82	920.84	835.63
#别墅、高档公寓	Villas and Apartment	31.75	40.72	225.50	203.24
办公楼	Office Building	81.74	57.47	102.18	124.29
商业营业用房	Commercial Building	32.39	51.51	102.61	155.07
其 他	Others	71.69	48.38	121.23	160.60
新增固定资产	**Newly Increased Fixed Assets**	**151.06**	**477.39**	**1 054.02**	**1 058.94**
资金来源合计	**Total Capital Source**	**670.83**	**778.16**	**2 618.00**	**2 775.76**
上年末结余资金	Balance at End of Previous Year	112.00	113.48	628.12	598.87
本年资金来源小计	Sub-total Capital Source of this Year	558.83	664.68	1 989.88	2 176.89
国内贷款	Domestic Loans	122.63	155.37	483.03	575.10
利用外资	Foreign Capital Utilized	51.81	28.11	40.54	55.96
#外商直接投资	Foreign Direct Investment	34.87	16.24	15.22	51.30
自筹资金	Self-Financed Capital	214.53	211.86	527.78	577.98
其他资金	Other Capital	169.86	269.34	938.52	967.85

表 17.4 主要年份房地产开发企业房屋建筑面积和造价
CONSTRUCTION AREA AND COST OF PROPERTY DEVELOPED BY REAL ESTATE COMPANIES IN MAIN YEARS

	指 标 Indicators	1995	2000	2005	2006
房屋施工面积（万平方米）	**Floor Area of Construction (10 000 sq. m.)**	**5 074.80**	**5 523.23**	**10 462.39**	**10 938.75**
住 宅	Residence	3 843.22	4 263.50	8 091.85	7 988.73
# 别墅、高档公寓	Villas and Apartment	246.47	254.11	1 652.89	1 381.80
办公楼	Office Building	634.46	515.10	630.38	723.78
商业营业用房	Commercial Building	274.68	438.47	951.58	1 074.06
其 他	Others	322.44	306.16	788.58	1 152.18
房屋竣工面积（万平方米）	**Floor Area Completed (10 000 sq. m.)**	**700.39**	**1 643.62**	**3 095.74**	**3 274.27**
住 宅	Residence	529.77	1 388.01	2 739.91	2 699.11
# 别墅、高档公寓	Villas and Apartment	75.50	66.38	419.44	343.99
办公楼	Office Building	30.82	95.93	87.05	108.53
商业营业用房	Commercial Building	50.74	100.16	112.19	239.39
其 他	Others	89.06	59.52	156.59	227.24
房屋竣工价值(亿元)	**Value of Building Completed (100 million yuan)**	**102.55**	**355.79**	**946.77**	**1 011.31**
住 宅	Residence	72.21	270.29	811.02	799.75
# 别墅、高档公寓	Villas and Apartment	18.41	20.66	214.64	178.81
办公楼	Office Building	9.48	45.41	57.37	71.55
商业营业用房	Commercial Building	7.88	24.29	38.50	82.16
其 他	Others	12.99	15.80	39.88	57.85
竣工房屋平均造价（元/平方米）	**Average Construction Cost (yuan/sq. m.)**	**1 464**	**2 164**	**3 058**	**3 089**
住 宅	Residence	1 363	1 947	2 960	2 963
# 别墅、高档公寓	Villas and Apartment	2 438	3 112	5 117	5 198
办公楼	Office Building	3 075	4 733	6 591	6 593
商业营业用房	Commercial Building	1 552	2 425	3 432	3 432
其 他	Others	1 458	2 654	2 547	2 546

表 17.5 商品房屋建筑面积(2006) FLOOR AREA OF COMMODITY HOUSING

指 标	Indicators	合 计 Total	其 中 of which 内环线以内 Inside Inner-Ring	内、外环线间 Between Inner-Ring and Out-Ring	外环线以外 Outside Out-Ring
房屋施工面积(万平方米)	**Floor Area Under Construction (10 000 sq. m.)**	**10 938.75**	**1 950.73**	**3 490.05**	**5 497.98**
住 宅	Residence	7 988.73	978.99	2 517.45	4 492.29
# 别墅、高档公寓	Villas and Apartment	1 381.80	310.90	425.75	645.15
其他住宅	Other Residence	6 606.93	668.09	2 091.70	3 847.13
办公楼	Office Building	723.78	406.21	254.8	62.76
商业营业用房	Commercial Building	1 074.06	256.44	324.62	493.00
其 他	Others	1 152.19	309.08	393.18	449.93
新开工面积(万平方米)	**Floor Area Started (10 000 sq. m.)**	**2 781.34**	**244.19**	**828.85**	**1 708.30**
住 宅	Residence	2 112.10	102.50	614.04	1 395.56
# 别墅、高档公寓	Villas and Apartment	280.90	18.96	113.07	148.87
其他住宅	Other Residence	1 831.20	83.54	500.97	1 246.69
办公楼	Office Building	154.76	79.70	57.44	17.62
商业营业用房	Commercial Building	239.06	29.47	54.28	155.31
其 他	Others	275.42	32.52	103.09	139.81
房屋竣工面积(万平方米)	**Floor Area Completed (10 000 sq. m.)**	**3 274.27**	**372.160**	**1 096.75**	**1 805.35**
住 宅	Residence	2 699.11	242.08	909.58	1 547.46
# 别墅、高档公寓	Villas and Apartment	343.99	57.89	122.85	163.26
其他住宅	Other Residence	2 355.12	184.20	786.73	1 384.2
办公楼	Office Building	108.53	46.67	41.90	19.96
商业营业用房	Commercial Building	239.39	40.00	65.73	133.66
其 他	Others	227.23	43.41	79.55	104.27
房屋竣工价值(亿元)	**Value of Building Completed (100 million yuan)**	**1 011.31**	**152.45**	**336.53**	**522.34**
住 宅	Residence	799.75	82.90	265.05	451.79
# 别墅、高档公寓	Villas and Apartment	178.81	29.71	63.44	85.66
其他住宅	Other Residence	620.94	53.20	201.61	366.13

表 17.5 续表 continued

指　标	Indicators	合　计 Total	其中 of which 内环线以内 Inside Inner-Ring	内、外环线间 Between Inner-Ring and Out-Ring	外环线以外 Outside Out-Ring
办公楼	Office Building	71.55	31.87	27.01	12.68
商业营业用房	Commercial Building	82.16	20.86	23.71	37.59
其　他	Others	57.85	16.82	20.76	20.28
商品房销售面积（万平方米）	**Sold Area of Commodity Housing (10 000 sq. m.)**	**3 025.40**	**463.41**	**1 070.00**	**1 491.98**
住　宅	Residence	2 615.49	314.85	951.08	1 349.56
#别墅、高档公寓	Villas and Apartment	498.56	103.68	184.22	210.66
其他住宅	Other Residence	2 116.93	211.17	766.86	1 138.90
办公楼	Office Building	139.05	73.50	45.47	20.09
商业营业用房	Commercial Building	188.51	32.70	58.46	97.35
其　他	Others	82.35	42.37	14.99	24.99
商品房销售额（亿元）	**Sales Volume of Commodity Housing (100 million yuan)**	**2 177.08**	**459.72**	**809.36**	**908.00**
住　宅	Residence	1 841.04	309.27	718.25	813.53
#别墅、高档公寓	Villas and Apartment	540.19	126.72	201.75	211.72
其他住宅	Other Residence	1 300.85	182.55	516.50	601.80
办公楼	Office Building	167.95	101.96	46.67	19.31
商业营业用房	Commercial Building	122.13	23.05	37.33	61.75
其　他	Others	45.95	25.43	7.12	13.40
房屋出租面积（万平方米）	**Leasing Area of Buildings (10 000 sq. m.)**	**977.77**	**452.08**	**454.15**	**71.54**
住　宅	Residence	78.63	42.65	27.38	8.60
#别墅、高档公寓	Villas and Apartment	68.88	37.57	26.93	4.38
其他住宅	Other Residence	9.75	5.08	0.44	4.22
办公楼	Office Building	332.91	249.80	76.71	6.40
商业营业用房	Commercial Building	234.85	140.43	76.26	18.16
其　他	Others	331.39	19.20	273.80	38.38

表 17.6 主要年份商品房销售和出租情况
COMMODITY HOUSING SOLD AND LEASED IN MAIN YEARS

	指 标 Indicators	1995	2000	2005	2006
商品房销售面积（万平方米）	**Sold Area of Commodity Housing (10 000 sq. m.)**	**567.66**	**1 557.87**	**3 158.87**	**3 025.40**
住 宅	Residence	536.31	1 445.87	2 845.70	2 615.49
#别墅、高档公寓	Villas and Apartment	16.31	53.44	449.38	498.56
办公楼	Office Building	4.03	47.76	97.89	139.05
商业营业用房	Commercial Building	6.89	54.54	150.20	188.51
其 他	Others	20.43	9.70	65.09	82.35
商品房销售额（亿元）	**Sales Volume of Commodity Housing (100 million yuan)**	**146.01**	**555.45**	**2 161.30**	**2 177.08**
住 宅	Residence	132.83	480.97	1 906.05	1 841.04
#别墅、高档公寓	Villas and Apartment	10.98	32.65	390.05	540.19
办公楼	Office Building	2.28	44.05	116.17	167.95
商业营业用房	Commercial Building	2.85	27.87	106.65	122.13
其 他	Others	8.05	2.56	32.43	45.96
商品房出租面积（万平方米）	**Commodity Housing Leased (10 000 sq. m.)**	**50.95**	**358.38**	**889.63**	**977.77**
住 宅	Residence	18.34	59.29	94.44	78.63
#别墅、高档公寓	Villas and Apartment	2.61	37.43	61.55	68.88
办公楼	Office Building	7.34	156.15	300.04	332.91
商业营业用房	Commercial Building	11.19	62.04	204.53	234.85
其 他	Others	14.08	80.91	290.62	331.38

表 17.7 每百户城市居民家庭房屋产权构成(2004～2006)
PROPERTY RIGHT STRUCTURE OF TOWNSMAN TENEMENT PER HUNDRED HOUSEHOLDS

单位:%

	类 别 Types	2004	2005	2006
每百户城市居民家庭房屋产权构成	**Property Right Structure of Townsman Tenement per hundred households**	**100**	**100**	**100**
租赁公房	Leasehold Public Tenement	25.9	25.5	23.8
租赁私房	Leasehold Private Tenement	0.7	1.1	1.3
原有私房	Inhere Private Tenement	2.2	2.4	1.3
房改私房	Reformed Private Tenement	42.9	40.4	40.4
商品房	Commercial Tenement	27.8	30.5	32.4
其 他	Others	0.5	0.1	0.8

表 17.8 房屋拆迁情况(1995～2006) BUILDINGS RESETTLEMENT

年 份 Year	拆迁户数(户) Quantity of Resettlements (unit)	其中 of which #居民住宅 Residence	拆迁面积(万平方米) Floor Area Resettled (10 000 sq. m.)	其中 of which #居民住宅 Residence
1995	75 777	73 695	322.77	253.90
1996	89 132	86 481	342.95	258.86
1997	79 857	77 388	479.67	363.16
1998	78 205	75 157	452.22	343.94
1999	75 185	73 709	342.50	248.17
2000	70 606	68 293	365.77	288.35
2001	73 728	71 909	515.65	386.66
2002	101 097	98 714	644.53	485.00
2003	80 858	79 077	584.93	475.47
2004	42 415	41 552	308.40	232.52
2005	75 857	74 483	1 222.53	851.85
2006	81 126	76 874	1 516.85	848.35

①本表至表 17.11 数据由市房屋土地资源管理局提供。
②此表的统计范围为下表 10 个中心城区。 下表同。
❶Data in table 17.7 to 17.11 are provided by Shanghai Municipal Building and Land Administration Bureau.
❷The scope of statistics in this table is 10 central urban districts, same as the fllowing table, in which the names of districts are listed.

表 17.9 各区房屋拆迁情况(2006) BUILDINGS RESETTLEMENT IN DIFFERENT DISTRICTS

地 区	District	拆迁户数(户) Quantity of Resettlements (unit)	其中 of which #居民住宅 Residence	拆迁面积(万平方米) Floor Area Resettled (10 000 sq. m.)	其中 of which #居民住宅 Residence
总 计	**Total**	**81 126**	**76 874**	**1 516.85**	**848.35**
#浦东新区	Pudong New Area	12 484	12 297	338.94	268.21
黄 浦 区	Huangpu	9 940	9 395	48.82	36.46
卢 湾 区	Luwan	4 947	4 869	18.07	10.56
徐 汇 区	Xuhui	2 727	2 520	31.67	14.17
长 宁 区	Changning	1 628	1 466	20.13	9.07
静 安 区	Jing'an	2 308	2 253	9.54	7.58
普 陀 区	Putuo	3 903	3 812	43.74	15.33
闸 北 区	Zhabei	7 465	7 447	23.06	23.04
虹 口 区	Hongkou	5 320	4 795	24.95	16.59
杨 浦 区	Yangpu	6 637	6 637	16.93	16.93

表 17.10 主要年份土地使用权出让情况
LEASE OF LAND PLOT TENURE IN MAIN YEARS

指 标	Indicators	1995	2000	2005	2006
出让地块（幅）	**Leased Plot (piece)**	**499**	**1 325**	**1 539**	**2 611**
出让面积（万平方米）	**Leased Area (10 000 sq. m.)**	**1 245.42**	**2 183.22**	**6 491.34**	**7 680.13**
区	District	875.11	1 259.94	5 791.41	7 424.17
#浦东新区	Pudong New Area	646.76	534.29	555.00	546.25
县	County	370.31	923.28	144.93	255.96
可建面积（万平方米）	**Area Suitable for Construction (10 000 sq. m.)**	**1 343.99**	**3 502.73**	**6 699.04**	**8 398.51**
住 宅	Residence	887.60	1 912.31	3 299.54	1 987.06
商业服务	Commercial Service	1.27	92.96	516.47	295.07
工矿仓储	Storege of Industry	424.46	1 417.67	2 734.35	5 940.81
其 他	Others	30.66	79.79	148.68	175.57

注：1995 年以前为外销地块，2000 年起包括内销和外销地块。
Note: The figures before 1995 are of the plots leased to foreigners, and since 2000, the plots leased to domestic leases have been included.

表 17.11 存量房交易情况（1994～2006）
EXCHANGE OF SECOND - HAND HOUSES

年 份 Year	成交套数 （套） Houses Traded (set)	成交面积 （万平方米） Areas Traded (10 000 sq. m.)	其 中 of which		
			住 宅 Residence	办公楼 Office	商业营业用房 Commerce
1994	2 821	31.76	10.59		
1995	4 176	60.87	19.70		
1996	4 689	82.29	25.09		
1997	9 180	162.40	87.68	23.95	14.95
1998	24 501	315.23	197.56	21.49	18.28
1999	44 234	510.84	336.69	37.63	14.61
2000	96 348	778.52	648.23	39.48	21.65
2001	164 598	1 422.43	1 031.48	56.99	57.24
2002	204 239	1 790.50	1 341.60	65.70	91.80
2003	263 297	2 306.28	1 807.57	105.14	114.28
2004	303 291	2 726.70	2 222.24	117.12	121.39
2005	189 896	1 971.50	1 608.20	88.10	78.00
2006	184 194	1 706.81	1 375.22	67.35	46.53

表 17.12　各区县房地产开发建设和经营情况(2006)
INVESTMENT AND OPERATION IN REAL ESTATE DEVELOPMENT BY DISTRICTS AND COUNTY

单位:万平方米 (10 000 sq. m.)

地区	District	施工面积 Floor Area of Construction	竣工面积 Floor Area Completed	其中 of which #住宅 Residential Housing
全　市	**Total**	**10 938.75**	**3 274.27**	**2 699.11**
浦东新区	Pudong New Area	2 204.65	779.65	597.52
黄浦区	Huangpu	274.23	26.11	15.26
卢湾区	Luwan	93.14	28.96	20.71
徐汇区	Xuhui	378.11	85.68	69.49
长宁区	Changning	328.92	53.70	46.02
静安区	Jing'an	170.65	23.51	15.95
普陀区	Putuo	563.25	245.56	204.27
闸北区	Zhabei	239.00	64.64	57.98
虹口区	Hongkou	364.22	80.75	44.25
杨浦区	Yangpu	538.12	60.12	55.74
宝山区	Baoshan	1 231.3	384.52	341.52
闵行区	Minhang	866.65	263.95	239.83
嘉定区	Jiading	631.89	236.07	190.14
金山区	Jinshan	229.00	62.26	55.24
松江区	Songjiang	1 123.41	313.17	245.78
青浦区	Qingpu	367.94	136.7	95.56
南汇区	Nanhui	977.87	285.54	268.34
奉贤区	Fengxian	306.76	141.18	133.42
崇明县	Chongming	49.64	2.20	2.09

表 17.12 续表 continued

单位:万平方米 (10 000 sq. m.)

地　区 District		实际销售面积 Areas Sold	其中 of which #住宅 Residential Housing	实际销售额(亿元) Sales Volume (100 million yuan)	其中 of which #住宅 Residential Housing
全　市	**Total**	**3 025.40**	**2 615.49**	**2 177.08**	**1 841.04**
浦东新区	Pudong New Area	640.81	558.10	503.06	436.42
黄 浦 区	Huangpu	54.63	24.77	42.42	26.41
卢 湾 区	Luwan	17.22	10.89	17.29	13.88
徐 汇 区	Xuhui	87.11	77.72	90.05	77.47
长 宁 区	Changning	47.79	38.09	62.89	49.15
静 安 区	Jing'an	27.34	9.29	31.41	9.49
普 陀 区	Putuo	233.40	174.14	168.36	117.37
闸 北 区	Zhabei	86.34	83.27	70.43	67.11
虹 口 区	Hongkou	92.43	59.61	89.49	54.78
杨 浦 区	Yangpu	132.41	121.05	102.97	91.79
宝 山 区	Baoshan	345.35	322.98	231.38	212.83
闵 行 区	Minhang	227.36	220.79	143.30	138.81
嘉 定 区	Jiading	193.09	176.53	118.35	104.03
金 山 区	Jinshan	50.55	41.50	23.61	15.96
松 江 区	Songjiang	360.49	318.56	229.26	206.22
青 浦 区	Qingpu	114.90	87.96	85.32	67.75
南 汇 区	Nanhui	209.02	188.08	114.54	100.47
奉 贤 区	Fengxian	98.56	95.63	49.70	47.93
崇 明 县	Chongming	6.60	6.53	3.25	3.20

上 / 海 / 统 / 计 / 年 / 鉴

主要统计指标解释

■ 房地产开发投资

指各种登记注册类型的房地产开发公司、商品房建设公司及其他房地产开发法人单位和附属于其他法人单位实际从事房地产开发或经营活动的单位统一开发的包括统代建、拆迁还建的住宅、厂房、仓库、饭店、宾馆、度假村、写字楼、办公楼等房屋建筑物和配套的服务设施，土地开发工程(如道路、给水、排水、供电、供热、通讯、平整场地等基础设施工程)的投资；不包括单纯的土地交易活动。

■ 施工面积

指报告期内施工的全部房屋建筑面积。包括本期新开工的面积和上期开工跨入本期继续施工的房屋面积，以及上期已停建在本期恢复施工的房屋面积。本期竣工和本期施工后又停缓建的房屋，其建筑面积仍计入本期房屋施工面积中。

■ 竣工面积

指在报告期内房屋建筑按照设计要求已经全部完工，达到住人和使用条件，经验收鉴定合格(或达到竣工验收标准)，正式移交使用单位的各栋房屋建筑面积的总和。

■ 房屋建筑面积竣工率

指一定时期内房屋竣工面积占同期房屋施工面积的比率。该指标从房屋建筑施工速度的角度反映投资效果的指标。

■ 别墅、高档公寓

指建筑造价和销售价格明显高于一般商品住宅的商品住宅。别墅一般指地处郊区，独立成栋的商品住宅；高档公寓一般指地处市内高尚社区，高层或多层的商品住宅。别墅、高档公寓的确定标准：一是经有房地产投资计划审批权的主管部门审批建设的别墅、高档公寓开发项目；二是销售价格高于当地同等地段商品住宅平均销售价格一倍以上的别墅、公寓开发项目。该指标可以分析房地产投资结构，反映高收入家庭商品住宅的供求平衡情况。

SHANGHAI STATISTICAL YEARBOOK

EXPLANATORY NOTES TO MAJOR STATISTICAL INDICATORS

□ Investment in Real Estate Development

It includes the investment by the real estate development companies, commercial buildings construction companies and other real estate development units of various types of ownership in the construction of house buildings, such as residential buildings, factory buildings, warehouses, hotels, guesthouses, holiday villages, office buildings, and the complementary service facilities and land development projects, such as roads, water supply, water drainage, power supply, heating, telecommunications, land leveling and other projects of infrastructure. It excludes the activities in simple land transactions.

□ Floor Area of under Construction

Floor Area of Construction refers to total floor space of all buildings under construction during the reference period, including floor space of newly started buildings during the reference period, floor space of construction extended from the previous period to the current period, and floor space of construction suspended during the previous period and resumed in the current period. Floor space of construction completed in the current period, and floor space of construction started and then suspended in the current period are also included in the floor space under construction of the current year.

□ Floor Area Completed

Floor Area Completed refers to the floor space of all buildings completed in the reference period, which have been appraised and accepted(or come up to the designed standards) and have been transferred to the owners for use.

□ Completion Rate of Floor Space of Buildings

Completion Rate of Floor Space of Buildings refers to the ratio of the floor space of buildings completed in certain period of time to the floor space of buildings under construction in the same period. This indicator reflects the investment result from the perspective of the speed of construction.

□ Villas High–Grade Apartments

Villas, High–Grade Apartments refers to commercial houses whose construction costs and marketing prices are significantly higher than ordinary housing. Villas are independent structures generally located in the suburbs; high–grade apartments are multi–story buildings located in elegant urban neighborhoods. Criteria for villas and high–grade apartments include: 1) projects for the construction of villas or high–grade apartments have to be approved by competent departments in charge of real estate development and investment plans, and 2) prices for projects on villas or high–grade apartments are higher by over 100% compared with the average prices of ordinary commercial housing projects in similar location. This indicator helps to analyze the investment structure of the real estate industry and the demand and supply of housing for high–income households.

第十八篇

CHAPTER 18

科学技术

SCIENCE AND TECHNOLOGY

表 18.1　主要年份科技活动主要指标
MAIN INDICATORS OF SCIENTIFIC AND TECHNOLOGICAL ACTIVITIES IN MAIN YEARS

年　份 Year	科技活动机构数（个） Number of Scientific & Technological Research Institutions (unit)	科技活动人员（万人） Personnel Engaged in Scientific and Technological Activities (10 000 persons)	科技活动经费筹集总额（亿元） Funds Financed for Scientific and Technological Research (100 million yuan)	科技活动经费支出总额（亿元） Expenditures of Scientific and Technological Research (100 million yuan)
1980	551			
1985	816	15.12	19.91	13.37
1990	1 053	19.34	32.47	28.25
1995	1 266	18.25	122.49	114.22
1996	1 018	19.11	127.41	134.37
1997	1 133	17.99	153.77	165.61
1998	1 022	18.72	140.24	177.62
1999	915	16.25	153.05	198.00
2000	894	16.31	201.45	221.38
2001	826	15.19	218.18	247.22
2002	848	15.18	243.99	278.37
2003	839	15.07	274.25	304.48
2004	1 050	18.28	362.50	364.94
2005	1 114	19.67	453.94	419.34
2006	1 162	20.07	485.13	434.57

注：本表从 2003 年起包括高校的人文社科类数据。
Note: Starting from 2003, it includes data of humanities and social science of higher education.

表 18.2　主要年份研究与试验发展(R&D)经费与科技经费支出
EXPENDITURES ON R&D AND EXPENDITURES OF SCIENTIFIC AND TECHNOLOGICAL RESEARCH IN MAIN YEARS

年　份 Years	研究与试验发展经费支出(亿元) Expenditures on R&D (100 million yuan)	研究与试验发展经费支出相当于上海市生产总值比例(%) R&D as Percentage of Gross Domestic Product (%)	地方财政科技经费支出（亿元） Local Fiscal Expenditures of Scientific and Technological Research (100 million yuan)	科技经费支出占地方财政支出比重(%) Percentage of Expenditures on Scientific and Technological Research in Local Fiscal (%)
1978	1.32	0.48		
1980	2.04	0.65	1.38	7.2
1985	4.62	0.99	2.49	5.4
1990	10.13	1.36	2.44	3.2
1995	32.60	1.30	5.12	2.0
1996	40.96	1.38	5.63	1.7
1997	49.76	1.45	7.65	1.8
1998	55.69	1.47	8.28	1.7
1999	63.75	1.52	10.82	2.0
2000	76.73	1.61	10.08	1.6
2001	88.08	1.69	12.39	1.7
2002	102.36	1.78	15.25	1.7
2003	128.92	1.93	19.84	1.8
2004	170.28	2.11	39.32	2.8
2005	213.77	2.33	79.34	4.8
2006	256.78	2.48	94.89	5.2

①本表数据由上海市财政局提供。
②研究与试验发展经费支出为全社会口径。
③2004 年起地方财政科技经费支出口径范围扩大至其他系统(包括区县)财政安排的事业费中对科技的支出。
❶Data in this table are provided by Shanghai Municipal Finance Bureau.
❷Expenditures in R&D cover the total society.
❸Since 2004, the scope of Local Fiscal Expenditures of Scientific and Technological Research has extended to other expenditures on science and technology arranged by finance department of other economy(including districts and counties).

表 18.3 主要年份科技活动基本情况
BASIC STATISTICS OF SCIENTIFIC AND TECHNOLOGICAL ACTIVITIES IN MAIN YEARS

指标	Indicators	2000	2002	2005	2006
科技机构数（个）	**Number of Scientific and Technological Research Institutions (unit)**	**1 232**	**1 127**	**1 114**	**1 162**
#科研机构	Research Institutions	304	281	266	262
高等院校	Institutions of Higher Education	326	346	225	237
大中型工业企业	Large and Medium Industrial Enterprises	264	247	326	355
科技活动人员数（万人）	**Personnel Engaged in Scientific and Technological Activities (10 000 persons)**	**20.17**	**17.89**	**19.67**	**20.07**
#科学家、工程师	Scientists and Engineers	13.36	12.56	14.55	15.04
科技活动经费筹集总额（亿元）	**Funds for Scientific and Technological Research (100 million yuan)**	**247.14**	**278.32**	**453.94**	**485.13**
政府资金	Government Allocation	46.90	62.77	99.60	100.63
事业资金	Undertaking Funds	17.65	12.70	9.90	7.35
企业资金	Self-raised Funds	146.68	181.12	324.22	323.50
银行贷款	Bank Loans	22.42	11.38	6.73	34.30
其他收入	Others	13.49	10.35	13.49	19.35
科技活动经费支出总额（亿元）	**Expenditures of Scientific and Technological Research Funds (100 million yuan)**	**221.38**	**272.93**	**419.34**	**434.57**
#劳务费	Service Fees	52.02	64.62	86.80	97.20
固定资产购建费	Purchasing Fixed Assets	38.68	68.12	106.14	107.98
#研究与试验发展经费支出	**Expenditures on R&D**	**76.73**	**102.36**	**213.77**	**256.78**
基础研究	Basic Research	4.79	7.02	10.64	14.00
应用研究	Applied Research	17.53	23.31	32.33	40.98
试验发展	Experimental Development	54.41	72.03	170.80	201.80
科技成果登记数(项)	**Number of Achievements Registered in Scientific and Technological Activities(item)**	**1 102**	**1 338**	**1 701**	**1 953**
科技成果获奖数(项)	**Number of Achievements Awarded(item)**	**287**	**344**	**362**	**351**
#国家科技成果奖	National Award for Achievements in Science and Technology	21	31	44	42
上海科技进步奖	Shanghai Scientific and Technological Progress Prize	266	313	318	309
专利申请受理量(件)	**Patent Applications(piece)**	11 318	12 777	32 741	36 042
专利申请授权量(件)	**Patent Certified(piece)**	4 048	5 371	12 603	16 602

①本表为全社会口径。
②科研机构统计范围包括区县级及以上的科技机构数，高等院校包括理工农医类和人文社科类科技机构数。
③ 本表部分数据由上海市科委以及市知识产权局提供。
❶All the indicators of this table cover the total society.
❷The statistical scale of Research Institutions include those of districts and counties and above. Institutions of Higher education include the institutions of Science, Engineering, Agriculture, Medicine Science, Humanities and Social Science.
❸Part of the data in this table are provided by Shanghai Science and Technology Commission and Shanghai Intellectual Property Bureau.

表 18.4 主要年份国有企事业单位各类专业人员
PROFESSIONAL AND TECHNICAL PERSONNEL IN STATE-OWNED ENTERPRISES AND INSTITUTIONS IN MAIN YEARS

单位:万人(10 000 persons)

类别	Types	1990	2000	2005	2006
总　计	**Total**	**86.16**	**71.03**	**71.99**	**72.72**
工程技术人员	Engineering	26.30	17.07	19.60	19.65
农业技术人员	Agriculture	0.37	0.31	0.30	0.22
科学研究人员	Scientific Research	2.55	1.76	1.62	1.82
卫生技术人员	Medical Professionals	9.07	9.00	9.22	9.11
教学人员	Teaching	20.12	16.55	16.42	16.41
经济人员	Economic	14.07	10.17	11.94	12.92
财会人员	Financial Accounting	7.46	7.63	6.46	6.57
统计人员	Statistical	1.76	0.78	0.66	0.62
翻译人员	Translator	0.41	0.21	0.17	0.16
新闻出版、播音人员	Media and Publishing	0.55	0.59	0.77	0.77
艺术人员	Art Personnel	0.55	0.40	0.49	0.44
其他专业人员	Others	2.95	6.56	4.34	4.03
在总计中:高级专业人员	**Of Total:Senior and Intermediate**	**4.72**	**6.43**	**7.31**	**7.55**
工程技术人员	Engineering	2.05	2.17	2.16	2.17
农业技术人员	Agriculture	0.01	0.02	0.04	0.03
科学研究人员	Scientific Research	0.51	0.55	0.58	0.63
卫生技术人员	Medical Professionals	0.38	0.64	0.86	0.89
教学人员	Teaching	0.90	1.96	2.44	2.60
经济人员	Economic	0.10	0.32	0.43	0.45
财会人员	Financial Accounting	0.04	0.08	0.11	0.12
统计人员	Statistical	…	0.01	0.01	0.01
新闻出版、播音人员	Media and Publishing	0.07	0.12	0.13	0.14
翻译人员	Translator	0.02	0.02	0.14	0.01
艺术人员	Art Personnel	0.12	0.12	0.11	0.12
其他专业人员	Others	0.52	0.33	0.30	0.38
平均每万职工拥有专业技术人员(人)	**Professional and Technical Personnel Per 10 000 Employees(person)**	**2 169**	**3 099**	**4 630**	**4 968**

注:本表至表 18.6 数据由市委组织部提供。
Note: Data in this table to table 19.6 are provided by the Organization Department of Shanghai Committee of the Commist Party of China.

表 18.5 国有企事业单位各类专业人员(2006)
PROFESSIONAL AND TECHNICAL PERSONNEL IN STATE-OWNED ENTERPRISES AND INSTITUTIONS

单位:万人(10 000 persons)

类别	Types	合计 Total	其中 of which #女性 Female	按专业技术职务分 By Profession 高级 Senior	中级 Medium	初级 Junior	未聘 Not Appointed
总计	**Total**	**72.72**	**33.52**	**7.55**	**26.10**	**28.30**	**10.77**
工程技术人员	Engineering	19.65	4.18	2.17	6.46	7.49	3.53
农业技术人员	Agriculture	0.22	0.06	0.03	0.07	0.11	0.01
科学研究人员	Scientific Research	1.82	0.64	0.63	0.64	0.40	0.15
卫生技术人员	Medical Professionals	9.11	6.60	0.89	2.49	5.40	0.33
教学人员	Teaching	16.41	10.50	2.60	8.65	4.63	0.53
经济人员	Economic	12.92	4.84	0.45	3.71	4.29	4.47
财会人员	Financial Accounting	6.57	4.24	0.12	1.85	3.85	0.75
统计人员	Statistical	0.62	0.37	0.01	0.14	0.27	0.20
翻译人员	Translator	0.16	0.08	0.01	0.07	0.05	0.03
新闻出版、播音人员	Media, Publishing & Announcer	0.77	0.36	0.14	0.28	0.24	0.11
艺术人员	Culture & Art	0.44	0.15	0.12	0.16	0.12	0.04
其他专业人员	Others	4.03	1.50	0.38	1.58	1.45	0.62

表 18.5 续表 continued

单位:万人(10 000 persons)

类别	Types	按学历分 By Education Background 大学本专科及以上 College and university above	中等专业 Specialized Secondary School	高中及以下 Senior Middle School and below	按年龄分 By Age 45岁及以下 45 and below	46~54岁 46~54	55岁及以上 55 and above
总计	**Total**	**57.06**	**10.64**	**5.02**	**52.45**	**15.33**	**4.94**
工程技术人员	Engineering	15.65	2.24	1.76	14.81	3.55	1.29
农业技术人员	Agriculture	0.15	0.05	0.02	0.16	0.04	0.02
科学研究人员	Scientific Research	1.68	0.07	0.07	1.32	0.35	0.15
卫生技术人员	Medical Professionals	5.31	3.59	0.21	6.53	2.32	0.26
教学人员	Teaching	15.24	0.99	0.18	12.55	2.55	1.31
经济人员	Economic	9.86	1.56	1.50	9.09	2.85	0.98
财会人员	Financial Accounting	4.67	1.34	0.56	4.95	1.44	0.18
统计人员	Statistical	0.37	0.15	0.10	0.41	0.18	0.03
翻译人员	Translator	0.16	…	…	0.09	0.06	0.01
新闻出版、播音人员	Media, Publishing & Announcer	0.72	0.02	0.03	0.52	0.17	0.08
艺术人员	Culture & Art	0.23	0.12	0.09	0.23	0.14	0.07
其他专业人员	Others	3.02	0.51	0.50	1.79	1.68	0.56

表 18.6 集体经济单位各类专业人员（2006）
PROFESSIONAL AND TECHNICAL PERSONNEL IN OTHER ECONOMIC ORGANS

单位：人(person)

类别	Types	合计 Total	其中 of which #女性 Female	按专业技术职务分 By Professional Titles 高级 Senior	中级 Medium	初级 Junior	未聘 Not Appointed
总计	**Total**	**27 387**	**14 025**	**570**	**7 266**	**18 501**	**1 050**
工程技术人员	Engineering	2 856	455	116	1 036	1 580	124
农业技术人员	Agriculture	1 453	175	14	521	851	67
科学研究人员	Scientific Research	15	4	2	5	6	2
卫生技术人员	Medical Professionals	14 028	9 714	249	3 243	10 405	131
教学人员	Teaching	335	215	1	81	253	
其他专业人员	Others	8 700	3 462	188	2 380	5 406	726

表 18.6 续表 continued

单位：人(person)

类别	Types	按学历分 By Education Background 高等院校 Higher Education	中等专业 Specialized Secondary School	高中及以下 Senior Middle School and below	按年龄分 By Age 45岁及以下 45 and below	46～55岁 46～55	55岁及以上 55 and above
总计	**Total**	**12 421**	**10 171**	**4 795**	**14 494**	**10 378**	**2 515**
工程技术人员	Engineering	1 413	586	857	1 526	891	439
农业技术人员	Agriculture	347	534	572	494	660	299
科学研究人员	Scientific Research	8	2	5	6	7	2
卫生技术人员	Medical Professionals	6 385	6 486	1 157	8 195	5 146	687
教学人员	Teaching	154	154	27	193	109	33
其他专业人员	Others	4 114	2 409	2 177	4 080	3 565	1 055

注：本表包括集体事业和企业单位人数。
Note: The figures include employees at collective and public service organizations and enterprises.

表 18.7 各类技术合同项目（1991～2006）
VARIOUS TECHNOLOGICAL CONTRACTS

单位：项(item)

年 份 Year	项 目 Item	其 中 of which 技术开发 Technological Development	技术转让 Technological Transfer	技术咨询 Technological Consulting	技术服务 Technological Service
1991	25 023	3 038	1 992	3 203	16 790
1992	32 731	3 501	2 159	4 200	22 871
1993	25 507	2 517	1 389	3 671	17 930
1994	25 099	2 368	941	4 215	17 575
1995	21 213	1 915	775	3 672	14 851
1996	20 074	1 841	823	3 821	13 589
1997	18 863	1 643	1 037	3 569	12 614
1998	18 364	1 206	919	3 235	13 004
1999	19 721	1 158	937	3 993	13 633
2000	20 974	1 561	888	3 905	14 620
2001	23 816	2 385	1 294	5 012	15 125
2002	26 010	2 984	1 156	4 983	16 887
2003	27 292	3 512	2 112	5 306	16 362
2004	27 327	4 398	2 453	4 814	15 662
2005	30 290	5 256	2 444	4 753	17 837
2006	28 191	6 165	2 172	3 592	16 262

注：表 18.7 至表 18.8 数据由市技术市场管理办公室提供。
Note: Data in table 18.7 to table 18.8 are provided by Shanghai Technology Market Administrative Office.

表 18.8 各类技术合同成交金额（1991～2006）
TOTAL CONTRACTED VALUE IN VARIOUS TECHNOLOGICAL CONTRACTS

单位：亿元(100 million yuan)

年 份 Year	成交金额 Contracted Value	其 中 of which 技术开发 Technological Development	技术转让 Technological Transfer	技术咨询 Technological Consulting	技术服务 Technological Service
1991	9.33	2.15	1.90	0.55	4.72
1992	15.25	3.56	1.33	0.99	9.37
1993	20.32	3.03	2.00	2.16	13.13
1994	22.09	3.31	1.08	2.08	15.62
1995	23.04	4.14	1.57	2.12	15.21
1996	25.65	4.38	1.50	2.81	16.97
1997	28.76	5.72	2.14	3.28	17.61
1998	31.41	4.55	2.58	2.44	21.85
1999	36.63	3.68	3.50	3.24	26.21
2000	73.90	9.96	36.44	3.51	23.99
2001	106.16	28.24	50.71	4.63	22.58
2002	120.22	45.40	46.18	4.63	24.01
2003	142.78	50.96	50.79	6.11	34.92
2004	171.70	61.31	42.32	6.00	62.07
2005	231.73	87.47	110.08	6.42	27.76
2006	344.43	142.79	165.18	7.60	28.86

表 18.9 科技成果（1994～2006）
ACHIEVEMENTS IN SCIENTIFIC AND TECHNICAL RESEARCH

单位：项（item）

年 份 Year	科技成果 Achievements in Science and Technology	按成果水平分 By Level of Achievements				
		国际领先 Being First Created in the World	国际先进 Attaining Advanced World Levels	国内领先 Being First Created in China	国内先进 Attaining Advanced Domestic Levels	其 他 Others
1994	1 715	9	386	677	643	
1995	1 350	6	326	525	470	23
1996	1 094	10	348	477	234	25
1997	1 193	8	434	538	181	32
1998	1 305	30	494	539	210	32
1999	1 252	41	457	536	193	25
2000	1 102	45	462	452	117	26
2001	1 338	78	542	444	116	158
2002	1 418	65	603	463	106	181
2003	1 508	71	532	481	155	269
2004	1 629	147	669	480	155	178
2005	1 701	123	629	588	189	172
2006	1 953	250	675	655	191	182

表 18.9 续表 continued

单位：项（item）

年 份 Year	按成果分 By Type of Achievements			按推广应用分 By Populization	
	基础理论成果 Fundamental Theory Research Results	应用技术成果 Application of Technological Achievements	软科学成果 Soft Scientific Achievements	已推广应用 Been Populized	未应用 Not Been Populized
1997	118	978	97	959	234
1998	156	1 036	113		
1999	80	1 054	118	835	219
2000	79	953	70	809	293
2001	81	1 196	61	940	256
2002	110	1 250	58	961	289
2003	97	1 281	130	1 045	236
2004	70	1 488	71	1 204	284
2005	61	1 555	85	1 261	294
2006	52	1 799	102	1 506	293

注：本表数据由市科学技术委员会提供。
Note: Data in this table are provided by Shanghai Science and Technology Commission. (the same to the next table)

表 18.10 主要年份获得科技成果奖励情况
ACHIEVEMENTS AWARDED IN SCIENTIFIC AND TECHNOLOGICAL RESEARCH IN MAIN YEARS

单位：项（item）

指 标	Indicators	1995	2000	2005	2006
一、科技成果获奖总数	**Number of Achievements Awarded**	**335**	**287**	**362**	**351**
1. 获国家科技成果奖	National Award	59	21	44	42
#国家科学技术进步奖	Science and Technology Progress Award	45	17	34	33
国家技术发明奖	Technological Invention Award	7	1	3	5
国家自然科学奖	Natural Science Award	7	3	7	4
2. 获上海科技进步奖	Shanghai Award	276	266	318	309

表 18.11 主要年份专利申请量
PATENT APPLICATIONS IN MAIN YEARS

单位：件(item)

指 标	Indicators	1990	2000	2005	2006
总 计	**Total**	**1 526**	**11 337**	**32 741**	**36 042**
按种类分	**By Type of Patents**				
发 明	Inventions	297	4 713	10 441	12 050
实用新型	Utility Models	1 049	2 760	8 711	9 881
外观设计	Exterior Designs	180	3 864	13 589	14 111
按对象分	**By Applicant**				
非职务发明创造	Non-position Patents	846	2 137	4 829	5 384
职务发明创造	Position Patents	680	9 200	27 912	30 658
大专院校	Universities and Colleges	87	618	2 955	3 066
科研单位	Research Institutions	153	613	1 522	1 428
工矿企业	Industrial and Mining Enterprises	354	7 936	22 880	24 835
机关团体	Government Agencies and Organizations	86	33	555	1 329

注：本表由市知识产权局提供(下同)。
Note: Data in this table are provided by Shanghai Intellectual Property Bureau (the same to the next table).

表 18.12 主要年份专利授权量
PATENTS CERTIFIED IN MAIN YEARS

单位：件(item)

指 标	Indicators	1990	2000	2005	2006
总 计	**Total**	**924**	**4 050**	**12 603**	**16 602**
按种类分	**By Type of Patents**				
发 明	Inventions	99	304	1 997	2 644
实用新型	Utility Models	769	2 083	4 437	6 739
外观设计	Exterior Designs	56	1 663	6 169	7 219
按对象分	**By Applicant**				
非职务发明创造	Non-position Patents	502	1 516	2 222	2 360
职务发明创造	Position Patents	422	2 534	10 381	14 242
大专院校	Universities and Colleges	81	183	1 096	1 586
科研单位	Research Institutions	145	215	645	864
工矿企业	Industrial and Mining Enterprises	156	2 101	8 486	11 503
机关团体	Government Agencies and Organizations	40	35	154	289

表 18.13 主要年份研究与试验发展(R&D)经费按执行部门分类
EXPENDITURES ON R&D GROUPED BY EXECUTIVE DEPARTMENT IN MAIN YEARS

单位:亿元(100 million yuan)

指 标	Indicators	2000	2005	2006
总 计	**Total**	**76.73**	**213.77**	**256.78**
科研机构	Research Institutions	25.58	44.91	52.07
高等院校	Institutions of Higher Education	7.43	23.72	26.51
企 业	Enterprises	41.44	143.86	177.07
#工业企业	Industrial Enterprises	34.78	125.76	161.43
#大中型工业企业	Large and Medium Industrial Enterprises	30.98	111.52	133.80
其 他	Others	2.28	1.28	1.13

注：本表数据由上海市财政局提供。
Note: Data in this table are provided by Shanghai Municipal Finance Bureau.

表 18.14 主要年份自然科学研究与技术开发机构课题情况
PROJECTS OF NATURAL SCIENCE RESEARCH AND TECHNOLOGICAL DEVELOPMENT INSTITUTIONS IN MAIN YEARS

年 份 Year	机构数 (个) Number of Institutions (unit)	课题数 (项) Number of Projects (item)	投入经费 (万元) Funds Invested (10 000 yuan)	投入人力 (人年) Manpower Input (person-year)	其 中 of which #科学家和工程师 Scientists and Engineers
1985	220	6 398	21 235	22 349	
1990	229	8 339	33 061	23 279	16 292
1991	231	8 504	37 736	23 970	17 402
1992	232	8 909	53 501	23 924	17 487
1993	230	6 926	54 480	20 489	14 951
1994	229	6 268	66 158	17 023	13 275
1995	230	6 544	80 957	17 531	13 811
1996	233	5 538	90 504	17 434	14 465
1997	232	5 481	117 199	17 507	14 453
1998	230	5 554	122 513	16 713	13 466
1999	225	5 135	125 620	16 396	13 360
2000	229	4 879	148 846	17 104	13 569
2001	221	4 468	210 910	16 972	13 821
2002	218	4 393	251 837	15 523	11 710
2003	216	4 473	282 865	17 058	11 849
2004	212	4 540	330 063	17 299	12 045
2005	206	4 416	425 266	18 924	12 542
2006	202	4 585	494 657	19 008	12 905

注：本表数据由市科学技术委员会提供。
Note: Data in this table are provided by Shanghai Science and Technology Commission.

表 18.15 自然科学研究与技术开发机构课题情况(2006)
STATISTICS OF PROJECTS OF NATURAL SCIENCE RESEARCH AND DEVELOPMENT INSTITUTIONS

类别	Types	机构数(个) Number of Institutions (unit)	课题数(项) Number of Projects (item)	投入经费(万元) Funds Invested (10 000 yuan)	投入人力(人年) Manpower Input (person-year)
总计	**Total**	**202**	**4 585**	**494 657**	**19 008**
按学科分	**Grouped by Subject**				
自然科学	Natural Science	17	1 623	71 653	1 953
农业科学	Agriculture Science	19	451	8 068	684
医学科学	Medical Science	16	355	12 100	885
工程科学与技术	Engineering Science and Technology	146	2 128	402 642	15 430
社会与人文科学	Social Science and Humanities	4	28	194	56
按行业分	**By Sector**				
制造业	Manufacturing	112	1 452	312 679	11 657
建筑业	Construction	4	91	1 181	205
交通运输、仓储和邮政业	Transportation, Warehousing and Post	4	22	329	73
科学研究、技术服务和地质勘查业	Scientific Research, Technical Service and Geological Prospecting	39	2 033	150 915	4 981
水利、环境和公共设施管理业	Water Conservancy, Environment and Public Facility Management	8	188	4 388	365
卫生、社会保障和社会福利业	Health, Social Security and Welfare	13	303	6 763	609
文化、体育和娱乐业	Culture, Sports and Entertainment	2	31	6 705	371

注：本表数据由市科学技术委员会提供(下表同)。
Note: Data in this table are provided by Shanghai Science and Technology Commission. (the same to next table)

表 18.16 自然科学研究与技术开发机构论文与著作情况 (2006)
PAPERS AND WORKS OF NATURAL SCIENCE RESEARCH AND TECHNOLOGICAL DEVELOPMENT INSTITUTIONS

类别	Types	论文(篇) Papers (piece)	其中 of which #国外发表 Published Abroad	科技著作(种) Scientific and Technological Works (sort)
总计	**Total**	**6 659**	**2 166**	**88**
按学科领域分	**Grouped by the Domain of Subject**			
自然科学	Natural Science	2 639	1 476	18
农业科学	Agriculture Science	603	16	21
医学科学	Medical Science	900	113	13
工程科学与技术	Engineering Science and Technology	2 516	561	34
社会与人文科学	Social and Humanities Science	1		2
按行业分	**By Sector**			
#农、林、牧、渔业	Farming, Forestry, Animal Husbandry and Fishery	575	22	17
制造业	Manufacturing	1 509	291	30
电力、燃气及水的生产和供应业	Electric Power, Steam and Water Production and Supply	31		
建筑业	Construction	171	7	6
科学研究、技术服务和地质勘查业	Scientific Research, Technical Service and Geological Prospecting	3 448	1 736	17
卫生、社会保障和社会福利业	Health, Social Security and Welfare	736	103	10

表 18.17 主要年份区县级以上国有单位独立研究与开发机构从事科技活动的科学家和工程师
SCIENTISTS AND ENGINEERS ENGAGED IN SCIENTIFIC AND TECHNOLOGICAL ACTIVITIES OF STATE-OWNED INDEPENDENT RESEARCH AND DEVELOPMENT INSTITUTIONS ABOVE DISTRICT AND COUNTY LEVEL IN MAIN YEARS

单位：人(person)

类 别	Types	1990	2000	2005	2006
总 计	**Total**	**40 962**	**25 699**	**23 233**	**23 299**
按隶属关系分	**Grouped by Subordination**				
中国科学院	The Chinese Academy of Science	6 091	3 810	2 973	2 907
国务院部门	Departments of the State Council	19 261	13 129	6 897	13 043
地 方	Local	15 610	8 760	13 363	7 349
按领域分	**By Subjects**				
自然科学	Natural Science	39 130	24 160	21 631	21 584
科技信息文献	Scientific & Technological Information & Documents	754	732	784	875
社会与人文科学	Social Sciences and Humanities	1 078	807	818	840

注：本表及表 18.18 数据由市科学技术委员会提供。
Note: Data in this table and table 18.18 are provieded by Shanghai Science and Technology Commission.

表 18.18 区县级以上国有单位独立研究与开发机构人员(2006)
PERSONNEL OF STATE-OWNED INDEPENDENT RESEARCH AND DEVELOPMENT INSTITUTIONS ABOVE DISTRICT AND COUNTY LEVEL

单位：人(person)

类 别	Types	从事科技活动人员 Personnel Engaged in Scientific and Technological Activities	其中 of which			
			#科学家和工程师 Scientists and Engineers	#研究生 Post-graduates	#大 学 University and College	#大 专 Specialized Institutions of Higher Education
总 计	**Total**	**36 857**	**23 299**	**6 591**	**14 403**	**6 833**
按隶属关系分	**Grouped by Subordination**					
中国科学院	The Chinese Academy of Science	3 793	2 907	1 544	1 128	494
国务院部门	Departments of the State Council	22 318	13 043	3 021	9 160	3 727
地 方	Local	10 746	7 349	2 026	4 115	2 612
按领域分	**By Subject**					
自然科学	Natural Science	34 557	21 584	5 956	13 635	6 247
科技情报文献	Scientific & Technological Information & Documents	1 249	875	133	470	398
社会与人文科学	Social Sciences and Humanities	1 051	840	502	298	188

表 18.19 主要年份区县级属研究与开发机构状况
RESEARCH AND DEVELOPMENT INSTITUTIONS AT DISTRICT AND COUNTY LEVEL IN MAIN YEARS

指标	Indicators	1990	2000	2005	2006
机构数（个）	Number of Institutions (unit)	28	35	21	21
从业人员（人）	Number of Employees (person)	1 175	1 261	1 033	1 020
#科学家和工程师	Scientists and Engineers	339	504	346	332
技术员	Technicians	378	198	352	363
经费支出（万元）	Expenditures (10 000 yuan)	770	7 343	14 665	10 564

表 18.20 主要年份民营科技企业状况
SCIENTIFIC AND TECHNOLOGICAL RESEARCH INSTITUTIONS RUN BY LOCAL PEOPLE IN MAIN YEARS

指标	Indicators	2000	2005	2006
机构数（个）	**Number of Institutions (unit)**	**12 316**	**16 128**	**15 131**
#集体单位	Collective-owned Units	1 401	539	369
从业人员（万人）	**Employment (10 000 persons)**	**26**	**54**	**62**
#从事科技活动人员	Scientific & Technological Personnel	13	19	22
#科学家和工程师	Scientists & Engineers	9	11	12
技术员	Technicians	4	8	10
总产值(亿元)	Gross Output Value(100 million yuan)	311	2 961	3 517
利润总额(亿元)	Total Pre-tax Profits(100 million yuan)	48	193	240
税金总额(亿元)	Total Tax and Duties(100 million yuan)	29	166	215
创汇(亿美元)	Foreign Exchange Income (100 million USD)	3	96	133
资产总额(亿元)	Total Assets(100 million yuan)	1 064	4 087	5 074
科技投入(亿元)	Input Value of Science and Technology (100 million yuan)	34.00	60.89	114.46
总收入（亿元）	Revenue(100 million yuan)	811	4 140	5 024
总支出（亿元）	Expenditures (100 million yuan)	713	3 829	4 639
专利申请量(件)	Patent Applications(piece)	452	8 010	9 048
专利授权量(件)	Patent Certified(piece)	1 169	3 970	4 111

①本表统计范围是指经上海市科委确认的独立核算国有、集体、个体、私营以及国有与集体联营等科技经营机构。
②"科技投入"2005 年按照国家规定的"科学研究与试验发展经费"口径填报。
❶Figures of Scientific and Technological Institutions in this table are the enterprises with independent accounting systems such as state-owned, collective-owned, individual, private and state-collective joint units certified by Shanghai Science and Technology Commission.
❷Data of Input Value of Science and Technology in 2005 are reported according to the scope of science research and experiment development which are authorized by the country.

表 18.21 高等学校科技活动人员（2006）
SCIENTIFIC AND TECHNOLOGICAL PERSONNEL OF INSTITUTIONS OF HIGHER EDUCATION

单位：人(person)

指 标	Indicators	合 计 Total	其 中 of which #自然科学 Natural Science	#工程与技术 Engineering and Technology	#医学科学 Medical Science	#农业科学 Agriculture Science	#其 他 Others
总 计	**Total**	**26 701**	**3 288**	**8 729**	**11 394**	**230**	**3 060**
按职称分	**By Professional Title**						
高 级	Senior	9 150	1 676	3 603	3 233	103	535
中 级	Medium	9 966	1 142	3 541	4 086	55	1 142
初 级	Junior	6 448	340	1 302	3 818	71	917
按技术等级分	**By Technical Level**						
#科学家和工程师	Scientists and Engineers	25 564	3 158	8 446	11 137	229	2 594

①本表至表 18.23 数据由市教育委员会提供。
②本表统计范围是指高等学校中理工农医类口径。
❶Data in this table to table 18.23 are provided by Shanghai Education Commission.
❷Figures of scientific and technological personnel in this table refer to those of science, engineering, agriculture.

表 18.22 主要年份高等学校研究与开发状况
R&D BY INSTITUTIONS OF HIGHER EDUCATION IN MAIN YEARS

指 标	Indicators	1990	2000	2005	2006
科技活动机构数（个）	**R&D Institutions (unit)**	**370**	**326**	**173**	**178**
科技活动人员数（人）	**Technological Personnel (person)**	**53 013**	**49 402**	**23 792**	**26 701**
自然科学	Natural Science	7 901	5 012	2 600	3 288
工程与技术	Engineering and Technology	17 976	15 854	8 109	8 729
医学科学	Medical Science	12 116	15 817	10 210	11 394
农业科学	Agriculture Science	415	441	192	230
社会与人文科学	Social Science and Humanities	9 199	8 994		
其 他	Others	5 406	3 284	2 681	3 060
R&D 人员数（人年）	**R&D Personnel (person-Year)**	**18 658**	**13 526**	**11 751**	**13 517**
#科学家和工程师	Scientists & Engineers	15 278	13 055	11 637	13 071
#高级职务	Personnel with Senior Titles	5 363	6 212	7 258	6 501
课题数（个）	**Number of Projects (unit)**	**8 801**	**12 827**	**17 507**	**19 541**
课题投入人数（万人年）	**Personnel Engaged in Projects (10 000 person-year)**	**1.21**	**1.71**	**1.43**	**1.60**
课题投入经费（亿元）	**Funds Financed (100 million yuan)**	**1.36**	**13.56**	**35.53**	**39.41**
课题经费支出（亿元）	**Expenditures (100 million yuan)**	**1.11**	**10.64**	**30.93**	**34.65**

①本表统计范围是指高等学校中理工农医类口径。
②从 2005 年起，科技活动机构数统计口径为上级主管部门批准的科技活动机构。
❶Figures of scientific and technological personnel in this table refer to those of science, engineering, agriculture and medicine of higher education.
❷Since 2005, R&D institutions refer to institutions which are authorized by superior administrative department.

表 18.23 高等学校 R&D 人员、机构及课题情况（2006）
PERSONNEL, INSTITUTIONS AND PROJECTS OF R&D IN INSTITUTIONS OF HIGHER EDUCATION

指 标	Indicators	合 计 Total	其 中 of which #自然科学 Natural Science	#工程与技术 Engineering and Technology	#医学科学 Medical Science	#农业科学 Agriculture Science
R&D 人员数（人年）	R&D Personnel（person-year）	13 517	2 024	6 614	4 637	242
R&D 机构数（个）	R&D Institutions（unit）	178	34	59	81	4
R&D 机构人员（人）	R&D Institutions Personnel（person）	5 659	1 309	1 858	2 442	50
课题数（个）	Number of Projects（unit）	19 541	3 375	11 235	4 383	548
课题投入人数（人年）	Personnel Engaged in Projects（person-year）	16 021	2 399	7 839	5 496	287
课题投入经费（万元）	Funds Financed(10 000 yuan）	3 940 557	529 217	2 974 576	380 544	56 220
课题经费支出（万元）	Expenditures（10 000 yuan）	3 464 798	470 196	2 688 304	274 085	32 213

注：本表统计范围是指高等学校中理工农医类口径。
Note: Figures of scientific and technological personnel in this table refer to those of science, engineering, agriculture and medicine of higher education.

表 18.24 各级科协机构和人员（2006）
INSTITUTIONS AND PERSONNEL OF SCIENCE AND TECHNOLOGY ASSOCIATIONS AT VARIOUS LEVELS

指 标	Indicators	市级科协 Municipal Level Associations	区级科协 District Level Associations	县级科协 County Level Associations
机构数（个）	Number of Institutions（unit）	1	18	1
人 员（人）	Personnel（person）	68	335	8
各级学会在册个数（个）	Number of Societies Registered（unit）	179	395	28

表 18.24 续表 continued

指 标	Indicators	机构数(个) Number of Institutions (unit)	个人会员(万人) Individual Members (10 000 persons)	团体会员数(个) Organization Members (unit)	所属分科学会(个) Attached Associations (unit)
市级学会	Prefectural Societies	179	17.9	13 259	928

注：本表至表 18.27 数据由市科学技术协会提供。
Note: Data in this table to table 18.27 are provided by Shanghai Municipal Science and Technology Associations.

表 18.25 科协系统科普活动和科技培训情况（2006）
PROMOTING SCIENCE ACTIVITIES AND TRAINING PROGRAM ORGANIZED BY SCIENCE AND TECHNOLOGY ASSOCIATIONS

指 标	Indicators	合 计 Total	市科协 Municipal Level Associations	#区县科协 District and County Level Associations	学 会 Academies
科普活动	**Promoting Science Activities**				
科普讲座次数（次）	Lectures(time)	6 778	4 660	4 274	2 118
科普讲座参加人次（万人次）	Participants of Lectures(10 000 person-times)	10 111	10 063	61	48
科普展览次数(次)	Exhibitions(time)	1 089	875	860	214
科普展览参加人次（万人次）	Participants of Lectures(10 000 person-times)	190	117	76	73
科普宣传活动次数(次)	Popular Science Promotion Activities(time)	2 672	2 312	2 276	360
科技夏（冬）令营次数(次)	Technical Summer (Winter) Camps(time)	198	158	156	40
青少年科技竞赛次数(次)	Youth Technical Competitions(time)	756	704	700	52
培训班	**Training Classes**				
36 学时以上班数（个）	Classes of More Than 36 Learning Hours (unit)	1 620	856	745	764
培训人次（万人次）	Trainees (10 000 person-times)	19	10	10	9

表 18.26 科协系统出版物和科技服务情况（2006）
PUBLICATIONS AND CONSULATIVE ACTIVITIES OF SCIENCE AND TECHNOLOGY ASSOCIATIONS

指 标	Indicators	合 计 Total	市科协 Municipal Level Associations	#区县科协 District and County Level Associations	学 会 Academies
出版物	**Publications**				
主办科技期刊种数（种）	Academic Journals (sort)	82	1		81
年发行总数（万册）	Annual Issues (10 000 copies)	506	13		493
年发表论文(篇)	Number of Paper Published over the Year (piece)	14 000			14 000
编辑论文集种数（种）	Thesis Collections Edited (sort)	106	8		98
年发行总数（册）	Annual Issues (copy)	53 775	470		53 305
主办科技报纸种数（种）	Science and Technology Newspaper (sort)	7	2		5
年发行份数（万份）	Annual Circulation (10 000 pieces)	968	948		20
编著科技图书种数（种）	Science and Technology Books (sort)	272	211	9	61
年发行册数（万册）	Annual Issues (10 000 copies)	228	196	19	32
咨 询	**Consultation**				
完成技术咨询合同数（项）	Technical Contracts Completed (item)	1 882	1 082	793	800
无偿咨询项目数（项）	Free Consultation (item)	8 233	70	70	8 163
咨询合同实现金额（万元）	Technical Constracts Revenue (10 000 yuan)	83 284	80 850	78 170	2 434

表 18.27 科协系统学术交流情况（2006）
ACADEMIC EXCHANGES OF SCIENCE AND TECHNOLOGY ASSOCIATIONS

指 标	Indicators	合 计 Total	市科协 Municipal Level Associations	区县科协 District and County Level Associations	学 会 Academies
国内学术会议	**Domestic Academic Conferences**				
举办次数（次）	Times(time)	1 980	706	695	1 274
参加人次（人次）	Participants (person-times)	181 698	60 844	53 304	120 854
交流论文（篇）	Papers Exchanged (piece)	15 616	549		15 067
国际学术会议	**International Academic Conferences**				
举办次数（次）	Times(time)	88	8		80
中方参加人次（人次）	Chinese Participants (person-time)	16 118	2 000		14 118
中方交流论文（篇）	Chinese Papers Exchanged (piece)	4 067	99		3 968
外方参加人次（人次）	Overseas Participants (person-time)	2 575	251		2 324
外方交流论文（篇）	Overseas Papers Exchanged (piece)	1 301	40		1 261
接待科技来访团组	**Receiving Visiting Science and Technology Delegations**				
接待海外科技团组数（个）	Foreign Science and Technology Groups (unit)	301	26		275
接待海外来访人次（人次）	Foreign Visitors (person-time)	3 082	365		2 717
接待港澳台科技团组(个)	Science and Technology Groups from Hong Kang, Macao and Taiwan (unit)	118	31	28	87
接待港澳台来访人次(人次)	Visitors from Hong Kang, Macao and Taiwan (person-time)	1 155	230	126	925
双边学术会议	**Bilateral Academic Conferences**				
举办次数(次数)	Number of Meetings(time)	29	7		22
参加人数(人次)	Number of Participants(person-times)	2 173	1 020		1 153
交流论文(篇)	Number of Papers Exchanged(piece)	397	48		349
港澳台地区学术会议	**Number of Academic Meetings Related with Hongkang, Macao**				
举办次数(次)	Number of Meetings(time)	3	1		2
参加人次(人次)	Number of Participants(person-times)	315	200		115
交流论文(篇)	Number of Papers Exchanged(piece)	108	20		88
海峡两岸地区学术会议	**Number of Academic Meetings Related with Mainland and Taiwan**				
举办次数(次)	Number of Meetings(time)	6	1		5
参加人次(人次)	Number of Participants(person-times)	513	64		449
交流论文(篇)	Number of Papers Exchanged(piece)	98	20		78
外派科技团组	**Dispatching Science and Technology Delegations Abroad**				
外派团组数（个）	Number of Delegations Sent Abroad (unit)	98	17		81
外派总人次（人次）	Number of People Sent Abroad (person-time)	778	79		699
#参加国际会议	Attending International Conferences	268	7		261
参加展览、技贸活动	Attending Exhibition and Technical Trade	79	10		69
派往港澳台地区科技团组	**Number of Delegations Sent to Hongkong, Macao and Taiwan**				
派出团组数(个)	Number of Delegations Sent Abroad (unit)	92	59	55	33
派出总人次(人次)	Number of People Sent Abroad (person-time)	466	171	111	295

表 18.28 规模以上工业企业技术开发机构和人员（2006）
TECHNICAL DEVELOPMENT ORGANIZATIONS AND PERSONNEL OF INDUSTRIAL ENTERPRISES ABOVE THE SET SCALE

类 别	Types	技术开发机构数(个) Technological Development Institutions (unit)	从事技术开发人员(万人) Tech. Development Personnel (10 000 persons)	其 中 of which #科学家和工程师 Scientists & Engineers
总 计	**Total**	**558**	**8.58**	**6.01**
一、按隶属关系分	**Grouped by Subordination**			
中央单位	Central Units	52	2.35	1.97
地方单位	Local Units	506	6.23	4.04
二、按登记注册类型分	**By Registration Categories**			
#国有企业	State-owned	71	1.24	0.85
股份制及其他有限公司	Share-holding and Other Companies with Limited Liabilities	170	2.70	1.95
外资企业	Foreign Funded	206	3.77	2.66
#国有及国有控股企业	Enterprises Owned by the State or with the State Holding Major Shares	302	5.57	3.93
三、按企业规模分	**By Size of Enterprises**			
大型企业	Large	95	3.33	2.62
中型企业	Medium	260	3.37	2.16
小型企业	Small	203	1.88	1.22
四、按行业分	**By Sectors**			
#高技术产业	**High Technology Industry**	**167**	**2.47**	**1.83**
信息化学品制造	Information Chemical Product Manufacturing	1	…	…
医药制造业	Medicine Manufacturing	55	0.41	0.27
航空航天器制造	Aviation and Aircraft Manufacturing	12	0.11	0.10
电子及通信设备制造业	Electronic and Communicantion Equipment Manufacturing	61	1.29	0.99
电子计算机及办公设备制造业	Electronic Computer and Office Equipment Manufacturing	14	0.27	0.21
医疗设备及仪器仪表制造业	Medical Machinery amd Measuring Instrument Manufacturing	24	0.39	0.27
#六个重点发展工业行业	**Six Key Industries**	**402**	**6.65**	**4.77**
电子信息产品制造业	Electronic Information Product Manufacturing	96	1.74	1.32
汽车制造业	Automobile Manufacturing	41	0.81	0.58
石油化工及精细化工制造业	Petrochemical and Fine Chemical Products Manufacturing	71	0.60	0.42
精品钢材制造业	Fine Steel Manufacturing	12	0.91	0.74
成套设备制造业	Equipment Complex Manufacturing	117	2.11	1.40
生物医药制造业	Bio-medicine Manufacturing	65	0.48	0.31

表 18.28 续表 continued

类别	Types	技术开发机构数(个) Technical Development Organizations	从事技术开发人员(人) Tech. Development Personnel (persons)	其中 of which #科学家和工程师 Scientists & Engineers
总　计	**Total**	**558**	**85 799**	**60 061**
按工业行业分	**By Sectors**			
制造业	**Manufacture Industry**	**549**	**83 092**	**57 585**
#石油和天然气开采业	Petroleum and Natural Gas Exploiting		63	54
农副食品加工业	Farm and Sideline Products Processing	6	167	84
食品制造业	Food Manufacturing	11	827	449
饮料制造业	Beverage Manufacturing	1	122	52
烟草制品业	Tabacco Manufacturing	1	357	196
纺织业	Textile	7	1 263	648
纺织服装、鞋、帽制造业	Garments,Shoes and Accessories Manufacturing	3	152	31
木材加工及木、竹、藤、棕、草制品业	Timber Processing and Timber, Bamboo, Rattan, Coir and Straw Products Manufacturing	3	159	104
家具制造业	Furniture Manufacturing		329	161
造纸及纸制品业	Paper-making and Paper Products Manufacturing		88	46
印刷业和记录媒介的复制	Printing and Record Duplicating	6	701	415
文教体育用品制造业	Stationary,Education and Sports Goods Manufacturing	6	401	153
石油加工、炼焦及核燃料加工业	Oil Processing,Coking and Nuclear	7	1 717	1 437
化学原料及化学制品制造业	Raw Chemical Materials and Chemical	78	4 858	3 125
医药制造业	Medicine Manufacturing	55	4 085	2 674
化学纤维制造业	Chemical Fiber Manufacturing	1	33	20
橡胶制品业	Rubber Products Manufacturing	6	761	405
塑料制品业	Plastic Products Manufacturing	10	780	514
非金属矿物制品业	Nonmetal Mineral Products	10	2 003	1 035
黑色金属冶炼及压延加工业	Smelting and Pressing of Ferrous Metals	12	9 141	7 400
有色金属冶炼及压延加工业	Smelting and Pressing of Nonferrous Metals	5	401	201
金属制品业	Metal Products Manufacturing	10	950	670
通用设备制造业	General Equipment Manufacturing	57	10 427	6 882
专用设备制造业	Special Purpose Equipment Manufacturing	36	5 487	3 461
交通运输设备制造业	Transportation Equipment Manufacturing	60	12 395	9 080
电气机械及器材制造业	Electric Machinery Equipments and Manufacturing	64	6 132	3 772
通信设备、计算机及其他电子设备制造业	Communications Equipments,Computer and Other Electronic Equipment Manufacturing	73	15 339	11 751
仪器仪表及文化、办公用机械制造业	Instruments,Meters,Culture and Office Equipments Manufacturing	20	3 705	2 554
工艺品及其他制造业	Artworks and Other Manufacturing	1	224	211
电力、燃气及水的生产和供应业	**Production and Supply of Power, Gas and Water**	**9**	**2 707**	**2 476**
电力、热力的生产和供应业	Production and Supply of Electricity and Thermal Power	6	2 236	2 175
燃气生产和供应业	Production and Supply of Gas	1	256	161
水的生产和供应业	Production and Supply of Water	2	215	140

表 18.29 规模以上工业企业技术开发经费来源（2006）
TECHNICAL DEVELOPMENT FUNDS OF INDUSTRIAL ENTERPRISES ABOVE THE SET SCALE

单位：亿元(100 million yuan)

类别	Types	当年筹集额 Funds of 2006	其中 of which #政府资金 Government Capital	#银行贷款 Bank Loans	#企业自筹 Self-raised Funds
总计	**Total**	**289.09**	**8.70**	**32.33**	**242.07**
一、按隶属关系分	**Grouped by Subordination**				
中央单位	Central Units	56.64	4.48	0.10	50.99
地方单位	Local Units	232.45	4.22	32.23	191.08
二、按登记注册类型分	**By Registration Categories**				
#国有企业	State-owned	19.95	1.54	0.35	17.58
股份制及其他有限公司	Share-holding and Other Companies with Limited Liabilities	74.45	2.15	1.56	70.07
外资企业	Foreign Funded	179.23	2.28	29.34	143.07
#国有及国有控股企业	Enterprises Owned by the State or with the State Holding Major Shares	176.41	6.67	1.97	166.34
三、按企业规模分	**By Size of Enterprises**				
大型企业	Large	150.24	5.64	27.65	112.76
中型企业	Medium	104.57	1.89	1.66	100.40
小型企业	Small	34.27	1.17	3.02	28.91
四、按行业分	**By Sectors**				
#高技术产业	**High Technology Industry**	**96.61**	**3.26**	**28.21**	**60.90**
信息化学品制造	Information Chemical Product Manufacturing	0.14			0.14
医药制造业	Medicine Manufacturing	13.18	0.26	0.51	12.27
航空航天器制造	Aviation and Aircraft Manufacturing	2.44	0.91		1.38
电子及通信设备制造业	Electronic and Communicantion Equipment Manufacturing	68.14	1.76	27.64	38.55
电子计算机及办公设备制造业	Electronic Computer and Office Equipment Manufacturing	6.98	0.09	0.05	3.10
医疗设备及仪器仪表制造业	Medical Machinery and Measuring Instrument Manufacturing	5.73	0.25	0.01	5.44
#六个重点发展工业行业	**Six Key Industries**	**245.20**	**8.32**	**30.17**	**201.29**
电子信息产品制造业	Electronic Information Product Manufacturing	79.19	2.07	28.05	45.12
汽车制造业	Automobile Manufacturing	62.43	0.56	0.20	61.63
石油化工及精细化工制造业	Petrochemical and Fine Chemical Products Manufacturing	12.34	0.23	0.11	11.94
精品钢材制造业	Fine Steel Manufacturing	17.27	0.24	0.08	16.89
成套设备制造业	Equipment Complex Manufacturing	59.82	4.93	1.18	52.55
生物医药制造业	Bio-medicine Manufacturing	14.15	0.28	0.56	13.17

表 18.29 续表 continued

单位:万元(10 000 yuan)

类别	Types	当年筹集额 Funds of 2006	其中 of which #政府资金 Government Allocation	#银行贷款 Bank Loans	#企业自筹 Self-raised Funds
总　计	**Total**	**2 890 899**	**87 027**	**323 301**	**2 420 695**
制造业	**Manufacture Industry**	**2 849 069**	**87 004**	**323 301**	**2 378 912**
#石油和天然气开采业	Petroleum and Natural Gas Exploiting	10 441			10 441
农副食品加工业	Farm and Sideline Products Processing	2 127	208	360	1 559
食品制造业	Food Manufacturing	5 539	55	300	5 184
饮料制造业	Beverage Manufacturing	3 713			3 713
烟草制品业	Tabacco Manufacturing	16 367			16 367
纺织业	Textile	12 394	411		10 485
纺织服装、鞋、帽制造业	Garments, Shoes and Accessories Manufacturing	2 901		1 000	1 901
木材加工及木、竹、藤、棕、草制品业	Timber Processing and Timber, Bamboo, Rattan, Coir and Straw Products Manufacturing	2 782	20	820	1 890
家具制造业	Furniture Manufacturing	15 196			15 196
造纸及纸制品业	Paper-making and Paper Products Manufacturing	684			684
印刷业和记录媒介的复制	Printing and Record Duplicating	9 555	60	271	9 224
文教体育用品制造业	Stationary, Education and Sports Goods Manufacturing	2 649			2 649
石油加工、炼焦及核燃料加工业	Oil Processing, Coking and Nuclear	21 776	545		20 735
化学原料及化学制品制造业	Raw Chemical Materials and Chemical	110 003	2 096	1 485	106 191
医药制造业	Medicine Manufacturing	131 836	2 590	5 100	122 748
化学纤维制造业	Chemical Fiber Manufacturing	311	15	200	96
橡胶制品业	Rubber Products Manufacturing	24 014	96		23 818
塑料制品业	Plastic Products Manufacturing	23 053	364	5 840	15 578
非金属矿物制品业	Nonmetal Mineral Products	30 653	502	200	29 915
黑色金属冶炼及压延加工业	Smelting and Pressing of Ferrous Metals	172 710	2 435	770	168 869
有色金属冶炼及压延加工业	Smelting and Pressing of Nonferrous Metals	9 680	90	956	8 549
金属制品业	Metal Products Manufacturing	24 068	45	1 000	23 023
通用设备制造业	General Equipment Manufacturing	402 791	8 545	14 066	377 750
专用设备制造业	Special Purpose Equipment Manufacturing	87 881	2 540	2 600	82 651
交通运输设备制造业	Transportation Equipment Manufacturing	761 459	42 077	1 973	707 717
电气机械及器材制造业	Electric Machinery Equipments and Manufacturing	164 589	3 562	7 366	153 631
通信设备、计算机及其他电子设备制造业	Communications Equipments, Computer and Other Electronic Equipment Manufacturing	745 012	18 482	276 914	410 366
仪器仪表及文化、办公用机械制造业	Instruments, Meters, Culture and Office Equipments Manufacturing	49 892	2 265	80	44 987
工艺品及其他制造业	Artworks and Other Manufacturing	4 900		2 000	2 900
电力、燃气及水的生产和供应业	**Production and Supply of Power, Gas and Water**	**41 829**	**23**		**41 783**
电力、热力的生产和供应业	Production and Supply of Electricity and Thermal Power	40 238			40 238
燃气生产和供应业	Production and Supply of Gas	565			565
水的生产和供应业	Production and Supply of Water	1 026	23		980

表 18.30 规模以上工业企业技术开发项目与技术开发经费支出情况（2006）
TECHNICAL DEVELOPMENT PROJECTS AND EXPENDITURES OF INDUSTRIAL ENTERPRISES ABOVE THE SET SCALE

类 别	Types	项目数（项）Number of Projects (item)	技术开发经费支出（亿元）Expenditures of Technological Development (100 million yuan)	其中 of which #新产品开发经费支出 on New Products Development	#研究与试验发展经费支出 Expenditures on R&D
总　计	**Total**	**6 930**	**290.84**	**153.43**	**146.28**
一、按隶属关系分	**Grouped by Subordination**				
中央单位	Central Units	1 990	59.53	28.28	37.90
地方单位	Local Units	4 940	231.31	124.61	108.38
二、按登记注册类型分	**By Registration Categories**				
#国有企业	State-owned	1 217	22.84	8.84	7.82
股份制及其他有限公司	Share-holding and Other Companies with Limited Liabilities	2 423	77.77	41.58	35.46
外资企业	Foreign Funded	2 602	174.70	94.45	97.47
#国有及国有控股企业	Enterprises Owned by the State or with the State Holding Major Shares	5 136	184.83	98.84	96.73
三、按企业规模分	**By Size of Enterprises**				
大型企业	Large	2 137	137.21	75.85	78.16
中型企业	Medium	2 813	119.04	59.54	54.86
小型企业	Small	1 980	34.59	18.04	13.26
四、按行业分	**By Sectors**				
#高技术产业	**High Technology Industry**	**1 591**	**88.64**	**45.91**	**45.51**
信息化学品制造	Information Chemical Product Manufacturing	4	0.13	0.12	0.12
医药制造业	Medicine Manufacturing	519	14.06	7.09	9.42
航空航天器制造	Aviation and Aircraft Manufacturing	42	3.15	2.55	1.94
电子及通信设备制造业	Electronic and Communicantion Equipment Manufacturing	522	54.40	27.82	25.25
电子计算机及办公设备制造业	Electronic Computer and Office Equipment Manufacturing	79	10.59	5.00	4.92
医疗设备及仪器仪表制造业	Medical Machinery amd Measuring Instrument Manufacturing	425	6.31	3.33	2.86
#六个重点发展工业行业	**Six Key Industries**	**5 016**	**243.04**	**130.57**	**128.58**
电子信息产品制造业	Electronic Information Product Manufacturing	799	68.59	34.88	32.13
汽车制造业	Automobile Manufacturing	715	65.47	39.63	34.17
石油化工及精细化工制造业	Petrochemical and Fine Chemical Products Manufacturing	664	13.23	6.41	5.90
精品钢材制造业	Fine Steel Manufacturing	959	17.82	4.80	12.23
成套设备制造业	Equipment Complex Manufacturing	1 229	62.86	37.10	34.20
生物医药制造业	Bio-medicine Manufacturing	650	15.07	7.75	9.95

注：技术开发经费支出和研究与发展经费支出包括科研基建费支出。
Note: The Expenditure of Technology Development and R&D comprises the payout of infrastructure for scientific research.

表 18.30 续表 continued

类　别	Types	项目数（项） Number of Projects (item)	技术开发经费支出（万元） Expenditures of Technical Development (100 million yuan)	其　中 of which #新产品开发经费支出 New Products Development	#研究与试验发展经费支出 Expenditures on R&D
总　计	**Total**	**6 930**	**2 908 445**	**1 534 316**	**1 462 803**
制造业	**Manufacture Industry**	**6 641**	**2 865 490**	**1 531 480**	**1 449 991**
#石油和天然气开采业	Petroleum and Natural Gas Exploiting	6	10 441		9 079
农副食品加工业	Farm and Sideline Products Processing	12	3 123	1 432	1 640
食品制造业	Food Manufacturing	63	8 633	2 592	4 509
饮料制造业	Beverage Manufacturing	12	3 909	2 499	1 939
烟草制品业	Tabacco Manufacturing	79	17 683	805	6 284
纺织业	Textile	114	12 698	8 422	7 834
纺织服装、鞋、帽制造业	Garments, Shoes and Accessories Manufacturing	7	4 558	2 797	634
木材加工及木、竹、藤、棕、草制品业	Timber Processing and Timber, Bamboo, Rattan, Coir and Straw Products Manufacturing	7	2 970	628	269
家具制造业	Furniture Manufacturing	17	16 428	15 057	15 027
造纸及纸制品业	Paper-making and Paper Products Manufacturing	8	1 358	497	537
印刷业和记录媒介的复制	Printing and Record Duplicating	73	11 917	3 865	3 430
文教体育用品制造业	Stationary, Education and Sports Goods Manufacturing	44	3 349	1 097	1 669
石油加工、炼焦及核燃料加工业	Oil Processing, Coking and Nuclear	222	19 257	5 232	9 792
化学原料及化学制品制造业	Raw Chemical Materials and Chemical	513	127 024	63 672	54 437
医药制造业	Medicine Manufacturing	519	140 572	70 880	94 150
化学纤维制造业	Chemical Fiber Manufacturing	2	309	309	305
橡胶制品业	Rubber Products Manufacturing	52	24 336	20 679	19 494
塑料制品业	Plastic Products Manufacturing	84	29 052	16 189	7 452
非金属矿物制品业	Nonmetal Mineral Products	167	36 459	15 967	9 446
黑色金属冶炼及压延加工业	Smelting and Pressing of Ferrous Metals	959	178 241	47 984	122 257
有色金属冶炼及压延加工业	Smelting and Pressing of Nonferrous Metals	38	11 914	5 408	1 238
金属制品业	Metal Products Manufacturing	140	27 116	7 294	5 895
通用设备制造业	General Equipment Manufacturing	798	406 117	250 146	213 892
专用设备制造业	Special Purpose Equipment Manufacturing	457	95 484	70 159	49 062
交通运输设备制造业	Transportation Equipment Manufacturing	881	812 978	465 894	413 956
电气机械及器材制造业	Electric Machinery Equipments and Manufacturing	441	155 445	99 351	72 764
通信设备、计算机及其他电子设备制造业	Communications Equipments, Computer and Other Electronic Equipment Manufacturing	579	643 742	324 506	299 134
仪器仪表及文化、办公用机械制造业	Instruments, Meters, Culture and Office Equipments Manufacturing	343	59 413	27 680	23 427
工艺品及其他制造业	Artworks and Other Manufacturing	4	868	439	439
电力、燃气及水的生产和供应业	**Production and Supply of Power, Gas and Water**	**289**	**42 955**	**2 837**	**12 812**
电力、热力的生产和供应业	Production and Supply of Electricity and Thermal Power	230	41 104	2 807	12 400
燃气生产和供应业	Production and Supply of Gas	32	645		83
水的生产和供应业	Production and Supply of Water	27	1 206	30	329

表 18.31 规模以上工业企业其他技术活动费用支出情况（2006）
SPECIAL TECHNICAL PROJECT FUNDS OF INDUSTRIAL ENTERPRISES ABOVE THE SET SCALE

单位：亿元（100 million yuan）

类 别	Types	技术改造经费支出 Expenditures of Technical Transformation	技术引进经费支出 Expenditures of Technical Introduction	购买国内技术支出 Expenditures of Buying Domestic Technology
总　计	**Total**	**127.94**	**42.30**	**15.59**
一、按隶属关系分	**Grouped by Subordination**			
中央单位	Central Units	71.68	20.81	13.75
地方单位	Local Units	56.27	21.49	1.84
二、按登记注册类型分	**By Registration Categories**			
#国有企业	State-owned	9.44	1.28	0.64
股份制及其他有限公司	Share-holding and Other Companies with Limited Liabilities	75.39	19.66	13.74
外资企业	Foreign Funded	36.52	20.54	0.79
#国有及国有控股企业	Enterprises Owned by the State or with the State Holding Major Shares	114.79	28.23	15.09
三、按企业规模分	**By Size of Enterprises**			
大型企业	Large	92.16	23.25	9.40
中型企业	Medium	21.71	13.80	0.62
小型企业	Small	14.07	5.25	5.57
四、按行业分	**By Sectors**			
#高技术产业	**High Technology Industry**	**8.19**	**11.92**	**0.87**
信息化学品制造	Information Chemical Product Manufacturing	0.08	0.02	
医药制造业	Medicine Manufacturing	0.82	0.19	0.42
航空航天器制造	Aviation and Aircraft Manufacturing	1.34	0.44	0.12
电子及通信设备制造业	Electronic and Communicantion Equipment Manufacturing	4.65	10.68	0.26
电子计算机及办公设备制造业	Electronic Computer and Office Equipment Manufacturing	0.48	0.15	
医疗设备及仪器仪表制造业	Medical Machinery amd Measuring Instrument Manufacturing	0.81	0.43	0.07
#六个重点发展工业行业	**Six Key Industries**	**111.45**	**38.46**	**15.29**
电子信息产品制造业	Electronic Information Product Manufacturing	6.18	11.08	0.28
汽车制造业	Automobile Manufacturing	22.31	2.83	0.27
石油化工及精细化工制造业	Petrochemical and Fine Chemical Products Manufacturing	29.05	0.23	0.17
精品钢材制造业	Fine Steel Manufacturing	36.61	16.48	12.69
成套设备制造业	Equipment Complex Manufacturing	16.08	7.48	1.46
生物医药制造业	Bio-medicine Manufacturing	1.22	0.37	0.42

表 18.31 续表 continued

单位:万元 (10 000 yuan)

类 别	Types	技术改造经费支出 Expenditures of Technical Transformation	技术引进经费支出 Expenditures of Technical Introduction	购买国内技术支出 Expenditures of Buying Domestic Techniology
总 计	**Total**	**1 279 447**	**423 012**	**155 898**
制造业	**Manufacture Industry**	**1 250 300**	**423 012**	**155 898**
#农副食品加工业	Farm and Sideline Products Processing	1 733		100
食品制造业	Food Manufacturing	515	325	
饮料制造业	Beverage Manufacturing	609		
烟草制品业	Tabacco Manufacturing	22 450		
纺织业	Textile	4 033	1 053	36
纺织服装、鞋、帽制造业	Garments, Shoes and Accessories Manufacturing	1 660		
木材加工及木、竹、藤、棕、草制品业	Timber Processing and Timber, Bamboo, Rattan, Coir and Straw Products Manufacturing	630		30
造纸及纸制品业	Paper-making and Paper Products Manufacturing		142	
印刷业和记录媒介的复制	Printing and Record Duplicating	7 932	2 824	1 198
文教体育用品制造业	Stationary, Education and Sports Goods Manufacturing	600		
石油加工、炼焦及核燃料加工业	Oil Processing, Coking and Nuclear	249 071		1 222
化学原料及化学制品制造业	Raw Chemical Materials and Chemical	43 816	2 907	517
医药制造业	Medicine Manufacturing	8 214	1 928	4 152
化学纤维制造业	Chemical Fiber Manufacturing	187		
橡胶制品业	Rubber Products Manufacturing	10 768	807	150
塑料制品业	Plastic Products Manufacturing	11 478	642	12
非金属矿物制品业	Nonmetal Mineral Products	8 250	3 520	40
黑色金属冶炼及压延加工业	Smelting and Pressing of Ferrous Metals	366 097	164 778	126 860
有色金属冶炼及压延加工业	Smelting and Pressing of Nonferrous Metals	1 698		
金属制品业	Metal Products Manufacturing	14 495	1 408	20
通用设备制造业	General Equipment Manufacturing	77 676	51 942	1 837
专用设备制造业	Special Purpose Equipment Manufacturing	69 918	4 859	3 034
交通运输设备制造业	Transportation Equipment Manufacturing	253 595	42 547	11 957
电气机械及器材制造业	Electric Machinery Equipments and Manufacturing	38 778	32 486	1 423
通信设备、计算机及其他电子设备制造业	Communications Equipments, Computer and Other Electronic Equipment Manufacturing	51 360	106 840	2 579
仪器仪表及文化、办公用机械制造业	Instruments, Meters, Culture and Office Equipments Manufacturing	4 725	4 007	732
电力、燃气及水的生产和供应业	**Production and Supply of Power, Gas and Water**	**29 148**		
电力、热力的生产和供应业	Production and Supply of Electricity and Thermal Power	13 564		
燃气生产和供应业	Production and Supply of Gas	4 596		
水的生产和供应业	Production and Supply of Water	10 988		

表 18.32　规模以上工业企业新产品开发情况（2006）
NEW PRODUCTS DEVELOPMENT OF INDUSTRIAL ENTERPRISES ABOVE THE SET SCALE

单位：亿元（100 million yuan）

类　别	Types	新产品产　值 Output Value of New Products	新产品主　营业务收入 Prime Operating Revenue	其中 of which #新产品出　口 Exports of New Products
总　计	**Total**	**4 112.36**	**4 285.69**	**1 186.42**
一、按隶属关系分	**Grouped by Subordination**			
中央单位	Central Units	971.04	949.30	306.31
地方单位	Local Units	3 141.32	3 336.39	880.12
二、按登记注册类型分	**By Registration Categories**			
#国有企业	State-owned	141.13	132.75	23.77
股份制及其他有限公司	Share-holding and Other Companies with Limited Liabilities	772.61	770.67	154.10
外资企业	Foreign Funded	3 095.97	3 318.10	994.14
#国有及国有控股企业	Enterprises Owned by the State or with the State Holding Major Shares	2 421.40	2 572.25	398.55
三、按企业规模分	**By Size of Enterprises**			
大型企业	Large	2 747.64	2 908.22	692.92
中型企业	Medium	1 197.98	1 204.57	463.61
小型企业	Small	166.74	172.91	29.89
四、按行业分	**By Sectors**			
#高技术产业	**High Technology Industry**	**1 534.96**	**1 569.46**	**764.85**
信息化学品制造	Information Chemical Product Manufacturing	0.88	0.03	
医药制造业	Medicine Manufacturing	45.31	59.16	2.83
航空航天器制造	Aviation and Aircraft Manufacturing	4.23	4.63	0.01
电子及通信设备制造业	Electronic and Communicantion Equipment Manufacturing	570.96	568.18	265.63
电子计算机及办公设备制造业	Electronic Computer and Office Equipment Manufacturing	875.65	898.56	485.89
医疗设备及仪器仪表制造业	Medical Machinery amd Measuring Instrument Manufacturing	37.92	38.89	10.49
#六个重点发展工业行业	**Six Key Industries**	**3 651.95**	**3 827.55**	**1 041.36**
电子信息产品制造业	Electronic Information Product Manufacturing	1 453.37	1 475.23	741.04
汽车制造业	Automobile Manufacturing	888.87	1 054.03	15.02
石油化工及精细化工制造业	Petrochemical and Fine Chemical Products Manufacturing	244.03	254.30	8.37
精品钢材制造业	Fine Steel Manufacturing	328.55	328.13	29.99
成套设备制造业	Equipment Complex Manufacturing	684.27	650.52	242.54
生物医药制造业	Bio-medicine Manufacturing	52.86	65.34	4.40

注：新产品包括：1. 经国家级或市经委认证并颁发给新产品证书，且在新产品证书规定的有效期内生产的产品。 2. 未经国家级或市经委等有关部门认证的产品，这些产品在报告期内由企业根据新产品定义自行定义，而且各类产品投入批量生产跟踪 2 至 5 年的产品。

Note: New Products refer to, 1. The products under the authentication of national or municipal economic committee and produced during the period of validity limited by the certificate. 2. Other products defined by enterprises in the report period complying with the definition of new products which have been batch produced for 2 to 5 years.

表 18.32 续表 continued

单位:万元 (10 000 yuan)

类别	Types	新产品产值 Output Value of New Products	新产品主营业务收入 Prime Operating Revenue	其中 of which #新产品出口 Exports of New Products
总　计	**Total**	**41 123 615**	**42 856 937**	**11 864 228**
制造业	**Manufacture Industry**	**41 123 615**	**42 856 937**	**11 864 228**
#农副食品加工业	Farm and Sideline Products Processing	20 027	21 033	
食品制造业	Food Manufacturing	89 876	90 841	8 990
饮料制造业	Beverage Manufacturing	13 692	11 600	120
烟草制品业	Tabacco Manufacturing	228 035	283 109	
纺织业	Textile	159 196	154 116	22 258
纺织服装、鞋、帽制造业	Garments, Shoes and Accessories Manufacturing	59 723	57 091	22 711
木材加工及木、竹、藤、棕、草制品业	Timber Processing and Timber, Bamboo, Rattan, Coir and Straw Products Manufacturing	5 743	5 910	27
家具制造业	Furniture Manufacturing	460 984	479 252	113 775
造纸及纸制品业	Paper-making and Paper Products Manufacturing	26 749	26 251	
印刷业和记录媒介的复制	Printing and Record Duplicating	140 776	139 509	2 166
文教体育用品制造业	Stationary, Education and Sports Goods Manufacturing	24 236	20 077	4 347
石油加工、炼焦及核燃料加工业	Oil Processing, Coking and Nuclear	1 276 858	1 371 883	2 585
化学原料及化学制品制造业	Raw Chemical Materials and Chemical	1 220 421	1 215 850	88 311
医药制造业	Medicine Manufacturing	453 148	591 632	28 348
化学纤维制造业	Chemical Fiber Manufacturing	2 844	2 957	2 432
橡胶制品业	Rubber Products Manufacturing	223 469	224 139	74 951
塑料制品业	Plastic Products Manufacturing	173 598	176 674	8 891
非金属矿物制品业	Nonmetal Mineral Products	170 283	169 815	63 177
黑色金属冶炼及压延加工业	Smelting and Pressing of Ferrous Metals	3 285 526	3 281 295	299 914
有色金属冶炼及压延加工业	Smelting and Pressing of Nonferrous Metals	150 821	132 321	9 301
金属制品业	Metal Products Manufacturing	235 206	233 584	148 924
通用设备制造业	General Equipment Manufacturing	4 292 980	4 311 239	1 148 582
专用设备制造业	Special Purpose Equipment Manufacturing	735 495	711 001	100 826
交通运输设备制造业	Transportation Equipment Manufacturing	10 858 769	12 198 972	1 405 539
电气机械及器材制造业	Electric Machinery Equipments and Manufacturing	1 975 393	1 888 347	620 424
通信设备、计算机及其他电子设备制造业	Communications Equipments, Computer and Other Electronic Equipment Manufacturing	14 248 920	14 457 735	7 333 040
仪器仪表及文化、办公用机械制造业	Instruments, Meters, Culture and Office Equipments Manufacturing	581 200	590 908	351 280
工艺品及其他制造业	Artworks and Other Manufacturing	8 100	8 247	1 760

表 18.33 主要年份大中型工业企业技术开发情况
TECHNOLOGICAL DEVELOPMENT PROJECTS OF LARGE AND MEDIUM INDUSTRIAL ENTERPRISES IN MAIN YEARS

指 标	Indicators	1990	2000	2005	2006
技术开发机构数（个）	**Technological Development Institutions (unit)**	**383**	**264**	**257**	**355**
从事技术开发人员数（万人）	**Technological Development Personnel (10 000 persons)**	**6.45**	**7.48**	**5.89**	**6.70**
#科学家和工程师	Scientists and Engineers	2.50	4.33	4.09	4.78
研究与发展人员	Research and Development Personnel		2.63	2.67	3.47
经费筹集额(亿元)	**Funds (100 million yuan)**	**12.50**	**122.64**	**215.31**	**254.82**
技术开发经费支出(亿元)	**Expenditures of Technical Development (100 million yuan)**	**10.72**	**100.78**	**231.86**	**256.25**
各项技术专款(亿元)	**Special Technology Funds (100 million yuan)**	**30.89**	**117.47**	**190.52**	**174.40**
技术改造经费支出	Expenditures on Technological Transformation	18.61	75.31	139.66	113.87
技术引进经费支出	Expenditures on Technological Introduction	11.28	39.00	42.45	37.05
用于消化吸收的经费	Expenditures on Technological Digesting and Absorbing	0.31	2.41	4.81	13.46
购买国内技术支出	Expenditures on Buying Domestic Technology	0.70	0.75	3.59	10.02
技术开发项目数（项）	**Number of Projects (item)**	**3 107**	**5 140**	**4 025**	**4 950**
项目组人员（人）	**Personnel of Project Groups (person)**		**45 254**	**302 509**	**40 867**
#科学家和工程师	Scientists and Engineers		29 965	28 450	33 391
项目经费支出（内部）(亿元)	**Expenditure on Projects (Internal) (100 million yuan)**	**5.43**	**63.72**	**109.40**	**120.18**
新产品主营业务收入(亿元)	**Prime Operating Revenue(100 million yuan)**	**127.63**	**1 351.69**	**3 153.10**	**3 945.62**
#新产品出口	New Products Exported		197.41	908.87	4 112.78
新产品产值(亿元)	**Taxes of New Products(100 million yuan)**	**130.34**	**1 355.19**	**312.88**	**3 945.62**

表 18.34 大中型工业企业技术开发情况(2006)
TECHNOLOGICAL DEVELOPMENT PROJECTS OF LARGE AND MEDIUM INDUSTRIAL ENTERPRISES

类 别	Types	从事技术开发的人员数(万人) Technological Development Personnel (10 000 persons)	技术开发经费支出(亿元) Expenditures of Technical Development (100 million yuan)	其中 of which #新产品开发经费支出 Expenditures on New Products Development	研究与试验发展经费支出 Expenditures on R&D
总 计	**Total**	**6 695**	**256.25**	**135.39**	**133.02**
一、按隶属关系分	**Grouped by Subordination**				
中央单位	Central Units	2 246	58.26	27.97	37.10
地方单位	Local Units	4 450	198.00	107.42	95.92
二、按登记注册类型分	**By Registration Categories**				
#国有企业	State-owned	1 051	19.10	7.60	7.21
股份制及其他有限公司	Share-holding and Other Companies with Limited Liabilities	2 129	69.06	36.71	31.32
外资企业	Foreign Funded	3 101	158.53	86.14	91.35
#国有及国有控股企业	Enterprises Owned by the State or with the State Holding Major Shares	4 699	171.13	92.14	90.88
三、按行业分	**By Sectors**				
制造业	**Manufacture Industry**	**6 427**	**251.96**	**135.11**	**131.74**
#农副食品加工业	Farm and Sideline Products Processing	11	0.24	0.11	0.13
食品制造业	Food Manufacturing	38	0.69	0.19	0.39
饮料制造业	Beverage Manufacturing	11	0.38	0.24	0.19
烟草制品业	Tabacco Manufacturing	36	1.77	0.08	0.63
纺织业	Textile	95	0.97	0.64	0.65
纺织服装、鞋、帽制造业	Garments, Shoes and Accessories Manufacturing	7	0.12	0.11	0.06
家具制造业	Furniture Manufacturing	33	1.64	1.50	1.50
造纸及纸制品业	Paper-making and Paper Products Manufacturing	9	0.14	0.05	0.05
印刷业和记录媒介的复制	Printing and Record Duplicating	67	1.13	0.32	0.33
文教体育用品制造业	Stationary, Education and Sports Goods Manufacturing	35	0.26	0.09	0.14
石油加工、炼焦及核燃料加工业	Oil Processing, Coking and Nuclear	169	1.92	0.52	0.98
化学原料及化学制品制造业	Raw Chemical Materials and Chemical	312	9.21	4.60	3.67
医药制造业	Medicine Manufacturing	263	11.65	5.36	8.06
化学纤维制造业	Chemical Fiber Manufacturing				
橡胶制品业	Rubber Products Manufacturing	51	2.08	1.90	1.79
塑料制品业	Plastic Products Manufacturing	34	1.16	0.94	0.42
非金属矿物制品业	Nonmetal Mineral Products	119	1.47	0.90	0.62
黑色金属冶炼及压延加工业	Smelting and Pressing of Ferrous Metals	849	17.23	4.57	11.94
有色金属冶炼及压延加工业	Smelting and Pressing of Nonferrous Metals	28	0.51	0.31	0.07
金属制品业	Metal Products Manufacturing	69	2.31	0.54	0.55
通用设备制造业	General Equipment Manufacturing	831	34.86	22.26	20.13
专用设备制造业	Special Purpose Equipment Manufacturing	357	7.70	5.64	3.88
交通运输设备制造业	Transportation Equipment Manufacturing	1 117	78.59	45.07	40.34
电气机械及器材制造业	Electric Machinery Equipments and Manufacturing	428	11.90	7.95	5.51
通信设备、计算机及其他电子设备制造业	Communications Equipments, Computer and Other Electronic Equipment Manufacturing	1 207	59.54	29.30	27.91
仪器仪表及文化、办公用机械制造业	Instruments, Meters, Culture and Office Equipments Manufacturing	230	4.34	1.82	1.78
工艺品及其他制造业	Artworks and Other Manufacturing	19			
电力、燃气及水的生产和供应业	**Production and Supply of Power, Gas and Water**	**268**	**4.29**	**0.28**	**1.28**
电力、热力的生产和供应业	Production and Supply of Electricity and Thermal Power	223	4.11	0.28	1.24
燃气生产和供应业	Production and Supply of Gas	26	0.06		0.01
水的生产和供应业	Production and Supply of Water	20	0.12		0.03

表 18.35 质量技术监督机构情况(2002 ~2006)
THE INSTITUTIONS OF QUALITY AND TECHNICAL SUPERVISION

	类 别 Types	2002	2003	2004	2005	2006
机构数(个)	**Number of Institutions (unit)**	**42**	**52**	**51**	**62**	**61**
按地区分	By Districts					
市 级	Municipal Level	10	10	9	10	9
区县级	Districts Level	32	42	42	52	52
按性质分	By Charactors					
行政管理机构	Administrations	20	20	20	21	21
事业单位	Public Service Organization	22	32	31	41	40
从业人员(人)	**Personnel (person)**	**2 490**	**2 678**	**2 651**	**3 177**	**3 171**
公务员	Official	567	574	601	771	793
管理人员	Management People	353	295	236	286	281
专业技术人员	Professional	930	1 154	1 227	1 544	1 557
其他人员	Other People	640	655	587	576	540
计量检定、测试与执法	**Metrological Check, Testing and Enforcement**					
计量标准(项)	**Metrology Criterion (item)**	**766**	**772**	**643**	**657**	**986**
建立在国家法定计量检定机构的社会公用计量标准	Public Measurement Standards Set by the State Metrological Authority	410	415	437	443	672
授权建立的社会公用计量标准	Authorized Public Measurement Standard	13	3	1	1	2
建立在部门、企事业单位的最高计量标准	Measurment Standard Set by Government Department and Corporations	343	354	205	213	312
授权法定计量技术机构(个)	Authorized Metroloical Institutions (unit)	34	35	41	41	36
计量检定员(人)	**Measurement Inspectors (person)**	**1 189**	**1 171**	**1 496**	**1 064**	**1 360**
全年完成计量检定、测试(万台、万件)	Number of Products that Underwent measurement Inspection in the year (10 000 unit)	378.12	437.88	395.30	426.39	428.00
产品质量监督检查	**Supervision and Inspection of Products Quality**					
抽查产品品种(种)	Product types of Spot Test (type)	2 437	2 942	2 781	3 626	3 193
抽查工业企业(个)	Industrial Enterprises of Spot test (unit)	2 228	2 467	2 630	2 742	2 875

注：本表数据由上海市质量技术监督局提供。
Note: Data in this table are provided by Shanghai Municipal Bureau of Quality and Technical Supervision.

上 / 海 / 统 / 计 / 年 / 鉴

主要统计指标解释

■ 专业技术人员

指事业、企业单位中已被聘任专业技术职务的从事专业技术工作和专业技术管理的人员，以及虽未被聘任专业技术职务，但现在专业技术岗位上工作的人员。

■ R&D

是“科学研究与试验发展”(Research and Development)的英文缩写。其含义是指在科学技术领域，为增加知识总量，以及运用这些知识去创造新的应用进行的系统的创造性的活动。R&D 包括基础研究、应用研究、试验发展三类活动。

■ 基础研究

指为了获得关于现象和可观察事实的基本原理的新知识(揭示客观事物的本质、运动规律，获得新发现、新学说)而进行的实验性或理论性研究，它不以任何专门或特定的应用或使用为目的。其成果以科学论文和科学著作为主要形式。用来反映知识的原始创新能力。

■ 应用研究

指为获得新知识而进行的创造性研究，主要针对某一特定的目的或目标。应用研究是为了确定基础研究成果可能的用途，或是为达到预定的目标探索应采取的新方法(原理性)或新途径。其成果形式以科学论文、专著、原理性模型或发明专利为主。用来反映对基础研究成果应用途径的探索。

■ 试验发展

指利用从基础研究、应用研究和实际经验所获得的现有知识，为产生新的产品、材料和装置，建立新的工艺、系统和服务，以及对已产生和建立的上述各项作实质性的改进而进行的系统性工作。其成果形式主要是专利、专有技术、具有新产品基本特征的产品原型或具有新装置基本特征的原始样机等。在社会科学领域，试验发展是指把通过基础研究、应用研究获得的知识转变成可以实施的计划(包括为进行检验和评估实施示范项目)的过程。人文科学领域没有对应的试验发展活动。主要反映将科研成果转化为技术和产品的能力，是科技推动经济社会发展的物化成果。

■ 发　明

指对产品、方法或者其改进所提出的新的技术方案。是国际通行的反映拥有自主知识产权技术的核心指标。

■ 实用新型

指对产品的形状、构造或者其结合所提出的适于实用的新的技术方案。反映具有一定技术含量的技术成果情况。

■ 外观设计

指对产品的形状、图案、色彩或者其结合所作出的富有美感并适于工业上应用的新设计。反映拥有自主知识产权的外观设计成果情况。

■ 独立研究与开发机构

指有明确的任务和研究方向，有一定学术水平的业务骨干和一定数量的研究人员，具有研究、开发、开展学术工作的基本条件，主要进行科学研究与技术开发活动，并且在行政上有独立的组织形式，财务上独立核算盈亏，有权与其他单位签订合同，在银行有单独户头的单位。

■ 科学家和工程师

指科技活动人员中具有高、中级技术职称(职务)的人员和不具有高、中级技术职称(职务)的大学本科及以上学历人员。

■ 科技活动

指在自然科学、农业科学、医药科学、工程与技术科学、人文与社会科学领域(简称科学技术领域)中，与科技知识的产生、发展、传播和应用密切相关的有组织的活动。可分为研究与试验发展(R&D)、研究与试验发展成果应用及相关的科技服务三类活动。该定义是联合国教科文组织考虑成员国特别是发展中国家开展科技统计工作的需要，而对科技活动所作的统计界定。

■ 科技活动人员

指直接从事科技活动、以及专门从事科技活动管理和为科技活动提供直接服务，累计从事科技活动的时间占全年制度工作时间 10%及以上的人员。(1)直接从事科

主要统计指标解释

技活动的人员，包括：在独立核算的科学研究与技术开发机构、高等学校、各类企业及其他事业单位内设的研究室、实验室、技术开发中心及中试车间(基地)等机构中从事科技活动的研究人员、工程技术人员、技术工人及其它人员；虽不在上述机构工作，但编入科技活动项目(课题)组的人员；科技信息与文献机构中的专业技术人员；从事论文设计的研究生等。(2)专门从事科技活动管理和为科技活动提供直接服务的人员包括：独立核算的科学研究与技术开发机构、科技信息与文献机构、高等学校、各类企业及其他事业单位主管科技工作的负责人，专门从事科技活动的计划、行政、人事、财务、物资供应、设备维护、图书资料管理等工作的各类人员，但不包括保卫、医疗保健人员、司机、食堂人员、茶炉工、水暖工、清洁工等为科技活动提供间接服务的人员。该指标用来反映投入科技活动人力的规模。

■ 新产品

指采用新技术原理、新设计构思研制、生产的全新产品，或在结构、材质、工艺等某一方面比原有产品有明显改进，从而显著提高了产品性能或扩大了使用功能的产品。既包括政府有关部门认定并在有效期内的新产品，也包括企业自行研制开发、在统计规定的新产品跟踪期限内的产品。跟踪期限规定如下：装备类跟踪五年，消费品类跟踪二年，其他类跟踪三年。用来反映科技产出及对经济增长的直接贡献。

■ 专　利

是专利权的简称，是对发明人的发明创造经审查合格后，由专利局依据专利法授予发明人和设计人对该项发明创造享有的专有权。包括发明、实用新型和外观设计。反映拥有自主知识产权的科技和设计成果情况。

■ 科技活动经费筹集

指从各种渠道筹集到的计划用于科技活动的经费，包括政府资金、事业资金、企业资金、银行贷款和其他收入等。反映各社会经济主体对促进科技进步所作的努力。

■ 政府资金

指从各级政府部门获得的计划用于科技活动的经费，包括科学事业费、科技三项费、科研基建费、科学基金、教育等部门事业费中计划用于科技活动的经费以及政府部门预算外资金中计划用于科技活动的经费等。

SHANGHAI STATISTICAL YEARBOOK

EXPLANATORY NOTES TO MAJOR STATISTICAL INDICATORS

□ Professional and Technical Personnel

Professional and Technical Personnel refer to professional, technical and managerial staff members in institutions or enterprises who not only have professional and technical titles but also hold professional and technical posts. They also include those who work on professional and technical posts but do not have professional and technical titles.

□ R&D

R&D is an abbreviation which stands for 'Science Research and Experimental Development', which means systematic and creative endeavors aimed at expanding the overall volume of knowledge and applying the knowledge in systematic creation. R&D includes basic studies, application research and experimental development.

□ Basic Research

Basic Research refers to empirical or theoretical research aiming at obtaining new knowledge on the fundamental principles of phenomena of observable facts to reveal the nature and law of movement of objects and to acquire new discoveries or new theories. Basic research takes no specific or designated application as the aim of the research. Results of basic research are mainly released or disseminated in the form of scientific papers or monographs. This indicator reflects the original innovation capacity of knowledge.

□ Applied Research

Applied Research refers to creative research aiming at obtaining new knowledge on a specific objective or target. Purpose of the applied research is to identify the possible use of results from basic research, or to explore new (fundamental) methods or new approaches. Results of applied research are expressed in the form of scientific papers, monographs, fundamental models or invention patents. This indicator reflects the exploration of ways to apply the results of basic research.

□ Experiments Development

Experiments Development refer to systematic activities aiming at using the knowledge from basic and applied researches or from practical experience to develop new products, materials and equipment, to establish new production process, systems and services, or to make substantial improvement on the existing products, process or services. Results of experiment and development activities are embodied in patents, exclusive technology, and monotype of new products or equipment. In social sciences, experiment and development activities refer to the process of converting the knowledge from basic or applied researches into feasible programmes (including conduct of demonstration projects for assessment and evaluation). There are no experiment and development activities in the science of humanities. This indicator reflects the capability of transferring the results of S&T into technique and products, which is the materialized measurement of S&T pushing forward the economic and social development.

□ Invention

Inventions refer to the new technical proposals to the products or methods or their modifications. This is universal core indicator reflecting the technologies with independent intellectual property.

□ Utility Models

Utility Models refer to the practical and new technical proposals on the shape and structure of the product or the combination of both. This indicator reflects the condition of technological results with certain technical content.

□ Exterior Design

Designs refer to the aesthetics and industrially applicable new designs for the shape, pattern and color of the product, or their combinations. This indicator reflects the appearance design achievements with independent intellectual property.

□ Independent Research and Development Institutions

Independent Research and Development Institutions refer to the state-owned institutions which have direct mission and research purpose, a certain research level and quantities of personnel, favorable conditions for R&D and engaging in scientific research and technological development. The institutions also

EXPLANATORY NOTES TO MAJOR STATISTICAL INDICATORS

have their own independent organization, accounting system authority to sign contract with other units, and their own accounts in banks.

□ Scientists and Engineers

Scientists and Engineers refer to persons engaged in S&T activities who have obtained titles of senior and middle level professional positions, and those without such position but have completed university or higher education.

□ Scientific and Technological Activities (S&T Activities)

Scientific and Technological Activities (S&T Activities) refer to organized activities which are closely related with the creation, development, dissemination and application of the scientific and technical knowledge in the fields of natural sciences, agricultural sciences, medical sciences, engineering and technological sciences, humanities and social sciences (referred to as scientific and technological fields). S&T activities can be classified into 3 categories: research and development (R&D) activities, application of R&D results, and related S&T services. This statistical definition is made by UNICHIEF for scientific and technological activities to meet the need of carrying out statistical work in this field for its member countries in particular those developing countries.

□ Personnel Engaged in S&T Activities

Personnel Engaged in S&T Activities refer to personnel directly engaged in S&T activities, in the management of S&T activities, and in providing direct service to S&T activities, who spend over 10% of the total working hours in a year in S&T activities. (1) Personnel directly engaged in S&T activities include researchers, engineers, technicians and other related personnel engaged in S&T activities in independent-accounting R&D institutions, institutions of higher learning, and in research institutes, laboratories, technology development centers and central experiment workshops under enterprises and institutions. Also included are people working in S&T information archiving institutes, and graduate students working on the design of their thesis. (2) Personnel engaged in the management of S&T activities and in providing direct service to S&T activities include senior management people responsible for S&T activities in independent-accounting R&D institutions, S&T information archiving institutes, institutions of higher learning, and in enterprises and institutions where S&T activities are undertaken. Also included are people responsible for the planning, administration, personnel management, financial management, logistics supply, equipment maintenance, information and library management that are related with S&T activities. People providing indirect services are excluded, such as security, medical service, drivers, plumbers, cleaners and those providing catering and related service. This indicator reflects the size of personnel engaged in S&T activities.

□ New Products

New Products refer to new products produced with new technology and new design, or products that represent noticeable improvement in terms of structure, material, or production process so as to improve significantly the character or function of the older versions. They include new products certified by relevant government agencies within the period of certification, as well as new products designed and produced by enterprises within the new product track time limit prescribed by the statistical regulations. The new product track time limit is prescribed as following: equipment products 5 years, consumption products 2 years, other products 3 years. This indictor reflects the direct contribution of S&T output to economic growth.

□ Patent

Patent is an abbreviation for the patent right and refers to the exclusive right of ownership by the inventors or designers for the creation or inventions, given from the patent offices after due process of assessment and approval in accordance with the Patent Law. Patents are granted for inventions, utility models and designs. This indicator reflects the achievements of S&T and design with independent intellectual property.

□ Funding for S&T Activities

Funding for S&T Activities refers to funds obtained from various sources for S&T activities, including government funds, self-raised funds by institutions, self-raised funds by enterprises, loans from banks and other funds. This indicator reflects the efforts made by various social economic entities in promoting the development of S&T.

□ Government Funds

Government Funds refer to funds obtained from govern-

EXPLANATORY NOTES TO MAJOR STATISTICAL INDICATORS

ment agencies at all levels to be used for S&T activities, including fund for scientific undertakings, 3 kinds of fund for S&T activities, fund for capital construction for scientific researches, science fund, funds from education expenditures by education departments for S&T activities, and extra-budget fund from government agencies for S&T activities.

第十九篇

CHAPTER 19

环境保护治理

ENVIRONMENT
PROTECTION
AND TREATMENT

表 19.1 环保投入和"三废"综合利用(1990～2006)
INVESTMENT ON ENVIRONMENT PROTECTION AND WASTE GAS, WASTE WATER AND SOLID WASTES UTILIZED

单位:亿元(100 million yuan)

年份 Year	环境保护投资 Investment on Environment Protection	其中 of which: #城市环境基础设施建设投资 Urban Environment Infrastructure Investment	环境保护投资相当于全市生产总值比例(%) Investment on Environment Protection as Percentage of Gross Domestic Product(%)	"三废"综合利用产品产值 Output Value of Products Made from Utilization of Waste Gas, Waste Water and Solid Wastes	自然保护区覆盖率(%) Coverage Rate of Natural Preservation Areas(%)
1990				2.06	
1991	7.60		0.90	2.67	
1992	15.20		1.40	3.94	
1993	32.13		2.10	5.36	
1994	39.09		2.00	5.95	
1995	46.49		1.90	6.63	
1996	68.83		2.40	7.55	
1997	82.35		2.50	12.15	
1998	102.13		2.80	8.01	
1999	111.57		2.80	8.69	
2000	141.91		3.10	9.16	7.8
2001	152.93		3.10	5.00	10.5
2002	162.39	126.99	3.00	7.25	11.8
2003	191.53	144.05	3.10	7.13	11.8
2004	225.37	166.90	3.03	13.04	11.8
2005	281.18	201.01	3.07	9.11	11.8
2006	310.85	177.81	3.00	9.72	11.8

注:本表至 19.8 数据由上海市环境保护局提供。
Note: Data in this table to table 19.8 are provided by Shanghai Environmental Protection Bureau.

表 19.2 主要年份工业固体废弃物防治
PREVENTION AND CURE OF INDUSTRIAL SOLID WASTES IN MAIN YEARS

指标	Indicators	2000	2005	2006
工业固体废弃物产生量(万吨)	Volume of Industrial Solid Wastes Produced (10 000 tons)	1 354.74	1 963.62	2 063.19
#危险废物	Dangerous Wastes	28.32	48.77	40.79
工业废弃物综合利用量(万吨)	Volume of Industrial Wastes Treated and Utilized (10 000 tons)	1 515.90	1 891.62	1 953.11
#危险废物	Dangerous Wastes	27.05	38.21	29.13
工业废弃物综合利用率(%)	Ratio of Industrial Wastes Treated and Utilized (%)	93.26	96.31	94.66
工业固体废物处置量(万吨)	Volume of Industrial Solid Wastes Disposed (10 000 tons)	90.96	64.66	103.22
#危险废物	Dangerous Wastes	1.08	9.64	14.10

表 19.3 水环境保护(1991～2006)
WATER ENVIRONMENT PROTECTION

年份 Year	废水排放总量(亿吨) Total Waste Water Discharged (100 million tons)	其中 of which		废水化学需氧量排放总量(万吨) Total Emission of Oxygen of Waste Water Needed by Chemistry (10 000 tons)	其中 of which	
		工业 Industrial Waste Water	生活及其他 Residential Waste Water		工业 Industrial Waste Water	生活及其他 Residential Waste Water
1991	19.58	13.25	6.33		24.75	
1992	20.28	13.70	6.58		19.60	
1993	20.32	12.81	7.51		16.76	
1994	20.37	11.81	8.56		16.37	
1995	22.45	11.61	10.84		12.29	
1996	22.85	11.41	11.44	27.46	12.16	15.30
1997	21.10	9.99	11.11	38.55	11.70	26.85
1998	20.81	9.00	11.81	36.55	9.63	26.92
1999	20.28	8.52	11.76	34.98	8.92	26.06
2000	19.37	7.25	12.12	31.87	6.93	24.94
2001	19.50	6.80	12.70	30.48	5.27	25.21
2002	19.21	6.49	12.72	32.96	4.78	28.18
2003	18.22	6.11	12.11	28.38	4.38	24.00
2004	19.34	5.64	13.70	29.38	3.76	25.62
2005	19.97	5.11	14.86	30.44	3.66	26.78
2006	22.37	4.83	17.54	30.20	3.53	26.67

表 19.3 续表 continued

年份 Year	工业废水排放达标量(万吨) Volume of Industrial Waste Water Meeting Discharge Standard (10 000 tons)	工业废水排放达标率(%) Ratio of Standard Industrial Waste Water Discharged to the Total Discharge(%)	工业重复用水量(万吨) Volume of Interative Used Water by Industry (10 000 tons)	污水处理厂数(个) Number of Sewage Disposal Plants (unit)	污水处理厂污水处理量(万吨) Volume of Sewage Disposed by Sewage Disposal Plants (10 000 tons)
1991	86 594	65.3		17	11 984
1992	90 559	66.1	384 830	13	13 246
1993	90 721	70.8	390 629	16	14 133
1994	83 683	70.8	427 236	17	12 644
1995	89 365	77.0	445 391	17	14 665
1996	99 721	87.4	486 278	20	12 876
1997	86 568	86.6	495 622	22	14 790
1998	79 356	88.2	475 656	22	15 605
1999	76 664	89.9	605 772	22	17 479
2000	67 553	93.2	592 055	27	23 028
2001	64 876	95.4	709 913	26	29 487
2002	61 521	94.9	654 133	27	30 658
2003	58 020	94.9	690 068	30	39 891
2004	54 255	96.3	750 803	37	95 301
2005	49 590	97.1	886 503	42	117 833
2006	47 146	97.5	843 970	43	155 726

表 19.4 大气环境保护(1991～2006)
ATMOSPHERE ENVIRONMENT PROTECTION

年 份 Year	废 气 排放总量 (亿标立方米) Total Waste Gas Emission (100 million cu. m)	其 中 of which		烟尘排放总量(万吨) Total Emission of Smoke and Dust (10 000 tons)	其 中 of which	
		工 业 Industrial Sector	生活及其他 Residential Sector and Others		工 业 Industrial Sector	生活及其他 Residential Sector and Others
1991	4 617	4 000	617	21.54	14.68	6.86
1992	5 110	4 418	692	22.50	14.81	7.69
1993	4 231	3 859	371	18.93	14.80	4.13
1994	4 577	4 184	393	18.45	14.08	4.37
1995	5 095	4 625	471	20.78	13.33	7.45
1996	5 132	4 757	375	15.78	14.77	1.01
1997	5 249	4 755	494	17.08	13.38	3.70
1998	5 493	4 912	580	15.63	10.74	4.89
1999	5 480	4 947	533	13.57	9.00	4.57
2000	6 398	5 755	643	14.12	8.32	5.80
2001	7 620	6 964	656	13.52	6.23	7.29
2002	7 902	7 440	462	10.74	5.60	5.14
2003	8 391	7 799	592	11.54	4.97	6.57
2004	9 466	8 834	632	12.27	5.25	7.02
2005	9 103	8 482	621	11.52	4.95	6.57
2006	10 045	9 428	617	11.29	4.73	6.56

表 19.4 续表 continued

年 份 Year	废气二氧化硫排放总量 (万吨) Total Emission of SO_2 (10 000 tons)	其 中 of which		工业废气二氧化硫去除量 (万吨) SO_2 Dispeled from Industrial Waste Gas (10 000 tons)	工业烟尘去除量 (万吨) Industrial Smoke and Dust Dispeled (10 000 tons)	工业粉尘去除量 (万吨) Industrial Powder and Dust Dispeled (10 000 tons)
		工 业 Industrial Sector	生活及其他 Residential Sector and Others			
1991	47.92	33.87	14.05	4.13	255.60	89.05
1992	51.36	35.62	15.74	3.90	258.49	117.86
1993	44.12	35.67	8.45	3.70	279.15	123.44
1994	45.19	36.24	8.95	3.47	306.39	123.61
1995	53.41	38.15	15.26	3.34	325.16	117.72
1996	54.00	43.30	7.70	5.58	403.95	89.11
1997	50.85	43.62	7.23	4.16	359.85	141.80
1998	48.89	39.09	9.80	3.11	273.54	151.77
1999	40.31	31.09	9.22	3.36	261.04	184.61
2000	46.49	32.68	13.81	3.77	308.35	218.08
2001	47.26	30.00	17.26	2.14	326.35	263.89
2002	44.66	32.49	12.17	5.58	366.44	301.92
2003	43.54	30.07	13.47	4.86	402.89	348.02
2004	47.31	34.95	12.36	5.53	655.27	208.07
2005	51.28	37.52	13.76	7.49	574.24	150.53
2006	50.80	37.43	13.37	9.45	520.54	146.80

表 19.5 主要年份环境空气状况
AMBIENT AIR CONDITION IN MAIN YEARS

指 标	Indicators	2000	2005	2006
中心城区二氧化硫年日平均值（毫克/立方米）	Annual Daily Mean Concentration of SO_2 in Urban Area (mg/m^3)	0.045	0.061	0.055
中心城区二氧化氮年日平均值（毫克/立方米）	Annual Daily Mean Concentration of NO_2 in Urban Area (mg/m^3)	0.090	0.061	0.051
中心城区可吸入颗粒平均浓度（毫克/立方米）	Mean Concentration of Inhalable Particulate in Urban Area (mg/m^3)		0.088	0.086
降水 PH 平均值	Rain PH Value	5.19	4.93	4.73
酸雨频率(%)	Frequency of Acid Rain (%)	26.0	40.0	56.4
环境空气质量优良天数(天)	Number of Days with Good Ambient Air Quality (day)	295	322	324
环境空气质量优良率(%)	Rate of Good Ambient Air Quality (%)	80.8	88.2	88.8

表 19.6 主要年份声环境及治理
NOISE ENVIRONMENT AND TREATMENT IN MAIN YEARS

指 标	Indicators	2000	2005	2006
区域环境噪声平均等效声级	**Average Equivalent Sound Level of Area Ambient Noise**			
昼间时段(LeqdB(A))	Daytime (LeqdB(A))	56.6	57.3	56.6
夜间时段(LeqdB(A))	Nighttime (LeqdB(A))	49.2	49.8	49.7
交通环境噪声平均等效声级	**Average Equivalent Sound Level of Traffic Noise**			
昼间时段(LeqdB(A))	Daytime (LeqdB(A))	70.5	72.0	72.0
夜间时段(LeqdB(A))	Nighttime (LeqdB(A))	64.1	65.8	64.9

表 19.7 城市环境卫生情况(1978～2006)
URBAN ENVIRONMENTAL SANITATION

年 份 Year	清运垃圾 (万吨) Garbage Disposal Cleared (10 000 tons)	其 中 of which		清运粪便 (万吨) Excrements Disposal Cleared (10 000 tons)
		生活垃圾 Residential Garbage	建筑垃圾 Construction Garbage	
1978	214	108	106	418
1979	250	125	126	374
1980	272	131	141	331
1981	272	146	126	329
1982	296	169	127	325
1983	280	166	113	311
1984	308	185	123	272
1985	305	196	109	252
1986	328	226	102	263
1987	325	229	97	262
1988	329	240	89	249
1989	344	250	94	246
1990	382	279	103	243
1991	393	296	97	229
1992	428	301	127	242
1993	488	335	152	234
1994	558	358	200	240
1995	668	372	296	216
1996	736	419	317	217
1997	755	454	301	227
1998	824	470	353	218
1999	767	500	267	172
2000	858	641	217	256
2001	901	644	257	219
2002	760	467	293	238
2003	800	585	215	251
2004	802	610	192	258
2005	777	622	155	254
2006	805	658	146	247

表 19.8 环境卫生设施(1978 ~ 2006)
URBAN ENVIRONMENTAL SANITATION

年 份 Year	公共厕所 (座) Public Lavatories (unit)	生活垃圾收集箱(座) Collection Cans of Residential Garbage(unit)	废物箱 (只) Trash Cans (unit)	倒粪站 (座) Excrements Stations (unit)	化粪池 (只) Septic Tanks (unit)
1978	706	13 840	2 333	3 303	25 540
1979	696	12 695	3 151	3 382	25 915
1980	713	15 707	3 402	3 445	26 754
1981	740	17 905	2 546	3 464	27 407
1982	760	18 824	2 821	3 484	28 652
1983	778	17 859	2 733	3 467	29 977
1984	798	20 384	3 890	3 481	30 943
1985	952	22 870	5 700	3 470	33 477
1986	950	31 142	5 983	3 537	39 175
1987	978	37 751	6 341	3 587	40 042
1988	992	42 802	5 117	3 342	41 171
1989	1 057	46 149	5 276	3 107	41 349
1990	1 016	46 368	4 921	2 973	43 655
1991	1 033	40 309	4 980	3 006	43 089
1992	1 048	44 752	4 961	2 655	43 694
1993	1 104	46 741	5 756	2 732	43 323
1994	1 100	50 292	6 993	2 739	43 125
1995	1 100	48 563	9 019	2 532	43 151
1996	1 112	51 456	9 522	2 412	38 657
1997	1 120	53 643	12 735	2 207	44 440
1998	1 203	59 498	15 968	2 127	41 760
1999	1 311	66 067	17 326	2 192	44 694
2000	2 215	22 470	23 189	2 045	46 921
2001	2 406	17 694	24 672	1 890	47 500
2002	3 776	26 787	29 517	1 846	49 220
2003	3 468	27 814	31 272	1 709	48 831
2004	3 640	28 649	34 571	1 611	47 579
2005	3 640	28 388	39 539	1 689	47 424
2006	3 746	29 812	44 888	2 253	46 217

上/海/统/计/年/鉴

主要统计指标解释

■ “三废”综合利用产品产值

指报告期内利用“三废”作为主要原料生产的产品价值(现行价);已经销售或准备销售的应计算产品价值,留作生产自用的不应计算产品价值。

■ 自然保护区

指对有代表性的自然生态系统、珍稀濒危野生动植物物种的天然分布区、水源涵养区、有特殊意义的自然历史遗迹等保护对象所在的陆地、陆地水体或海域,依法划出一定面积进行特殊保护和管理的区域。以县及县以上各级人民政府正式批准建立的自然保护区为准(包括“六五”以前由部门或“革委会”批准且现仍存在的自然保护区)。风景名胜区、文物保护区不计在内。自然保护区分国家级、省级、地市级和县级。按主管部门分属:环保、林业、农业、地矿、海洋、水利和其他部门。

■ 工业固体废弃物产生量

指报告期内企业在生产过程中产生的固体状、半固体状和高浓度液体状废弃物的总量,包括危险废物、冶炼废渣、粉煤灰、炉渣、煤矸石、尾矿、放射性废物和其他废物等;不包括矿山开采的剥离废石和掘进废石(煤矸石和呈酸性或碱性的废石除外)。酸性或碱性废石指采掘的废石其流经水、雨淋水的pH值小于4或pH值大于10.5者。

■ 危险废物

指列入国家危险废物名录或根据国家规定的危险废物鉴别标准和鉴别方法认定的,具有爆炸性、易燃性、易氧化性、毒性、腐蚀性、易传染疾病等危险特性之一的废物。

■ 工业废弃物综合利用量

指报告期内企业通过回收、加工、循环、交换等方式,从废弃物中提取或者使其转化为可以利用的资源、能源和其他原材料的废弃物量(包括当年利用往年的工业废弃物贮存量),如用作农业肥料、生产建筑材料、筑路等。综合利用量由原产生废弃物的单位统计。

■ 工业废弃物综合利用率

指工业废弃物综合利用量占工业废弃物产生量(包括综合利用往年贮存量)的百分率。计算公式为:

$$\text{工业废弃物综合利用率} = \frac{\text{工业废弃物综合利用量}}{\text{工业废弃物产生量} + \text{综合利用往年贮存量}} \times 100\%$$

■ 工业固体废物处置量

指报告期内企业将固体废物焚烧或者最终置于符合环境保护规定要求的场所,并不再回取的工业固体废物量(包括当年处置往年的工业固体废物贮存量)。处置方式有填埋(其中危险废物应安全填埋)、焚烧、专业贮存场(库)封场处理、深层灌注、回填矿井及海洋处置(经海洋管理部门同意投海处置)等。

■ 工业废水排放量

指经过企业厂区所有排放口排到企业外部的工业废水量。包括生产废水、外排的直接冷却水、超标排放的矿井地下水和与工业废水混排的厂区生活污水,不包括外排的间接冷却水(清污不分流的间接冷却水应计算在内)。

■ 工业废水排放达标量

指报告期内废水中各项污染物指标都达到国家或地方排放标准的外排工业废水量,包括未经处理外排达标的,经废水处理设施处理后达标排放的,以及经污水处理厂处理后达标排放的。

■ 工业废水排放达标率

指工业废水排放达标量占工业废水排放量的百分率,计算公式为:

$$\text{工业废水排放达标率} = \frac{\text{工业废水排放达标量}}{\text{工业废水排放量}} \times 100\%$$

■ 工业废气排放量

指企业厂区内燃料燃烧和生产工艺过程中产生的各种排入空气的含有污染物的气体总量,按标准状态〔273K,101 325Pa〕计算。测算公式为:

$$\text{工业废气排放量} = \text{燃料燃烧过程中废气排放量} + \text{生产工艺过程中废气排放量}$$

■ 工业二氧化硫排放总量

指报告期内企业在燃料燃烧和生产工艺过程中排入

主要统计指标解释

大气的 SO_2 总量,计算公式为:

工业二氧化硫排放量 = 燃料燃烧过程中二氧化硫排放量 + 生产工艺过程中二氧化硫排放量

■ 工业烟尘排放量

指企业厂区内燃料燃烧过程中产生的烟气中夹带的颗粒物排放量。

■ 酸雨频率

指酸雨出现的次数占降水出现次数的比例,通常称PH值小于5.6的降水为酸雨。

■ 生活垃圾清运量

指报告期内收集和运送到垃圾处理厂(场)的生活垃圾数量。生活垃圾指城市日常生活或为城市日常生活提供服务的活动中产生的固体废物以及法律行政规定的视为城市生活垃圾的固体废物。包括:居民生活垃圾、商业垃圾、集市贸易市场垃圾、街道清扫垃圾、公共场所垃圾和机关、学校、厂矿等单位的生活垃圾。

EXPLANATORY NOTES TO MAJOR STATISTICAL INDICATORS

□ Output Value of Products Made from Utilization of Waste Gas, Waste Water and Solid Wastes

Output Value of Products Made from Utilization of Waste Gas, Waste Water and Solid Wastes refers current value of products with waste gas, waste water and solid wastes as main materials of production. Products sold and ready to sell shall be included while those produced for own use shall not be included.

□ Natural Preservation

Natural Preservation refers to all the land, water areas on land and sea areas are under special protection or management due to the possession of representative natural ecological system, natural distribution of rare and dying out animal zones, water-resource conservation areas, and natural historical relics. Also included are natural reserves formally approved by people's governments at various levels at and above county level (including those approved before the Sixth-five-year Program and still active natural reserves).Scenic spots and historical sites and zones for preservation of cultural relics are not included. Natural reserves are classified as national level, provincial level, prefecture level and county level ones. They are under the jurisdiction of different departments, such as: environment protection, forestry, agriculture, geological and mining, oceanic and water conservancy and so on.

□ Industrial Solid Wastes Produced

Industrial Solid Wastes Produced refers to total volume of solid, semi-solid and high concentration liquid residues produced by industrial enterprises from production process in a given period of time, including hazardous wastes, slag, coal ash, gangue, tailings, radioactive residues and other wastes, but excluding stones stripped or dug out in mining (gangue and acid or alkaline stones not included). A stone is acid or alkaline depending on the pH value of the water below 4 or above 10.5 when the stone is in, or soaked by, the water.

□ Dangerous Wastes

Dangerous Wastes refers to those included in the national hazardous wastes catalogue or specified as any one of the following properties in the national hazardous wastes identification standards: explosive, ignitable, oxidizable, toxic, corrosive or liable to cause infectious diseases or lead to other dangers.

□ Industrial Wastes Treated and Utilized

Industrial Wastes Treated and Utilized refers to volume of wastes from which useful materials can be extracted or which can be converted into usable resources, energy or other materials by means of reclamation, processing, recycling and exchange (including utilizing in the year the stocks of industrial wastes of the previous year). Examples of such utilizations include fertilizers, building materials and road materials. The information shall be collected by the producing units of the wastes.

□ Ratio of Industrial Wastes Treated and Utilized

Ratio of Industrial Wastes Treated and Utilized refers to the percentage of industrial wastes utilized over industrial wastes produced (including stocks of the previous years). It is calculated as:

$$\text{Ratio of industrial wastes treated and utilized} = \frac{\text{volume of industrial wastes utilized}}{\text{(industrial wastes produced + stock of previous years)}} \times 100\%$$

□ Industrial Solid Wastes Disposed

Industrial Solid Wastes Disposed refers to quantity of industrial solid wastes which are burnt or placed ultimately in the sites meeting the requirements for environmental protection and not salvaged or recycled (including disposition in the year of those wastes of previous years). The disposition includes landfill (Safe landfills should be conducted for hazardous wastes), incineration, containment spaces, deep underground disposal, backfill in mining pits and disposal at sea.

□ Volume of Industrial Waste Water Discharged

Volume of Industrial Waste Water Discharged refers to the volume of industrial waste water discharged, through all outlets, to the outside of industrial enterprises, including waste water produced, direct-cooling water, underground water from mines that does not meet the standard of discharge, and the domestic sewage mixed up with industrial waste water when discharged, but excluding discharged indirect-cooling water.

EXPLANATORY NOTES TO MAJOR STATISTICAL INDICATORS

□ Industrial Waste Water Meeting Discharge Standards

Industrial Waste Water Meeting Discharge Standards refers to volume of industrial waste water discharge which, with or without treatment, reaches national or local standards with regard to all pollutants.

□ Ratio of Standard Waste Water Discharged to the Total Discharge

Ratio of Standard Waste Water Discharged to the Total Discharge refers to the share of the volume of waste water up to the standard for discharge of the total volume. The formula is as follows:

$$\text{Ratio of Standard Waste Water Discharged to the Total Discharge} = \frac{\text{Volume of Waste Water up to the Standard for Discharge}}{\text{Volume of Industrial Waste Water Discharged}} \times 100\%$$

□ Volume of Waste Industrial Gas Emission

Industrial Waste Air Emission refers to discharge into atmosphere of waste air containing pollutants generated from fuel burning and production process in enterprises within a given period of time. It is calculated at standard status (273K, 101325Pa) as:

Industrial waste air emission=emission through fuel burning +emission through production process

□ SO_2 Emission through Industrial Activities

SO_2 Emission through Industrial Activities refers to volume of sulphur dioxide emission from fuel burning and production process by enterprises during a given period of time. It is calculated as:

SO_2 emission through industrial activities = SO_2 emission from fuel burning + SO_2 emission from production process

□ Industrial Smoke and Dust Emission

Industrial Soot Emission refers to volume of soot in smoke emitted in process of fuel burning inside factories.

□ Acid Rain Frequency

Acid Rain Frequency refers to the proportion of frequencies of acid rainfall to the total rainfall times. Rainfall is defined as acid rain when the PH value of its rainwater is small than 5.6.

□ Residential Garbage Disposal Cleared

Residential Garbage Disposal Cleared refers to volume of consumption wastes collected and transported to disposal factories or sites. Consumption wastes are solid wastes produced from urban households or from service activities for urban households, and solid wastes regarded by laws and regulations as urban consumption wastes, including those from households, commercial activities, markets, cleaning of streets, public sites, offices, schools, factories, mining units and other sources.

第二十篇

CHAPTER 20

教　育

EDUCATION

表 20.1 主要年份教育事业基本情况
BASIC STATISTICS OF EDUCATION IN MAIN YEARS

	指 标 Indicators	1990	2000	2005	2006
学校数(所)	**Quantity of Schools(unit)**	**3 928**	**2 212**	**1 694**	**1 659**
普通高等学校	Regular Institutions of Higher Education	50	37	60	60
普通中等学校	Secondary Schools	1 219	1 120	966	945
中等专业学校	Specialized Secondary Schools	110	84	81	81
职业中学	Vocational Secondary Schools	80	60	37	37
技工学校	Technical Worker Schools	317	115	41	33
普通中学	Regular Secondary Schools	712	861	807	794
高 中	Senior Secondary Schools	264	328	330	317
初 中	Junior Secondary Schools	448	533	477	477
普通小学	Primary Schools	2 630	1 021	640	626
特殊教育学校	Special Education Schools	29	34	28	28
教职工数(万人)	**Quantity of Teachers and Staff (10 000 persons)**	**24.95**	**22.66**	**21.59**	**21.29**
普通高等学校	Regular Institutions of Higher Education	7.06	6.01	7.09	7.17
普通中等学校	Secondary Schools	10.30	10.36	9.40	9.10
中等专业学校	Specialized Secondary Schools	1.49	1.27	1.09	1.06
职业中学	Vocational Secondary Schools	0.53	0.66	0.51	0.50
技工学校	Technical Worker Schools	1.66	0.77	0.34	0.21
普通中学	Regular Secondary Schools	6.62	7.66	7.46	7.33
普通小学	Primary Education Schools	7.48	6.13	4.94	4.86
特殊教育学校	Special Education Schools	0.11	0.16	0.16	0.16
专任教师(万人)	**Quantity of Full-time Teachers (10 000 persons)**	**14.14**	**12.80**	**13.10**	**13.31**
普通高等学校	Regular Institutions of Higher Education	2.58	2.05	3.18	3.39
普通中等学校	Secondary Schools	5.62	6.23	6.08	6.07
中等专业学校	Specialized Secondary Schools	0.66	0.53	0.53	0.52
职业中学	Vocational Secondary Schools	0.26	0.39	0.31	0.30
技工学校	Technical Worker Schools	0.57	0.30	0.12	0.12
普通中学	Regular Secondary Schools	4.13	5.01	5.12	5.14
高 中	Senior Secondary Schools	0.92	1.42	1.81	1.80
初 中	Junior Secondary Schools	3.21	3.59	3.31	3.34
普通小学	Primary Schools	5.88	4.43	3.74	3.75
特殊教育学校	Special Education Schools	0.06	0.09	0.10	0.10

①本篇资料除注明外均由上海市人民政府教育委员会提供。
②普通中学学校数中，完全中学 174 所，高级中学 143 所，初级中学 338 所，一贯制学校 139 所。
❶Data in this chapter are provided by Shanghai Municipal Education Commission except noting data.
❷In regular secondary schools, there are 174 whole secondary schools , 143 senior high schools , 338 junior high schools and 139 system schools.

表 20.1 续表 continued

指 标	Indicators	1990	2000	2005	2006
毕业生数（万人）	**Graduates (10 000 persons)**	**35.83**	**55.54**	**53.90**	**50.59**
普通高等学校	Regular Institutions of Higher Education	3.46	4.09	10.34	11.05
普通中等学校	Secondary Schools	18.69	32.63	32.55	28.60
中等专业学校	Specialized Secondary Schools	2.03	3.86	3.39	3.52
职业中学	Vocational Secondary Schools	1.61	3.99	2.34	2.00
技工学校	Technical Worker Schools	1.69	1.86	1.43	0.84
普通中学	Regular Secondary Schools	13.36	22.92	25.39	22.24
高　中	Senior Secondary Schools	3.04	7.18	10.10	10.21
初　中	Junior Secondary Schools	10.32	15.74	15.29	12.03
普通小学	Primary Schools	13.66	18.73	10.93	10.85
特殊教育学校	Special Education Schools	0.02	0.09	0.08	0.09
招生数（万人）	**New Student Enrollment (10 000 persons)**	**44.05**	**52.10**	**50.28**	**48.49**
普通高等学校	Regular Institutions of Higher Education	3.24	8.13	13.18	14.04
普通中等学校	Secondary Schools	22.61	33.58	26.67	23.50
中等专业学校	Specialized Secondary Schools	1.91	3.00	3.33	3.47
职业中学	Vocational Secondary Schools	1.86	2.44	1.84	1.76
技工学校	Technical Worker Schools	1.75	1.68	0.60	0.44
普通中学	Regular Secondary Schools	17.09	26.46	20.90	17.84
高　中	Senior Secondary Schools	3.40	7.84	9.94	7.00
初　中	Junior Secondary Schools	13.69	18.62	10.96	10.84
普通小学	Primary Schools	18.14	10.28	10.36	10.87
特殊教育学校	Special Education Schools	0.06	0.11	0.07	0.07
在校学生（万人）	**Student Enrollment (10 000 persons)**	**185.24**	**207.36**	**197.58**	**192.75**
普通高等学校	Regular Institutions of Higher Education	12.13	22.68	44.26	46.63
普通中等学校	Secondary Schools	62.59	105.28	99.30	92.25
中等专业学校	Specialized Secondary Schools	6.17	11.89	13.67	13.70
职业中学	Vocational Secondary Schools	3.66	8.48	5.76	5.33
技工学校	Technical Worker Schools	4.45	5.37	2.85	2.05
普通中学	Regular Secondary Schools	48.31	79.54	77.02	71.17
高　中	Senior Secondary Schools	9.80	23.94	30.82	27.17
初　中	Junior Secondary Schools	38.51	55.60	46.20	44.00
普通小学	Primary Schools	110.19	78.86	53.50	53.37
特殊教育学校	Special Education Schools	0.33	0.54	0.52	0.50

表 20.2 每万人口在校学生数、每个教师负担学生数(1978～2006)
STUDENTS ENROLLMENT PER 10 000 PERSONS AND STUDENTS TAUGHT

单位:人(person)

年 份 Year	平均每万人口在校学生数 Students Enrollment Per 10 000 Persons				平均每个教师负担学生数 Students Taught by Each Teacher		
	大学生 College and University	中专生 Speciallized Secondary School	中学生 Secondary School	小学生 Primary School	普通高等学校 Institution of Higher Education	普通中等学校 Regular Secondary School	普通小学 Primary School
1978	46	14	913	793	3	17	18
1979	60	21	722	777	4	16	19
1980	67	24	547	746	4	13	18
1981	78	25	429	716	5	11	17
1982	71	28	453	668	4	12	16
1983	66	30	436	669	4	10	16
1984	75	37	408	693	4	11	17
1985	89	49	396	692	4	12	17
1986	95	56	392	702	5	11	17
1987	98	56	386	715	5	11	17
1988	102	52	362	779	5	11	18
1989	99	50	361	831	5	11	19
1990	94	48	376	859	5	11	19
1991	91	47	398	865	5	12	19
1992	93	50	425	879	5	13	22
1993	101	58	445	901	6	14	21
1994	108	71	504	877	6	15	21
1995	110	83	556	843	7	16	20
1996	113	76	584	816	7	16	20
1997	118	85	570	785	8	16	20
1998	126	95	565	736	8	17	19
1999	142	99	584	664	9	17	19
2000	172	90	602	597	11	17	18
2001	211	91	605	545	13	16	17
2002	249	95	592	504	14	17	17
2003	282	102	562	483	16	16	17
2004	307	104	612	397	15	17	14
2005	325	101	566	393	14	16	14
2006	341	100	520	390	14	15	14

表 20.3　各级各类学校在校学生数(1978～2006)
STUDENTS ENROLLMENT BY VARIOUS SCHOOLS

单位:万人 (10 000 persons)

年　份 Year	普通高等学校 Institutions of Higher Education	普通中等学校 Secondary School	其　中　of which 中等专业学校 Specialized Secondary School	普通中学 Regular Secondary School	职业学校 Secondary Vocational School	技工学校 Technical Worker School	普通小学 Primary School	特殊教育学校 Special Education School
1978	5.06	101.81	1.55	100.26			87.06	0.18
1979	6.74	90.80	2.42	81.72		6.66	88.00	0.18
1980	7.67	71.68	2.81	62.71	0.29	5.87	85.47	0.18
1981	9.11	58.82	2.94	49.93	0.45	5.50	83.22	0.16
1982	8.39	61.69	3.30	53.53	0.85	4.01	78.88	0.16
1983	7.87	60.53	3.61	52.04	1.71	3.17	79.82	0.23
1984	8.99	61.01	4.48	49.18	3.07	4.28	83.47	0.21
1985	10.79	63.50	5.92	48.23	4.69	4.66	84.18	0.23
1986	11.77	64.82	6.86	48.31	4.71	4.94	86.56	0.25
1987	12.25	64.50	7.03	48.21	4.08	5.18	89.35	0.28
1988	12.82	61.20	6.52	45.68	3.69	5.31	98.39	0.30
1989	12.61	61.01	6.45	46.10	3.54	4.92	106.02	0.32
1990	12.13	62.59	6.17	48.31	3.66	4.45	110.19	0.33
1991	11.69	65.92	6.01	51.24	3.97	4.70	111.38	0.35
1992	11.95	70.84	6.41	54.77	4.90	4.76	113.37	0.38
1993	13.10	76.54	7.58	57.69	6.39	4.88	116.70	0.44
1994	14.04	87.23	9.23	65.56	7.54	4.90	113.98	0.52
1995	14.41	96.38	10.85	72.40	8.64	4.49	109.78	0.57
1996	14.79	99.97	9.95	76.23	9.12	4.67	106.46	0.62
1997	15.38	100.81	11.10	74.43	10.29	4.99	102.44	0.63
1998	16.51	102.53	12.38	73.85	10.72	5.58	96.14	0.52
1999	18.63	105.66	13.06	76.69	10.21	5.70	87.16	0.53
2000	22.68	105.28	11.89	79.54	8.48	5.37	78.86	0.54
2001	28.00	104.37	12.12	80.23	7.48	4.54	72.28	0.48
2002	33.16	103.59	12.66	78.97	7.56	4.40	67.24	0.55
2003	37.85	100.71	13.69	75.47	7.04	4.51	64.83	0.55
2004	41.57	106.94	14.05	82.78	6.43	3.68	53.74	0.54
2005	44.26	99.24	13.67	77.02	5.76	2.79	53.50	0.52
2006	46.63	92.25	13.70	71.17	5.33	2.05	53.37	0.50

表 20.4 主要年份教育经费支出
EDUCATIONAL FUNDS EXPENDITURE IN MAIN YEARS

单位：亿元(100 million yuan)

指 标	Indicators	2000	2005	2006
总 计	**Total**	**185.12**	**404.29**	**450.16**
#中 央	Central Government	44.53	97.23	79.43
地 方	Local Government	140.59	307.06	370.73
国家财政性教育经费	Government Appropriation for Education	142.10	266.95	295.12
#预算内教育经费	Budgetary	119.95	214.17	256.17
社会团体和公民个人办学经费	Funds of Social Organizations and Citizens for Running Schools	4.69	20.16	23.98
社会捐资和集资办学经费	Donations and Fund-raising for Running Schools	2.33	2.36	2.19
学费和杂费	Tuition and Miscellaneous Fee	21.17	74.68	71.22
其他教育经费	Other Educational Funds	14.83	40.14	57.65

表 20.5 主要年份各阶段教育实施情况
BASIC STATISTICS OF VARIOUS PHASES EDUCATION IN MAIN YEARS

单位：%

指 标	Indicators	2000	2005	2006
小 学	**Primary School**			
小学学龄儿童净入学率	Enrollment Rate of Schoolage Children	99.9	99.9	99.9
初 中	**Junior School**			
初中学生净入学率	Enrollment Rate of Students in Junior Secondary School Phase	99.9	99.9	99.9
高 中	**Senior School**			
初中毕业生升学率	Enrollment Quotas of Junior School Graduates	97.0	99.7	99.0
普通高中招生比例	Recruit Students Rate of Regular Senior Secondary Schools	51.00	58.68	55.00
高 校	**Institutions of Higher Education**			
普通高等学校录取率	Admission Rate of Students in Regular Institution of Higher Education	67.4	84.6	81.7

表 20.6 主要年份各级民办学校基本情况
BASIC STATISTICS OF CIVIL SCHOOLS IN MAIN YEARS

类　别	Types	1995	2000	2005	2006
民办高等学校	**Civil Institutions of Higher Education**				
学校数(所)	Schools (unit)	1	3	16	16
在校学生(万人)	Students Enrollment(10 000 persons)	0.04	0.67	6.69	7.86
专任教师(人)	Full-time Teachers(persons)	33	304	3 041	3 422
民办职业学校	**Civil Vocational Schools**				
学校数(所)	Schools (unit)	2	1	3	3
在校学生(万人)	Students Enrollment(10 000 persons)	0.04	0.08	0.14	0.14
专任教师(人)	Full-time Teachers(person)	4	30	97	95
民办中学	**Civil Secondary Schools**				
学校数(所)	Schools (unit)	29	155	129	126
班级数(个)	Class(unit)	151	1 842	2 293	2 331
在校学生(万人)	Students Enrollment(10 000 persons)	0.74	8.48	9.23	9.30
高　中	Senior school	0.42	4.54	3.53	3.56
初　中	Junior school	0.31	3.94	5.70	5.74
专任教师(人)	Full-time Teachers(person)	106	2 400	3 125	3 616
民办小学	**Civil Primary Schools**				
学校数(所)	Schools (unit)	11	35	19	22
班级数(个)	Class(unit)	147	987	839	950
在校学生(万人)	Students Enrollment(10 000 persons)	0.63	3.95	2.63	2.94
专任教师(人)	Full-time Teachers(person)	53	831	1 273	1 271
民办幼儿园	**Civil Kindergarten**				
学校数(所)	Schools (unit)	15	92	277	288
班级数(个)	Class(unit)	241	636	1 691	1 999
在校学生(万人)	Students Enrollment(10 000 persons)	0.31	1.77	4.22	4.80
专任教师(人)	Full-time Teachers(person)	148	1 056	3 139	3 840

表 20.7 民办学校(园)基本情况(2006)
BASIC STATISTICS OF CIVIL SCHOOLS

单位:人(person)

指 标	Indicators	学校数(所) School	毕业生数 Graduate	招生数 Students Recruited	在校生数 Students Enrollment	专任教师数 Full-time Teacher
普通高等学校	Institutions of Higher Education	16	14 810	27 510	78 556	3 422
普通中等专业学校	Specialized Secondary School	3	937	669	2 561	107
普通中学	Regular Secondary School	126	26 586	23 276	92 992	3 616
高 中	Senior School	82	12 158	8 498	35 616	1 050
初 中	Junior School	44	14 428	14 778	57 376	2 566
职业高中学校	Secondary Vocational School	3	460	411	1 442	95
普通小学	Primary School	22	5 190	6 808	29 391	1 271
幼儿园	Kindergarten	288	12 839	16 700	47 970	3 840

注：根据《民办教育促进法》的新规定，民办中、小学统计口径中扣除了公立转制学校。
Note: According to New Provision of Civil Education Advance Law, the Scope of Civil Secondary and Primary School excluded public schools transformed.

表 20.8 留学生情况(2002～2006)
STATISTICS OF STUDENT ABROAD

指 标	Indicators	2002	2003	2004	2005	2006
出国留学生人数(人)	Number of Students Studing Abroad(person)	13 150	13 041	8 497	8 783	10 582
自 费	Commoners	12 463	11 848	6 669	7 100	9 741
公 派	Public Mission	687	1 193	1 828	1 683	841
外国留学生人数(人)	Number of Foreign Students(person)	7 471	8 589	9 584	13 691	14 100
#自 费	Commoners	6 554	7 532	8 466	12 279	10 741
中国政府资助	Chinese Government Sustentation	702	805	764	934	815
学校间交换	Inter-school Communion	214	247	340	463	2 255

注：本表资料由上海市公安局、市教育委员会提供。
Note: Data in this table are provided by Shanghai Municipal Public Security Bureau and Shanghai Municipal Education Commission.

表 20.9 主要年份研究生人数
NUMBER OF GRADUATE STUDENTS IN MAIN YEARS

单位:人(person)

年 份 Year	获博士学位人数 Number of Doctor's Degrees Obtained	获硕士学位人数 Number of Master's Degrees Obtained	研究生 Postgraduates 毕业生数 Graduates 普通高等学校 Institutions of Higher Education	毕业生数 Graduates 研究所(院) Research Institutions (Academies)	招生数 New Students Enrollment 普通高等学校 Institutions of Higher Education	招生数 New Students Enrollment 研究所(院) Research Institutions (Academies)	在读人数 Students Enrollment 普通高等学校 Institutions of Higher Education	在读人数 Students Enrollment 研究所(院) Research Institutions (Academies)
1978			9		1 072		1 253	
1980			6		410		2 696	
1985	57	1 371	1 543	37	4 264	83	8 163	170
1990	300	2 746	2 953	369	2 803	324	8 533	1 035
1991	342	2 739	2 936	320	2 717	302	8 020	949
1992	343	2 124	2 262	264	3 323	345	8 858	997
1993	368	2 489	2 569	315	3 919	363	10 037	1 008
1994	442	2 363	2 608	251	4 665	465	11 905	1 185
1995	606	2 742	3 038	317	4 776	525	13 378	1 335
1996	627	3 233	3 537	323	5 915	592	15 307	1 528
1997	890	3 585	4 117	358	6 163	562	16 841	1 619
1998	1 090	3 552	4 253	389	7 281	593	19 499	1 663
1999	1 323	4 288	5 196	415	8 758	655	22 656	1 764
2000	1 307	4 546	5 435	433	11 796	856	28 582	2 032
2001	1 487	5 330	6 380	437	14 751	1 075	36 528	2 515
2002	1 655	6 067	7 481	445	17 848	1 363	45 713	3 183
2003	1 994	7 683	9 501	578	20 767	1 757	55 092	3 998
2004	2 678	10 580	12 788	681	23 545	1 789	64 747	4 690
2005	3 119	13 245	15 857	884	25 845	1 847	73 557	5 171
2006	3 772	15 957	18 833	1 098	28 250	1 849	81 487	5 419

注：2001 年前的获博士学位和获硕士学位的人数为当年毕业生人数。
Note: Number of Doctor's and Master's Degrees obtained refer to number of graduates in this year before 2001.

表 20.10 普通高等学校基本情况（2006） BASIC STATISTICS OF INSTITUTIONS OF HIGHER EDUCATION

类别 Types		学校(所) Institutions (unit)	毕业生数(人) Graduates (person)	招生数(人) New Students Enrollment (person)	在校学生人数(人) Students Enrollment (person)	教职员工(人) Staff and Workers (person)	其中 of which #专任教师 Full-time Teacher	其中 of which #正、副高级 Senior and Associate Title
总计	**Total**	**60**	**110 520**	**140 448**	**466 333**	**71 651**	**33 873**	**14 960**
#综合大学	Comprehensive Universities	3	15 358	17 552	69 684	19 275	7 646	4 272
理工院校	Science and Engineering	24	45 816	58 591	193 237	28 445	13 191	5 395
农林院校	Agriculture and Forestry	2	4 229	4 298	15 465	1 438	1 016	346
医药院校	Medical	2	748	2 346	5 852	1 351	493	150
师范院校	Teacher Training	2	8 406	9 566	35 990	7 017	3 266	1 581
语言院校	Linguistics and Literacy	2	3 904	4 002	13 094	1 608	886	314
财经院校	Economics and Finance	17	22 189	30 830	94 057	7 859	4 824	1 901
政法院校	Politics and Law	3	3 083	5 785	16 495	2 236	1 187	551
体育院校	Physical Culture	1	939	986	3 965	719	381	152
艺术院校	Art Schools	4	1 424	3 658	10 001	1 703	983	298

注：学生数中未包括在读研究生人数，在分类院校学生数中未包括成人高等学校中的普通本专科学生。

Note: Post-graduates do not included in the students enrollment. Undergraduates and junior college students in adult education schools do not includ in the students enrollment by types of colleges.

表 20.11 普通高等学校分科专任教师数（2006） FULL-TIME TEACHERS IN INSTITUTIONS OF HIGHER EDUCATION BY SUBJECTS

单位：人（person）

类别 Types		专任教师数 Full-time Teachers	其中 of which 正高级 Senior Title	副高级 Associate Title	中级 Junior Title	初级 Primary Title	无职称 Non-Title
总计	**Total**	**33 873**	**5 043**	**9 917**	**12 831**	**4 398**	**1 684**
哲学	Philosophy	880	137	262	333	104	44
经济学	Economics	2 262	350	706	886	237	83
法学	Law	2 089	256	587	776	357	113
教育学	Education	2 791	169	603	1 191	590	238
文学	Literature	7 930	781	1 907	3 157	1 468	617
历史学	History	372	111	111	101	27	22
理学	Science	3 338	762	1 171	1 085	204	116
工学	Engineering	10 273	1 858	3 454	3 801	898	262
农学	Agriculture	254	45	88	89	23	9
医学	Medical	1 471	247	342	563	237	82
管理学	Aduninistration	2 213	327	686	849	253	98

表 20.12 普通高等学校分科学生数（2006）
STUDENTS IN INSTITUTIONS OF HIGHER EDUCATION BY SUBJECTS

单位:人（person）

类 别	Types	毕业生人数 Graduates		招生人数 New Students Enrollment		在校学生人数 Students Enrollment	
		本 科 Undergraduate	专 科 Junior College	本 科 Undergraduate	专 科 Junior College	本 科 Undergraduate	专 科 Junior College
总 计	**Total**	**54 383**	**56 137**	**82 902**	**57 546**	**292 859**	**173 474**
哲 学	Philosophy	89		195		578	
经济学	Economics	4 684	5 178	8 556	3 876	28 914	13 215
法 学	Law	3 683	2 094	5 314	2 062	18 534	5 745
教育学	Education	1 670	409	1 658	927	6 439	2 078
文 学	Literature	7 474	12 016	14 019	12 763	46 316	39 731
历史学	History	224		207		800	
理 学	Science	4 939	59	7 062	45	26 252	132
工 学	Engineering	20 044	19 884	26 065	21 339	95 107	64 511
农 学	Agriculture	331	347	676	537	1 852	1 744
医 学	Medical	1 672	2 338	2 451	3 698	10 736	9 309
管理学	Management	9 573	13 810	16 699	12 299	57 331	37 009

表 20.13 中等专业学校基本情况（2006）
BASIC STATISTICS OF SPECIALIZED SECONDARY SCHOOLS

单位:人（person）

类 别	Types	毕业生数 Graduates	招生数 New Students Enrollment	在校学生 Students Enrollment	专业课专任教师 Full-time Teachers in professional course	其 中 of which	
						正副高级 Senior and Associate Title	中 级 Junior Title
总 计	**Total**	**35 194**	**34 690**	**137 012**	**2 793**	**612**	**1 412**
农业、林业	Agriculture, Forestry	1 020	611	3 320	37	8	23
资源与环境	Resource and Environment	668	747	3 651	13	4	5
能 源	Power	121	807	2 196	57	21	32
土木水利工程	Construction and Water Conservancy Engineering	2 084	2 037	7 626	161	36	78
加工制造	Machining and Manufacture	6 849	6 460	23 544	464	125	223
交通运输	Transport	1 552	3 341	10 096	253	58	123
信息技术	Information Technology	5 272	3 066	15 240	366	67	180
医药卫生	Health	2 316	4 894	15 496	305	69	185
商贸与旅游	Trade and Tour	7 105	5 846	26 144	123	31	62
财 经	Finance and Economics	3 350	2 905	12 180	235	48	119
文化艺术与体育	Arts and Physical Culture	2 902	1 805	11 193	564	111	265
社会公共事务	Society Commonality Business	1 795	1 149	4 879	50	7	25
其 他	Others	160	1 022	1 447	165	27	92

表20.14 各区、县普通中学基本情况（2006）
BASIC STATISTICS OF REGULAR SECONDARY SCHOOLS BY DISTRICT

地 区	District	学校（所） Schools (unit)	毕业生数（万人） Graduates (10 000 person)	招生数（万人） New Students Enrollment (10 000 persons)	在校学生（万人） Students Enrollment (10 000 persons)	教职员工（万人） Staff and Workers (10 000 persons)	其中 of which 专任教师 Full-time Teachers
总 计	**Total**	**794**	**22.24**	**17.83**	**71.17**	**7.33**	**5.14**
浦东新区	Pudong New Area	105	3.22	2.70	10.92	1.04	0.79
黄浦区	Huangpu	29	0.98	0.69	2.78	0.32	0.20
卢湾区	Luwan	16	0.44	0.28	1.17	0.14	0.10
徐汇区	Xuhui	45	1.53	1.18	4.72	0.46	0.32
长宁区	Changning	29	1.00	0.69	2.89	0.28	0.19
静安区	Jing'an	15	0.58	0.42	1.73	0.19	0.12
普陀区	Putuo	52	1.39	0.95	4.17	0.45	0.27
闸北区	Zhabei	41	1.32	0.91	3.71	0.40	0.27
虹口区	Hongkou	50	1.29	0.90	3.60	0.34	0.21
杨浦区	Yangpu	59	1.73	1.15	4.87	0.51	0.36
宝山区	Baoshan	52	1.19	1.11	4.15	0.39	0.30
闵行区	Minhang	56	1.22	1.16	4.44	0.55	0.40
嘉定区	Jiading	33	0.69	0.68	2.57	0.29	0.21
金山区	Jinshan	30	0.86	0.71	2.89	0.30	0.21
松江区	Songjiang	33	0.92	0.81	3.10	0.33	0.22
青浦区	Qingpu	29	0.72	0.69	2.62	0.25	0.19
南汇区	Nanhui	41	1.25	1.11	4.24	0.39	0.31
奉贤区	Fengxian	37	0.76	0.79	2.88	0.30	0.21
崇明县	Chongming	38	1.12	0.85	3.59	0.38	0.26
农 场	Farm	4	0.05	0.05	0.14	0.01	0.01

表20.15　各区、县普通中学初、高中学生基本情况(2006)
BASIC STATISTICS OF REGULAR JUNIOR AND SENIOR SCHOOLS' STUDENTS BY DISTRICTS AND COUNTIES

单位:万人 (10 000 persons)

地　区	District	毕业生数 Graduates		招生数 New Students Enrollment		在校学生 Students Enrollment	
		初　中 Junior	高　中 Senior	初　中 Junior	高　中 Senior	初　中 Junior	高　中 Senior
总　计	**Total**	**12.03**	**10.21**	**10.83**	**7.00**	**44.00**	**27.17**
浦东新区	Pudong New Area	1.76	1.46	1.76	0.94	7.10	3.82
黄浦区	Huangpu	0.47	0.50	0.32	0.37	1.43	1.35
卢湾区	Luwan	0.22	0.22	0.17	0.12	0.67	0.50
徐汇区	Xuhui	0.77	0.75	0.70	0.47	2.74	1.98
长宁区	Changning	0.50	0.50	0.39	0.30	1.66	1.24
静安区	Jing'an	0.28	0.30	0.23	0.19	0.96	0.77
普陀区	Putuo	0.66	0.73	0.54	0.42	2.29	1.88
闸北区	Zhabei	0.72	0.60	0.52	0.39	2.23	1.49
虹口区	Hongkou	0.63	0.66	0.46	0.44	1.92	1.68
杨浦区	Yangpu	0.86	0.87	0.59	0.55	2.64	2.23
宝山区	Baoshan	0.67	0.52	0.70	0.41	2.66	1.49
闵行区	Minhang	0.69	0.53	0.77	0.39	2.89	1.55
嘉定区	Jiading	0.38	0.31	0.47	0.22	1.74	0.83
金山区	Jinshan	0.52	0.34	0.46	0.25	1.99	0.90
松江区	Songjiang	0.52	0.40	0.52	0.29	2.04	1.06
青浦区	Qingpu	0.44	0.29	0.46	0.23	1.81	0.81
南汇区	Nanhui	0.78	0.46	0.69	0.42	2.83	1.41
奉贤区	Fengxian	0.44	0.31	0.55	0.24	2.03	0.85
崇明县	Chongming	0.68	0.43	0.48	0.37	2.26	1.34
农　场	Farm	0.03	0.02	0.04	0.01	0.11	0.03

表 20.16 各区、县职业中学基本情况(2006)
BASIC STATISTICS OF SECONDARY VOCATIONAL SCHOOLS BY DISTRICTS AND COUNTIES

地 区	District	学校(所) Schools (unit)	毕业生数 (人) Graduates (person)	招生数 (人) New Students Enrollment (person)	在校学生 (人) Students Enrollment (person)	教职员工 (人) Staff and Workers (person)	其中 of which #专任教师 Full-time Teachers
总 计	**Total**	**36**	**19 832**	**17 498**	**52 890**	**4 935**	**2 990**
浦东新区	Pudong New Area	6	4 769	4 745	11 824	684	505
黄 浦 区	Huangpu	3	1 690	778	3 643	678	347
卢 湾 区	Luwan	3	679	813	2 175	201	143
徐 汇 区	Xuhui	2	1 583	1 511	2 711	369	204
长 宁 区	Changning	2	985	740	2 599	298	177
静 安 区	Jing'an	1	303	617	2 400	278	172
普 陀 区	Putuo	1	1 358	681	2 066	260	154
闸 北 区	Zhabei	1	877	422	1 650	230	148
虹 口 区	Hongkou	1	1 442	1 576	6 619	418	209
杨 浦 区	Yangpu	1	1 021	629	2 659	257	173
宝 山 区	Baoshan	2	1 886	1 040	3 430	292	150
闵 行 区	Minhang	4	558	930	2 372	273	136
嘉 定 区	Jiading	1	110	131	291	75	56
金 山 区	Jinshan	1	49		33		
松 江 区	Songjiang	2	631	1 231	3 068	226	150
青 浦 区	Qingpu	1	755	197	1 601	98	56
南 汇 区	Nanhui		45	86	140	12	8
奉 贤 区	Fengxian		66	93	252		
崇 明 县	Chongming	3	953	1 228	3 104	273	193
农 场	Farm	1	72	50	253	13	9

表 20.17 各区、县普通小学基本情况(2006)
BASIC STATISTICS OF REGULAR PRIMARY SCHOOLS BY DISTRICTS AND COUNTIES

地 区 District		学校(所) Schools (unit)	毕业生数 (万人) Graduates (10 000 persons)	招生数 (万人) New Students Enrollment (10 000 persons)	在校学生 (万人) Students Enrollment (10 000 persons)	教职员工 (万人) Staff and Workers (10 000 persons)	其中 of which #专任教师 Full-time Teachers
总 计	**Total**	**626**	**10.85**	**10.87**	**53.37**	**4.86**	**3.75**
浦东新区	Pudong New Area	104	1.76	2.05	9.53	0.78	0.66
黄浦区	Huangpu	22	0.29	0.24	1.25	0.16	0.11
卢湾区	Luwan	14	0.15	0.13	0.67	0.10	0.06
徐汇区	Xuhui	44	0.71	0.66	3.40	0.26	0.21
长宁区	Changning	25	0.40	0.39	1.94	0.19	0.15
静安区	Jing'an	12	0.18	0.19	0.91	0.12	0.07
普陀区	Putuo	28	0.59	0.57	2.85	0.22	0.16
闸北区	Zhabei	35	0.50	0.43	2.20	0.23	0.17
虹口区	Hongkou	38	0.42	0.43	2.10	0.22	0.15
杨浦区	Yangpu	48	0.60	0.53	2.85	0.29	0.22
宝山区	Baoshan	59	0.76	0.86	4.04	0.35	0.30
闵行区	Minhang	43	0.74	0.90	4.03	0.35	0.28
嘉定区	Jiading	23	0.48	0.47	2.33	0.20	0.16
金山区	Jinshan	22	0.49	0.40	2.04	0.22	0.14
松江区	Songjiang	13	0.50	0.55	2.62	0.21	0.17
青浦区	Qingpu	22	0.47	0.45	2.33	0.21	0.16
南汇区	Nanhui	23	0.71	0.65	3.25	0.29	0.23
奉贤区	Fengxian	16	0.55	0.62	2.96	0.22	0.17
崇明县	Chongming	34	0.49	0.33	1.85	0.22	0.16
农 场	Farm	1	0.07	0.04	0.20	0.02	0.01

表 20.18 主要年份实验性示范性中学基本情况
BASIC STATISTICS OF SECONDARY CAMPUS SCHOOL IN MAIN YEARS

指 标	Indicators	1995	2000	2005	2006
学 校(所)	Schools(unit)	79	84	87	88
班级数(个)	Classes(unit)	2 481	2 584	3 145	3 098
在校学生(万人)	Students Enrollment(10 000 persons)	11.95	12.10	14.63	13.07
教职员工(万人)	Staff and Workers(10 000 persons)	1.33	1.40	1.51	1.49
#专任教师	Full-time Teachers	0.82	0.88	1.03	1.03

注：实验性示范性中学包括重点中学和寄宿制高级中学。
Note: Secondary campus school includs important secondary school and boarding high school.

表 20.19 主要年份幼儿园基本情况
BASIC STATISTICS OF KINDERGARTENS IN MAIN YEARS

指 标	Indicators	1990	2000	2005	2006
幼儿园(所)	Kindergartens(unit)	999	958	1 035	1 057
幼儿数(万人)	Children Enrollment(10 000 persons)	41.75	24.12	28.70	29.98
教职员工(万人)	Staff and Workers(10 000 persons)	4.35	2.52	2.79	3.04
#教 师	Teachers	2.79	1.50	1.7	1.88

表 20.20 主要年份特殊教育基本情况
BASIC STATISTICS OF SPECIAL EDUCATION IN MAIN YEARS

指 标	Indicators	1990	2000	2005	2006
学校(所)	Schools(unit)	29	34	28	28
毕业生数(人)	Graduates(person)	237	868	853	869
招生数(人)	New Students Enrollment(person)	561	1 141	692	675
在校学生(人)	Students Enrollment(person)	3 341	5 407	5 238	5 043
教职员工(人)	Staff and Workers(person)	1 053	1 584	1 598	1 614
#专任教师	Full-time Teachers	613	943	1 002	1 047

表 20.21　网络教育基本情况(2003～2006)
BASIC STATISTICS OF NETWORK EDUCATION

单位:人(person)

指　标	Indicators	2003	2004	2005	2006
网络教育毕业生数	**Graduates of Network Education**	**1 404**	**11 875**	**27 844**	**41 893**
普通生	Regular Students	1 309	2 992	7 467	18 583
成人生	Adult Students	95	8 883	20 377	23 310
网络教育招生数	Network Education New Student Enrollment	14 198	44 189	50 635	58 115
普通生	Regular Students	10 257	15 254	22 498	27 127
成人生	Adult Students	3 941	28 935	28 137	30 988
网络教育在校生数	Network Education Student Enrollment	29 472	119 721	135 445	142 173
普通生	Regular Students	23 461	36 982	58 161	65 265
成人生	Adult Students	6 011	82 739	77 284	76 908

表 20.22　分学科网络教育学生情况 (2006)
BASIC STATISTICS OF NETWORK EDUCATION STUDENTS BY SUBJECT

单位:人(person)

类　别	Types	毕业生人数 Graduates		招生人数 New Students Enrollment		在校学生人数 Student Enrollment	
		本　科 Undergraduate	专　科 Junior College	本　科 Undergraduate	专　科 Junior College	本　科 Undergraduate	专　科 Junior College
总　计	**Total**	**18 606**	**23 287**	**19 843**	**38 272**	**47 385**	**94 788**
经济学	Economics	2 534	353	2 836	705	7 954	1 262
法　学	Law	1 120	299	750	180	1 928	510
教育学	Education	1 371	341	1 708	738	4 310	2 009
文　学	Literature	2 707	2 992	3 097	1 987	7 646	5 548
历史学	History	109		55		135	
理　学	Science	1 403		831		1 726	
工　学	Engineering	2 803	1 164	1 947	2 428	4 930	5 744
医　学	Medical	285	217	758	1 671	2 129	4 319
管理学	Adncinistration	6 274	17 921	7 861	30 563	16 627	75 396

表 20.23 主要年份成人教育基本情况
BASIC STATISTICS OF ADULT EDUCATION IN MALN YEARS

类 别	Types	2000	2005	2006
成人高等教育	**Special Education**			
学校（所）	Schools (unit)	37	21	21
毕业生数(万人)	Graduates(10 000 persons)	3.10	5.64	1.50
招生数(万人)	New Students Enrollment(10 000 persons)	4.22	6.50	6.78
在校学生(万人)	Students Enrollment(10 000 persons)	11.49	14.72	19.46
专任教师(万人)	Full-time Teachers(10 000 persons)	0.30	0.15	0.16
成人中等教育	**Adult Secondary Education**			
学校（所）	Schools (unit)	459	65	52
毕业生数(万人)	Graduates(10 000 persons)	13.65	2.78	2.01
招生数(万人)	New Students Enrollment(10 000 persons)	20.53	0.37	0.45
在校学生(万人)	Students Enrollment(10 000 persons)	18.22	4.11	3.32
专任教师(万人)	Full-time Teachers(10 000 persons)	0.46	0.09	0.06
成人职业技术培训	**Adult Technical Training**			
学校（所）	Schools (unit)	917	901	827
毕业生数(万人)	Graduates(10 000 persons)	81.42	19.82	29.66
在校学生(万人)	Students Enrollment(10 000 persons)	18.00	35.43	41.12
专任教师(万人)	Full-time Teachers(10 000 persons)	0.48	0.74	0.65

表 20.24 各级各类成人学校基本情况（2006）
BASIC STATISTICS OF ADULT SCHOOLS AT VARIOUS LEVELS

类 别	Types	学校数（所） Schools (unit)	毕业生人数（万人） Graduates (10 000 persons)	招生数（万人） New Students Enrollment (10 000 persons)	在校学生人数（万人） Students Enrollment (10 000 persons)	教职员工人数（万人） Staff and Workers (10 000 persons)	其中 of which 专任教师 Full-time Teachers
成人高等教育	**Adult Higher Education**	**21**	**1.50**	**6.78**	**19.46**	**0.31**	**0.16**
广播电视大学	Broadcasting and TV Universities	1	0.02		0.02	0.03	0.02
职工高等学校	Staff Higher Education Schools	16	0.20	0.83	2.30	0.24	0.12
管理干部学院	Institutes for Administrative Officials	4	0.02	0.11	0.29	0.04	0.02
普通高等学校办	Run by Regular High Education Institutions	(79)	1.26	5.84	16.85		
函 授	Correspondence Programs	(14)	0.19	0.62	2.23		
业 余	Spare Time	(42)	0.45	4.81	13.49		
脱 产	Full Time	(23)	0.62	0.41	1.13		
成人中等教育	**Adult Secondary Education**	**52**	**2.01**	**0.45**	**3.32**	**0.12**	**0.06**
成人中等专业学校	Specialized Secondary Schools	37	0.57	0.45	1.07	0.08	0.04
成人中学	Adult Spare-time Secondary Schools	15	1.44		2.25	0.04	0.02
成人职业技术学校	**Adult Technical Secondary Schools**	**827**	**29.66**		**41.12**	**1.55**	**0.65**

注："( )"指高等院校举办的各类成人教学点数据。成人中学、成人初等学校在校学生数均为在校注册学生数；成人技术培训在校学生数为培训期超过半年的累计注册学生数。

Note: The figures with"( )" refer to the number of the adult education places conducted by higher education institutions. Students enrollment of adult spare-time secondary schools and adult junior schools refers to the number of students registered at school. Students Enrollment of adult technical secondary schools refers to accumulative total number of students registered at schools who has been trained more than half a year.

表 20.25 上海国际学校一览（2006）
SHANGHAI INTERNATIONAL SCHOOLS

学校名称 Name of School		地 址 Address	
上海美国学校	Shanghai American School	闵行区金丰路 258 号	No. 258 Jinfeng Road, Minhang District
上海日本人学校	Shanghai Japanese School	闵行区虹梅路 3185 号	No. 3185 Hongmei Road, Minhang District
耀中上海国际学校	Yaozhong Shanghai International School Hongqiao Campus	长宁区水城路 11 号	No. 11 Shuicheng Road, Changning District
宋庆龄幼儿园国际部	International Section of Songqinglin Kindergarten	长宁区虹梅北路 3908 号	No. 3908 Hongmei Road N. Changning District
上海德国学校	Shanghai German School	青浦区诸光路 399 弄 30 号	Lane 399, 30 Zhuguang Road, Xujing Towm, Qingpu District
上海法国学校	Shanghai French School	青浦区诸光路 399 弄 30 号	Lane 399, 30 Zhuguang Road, Xujing Towm, Qingpu District
上海英国学校	Shanghai British School	沪南公路 2729 弄 600 号（康桥半岛）	Lane 2729, 600 Hunan Highway (Cambridge Peninsula)
上海协和国际学校	Shanghai Xiehe International School	浦东金桥明月路 999 号	No 345, Huangyang Road, Jingqiao Pudong
上海长宁国际学校	Shanghai Changning	长宁区江苏路 261 弄 79 号	No. 79, Lane 261, Jiangsu Road Changning District
上海新加坡国际学校	Shanghai Singapore International	闵行区纪翟路 288 号	No. 288 Jizhai Road, Minhang District School
上海虹桥国际学校	Shanghai Hongqiao International School	长宁区虹桥路 2381 号	No. 2381 Hongqiao Road, Changning District
上海韩国学校	Shanghai Korea School	闵行区华漕镇联友路 555 号	No. 555, Lianyou Road, Caohua Town Minhang District
上海美丘第一幼儿园	Shanghai Meiqiu No. 1 Kindergarten	闵行区虹许路 788 号(名都城)	No. 788 Hongxu Road, Minhang District
奥伊斯嘉上海日本语幼儿园	Shanghai Japanese Kindergarten	长宁区茅台路 715 弄 20 号	No. 20 Lane 715 Maotai Road
东进上海日本人幼儿园	Shanghai Dongjin Japanese Kindergarten	长宁区虹梅路 3081 号虹桥别墅内	Hongqiao Villa, No. 3081 Hongmei Road
上海恩吉尔幼儿园	Shanghai Angel Kindergarten	闵行区吴中路 2358 号	No. 2358 Wuzhong Road Minhang District
上海泰宁国际幼儿园	Taining International Kindergarten	徐汇区复兴西路 43 号	No. 43 Fuxing Road W
幼儿天地国际幼儿园	Kid's World International Kindergarten	复兴中路 524 号	No. 524 Fuxing Mid Road.
上海瑞金国际学校	Shanghai Ruijin International School	莘庄镇东闸路 189 号	No. 189 Dongzha Road, Xinzhuang Town
上海李文斯顿美国学校	Shanghai Livingston America School	长宁区甘溪路 580 号	No. 580 Ganxi Road Changning District
上海德威英国国际学校	Shanghai Sulwich College	浦东金桥蓝桉路 222 号	No. 222 Lan'an Road, Jinqiao, Pudong District
上海中学国际部	International Section of Shanghai Middle School	徐汇区上中路 400 号	No. 400 Shangzhong Road
华东师范大学二附中国际部	The International Section of the No. 2 Middle School Attached to East China Normal University	浦东晨晖路 555 号	No. 555, Chenhui Road, Pudong
上海外国语大学附中国际部	The International Section of the Middle School Attached to Shanghai International Studies University	中山北一路 295 号	No. 295 Zhongshan Road N1
进才中学国际部	The International Section of Jincai High School	丁香路 129 号	No. 129 Dingxiang Road
上海西华国际学校	Shanghai Xihua International School	青浦区联名路 555 号	No. 555, Lianming Road, Qingpu District

上 / 海 / 统 / 计 / 年 / 鉴

主要统计指标解释

■ 学　校

指按国家规定的设置标准和审批程序批准设立的，招收适龄人口实施各级各类教育活动的教育机构。

■ 普通高等学校

指按照国家规定的设置标准和审批程序批准举办的，通过全国普通高等学校统一招生考试，招收高中毕业生为主要培养对象，实施高等教育的全日制大学、独立设置的学院和高等专科学校、高等职业学校和其他机构。

大学、独立设置的学院主要实施本科层次以上教育，高等专科学校、高等职业学校实施专科层次教育，其他机构是承担国家普通招生计划任务不计校数的机构。包括普通高等学校分校和批准筹建的普通高等学校等。

■ 成人高等学校

指按国家规定的设置标准和审批程序举办的，通过全国成人高等教育统一招生考试，招收高中毕业或同等学历的人员为主要培养对象，利用函授、业余、脱产的多种形式对其实施高等学历教育的学校。包括：职工高等学校、农民高等学校、管理干部学院、教育学院、独立函授学院、广播电视大学、其他机构等。

■ 民办的其他高等教育机构

指经省、自治区、直辖市教育行政部门审批并颁发办学许可证，但不具有颁发学历文凭资格的实施高等教育的单位。学历文凭考试机构是指民办的经教育行政部门专门批准，进行全日制高等教育的其他高等教育机构。

■ 中等专业学校

指经县或县以上教育行政部门批准设立，招收初中毕业生实施中等专业课程教育的教学机构。

■ 职业中学(职业高中、职业初中)

指经县或县以上教育行政部门批准设立，招收小学或初中毕业生实施中等职业技术教育的教学机构。按学校性质类别可分为：独立设置的职业中学(包括：职业初中、职业高中、职业初高中合设学校)；附设有普通中学班的职业中学。

■ 普通中学(普通高中、普通初中)

普通中学分为普通高级中学和普通初级中学两个阶段。普通初级中学是指独立设置的招收小学毕业的适龄人口进行初级中等基础教育的机构；普通高级中学是指独立设置的招收初中毕业的适龄人口进行高级中等基础教育的机构；完全中学是指普通初、高中合设的教育机构；一贯制学校是指在一所学校连续实施中小学教育的机构。其中包括实施九年义务教育的九年一贯制学校和实施高中教育的十二年一贯制学校。(说明：一贯制学校的办学条件如能划分为小学、初中、高中，则分开填报；如不能划分清楚，可按就高不就低的方法填入初中、高中报表中，不能重复填写。)

■ 普通小学

指由区或区以上教育行政部门批准，招收学龄儿童实施初等教育的教学机构。

■ 幼儿园

指招收三周岁以上(含三周岁)学龄前幼儿，对其进行保育和教育的单位。

■ 特殊教育学校

指本市独立设置的招收盲聋哑和智残儿童，以及其他特殊需要的儿童、青少年进行普通或职业初、中等教育的教学机构。

■ 小学学龄儿童净入学率

小学学龄人口中正在接受小学教育人数所占比重。

■ 初中学生净入学率

是指初级中学(普通初中和职业初中)在校学生总数占初中学龄人口数的比重。

■ 国家财政性教育经费

包括国家财政预算内教育经费，各级政府征收用于教育的税费，企业办学校教育经费，校办产业、勤工俭学

主要统计指标解释

和社会服务收入用于教育的经费。

预算内教育经费

指中央、地方各级财政或上级主管部门在年度内安排，并计划拨到教育部门和其他部门主办的各级各类学校、教育事业单位，列入国家预算支出科目的教育经费，包括教育事业拨款、科研经费拨款、基建拨款和其他经费拨款。

SHANGHAI STATISTICAL YEARBOOK

EXPLANATORY NOTES TO MAJOR STATISTICAL INDICATORS

□ School

School Institutions refer to education establishment set up according to the government evaluation and approval procedures, enrolling population of the right age, providing various phase education activity.

□ Regular Institutions of Higher Education

Regular Institutions of Higher Learning refer to educational establishments set up according to the government evaluation and approval procedures, enrolling graduates from senior secondary schools and providing higher education courses and training for senior professionals. They include full-time universities, colleges, high professional schools, high professional vocational schools and others.

Universities and colleges are mainly providing undergraduate courses; those high professional schools and high professional vocational schools are mainly providing professional trainings; and others refer to educational establishments, which are responsible for enrolling students but not covered in the total number of schools, including: branch schools of universities and colleges, and universities and colleges that have been proved and prepared to construct.

□ Institutions of Higher Education for Adults

Institution of Higher Learning for Adults refer to educational establishments, set up in line with relevant rules approved by the government, enrolling personnel with senior secondary schools or equivalent education, and providing higher education courses in many forms of correspondence, spare time, or full time for adults. Institutions of higher schools for adults include schools of higher educations for staff and workers, schools of higher education for peasants, colleges for management cadres, pedagogical colleges, independent correspondence colleges, Radio and TV universities and other educational establishment, etc.

□ Civil Other Institution of Higher Education

Civil Other Institution of Higher Education refer to educational establishment set up according to rules approved and permitted by educational administration department of municipal government and not be provided with qualification to awarding diploma.

□ Specialized Secondary schools

Specialized Secondary schools refer to educational establishment set up according to approval and permission by educational administration department of district and above government, enrolling graduates from junior secondary schools and providing secondary professional education courses.

□ Vocational Secondary Schools (senior secondary schools and junior secondary schools)

Vocational Secondary Schools (senior secondary schools and junior secondary schools) refer to educational establishment set up according to approval and permission by educational administration department of district and above government, enrolling graduates from primary schools and junior secondary schools and providing secondary vocational education courses.

□ Regular Secondary Schools (senior secondary schools and junior secondary schools)

Regular Secondary Schools (senior secondary schools and junior secondary schools) are classified as senior secondary schools and junior secondary schools. Junior Secondary Schools refer to educational establishment enrolling graduates from primary schools and providing junior secondary educational courses. Senior Secondary Schools refer to educational establishment enrolling graduates from junior secondary schools and providing higher secondary educational courses.

□ Primary Schools

Primary Schools refer to educational establishment set up according to approval and permission by educational administration department of district and above government, enrolling graduates from children of school age and providing primary educational courses.

□ Kindergartens

Kindergartens refer to nursery and education establishment, enrolling children in 3 years old and above.

EXPLANATORY NOTES TO MAJOR STATISTICAL INDICATORS

□ Special Education Schools

Special Education Schools refer to educational establishments set up independently, enrolling blind, deaf, dumb, amentia or other special children, and educational establishment, providing regular or vocational junior and senior secondary education for hobbledehoy.

□ Enrollment Rate of Schoolage Children

Enrollment Rate of Schoolage Children refers to the proportion of school age children enrolled at schools to the total number of school age children both in and outside schools.

□ Enrollment rate of Schoolage Children

Enrollment rate of Schoolage Children refers to the proportion of students in junior secondary schools to the total number of junior school age students.

□ Enrollment Rate of Students in Junior Secondary School Phase

Enrollment Rate of Students in Junior Secondary School Phase refers to the proportion of students in junior secondary schools to the total number of junior school age students.

□ Budgetary Fund for Education

Budgetary Fund for Education refers to education fund that is planned to allocate to various schools and education institutions by central and local financial departments at various levels within the reference year, which is within the state budgetary expenditure, including: appropriate funds for education, science and research, capital construction and others.

第二十一篇

CHAPTER 21

卫生、社会保障和社会福利业

HEALTH, SOCIAL SECURITY AND SOCIAL WELFARE

表 21.1 卫生事业基本情况(1978～2006)
BASIC STATISTICS OF PUBLIC HEALTH

年份 Year	卫生机构数(个) Health Care Institutions (unit)	其中 of which #医院 Hospital	卫生技术人员(万人) Medical Professionals (10 000 persons)	其中 of which #医生 Doctors	卫生机构床位数(万张) Hospital Beds (10 000 beds)	其中 of which #医院 Hospital	每万人口医生数(人) Doctors per 10 000 Persons (person)	每万人口医院床位数(张) Hospital Beds per 10 000 Persons (bed)
1978	4 823	388	8.50	3.35	5.47	4.68	31	43
1979	5 627	394	8.88	3.58	5.56	4.78	32	42
1980	6 067	399	9.41	3.92	5.80	4.94	34	43
1981	6 337	403	9.57	4.37	5.84	4.99	38	43
1982	6 445	408	9.88	4.72	5.93	5.11	40	43
1983	6 451	415	10.09	4.87	6.00	5.20	41	44
1984	6 318	420	10.24	4.84	6.16	5.34	40	44
1985	7 245	405	10.42	4.85	6.02	5.32	40	44
1986	7 306	419	10.71	4.91	6.22	5.47	40	44
1987	7 330	431	11.00	5.05	6.38	5.60	40	45
1988	7 471	444	11.46	5.40	6.79	5.89	43	47
1989	7 550	460	11.65	5.73	6.87	6.04	45	47
1990	7 690	462	11.84	5.82	6.96	6.21	45	48
1991	7 554	463	11.92	5.89	7.01	6.31	46	49
1992	7 363	454	11.82	5.88	7.07	6.42	46	50
1993	6 077	486	11.53	5.75	7.12	6.75	44	52
1994	5 606	497	11.20	5.52	7.20	6.81	43	53
1995	5 286	485	11.06	5.37	7.10	6.69	41	52
1996	5 200	477	10.95	5.24	7.00	6.73	40	52
1997	5 028	474	10.89	5.13	7.00	6.78	34	52
1998	4 637	473	10.84	5.03	7.02	6.83	39	52
1999	4 620	465	10.81	5.06	7.24	7.06	39	54
2000	4 400	459	10.71	4.99	7.53	7.31	38	55
2001	3 813	432	10.51	4.85	7.88	7.63	37	58
2002	2 422	436	10.16	4.38	8.15	8.13	33	61
2003	2 319	452	10.22	4.41	8.44	8.11	33	60
2004	2 577	489	10.17	4.38	8.64	8.50	32	63
2005	2 527	487	10.35	4.40	9.08	8.93	32	66
2006	2 519	505	10.90	4.55	9.44	9.28	33	68

① 本表至表 21.13 的数据由市卫生局提供。
② 2002 年开始,卫生指标按照新的《中国卫生统计调查制度》统计。其中,医生为执业医师和执业助理医师;护师、护士为注册护士。
❶ Data in table 21.1 to 21.13 are provided by Shanghai Municipal Health Bureau.
❷ Since 2002, Statistics of health care are based on "China Health Care Statistical Investigation System". Of which, Doctors refer to medical practitioners, senior and junior nurses refer to registered nurses.

表21.2 主要年份卫生事业基本情况
BASIC STATISTICS OF PUBLIC HEALTH IN MAIN YEARS

指 标	Indicators	1990	2000	2005	2006
全 市	**Total**				
机构数（个）	Institutions（unit）	7 690	4 400	2 527	2 519
#医 院	Hospitals	462	459	487	505
门诊部、所、卫生所、医务室、护理站	Out-patient Departments, Clinics, Infirmaries and Nursing Stations	6 947	3 769	1 923	1 895
妇幼保健所	Maternity and Child Care Centers	23	10	13	13
专科疾病防治所	Special Disease Stations	41	16	13	14
急救中心（站）	First-aid Centers		12	12	12
疾病预防控制中心	Disease Prevention and Control Centers	33	28	22	22
床位数（万张）	Hospital Beds（10 000 beds）	6.96	7.53	9.08	9.44
#医 院	Hospitals	6.21	7.31	8.93	9.28
工作人员（万人）	Personnel（10 000 persons）	15.85	14.67	13.20	13.8
#卫生技术人员	Medical Professionals	11.84	10.71	10.35	10.90
#医 生	Doctors	5.82	4.99	4.40	4.55
护师、护士	Senior and Junior Nurses	3.66	3.83	3.94	4.22
药剂人员	Pharmacists	0.73	0.68	0.61	0.66
检验人员	Laboratory Technicians	0.54	0.50	0.52	0.53
县及县以上医院	**Hospitals at County Level and Above**				
机构数（个）	Hospitals（unit）	206	194	257	277
床位数（万张）	Hospital Beds（10 000 beds）	5.01	5.80	7.06	7.29
工作人员（万人）	Personnel（10 000 persons）	8.25	9.50	9.46	9.88
#卫生技术人员	Medical Professionals	6.04	7.03	7.4	7.79
#医 生	Doctors	2.21	2.72	2.78	2.90
平均每万人口拥有	**Owned by Every 10 000 Persons**				
床位数（张）	Hospital Beds（bed）	54	57	67	69
#医 院	Hospitals	48	55	66	68
#县及县以上医院	Hospitals at County Level and Above	39	44	52	53
卫生技术人员（人）	Medical Professionals（person）	92	81	76	80
#医 生	Doctors	45	38	32	33
护师、护士	Senior and Junior Nurses	29	29	29	31

表21.3　各区、县医院基本情况(2006)
STATISTICS OF HOSPITALS BY DISTRICTS AND COUNTIES

地　区	District	医院数(个) Hospitals (unit)	床位数(张) Hospital Beds (bed)	卫生技术人员(人) Medical Professionals (person)	其　中 of which #医　生 Doctors	#护师、护士 Senior and Junior Nurses
总　计	**Total**	**505**	**92 800**	**97 194**	**38 698**	**40 326**
浦东新区	Pudong New Area	53	7 452	9 232	4 041	3 793
黄 浦 区	Huangpu	23	5 213	7 793	3 148	3 238
卢 湾 区	Luwan	15	4 170	5 341	1 980	2 228
徐 汇 区	Xuhui	33	12 366	12 765	4 452	5 675
长 宁 区	Changning	28	3 264	4 168	1 593	1 766
静 安 区	Jing'an	19	4 508	6 867	2 439	2 981
普 陀 区	Putuo	20	4 495	5 059	2 148	2 046
闸 北 区	Zhabei	22	4 637	4 593	1 862	1 835
虹 口 区	Hongkou	33	6 731	6 935	2 718	2 863
杨 浦 区	Yangpu	30	5 852	6 214	2 480	2 740
宝 山 区	Baoshan	28	4 325	4 425	1 876	1 897
闵 行 区	Minhang	33	5 373	4 067	1 634	1 642
嘉 定 区	Jiading	27	2 585	2 838	1 216	1 129
金 山 区	Jinshan	19	3 206	3 294	1 262	1 342
松 江 区	Songjiang	23	3 886	2 660	1 123	1 105
青 浦 区	Qingpu	19	1 784	2 201	936	896
南 汇 区	Nanhui	25	4 755	3 414	1 401	1 171
奉 贤 区	Fengxian	25	4 598	2 628	1 190	971
崇 明 县	Chongming	30	3 600	2 700	1 199	1 008

表21.4 各类卫生机构、床位及人员数(2006)
VARIOUS HEALTH CARE INSTITUTIONS,BEDS AND PERSONNEL

机构类别	Type of Institutions	机构数(个) Health Care Institutions (unit)	床位数(张) Beds (bed)	人员数(人) Personnel (person)
总　计	**Total**	**2 519**	**94 387**	**138 002**
医疗机构合计	Medical Institutions	2 444	93 199	131 935
#医　院	Hospitals	505	92 800	122 433
综合医院	Comprehensive Hospitals	157	45 702	70 309
中医医院	Hospitals of Traditional Chinese Medicine	16	4 033	6 970
中西医结合医院	Hospitals of Combination of Chinese and Western Medicine	4	1 534	2 585
专科医院	Special Diseases Hospitals	73	17 870	15 440
妇幼保健院	Maternity and Child Care Place	9	1 135	2 003
专科疾病防治院	Specialized Disease Prevention & Treatment Institution	5	154	576
社区卫生服务中心	Community Health Care Centers	179	15 233	20 527
乡镇卫生院	Township Hospitals	49	4 640	3 078
护理院	Nursing Hospitals	13	2 499	945
疗养院	Sanatoriums	2	332	184
门诊部、所	Out-patient Departments	223	41	2 213
卫生所、医务室、护理站	Clinics, Infirmaries and Nursing Stations	1 672		4 663
妇幼保健所	Maternity and Child Care Centers	13	3	557
专科疾病防治所	Special Disease Stations	14	23	712
急救中心(站)	First-aid Centers	12		1 050
临床检验中心	Clinical Laboratory Centers	3		123
疾病预防控制中心	Disease Prevention and Control Centers	22		2 984
卫生监督所	Health Supervision Centers	20		1 208
医学科学研究机构	Institutions of Medical Science	10		651
其他卫生机构	Other Health Care Institutions	23	1 188	1 224

表 21.4 续表 continued

机构类别	Type of Institutions	其中 of which		
		#卫生技术人员 Medical Professionals	其中 of which	
			#医生 Doctors	#护师、护士 Senior and Junior Nurses
总计	**Total**	**109 009**	**45 511**	**42 216**
医疗机构合计	Medical Institutions	105 119	43 742	41 917
#医院	Hospitals	97 194	38 698	40 326
综合医院	Comprehensive Hospitals	55 965	21 264	24 849
中医医院	Hospitals of Traditional Chinese Medicine	5 704	2 309	2 129
中西医结合医院	Hospitals of Combination of Chinese and Western Medicine	2 000	750	740
专科医院	Special Diseases Hospitals	11 588	3 746	5 734
妇幼保健院	Maternity and Child Care Place	1 657	623	801
专科疾病防治院	Specialized Disease Prevention & Treatment Institution	392	185	130
社区卫生服务中心	Community Health Care Centers	16 775	8 337	5 073
乡镇卫生院	Township Hospitals	624	1 312	632
护理院	Nursing Hospitals	2 489	172	238
疗养院	Sanatoriums	80	21	33
门诊部、所	Out-patient Departments	1 670	820	531
卫生所、医务室、护理站	Clinics, Infirmaries and Nursing Stations	4 663	3 259	808
妇幼保健所	Maternity and Child Care Centers	445	294	70
专科疾病防治所	Special Disease Stations	544	345	109
急救中心(站)	First-aid Centers	462	305	40
临床检验中心	Clinical Laboratory Centers	61		
疾病预防控制中心	Disease Prevention and Control Centers	2 190	1 334	93
卫生监督所	Health Supervision Centers	931	206	7
医学科学研究机构	Institutions of Medical Science	224	133	4
其他卫生机构	Other Health Care Institutions	545	96	195

表 21.5 医疗机构病床使用情况(2006)
STATISTICS OF HOSPITAL BED USAGE IN MEDICAL TREATMENT INSTITUTION

机构类别	Types	平均开放床位数(张) Average Beds Opened(bed)	病床周转次数(次) Turnover Times of Beds(times)	病床使用率(%) Usage Rate of Beds(%)	出院者平均住院日(日) Average Days to Inpatient be in Hospital(day)
总　计	**Total**	**95 935.77**	**18.61**	**93.52**	**16.69**
卫生部门	Medical Institutions	79 070.64	19.38	95.74	16.52
#医　院	Hospital	78 203.47	19.53	95.59	16.63
#综合医院	Comprehensive Hospitals	37 919.95	26.87	98.10	13.20
中(西)医医院	Hospitals of Chinese and Western Medicine	5 490.98	19.77	95.25	17.51
社区卫生服务中心(站)	Community Health Care Centers	14 723.65	9.37	85.57	28.69
卫生院	Township Hospitals	4 398.38	10.90	74.14	23.70
护理院	Nursing Hospitals	867.17	5.39	109.48	69.74
其他部门	Other Departments	16 865.12	15.04	83.12	17.72

表 21.6 家庭病床情况(2006)
FAMILY SICKBEDS

机构类别	Types	开展工作机构数(个) Running Institutions (unit)	上门诊疗总次数(次) Total Times of Family Call (time)	年底实有病床数(张) Year-end Sickbeds (bed)	年内开设总病床数(张) Sickbeds Set up in 2006 (bed)
总　计	**Total**	**171**	**1 016 193**	**19 830**	**41 875**
县及县以上医院	Hospitals	36	160 241	2 729	5 150
社区卫生服务中心	Community Health-care Centers	118	834 629	16 664	36 340
乡镇卫生院	Rural Township Hospitals	17	21 323	437	385

表21.7 医疗机构诊疗人次和入院人数（2006）
PATIENTS TREATED AND INPATIENTS IN MEDICAL TREATMENT INSTITUTION

机构类别	Types	诊疗人次（万人次）Total Patients Treated（10 000 person-times）	其中 of which #门、急诊 Outpatients and Emergency Patients	入院人数（万人）Inpatients（10 000 persons）	每百诊次的入院人数（人）Inpatients Per 100 Patient-times（person）
总　计	**Total**	**11 682.37**	**11 491.31**	**179.01**	**1.5**
卫生部门	Public Health Sector	10 481.13	10 298.21	153.60	1.5
医　院	Hospitals	10 343.72	10 163.71	153.60	1.5
综合医院	Comprehensive Hospitals	4 569.56	4 529.93	102.16	2.2
中(西)医医院	Hospitals of Chinese(Western) Medicine	918.53	915.62	10.92	1.2
传染病医院	Infectious Diseases Hospitals	20.95	20.95	0.91	4.3
精神病医院	Mental Hospitals	76.75	73.60	1.07	1.4
结核病医院	Tuberculosis Hospitals	30.52	26.26	2.22	7.3
妇幼保健院	Hospitals for Maternity and Child Care	259.00	247.34	8.24	3.2
肿瘤医院	Tumor Hospitals	44.47	44.47	1.58	3.6
儿童医院	Children's Hospitals	255.71	250.01	4.06	1.6
其他专科医院	Other Specialized Hospitals	231.30	231.30	3.40	1.5
社区卫生服务中心	Community Health-care Centers	3 706.44	3 595.88	13.77	0.4
乡镇卫生院	Township Hospitals	215.55	213.41	4.80	2.2
护理院	Nurse Hospitals	14.94	14.94	0.47	3.1
其他医疗机构	Other Medical Facilities	131.83	128.92		
其他卫生事业机构	Other Health Utilities	5.58	5.58		
工业及其他部门	Industry and Other Sectors	1 201.24	1 193.10	25.41	2.1

表21.8 主要年份公民献血、用血情况
BASIC STATISTICS OF BLOOD DONATION AND USE IN MAIN YEARS

指　标	Indicators	1995	2000	2005	2006
无偿(义务)献血(万人份)	Volunteer or Compulsory Blood Offer (10 000 person unit)	24.03	35.19	36.46	39.95
临床用血量(万人份)	Clinic Blood Use Volum (10 000 person unit)	52.20	34.70	34.97	37.32

注：2005，2006年公民献血全部为无偿献血。
Note: Blood offer of citizens refers to volunteer blood offer in 2005 and 2006.

表 21.9 前十位疾病死亡原因和构成(2006)
THE TOP 10 DEATH-CAUSING DISEASES AND COMPOSITION

死亡原因	Cause of Death	死亡专率(1/10万) Death Rate(1/100 000)	占死亡总数(%) Percentage of Total Death(%)
循环系病	Circulation Diseases	243.58	33.96
肿　瘤	Tumor	225.56	31.45
呼吸系病	Respiratory System Diseases	81.11	11.31
损伤和中毒	Damage and Poisoning	42.19	5.88
内分泌营养代谢病	Endocrine-Immunity-Metabolic Diseases	29.28	4.08
消化系病	Digestive System Diseases	19.37	2.70
传染病及寄生虫病	Infectious & Parasitic Diseases	12.16	1.69
精神系病	Psychosis	8.35	1.16
泌尿生殖系病	Genitourinary Diseases	7.58	1.06
神经系病	Nervous System Disease	7.09	0.99

表 21.10 婴儿前五位疾病死亡原因和构成(2006)
THE TOP 5 INFANT DEATH-CAUSING DISEASES AND COMPOSITION

死亡原因	Cause of Death	死亡专率(1/10万) Death Rate (1/100 000)	占死亡总数 (%) As Percentage of Total Death(%)
先天异常	Born Abnormity	483.53	68.70
新生儿病	Newborn Diseases	145.47	20.67
损伤中毒	Damage and Poisoning	22.17	3.15
呼吸系病	Respiratory System Diseases	18.01	2.56
传染病及寄生虫病	Infectious & Parasitic Diseases	11.08	1.57

表21.11 主要年份婴儿死亡率、新生儿死亡率、孕产妇死亡率
DEATH RATE OF INFANT,NEW BORN,PREGNANT AND LYING-IN WOMAN IN MAIN YEARS

指 标	Indicators	1990	2000	2005	2006
婴儿死亡率(‰)	Death Rate of Infant(‰)	10.95	5.05	3.78	4.01
新生儿死亡率(‰)	Death Rate of New Born(‰)	7.17	3.09	2.47	2.60
孕产妇死亡率(1/10万)	Death Rate of Pregnant and Lying-in Woman(1/100 000)	23.76	9.61	1.40	8.31

表21.12 主要年份防病工作情况
BASIC STATISTICS OF DISEASE PREVENTION IN MAIN YEARS

指 标	Indicators	1990	2000	2005	2006
传染病发病总例数(甲、乙)(万例)	**Cases Of Contagious Diseases Reported (A,B)(10 000 cases)**	**4.56**	**3.58**	**3.22**	**2.78**
发病率(1/10万)	Disease Rate(1/100 000)	356.12	271.66	237.52	204.07
传染病死亡总人数(人)	Number Of Deaths Caused By Contagious Diseases (person)	95	179	153	97
死亡率(1/10万)	Death Rate (1/100 000)	0.74	1.36	1.13	0.71
结核病登记病人数(千例)	T. B. Patients Registered (1 000 cases)	7.27	3.09	2.75	2.47
登记患病率(‰)	Registered Disease Rate(‰)	0.57	0.23	0.20	0.18
结核病新发病人数(千例)	Newly Reported T. B. Cases(1 000 cases)	5.67	5.18	3.87	3.70
登记新发病率(1/万)	Registered Newly Diseased Rate (1/10 000)	4.43	3.94	2.86	2.71
结核病死亡人数(人)	Number Of Deaths Caused By T. B (person)	605	293	256	170
死亡率(1/10万)	Death Rate (1/100 000)	4.73	2.22	1.89	1.25
牙病受检人数(万人)	Number Of People Undergoing Tooth Disease Check (10 000 persons)		51.89	52.11	58.26
龋牙患病率(%)	Rate Of Caries Patients (%)		28.3	28.5	25.9
小学生视力不良率(%)	Rate Of Nearsight In Primary School (%)	16.5	26.0	29.2	31.1
初中生视力不良率(%)	Rate Of Nearsight In Junior High School (%)	39.8	55.0	62.1	63.6
高中生视力不良率(%)	Rate Of Nearsight In Senior High School (%)	68.4	78.5	81.5	82.1
"五苗"接种率(%)	Rate Of "Four Vaccines" Recipients(%)	98.6	99.7	99.4	99.3
乙肝疫苗全程接种率(%)	Rate Of Hepatitis-B Innoculation (%)		99.9	99.8	99.8

表21.13 主要年份妇幼卫生工作情况
BASIC STATISTICS OF GYNAECOLOGY AND PAEDIATRICS IN MAIN YEARS

指 标	Indicators	1990	2000	2005	2006
妇女病普查人数(万人)	**Number Of People Surveyed For Female Diseases (10 000 persons)**	**49.90**	**40.27**	**55.76**	**56.17**
患病率(%)	Rate of Sufferers (%)	42.9	35.0	26.0	25.0
治疗率(%)	Rate of Patients Treated (%)	80.1	91.1	95.9	96.5
胎儿娩出顺产数(万人)	Number of Smooth Delivery (10 000 persons)	8.04	4.05	5.73	7.16
顺产率(%)	Rate of Smooth Delivery (%)	59.4	47.5	45.6	49.2
出生低体重儿(人)	Number of Low-weight Newborns (person)		2 567	4 303	5 083
占活产总数(%)	Proportion in All Deliveries (%)		3.0	3.4	3.5
出生缺陷人数(人)	Number of Newborns with Innate Problems (person)		764	1 163	1 370
出生缺陷率(‰)	Rate of Disabled among All Deliveries (‰)		8.96	9.30	9.40
0~6岁儿童保健管理率(%)	Rate of Children, 0~6 Years Old under Health Programm (%)	78.3	94.3	95.0	95.8
0~6岁儿童眼保健率(%)	Rate of 0~6 Year-olds under Eye-Health Program (%)		81.8	93.7	95.1
0~6岁儿童听力保健率(%)	Rate of 0~6 Year-olds under Ear-Health Program (%)		83.7	84.9	91.3
0~6岁儿童口腔保健率(%)	Rate of 0~6 Year-olds under Mouth-Health Program (%)		88.6	98.4	97.3
0~6岁儿童贫血患病率(%)	Rate of 0~6 Year-olds Suffering From Anemia (%)		6.0	2.2	4.2
婚前检查人数(万人)	Number of People Undergoing Pre-marriage Checkup (10 000 persons)	19.69	17.36	1.76	6.85
婚检率(%)	Rate of Pre-marriage Checkup Recipients (%)	97.4	98.4	9.2	22.4

表21.14 主要年份社会保险参保人数
NUMBER OF PARTICIPANTS IN SOCIAL INSURANCE IN MAIN YEARS

单位:万人(10 000 persons)

指标	Indicators	2000	2005	2006
城镇基本养老保险	**Urban Basic Pension Insurance**			
城镇职工	Urban Staff and Workers	431.27	436.52	460.75
个体工商户和自由职业人员	Individual Businessman	9.82	18.26	16.97
领取养老金的离退休人员	Retired Veteran Cadres and Retired Staff and Workers with Pensions	234.23	279.72	294.69
城镇基本医疗保险	**Urban Basic Medicare**			
城镇职工	Urban Staff and Workers	364.59	434.51	436.63
个体工商户和自由职业人员	Individual Businessman and Professionals		18.26	16.97
享受医保的离退休人员	Retired Veteran Cadres and Retired Staff and Workers with Medicare	202.14	279.11	294.04
城镇职工失业保险	**Unemployment Insurance of Urban Staff and Workers**	**434.86**	**466.06**	**476.41**
城镇职工生育保险	**Generational Insurance of Urban Staff and Workers**		**539.27**	**555.09**
城镇职工工伤保险	**Work Injury Insurance of Urban Staff and Workers**		**523.71**	**538.96**
农村社会养老保险	Rural Social Pension Insurance	121.00	101.34	83.71
小城镇社会保险	Town Social Insurance		110.16	139.80
来沪从业人员综合保险	General Insurance of Employment of Migratory Population		247.70	279.00
高龄无保障老人保险	Insurance of Old Ages without Living Sccuriey			6.28
少儿住院基金	Medicare Fund of Children	212.47	181.09	180.13

注：本表数据由市劳动和社会保障局、市医疗保险局、市红十字会提供。
Note: Data in this table are provided by Shanghai Municipal Labour and Social Security Bureau, Shanghai Municipal Medicare and Insurance Bureau and Red Cross Society of China Shanghai Municipal Branch.

表21.15 主要年份社会保障标准
SOCIAL SECURITY STANDARD IN MAIN YEARS

单位:元(yuan)

指标	Indicators	2000	2005	2006
职工工资最低标准	Minimum Standard of Wages of Staff and Workers	445	690	750
城镇基本养老金最低标准	Minimum Standard of Urban Basic Pension Insurance	460	460	460
城镇居民生活保障最低标准	Minimum Standard of Living Security	280	300	320

注：本表数据由市劳动和社会保障局、市民政局提供。
Note: Data in this table are provided by Shanghai Municipal Labour and Social Security Bureau and Shanghai Civil Affairs Bureau.

表 21.16 优抚、救济对象享受国家定期抚恤补助、救济情况（1980～2006）
PERSONS ENJOYING REGULAR SUBSIDIES AND COMMISERATION FROM THE STATE

单位：万人（10 000 persons）

年份 Year	合计 Total	伤残抚恤 Pension for the Disabled	烈军属抚恤 Pension for Families of Martyr	复退军人定期补助 Subsidies for Ex-servicemen	享受国家定期救济人数 Number of People Receiving Regular Relief from the State	其中 of which 社会困难户定期救助 Subsidies for Impoverished Residents	精减退职老职工救济 Almsgiving for Retirees and Laid-off Workers	最低生活保障对象 People Under City's Basic Provision Protection
1980	1.44	0.69			0.75	0.38	0.37	
1981	1.60	0.70			0.90	0.46	0.44	
1982	1.98	0.74	0.24	0.22	0.78	0.42	0.36	
1983	1.99	0.76	0.26	0.24	0.73	0.40	0.33	
1984	2.05	0.78	0.29	0.27	0.70	0.39	0.32	
1985	2.11	0.78	0.23	0.37	0.73	0.43	0.30	
1986	2.60	0.80	0.26	0.49	1.05	0.76	0.29	
1987	2.50	0.82	0.25	0.59	0.84	0.55	0.29	
1988	2.50	0.82	0.24	0.62	0.82	0.54	0.28	
1989	2.76	0.84	0.23	0.65	1.04	0.76	0.28	
1990	2.81	0.86	0.22	0.68	1.05	0.77	0.28	
1991	2.72	0.83	0.21	0.71	0.97	0.70	0.27	
1992	3.10	0.83	0.20	0.71	1.36	1.10	0.26	
1993	3.10	0.83	0.19	0.70	1.38	1.13	0.25	
1994	3.12	0.83	0.18	0.70	1.41	1.17	0.24	
1995	3.11	0.82	0.17	0.69	1.43	1.19	0.24	
1996	3.20	0.81	0.17	0.68	1.54	1.31	0.23	
1997	2.68	0.80	0.15	0.69	1.04	0.84	0.20	
1998	3.22	0.79	0.15	0.66	1.62	0.38		1.24
1999	6.87	0.77	0.12	0.65	5.33	0.74	0.19	4.40
2000	22.26	0.76	0.12	0.66	20.72	0.94	0.18	19.60
2001	39.46	0.75	0.11	0.63	37.97	0.76	0.17	37.04
2002	51.47	0.74	0.11	0.59	50.03		0.17	49.86
2003	56.50	0.73	0.11	0.59	55.07			55.07
2004	50.87	0.72	0.12	0.57	49.46			49.46
2005	49.23	0.71	0.36	0.52	47.64			47.64
2006	49.58	0.71	0.73	0.47	47.67			47.67

注：本表至表 21.19 数据由市民政局提供。
Note: Data in this table to table 21.19 are provided by Shanghai Civil Affairs Bureau.

表21.17 社会福利院、儿童福利院、社会福利医院和收养性老年福利机构情况(1980～2006)
INSTITUTIONS OF SOCIAL WELFARE, CHILDREN WELFARE, ADOPTIVE SENIORS WELFARE INSTITUTIONS AND SOCIAL WELFARE HOSPITALS IN MAIN YEARS

年 份 Year	社会福利院 Social Welfare Institutions			儿童福利院 Children Welfare Homes		
	单 位 (个) Units (unit)	床位数 (张) Beds (bed)	收养人数 (人) Person Housed (year-end) (person)	单 位 (个) Units (unit)	床位数 (张) Beds (bed)	收养人数 (人) Children Housed (year-end) (person)
1980	9	1 555	1 337	2	600	559
1981	9	1 621	1 313	2	650	634
1982	9	1 525	1 495	2	650	672
1983	9	1 644	1 491	2	600	676
1984	10	1 948	1 635	2	600	633
1985	10	1 727	1 630	2	580	625
1986	10	1 697	1 648	2	550	612
1987	10	1 991	1 770	2	378	449
1988	13	2 189	1 790	2	387	458
1989	14	2 418	2 012	2	538	481
1990	15	2 679	2 019	2	589	586
1991	14	2 687	2 138	2	611	592
1992	14	2 776	2 431	2	665	651
1993	14	2 874	2 554	2	708	690
1994	15	2 931	2 648	2	878	862
1995	15	3 006	2 722	2	988	919
1996	17	3 294	2 866	2	988	943
1997	21	4 012	3 441	2	988	946
1998	24	4 596	3 678	2	1 004	984
1999	20	4 215	3 498	2	981	958
2000	23	4 884	4 137	2	1 100	1 092
2001	26	5 570	4 410	2	1 221	1 221
2002	27	5 590	4 760	3	1 491	1 429
2003	26	5 818	4 779	2	1 087	1 512
2004	26	5 876	4 848	6	1 300	1 893
2005	23	5 999	4 809	6	2 016	1 986
2006	25	6 583	5 024	6	1 252	2 142

表21.17 续表 continued

年 份 Year	社会福利医院 Social Welfare hospitals			收养性老年福利机构 Adoptive Seniors Welfare Institutions			
	单 位（个）Units (unit)	床位数（张）Beds (bed)	收养人数（人）Patients Housed (person)	机 构（个）Institutions (unit)	床位数（张）Beds (bed)	收养人数（人）Person Housed (person)	其 中 of which #老 人 Elder
1980	3	1 475	1 424	42		630	
1981	3	1 460	1 430	53		762	
1982	3	1 490	1 422	58		1 022	
1983	3	1 490	1 432	90		1 402	
1984	3	1 460	1 380	135		2 328	
1985	3	1 480	1 360	199	3 870	3 038	2 786
1986	3	1 510	1 354	249	4 655	3 446	3 100
1987	3	1 497	1 342	277	5 520	4 262	3 893
1988	3	1 497	1 313	322	5 969	4 754	4 429
1989	3	1 433	1 324	349	6 281	5 129	4 835
1990	3	1 497	1 298	332	6 275	5 031	4 452
1991	3	1 391	1 285	341	6 731	5 763	5 642
1992	3	1 510	1 404	351	7 002	6 035	5 655
1993	3	1 510	1 394	331	7 143	6 365	5 934
1994	3	1 510	1 392	333	7 533	6 838	6 541
1995	3	1 510	1 409	330	8 576	7 405	6 633
1996	3	1 510	1 429	333	10 270	8 361	7 867
1997	3	1 500	1 452	323	11 253	9 295	8 647
1998	3	1 500	1 455	339	13 958	11 122	10 826
1999	3	1 710	1 703	331	16 526	12 698	12 013
2000	3	1 840	1 779	398	22 244	16 988	16 541
2001	3	1 894	1 894	378	23 627	17 363	16 923
2002	3	1 917	1 901	417	33 413	20 900	20 309
2003	3	1 680	1 881	422	36 791	23 451	22 682
2004	3	1 780	1 829	414	33 891	26 993	25 902
2005	3	1 811	1 811	450	43 131	31 301	30 181
2006	3	1 860	1 796	479	52 427	35 946	34 447

表21.18 主要年份社会福利事业机构数和职工人数
NUMBER OF SOCIAL WELFARE INSTITUTIONS AND STAFF AND WORKERS IN MAIN YEARS

指 标	Indicators	2000	2005	2006
机构数(个)	**Total Institutions(unit)**			
收养性福利单位	Adopting Social Welfare Institutions	427	483	515
优抚类	Subsidy	1	1	1
福利类	Welfare	426	482	514
社会福利企业	Social Welfare Enterprises	3 352	2 230	2 036
优抚安置单位	Subsidy and Arrangement Institution	45	46	42
救助类单位	Salvation Institution	16	22	22
殡仪服务单位	Funeral and Interment Service Institution	68	75	76
福利彩票发行单位	Issue Institution of Welfare Lottery	16	19	18
社区服务单位	Community Service Institutions	92	104	122
职工人数(人)	**Staff and Workers (person)**			
收养性福利单位	Adopting Social Welfare Institutions	7 793	12 105	13 738
优抚类	Subsidy	35	41	46
福利类	Welfare	7 758	12 064	13 692
社会福利企业	Social Welfare Enterprises	177 260	111 220	103 314
优抚安置单位	Subsidy and Anargment Institution	745	768	737
救助类单位	Salvation Institution	472	457	455
殡仪服务单位	Funeral and Interment Service Institution	2 577	3 078	2 999
福利彩票发行单位	Issue Institution of Welfare Lottery	86	73	77
社区服务单位	Community Service Institutions	1 014	1 247	1 696

表21.19 收养类机构基本情况(2006)
BASIC FACTS ABOUT THE ADOPTIVE WELFARE INSTITUTIONS

福利机构名称	Name of Welfare Institutions	机构数(个) Institutions (unit)	年末职工人数(人) Staff and Workers (person)	床位数(张) Beds (bed)	年末收养人数(人) Person Housed (year-end) (person)	其中 of which #老年人 Elder
总　计	**Total**	**515**	**13 738**	**62 584**	**45 333**	**39 441**
政府办	**By Governments**					
社会福利院	Social Welfare Homes	25	1 830	6 583	5 024	4 428
市　级	Prefectural Level	4	677	1 614	1 441	983
浦东新区	Pudong New Area	1	90	200	200	200
黄浦区	Huangpu	2	165	370	368	352
徐汇区	Xuhui	2	202	492	421	414
长宁区	Changning	2	88	244	148	148
普陀区	Putuo	1	76	234	234	234
闸北区	Zhabei	1	30	317	252	246
虹口区	Hongkou	2	164	420	378	378
杨浦区	Yangpu	1	55	320	300	300
宝山区	Baoshan	1	47	200	144	40
闵行区	Minhang	2	71	590	577	577
嘉定区	Jiading					
松江区	Songjiang	1	19	300	239	236
青浦区	Qingpu	3	73	870	133	131
南汇区	Nanhui	1	15	210	1	1
奉贤区	Fengxian	1	58	202	188	188
儿童福利院	Children's Welfare Homes	6	642	1 252	2 142	
市儿童福利院	Shanghai Children's Welfare Home	1	431	1 000	1 930	
徐汇区儿童福利院	Capibility Rehabilitation Institution of Xuhui	3	102	102	92	
虹口区儿童福利院	Capibility Rehabilitation Institution of Hongkou	2	109	150	120	
社会福利医院	Social Welfare Hospitals Homes	3	603	1 860	1 796	443
荣誉军人康复院	Convalescent Homes for Honored Ex-servicemen	1	46	50	13	13
社会办	**By Social**					
城镇老年福利机构	Urban Senile Welfare Homes	243	5 789	23 410	16 508	16 387
农村老年福利机构	Rural Senile Welfare Homes	236	4 696	29 017	19 438	18 060

表21.20 红十字会基本情况(2004～2006)
BASIC STATISICS ON RED CROSS SOCIETY OF CHINA SHANGHAI MUNICIPAL BRANCH

指 标	Indicators	2004	2005	2006
红十字会组织机构	**Institutions(unit)**			
红十字会各级组织机构(个)	Organizing Instituntions(unit)	3 140	2 934	3 341
红十字会医疗机构(个)	Medical Institutions(unit)	63	67	70
志愿工作管理机构(个)	Administrative Institutions on Voluntary Work(unit)	54	20	1
红十字会会员人数(万人)	**Number of Member (10 000 persons)**	**66.69**	**61.62**	**54.61**
#青少年会员(万人)	Hobbledehoy Member(10 000 persons)	43.88	37.16	37.30
团体会员单位(个)	Team Member(unit)	1 124	970	3 485
社区服务工作	**Community Service**			
社区公益服务站点(个)	Community Commonweal Service Station (unit)	1 581	1 589	2 293
社区志愿者人数(万人)	Number of Volunteer (10 000 persons)	1.55	1.75	2.56
组织各种宣传活动	**Times of Publicizing Activity(time)**			
在报刊登载宣传文章(篇)	Articles on Newspaper and Periodical (piece)	610	831	647
电视台播报宣传节目(条/次)	Programs on Television (piece/time)	235	459	313
参加艾滋病预防宣传救助活动人次数(万人次)	Person-time Attended AIDs Prevention Activities (10 000 person-times)	17.02	9.86	6.56
参加普及宣传无偿献血活动人次数(万人次)	Person-time Attended Publicizing Volunteer Blood Donation Activiies (10 000 person-times)			4.45
卫生救护工作	**Sanitation Rescue**			
救护普及培训(人次)	Rescue Popularization Training(person-time)	26.74	24.72	29.76
救护师资培训(人次)	Rescue Teachers Training	356	304	1 534
造血干细胞捐献工作	**Contributing Trunk Cell**			
当年参加造血干细胞捐献库人数(万人)	Number of Subscribers (10 000 persons)	4.54	5.60	6.41
患者检索人次(人次)	Person-times of Patient Researches (person-times)	288	1 942	113
配型相合人数(人)	Matching(person)	44	316	70
累计移植人数(人)	Transplanting(person)	46	68	87
遗体捐献工作	**Contributing Reliquiae**			
遗体捐献登记站(个)	Register Center(unit)	27	27	27
遗体捐献接收站(个)	Accepting Center(unit)	8	8	8
全年接受捐献遗体登记(人)	Number of Contributing Reliquiae(Person)	1 335	1 284	1 492
全年接受角膜捐献登记(人)	Number of Contributing Cornea(Person)	197	133	146
社会赈济和社区救助工作	**Working on Social Relieving**			
社会赈济救济投入(万元)	Social Relieve Devotion (10 000 yuan)	3 695.41	10 635.36	5 877.42
受益人数(万人)	Number of Beneficiaries(10 000 persons)	3.08	3.04	3.03
社区救助款物投入(万元)	Community Salvation Devotion (10 000 yuan)	1 232.30	1 538.12	3 010.10
受益人数(万人)	Number of Beneficiaries(10 000 persons)	2.65	2.87	4.29

①2005 年,救助投入款项中包括年初为东南亚海啸筹集的捐款 5 461 万元。
②本表数据由市红十字会提供。
❶Salvation Devotion Funds includs the donation of fifty four million six hundred and ten thousand yuan for South-east Aisa Tsunami in early 2005.
❷Data in this table are provided by Red Cross Society of China Shanghai Municipal Branch.

上 / 海 / 统 / 计 / 年 / 鉴

主要统计指标解释

■ 卫生机构

是指从卫生行政部门取得《医疗机构执业许可证》，或从民政、工商行政、机构编制管理部门取得法人单位登记证书，为社会提供医疗保健、疾病控制、卫生监督服务或从事医学研究、医学教育等卫生单位和卫生社会团体。

■ 医疗机构

是指根据《医疗机构管理条例》的规定，经登记取得《医疗机构执业许可证》的机构。包括医院、社区卫生服务中心(站)、卫生院、门诊部、诊疗所、医务室、村卫生室、妇幼保健院(所、站)、专科疾病防治院(所、站)、急救中心、临床检验中心。

■ 医　院

指设有固定床位，能收容病人住院并能为病人提供医疗、护理服务的医疗机构，包括县及县以上医院、农村乡卫生院和其他医院三部分。县及县以上医院按业务性质不同分为综合医院和专科医院。

■ 卫生技术人员

指从事卫生技术工作并在卫生事业机构领取劳动报酬的专业人员。包括中医师、西医师、中西医结合高级医师、护师、中药师、西药师、检验师、其他技师、中医士、西医士、护士、助产士、中药剂士、西药剂士、检验士、其他技士、其他中医、护理员、中药剂员、西药剂员、检验员、其他初级卫生技术人员。

■ 医　生

指在医疗、预防保健机构工作且取得《执业医师证书》的执业医师和执业助理医师。

■ 优抚对象

优抚指政府对革命烈士家庭、病故残疾工作人员以及参战负伤致残的民兵、民工的抚恤和人民群众对其的优待。优抚对象包括革命烈士家属、因公牺牲和病故军人家属、革命伤残人员、现役军属、退伍红军老战士、红军失散人员、复员军人、退伍军人、在职退役军人、在乡退役军人、带病回乡退伍军人、复退军人精神病员、孤老优抚对象等。

■ 社会福利事业单位

指集中收养社会孤老、残、幼的机构。包括由民政部门管理的社会福利院、儿童福利院、精神病人福利院和城镇集体办的福利院，以及农村集体办的敬老院。

■ 基本养老保险

1. (参保)职工人数：指报告期末按照国家法律、法规和有关政策规定参加基本养老保险并在社保经办机构已建立缴费记录档案的职工人数，包括中断缴费但未终止养老保险关系的职工人数，不包括只登记未建立缴费记录档案的人数。

2. (参保)离退休人员人数：指报告期末参加基本养老保险的离休、退休和退职人员的人数。

3. 基本养老保险基金收入：指根据国家有关规定，由纳入基本养老保险范围的缴费单位和个人按国家规定的缴费基数和缴费比例缴纳的养老保险基金，以及通过其他方式取得的形成基金来源的收入。包括单位和职工个人缴纳的基本养老保险费、基本养老保险基金利息收入、上级补助收入、下级上解收入、转移收入、财政补贴和其他收入。

4. 基本养老保险基金支出：指按照国家政策规定的开支范围和开支标准从养老保险基金中支付给参加基本养老保险的离休、通休、退职人员个人的养老金、丧葬抚恤补助，以及由于保险关系转移、上下级之间调剂资金等原因而发生的支出。包括离休金、退休金、退职金、各种补贴、医疗费、死亡丧葬补助费、抚恤救济费、社会保险经办机构管理费、补助下级支出、上解上级支出、转移支出、其他支出等。

5. 基本养老保险基金累计结余：指截止报告期末基本养老保险基金收支相抵后的累计余额。

■ 基本医疗保险

1. 参保人数：指报告期末按国家有关规定参加基本医疗保险的人数。包括参加保险的职工人数和退休人员人数。

2. 基金收入：指根据国家有关规定，由纳入基本医疗保险范围的缴费单位和个人，按国家规定的缴费基数和缴费比例缴纳的基金，以及通过其他方式取得的形成基金来源的款项，包括：单位缴纳的社会统筹基金收入、个

主要统计指标解释

人缴纳的个人账户基金收入、财政补贴收入、利息收入、其他收入。

3. 基金支出：指按照国家政策规定的开支范围和开支标准从社会统筹基金中支付给参加基本医疗保险的职工和退休人员的医疗保险待遇支出，和从个人帐户基金中支付给参加基本医疗保险的职工和退休人员的医疗费用支出，以及其他支出。包括：住院医疗费用支出、门急诊医疗费用支出、个人账户基金支出、其他支出。

4. 基金累计结余：指截止报告期末基本医疗保险的社会统筹和个人帐户基金累计结余金额。包括银行存款、财政专户、债券投资和其他。

■ 失业保险

1. 参保人数：指报告期末按照国家法律、法规和有关政策规定参加了失业保险的城镇企业事业单位的职工及地方政府规定参加失业保险的其他人员的人数。

2. 失业保险基金收入：指按照规定从企业、事业及其他单位筹集的失业保险费及其他并入失业保险基金收入的总额。包括单位和个人缴纳的失业保险费、失业保险基金利息收入、上级补助收入、下级上解收入、转移收入、财政补贴和其他收入。

3. 失业保险基金支出：指报告期内为保障失业人员和下岗职工基本生活、促进其再就业等支出的基金总额。包括失业救济金、医疗费、死亡丧葬补助费、抚恤救济费、转业训练费支出、失业保险经办机构管理费、补助下级支出、上解上级支出、转移支出和其他支出。

4. 基金累计结余：指截止报告期末失业保险基金收支相抵后的累计余额。

■ 工伤保险

1. 参加保险人数：指报告期末依据国家有关规定参加工伤保险的职工人数。

2. 享受保险待遇人数：指劳动者因工负伤致残、死亡或因患职业病致残，根据有关规定享受工伤保险待遇职工或供养直系亲属人数。包括伤残人数、职业病人数、因工死亡人数、供养直系亲属人数。

3. 基金收入：指根据国家有关规定，由参加工伤保险的单位按国家规定的缴费基数和缴费比例缴纳的工伤保险基金，以及通过其他形式取得的形成基金来源的款项。包括：单位缴纳的社会统筹基金收入、财政补贴收入、利息收入、其他收入。

4. 基金支出：指按照国家政策规定的开支范围和开支标准从工伤保险基金中支付给参加工伤保险的人员及供养直系亲属工伤保险待遇支出及其他支出。包括工伤医疗费、伤残补助金、工亡补助金、护理费、丧葬补助费、工伤预防费用、职业康复费用和其他支出。

5. 基金累计结余：指截止报告期末工伤保险基金累计结余金额。包括银行存款、财政专户、债券投资和其他。

■ 生育保险

1. 参保人数：指报告期末依据有关规定参加生育保险的职工人数。

2. 基金收入：指根据国家有关规定，由参加生育保险的单位按照国家规定的缴费基数和缴费比例缴纳的生育保险基金，以及通过其他方式取得的形成基金来源的款项，包括：单位缴纳的基金收入、利息收入和其他收入。

3. 基金支出：指按照国家政策规定的开支范围和开支标准，从生育保险基金中支付给参加生育保险的职工，因妊娠、分娩和计划生育手术而享受的待遇及其他支出。包括：生育津贴、医疗费用支出及其他支出。

4. 基金累计结余：指截止报告期末生育保险基金累计结余金额。包括银行存款、财政专户、债券投资和其他。

SHANGHAI STATISTICAL YEARBOOK

EXPLANATORY NOTES TO MAJOR STATISTICAL INDICATORS

□ Health Care Institutions

Health Care Institution refers to medical institutions and corporations providing health care, disease control and medical supervision service or engaged in medical research and medical education, which obtain Medical Institution Practice License from Medical Administration or Corporative Registration Certificate from Civil Administration, Commercial Administration or Organizational Management Administration.

□ Medical Institutions

Medical Institutions refer to institutions which register Medical Institution Practice License according to Medical Institution Management Regulation, including hospitals, community medical service centers, medical house, clinics, dispensaries, medicine rooms, village medicine rooms, hospitals for maternity and kids care, special disease cure hospitals, first-aid center, clinical inspection centers.

□ Hospitals

Hospitals refer to medical institutions with permanent hospital beds, which are able to take in patients and provide them with medical and nursing services. Hospitals are classified into three categories: hospitals at or above the county level, hospitals of rural townships, and other hospitals. Hospitals at or above county level are divided into comprehensive and specialized hospitals.

□ Medical Professionals

Medical Professionals refer to those professionals engaged in medical work and receive salaries from medical institutions, including doctors of Chinese and Western medicine, senior doctors of integrated Chinese-Western medicine, head nurses, pharmacists of Chinese and Western medicine, laboratory specialists , other specialists, junior doctors of Chinese and Western medicine, nurses, midwives, druggists of Chinese and Western medicine, laboratory technicians, other technicians, other practitioners of Chinese medicine, nursing attendants, pharmacological workers of Chinese and Western medicine, laboratory workers and other primary medical personnel.

□ Doctors

Doctors refer to certified physicians and certified assistant physicians with certifications working in medical and health care and prevention agencies.

□ Persons Entitled to Special Care

Special Care is offered by the government to the family member of the martyrs, disabled or demobilized servicemen or laborers who were injured on duty. Entitled to the special care are family members of the revolutionary martyrs, family members of servicemen who dies on duty or died of an illness, disabled servicemen, family members of servicemen on active service, retired veteran Red Army soldiers, scattered Red Army soldiers, demobilized servicemen, ex-servicemen, servicemen who were demobilized while on duty, ex-servicemen back to their rural homes, ex-servicemen who were demobilized because of an illness and have gone back to their rural homes, ex-servicemen who suffer from mental illness and elderly persons with no family.

□ Social Welfare Institutions

Social Welfare Institutions refer to institutions taking care of old people without children, handicapped people and orphans. They include social welfare institutions run by civil affairs departments, children's welfare institutions, welfare institutions for mental patients, and collectively-run old people's homes in rural areas.

□ Basic Pension Insurance

1. Number of staff and workers covered refer to staff and workers participating in basic pension insurance programme in line with national laws, regulations and related policies by the end of reference period, who have already had payment records in social security management agencies, including those who interrupt payment without terminating the insurance programme. Those who have registered in the programme with no payment records are not included.

2. Number of retirees participating in basic pension insurance programme refer to number of retirees participating in basic pension insurance programme by the end of reference period.

3. Revenue of basic pension insurance refer to payments

EXPLANATORY NOTES TO MAJOR STATISTICAL INDICATORS

made by employers and individuals participating in pension insurance programs in accordance with the basis and proportion stipulated in state regulations, and income from other sources that become source of pension insurance fund, including the premium paid by employers and staff and works, interest income, subsidies from higher level agencies, income as transfer from subordinate agencies, transferred income, government financial subsidies and other income.

4. Expenses of basic pension insurance refer to payment made to those retired and resigned people covered in pension insurance program in terms of pension or compensation within the scope and standards of expenditure according to related national policies, and expenditure occurred due to shift of the insurance relationship or adjustment of funds among agencies, including pension for resigned people, pension for retired people, pension for people quitting jobs, various subsidies, medical fees, funeral subsidies, compensation pension, management fees for social security agencies, expenses on subsidies to lower subordinates, expenses as transfer to agencies at higher level, transferred expenditure and other expenditure.

5. Balance of basic pension insurance refers to the balance of basic pension insurance at the end of the reference period after deducting expenses from revenue.

□ Basic Medicare

1. Number of people participating in the insurance programme refers to people participating in the basic medical care insurance programme according to related regulations by the end of reference period, including number of staff and workers and retirees participating in this insurance programme.

2. Revenue of insurance programme refer to payments made by employers and individuals participating in medical care insurance programs in accordance with the basis and proportion stipulated in state regulations, and income from other sources that become source of medical insurance fund, including income of social comprehensive funds paid by employers, income from individual accounts, government financial subsidies, interest income and other income.

3. Expenses of insurance programme refer to payment made from social comprehensive funds to those retired and resigned people covered in basic medical care insurance within the scope and standards of expenditure according to related national policies, and medical care payment made from individual accounts to staff and workers and retirees, and other expenses, including medical expenses of hospital inpatients, medical expenses for outpatients and emergency patients, payment from individual accounts and other expenditure.

4. Balance of basic medical care insurance refer to the balance of medical care insurance of social comprehensive funds and individual accounts at the end of the reference period, including bank savings, special fiscal accounts, investment in bonds and others.

□ Unemployment Insurance

1. Number of people covered refers to staff and workers in urban enterprises or institutions who have participated in unemployment insurance programme in line relevant policies and regulations, and other people who have participated according to local government regulations, by the end of reference period.

2. Revenue of unemployment insurance refer to payments made by employers and individuals participating in unemployment insurance programme in accordance with relevant regulations and other income contributed to this programme, including unemployment insurance premium made by employers and individuals, interest income, subsidies from higher level agencies, income as transfer from subordinate agencies, transferred income, government financial subsidies and other income.

3. Expenses of unemployment insurance refer to total expenses during the reference period to guarantee the basic livelihood of unemployed people and laid-off staff and workers and to encourage their re-employment. Included are unemployment relief, medical fees, funeral subsidies, compensation pension, training expenses, management fees for unemployment insurance agencies, subsidies to lower level agencies, expenses as transfer to higher level agencies, transferred expenditure and other expenditure.

4. Balance of unemployment insurance refer to the balance of unemployment revenue deducting unemployment expenses at the end of the reference period.

□ Work Injury Insurance

1. Number of people covered refers to staff and workers who have participated in work injury insurance programme in line with relevant national regulations.

2. Number of beneficiaries refers to staff and workers and their direct dependents who can, in line with relevant regulations, benefit from work injury insurance, as a result of work injury leading to disability or death of the staff/worker, or occupational

EXPLANATORY NOTES TO MAJOR STATISTICAL INDICATORS

disease leading to disability. Included in this category are number of injured and disabled people, number of people with occupational diseases, number of deaths at work places, and number of direct dependents.

3. Revenue of work injury insurance refer to payments made by employers participating in work injury insurance programs in accordance with the basis and proportion stipulated in state regulations, and income from other sources that become source of work injury insurance fund, including income of social comprehensive funds paid by employers, government financial subsidies, interest income and other income.

4. Expenses of work injury insurance refer to payments made from work injury insurance funds to those who participated in the work injury insurance programme and their direct dependents within the scope and standards of expenditure according to related national policies, and other expenditure, including medical fees for work injury, injury and disability subsidies, death subsidies, nursing fees, funeral subsidies, injury prevention fees, rehabilitation fees for occupational diseases and other expenditure.

5. Balance of work injury insurance refer to the balance of the work injury funds at the end of the reference period, including bank savings, special fiscal account, investment in bonds and others.

□ Generational Insurance

1. Number of people covered refers to staff and workers who have participated in generational insurance programme according to relevant regulation at the end of the reporting period.

2. Revenue of generational insurance refers to payments made by employers participating in maternity insurance programs in accordance with the basis and proportion stipulated in state regulations, and income from other sources that become source of maternity insurance fund, including income of funds paid by employers, interest income and other income.

3. Expenses of generational insurance refer to payments made from maternity insurance funds to staff and workers who participated in maternity insurance programme within the scope and standards of expenditure according to related national policies, expenses paid for pregnancy, child delivery or surgeries related to family planning, and other expenditure, including allowance for child bearing, medical fees and other expenditure.

4. Balance of the generational insurance refers to the balance of the maternity insurance funds at the end of reference period, including bank savings, special fiscal account, investment in funds and others.

第二十二篇

CHAPTER 22

文化和体育

CULTURE AND SPORTS

表22.1 主要年份文化机构数
NUMBER OF CULTURAL INSTITUTIONS IN MAIN YEARS

单位:个(unit)

年份 Year	图书馆 Libraries	群众文化活动机构 Mass Culture	艺术教育事业 Art Education	文艺科研 Art Research	文物保护机构 Agency of Historic Relics Preservation	档案机构 Archives Institutions
1978	23	364	3		7	
1980	21	367	2	2	8	
1985	46	369	3	2	9	
1986	49	403	3	2	11	
1987	50	407	3	2	13	127
1988	54	416	3	2	16	125
1989	52	405	3	2	19	134
1990	51	410	3	2	18	137
1991	31	397	3	2	18	671
1992	31	394	3	2	20	745
1993	31	376	3	2	21	720
1994	31	371	3	2	23	
1995	31	332	3	2	23	768
1996	32	348	4	2	24	674
1997	32	352	4	2	24	681
1998	32	355	4	2	23	643
1999	32	349	4	2	24	994
2000	31	340	4	2	24	792
2001	32	276	3	2	23	614
2002	32	270	1	2	26	652
2003	35	261	1	2	26	656
2004	28	251	1	2	99	513
2005	28	248	1	2	106	545
2006	28	250	1	2	106	466

①本表数据由市文化广播影视管理局、市文物管理委员会、市档案局提供。
②自2004年始文物保护机构中包括系统外的机构数。
❶Data in this table are provided by Shanghai Municipal Culture, Radio, Film and TV Administration, Shanghai Municipal Committee of Culture Heritage and Shanghai Municipal Archives.
❷Agency of Historic Relics Preservation refers to total number of Agency Bureau since 2004.

表 22.2 影剧院、艺术表演场所、艺术表演团体数(1978~2006)
NUMBER OF CINEMAS,THEATRES AND ART PERFORMANCE TROUPES

单位:个(unit)

年　份 Year	电影放映单位 Film Projection Units	其中 of which #影、剧院 Cinemas and Theatres	艺术表演场所 Art Performance Places	其中 of which #剧　院 Theatres	#书　场 Storytelling Places	艺术表演团体 Art Performance Troupes
1978	803	109	31	26	4	17
1979	799	115	46	32	5	45
1980	770	119	47	43	6	48
1981	804	127	60	56	6	49
1982	815	134	31	48	6	46
1983	822	140	54	49	8	46
1984	815	146	54	48	8	44
1985	847	156	52	47	8	44
1986	859	169	53	49	9	42
1987	890	199	51	48	8	42
1988	734	215	53	50	8	40
1989	579	213	52	49	8	37
1990	577	211	49	46	8	38
1991	548	229	51	47	9	38
1992	530	249	51	47	9	37
1993	462	254	49	40	9	34
1994	462	254	47	39	8	35
1995	452	249	43	35	7	31
1996	488	280	45	38	7	31
1997	466	263	45	38	7	31
1998	445	242	44	39	5	29
1999	445	242	44	41	4	29
2000	445	242	44	39	5	29
2001	370	273	41	35	3	28
2002	370	273	37	31	2	28
2003	328	238	180	174	4	72
2004	311	225	177	163	7	75
2005	236	193	160	150	5	85
2006	245	186	148	137	2	97

①本表数据由市文化广播影视管理局提供。
②2003 年起文化统计范围扩大到全行业。
❶Data in this table are provided by Shanghai Municipal Culture, Radio, Film and TV Administration.
❷The scope of statistics to culture expands to total sectors in 2003.

表 22.3 主要年份主要文化机构从业人员数
NUMBER OF EMPLOYEES IN MAJOR CULTURAL INSTITUTIONSS IN MAIN YAERS

单位：人(person)

机构类别	Category of Institution	2000	2005	2006
总　计	**Total**	**217 572**	**248 038**	**245 014**
艺术机构	Art	4 759	6 222	6 145
图书馆	Libraries	2 513	2 597	2 425
档案机构	Archives Institution	2 330	1 916	2 418
群众文化活动机构	Mass Culture	3 874	3 832	3 756
文物保护机构	History Relic	1 136	1 661	2 278
文化娱乐机构	Cultural and recreational Institutions	63 297	64 659	62 992
新闻出版机构	Institutions Engaged in News and Publishing	138 492	167 101	164 659
其他文化机构	Other Cultural Institutions	1 171	50	623

注：本表数据由市文化广播影视管理局、市文物管理委员会、市档案局、市新闻出版局提供(下表同)。
Note: Data in this table are provided by Shanghai Municipal Culture, Radio, Film and TV Administration, Shanghai Municipal Committee of Culture Heritage, Shanghai Municipal Archives Bureau and Shanghai Municipal Press and Publication Bureau. (same as follows)

表 22.4 主要文化机构和人员数(2006)
MAJOR CULTURAL INSTITUTIONS AND PERSONNEL

机构类别	Category of Institution	机构数(个) Institutions(unit)	从业人数(人) Employees(person)
艺术机构	**Art**	**254**	**6 145**
艺术表演团体	Art Performance Troupes	97	3 727
艺术表演场所	Art Centers	148	2 031
#剧场、影剧院	Theaters and Music Halls	137	1 727
书场、曲艺场	Storytelling Places, Recitation and Ballad Places	2	49
杂技、马戏场	Acrobatics, Circus Places	1	84
音乐厅	Concert Halls	1	12
艺术创作机构	Art Inditing	4	115
艺术展览机构	Art Exhibition	2	159
艺术教育机构	Art Education	1	51
文艺科研机构	Art Research	2	62
图书馆	**Libraries**	**28**	**2 425**
#少儿图书馆	Libraries for Children	5	113
档案机构	**Archives Institution**	**466**	**2 418**
群众文化活动机构	**Mass Culture**	**250**	**3 756**
群众艺术馆	Mass Art Centers	1	54
文化馆	Cultural Centers	29	1 142
文化站	Cultural Stations	220	2 560
文物保护机构	**Historical Relic**	**113**	**2 278**
文物保护管理机构	Agency of Historical Relics Protection	5	91
博物馆	Museums	106	2 075
文物商店	Cultural Relic Shop	2	112
文化娱乐机构	**Cultural and Recreational Institutions**	**4 240**	**62 992**
新闻出版机构	**Institutions Engaged in News and Publishing**	**13 074**	**164 659**

表 22.5 群众艺术馆和文化馆(站)情况（2006）
MASS ART AND CULTURAL CENTERS

指 标	Indicators	合 计 Total	群众艺术馆 Mass Art Centers	文化馆 Cultural Centers	文化站 Cultural Stations
单位数（个）	Number of Units (unit)	250	1	29	220
从业人员(人)	Employees (person)	3 756	54	1 142	2 560
组织活动	Organizing Activity				
文艺活动（次）	Literary Activity(time)	47 458	116	856	46 486
各类理论研讨（次）	Theoretics Conference(time)	99	6	93	
各类讲座（次）	Chair(time)	162	6	156	
举办训练班	Conducting Training Courses				
班 次（次）	Number of Classes (time)	28 739	33	1 908	26 798
结业人次（万人次）	Persons Completing the Courses (10 000 person-times)	56.3	0.4	2.3	53.6
举办展览个数（个）	Exhibitions Conducted (unit)	2 256	9	240	2 007

注：本表至表22.15数据由市文化广播影视管理局提供。
Note: Data in table 22.5 to 22.15 are provided by Shanghai Municipal Culture, Radio, Film and TV Administration..

表 22.6 艺术表演团体情况（2006）
BASIC STATISTICS OF ART TROUPES

类 别	Types	剧团数（个） Troupes (unit)	从业人员（人） Employees (person)	国内演出场次(场) Times of Domestic Performance (time)	观众人数（万人次） Spectators (10 000 person times)
总 计	**Total**	**97**	**3 727**	**17 308**	**7 151**
按隶属关系分	**By Administrative Relationship**				
市 级	Perfectural level	29	2 850	6 844	3 652
区 级	District level	67	861	10 282	3 279
县 级	County level	1	16	182	220
按剧种分	**By Type of Drama**				
话剧、儿童剧、滑稽剧团	Drama, Children's Play & Comedy Troupes	15	674	1 121	844
歌剧、舞剧、歌舞剧团	Opera and Dance Troupes	9	541	562	674
乐团、歌舞团、轻音乐团	Philharmonic, Song & Dance, Light Music Troupes	14	443	948	409
戏曲剧团	Local Opera Troupes	27	1 230	7 674	2 034
曲艺、杂技、木偶、皮影团	Recitation & Ballad, Acrobatics & Cirus, Puppet Show, Shadow Puttet	14	647	5 398	2 443
综合性艺术表演团体	Comprehensive Art Troupe	18	192	1 605	747

表 22.7 艺术表演场所基本情况(2006)
ART PERFORMANCE PLACES

类别 Types		机构数(个) Institutions (unit)	从业人员(人) Employees (person)	座席数(个) Seats (unit)	演(映)出场次(场) Number of Art Projections & Performances (time)	其中 of which #艺术演出场次 Number of Art Performances	观众人次(万人次) Spectators (10 000 person-times)	其中 of which #艺术演出场次 Number of Art Performances
总　计	**Total**	**148**	**2 031**	**115 948**	**35 440**	**12 500**	**1 080.9**	**629.7**
市　级	Municipal Level	19	758	28 359	3 931	3 779	271.6	267.0
#上海大剧院	Shanghai Grand Theater	1	190	2 664	738	738	41.0	41.0
上海音乐厅	Shanghai Concert Hall	1	68	1 185	176	176	10.4	10.4
贺绿汀音乐厅	He Luting Concert Hall	1	12	744	161	161	22.2	22.2
上海商城剧院	Shanghai Center Theater	1	13	991	381	347	34.3	31.2
上海话剧艺术中心	Shanghai Dramatic Arts Center	1	50	652	482	482	9.8	9.8
上海戏剧学院实验剧院	Expenrimental Theater of Shanghai Theater	1	9	908	29	27	2.0	1.9
上海美琪大戏院	Shanghai Majestic Theater	1	56	1 328	194	194	21.2	21.2
逸夫舞台	Yifu Theater	1	30	928	356	356	27.3	27.3
兰心大戏院	Lyceum Theater	1	34	681	237	236	9.1	9.1
上海艺海剧院	Shanghai Yihai Theater	1	20	999	157	157	12.5	12.5
上海马戏城	Shanghai Circus World	1	84	2 252	491	491	32.1	32.1
上海体育馆	Shanghai Stadium	1	131	12 216	51	51	42.0	42.0
区　级	District Level	119	1 224	76 769	29 928	8 497	763.6	351.7
#中国大戏院	China Theater	1	26	400	70	70	3.6	3.6
县　级	County Level	10	49	10 820	1 581	224	45.7	11.0

表 22.8 博物馆、纪念馆情况(2006) STATISTICS OF MUSEUMS AND MEMORIALS

指 标 Indicators		机构数(个) Quantity (unit)	馆内藏品实际数量 Real Quantity of Collections (万件) (10 000 pieces)	#一至三级藏品 Collections of Class One to Three	展览活动(个) Exhibit Activity (unit)	参观人次(万人次) Visiting Person-times (10 000 person-times)
总 计	**Total**	**106**	**75.64**	**18.14**	**196**	**1 114.5**
综合性	Comprehensive	15	1.83	0.68	61	309.7
历史类	Historical	15	8.10	2.36	24	275.8
艺术类	Art	6	12.91	12.88	20	115.3
科学类	Scientific	3	26.66	0.40	10	300.6
人物类	Character	18	10.17	1.80	34	39.1
行业类	Industrial	37	13.68	0.02	38	69.3
高校类	University	12	2.29	…	9	4.7

注：本表由市文物管理委员会提供(下表同)。
Note: Data in this table are provided by Municipal Historical Relic Administrative Committee.

表 22.9 文物保护维修情况(2002～2006) PRESERVATION AND MAINTAIN OF HISTORICAL RELICS

指 标 Indicators		2002	2003	2004	2005	2006
保护维修项目数(个)	Items of Preservation and Maintaining (item)	27	28	30	44	63
#国家级	National	4	5	5	4	10
市 级	Municipal	18	15	14	18	23
维修面积(万平方米)	Areas of Maintaining (10 000 sq. m)	2.3	2.5	2.2	2.3	17.4
项目总预算(万元)	Aggregate Budget of Items (10 000 yuan)	1 900	3 899	9 693	19 650	44 702
#专项补助	Special Assistance	736	920	582	934	765
已拨入专项补助(万元)	Special Assiatance Appropriated (10 000 yuan)	644	900	396	1 209	520
当年保护维修支出(万元)	Expend on Preservation and Maintaining (10 000 yuan)	1 102	2 474	8 400	19 571	30 145

表 22.10　电视台和广播电台情况(2006)
TELEVISION STATIONS AND BROADCASTING STATIONS

类　别 Types		节目套数(套) Programs(set)	公共节目播出时间(小时) Playing Hours of Public Program (hour)	其中 of which #自办节目 Self-produced Programs	全年制作节目时间(小时) Annual Production of Programs(hour)
电视台	**Television Stations**	**25**	**159 550**	**78 634**	**66 275**
市级电视台	Municipal Level	16	117 468	66 417	55 232
#上海教育电视台	Shanghai Educational Television Station	1	6 935	1 402	901
区县级电视台	Distric Level	9	42 082	12 217	11 043
广播电台	**Broadcasting Stations**	**21**	**129 740**	**101 712**	**90 582**
市级广播电台	Municipal Level	11	77 174	70 959	76 016
区县级广播电台	Distric Level	10	52 566	30 753	14 566

注：本表至表 22.17 数据由市文化广播影视管理局提供。
Note: Data in this table to table 22.17 are provided by Shanghai Municipal Administration of Culture, Radio, Film & TV.

表 22.11　电视和广播公共节目播出时间（2006）
PLAYING HOURS OF TELEVISION AND BROADCASTING PUBLIC PROGRAMS

单位:小时(hour)

类　别 Types		电视台 Television Stations 合计 Total	市级 Municipal Level	区县级 Distric Level	广播电台 Broadcasting Stations 合计 Total	市级 Municipal Level	区县级 Distric Level
总　计	**Total**	**159 550**	**117 468**	**42 082**	**129 740**	**77 174**	**52 566**
新闻资讯类节目	News Program	20 861	16 306	4 555	33 888	20 951	12 937
专题服务类节目	Subject Service Program	27 163	23 057	4 106	18 395	12 509	5 886
综艺类节目	Recreational and Artistic Program	20 706	19 835	871	45 601	31 606	13 995
影视剧类节目	Film and TV Program	56 538	34 806	21 732			
广播剧类节目	Broadcasting Drama Program				9 740	2 372	7 368
广告类节目	Advertising Program	20 081	13 294	6 787	14 099	9 736	4 363
其他类节目	Others	14 201	10 170	4 031	8 017		8 017

表 22.12　主要年份有线电视基本情况
BASIC STATISTICS ON CABLE TELEVISION IN MAIN YEARS

指　标 Indicators		2000	2005	2006
有线电视总用户数(万户)	Subscribers(10 000 households)	303.00	435.13	477.20
有线电视入户率(%)	Popularity Rate(%)	64.5	88.7	96.1
有线广播电视传输网络干线总长(公里)	Lines Total (kilometer)	604	21 174	28 551

表22.13 电影摄制、译制和放映情况(1978～2006)
PRODUCTION, DUBBING AND SHOWING OF FILMS

年份 Year	摄制和译制电影片 Production and Dubbing				电影放映 Film Showing			
	故事片(部) Feature Films (film)	美术片(本) Cartoons (reel)	科学教育片(本) Popular Science Films (reel)	译制片(本) Dubbed Films (reel)	放映场次(万场) Showing (10 000 times)	其中 of which #影、剧院 At Cinemas and Theatres	观众人次(万人次) Spectators (10 000 person-times)	其中 of which #影、剧院 At Cinemas and Theatres
1978	10	24	84	275	35	17	27 405	15 291
1979	14	25	95	315	40	20	32 763	29 743
1980	17	30	105	382	39	20	29 304	18 039
1981	17	32	109	289	38	19	26 823	16 203
1982	19	35	112	604	38	20	25 828	15 586
1983	19	34	116	666	37	20	25 204	15 124
1984	19	40	117	633	36	21	24 149	15 539
1985	15	43	140	426	34	21	21 885	14 748
1986	19	38	150	450	36	24	23 220	16 720
1987	17	38	151	378	37	28	21 985	17 067
1988	13	29	156	501	38	30	20 461	16 742
1989	17	29	140	398	37	32	20 776	18 216
1990	16	47	142	340	38	33	19 351	17 021
1991	17	37	146	272	36	31	15 766	13 615
1992	17	42	146	325	29	25	9 145	8 089
1993	16	35	91	251	16	14	3 862	3 332
1994	14	13	69	162	22	20	4 001	3 617
1995	17	37	22	266	23	20	4 419	3 913
1996	10	58	6	283	27	25	4 420	3 783
1997	11	17	8	312	25	23	3 670	3 023
1998	4	16	6	271	23	21	2 924	2 451
1999	17	10	14	372	20	19	2 055	1 678
2000	10	500	12	438	18	17	1 794	1 452
2001	12	2	8	237	18	17	1 553	1 315
2002	10	2	11	204	20	17	1 198	921
2003	9	10	2	216	20	19	971	870
2004	12	1		18	24	23	1 364	1 183
2005	13			15	28	26	1 509	1 323
2006	9			24	27	26	1 254	1 173

表 22.14 区、县文化娱乐机构情况(2006)
CULTURE AND ENTERTAINMENT UNDERTAKINGS BY DISTRICTS AND COUNTIES

单位:个(unit)

地 区	District	合 计 Total	其 中 of which #歌舞娱乐场所 Singing & Dancing Rooms	#游戏电子游艺经营场所 Video Games Rooms	#其他娱乐场所 Other Places	#网 吧 Internet Bar
总 计	**Total**	**4 240**	**1 725**	**460**	**533**	**1 434**
市 级	Prefectural Level	558	56		10	404
浦东新区	Pudong New Area	674	249	148	104	173
黄 浦 区	Huangpu	99	45	8	16	30
卢 湾 区	Luwan	115	46	9	45	15
徐 汇 区	Xuhui	216	68	14	66	68
长 宁 区	Changning	196	113	5	38	40
静 安 区	Jing'an	86	57	5	4	20
普 陀 区	Putuo	177	67	24	12	74
闸 北 区	Zhabei	159	70	14	14	61
虹 口 区	Hongkou	164	51	31	27	55
杨 浦 区	Yangpu	172	69	19	8	76
宝 山 区	Baoshan	216	109	28	4	75
闵 行 区	Minhang	363	163	60	50	90
嘉 定 区	Jiading	179	88	22	6	63
金 山 区	Jinshan	122	62	12	18	30
松 江 区	Songjiang	211	115	14	29	53
青 浦 区	Qingpu	134	86	3	19	26
南 汇 区	Nanhui	202	103	30	34	35
奉 贤 区	Fengxian	127	60	12	23	32
崇 明 县	Chongming	70	48	2	6	14

表22.15 各区、县艺术表演场所、图书馆、群艺馆、文化馆基本情况(2006)
ART PERFORMANCE PLACES,LIBRARIES, MASS ART CENTERS AND CULTURE CENTERS BY DISTRICS AND COUNTIES

地区 District		艺术表演场所 Art Performance Place		公共图书馆 Libraries		群艺馆、文化馆(个) Mass Art Centers and Culture Centers (unit)
		个数(个) Number (unit)	座席数(个) Seat (unit)	个数(个) Number (unit)	读者人数(万人次) Readers (10 000 person-times)	
总计	**Total**	**148**	**115 948**	**28**	**1 342.41**	**30**
市级	Municipal Level	19	28 359	2	211.73	1
浦东新区	Pudong New Area	14	9 220	1	159.93	4
黄浦区	Huangpu	4	2 862	1	104.41	1
卢湾区	Luwan	1	600	1	49.38	1
徐汇区	Xuhui			1	73.31	2
长宁区	Changning	3	1 110	2	51.43	2
静安区	Jing'an			1	59.59	1
普陀区	Putuo			2	118.86	3
闸北区	Zhabei	3	1 895	2	60.41	2
虹口区	Hongkou	1	861	2	53.33	2
杨浦区	Yangpu	2	2 117	3	97.80	1
宝山区	Baoshan	7	1 832	1	77.70	2
闵行区	Minhang	12	6 614	1	19.38	1
嘉定区	Jiading	9	4 052	1	28.33	1
金山区	Jinshan	6	3 995	1	10.42	1
松江区	Songjiang	6	4 618	1	44.53	1
青浦区	Qingpu	18	12 503	2	21.01	1
奉贤区	Fengxian	17	12 562	1	36.06	1
南汇区	Nanhui	16	11 928	1	23.00	1
崇明县	Chongming	10	10 820	1	41.80	1

表 22.16 文化娱乐机构基本情况(2006)
BASIC STATISTICS OF CULTURE AND ENTERTAINMENT INSTITUTIONS

类别	Types	从业人员(人) Employees (person)	主营营业收入(万元) Major Business Revenue (10 000 yuan)	主营业务利润(万元) Major Business Profits (10 000 yuan)	房屋建筑面积(万平方米) Floor Space of Buildings (10 000 sq. m)
总计	**Total**	**62 992**	**773 133**	**240 534**	**384.60**
歌舞娱乐场所	Singing & Dancing Rooms	33 586	218 797	44 056	247.40
游戏电子游艺经营场所	Gaming Rooms	2 801	12 375	3 706	30.90
其他娱乐场所	Other Places	13 523	102 252	18 403	52.60
网吧	Internet Bar	8 556	57 933	8 793	50.00
其他	Others	4 526	381 776	165 573	3.70

表 22.17 公共图书馆情况(2006)
PUBLIC LIBRARIES

指标	Indicators	合计 Total	市级 Munnicipal Level	区级 District Level	县级 County Level
机构数(个)	Institutions (unit)	28	2	25	1
从业人员(人)	Employees (person)	2 425	1 287	1 098	40
总藏量(万册、件)	Collection (10 000 copies)	6 062.44	5 172.23	848.90	41.31
#图书	Books	2 170.19	1 320.71	808.29	41.19
报刊	Newspaper and Magzines	304.02	290.90	13.11	0.01
本年新购藏量(万册、件)	Publications Newly Bought (10 000 copies)	117.50	51.70	63.15	2.65
#图书	Books	102.68	42.09	58.06	2.53
建筑面积(万平方米)	Floor Space of Buildings (10 000 sq. m)	23.52	12.27	10.54	0.71
书库	Stack Room	7.94	5.83	1.95	0.16
阅览室	Reading Room	4.53	1.33	3.05	0.15
阅览座位(个)	Seats in Reading Room (unit)	14 184	2 352	11 332	500
图书借阅情况	Books Lending				
人次(万人次)	Readers (10 000 person-times)	1 342.41	211.73	1 088.88	41.80
册数(万册次)	Books (10 000 copy-times)	1 086.92	229.81	831.41	25.70
信息化装备	Information Equipment				
计算机(台)	Computer (unit)	4 534	2 308	2 156	70
共享工程服务点(个)	Communion Services Spot (unit)	420	420		
为读者举办各种活动	Activities Held for Readers				
次数(次)	Times (time)	4 809	809	3 978	22
参加人次(万人次)	Participants (10 000 person-times)	112.23	31.51	79.72	1.00

表 22.18 图书出版数量(1978～2006)
BOOKS PUBLISHED

年份 Years	种数 (种) Number of Publications (type)	其中 of which #新出版 Newly Published	总印数 (亿册) Total Printed (100 million copies)	总印张数 (亿印张) Total Ptrinted Signatures (100 million signatures)
1978	1 666	1 332	3.92	12.19
1979	2 040	1 563	4.58	15.54
1980	2 338	1 804	5.62	17.73
1981	2 801	1 949	6.01	22.89
1982	3 395	2 057	6.07	21.76
1983	3 653	2 254	4.65	21.31
1984	3 848	2 328	5.37	25.58
1985	4 176	2 634	4.96	23.95
1986	4 531	3 045	3.66	17.81
1987	5 103	3 151	4.26	19.84
1988	5 538	3 658	4.33	19.04
1989	6 765	4 960	3.28	14.52
1990	7 767	4 887	2.98	14.66
1991	8 141	4 756	3.11	17.30
1992	8 095	4 179	2.75	17.19
1993	7 721	4 272	2.26	15.34
1994	7 812	4 382	2.35	17.01
1995	8 338	4 185	2.44	17.92
1996	9 234	4 445	2.79	20.1
1997	9 928	4 844	2.70	18.00
1998	10 718	5 083	2.83	18.69
1999	11 381	5 880	2.68	18.69
2000	12 682	6 936	2.54	19.05
2001	14 000	7 947	2.68	21.24
2002	14 537	8 156	2.59	21.38
2003	15 636	8 726	2.74	23.27
2004	16 449	9 391	2.67	23.54
2005	16 504	9 286	2.59	23.65
2006	17 283	9 338	2.54	24.86

注：本表数据至表 22.25 的数据由市新闻出版局提供。
Note: Data in table 22.18 to 22.25 are provided by Shanghai Municipal Press and Publication Bureau.

表 22.19 期刊出版数量(1978～2006)
PERIODICALS PUBLISHED

年份 Years	种数 (种) Number of Publications (type)	每期平均印数 (万册、份) Average Publications Issued (10 000 copies)	总印数 (亿册) Total Printed (100 million copies)	总印张数 (亿印张) Total Printed Signatures (100 million signatures)
1978	42	459	0.47	1.12
1979	90	721	0.73	2.08
1980	126	1 061	1.22	3.37
1981	266	1 873	2.03	5.95
1982	308	2 203	2.31	6.37
1983	349	2 572	2.51	7.07
1984	402	3 502	3.10	8.56
1985	491	3 424	3.45	9.21
1986	541	3 073	3.03	8.17
1987	546	3 058	3.13	8.05
1988	535	2 624	2.66	6.63
1989	527	1 793	1.86	4.58
1990	522	1 735	1.73	4.24
1991	504	1 749	1.79	4.44
1992	527	1 794	1.84	4.59
1993	535	1 668	1.82	4.95
1994	556	1 569	1.72	4.87
1995	565	1 583	1.78	5.3
1996	582	1 530	1.66	5.14
1997	587	1 513	1.66	5.35
1998	591	1 503	1.65	5.81
1999	606	1 493	1.78	6.87
2000	613	1 489	1.85	7.38
2001	616	1 413	1.85	7.58
2002	621	1 332	1.80	7.77
2003	626	1 335	1.83	8.51
2004	612	1 184	1.93	8.94
2005	612	1 130	1.90	8.96
2006	616	1 125	1.83	8.76

表 22.20 报纸出版数量(1978 ~ 2006)
NEWSPAPER PUBLISHED

年 份 Years	种 数 (种) Number of Publications (type)	每期平均印数 (万份) Average Publication Issued (10 000 copies)	总印数 (亿册) Total Printed (100 million copies)	总印张数 (亿印张) Total Printed Signatures (100 million signatures)
1978	5	257	6.41	6.20
1979	8	349	7.32	7.08
1980	12	464	8.55	8.20
1981	15	640	10.28	9.77
1982	31	936	14.93	13.13
1983	34	1 185	18.13	15.49
1984	41	1 429	19.63	16.57
1985	89	1 656	19.54	17.07
1986	93	1 750	19.94	18.37
1987	90	2 003	22.45	20.49
1988	83	1 958	21.38	22.07
1989	81	1 477	15.85	16.25
1990	81	1 510	16.16	16.76
1991	75	1 506	18.48	19.16
1992	77	1 506	24.76	24.76
1993	81	1 506	32.27	32.27
1994	87	1 369	30.43	30.43
1995	86	1 358	19.04	34.00
1996	87	1 357	18.93	36.96
1997	87	1 397	19.34	43.19
1998	80	1 441	19.73	49.84
1999	75	1 311	18.42	46.26
2000	103	1 135	16.77	44.57
2001	101	1 060	16.98	47.67
2002	101	983	16.46	51.42
2003	101	886	17.05	66.13
2004	103	939	19.71	83.66
2005	102	903	19.06	89.94
2006	101	850	17.89	87.33

表 22.21 主要年份新闻出版机构和人员数
NUMBER OF INSTITUTIONS AND EMPLOYEES ENGAGED IN NEWS AND PUBLISHING IN MAIN YEARS

指 标	Indicators	2000	2005	2006
图书出版机构	**Publishing Houses**			
机构数（个）	Institutions (unit)	37	39	39
从业人员（人）	Employee (person)	3 666	3 874	3 874
书刊印刷机构	**Printing Houses**			
机构数（个）	Institutions (unit)	4 543	4 971	5 281
从业人员（万人）	Employee (10 000 persons)	11.54	14.03	13.62
发行机构	**Issuing Houses**			
机构数（个）	Institutions (unit)	6 743	7 146	7 754
从业人员（万人）	Employee (10 000 persons)	1.94	2.29	2.46

注：发行机构数中包括发行网点数。
Note: Issuig Houses include number of net places.

表 22.22 图书出版数量(2006)
BOOKS PUBLISHED

类 别	types	种 数（种）Number of Publications (type)	其中 of which #新出版 Newly Published	总印数（万册）Total Printed (10 000 copies)	总印张数（万印张）Total Printed Signatures (10 000 signatures)
总 计	**Total**	**17 283**	**9 338**	**25 433**	**2 486 373**
书 籍	**Books**	**14 629**	**8 467**	**15 761**	**1 824 412**
哲学、社会科学	Philosophy and Social Science	3 436	2 236	2 021	339 736
文化教育	Culture and Education	5 740	2 700	8 744	924 890
文学艺术	Literature and Art	2 618	1 698	2 527	309 709
自然科学技术	Natural Science and Technology	2 239	1 400	1 521	211 319
少年儿童读物	Children's Reading Materials	596	433	948	38 758
课 本	**Textbooks**	**2 470**	**740**	**9 319**	**654 528**
#大专课本	University and College	727	259	1 059	182 193
中专技校教材	Specialized Secondary and Technical Worker School	95	42	68	7 490
中学课本	Secondary School	591	111	4 311	302 023
小学课本	Primary School	442	105	3 525	116 851
业余教育课本	Spare-time Education	48	4	47	6 152
教学用书	Teaching References	567	219	309	39 818
图 片	**Pictures**	**184**	**131**	**353**	**7 279**

注：在 2 486 373 万总印张数中，还包括 154 万印张的国标、部标、影印书、活页文选等附录。
Note: Among the total 2 486 373 million printed signatures, there are also 154 million printed signatures of appendixes such as National Standards, Ministry Standards, photocopy books, loose-leaf analecta, etc.

表 22.23 期刊出版数量(2006)
PERIODICALS PUBLISHED

类 别 Types		种 数 (种) Number of Publications (type)	出版期数 (期) Number of Issue (issue)	总印数 (万册、份) Total Printed (10 000 copies)	总印张数 (万印张) Total Printed Signatures (10 000 signatures)
总 计	**Total**	**616**	**5 756**	**18 335**	**876 030**
综 合	Comprehensive	9	91	171	17 228
哲学、社会科学	Philosophy and Social Science	116	1 330	3 703	177 250
自然科学技术	Natural Science and Technology	362	2 821	2 591	210 207
文化教育	Culture and Education	77	860	2 194	135 133
文学艺术	Literature and Art	36	413	8 381	302 443
少年儿童读物	Children's Reading Materials	15	229	1 287	33 408
画 刊	Pictorial	1	12	9	361

表 22.24 报纸出版数量(2006)
NEWSPAPER PUBLISHED

类 别 Types		种 数 (种) Number of Publications (type)	期 数 (期) Issue (issue)	每期平均印数 (万份) Average Publication Per Issue (10 000 copies)	总印数 (万份) Total Printed (10 000 copies)	总印张数 (万印张) Total Printed Signatures (10 000 signatures)
总 计	**Total**	**101**	**10 982**	**850**	**178 928**	**8 732 830**
综合报	Comprehensive	19	4 805	486	142 109	7 308 929
专业报	Specialized	82	6 177	364	36 819	1 423 901

表 22.25 音像电子出版数量 (2006)
AUDIO, VIDEO AND ELECTRON PUBLISHED

类 别 Types		种 数 (种) Number of Publications (type)	出版数量 (万张、万盒) Number of Publications (10 000 piece box)	发行数量 (万张、万盒) Number of Issue (10 000 piece box)	发行总金额 (万元) Total Values (10 000 yuan)
总 计	**Total**	**4 790**	**7 067.86**	**3 474.81**	**24 407.22**
电子出版物	Electronic Publication	327	3 069.55	375.89	4 553.31
数码激光视盘	DVD	493	707.75	614.82	2 615.89
高密度激光视盘	VCD	235	136.62	84.21	926.04
录像带	Video	13	0.65	0.39	10.02
激光唱盘	CD	1 454	557.17	478.02	5 204.91
录音带	Tape	2 172	2 536.01	1 867.66	10 640.18
其 他	Others	96	60.11	53.82	456.87

表 22.26 档案机构基本情况(2006)
BASIC STATISTICS OF ARCHIVE INSTITUTIONS

指 标	Indicators	合 计 Total	档案馆 Archives Library	其中 Of which 综 合 Comprehensive	档案室(处、科) Archives
机构数(个)	**Number of Institutions(unit)**	**466**	**41**	**20**	**405**
从业人员(人)	**Employees(person)**	**2 418**	**721**	**443**	**1 446**
专 职	Full-time	1 647	721	443	675
兼 职	Part-time	771			771
馆藏档案	**Archives Collected**				
全 宗(个)	Overall Rolls(unit)	5 923	5 201	5 157	722
案 卷(万卷)	Rolls(10 000 rolls)	1 259	859	748	400
以件为保管单位档案(万件)	Archives (Piece as Unit) (10 000 unit)	141	24	44	118
录音、录像、影片档案(万盘)	Recprd, Video and Film (10 000 disks)	5.66	1.32	8.14	4.30
照片档案(万张)	Photo Records(10 000 pieces)	88.50	47.96	36.40	40.54
底图(万张)	Base Maps(10 000 pieces)	1 275.23	186.28	2.00	1 088.95
电子档案(万张)	Electronic Records(10 000 disks)				
磁 盘	Disks	2.34	0.07	0.01	2.27
光 盘	Compact Discs	3.19	1.71	0.29	1.48
微缩胶片	Microfilm				
开窗卡(万张)	Open Window Card(10 000 pieces)	67.36	43.32	22.82	24.04
档案利用	**Records Utilized**				
已开放档案	Records Opened				
案 卷(万卷)	Rolls(10 000 rolls)	180.79	180.79	180.16	
开放档案目录(万条)	Catalog of Records Opened(10 000 pieces)				
案卷级	Roll Grade	130.35	130.35	130.08	
文件级	Document Grade	31.14	31.14	31.14	
本年利用档案	Records Utilized This Year				
卷次(万卷次)	Roll-times(10 000 roll-times)	91.67	68.34	59.19	23.33
件次(万件次)	Piece-times(10 000 piece-times)	28.17	0.22	0.15	27.95
人次(万人次)	Person-times(10 000 person-times)	27.88	16.39	10.49	11.49

①本表数据由市档案局提供。
②至 2006 年末全市有档案行政管理部门 20 个，专职从业人员 251 人。
❶Data in this table are provided by Shanghai Municipal Archives Bureau.
❷By the end of 2006, there are 20 administration institutions of archive and 251 full – time employees in total city.

表22.27　等级裁判员、运动员人数和运动员破纪录情况(1978~2006)
CERTIFIED REFEREES,ATHLETES AND RECORD-BREAKING

单位:人(person)

年份 Year	等级裁判员 Certified Referees	其中 of which 国际裁判 International Referees	等级运动员 Certified Athletes	其中 of which 国际运动健将 International Master Athletes	打破上年全国最高纪录 Break the Highest National Record of the Preceding Year 人 Person	队 Team	次 Time	项 Item
1978	268	5	1 957		25	4	77	20
1979	2 423		1 899		8	4	38	25
1980	1 610		1 871		51		164	50
1981	1 949	2	1 447		27	4	76	36
1982	1 250	3	1 367		13		19	11
1983	733	2	1 056		14		36	21
1984	1 244		2 635	4	15	2	33	16
1985	1 558		1 231	10	17	4	46	19
1986	980	4	1 412	17	21	7	47	31
1987	1 265	3	1 217	8	24		64	23
1988	828	5	1 100	7	15	2	41	25
1989	1 116	3	1 319		6		9	8
1990	1 110	4	1 455	4	13		18	18
1991	904	1	1 601	8	4		7	7
1992	805		782		58	8	99	82
1993	358	3	1 078	8	60	8	102	86
1994	520		1 570	12	20	2	34	21
1995	523	2	960	11	16	1	74	34
1996	1 310		1 159	12	20	2	8	8
1997	699	1	1 235	8	31	8	75	59
1998	1 175	2	1 996	15	12	10	30	29
1999	1 127		1 903		15	3	6	6
2000	880				3		4	3
2001	968		1 338	8	2	1	5	3
2002	459	2	991	7				
2003	535		1 189	18				
2004	301		524	12				
2005	357		793	5				
2006	274	5	699	18				

注：本表至表22.36数据由市体育局提供。等级裁判员和等级运动员均为当年发展数。

Note: Data in table 22.27 to 22.36 are provided by Shanghai Municipal Sports Bureau. Data of Certified Referees and Certified Athletes refer to those newly developed of each year.

表 22.28 主要年份优秀运动员、教练员情况
BASIC STATISTICS ON EXCELLENT ATHLETES AND COACHES IN MAIN YEARS

指 标	Indicators	2000	2005	2006
优秀运动员(人)	Excellent Athletes(person)	899	1 248	1 036
#女运动员	Women	402	535	498
优秀运动队专职教练员(人)	Full-time Coaches(person)	196	240	179
#女专职教练员	Women	30	59	40

表 22.29 体育系统职工人数(2006)
STAFF AND WORKERS IN SPORTS SECTORS

单位:人 (person)

指 标	Indicators	总 计 Total	其中 of which #优秀运动队 Excellent Sports Teams	#体育运动学校 Physical Education and Sports Schools	#普通业余体校 Popular Sparetime Sports School	#公共体育场(馆) Public Stadiums and Gymnasiums
总 计	**Total**	**6 368**	**1 401**	**455**	**1 458**	**1 464**
#专职教练员	Full-time Coaches	787	46	40	615	67
运动员	Athletes	1 036	868	122	36	10
管理干部	Administraive Staff	1 721	241	101	339	553
专职教师	Full-time Teachers	198	43	60	95	
科技人员	Scientific and Technical Personnel	81	67	2	10	1
医务人员	Medical Personnel	65	36	14	9	3

表 22.30 主要年份群众体育健身活动场所情况
MASS PHYSICAL ACTIVITIES IN MAIN YEARS

指 标	Indicators	2000	2005	2006
社区体育健身设施数(个)	Number of Community Fitness Facilities (unit)	1 354	4 604	4 926
#健身点	Fitness Centers	1 271	4 345	4 537
社区健身场地面积(万平方米)	Area of Communtiy Fitness Space (10 000 sq. m)	65	295	300
社区公共运动场(个)	Number of Community Public Playground(unit)		76	130
社区公共运动场面积(万平方米)	Area of Community Public Playground(10 000 sq. m)		16.4	199.1

表 22.31 主要年份上海与国外体育活动交流情况
SPORTS EXCHANGES WITH FOREIGN COUNTRIES IN MAIN YEARS

指 标	Indicators	2000	2005	2006
来上海的外国体育团体	**Sports Groups From Foreign Countries**			
次数(次)	Times (time)	112	88	95
人数(人次)	Persons (person time)	4 623	5 969	6 775
上海派出的体育团体	**Sports Groups Sent By Shanghai**			
次数(次)	Times (time)	108	114	110
人数(人次)	Persons (person time)	981	1 213	1 005

表22.32 举办运动会(比赛)和全民健身活动情况(2006)
BASIC STATISTICS IN ATHLETIC MEETINGS AND MASS PHYSICAL ACTIVITIES

地区	District	运动会和比赛次数(次) Number of Sports Meetings (time)	其中 of which: 综合运动会 Comprehensive Sports Meetings	其中 of which: 单项比赛 Single Game	举办全民健身活动情况 Mass Physical Activities: 活动次数(次) Number of Activities (time)	其中 of which: 千人以上活动 above 1000 Persons	参加活动人次(万人) Person Time of Activities (10 000 persons)
总计	**Total**	**936**	**71**	**865**	**5 244**	**2 622**	**216.09**
市直属	Municipal Level	268	3	265	200	48	100.00
浦东新区	Pudong New Area				50	20	3.00
黄浦区	Huangpu						
卢湾区	Luwan	33	1	32	29	3	1.78
徐汇区	Xuhui						
长宁区	Changning	17	2	15	21	1	2.10
静安区	Jing'an	15	1	14	20	5	3.20
普陀区	Putuo	13	5	8	12	3	1.15
闸北区	Zhabei	6	1	5	60	10	12.60
虹口区	Hongkou	44	1	43	80	4	20.00
杨浦区	Yangpu	41		41	26	5	12.00
宝山区	Baoshan	346	41	305	605	1	0.54
闵行区	Minhang						
嘉定区	Jiading	29	13	16	32	1	7.00
金山区	Jinshan	18	2	16	30	10	2.00
松江区	Songjiang	31		31	13	2	36.29
青浦区	Qingpu	33	1	32	25	8	5.00
南汇区	Nanhui	22		22	5	1	8.00
奉贤区	Fengxian	0			36		0.23
崇明县	Chongming	20		20	4 000	2 500	1.20

表 22.33 第五次体育场地普查情况
STATISTICS OF THE FIFTH PALAESTRA CENSUS

类 别 Types		体育场地（个） Palaestra (unit)	其 中 of which		体育场地面积 Area of Palaestra（万平方米）(10 000 sq. m.)	其 中 of which	
			标准场地 Standard Palaestra	非标准场地 Nonstandard Palaestra		标准场地 Standard Palaestra	非标准场地 Nonstandard Palaestra
总 计	**Total**	**14 425**	**6 451**	**7 974**	**2 926.16**	**2 548.25**	**377.91**
按系统分	By System						
教育系统	Education System	5 246	3 914	1 332	920.88	764.22	156.66
高等院校	University and College	1 138	1 059	79	181.74	174.17	7.57
中专技校	Technical Secondary School	300	194	106	44.48	35.62	8.86
中小学	Middle and Primary School	3 808	2 661	1 147	694.66	554.43	140.23
体育系统	Sports System	380	327	53	190.44	185.04	5.40
其他系统	Other System	8 663	2 167	6 496	1 807.33	1 595.58	211.75
其 他	Others	136	43	93	7.51	3.41	4.10

表 22.33 续表 continued

类 别 Types		体育场地从业人员 Employees of Palaestra（人）(person)	其 中 of which		标准体育场地观众席位 Quantity of Seats of Standard Palaestra（万个）(10 000 units)	非标准体育场地设施数（件） Quantity of Establishment in Nonstandard Palaestra	
			标准场地 Standard Palaestra	非标准场地 Nonstandard Palaestra		室内设施 Indoors Establishment	室外设施 Outdoors Establishment
总 计	**Total**	**22 542**	**15 785**	**6 757**	**38.17**	**5 093**	**60 506**
按系统分	By System						
教育系统	Education System	4 257	3 277	980	4.80	1 145	3 675
高等院校	University and College	822	768	54	0.36	82	236
中专技校	Technical Secondary School	215	162	53	3.38	55	260
中小学	Middle and Primary School	3 220	2 347	873	8.54	1 008	3 179
体育系统	Sports System	3 456	3 293	163	30.78	63	461
其他系统	Other System	14 571	9 020	5 551	2.58	3 841	55 869
其 他	Others	258	195	63	0.01	44	501

注：第五次体育场地普查时间为 2003 年。
Note: The fifth Palaestra census was held in 2003.

表22.34　第五次体育场地普查分区县情况
STATISTICS OF THE FIFTH PALAESTRA CENSUS BY DISTRICTS AND COUNTIES

地　区 District		标准体育场地 Standard Palaestra (个) (unit)	其中 of which 公益性 Nonprofit	非标准体育场地 Nonstandard Palaestra (个) (unit)	其中 of which 公益性 Nonprofit	体育场地面积(万平方米) Area of Palaestra(10 000 sq. m.) 标准场地 Standard Palaestra	非标准场地 Nonstandard Palaestra
总　计	**Total**	**6 451**	**5 414**	**7 974**	**7 529**	**2 548.25**	**377.91**
浦东新区	Pudong New Area	923	795	1 441	1 401	908.66	51.68
黄浦区	Huangpu	166	135	312	302	10.51	7.33
卢湾区	Luwan	122	58	249	211	8.32	11.87
徐汇区	Xuhui	508	406	734	689	73.22	32.02
长宁区	Changning	349	193	385	275	28.93	10.46
静安区	Jing'an	71	33	157	157	8.47	8.69
普陀区	Putuo	268	230	379	358	36.99	21.19
闸北区	Zhabei	239	208	287	281	28.36	13.45
虹口区	Hongkou	288	244	340	326	41.07	15.32
杨浦区	Yangpu	350	321	482	473	59.58	31.26
宝山区	Baoshan	443	429	391	388	75.00	19.16
闵行区	Minhang	499	416	589	534	167.64	40.03
嘉定区	Jiading	322	299	373	359	143.26	12.77
金山区	Jinshan	201	170	189	188	37.12	7.98
松江区	Songjiang	400	347	323	307	178.54	33.46
青浦区	Qingpu	553	482	565	517	446.54	20.33
南汇区	Nanhui	325	287	219	214	175.85	9.79
奉贤区	Fengxian	243	203	425	416	51.94	23.40
崇明县	Chongming	181	158	134	133	68.25	7.72

表 22.35 国民体质监测指标均值(身体形态)
AVERAGE VALUE OF NATIONAL PHYSIQUE MONITORING INDICATORS (BODY SHAPE)

年龄组	Age Group	平均身高(厘米) Average Stature (cm) 第一次监测结果 Results of First Monitoring 男性 Male	第一次监测结果 女性 Female	第二次监测结果 Results of Second Monitoring 男性 Male	第二次监测结果 女性 Female	平均体重(千克) Average Weight (kg) 第一次监测结果 Results of First Monitoring 男性 Male	第一次监测结果 女性 Female	第二次监测结果 Results of Second Monitoring 男性 Male	第二次监测结果 女性 Female
3~6岁幼儿组	**3~6 Infant Group**								
3岁	3 Years Old	100.3	99.2	101.9	100.6	15.9	15.2	16.7	16.2
4岁	4 Years Old	107.5	105.9	108.1	106.7	18.3	17.4	18.9	18.0
5岁	5 Years Old	114.1	112.7	114.5	113.4	20.6	19.6	21.3	20.4
6岁	6 Years Old	119.8	118.7	119.9	118.7	23.3	22.0	23.6	22.2
7~22岁学生组	**7~22 Student Group**								
7岁	7 Years Old	125.4	124.6	126.4	125.9	25.6	24.2	26.5	25.1
8岁	8 Years Old	130.8	129.9	131.9	131.6	28.3	26.7	29.3	27.8
9岁	9 Years Old	135.9	136.0	137.5	137.4	31.1	29.9	33.5	31.0
10岁	10 Years Old	140.7	142.6	142.2	143.5	34.2	33.9	36.5	34.8
11岁	11 Years Old	146.2	148.8	147.9	149.6	37.5	38.5	41.5	39.3
12岁	12 Years Old	154.9	154.6	156.2	155.6	44.3	43.3	46.7	44.5
13岁	13 Years Old	164.8	157.2	164.8	157.5	49.2	46.1	52.1	46.6
14岁	14 Years Old	167.3	159.1	169.6	160.2	53.8	48.5	56.2	49.5
15岁	15 Years Old	169.8	160.0	171.3	160.2	57.7	50.3	58.4	51.4
16岁	16 Years Old	172.2	160.1	172.4	161.0	60.1	50.7	60.7	52.6
17岁	17 Years Old	172.4	160.2	173.0	161.4	61.8	51.8	62.3	52.3
18岁	18 Years Old	172.5	159.9	173.2	160.7	62.2	52.0	63.3	53.1
19岁	19 Years Old	172.1	161.1	174.0	161.7	60.5	51.1	66.0	54.4
20岁	20 Years Old			172.6	161.6			64.8	53.4
21岁	21 Years Old			173.1	161.1			65.9	53.1
22岁	22 Years Old			172.9	161.3			65.7	52.6
20~59岁成人组	**20~59 Adult Group**								
20~24岁	20~24 Years Old	172.0	160.3	172.3	160.4	65.1	52.6	66.2	52.9
25~29岁	25~29 Years Old	171.3	159.6	171.5	159.6	65.9	53.9	67.9	54.0
30~34岁	30~34 Years Old	171.2	159.6	170.8	159.5	67.4	55.4	69.0	55.3
35~40岁	35~40 Years Old	170.5	159.3	170.6	159.2	67.6	57.3	69.5	56.7
40~44岁	41~44 Years Old	170.1	158.8	169.9	159.0	68.1	58.5	69.5	58.9
45~49岁	45~49 Years Old	169.5	158.0	169.2	158.4	68.6	59.5	69.5	59.2
50~54岁	50~54 Years Old	168.6	157.3	168.3	157.3	68.7	59.4	68.7	59.2
55~59岁	55~59 Years Old	167.4	156.0	167.6	156.2	67.0	59.1	68.5	59.4
60~69岁老年组	**60~69 Old Group**								
60~64岁	60~64 Years Old	165.5	154.0	166.3	154.6	65.1	58.0	67.4	59.0
65~69岁	65~69 Years Old	164.2	153.0	165.4	153.7	63.1	57.6	65.9	58.3

注：本表中第一次体质监测为2000年，第二次体质监测为2005年。
Note: The first national physique monitoring was held in 2000, while the second one was held in 2005.

表 22.36 国民体质监测指标均值（身体机能、素质）
AVERAGE VALUE OF NATIONAL PHYSIQUE MONITORING INDICATORS (BODY ENGINERY AND DAITHESIS)

年龄组	Age Group	肺活量（毫升） vital capacity (ml.) 第一次监测结果 Results of First Monitoring 男性 Male	女性 Female	第二次监测结果 Results of Second Monitoring 男性 Male	女性 Female	握力（千克） Grip (kg) 第一次监测结果 Results of First Monitoring 男性 Male	女性 Female	第二次监测结果 Results of Second Monitoring 男性 Male	女性 Female
7～22 岁学生组	**7～22 Student Group**								
7 岁	7 Years Old	1 231	1 121	1 150	1 055	6.8	5.5	10.7	9.5
8 岁	8 Years Old	1 407	1 281	1 356	1 282	8.3	7.4	12.6	11.2
9 岁	9 Years Old	1 574	1 413	1 557	1 508	9.5	8.3	14.5	13.0
10 岁	10 Years Old	1 767	1 635	1 716	1 596	12.0	12.1	16.9	15.3
11 岁	11 Years Old	1 961	1 822	1 963	1 788	14.2	13.2	18.9	17.2
12 岁	12 Years Old	2 262	2 014	2 384	2 014	18.4	16.2	23.9	20.2
13 岁	13 Years Old	2 679	2 177	2 741	2 076	25.6	18.7	30.3	21.7
14 岁	14 Years Old	2 997	2 283	3 053	2 247	30.6	20.2	35.5	22.9
15 岁	15 Years Old	3 287	2 360	3 387	2 304	33.5	20.5	37.8	24.1
16 岁	16 Years Old	3 425	2 420	3 635	2 383	36.3	22.0	39.7	24.0
17 岁	17 Years Old	3 683	2 454	3 741	2 464	36.9	22.1	41.6	24.8
18 岁	18 Years Old	3 675	2 492	3 748	2 497	39.3	22.1	42.5	25.5
19 岁	19 Years Old	3 922	2 883	3 730	2 338			41.1	25.4
20 岁	20 Years Old			3 750	2 344			42.0	25.4
21 岁	21 Years Old			3 784	2 379			43.1	26.0
22 岁	22 Years Old			3 878	2 471			43.3	25.0
20～59 岁成人组	**20～59 Adult Group**								
20～24 岁	20～24 Years Old	3 834	2 565	3 854	2 587	47.1	26.5	46.0	27.0
25～29 岁	25～29 Years Old	3 687	2 494	3 860	2 582	47.6	27.8	48.0	28.0
30～34 岁	30～34 Years Old	3 639	2 483	3 733	2 558	47.6	28.2	48.4	28.9
35～40 岁	35～40 Years Old	3 469	2 328	3 647	2 456	47.9	28.7	48.4	29.3
40～44 岁	41～44 Years Old	3 315	2 290	3 457	2 343	46.6	28.1	47.6	29.0
45～49 岁	45～49 Years Old	3 156	2 179	3 294	2 268	46.2	27.4	46.4	28.4
50～54 岁	50～54 Years Old	3 006	2 046	3 129	2 146	44.2	26.1	45.0	27.0
55～59 岁	55～59 Years Old	2 872	1 912	3 008	2 037	42.1	25.3	43.0	26.1
60～69 岁老年组	**60～69 Old Group**								
60～64 岁	60～64 Years Old	2 490	1 660	2 717	1 832	38.6	23.0	39.7	24.4
65～69 岁	65～69 Years Old	2 261	1 540	2 512	1 680	34.8	21.8	36.7	22.9

注：本表中第一次体质监测为 2000 年，第二次体质监测为 2005 年。
Note: The first national physique monitoring wsa held in 2000, while the second one was held in 2005.

上 / 海 / 统 / 计 / 年 / 鉴

主要统计指标解释

■ 文化机构

是指专门从事文化工作具有法人资格，独立核算的事业，企业单位，以及单独核算，附属于事业单位的经营性专业文化活动单位。包括从事艺术、图书馆、档案馆、群众文化、文物保护、艺术教育、艺术研究、文化娱乐、新闻出版等机构，以及其他文化机构。

■ 电影放映单位

指具有放映机器设备、固定或不固定的放映场所与专职或兼职的放映技术人员，经有关部门登记批准，经常为一定的观众对象放映电影的机构。包括电影院、影剧院、开放礼堂、俱乐部、放映队、对内礼堂俱乐部。

■ 艺术表演团体

指从事戏曲、音乐、舞蹈、杂技等专业艺术表演，有独立账户的单位，不包括半工半艺、半农半艺和民间职业剧团。该指标主要反映上海专业艺术表演团体发展规模水平。

■ 艺术表演观众人次

指售票、包场演出或民族地区免费演出的艺术表演观众人次数，不包括彩排审查和内部观摩演出的观看人次数。该指标主要反映上海观看专业艺术表演团体演出的效益规模。

■ 等级运动员人数

指经考核正式批准授予等级运动员称号的人数。运动员等级分为国际级运动健将、运动健将、一级运动员、二级运动员、三级运动员、少年级运动员。该指标主要反映运动员队伍的技术质量水平。

■ 等级裁判员人数

指经考核正式批准授予等级裁判员称号的人数。裁判员等级分为国际裁判、国家级裁判、一级裁判、二级裁判、三级裁判。该指标主要反映裁判员队伍的技术质量水平。

SHANGHAI STATISTICAL YEARBOOK

EXPLANATORY NOTES TO MAJOR STATISTICAL INDICATORS

□ Cultural Institutions

Cultural Institution refers to undertaking and business institutions which specialize in cultural work and have legal personality and independent accounting system, and those professional cultural institutions attached to undertaking institutions and have independent accounting system. It includes institutions specialize in art, library, archives, mass culture, historical relic protection, art education, art research, entertainment, news and publication and other cultural institutions.

□ Film Projection Units

Film Projection Units refer to units with film projection equipments, full or part–time projectionists, permanent or non–permanent places, approved by related administrative departments to show films regularly for certain groups of audience, including cinemas, theaters, public auditoriums, clubs, film projection teams, and interior auditorium clubs.

□ Art Performance Troupe

Art Performance Troupe refers to the troupe which is engaged in drama, opera, music, dance, acrobatics or other art performance, opens independent accounts with banks and has self–supporting accounting system; excluding the troupes which are engaged partly in industrial or agricultural activities, partly in art performance and the professional troupes organized by the people. This indicator reflects the development of Shanghai's professional art troupes.

□ Number of Spectators at Art Performance

Number of Spectators at Art Performance refers to the number of attendants at commercial shows, completely booked shows or free shows given in minority national areas, and does not include the number of spectators at rehearsals for examination and internal shows for study. This indicator reflects beneficial results of spectators at Professional Art Performance.

□ Number of Certified Athletes

Number of Certified Athletes refers to the number of athletes who have been given titles through examination. The titles of athletes include international masters of sports, masters of sports, first–grade, second–grade and third–grade sportsmen and young athletes. This indicator reflects skill of the athletes.

□ Number of Certified Referees

Number of Certified Referees refers to the number of referees who have been given titles after examination. They are classified as international referees, national referees and referees of the first, second and third grades. This indicator reflects the skill of referees.
international referees, national referees and referees of the first, second and third grades. This indicator reflects the skill of referees.

第二十三篇
CHAPTER 23

法律、公证和其他
LAWS, NOTARY AND OTHERS

表23.1 主要年份律师、公证及调解工作基本情况
BASIC STATISTICS OF LAWYERS, NOTARIZATIONS AND MEDIATIONS IN MAIN YEARS

指 标	Indicators	1990	2000	2005	2006
律师工作	**Lawyers**				
法律律师事务所（个）	Law Offices (unit)	60	415	682	741
专职工作人员（人）	Full-time Staff (person)	815	5 127	9 414	11 141
#专职律师	Full-time Lawyers	644	3 522	6 626	7 366
取得法律职业资格（人）	Qualified Law Occupation (person)	2 338	4 642	7 129	7 896
#专职律师	Full-time Lawyers	628	3 522	6 626	7 366
兼职律师	Part-time Lawyers	913	731	503	530
全年办理	**Total Transacted**				
民事案件诉讼代理（万件）	Civil Lawsuit(10 000 cases)	1.64	3.71	6.75	6.80
刑事诉讼辩护及代理（万件）	Criminal Lawsuit and Vindication(10 000 cases)	0.75	1.13	1.27	1.47
经济案件诉讼代理（万件）	Economic Lawsuit(10 000 cases)		3.34	2.23	2.15
非诉讼法律事务（万件）	Non-litigation Action(10 000 cases)	0.39	2.65	3.36	4.65
解答法律询问(万人次)	Legal Advisory Services (10 000 person times)	5.53	10.36	10.18	12.56
代写法律事务文书（万件）	Legal Documents Written on Behalf of Clients (10 000 cases)	1.2	1.92	2.15	2.56
行政案件诉讼代理（万件）	Administrative Lawsuit(10 000 cases)		0.12	0.15	0.16
公证工作	**Notarizations**				
公证处（个）	Notarial Offices (unit)	23	22	22	22
公证人员（人）	Notarial Personnel (person)	294	366	470	528
#公证员	Notaries	115	243	270	283
办理公证文书（万件）	Documents Notarized (10 000 cases)	13.68	47.72	41.58	40.41
#国内经济合同公证	Domestic Economic Contracts Notarized	1.21	18.73	10.48	9.69
在办理公证文书中	Documents Notarizing				
涉外公证（万件）	Foreign (10 000 cases)	10.41	19.93	21.39	22.26
国内公证（万件）	Domestic (10 000 cases)	3.27	27.79	19.36	17.16
公证费收入（万元）	Revenue of Notarial Fees (10 000 yuan)	472	11 276	34 646	31 064
人民调解工作	**People's Mediation**				
专职司法助理员（人）	Full-time Judicial Assistants (person)	386	416	608	736
人民调解委员会（万个）	People's Mediation Committees(10 000 units)	1.18	0.89	0.62	0.59
调解人员（万人）	Mediators (10 000 persons)	5.50	3.55	3.58	3.13
调解民间纠纷（万件）	Civil Disputes Mediated (10 000 cases)	8.11	6.37	8.15	9.09

①本表至表23.4的数据由市司法局提供。
②办理公证文件中包括涉及港、澳、台公证文件。
❶Data in this table to table 23.4 are provided by Shanghai Municipal Justice Bureau.
❷The number of notarized documents handled included Hong Kong, Macao, and Taiwan's.

表 23.2　主要年份国内公证文书分类情况
DOMESTIC NOTARIAL DOCUMENTS BY TYPE IN MAIN YEARS

单位：件(case)

指　标	Indicators	1990	2000	2005	2006
总　计	**Total**	**32 677**	**277 949**	**193 618**	**171 598**
经济公证	**Business Notarized**	**12 144**	**187 304**	**104 793**	**96 867**
# 购销合同	Purchases and Sales Contracts	21	5	384	1
贷款合同	Loans Contracts	427	80 980	53 902	30 484
招标、投标	Bidding	139	55	286	103
劳务合同	Labour Contracts	1 836	4 982	35	103
建筑工程承包	Construction Project Contracts	230	3	16	45
农、林、牧、副、渔业承包	Farming, Forestry, Animal Husbandry, Sideline Production and Fishery Contracts	1 817	38	23	48
财产租赁	Property Leases	3 213	22	364	35
法人资格	Legal Person Identification	453	109	49	109
法人委托书	Legal Person Certificate of Entrustment	289	227	12 791	6 795
民事公证	**Civil Legal Relations Notarized**	**20 533**	**90 645**	**88 825**	**74 731**
# 收　养	Child Adoption	178	15	154	84
解除收养	Adoption Renouncements	54	5	97	70
继承权	Rights of Inheritance	1 599	5 217	9 642	11 281
遗　嘱	Testaments	898	1 709	3 900	3 759
产　权	Porperty Rights	708	824	152	114
亲属关系	Kinship Confirmation	259	1 798	406	465
房屋买卖	Purchases and Sales of House	1 429	599	263	162
房屋租赁	House Leases	436	61	12	17
留学协议	Study Abroad Contracts	1 239	883	212	274
遗赠扶养协议	Donations and Family Fostering	91	260	39	28
委托书	Certificate of Entrustment	521	4 520	48 252	29 977
赠与书	Presentation Documents	1 583	5 196	1 462	1 832
声明书	Declarations	451	10 424	5 040	5 092
宅基使用协议	Rights to Housing Site	1 856	123	3	3
其他民事协议	Other Civil Agreements	5 473	15 552	4 451	2 839

表 23.3　主要年份涉外公证文书分类情况
FOREIGN-RELATED NOTARIAL DOCUMENTS BY TYPE IN MAIN YEARS

单位:件（case）

类别	Types	1990	2000	2005	2006
总　计	**Total**	**104 076**	**199 323**	**213 868**	**222 624**
出　生	Births	18 739	28 535	23 563	25 187
学　历	Schoolihg	13 762	21 644	7 607	9 370
经　历	Personal Histories	8 442	4 025	1 943	1 811
生存、居住	Survival and Residence	178	355	596	115
死　亡	Deaths	180	723	608	641
收　养	Children Adoption	27	171	41	41
亲属关系	Kinship	16 870	22 488	17 731	18 096
婚姻状况	Marriages	15 704	20 274	11 231	9 371
继承权	Rights of Inheritance	19	12	1 070	21
遗　嘱	Testaments	3	9	1 263	13
委托书	Trust Deeds	106	2 484	8 833	5 973
声明书	Declarations	2 410	1 285	3 120	4 076
受、未受刑事处分	Criminal Records & Uncriminal Records	13 269	20 669	18 289	14 597
文本相符	Confirmation of Copies and Photo-Offset Copies to Originals	359	23 645	46 127	29 291
其　他	Others	14 008	53 004	71 846	104 021

表 23.4　主要年份民间纠纷调解分类情况
CIVIL DISPUTES MEDIATED BY TYPE IN MAIN YEARS

单位:件（case）

类别	Types	1990	2000	2005	2006
总　计	**Total**	**81 076**	**63 653**	**81 495**	**90 940**
#婚姻家庭	Family Disputes	42 426	19 722	20 074	22 211
邻　里	Neighbor Disputes	22 658	25 064	33 244	34 975
赔　偿	Compensation	1 909	2 483	4 451	5 594
房屋宅基地	Housing and Housing Sites	9 671	10 359	11 341	11 568

表 23.5 主要年份公安机关立案的刑事案件情况
CRIMINAL CASES REGISTERED IN PUBLIC SECURITY ORGANS IN MAIN YEARS

单位：起（times）

类别	Types	2000	2005	2006
总　计	**Total**	**104 946**	**127 757**	**139 060**
杀　人	Homicide	252	246	229
伤　害	Injury	1 553	2 041	2 166
抢　劫	Robbery	3 033	2 539	2 698
强　奸	Rape	396	376	391
诈　骗	Fraud	8 425	9 999	11 975
盗　窃	Larceny	77 912	96 305	101 817
其　他	Others	13 375	16 251	19 784

注：本表至表 23.9 的数据由市公安局提供。
Note: Data in table 23.5 to 23.9 are provided by Shanghai Municipal Public Security Bureau.

表 23.6 主要年份公安机关查处治安案件情况
OFFENSE CASES AGAINST PUBLIC ORDER HANDLED BY PUBLIC SECURITY ORGANS IN MAIN YEARS

单位：起（times）

类别	Types	2000	2005	2006
总　计	**Total**	**194 141**	**322 393**	**572 280**
#扰乱工作、公共秩序	Disturbing Work and Public Order	23 568	20 825	30 731
结伙斗殴、寻衅滋事	"Gang Fighting or Picking Quarrels and Making Trouble"	3 373	3 049	6 098
阻碍国家工作人员执行职务	Obstructing the Goverment Workers to Perform Their Duty	1 029	929	1 400
殴打他人	Beating Other Body	16 973	24 551	86 768
骗取、抢夺、敲诈勒索财物	Defrauding, Snatching or Extoring and Racketeering Valuables	2 936	6 963	21 954
故意损坏公私财物	Intentionally Damaging Public or Private Valuables	681	2 201	2 519
伪造倒卖票券、证件	Forging and Fraudulently Selling Bills or Certificates	5 551	368	604
卖淫、嫖娼	Prostitution or Going Whoring	4 631	8 771	9 929
赌　博	Gambling	17 464	46 709	51 861

注：2005 年起公安部对治安查处数的统计口径作了调整，将之前的接受并处理结束的案件数，扩大概念至只要介入调查就作为查处数。
Note: Since 2005, The Ministry of Public Security has adjusted the statistical scale of oftense cases against public order handled. The concept has been extended from the cases accepted and handled to the cases had been involved into investigation.

表 23.7 交通事故和火灾情况 (1980～2006)
BASIC STATISTICS OF TRAFFIC ACCIDENTS AND FIRES

年份 Year	交通事故 Traffic Accidents				火灾 Fires			
	次数（万次）Number (10 000 times)	死亡人数（人）Death (person)	受伤人数（万人）Injuries (10 000 persons)	损失折款（万元）Losses Converted -into Cash (10 000 yuan)	次数（万次）Number (10 000 times)	死亡人数（人）Death (person)	受伤人数（人）Injuries (person)	损失折款（万元）Losses Converted -into Cash (10 000 yuan)
1980	1.10	445	1.01	96	0.08	17	126	457
1981	1.18	507	1.06	119	0.09	33	81	202
1982	0.83	434	0.77	98	0.07	33	76	255
1983	0.73	443	0.70	99	0.06	24	67	533
1984	0.83	503	0.75	123	0.05	21	71	177
1985	0.71	687	0.57	318	0.05	30	74	374
1986	0.84	678	0.62	576	0.06	25	54	790
1987	1.01	811	0.67	959	0.06	51	56	575
1988	0.84	707	0.56	1 117	0.06	58	53	460
1989	0.75	652	0.49	1 137	0.03	30	30	394
1990	0.76	608	0.47	1 345	0.21	45	137	1 868
1991	0.75	594	0.45	1 530	0.17	38	112	937
1992	0.45	591	0.18	2 029	0.17	40	57	2 742
1993	0.81	699	0.29	4 652	0.14	73	128	2 252
1994	1.26	722	0.33	8 337	0.11	51	95	2 378
1995	1.67	788	0.38	12 077	0.11	47	86	2 100
1996	2.01	783	0.44	13 462	0.09	87	96	2 206
1997	2.16	780	0.58	13 682	0.74	51	138	2 639
1998	2.40	781	0.65	15 186	0.72	42	114	2 205
1999	2.61	726	0.78	15 924	0.66	43	90	1 487
2000	4.13	1 492	1.61	20 391	0.52	40	57	1 919
2001	4.21	1 503	1.57	23 883	0.32	31	65	966
2002	4.71	1 400	1.57	30 052	0.60	39	58	1 313
2003	5.42	1 406	1.12	39 721	0.58	47	85	1 724
2004	2.71	1 543	1.13	19 149	0.51	30	47	1 681
2005	0.92	1 393	0.88	7 961	0.43	54	84	1 731
2006	0.66	1 231	0.67	3 292	0.45	45	54	2 292

注：2000 年开始，火灾统计口径为受理数，2004 年新交通法实施后，交通事故认定标准有所变化。
Note: From 2000, statistics of fires refer to the number of fires handled There are some changes in the congnizance standard of traffic accident after the new Taraffic law was carried out in 2004.

表 23.8 交通事故情况(2006)
BASIC STATISTICS OF TRAFFIC ACCIDENTS

类 别	Types	发生数 (起) Number (case)	死亡人数 (人) Death (person)	受伤人数 (人) Injuries (person)	损失折款 (万元) Losses Converted -into Cash (10 000 yuan)
总 计	**Total**	**6 584**	**1 231**	**6 662**	**3 292**
#死亡事故	Death Accident	1 150	1 231	433	818
伤人事故	Injury Accident	5 043		6 229	1 674
机动车	Motor-driven Vehicles	4 644	905	4 867	3 070
#汽 车	Automobiles	3 549	708	3 634	2 819
摩托车	Motorcycles	998	167	1 148	172
非机动车	Non-motor-driven Vehicles	1 347	168	1 318	107
#自行车	Bicycles	663	99	626	50
行人乘车人	Pedestrians and Passengers	497	102	423	45
其 他	Others	96	56	54	70

表 23.9 火灾事故情况(2006)
BASIC STATISTICS OF FIRES

指 标	Indicators	合 计 Total	按事故发生程度分 By Serious Degree of Fires		
			特 大 Extraordinarily serious	重 大 Serious	一 般 Ordinary
次 数(起)	Number (case)	4 526	1	5	4 520
死亡人数(人)	Deaths (person)	45		3	42
受伤人数(人)	Injuries (person)	54		4	50
损失折款(万元)	Losses Converted into Cash (10 000 yuan)	2 292	295	283	1 714
平均每起事故损失(万元)	Average Loss per Fire (10 000 yuan)	0.50	295.24	56.59	0.38

表 23.10 检察院直接立案侦查案件情况(2006)
CASES UNDER DIRECT INVESTIGATION BY PROCURATOR'S OFFICES

类别	Types	受案(件) Cases Accepted (case)	立案件数(件) Number of Cases Registered (case)	立案人数(人) Person of Cases Registered (person)	侦查终结件数(件) Number of Cases Settled (case)	侦查终结人数(人) Person of Cases Settled (person)
总 计	**Total**	**1 921**	**474**	**524**	**466**	**507**
贪污贿赂案件	**Number of Cases on Corruption and Bribery**	**1 713**	**446**	**494**	**436**	**476**
贪 污	Corruption	647	118	129	124	135
贿 赂	Bribery	942	294	328	270	296
挪用公款	Misappropriation of Public Funds	81	32	33	40	41
集体私分	Collective Illegal Possession of Publice Funds	19	1	1		
巨额财产来源不明	Unstated Source of Large Properties	22				
其 他	Others	2	1	3	2	4
渎职侵权案件	**Number of Cases on Abuse and Dereliction of Duty**	**208**	**28**	**30**	**30**	**31**
滥用职权	Abuse of Power	91	10	10	12	12
玩忽职守	Dereliction of Duty	33	7	7	9	9
徇私舞弊	Fraudulent Practice	64	11	13	9	10
侵犯公民权利	Offences Against Citizens' Rights	18				
其 他	Others	2				

注：本表至表 23.12 由市检察院提供。
Note: Data in table 23.10 to 23.12 are provided by Shanghai Municipal People's Procurator's Offices.

表 23.11 检察院民事、行政案件办理情况(2006)
CIVIL CASES AND ADMINISTRATIVE CASES HANDLED BY PROCURATOR'S OFFICES

单位:件(case)

类别	Types	受案 Cases Accepted	审查处理 Cases Investigated	其中 of which: 立案 Cases Registered	结案处理 Cases Settled	其中 of which: 抗诉 Appeals Rejected
总 计	**Total**	**1 397**	**1 410**	**478**	**512**	**58**
民事案	**Civil Cases**	**1 291**	**1 294**	**459**	**491**	**58**
#合同纠纷案	Contract Disputes	365	377	178	185	23
权益纠纷案	Rights and Interests Disputes	218	223	55	69	8
劳动争议	Labour Disputes	134	129	33	47	8
婚姻家庭、继承纠纷案	Marriages and Inheritance Disputes	82	85	30	29	3
行政案	**Administrative Cases**	**106**	**116**	**19**	**21**	

表 23.12 检察院申诉案件处理情况(2006) APPEALS HANDLED BY PROCURATOR'S OFFICES

单位:件(case)

类别	Types	受案 Cases Accepted	审查处理 Cases Investigated	其中 of which: 分送本院其他部门 Dilivering to Other Department of Such Procurator's Offices
总计	**Total**	**8 667**	**8 655**	**2 159**
首次申诉	**Appeals First Time**	**5 085**	**5 075**	**1 868**
#不服不立案	Appeals Against Rejection of the Case	225	224	207
不服刑事拘留	Appeals Against Criminal Detention	1	1	
不服逮捕	Appeals Against Arrest	4	4	2
不服刑事判决	Appeals Against Judgment of Criminal Case	219	214	17
不服民事行政裁决	Appeals Against Aadminnistration Arbitrament of Civil Case	1 813	1 809	1 369
不服劳教	Appeals Against Judgment of Reeducation Through Labor	9	9	
重复申诉	**Appeals Repeated**	**3 582**	**3 580**	**291**

表 23.12 续表 continued

单位:件(case)

类别	Types	其中 of which: 移送其他检查院 Removing to Other Procurator's Offices	移送公安机关 Removing to Public Security Organs	移送其他机关 Removing to Other Organs	直接答复 Direct Reply
总计	**Total**	**2 671**	**436**	**2 509**	**366**
首次申诉	**Appeals First Time**	**1 127**	**281**	**1 208**	**285**
#不服不立案	Appeals Against Rejection of the Case	9	1		5
不服刑事判决	Appeals Against Judgment of Criminal Case	36		22	9
不服民事行政裁决	Appeals Against Aadminnistration Arbitrament of Civil Case	271		50	106
不服劳教	Appeals Against Judgment of Reeducation Through Labor	1	3		5
重复申诉	**Appeals Repeated**	**1 544**	**155**	**1 301**	**81**

表 23.13 法院各类案件办理情况(2006)
CASES HANDLED BY COURTS

单位:件(case)

类别	Types	收案 Cases Accepted	结案 Cases Settled	其中 of which 判决 Judgement	裁定 Arbitration	调解 Mediation
一审刑事案件	**First Trial Criminal Cases**	**18 002**	**17 892**	**17 674**		**19**
#侵犯公民人身权利、民主权利罪	Offences Against Citizens' Personal and Democratic Rights	2 344	2 330	2 170		19
侵犯财产罪	Offences Against Properties	9 890	9 865	9 837		
妨碍社会管理秩序罪	Offences Against Social Management of Order	3 326	3 292	3 282		
一审民事案件	**First Trial Civil Cases**	**184 162**	**181 473**	**70 309**	**65 920**	**42 309**
婚姻家庭、继承案件	Marriages and Inheritance Cases	28 395	28 032	8 942	5 909	12 723
婚姻家庭案件	Marriages and Fimily Cases	26 725	26 417	8 466	5 609	11 911
继承案件	Inheritance Cases	1 670	1 615	476	300	812
合同纠纷案件	Contract Disputes Cases	126 792	124 902	48 511	50 274	24 050
#买卖合同纠纷	Trade Contracts	19 811	19 912	7 540	6 364	5 388
房地产开发经营合同纠纷	Real Estate Development Contracts	5 854	5 853	3 567	1 424	816
借款合同纠纷	Loan Contracts	16 754	16 090	8 427	3 413	3 815
租赁合同纠纷	Lease Contract	8 581	8 476	3 528	3 478	1 415
劳动争议	Labor Disputes	10 681	10 166	4 777	2 885	2 414
劳务合同	Labor Contracts	1 055	1 024	370	381	252
权属、侵犯纠纷及其他民事案件	Disputes of Right Infringement of Right and Other Civil Affaires	28 975	28 539	12 856	9 737	5 536
#所有权及与所有权相关权力纠纷	Ownership and Related Rights	12 394	12 329	5 269	4 348	2 508
票据、证券权益纠纷	Disputes of Bill and Securities Disputes	577	625	329	161	123
股东权纠纷	Shareholder Rights	835	834	371	311	80
人身权纠纷	Personal Rights	10 479	10 202	5 449	2 001	2 692
其他民事案件	Other Civil Cases	4 690	4 549	1 438	2 916	133
一审行政案件	**First Trial Administrative Cases**	**1 990**	**1 983**	**853**	**1 136**	**2**

注:本表至表 23.15 数据由市高级人民法院提供。
Note: Data in this table to table 23.15 are provided by Shanghai Municipal Senior Court.

表 23.14 法院执行案件情况(2006) CASES EXECUTED BY COURTS

单位:件(case)

类别 Types		收案 Cases Accepted	结案 Cases Settled	其中 of which 自动履行 Automatic Performance	和解 Mediation	强制执行 Compellent Execution
总计	**Total**	**86 226**	**85 110**	**31 069**	**13 062**	**11 751**
刑事	Criminal Cases	5 669	5 316	1 084	38	655
民事	Civil Cases	68 835	67 914	24 416	11 942	8 987
行政	Administrative Cases	104	108	27	1	55
行政非诉审查与执行	Non-litigious Investigation and Execution of Administration	3 463	3 498	1 532	220	156
仲裁	Arbitration	7 277	7 359	3 895	587	1 847
公证债权文书	Notary Creditor's Rights	872	908	115	272	47
其他	Others	6	7		2	4

表 23.15 法院各类案件结案情况(2003~2006) CASE ENDED BY COURTS

单位:起(time)

类别 Types		2003	2004	2005	2006
总计	**Total**	**243 980**	**255 427**	**283 230**	**311 493**
刑事案件	Criminal Cases	14 346	15 860	17 353	19 579
婚姻家庭、继承案件	Marriages and Inheritance Cases	32 901	28 453	28 563	29 111
合同纠纷案件	Contract Disputes Cases	101 298	115 138	128 118	138 130
权属、侵犯纠纷及其他民事案件	Disputes of Right Infringement of Right and Other Civil Affairs	22 625	26 598	31 153	32 455
行政案件	Administrative Cases	2 244	2 713	3 016	2 961
申诉、申请再审	Second Trial on Appeals and Requisition	4 050	4 157	4 023	4 145
司法赔偿	Justice Compensation	9	3	6	2
执行案件	Executed Cases	66 507	62 505	70 998	85 110

表23.16 查处广告违法情况(2005~2006)
ILLEGAL ADVERTISEMENT PUNISHED

指 标 Indicators		2005 查处案件数(件) Case Punished (case)	2005 罚没款(万元) Amercement (10 000 yuan)	2006 查处案件数(件) Case Punished (case)	2006 罚没款(万元) Amercement (10 000 yuan)
总 计	**Total**	**827**	**1 025.65**	**1 471**	**1 185**
药 品	Leechdom	42	49.99	89	92
食 品	Foodstuff	186	117.35	302	105
保健品	Health Product	11	11.4	15	7
化妆品	Cosmetic	40	11.28	93	33
医疗服务	Medical Service	106	95.61	255	93
房地产	Real Estate	74	114.73	136	297
家 电	Household Appliance	5	11.82	21	61
其 他	Others	363	613.47	560	497

注:表23.16~23.18由市工商行政管理局提供。
Note: Data in table 23.16 to 23.18 were supplied by Shanghai Administration of Industry and Commerce.

表23.17 商标认定情况(2005~2006)
TRADEMARK CONFIRMED

单位:起(time)

指 标	Indicators	2005	2006
经认定的上海市著名商标数	Quantity of Confirmed Shanghai Famous Trademarks	126	178
上海市著名商标累计有效数	Accumulative Quantity of Shanghai Famous Trademarks	318	440

表23.18 查处商标违法情况(2004~2006)
ILLEGAL TRADEMARK PUNISHED

指 标	Indicators	2004	2005	2006
查处商标违法案件(件)	Illegal Trademark Punished (case)	1 104	1 227	2 217
#商标侵权案件	Trademark Tort Case	1 010	1 108	2 076
处罚款(万元)	Amercement(10 000 yuan)	1 059	1 088	1 488
收缴和消除侵权商标标识(万件)	Confiscated and Eliminated Tortious Trademark Signs (10 000 cases)	150	162	160
移送司法机关案件(件)	Case Removed to Judicial Organ (case)	5	11	9

上 / 海 / 统 / 计 / 年 / 鉴

主要统计指标解释

律 师

指依法取得律师执业证书，担任法律顾问，民事（刑事、行政）案件代理人、刑事案件辩护人、办理非诉讼业务，解答法律询问，代写法律事务文书等，为社会提供法律服务的人员。

公证人员

指在国家机关依法办理公证事务的司法人员。包括公证员、助理公证员和在公证处工作的其他人员。

办理公证文书

指公证处根据当事人申请，依照事实和法律，按照法定程序制作的，具有法律效力的司法证明文书。根据公证书用途和使用地，公证书分为国内公证书、国内经济公证书、涉外民事公证书、涉外经济公证书四类。

调解民间纠纷

指调解委员会按照法律规定，根据自愿原则，用说服教育的方法调解民间发生的有关民事权利和义务争执的件数，包括调解成功数和调解未成功数。该指标主要反映人民调解委员会的工作量。

立 案

指人民检察院对受理的报案、控告、举报或自首及自行发现的犯罪线索、犯罪嫌疑人进行初步调查后，认为存在职务犯罪事实和应追究刑事责任，并决定作为刑事案件进行侦查的诉讼活动，是追究犯罪的开始。该指标主要反映人民检察院依法将职务犯罪线索作为刑事案件进行侦查的诉讼活动。

申 诉

指经检察机关信访部门审查处理后，移送到检察机关申诉部门的申诉案件，包括不服检察机关处理决定和不服法院刑事判决和裁定的申诉的案件。

SHANGHAI STATISTICAL YEARBOOK

EXPLANATORY NOTES TO MAJOR STATISTICAL INDICATORS

□ Lawyers

Lawyers are certified legal workers according to law, and who are employed by legal counseling firms to act as legal advisers, agents in criminal or civil lawsuits, or defenders in criminal lawsuits, or to handle non–litigious legal affairs, to advise on matters of law or to write legal papers for others, and provide service to the public.

□ Notarial Personnel

Notary Personnel are judicial workers of the state notary organs handling notarization work according to law. They include notaries, assistant notaries, and other people working in notary firms.

□ Notarized Documents

Notary Documents refer to the judicatory notary documents drawn up by the request of the party and are in accordance with facts and laws and following certain legal proceedings. According to usage and locality, the notary documents are divided into following 4 types: domestic notary documents, domestic economic notary documents, foreign–related civil notary documents and foreign–related economic notary documents.

□ Civil Disputes Mediated

Civil Disputes Mediated refers to number of cases made by mediation committees in mediating in civil disputes concerning civil rights and duties through persuasion and education in accordance with the provisions of law on a voluntary basis, so as to solve disputes by helping the parties involved come to an agreement and understanding, including those unsuccessful ones. This indicator reflects the workload of the mediation committees.

□ Registered Cases

Registered Cases refer to the decision made by the people's procuratorate office on reported cases, prosecution, impeachment, surrender, self–found criminal clues or suspects after initial investigation to confirm the act of crime and to start legal proceedings of the case as criminal case.

□ Appeals

Appeals refer to cases transferred to the appeal departments of procurator's offices after initial review by departments dealing with complaint letters and calls of the public. Included are appeals against decisions made by procurator's offices and appeals against court rules and verdicts.

第二十四篇

CHAPTER 24

浦东新区

PUDONG NEW AREA

表 24.1 主要年份人口、从业人员、工资和婚姻情况
POPULATION, EMPLOYMENT, WAGES AND MARRIAGE IN MAIN YEARS

指 标	Indicators	2000	2005	2006
年末总人口（万人）	**Year-end Population (10 000 persons)**	**164.87**	**184.81**	**187.56**
按性别分	Grouped by Sex			
男 性	Male	82.75	93.12	94.45
女 性	Female	82.12	91.69	93.11
按农业、非农业分	Grouped by Agriculture and Non-agriculture			
农业人口	Agriculture	30.30	14.64	12.32
非农业人口	Non-agriculture	134.57	170.17	175.24
人口密度（人/平方公里）	Density of Population (person/sq. km)	3 091	3 245	3 293
总户数（万户）	Total Households (10 000 households)	60.52	68.95	70.11
每户平均人口（人）	Average Persons Per Household (person)	2.72	2.68	2.68
人口自然变动	**Natural Change of Population**			
出生人口（人）	Number of Birth (person)	8 229	12 363	12 708
出生率（‰）	Birth Rate (‰)	5.07	6.76	6.83
死亡人口（人）	Number of Death (person)	11 007	13 423	12 910
死亡率（‰）	Death Rate (‰)	6.78	7.34	6.93
自然增长率（‰）	Natural Growth Rate (‰)	-1.71	-0.58	-0.10
人口迁移变动	**Migration**			
迁入人口（人）	Inflows (person)	160 975	128 476	106 408
迁入率(‰)	Rate of Inflows (‰)	99.10	70.3	57.20
迁出人口（人）	Outflows (person)	103 486	88 315	78 638
迁出率（‰）	Rate of Outflows (‰)	63.70	48.3	42.20
净迁移率（‰）	Net Migration Rate (‰)	35.40	21.96	14.90
从业人员（万人）	Employees(10 000 persons)	104.05	144.08	146.71
职工人数（万人）	Staff and Workers (10 000 persons)	67.75	70.16	66.57
职工工资总额（亿元）	Wages of Staff and Workers (100 million yuan)	120.59	235.03	278.91
职工平均工资（元）	Average Annual Wages of Staff and Workers (yuan)	17 607	33 186	41 725
婚姻登记	**Marriages**			
准予登记结婚（对）	Marriage Registration Permitted (couples)	11 083	14 602	24 361
离婚登记（对）	Divorces (couples)	2 102	4 402	5 378

注：本篇数据除工业、投资外均由浦东新区统计局提供。
Note: Data in this chapter except that of industry and investment are provided by Shanghai Pudong New Area Statistical Bureau. .

表 24.2 主要年份增加值和指数
VALUE ADDED AND INDEX IN MAIN YEARS

指标	Indicators	2000	2005	2006
增加值（亿元）	**Value Added（100 million yuan）**	**920.63**	**2 108.79**	**2 365.33**
第一产业	Primary Industry	5.72	6.09	5.88
第二产业	Secondary Industry	488.60	1 070.96	1 194.47
工业	Industry	445.43	1 009.74	1 133.76
建筑业	Construction	43.17	61.49	60.71
第三产业	Tertiary Industry	426.31	1 031.74	1 164.98
构成（%）	**Composition（%）**	**100**	**100**	**100**
第一产业	Primary Industry	0.6	0.3	0.2
第二产业	Secondary Industry	53.1	50.8	50.5
工业	Industry	48.4	47.9	47.9
建筑业	Construction	4.7	2.9	2.6
第三产业	Tertiary Industry	46.3	48.9	49.3
增加值指数（以1990年为100）	**Index of Value Added（1990 =100）**	**633.5**	**1 315.9**	**1 492.2**
第一产业	Primary Industry	139.1	140.0	132.9
第二产业	Secondary Industry	506.5	1 059.4	1 187.6
第三产业	Tertiary Industry	1 084.9	2 253.0	2 591.0
增加值指数（以上年为100）	**Index of Value Added（preceding year =100）**	**116.5**	**112.1**	**113.4**
第一产业	Primary Industry	104.9	96.0	94.9
第二产业	Secondary Industry	115.2	110.5	112.1
第三产业	Tertiary Industry	119.6	114.0	115.0

表24.3 主要年份城市基础设施投资额和公用事业情况
INVESTMENT IN URBAN INFRASTRUCTURE AND PUBLIC UTILITIES IN MAIN YEARS

指 标	Indicators	2000	2005	2006
城市基础设施投资额（万元）	**Investment in Urban Infrastructure（10 000 yuan）**	**545 081**	**1 259 548**	**1 560 384**
电力建设	Power Generation Facilities Construction	43 043	75 089	278 704
交通邮电	Transpotation and Post	233 014	800 236	905 210
公用设施	Public Facilities	269 024	384 223	376 470
自来水	**Tap Water**			
自来水管道长度（公里）	Length of Tap Water Pipelines（km）	2 636	3 100	3 617
自来水生产能力（万吨/日）	Tap Water Supply Capacity（10 000 tons/day）	171.98	171.20	189.60
售水量（万吨）	Sales of Tap Water（10 000 tons）	33 014	41 926	44 475
#生活用水	Residential Use	17 655	21 749	29 689
液化石油气	**Liquefied Petroleum Gas**			
销售量（万吨）	Sales（10 000 tons）	3.58	5.20	4.69
#家庭用	Family Use	2.80	5.00	3.36
家庭用液化气户数（万户）	Liquefied Petroleum Gas Users(10 000 households)	45.55	45.90	46.30
道 路	**Road**			
铺装道路长度（公里）	Length of Paved Road（km）	835	960	962
铺装道路面积（万平方米）	Area of Paved Road（10 000 sq. m）	1 180	1 704	1 710
交 通	**Traffic**			
年末实有公交线路条数（条）	Length of Public Traffic（year-end）（route）	169	176	177
年末实有公交线路长度（公里）	Lines of Public Traffic Routes（year-end）（km）	4 030	4 194	4 402
年末运营公共车辆（辆）	Public Transportation Vehicles（year-end）（vehicle）	3 025	3 616	3 453
客运总量（亿人次）	Passengers Volume（100 million person-times）	5.0	6.3	6.4
城市绿化	**Urban Greenbelt**			
园林绿地面积（公顷）	Area of Parks and Green Areas（hectare）	3 830	8 440	8 739
人均公共绿地面积（平方米）	Per Capita Public Green Area（sq. m）	11.00	24.42	24.21
绿化覆盖率（%）	Green Area Coverage（%）	30.2	37.8	37.4
公园数（个）	Number of Parks（nuit）	12	17	17

注：自来水管道长度包括系统外单位。
Note：Lengths of tap water pipelines include which are outside the system.

表 24.4 主要年份全社会固定资产投资主要指标
MAJOR INDICATORS OF TOTAL INVESTMENT IN FIXED ASSETS IN MAIN YEARS

	指 标 Indicators	2000	2005	2006
投资总额（亿元）	**Total Investment (100 million yuan)**	**351.06**	**693.62**	**659.97**
#房地产	Real Estate	111.18	287.92	257.81
在投资总额中	**In Total Investment**			
按构成分	Grouped by Use of Funds			
#建筑安装工程	Construction and Installation	165.70	351.06	345.12
设备、工具、器具购置	Purchase of Equipment and Instruments	92.21	103.97	121.39
按建设性质分	Grouped by Type of Construction			
#新 建	New Construction	174.55	300.29	313.35
改 建	Reconstruction	22.35	31.62	42.14
扩 建	Expansion	19.66	40.06	28.76
按三次产业分	Grouped by Type of Industry			
#第二产业	Secondary Industry	143.62	144.97	139.65
第三产业	Tertiary Industry	206.77	548.58	520.32
按经济类型分	Grouped by Economic Types			
#国有经济	State-owned	118.90	208.24	238.93
集体经济	Collective-owned	20.24	15.13	30.91
联营经济	Joint Owned	9.68	6.62	8.06
股份制经济	Shareholding	56.85	243.19	174.38
外商投资经济	Foreign Funded	104.75	112.22	113.18
港澳台商投资经济	Hong Kong, Macau and Taiwan Funded	26.98	35.05	37.40
房屋建筑面积（万平方米）	**Floor Space of Buildings (10 000 sq. m)**			
施工面积	Floor Space of Construction	1 576.48	2 483.56	2 555.22
#住 宅	Residential Housing	735.93	1 510.04	1 521.58
竣工面积	Floor Space Completed	570.36	615.37	879.26
#住 宅	Residential Housing	278.93	408.44	597.93
房屋建筑面积竣工率（%）	Rate of Floor Space Completed of Buildings(%)	36.2	24.8	34.4
资金来源合计（亿元）	**Total Capital Source(100 million yuan)**	**407.97**	**1 057.43**	**1 015.33**
上年末结余资金	Balance at End of Previous Year	67.81	170.99	162.5
本年资金来源小计	Sub-total Capital Source of the Year	340.16	886.44	852.83
#国家预算内资金	State Budgetarg Funds	4.21	16.05	18.85
国内贷款	Domestic Loans	94.78	166.05	256.66
利用外资	Foreign Capital Absorbed	41.38	61.96	48.45
自筹资金	Self-financial Capital	148.87	170.99	301.98
其他资金	Other Capital	50.92	246.99	226.89

表 24.5 主要年份财政、金融和保险情况
MAJOR FACT OF FINANCE AND INSURANCE IN MAIN YEARS

指 标	Indicators	2000	2005	2006
全部财政收入(亿元)	**Total Fiscal Revenue(100 million yuan)**	**103.21**	**494.94**	**587.49**
地方财政收入(亿元)	**Local Fiscal Revenue(100 million yuan)**	**56.40**	**155.31**	**178.31**
#区级财政收入	Fiscal Revenue at District Level	35.59	155.31	179.52
#增值税	Value-added Tax	4.43	27.59	33.46
营业税	Business Tax	12.22	52.88	62.71
个人所得税	Personal Income Tax	7.77	19.94	24.14
城市维护建设税	Tax on Urban Construction and Maintenance	1.16	2.43	2.62
房产税	Tax on Real Estate	1.34	3.52	4.52
企业所得税	Enterprise Income Tax	7.27	25.17	30.46
契 税	Contract Tax	0.71	20.24	14.43
地方财政支出(亿元)	**Local Government Expenditures(100 million yuan)**	**69.60**	**198.79**	**222.58**
#农业支出	Agriculture Expenditures	2.06	1.83	1.88
水利和气象支出	Water Conservancy and Weather Expenditures	0.74	1.15	1.49
城市维护费	Urban Maintenance	4.06	10.23	12.65
教育事业费	Expenditure on Education	9.56	18.85	20.76
医疗卫生支出	Expenditure on Health Care	2.99	4.49	5.31
行政管理费	Government Administration	2.14	5.58	6.99
教育费附加支出	Additional Education Expenditure	0.48	1.72	1.88
基本建设支出	Expenditures on Capital Construction	10.93	65.83	74.07
企业挖潜改造	Potential-tapping and Transformation of Enterprises	21.79	38.83	46.78
中资银行存款余额(亿元)	Saving Deposit Balance of Chinese Financial Institutions (100 million yuan)	1 046.81	3 705.44	3 293.70
中资银行贷款余额(亿元)	Loan Balance of Chinese Financial Institutions (100 million yuan)	891.59	2 366.61	3 060.26
中资保险费收入(亿元)	Premium Income(100 million yuan)	63.31	140.63	171.47
赔 款(亿元)	Indemnite Expenditure and Payment(100 million yuan)	7.06	23.16	26.17
赔款率(%)	Indemnitey and Premium Ratio(%)	11.2	16.5	15.3

表 24.6 主要年份农业主要指标
MAJOR INDICATORS OF AGRICULTURE IN MAIN YEARS

指标	Indicators	2000	2005	2006
户数（万户）	Households (10 000 households)	13.67	12.67	12.52
人口（万人）	Population (10 000 persons)	36.82	35.57	35.21
劳动力（万人）	Labour Force (10 000 persons)	19.86	19.66	19.51
外省市流入劳动力（人）	Labour Move in from Outside Shanghai (person)	91 268	265 223	314 539
第一产业	Primary Industry	14 743	16 453	15 006
第二产业	Secondary Industry	52 715	184 437	211 823
第三产业	Tertiary Industry	23 810	64 333	87 710
农业总产值（亿元）	**Gross Output Value of Agriculture (100 million yuan)**	**12.57**	**11.62**	**11.50**
种植业	Planting	5.96	6.68	6.74
林业	Forestry	0.13	2.54	2.28
牧业	Animal Husbandry	6.08	1.95	2.07
渔业	Fishery	0.40	0.45	0.42
上年末耕地面积（公顷）	Area of Cultivated Land (last year-end) (hectare)	12 799	9 483.2	8 848.9
当年减少耕地面积（公顷）	Decrease in Cultivated Area (hectare)	133	634.3	561.6
年末耕地面积（公顷）	Cultivated Areas (year-end) (hectare)	12 666	8 848.9	8 287.3
#水田	Paddy Fields	11 239	8 022.3	7 569.8
旱田	Dry Fields	1 427	826.6	717.5
主要农副产品产量	Output of Major Farm and Sideline Products			
粮食（万吨）	Grain (10 000 tons)	6.83	1.37	1.35
蔬菜（万吨）	Vegetables (10 000 tons)	32.17	30.09	27.08
水果（万吨）	Fruit (10 000 tons)	0.21	0.42	0.53
生猪饲养量（万头）	Hogs Raised (10 000 heads)	55.83	16.72	21.18
猪肉产量（万吨）	Pork (10 000 tons)	3.13	0.77	1.26
牛奶产量（万吨）	Cow Milk (10 000 tons)	3.06	1.27	1.05
鲜蛋产量（万吨）	Poulty Eggs (10 000 tons)	1.27	0.17	0.09
水产品（万吨）	Aquatic Products (10 000 tons)	0.31	0.23	0.24
#淡水产品	Freshwater Aquatic Products	0.25	0.23	0.24
农业机械总动力（万千瓦）	Total Power of Agricultural Machinery (10 000 kw)	6.39	1.86	1.61
机电排灌面积（万公顷）	Drainage and Irrigation Area Used by Machinery and Electricity (10 000 hectares)	1.08	0.15	0.14

表 24.7 主要年份工业企业主要指标
MAJOR INDICATORS OF INDUSTRIAL ENTERPRISES IN MAIN YEARS

指 标	Indicators	2000	2005	2006
工业总产值(亿元)	**Gross Output Value of Industry (100 million yuan)**	**1 793.14**	**3 763.14**	**4 306.13**
按轻、重工业分	Grouped by Light and Heavy Industry			
轻工业	Light Industry	439.02	756.83	805.77
重工业	Heavy Industry	1 354.12	3 006.31	3 500.36
按登记注册类型分	Grouped by Registration Categories			
国有经济	State-owned	300.12	85.18	134.04
集体经济	Collective-owned	56.84	33.79	33.71
其他经济	Others	1 436.18	3 644.17	4 138.38
#外商投资企业	Foreign Funded Units	795.43	2 161.63	2 361.97
按企业规模分	Grouped by Size of Enterprises			
大型企业	Large Enterprise	1 365.18	1 533.87	1 497.65
中型企业	Medium Enterprise	181.01	1 128.11	1 730.57
小型企业	Small Enterprise	246.95	1 101.16	1 077.91
出口交货值(亿元)	**Delivery Value of Industry Exports (100 million yuan)**	**436.61**	**1 209.75**	**1 347.43**
按轻、重工业分	Grouped by Light and Heavy Industry			
轻工业	Light Industry	122.42	260.33	272.31
重工业	Heavy Industry	314.18	949.42	1 075.12
按登记注册类型分	Grouped by Registration Categories			
国有经济	State-owned	44.94	10.66	37.3
集体经济	Collective-owned	4.49	1.74	1.24
其他经济	Others	387.18	1 197.36	1 308.89
#外商投资企业	Foreign Funded Units	270.44	911.43	867.88
按企业规模分	Grouped by Size of Enterprises			
大型企业	Large Enterprise	349.27	477.67	382.09
中型企业	Medium Enterprise	45.86	422.69	729.19
小型企业	Small Enterprise	41.48	309.39	236.15
工业企业经济指标	**Economic Indicators of Industrial Enterprises**			
年末资产总计(亿元)	Year-end Total Assets (100 million yuan)	3 028.13	3 742.57	4 432.93
年末负债合计(亿元)	Year-end Liability (100 million yuan)	1 354.44	2 046.11	2 332.94
主营业务收入(亿元)	Prime Operating Revenue(100 million yuan)	1 853.22	4 037.3	4 623.49
利润总额(亿元)	Pre-tax Profits (100 million yuan)	128.65	218.52	267.8
税金总额(亿元)	Tax and Duty (100 million yuan)	86.7	121.4	138.88
资金利税率(%)	Profits and Tax Total Assets (%)	7.11	9.08	9.17
成本费用利润率(%)	Profits/Cost and Expenses (%)	7.4	5.68	6.11
流动资产周转次数(次)	Turnover of Current Assets (time)	1.64	2.01	2.04

表 24.8 主要年份国内外贸易主要指标
MAJOR INDICATORS OF DOMESTIC AND FOREIGN TRADE IN MAIN YEARS

指 标	Indicators	2000	2005	2006
社会消费品零售总额（亿元）	**Total Retail Sales of Consumer Goods (100 million yuan)**	**215.17**	**414.99**	**400.02**
按用途分	Grouped by Types of Usage			
吃的商品	Food	81.55	104.27	125.88
穿的商品	Clothing	13.65	25.33	32.24
用的商品	Articles	117.94	283.74	240.83
烧的商品	Fuels	2.03	1.64	1.07
外商直接投资签约项目数（个）	**Contracted Projects of Foreign Direct Investment (unit)**	**693**	**1 734**	**1 446**
# 中外合资	Joint Venture	109	149	143
中外合作	Cooperative Operation	21	8	7
外商独资	Foreign Enterprise	563	1 574	1 292
外商直接投资合同金额（亿美元）	**Contracted Foreign Capital of Foreign Direct Investment (100 million USD)**	**28.84**	**56.54**	**48.42**
# 中外合资	Joint Venture	2.73	7.84	7.67
中外合作	Cooperative Operation	0.47	0.38	0.32
外商独资	Foreign Enterprise	25.63	42.20	39.56
进出口商品总额（亿美元）	**Total Value of Imports and Exports (100 million USD)**	**254.86**	**894.75**	**1 073.10**
出口总额	**Total Value of Exports**	**95.80**	**372.12**	**444.71**
# 一般贸易	Originary Trade	44.21	175.38	212.50
来料加工装配贸易	Processing and Assembly Trade with Customer Materials	11.37	45.21	32.35
进料加工贸易	Processing Trade with Imported Material	37.32	107.33	146.32
进口总额	**Total Value of Imports**	**159.06**	**522.63**	**628.39**
一般贸易	Originary Trade	71.91	186.52	198.72
来料加工装配贸易	Processing and Assembly Trade with Customer Materials	9.03	27.68	10.80
进料加工贸易	Processing Trade with Imported Material	22.85	63.82	95.92
外商投资企业作为投资进口的设备物品	Imported Equipment and Materials as Investment of Foreign Investment Enterprises	10.19	13.30	11.41

表 24.9 主要年份教育、卫生事业情况
STATISTICS OF EDUCATION AND HEALTH CARE IN MAIN YEARS

	指 标 Indicators	2000	2005	2006
学 校（所）	**Schools（umit）**			
高等学校	Institutions of Higher Education	3	6	6
中等专业学校	Specialized Secondary Schools	8	9	7
职业中学	Vocational Secondany Schools	8	5	5
普通中学	Regular Secondary Schools	100	103	105
小 学	Primary Schools	136	107	104
特殊教育学校	Special Education Schools	3	2	2
在校学生数（人）	**Student Enrollment（person）**			
高等学校	Institutions of Higher Education	11 940	41 034	43 435
中等专业学校	Specialized Secondary Schools	12 070	22 058	18 774
职业中学	Vocational Secondany Schools	18 423	13 027	849
普通中学	Regular Secondary Schools	108 448	114 322	109 193
小 学	Primary Schools	110 573	92 062	95 281
特殊教育学校	Special Education Schools	532	638	571
教职员工（人）	**Staff and Workers（person）**			
高等学校	Institutions of Higher Education	1 828	4 387	4 532
中等专业学校	Specialized Secondary Schools	1 207	1 383	1 278
职业中学	Vocational Secondany Schools	1 058	753	849
普通中学	Regular Secondary Schools	9 816	10 680	10 405
小 学	Primary Schools	8 826	7 909	7 820
特殊教育学校	Special Education Schools	125	149	153
卫生机构数（个）	**Health Care Institutions（unit）**	**586**	**630**	**651**
医院床位数（张）	**Hospital Beds（bed）**	**5 157**	**6 520**	**7 652**
卫生技术人员（人）	**Medical Technical Personnel（person）**	**6 900**	**9 794**	**10 427**
#医 生	Medical Practitioners	3 238	4 726	4 792
护师、护士	Senior and Junior Nurses	2 388	3 390	3 999
医院治疗人次（万人次）	**Total Patients Treated（10 000 person-times）**	**922.22**	**1 272.95**	**1 433.61**
#门、急诊	Out-patients and Emergency Patients	888.80	1 238.14	1 400.50
医院入院人数（万人次）	**In Patients（10 000 person-times）**	**17.02**	**15.98**	**16.12**
医院每百诊次的入院人数（人）	**In-patients/Per 100 Patient-times（person）**	**1.9**	**1.26**	**1.12**
医院病床使用率（%）	Utilization Rate of Hospital Beds（%）	101.51	102.66	102.30

(京)新登字041号

图书在版编目(CIP)数据

上海统计年鉴. 2007/上海市统计局编.
——北京：中国统计出版社，2007.6
ISBN 978-7-5037-5149-3

Ⅰ.上…
Ⅱ.上…
Ⅲ.统计资料-上海市-2007-年鉴
Ⅳ.C832.51-54

中国版本图书馆CIP数据核字(2007)第051662号

上海统计年鉴—2007

作　　者／上海市统计局
责任编辑／郑淼淼　范仲实
E-mail／yearbook@stats.gov.cn
执行编辑／钱文瑛　曹美芳
封面设计／蔡旭洲
出版发行／中国统计出版社
通信地址／北京市西城区三里河月坛南街75号　中国统计出版社
邮　　编／100826
电　　话／(010) 63376907
印　　刷／深圳宝峰印刷有限公司
经　　销／新华书店
开　　本／889×1240毫米1/16
字　　数／142.48万字
印　　张／34.25
印　　数／1～4000册
版　　别／2007年6月第1版
版　　次／2007年6月第1次印刷
书　　号／ISBN 978-7-5037-5149-3/F·2449
定　　价／360.00元